59th Annual Meeting of the Association for Computational Linguistics and the 11th International Joint Conference on Natural Language Processing (ACL-IJCNLP 2021)

Systems Demonstrations

Online
1-6 August 2021

ISBN: 978-1-7138-3310-9

Printed from e-media with permission by:

Curran Associates, Inc.
57 Morehouse Lane
Red Hook, NY 12571

Some format issues inherent in the e-media version may also appear in this print version.

Printed with permission by Curran Associates, Inc. (2021)

For permission requests, please contact the Association for Computational Linguistics at the address below.

Association for Computational Linguistics
209 N. Eighth Street
Stroudsburg, Pennsylvania 18360

Phone: 1-570-476-8006
Fax: 1-570-476-0860

acl@aclweb.org

Additional copies of this publication are available from:

Curran Associates, Inc.
57 Morehouse Lane
Red Hook, NY 12571 USA
Phone: 845-758-0400
Fax: 845-758-2633
Email: curran@proceedings.com
Web: www.proceedings.com

ACL-IJCNLP 2021

The Joint Conference of the 59th Annual Meeting of the Association for Computational Linguistics and the 11th International Joint Conference on Natural Language Processing

Proceedings of the System Demonstrations

August 1st - August 6th, 2021
Bangkok, Thailand (online)

Introduction

Welcome to the proceedings of the system demonstration track of the Joint Conference of the 59th Annual Meeting of the Association for Computational Linguistics and the 11th International Joint Conference on Natural Language Processing (ACL-IJCNLP) on August 1st - August 6th, 2021. ACL-IJCNLP 2021 will be an online conference.

The ACL-IJCNLP 2021 system demonstration track invites submissions ranging from early research prototypes to mature production-ready systems. We received 133 submissions, of which 43 were selected for inclusion in the program (acceptance rate of 32.3%) after reviewed by at least three members of the program committee. We would like to thank the members of the program committee for their timely help in reviewing the submissions.

Lastly, we thank the many authors that submitted their work to the demonstrations track. This year, the ACL conference is completely virtual. The demonstration paper will be presented through one pre-recorded talk and one live online QA session.

Best,
Heng Ji, Jong C. Park and Rui Xia
ACL-IJCNLP 2021 Demonstration Chairs

Organizing Committee:

Heng Ji, University of Illinois at Urbana and Champaign
Jong C. Park, Korea Advanced Institute of Science and Technology
Rui Xia, Nanjing University of Science and Technology

Program Committee:

Abdalghani Abujabal, Amazon Alexa AI
Rodrigo Agerri, University of the Basque Country UPV/EHU
Željko Agić, Unity Technologies
Roee Aharoni, Google
Khalid Al Khatib, Leipzig University
Malihe Alikhani, University of Pittsburgh
Miguel A. Alonso, Universidade da Coruña
Malik Altakrori, McGill University / MILA
Rafael Anchiêta, Federal Institute of Piauí
Diego Antognini, Swiss Federal Institute of Technology in Lausanne
Rahul Aralikatte, University of Copenhagen
Hiba Arnaout, Max Planck Institute for Informatics
Akari Asai, University of Washington
Awais Athar, European Bioinformatics Institute
Eleftherios Avramidis, German Research Center for Artificial Intelligence
Ioana Baldini, IBM Research
Siqi Bao, Baidu
Valerio Basile, University of Turin
Mohaddeseh Bastan, Stony Brook University
Timo Baumann, Universität Hamburg
Gábor Berend, University Of Szeged
Archna Bhatia, The Florida Institute for Human and Machine Cognition
Sumit Bhatia, IBM Research
Parminder Bhatia, Amazon
Wei Bi, Tencent AI Lab
Eduardo Blanco, University of North Texas
Rexhina Blloshmi, Sapienza University of Rome
Ansel Blume, University of Illinois at Urbana-Champaign
Bernd Bohnet, Google
Rishi Bommasani, Stanford University
Georgeta Bordea, Université de Bordeaux
Florian Boudin, Université de Nantes
Chris Brockett, Microsoft Research
Jill Burstein, Duolingo
Hongjie Cai, Nanjing University of Science and Technology
Andrew Caines, University of Cambridge
Daniel Campos, Microsoft
Ed Cannon, Expedia Group
Qingqing Cao, Stony Brook University
Yixin Cao, Nanyang Technological University
Jiarun Cao, University of Manchester
Thiago Castro Ferreira, Federal University of Minas Gerais
Guan-Lin Chao, Carnegie Mellon University

Kushal Chawla, University of Southern California
Hongshen Chen, JD.com
Shaowei Chen, Nankai University
Shizhe Chen, National de Recherche en Informatique et en Automatique
Chung-Chi Chen, National Taiwan University
Guanyi Chen, Utrecht University
Long Chen, Columbia University
Jiaoyan Chen, University of Oxford
Lu Chen, Shanghai Jiao Tong University
Jun Chen, Baidu
Yagmur Gizem Cinar, Amazon
Philip Cohen, Openstream Inc.
Shaobo Cui, Alibaba Group
Xinyu Dai, Nanjing University
Xiang Dai, University of Copenhagen
Alok Debnath, Factmata
Louise Deléger, Université Paris-Saclay
Shumin Deng, Zhejiang University
Yuntian Deng, Harvard University
Zixiang Ding, Nanjing University of Science and Technology
Carl Edwards, University of Illinois at Urbana-Champaign
Paulo Fernandes, Roberts Wesleyan College
Yi Fung, University of Illinois at Urbana Champaign
Fitsum Gaim, Korea Advanced Institute of Science and Technology
Sudeep Gandhe, Google Inc
Xiang Gao, Microsoft Research
Andrew Gargett, The Open University
Mozhdeh Gheini, University of Southern California
Asmelash Teka Hadgu, Lesan AI
Chi Han, ByteDance AI Lab
Maram Hasanain, Qatar University
Yun He, Texas A&M University
Matthew Henderson, PolyAI
Benjamin Hoover, IBM Research
Xiaodan Hu, University of Illinois at Urbana-Champaign
Hen-Hsen Huang, National Chengchi University
Julie Hunter, LINAGORA
Euijun Hwang, Korea Advanced Institute of Science and Technology
Ali Hürriyetoğlu, Koç University
Jeff Jacobs, Columbia University
Soyeong Jeong, Korea Advanced Institute of Science and Technology
Feng Ji, Tencent Inc
Zhuoxuan Jiang, Tencent Inc
Ridong Jiang, Institute for Infocomm Research
Joo-Kyung Kim, Amazon Alexa AI
Jung-Ho Kim, Korea Advanced Institute of Science and Technology
Varun Kumar, Amazon Alexa AI
Harshit Kumar, IBM Research
Tuan Lai, University of Illinois at Urbana-Champaign
Huije Lee, Korea Advanced Institute of Science and Technology
Jinchao Li, Microsoft Research

Sha Li, University of Illinois at Urbana-Champaign
Yanran Li, The Hong Kong Polytechnic University
Xintong Li, The Ohio State University
Manling Li, University of Illinois at Urbana-Champaign
Lizi Liao, National University of Singapore
Constantine Lignos, Brandeis University
Qian Liu, Beihang University
Yang Liu, Amazon
José Lopes, Heriot Watt University
Andrea Madotto, The Hong Kong University Of Science and Technology
Alex Marin, Microsoft Corporation
Junta Mizuno, The National Institute of Information and Communications Technology
Xiaoman Pan, Tencent AI Lab
Feifei Pan, Rensselaer Polytechnic Institute
Alexandros Papangelis, Amazon Alexa AI
ChaeHun Park, Korea Advanced Institute of Science and Technology
Oleksandr Polozov, Microsoft Research
Stephen Pulman, Apple Inc.
Eugénio Ribeiro, The Instituto de Engenharia de Sistemas e Computadores: Investigação e Desenvolvimento
Hassan Sawaf, Aixplain Inc.
Ethan Selfridge, LivePerson
Xiangqing Shen, Nanjing University of Science and Technology
Jiaming Shen, University of Illinois at Urbana-Champaign
Jisu Shin, Korea Advanced Institute of Science and Technology
Lei Shu, Amazon AWS AI
Hoyun Song, Korea Advanced Institute of Science and Technology
Kaitao Song, Nanjing University of Science and Technology
Alexander Spangher, University of Southern California
Shang-Yu Su, National Taiwan University
Chenkai Sun, University of Illinois at Urbana-Champaign
Jian Sun, Alibaba Group
Hisami Suzuki, Microsoft Corporation
Ivan Vulić, University of Cambridge
Zhenhailong Wang, University of Illinois at Urbana-Champaign
Jingjing Wang, Soochow University
Zhongqing Wang, Soochow University
Qingyun Wang, University of Illinois at Urbana-Champaign
Wen Wang, Alibaba Group
Spencer Whitehead, University of Illinois at Urbana-Champaign
Chien-Sheng Wu, Salesforce
Xianchao Wu, NVIDIA
Zhen Xu, Tencent PCG
Xiaohui Yan, Huawei
Min Yang, Shenzhen Institutes of Advanced Technology, Chinese Academy of Sciences
Yujiu Yang, Tsinghua University
Wonsuk Yang, Korea Advanced Institute of Science and Technology
Koichiro Yoshino, Nara Institute of Science and Technology
Dian Yu, University of California, Davis
Jianfei Yu, Nanjing University of Science and Technology
Pengfei Yu, University of Illinois at Urbana-Champaign

Qi Zeng, University of Illinois at Urbana-Champaign
Chengzhi Zhang, Nanjing University of Science and Technology
Zixuan Zhang, University of Illinois at Urbana-Champaign
Qi Zhang, Fudan University
Tiancheng Zhao, SOCO.AI
Deyu Zhou, Southeast University
Cangqi Zhou, Nanjing University of Science and Technology
Erion Çano, University of Vienna

Table of Contents

TexSmart: A System for Enhanced Natural Language Understanding

Lemao Liu, Haisong Zhang, Haiyun Jiang, Yangming Li, Enbo Zhao, Kun Xu, Linfeng Song, Suncong Zheng, Botong Zhou, Jianchen Zhu, Xiao Feng, Tao Chen, Tao Yang, Dong Yu, Feng Zhang, Zhanhui Kang, Shuming Shi*

Tencent AI

{texsmart, redmondliu, hansonzhang, shumingshi}@tencent.com

Abstract

This paper introduces TexSmart, a text understanding system that supports fine-grained named entity recognition (NER) and enhanced semantic analysis functionalities. Compared to most previous publicly available text understanding systems and tools, TexSmart holds some unique features. First, the NER function of TexSmart supports over 1,000 entity types, while most other public tools typically support several to (at most) dozens of entity types. Second, TexSmart introduces new semantic analysis functions like semantic expansion and deep semantic representation, that are absent in most previous systems. Third, a spectrum of algorithms (from very fast algorithms to those that are relatively slow but more accurate) are implemented for one function in TexSmart, to fulfill the requirements of different academic and industrial applications. The adoption of unsupervised or weakly-supervised algorithms is especially emphasized, with the goal of easily updating our models to include fresh data with less human annotation efforts. [1]

1 Introduction

The long-term goal of natural language processing (NLP) is to help computers understand natural language as well as we do, which is one of the most fundamental and representative challenges for artificial intelligence. Natural language understanding includes a broad variety of tasks covering lexical analysis, syntactic analysis and semantic analysis. In this paper we introduce TexSmart, a new text understanding system that provides enhanced named entity recognition (NER) and semantic analysis functionalities besides standard NLP modules. Compared to most previous publicly-available text understanding systems (Loper and Bird, 2002; OpenNLP; Manning et al., 2014; Gardner et al., 2018; Che et al., 2010; Qiu et al., 2013), TexSmart holds the following key characteristics:

- Fine-grained named entity recognition (NER)
- Enhanced semantic analysis
- A spectrum of algorithms implemented for one function, to fulfill the requirements of different academic and industrial applications

First, the fine-grained NER function of TexSmart supports over 1,000 entity types while most previous text understanding systems typically support several to (at most) dozens of coarse entity types (among which the most popular types are people, locations, and organizations). Large-scale fine-grained entity types are expected to provide richer semantic information for downstream NLP applications. Figure 1 shows a comparison between the NER results of a previous system and the fine-grained NER results of TexSmart. It is shown that TexSmart recognizes more entity types (e.g., work.movie) and finer-grained ones (e.g., loc.city vs. the general location type). Examples of entity types (and their important sub-types) which TexSmart is able to recognize include *people, locations, organizations, products, brands, creative work, time, numerical values, living creatures, food, drugs, diseases, academic disciplines, languages, celestial bodies, organs, events, activities, colors,* etc.

Second, TexSmart provides two advanced semantic analysis functionalities: semantic expansion, and deep semantic representation for a few entity types. These two functions are not available in most previous public text understanding systems. Semantic expansion suggests a list of related entities for an entity in the input sentence (as shown in Figure 1). It provides more information about the semantic meaning of an entity. Semantic expansion could also benefit upper-layer applications like web search (e.g., for query suggestion) and recommendation systems. For time and quantity entities, in addition to recognizing them from a sentence, TexSmart also tries to parse them into deep representations (as shown in Figure 1). This kind of deep representations is essential for some NLP applications. For example, when a chatbot is processing query

*Project lead and chief architect

[1]TexSmart is available at https://texsmart.qq.com/en, and the long version of this paper can be found in the technical report (Zhang et al., 2020).

Proceedings of the Joint Conference of the 59th Annual Meeting of the Association for Computational Linguistics and the 11th International Joint Conference on Natural Language Processing: System Demonstrations, pages 1–10, August 1st - August 6th, 2021.

(a)

No.	Entity	Type ID
1	Marvel	person
2	Los Angeles	location
3	24 months ago	time

(b) Semantic Expansion

No.	Entity	Type ID	Semantics
1	Captain Marvel	work.movie	{"related":["Batman","Superman","Wonder Woman", "Green Lantern","the flash","Aquaman","Spider-Man", "Green Arrow","Supergirl","Captain America"]}
2	Los Angeles	loc.city	{"related":["Toronto","Montreal","Vancouver","Ottawa", "Calgary","London","Paris","Chicago","Edmonton","Boston"]}
3	24 months ago	time.generic	{"value":[2019,3]}

Fine-grained NER   Deep Semantic Expression

Figure 1: Comparison between the NER results of a traditional text understanding system in (a) and the fine-grained NER and semantic analysis results provided by TexSmart in (b). The input sentence is "Captain Marvel was premiered in Los Angeles 24 months ago.". The screenshot was taken in Mar. 2021.

"please book an air ticket to London at 4 pm the day after tomorrow", it needs to know the exact time represented by "4 pm the day after tomorrow".

Third, a spectrum of algorithms is implemented for one task (e.g., part-of-speech tagging and NER) in TexSmart, to fulfill the requirements of different academic and industrial applications. On one side of the spectrum are the algorithms that are very fast but not necessarily the best in accuracy. On the opposite side are those that are relatively slow yet delivering state-of-the-art performance in terms of accuracy. Different application scenarios may have different requirements for efficiency and accuracy. Unfortunately, it is often very difficult or even impossible for a single algorithm to achieve the best in both speed and accuracy at the same time. With multiple algorithms implemented for one task, we have more chances to better fulfill the requirements of more applications.

One design principle of TexSmart is to put a lot of efforts into designing and implementing unsupervised or weakly-supervised algorithms for a task, based on large-scale structured, semi-structured, or unstructured data. The goal is to update our models easier to include fresh data with less human annotation efforts.

2 System Modules

Compared to most other public text understanding systems, TexSmart supports three unique modules, i.e., fine-grained NER, semantic expansion and deep semantic representation. Besides, traditional tasks supported by both TexSmart and many other systems include word segmentation, part-of-speech (POS) tagging, coarse-grained NER, constituency parsing, semantic role labeling, text classification and text matching. Below we first introduce the unique modules, and then describe the traditional tasks, followed by System Usage.

2.1 Key Modules

Since the implementation of fine-grained NER depends on semantic expansion, we first present semantic expansion, then fine-grained NER, and finally deep semantic representation.

2.1.1 Semantic Expansion

Given an entity within a sentence, the semantic expansion module suggests a list of entities related to the given entity. For example in Figure 1, the suggestion results for "Captain Marvel" include "Spider-Man", "Captain America", and other related movies. Semantic expansion attaches additional information to an entity mention, which could be leveraged by upper-layer applications for better understanding the entity and the source sentence. Possible applications of the expansion results include web search (e.g., for query suggestion) and recommendation systems.

Semantic expansion task was firstly introduced in Han et al. (2020), and it was addressed by a neural method. However, this method is not as efficient as one expected for some industrial applications. Therefore, we propose a light-weight alternative approach in TexSmart for this task.

This approach includes two offline steps and two online ones, as illustrated in Figure 2. During the offline procedure, Hearst patterns are first applied to a large-scale text corpus to obtain a is-a map (or called a hyponym-to-hypernym map) (Hearst, 1992; Zhang et al., 2011). Then a clustering algorithm is employed to build a collection of term clusters from all the hyponyms, allowing a hyponym to belong to multiple clusters. Each term cluster is labeled by one or more hypernyms (or called type names). Term similarity scores used in the clustering algorithm are calculated by a combination of word embedding, distributional similarity, and pattern-based methods (Mikolov et al., 2013; Song et al., 2018; Shi et al., 2010).

During the online testing time, clusters containing the target entity mention are first retrieved by referring to the cluster collection. Generally, there may be multiple (ambiguous) clusters containing the target entity mention and thus it is necessary to pick the best cluster through disambiguation. Once the best cluster is chosen, its members (or instances) can be returned as the expansion results.

Now the core challenge is how to calculate the

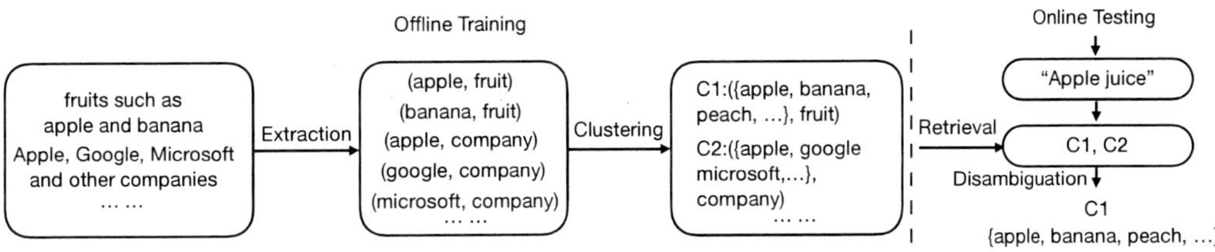

Figure 2: Key steps for semantic expansion: extraction, clustering, retrieval and disambiguation. The first two steps are conducted offline and the last two are performed online.

score of a cluster given an entity mention. We choose to compute the score as the average similarity score between a term in the cluster and a term in the context of the entity mention. Formally, suppose e is a mention in a sentence, context $\mathbf{C} = \{c_1, c_2, \cdots, c_m\}$ is a window of e within the sentence, and $\mathbf{L} = \{e_1, e_2, \cdots, e_n\}$ is a term cluster containing the entity mention (i.e., $e \in \mathbf{L}$). The cluster score is then calculated below:

$$\text{sim}(\mathbf{C}, \mathbf{L}; e) = \frac{1}{(m-1) \times (n-1)} \sum_{x \in \mathbf{C} \setminus \{e\}, y \in \mathbf{L} \setminus \{e\}} \cos(v_x, w_y) \quad (1)$$

where $\mathbf{C} \setminus \{e\}$ means excluding a subset $\{e\}$ from a set $\mathbf{C}$, v_x denotes the input word embedding of x, w_y denotes the output word embedding of y from a well-trained word embedding model, and cos is the cosine similarity function.

2.1.2 Fine-Grained NER

Generally, it is challenging to build a fine-grained NER system. Xu et al. (2020) create a fine-grained NER dataset for Chinese, but the number of its types is less than 20. A knowledge base (such as Freebase (Bollacker et al., 2008)) is utilized in Ling and Weld (2012) as distant supervision to obtain a training dataset for fine-grained NER. However, this dataset only includes about one hundred types whereas TexSmart supports up to one thousand types. Moreover, the fine-grained NER module in TexSmart does not rely on any knowledge bases and thus can be readily extended to other languages for which there is no knowledge base available.

Ontology To establish fine-grained NER in TexSmart, we need to define an ontology of entity types. The TexSmart ontology was built in a semi-automatic way, based on the term clusters in Figure 2. Please note that each term cluster is labeled by one or more hypernyms as type names of the cluster. We first conduct a simple statistics over the term clusters to get a list of popular type names (i.e., those having a lot of corresponding term clusters). Then we manually create one or more *formal types* from one popular type name and add the type name to the name list of the formal types. For example, formal type "work.movie" is manually built from type name "movie", and the word "movie" is added to the name list of "work.movie". As another example, formal types "language.human_lang" and "language.programming" are manually built from type name "language", and the word "language" is added to the name lists of both the two formal types. Each formal type is also assigned with a *sample instance list* in addition to a name list. Instances can be chosen manually from the clusters corresponding to the names of the formal type. To reduce manual efforts, the sample instance list for every type is often quite short. The supertype/subtype relation between the formal types are also specified manually. As a result, we obtain a type hierarchy containing about 1,000 formal types, each assigned with a standard id (e.g., work.movie), a list of names (e.g., "movie" and "film"), and a short list of example instances (e.g., "Star Wars"). The TexSmart ontology is available on the download page[2]. Figure 3 shows a sub-tree (with type id "loc.generic" as the root) sampled from the entire ontology.

Unsupervised method The unsupervised fine-grained NER method works in two steps. First, run the semantic expansion algorithm (referring to the previous subsection) to get the best cluster for the entity mention. Second, derive an entity type from the cluster.

For the best cluster obtained in the first step, it contains a list of terms as instances and is also labeled with a list of hypernyms (or type names). The final entity type id for the cluster is determined by a type scoring algorithm. The candidate types are those in the TexSmart ontology whose name lists contain at least one hypernym of the cluster. Please note that each entity type in the TexSmart ontology has been assigned with a name list and a sample instance list. Therefore the score of a candidate entity type can be calculated according to the information of the entity type and cluster.

This unsupervised method has a major drawback: It cannot recognize unknown entity mentions (i.e., entity mentions that are not in any of our term clusters).

[2] `https://ai.tencent.com/ailab/nlp/texsmart/en/download.html`

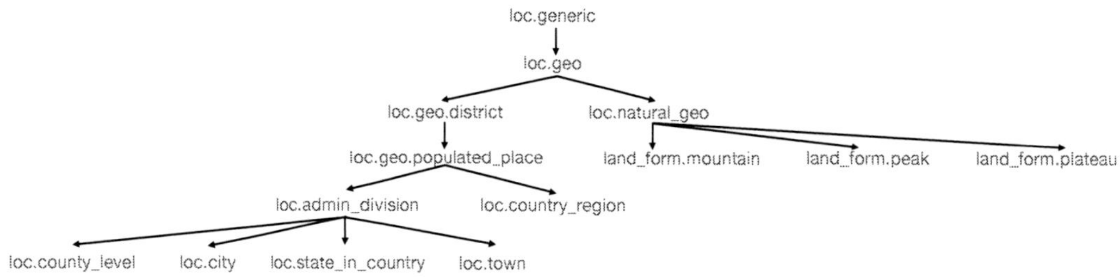

Figure 3: A sub-tree of the TexSmart ontology, with "loc.generic" as the root

Hybrid method In order to address the above issue, we propose a hybrid method for fine-grained NER. Its key idea is to combine the results of the unsupervised method and those of a coarse-grained NER model. We train a coarse-grained NER model in a supervised manner using an off-the-shelf training dataset (for example, Ontonotes dataset (Weischedel et al., 2013)). Given the supervised and unsupervised results, the combination policy is as follows: If the fine-grained type is compatible with the coarse type, i.e., the fine-grained one is a subtype of the coarse one, the fine-grained type is returned; otherwise the coarse type is chosen.

For example, assume that the entity mention "apple" in the sentence "...apple juice..." is determined as "food.fruit" by the unsupervised method and "food.generic" by the supervised model. The hybrid approach returns "food.fruit" according to the above policy. However, if the unsupervised method returns "org.company", the hybrid approach will return "food.generic" because the two types returned by the supervised method and the unsupervised method are not compatible.

Although both unsupervised and hybrid methods are described on top of the ontology manually defined above, they can actually be used for other ontologies such as those in FIGER and Ontonotes datasets, because most type names in these ontologies can be covered by our clusters obtained in semantic expansion as long as the training data is sufficient. In this sense, both methods are general in practice.

2.1.3 Deep Semantic Representation

For a time or quantity entity within a sentence, TexSmart can analyze its potential structured representation, so as to further derive its precise semantic meaning. For example in Figure 1, the deep semantic representation given by TexSmart for "24 months ago" is a structured string with a precise date in JSON format: {"value": [2019, 3]} if the screenshot time was Mar. 2021. Deep semantic representation is important for applications like task-oriented chatbots, where the precise meanings of some entities are required. So far, most public text understanding tools do not provide such a feature. As a result, applications using these tools have to implement deep semantic representation by themselves.

Some NLP toolkits make use of regular expressions or supervised sequence tagging methods to recognize time and quantity entities. However, it is difficult for those methods to derive structured or deep semantic information of entities. To overcome this problem, time and quantity entities are parsed in TexSmart by Context Free Grammar (CFG), which is more expressive than regular expressions. Its key idea is similar to that in Shi et al. (2015) and can be described as follows: First, CFG grammar rules are manually written according to possible natural language expressions of a specific entity type. Second, the Earley algorithm (Earley, 1970) is employed to parse a piece of text to obtain semantic trees of entities. Finally, deep semantic representations of entities are derived from the semantic trees.

2.2 Other Modules

Word Segmentation In order to support different application scenarios, TexSmart provides word segmentation results of two granularity levels: word level (or basic level), and phrase level. For phrase-level segmentation, some phrases (especially noun phrases) may contained as a unit. An unsupervised algorithm is implemented in TexSmart for both English and Chinese word segmentation. We choose an unsupervised method over supervised ones due to two reasons. First, it is at least 10 times faster. Second, its accuracy is good enough for most applications.

Part-of-Speech Tagging Part-of-Speech (POS) denotes the syntactic role of each word in a sentence, also known as word classes or syntactic categories and it is helpful for many downstream text understanding tasks such as parsing (Huang, 2008; Chen and Manning, 2014; Liu et al., 2018a). We implement three models among many popular ones for part-of-speech tagging (Ratnaparkhi, 1996; Huang et al., 2015; Li et al., 2021b): Log-linear based model (Ratnaparkhi, 1996), conditional random field (CRF) based model (Lafferty et al., 2001) and deep neural network (DNN) based model (Akbik et al., 2018; Liu et al., 2019). We denote them as: log_linear, crf and dnn, respectively.

Coarse-grained NER The difference between fine-grained and coarse-grained NERs is that the former involves more entity types with a finer granularity. We implement coarse-grained NER using supervised learning methods, including conditional random field (CRF) (Lafferty et al., 2001) based and deep neural network (DNN) based models (Akbik et al., 2018; Liu et al., 2019; Li et al., 2020).

Constituency Parsing We implement the constituency parsing model based on the work (Kitaev and Klein, 2018). Kitaev and Klein (2018) build the parser by combining a sentence encoder with a chart decoder based on the self-attention mechanism. Different from work (Kitaev and Klein, 2018) , we use pre-trained BERT model as the text encoder to extract features to support the subsequent decoder-based parsing. Our model achieves excellent performance and has low search complexity.

Semantic Role Labeling Semantic role labeling (also called shallow semantic parsing) tries to assign role labels to words or phrases in a sentence. TexSmart takes a sequence labeling model with BERT as the text encoder for semantic role labeling similar to Shi and Lin (2019). TexSmart supports semantic role labeling on both Chinese and English texts.

Text Classification Text Classification aims to assign a semantic label for an input text among a predefined label set. Text Classification is a classical task in NLP and it has been widely used in many applications, such as spam filtering, sentiment analysis and question classification. The predefined label set in TexSmart is available on the web page.[3]

Text Matching We implement two text matching algorithms in TexSmart: Linkage and ESIM (Chen et al., 2017). Linkage is an unsupervised algorithm designed by ourselves that incorporates synonymy information and word embedding knowledge to compute semantic similarity. Different from the previous models with complicated network architectures, ESIM carefully designs the sequential model with both local and global inference based on chain LSTMs and outperforms the counterparts.

3 System Usage

Two ways are available to use TexSmart: Calling the HTTP API directly, or downloading one version of the offline SDK. Note that for the same input text, the results from the HTTP API and the SDK may be slightly different, because the HTTP API employs a larger knowledge base and supports more text understanding tasks and algorithms. The detailed comparison between the SDK and the HTTP API is available in `https://ai.tencent.com/ailab/nlp/texsmart/en/instructions.html`.

Offline Toolkit (SDK) So far the SDK supports Linux, Windows, and Windows Subsystem for Linux (WSL). Mac OS support will be added in v0.3.0. Programming languages supported include C, C++, Python (both version 2 and version 3) and Java (version $\geq$ 1.6.0). Example codes for using the SDK with different programming languages are in the ./examples sub-folder. For example, the Python codes in ./examples/python/en_nlu_example1.py show how to use the TexSmart SDK to process an English sentence. The C++ codes in ./examples/c_cpp/src/nlu_cpp_example1.cc show how to use the SDK to analyze both an English sentence and a Chinese sentence.

HTTP API The HTTP API of TexSmart contains two parts: the text understanding API and the text matching API. The text understanding API can be accessed via HTTP-POST and the URL is available on the web page.[4] The text matching API is used to calculate the similarity between a pair of sentences. Similar to the text understanding API, the text matching API also supports access via HTTP-POST and the URL is available on the web page.[5]

4 System Evaluation

4.1 Settings

Semantic Expansion The performance of semantic expansion are evaluated based on human annotation. We first select at random 5,000 `<sentence, entity mention>` pairs (called SE pairs) from our test set of NER (to make sure that the entities selected are correct). Then our semantic expansion algorithm is applied to the SE pairs to generate a related-entity list for each pair. Top nine expansion results of each SE pair are then judged by human annotators in terms of quality and relatedness, with each result annotated by two annotators. For each result, a label of 2, 1, or 0 is assigned by each annotator. The three labels mean "highly related", "slightly related", and "not related" respectively. In calculating evaluation scores, the three labels are normalized to scores 100, 50, and 0 respectively. As there is no context for each expanded entity, it is challenging for human to annotate its ground-truth label. In fact, the overall disagreement rate between two annotators is 23.5%. To measure the quality of our model, we report the average score according to both annotators.

Fine-grained NER Ling and Weld (2012) provide a test set for fine-grained NER evaluation.

[3] `https://ai.tencent.com/ailab/nlp/texsmart/table_html/tc_label_set.html`.

[4] `https://texsmart.qq.com/api`

[5] `https://texsmart.qq.com/api/match_text`.

	SE		FGNER	
	ZH	EN	Base	Hybrid
Quality	79.5	80.5	45.9	53.8

Table 1: Semantic expansion (SE) and fine-grained NER (FGNER) evaluation results. SE is evaluated by human annotators and FGNER is evaluated by a variant of F1 score. Base denotes the supervised coarse NER model.

However, this dataset only contains about 400 sentences. In addition, it misses some important entities during human annotation, which is a common issue in building a dataset for evaluating fine-grained NER (Li et al., 2021a). Therefore, we create a larger fine-grained NER dataset, based on the Ontonotes 5.0 dataset. We ask three human annotators to label fine-grained types for each coarse-labeled entity. Since human annotators do not need to identify mentions from scratch, it would mitigate the missing entities issue to some extent. Furthermore, because it is too costly for three human annotators to annotate types from the entire ontology, we instead take a sub-ontology for human annotation which combines all types from Ling and Weld (2012) and Gillick et al. (2014), including 140 types in total. Due to ambiguous entities, there are indeed some disagreement annotations among three annotators but their overall agreement rate is respectful, i.e., the averaged pair-wise agreement rate is about 87.1% in terms of Mi-F1 scores.

	Parsing		SRL	
	EN	ZH	EN	ZH
F1	95.42	92.25	86.7	82.1
Sents/sec	16.60	16.00	10.2	11.5

Table 2: Evaluation results for constituency parsing and SRL. The decoding speed in is measured upon a GPU P40 machine.

To set the hybrid method for fine-grained NER, we select LUA (Li et al., 2020) as the coarse-grained NER model, which is trained on Ontonotes 5.0 training dataset (Weischedel et al., 2013). To compare fine-grained NER against coarse-grained NER, we report a variant of F1 measure for evaluation which only differs from standard F1 in matching count accumulation: if an output type is a fine-grained type and it exactly matches a gold fine-grained type, the matching count accumulates 1; if an output is a coarse grained type and it is compatible with a gold fine-grained type, the matching count accumulates 0.5.

POS Tagging We evaluate three POS tagging algorithms: log-linear, CRF, and DNN. They are all trained on the standard training datasets from PTB for English and CTB 9.0 for Chinese. We use their corresponding test sets to evaluate all the models.

Coarse-grained NER To ensure better generalization to industrial applications, we combine several public training sets together for English NER. They are CoNLL2003 (Sang and De Meulder, 2003), BTC (Derczynski et al., 2016), GMB (Bos et al., 2017), SEC_FILING (Alvarado et al., 2015), WikiGold (Balasuriya et al., 2009; Nothman et al., 2013), and WNUT17 (Derczynski et al., 2017). Since the label set for all these datasets are slightly different, we only maintain three common labels (Person, Location and Organization) for training and testing. For Chinese, we create a NER dataset including about 80 thousand sentences labeled with 12 entity types, by following a similar guideline to that of the Ontonotes dataset. We randomly split it into a training set and a test set with ratio of 3:1. We evaluate two algorithms for coarse-grained NER: CRF and DNN. For DNN, we implement the RoBERTa-CRF and Flair models. As we found RoBERTa-CRF performs better on the Chinese dataset while Flair is better on the English dataset, we report results of RoBERTa-CRF for Chinese and Flair for English in our experiments.

Constituency Parsing We conduct parsing experiments on both English and Chinese datasets. For English task, we use WSJ sections in Penn Treebank (PTB) (Marcus et al., 1993), and we follow the standard splits: the training data ranges from section 2 to section 21; the development data is section 24; and the test data is section 23. For Chinese task, we use the Penn Chinese Treebank (CTB) of the version 5.1 (Xue et al., 2005). The training data includes the articles 001-270 and articles 440-1151; the development data is the articles 301- 325; and the test data is the articles 271-300.

SRL Semantic role labeling experiments are conducted on both English and Chinese datasets. We use the CoNLL 2012 datasets (Pradhan et al., 2013) and follow the standard splits for the training, development and test sets. The network parameters of our model are initialized using RoBERTa. The batch size is set to 32 and the learning rate is $5{\times}10^{-5}$.

Text Matching Two text matching algorithms are evaluated: ESIM and Linkage. The datasets used in evaluating English text matching are MRPC[6] and QUORA[7]. For Chinese text matching, four datasets are involved: LCQMC (Liu et al., 2018b), AFQMC (Xu et al., 2020), BQ_CORPUS (Chen et al., 2018), and PAWS-zh (Zhang et al., 2019). We evaluate the quality

[6] `https://www.microsoft.com/en-us/download/details.aspx?id=52398`.

[7] `https://www.quora.com/q/quoradata/First-Quora-Dataset-Release-Question-Pairs`.

	POS Tagging						Coarse-grained NER			
	Log-linear		CRF		DNN		CRF		DNN	
	EN	ZH	EN	ZH	EN	ZH	EN	ZH	EN	ZH
F1	96.76	93.94	96.50	93.73	97.04	98.08	73.24	67.26	83.12	75.23
Sents/sec	3.9K		1.3K		149		1.1K		107	

Table 3: Evaluation results for some POS Tagging and coarse-grained NER algorithms in TexSmart on both English (EN) and Chinese (ZH) datasets. The English and Chinese NER datasets are labeled with 3 and 12 entity types respectively.

Algorithms	Sents/Sec	English		Chinese			
		MRPC	QUORA	LCQMC	AFQMC	BQ_CORPUS	PAWS-zh
ESIM	861	-	-	82.63	51.30	71.05	61.55
Linkage	1973	82.18	74.94	79.26	48.66	71.23	62.30

Table 4: Text matching evaluation results. ESIM is a supervised algorithm and it is trained on an in-house labeled dataset only for Chinese. Linkage is an unsupervised algorithm and it is trained for both English and Chinese.

and speed for both ESIM and Linkage algorithms in terms of F1 score and sentences per second, respectively. Since we have not trained the English version of ESIM yet, the corresponding evaluation results are not reported.

4.2 Evaluation Results

Table 1 shows the evaluation results of semantic expansion and fine-grained NER. For semantic expansion, it is shown that TexSmart achieves an accuracy of about 80.0 on both English and Chinese datasets. It is a pretty good performance. For fine-grained NER, it is observed that the hybrid approach performs much better than the supervised model (LUA).

Evaluation results for constituency parsing and semantic role labeling are summarized in Table 2. For constituency parsing, the F1 scores on the English and Chinese test sets are 95.42 and 92.25, respectively. The decoding speed depends on the input sentence length. It can process 16.6 and 16.0 sentences per second on our test sets. For SRL, the F1 scores on the English and Chinese test sets are 86.7 and 82.1 respectively and it processes about 10 sentences per second. The speed may be not efficient enough for some applications. As future work, we plan to design more efficient syntactic parsing and SRL algorithms.

The evaluation results for POS Tagging and coarse-grained NER are listed in Table 3. The speed values in this table are measured in sentences per second and they are measured upon a machine with `Platinum 8255C CPU @ 2.50GHz`. Please note that the speed results for Log-linear and CRF are obtained using one single thread, while the speed results for DNN are on 6 threads.

It is clear from the POS tagging results that the three algorithms form a spectrum. On one side of the spectrum is the log-linear algorithm, which is very fast but less accurate than the DNN algorithm. On the opposite side is the DNN algorithm, which achieves the best accuracy but are much slower than the other two algorithms. The CRF algorithm is in the middle of the spectrum.

Also from Table 3, we can see that the two coarse-grained NER algorithms form another spectrum. The CRF algorithm is on the high-speed side, while the DNN algorithm is on the high-accuracy side. Note that for DNN methods in this table, we employ a data augmentation method to improve their generalization abilities and a knowledge distillation method to speed up its inference (Hinton et al., 2015).

Table 4 shows the performance of two algorithms for text matching. We can see from this table that, in terms of speed, both algorithms are fairly efficient. Please note that the speed is measured in sentences per second using one single CPU from a machine with `Platinum 8255C CPU @ 2.50GHz`. In terms of accuracy, their performance comparison depends on the dataset being used. ESIM performs apparently better on the first two datasets, while slightly worse on the last one. Applications may need to test on their datasets before making decision between the two algorithms.

5 Conclusion

In this paper we have presented TexSmart, a text understanding system that supports fine-grained NER, enhanced semantic analysis, as well as some common text understanding functionalities. We have introduced the main functions of TexSmart and key algorithms for implementing the functions. We have also reported some evaluation results on major modules of TexSmart.

References

Alan Akbik, Duncan Blythe, and Roland Vollgraf. 2018. Contextual string embeddings for sequence labeling. In *COLING 2018, 27th International Conference on Computational Linguistics*, pages 1638–1649.

Julio Cesar Salinas Alvarado, Karin Verspoor, and Timothy Baldwin. 2015. Domain adaption of named entity recognition to support credit risk assessment. In *Proceedings of the Australasian Language Technology Association Workshop 2015*, pages 84–90.

Dominic Balasuriya, Nicky Ringland, Joel Nothman, Tara Murphy, and James R Curran. 2009. Named entity recognition in wikipedia. In *Proceedings of the 2009 Workshop on The People's Web Meets NLP: Collaboratively Constructed Semantic Resources (People's Web)*, pages 10–18.

Kurt Bollacker, Colin Evans, Praveen Paritosh, Tim Sturge, and Jamie Taylor. 2008. Freebase: a collaboratively created graph database for structuring human knowledge. In *Proceedings of the 2008 ACM SIGMOD international conference on Management of data*, pages 1247–1250.

Johan Bos, Valerio Basile, Kilian Evang, Noortje Venhuizen, and Johannes Bjerva. 2017. The groningen meaning bank. In Nancy Ide and James Pustejovsky, editors, *Handbook of Linguistic Annotation*, volume 2, pages 463–496. Springer.

Wanxiang Che, Zhenghua Li, and Ting Liu. 2010. Ltp: A chinese language technology platform. In *Coling 2010: Demonstrations*, pages 13–16.

Danqi Chen and Christopher Manning. 2014. A fast and accurate dependency parser using neural networks. In *Proceedings of the 2014 Conference on Empirical Methods in Natural Language Processing (EMNLP)*, pages 740–750.

Jing Chen, Qingcai Chen, Xin Liu, Haijun Yang, Daohe Lu, and Buzhou Tang. 2018. The BQ corpus: A large-scale domain-specific Chinese corpus for sentence semantic equivalence identification. In *Proceedings of the 2018 Conference on Empirical Methods in Natural Language Processing*.

Qian Chen, Xiao-Dan Zhu, Z. Ling, Si Wei, Hui Jiang, and Diana Inkpen. 2017. Enhanced lstm for natural language inference. In *ACL*.

Leon Derczynski, Kalina Bontcheva, and Ian Roberts. 2016. Broad twitter corpus: A diverse named entity recognition resource. In *Proceedings of COLING 2016, the 26th International Conference on Computational Linguistics: Technical Papers*, pages 1169–1179.

Leon Derczynski, Eric Nichols, Marieke van Erp, and Nut Limsopatham. 2017. Results of the wnut2017 shared task on novel and emerging entity recognition. In *Proceedings of the 3rd Workshop on Noisy User-generated Text*, pages 140–147.

Jay Earley. 1970. An efficient context-free parsing algorithm. *Communications of the ACM*, 13(2):94–102.

Matt Gardner, Joel Grus, Mark Neumann, Oyvind Tafjord, Pradeep Dasigi, Nelson F. Liu, Matthew Peters, Michael Schmitz, and Luke Zettlemoyer. 2018. AllenNLP: A deep semantic natural language processing platform. In *Proceedings of Workshop for NLP Open Source Software (NLP-OSS)*, pages 1–6, Melbourne, Australia. Association for Computational Linguistics.

Dan Gillick, Nevena Lazic, Kuzman Ganchev, Jesse Kirchner, and David Huynh. 2014. Context-dependent fine-grained entity type tagging. *arXiv preprint arXiv:1412.1820*.

Jialong Han, Aixin Sun, Haisong Zhang, Chenliang Li, and Shuming Shi. 2020. Case: Context-aware semantic expansion. In *AAAI*, pages 7871–7878.

Marti A Hearst. 1992. Automatic acquisition of hyponyms from large text corpora. In *Coling 1992 volume 2: The 15th international conference on computational linguistics*.

Geoffrey Hinton, Oriol Vinyals, and Jeff Dean. 2015. Distilling the knowledge in a neural network. *arXiv preprint arXiv:1503.02531*.

Liang Huang. 2008. Forest reranking: Discriminative parsing with non-local features. In *Proceedings of ACL-08: HLT*, pages 586–594.

Zhiheng Huang, Wei Xu, and Kai Yu. 2015. Bidirectional lstm-crf models for sequence tagging. In *Proceedings of ACL*.

Nikita Kitaev and D. Klein. 2018. Constituency parsing with a self-attentive encoder. In *ACL*.

John Lafferty, Andrew McCallum, and Fernando CN Pereira. 2001. Conditional random fields: Probabilistic models for segmenting and labeling sequence data.

Yangming Li, Lemao Liu, and Shuming Shi. 2020. Segmenting natural language sentences via lexical unit analysis. *arXiv preprint arXiv:2012.05418*.

Yangming Li, Lemao Liu, and Shuming Shi. 2021a. Empirical analysis of unlabeled entity problem in named entity recognition. In *Proceedings of ICLR*.

Yangming Li, Lemao Liu, and Kaisheng Yao. 2021b. Neural sequence segmentation as determining the leftmost segments. In *Proceedings of NAACL*.

Xiao Ling and Daniel S Weld. 2012. Fine-grained entity recognition. In *AAAI*, volume 12, pages 94–100.

Lemao Liu, Muhua Zhu, and Shuming Shi. 2018a. Improving sequence-to-sequence constituency parsing. In *Proceedings of the AAAI Conference on Artificial Intelligence*, volume 32.

Xin Liu, Qingcai Chen, Chong Deng, Huajun Zeng, Jing Chen, Dongfang Li, and Buzhou Tang. 2018b. LCQMC:a large-scale Chinese question matching corpus. In *Proceedings of the 27th International Conference on Computational Linguistics*.

Yinhan Liu, Myle Ott, Naman Goyal, Jingfei Du, Mandar Joshi, Danqi Chen, Omer Levy, Mike Lewis, Luke Zettlemoyer, and Veselin Stoyanov. 2019. Roberta: A robustly optimized bert pretraining approach. *arXiv preprint arXiv:1907.11692*.

Edward Loper and Steven Bird. 2002. Nltk: the natural language toolkit. In *Proceedings of the ACL-02 Workshop on Effective tools and methodologies for teaching natural language processing and computational linguistics*.

Christopher D Manning, Mihai Surdeanu, John Bauer, Jenny Rose Finkel, Steven Bethard, and David McClosky. 2014. The stanford corenlp natural language processing toolkit. In *Proceedings of 52nd annual meeting of the association for computational linguistics: system demonstrations*, pages 55–60.

Mitchell Marcus, Beatrice Santorini, and Mary Ann Marcinkiewicz. 1993. Building a large annotated corpus of english: The penn treebank.

Tomas Mikolov, Ilya Sutskever, Kai Chen, Greg S Corrado, and Jeff Dean. 2013. Distributed representations of words and phrases and their compositionality. *Advances in neural information processing systems*, 26:3111–3119.

Joel Nothman, Nicky Ringland, Will Radford, Tara Murphy, and James R Curran. 2013. Learning multilingual named entity recognition from wikipedia. *Artificial Intelligence*, 194:151–175.

OpenNLP. https://opennlp.apache.org.

Sameer Pradhan, Alessandro Moschitti, Nianwen Xue, Hwee Tou Ng, Anders Björkelund, Olga Uryupina, Yuchen Zhang, and Zhi Zhong. 2013. Towards robust linguistic analysis using ontonotes. In *Proceedings of the Seventeenth Conference on Computational Natural Language Learning*, pages 143–152.

Xipeng Qiu, Qi Zhang, and Xuan-Jing Huang. 2013. Fudannlp: A toolkit for chinese natural language processing. In *Proceedings of the 51st Annual Meeting of the Association for Computational Linguistics: System Demonstrations*, pages 49–54.

Adwait Ratnaparkhi. 1996. A maximum entropy model for part-of-speech tagging. In *Conference on empirical methods in natural language processing*.

Erik F Sang and Fien De Meulder. 2003. Introduction to the conll-2003 shared task: Language-independent named entity recognition. *arXiv preprint cs/0306050*.

Peng Shi and Jimmy Lin. 2019. Simple bert models for relation extraction and semantic role labeling. *arXiv preprint arXiv:1904.05255*.

Shuming Shi, Yuehui Wang, Chin-Yew Lin, Xiaojiang Liu, and Yong Rui. 2015. Automatically solving number word problems by semantic parsing and reasoning. In *Proceedings of the 2015 Conference on Empirical Methods in Natural Language Processing*, pages 1132–1142.

Shuming Shi, Huibin Zhang, Xiaojie Yuan, and Ji-Rong Wen. 2010. Corpus-based semantic class mining: distributional vs. pattern-based approaches. In *Proceedings of the 23rd International Conference on Computational Linguistics (Coling 2010)*, pages 993–1001.

Yan Song, Shuming Shi, Jing Li, and Haisong Zhang. 2018. Directional skip-gram: Explicitly distinguishing left and right context for word embeddings. In *Proceedings of the 2018 Conference of the North American Chapter of the Association for Computational Linguistics: Human Language Technologies, Volume 2 (Short Papers)*, pages 175–180.

Ralph Weischedel, Martha Palmer, Mitchell Marcus, Eduard Hovy, Sameer Pradhan, Lance Ramshaw, Nianwen Xue, Ann Taylor, Jeff Kaufman, Michelle Franchini, et al. 2013. Ontonotes release 5.0 ldc2013t19. *Linguistic Data Consortium, Philadelphia, PA*, 23.

Liang Xu, Xuanwei Zhang, Lu Li, Hai Hu, Chenjie Cao, Weitang Liu, Junyi Li, Yudong Li, Kai Sun, Yechen Xu, et al. 2020. Clue: A chinese language understanding evaluation benchmark. *arXiv preprint arXiv:2004.05986*.

Naiwen Xue, Fei Xia, Fu-Dong Chiou, and Marta Palmer. 2005. The penn chinese treebank: Phrase structure annotation of a large corpus. *Natural language engineering*, 11(2):207.

Fan Zhang, Shuming Shi, Jing Liu, Shuqi Sun, and Chin-Yew Lin. 2011. Nonlinear evidence fusion and propagation for hyponymy relation mining. In *Proceedings of the 49th Annual Meeting of the Association for Computational Linguistics: Human Language Technologies*, pages 1159–1168.

Haisong Zhang, Lemao Liu, Haiyun Jiang, Yangming Li, Enbo Zhao, Kun Xu, Linfeng Song, Suncong Zheng, Botong Zhou, Jianchen Zhu, et al. 2020. Texsmart: A text understanding system for fine-grained ner and enhanced semantic analysis. *arXiv preprint arXiv:2012.15639*.

Yuan Zhang, Jason Baldridge, and Luheng He. 2019. PAWS: paraphrase adversaries from word scrambling. *CoRR*, abs/1904.01130.

IntelliCAT: Intelligent Machine Translation Post-Editing with Quality Estimation and Translation Suggestion

Dongjun Lee[1], Junhyeong Ahn[1], Heesoo Park[1], Jaemin Jo[2]

[1]Bering Lab, Republic of Korea
[2]Sungkyunkwan University, Republic of Korea
{djlee, rkdrnf, heesoo.park}@beringlab.com, jmjo@skku.edu

Abstract

We present IntelliCAT, an interactive translation interface with neural models that streamline the post-editing process on machine translation output. We leverage two quality estimation (QE) models at different granularities: sentence-level QE, to predict the quality of each machine-translated sentence, and word-level QE, to locate the parts of the machine-translated sentence that need correction. Additionally, we introduce a novel translation suggestion model conditioned on both the left and right contexts, providing alternatives for specific words or phrases for correction. Finally, with word alignments, IntelliCAT automatically preserves the original document's styles in the translated document. The experimental results show that post-editing based on the proposed QE and translation suggestions can significantly improve translation quality. Furthermore, a user study reveals that three features provided in IntelliCAT significantly accelerate the post-editing task, achieving a 52.9% speedup in translation time compared to translating from scratch. The interface is publicly available at https://intellicat.beringlab.com/.

1 Introduction

Existing computer-aided translation (CAT) tools incorporate machine translation (MT) in two ways: post-editing (PE) or interactive translation prediction (ITP). PE tools (Federico et al., 2014; Pal et al., 2016) provide a machine-translated document and ask the translator to edit incorrect parts. By contrast, ITP tools (Alabau et al., 2014; Green et al., 2014a; Santy et al., 2019) aim to provide translation suggestions for the next word or phrase given a partial input from the translator. A recent study with human translators revealed that PE was 18.7% faster than ITP in terms of translation time (Green et al., 2014b) and required fewer edits (Do Carmo, 2020). However, many translators still prefer ITP over PE because of (1) high cognitive loads (Koehn, 2009) and (2) the lack of subsegment MT suggestions (Moorkens and O'Brien, 2017) in PE.

In this paper, we introduce IntelliCAT[1], a hybrid CAT interface designed to provide PE-level efficiency while retaining the advantages of ITP, such as subsegment translation suggestions. To mitigate the cognitive loads of human translators, IntelliCAT aims to automate common post-editing tasks by introducing three intelligent features: (1) quality estimation, (2) translation suggestion, and (3) word alignment.

Quality estimation (QE) is the task of estimating the quality of MT output without reference translations (Specia et al., 2020). We integrate QE into the CAT interface so that the human translator can easily identify which machine-translated sentences and which parts of the sentences require corrections. Furthermore, for words that require post-editing, our interface suggests possible translations to reduce the translators' cognitive load. Finally, based on word alignments, the interface aligns the source and translated documents in terms of formatting by transferring the styles applied in the source document (e.g., bold, hyperlink, footnote, equation) to the translated document to minimize the post-editing time. Our contributions are:

- We integrate state-of-the-art sentence-level and word-level QE (Lee, 2020) techniques into an interactive CAT tool, IntelliCAT.
- We introduce a novel words and phrases suggestion model, which is conditioned on both the left and right contexts, based on XLM-RoBERTa (Conneau et al., 2020). The model is fine-tuned with a modified translation language modeling (TLM) objective (Lample and Conneau, 2019).

[1]A demonstration video is available at https://youtu.be/mDmbdrQE9tc

Proceedings of the Joint Conference of the 59th Annual Meeting of the Association for Computational Linguistics and the 11th International Joint Conference on Natural Language Processing: System Demonstrations, pages 11–19, August 1st - August 6th, 2021.

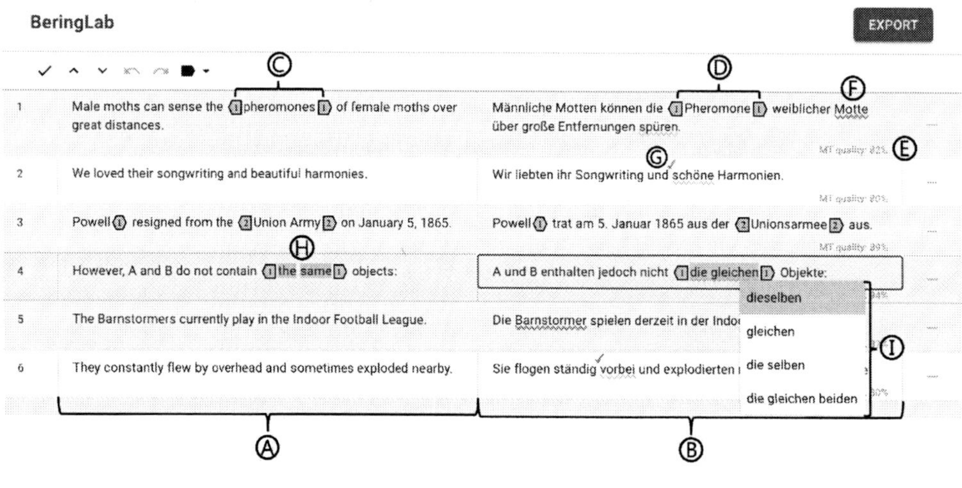

Figure 1: The IntelliCAT Interface. After a document (i.e., an MS Word file) is uploaded, (A) sentences from the original document (source) and (B) the initial MT output for each sentence (target) are shown side-by-side. (C) Formatting tags indicate where a specific style (identified by an integer style id) is applied and (D) are automatically inserted at the proper position of the MT output based on word alignments. (E) The interface shows the quality of each machine-translated sentence based on sentence-level QE. (F) Potentially incorrect words and (G) locations of missing words are highlighted based on word-level QE. When the user selects a sequence of words in the MT output, (H) the corresponding words in the source sentence are highlighted with a heat map, and (I) up to five alternative translations are recommended.

- We conduct quantitative experiments and a user study to evaluate IntelliCAT.

The experimental results on the WMT 2020 English-German QE dataset show that post-editing with the proposed QE and translation suggestion models could significantly improve the translation quality (−6.01 TER and +6.15 BLEU). Moreover, the user study shows that the three features provided by IntelliCAT significantly reduce post-editing time (19.2%), which led to a 52.6% reduction in translation time compared to translating from scratch. Finally, translators evaluate our interface to be highly effective, with a SUS score of 88.61.

2 Related Work

CAT Tool and Post-Editing In the localization industry, the use of CAT tools is a common practice for professional translators (Van den Bergh et al., 2015). As MT has improved substantially in recent years, approaches incorporating MT into CAT tools have been actively researched (Alabau et al., 2014; Federico et al., 2014; Santy et al., 2019; Herbig et al., 2020). One of the approaches is post-editing in which the translator is provided with a machine-translated draft and asked to improve the draft. Recent studies demonstrate that post-editing MT output not only improves translation productivity but also reduces translation errors (Green et al., 2013; Aranberri et al., 2014; Toral et al., 2018).

Translation Suggestion Translation suggestions from interactive translation prediction (ITP) (Alabau et al., 2014; Santy et al., 2019; Coppers et al., 2018) are conditioned only on the left context of the word to be inserted. Therefore, ITP has intrinsic limitations in post-editing tasks where the complete sentence is presented, and the right context of the words that need correction should also be considered. We propose a novel translation suggestion model in which suggestions are conditioned on both the left and right contexts of the words or phrases to be modified or inserted to provide more accurate suggestions when post-editing the complete sentence.

Cross-Lingual Language Model Cross-lingual language models (XLMs), which are language models pre-trained in multiple languages, have led to advances in MT (Lample and Conneau, 2019) and related tasks such as QE (Lee, 2020), automatic post-editing (Wang et al., 2020; Lee et al.,

2020), and parallel corpus filtering (Lo and Joanis, 2020). Accordingly, our QE and translation suggestion models are trained on top of XLM-R (Conneau et al., 2020), an XLM that shows state-of-the-art performance for a wide range of cross-lingual tasks. To the best of our knowledge, IntelliCAT is the first CAT interface that leverages XLM to assist human post-editing for MT outputs.

3 System Description

3.1 Overview

IntelliCAT is a web-based interactive interface for post-editing MT outputs (Figure 1). Once loaded, it shows two documents side-by-side: the uploaded original document (an MS Word file) on the left and the machine-translated document on the right. Each document is displayed as a list of sentences with *formatting tags* inserted, tags that show the style of the original document, including text styles (e.g., bold, italic, or hyperlinked) and inline contents (e.g., a media element or an equation).

The user can post-edit MT outputs on the right using the following three features: (1) sentence-level and word-level QE, (2) word or phrase suggestion, and (3) automatic tagging based on word alignments. The sentence-level QE shows the estimated MT quality for each sentence, and word-level QE highlights the parts of each machine-translated sentence that need correction. When the user selects a specific word or phrase, the top-5 recommended alternatives appear below, allowing the user to replace the selected words or insert a new word. Finally, the system automatically captures the original document style and inserts formatting tags in machine-translated sentences at the appropriate locations. After post-editing, the user can click on the export button to download the translated document with the original style preserved. A sample document and its translated document without human post-editing is presented in Appendix A.

3.2 Machine Translation

Our system provides MT for each sentence in the input document. We build our NMT model based on Transformer (Vaswani et al., 2017) using OpenNMT-py (Klein et al., 2017). As training data, the English-German parallel corpus provided in the 2020 News Translation Task (Barrault et al., 2020) is used. We use unigram-LM-based subword segmentation (Kudo, 2018) with a vocabulary size of 32K for English and German, respectively, and the remaining hyperparameters follow the base model of Vaswani et al. (2017).

3.3 Quality Estimation

Quality estimation (QE) is the task of estimating the quality of the MT output, given only the source text (Fonseca et al., 2019). We estimate the quality at two different granularities: sentence and word levels. Sentence-level QE aims to predict the human translation error rate (HTER) (Snover et al., 2006) of a machine-translated sentence, which measures the required amount of human editing to fix the the machine-translated sentence. By contrast, word-level QE aims to predict whether each word in the MT output is `OK` or `BAD` and whether there are missing words between each word.

Figure 1 demonstrates the use of QE in our interface. Based on the sentence-level QE, we show the MT quality for each machine-translated sentence computed as $1 - (predicted\ HTER)$. In addition, based on word-level QE, we show words that need to be corrected (with red or yellow underlines) or locations for missing words (with red or yellow checkmarks). To display the confidence of word-level QE predictions, we encode the predicted probability of the color of underlines and checkmarks (yellow for $P_{BAD} > 0.5$ and red for $P_{BAD} > 0.8$).

For QE training, we use a two-phase cross-lingual language model fine-tuning approach following Lee (2020), which showed the state-of-the-art performance on the WMT 2020 QE Shared Task (Specia et al., 2020). We fine-tune XLM-RoBERTa (Conneau et al., 2020) with a few additional parameters to jointly train sentence-level and word-level QEs. We train our model in two phases. First, we pre-train the model with a large artificially generated QE dataset based on a parallel corpus. Subsequently, we fine-tune the model with the WMT 2020 English-German QE dataset (Specia et al., 2020), which consists of 7,000 triplets consisting of source, MT, and post-edited sentences.

3.4 Translation Suggestion

As shown in Figure 1, when the user selects a specific word or phrase to modify or presses a hotkey (`ALT+s`) between words to insert a missing word, the system suggests the top-5 alternatives based on fine-tuned XLM-R.

XLM-R Fine-Tuning For translation suggestion, we fine-tune XLM-R with a modified translation language modeling (TLM) objective (Lample and Conneau, 2019), which is designed to better predict the masked spans of text in the translation. Following Lample and Conneau (2019), we tokenize source (English) and target (German) sentences with the shared BPE model (Sennrich et al., 2016), and concatenate the source and target tokens with a separation token (</s>). Unlike the TLM objective of Lample and Conneau (2019), which randomly masked tokens in both the source and target sentences, we only mask tokens in target sentences since the complete source sentence is always given in the translation task. We randomly replace $p\%$ ($p \in [15, 20, 25]$) of the BPE tokens in the target sentences by <mask> tokens and train the model to predict the actual tokens for the masks. In addition, motivated by SpanBERT (Joshi et al., 2020), we always mask complete words instead of sub-word tokens since translation suggestion requires predictions of complete words. As training data, we use the same parallel corpus that is used for MT training.

Inference To suggest alternative translations for the selected sequence of words, we first replace it with multiple <mask> tokens. The alternative translations may consist of sub-word tokens of varying lengths. Hence, we generate m inputs, where m denotes the maximum number of masks, and in the ith input ($i \in [1, ..., m]$), the selected sequence is replaced with i consecutive <mask> tokens. In other words, we track all cases in which alternative translations consist of 1 to m sub-word tokens. Then, each input is fed into the fine-tuned XLM-R, and <mask> tokens are iteratively replaced by the predicted tokens from left to right. In each iteration, we use a beam search with a beam size k to generate the top-k candidates. Finally, all mask prediction results from m inputs are sorted based on probability, and the top-k results are shown to the user.

3.5 Word Alignment and Automatic Formatting

To obtain word alignments, we jointly train the NMT model (§3.2) to produce both translations and alignments following Garg et al. (2019). One attention head on the Transformer's penultimate layer is supervised with an alignment loss to learn the alignments. We use Giza++ (Och and Ney, 2003) alignments as the guided labels for the training. As sub-word segmentation is used to train the NMT model, we convert the sub-word-level alignments back to the word-level. We consider each target word to be aligned with a source word if any of the target sub-words is aligned with the source sub-words.

We provide two features based on word alignment information. First, when the user selects a specific word or phrase in the machine-translated sentence, the corresponding words or phrases in the source sentence are highlighted using a heatmap. Second, formatting tags are automatically inserted at the appropriate locations in the machine-translated sentences. We use two types of tags to represent the formatting of the document: paired tags and unpaired tags. Paired tags represent styles applied across a section of text (e.g., bold or italic). To retain the style applied in the source sentence to the MT, we identify the source word with the highest alignment score for each target word and apply the the corresponding source word's style to the target word. By contrast, unpaired tags represent inline non-text contents such as media elements and equations. To automatically insert an unpaired tag in the MT, we identify the target word with the highest alignment score with the source word right before the tag and insert the corresponding tag after the target word.

4 Experiments

4.1 Model Evaluation

Experimental Setup To evaluate the performance of translation suggestions, we measure MT quality improvement when a sentence is corrected with the suggested words or phrases. We introduce two selection conditions (**Oracle QE** and **Predicted QE**) and two suggestion methods (**XLM-R** and **Proposed**). The selection conditions locate the words that need to be corrected in a sentence; in **Oracle QE** condition, the ground truth word-level QE label is used as a baseline, and in **Predicted QE** condition, our word-level QE model is used to identify the target words. The suggestion methods determine the words that the selected words should be replaced with. We test two suggestion models, the pre-trained XLM-R[2] and the proposed model, fine-tuned with the modified TLM objective, with three different suggestion sizes: top-1, top-3, and top-5.

Each of the QE and translation suggestion models was trained using two Tesla V100 GPUs. As an

[2]https://pytext.readthedocs.io/en/master/xlm_r.html

Model	(With Predicted QE) TER↓	BLEU↑	(With Oracle QE) TER↓	BLEU↑
Baseline (MT)	31.37	50.37	31.37	50.37
XLM-R (Conneau et al., 2020)				
Top-1	30.28 (-1.09)	50.78 (+0.41)	26.57 (-4.80)	56.02(+5.65)
Top-3	29.47 (-1.90)	50.89 (+0.52)	24.10 (-7.27)	60.28 (+9.91)
Top-5	28.75 (-2.62)	51.85 (+1.48)	22.78 (-8.59)	62.40 (+12.03)
Proposed				
Top-1	**29.04 (-2.33)**	**51.93 (+1.56)**	**24.26 (-7.11)**	**59.38 (+9.01)**
Top-3	26.69 (-4.68)	54.70 (+4.33)	19.08 (-12.29)	67.51 (+17.14)
Top-5	25.36 (-6.01)	56.52 (+6.15)	17.30 (-14.07)	70.50 (+20.13)

Table 1: TER and BLEU for machine-translated sentences (Baseline) and post-edited sentences (XLM-R and Proposed) based on word-level QE and translation suggestion.

evaluation dataset, we use the WMT 2020 English-German QE *dev* dataset (Specia et al., 2020). As evaluation metrics, we use the translation error rate (TER) (Snover et al., 2006) and BLEU (Papineni et al., 2002).

Experimental Result Table 1 shows the translation quality of (1) MT sentences (baseline), (2) post-edited sentences with XLM-R-based translation suggestion, and (3) post-edited sentences with the proposed translation suggestion model. When MT sentences are post-edited based on QE prediction with the top-1 suggestion, TER and BLEU are improved over the baseline by -2.33 and $+1.56$, respectively. This result suggests that our QE and translation suggestion models can be used to improve MT performance without human intervention. When the top-5 suggestions are provided, TER and BLEU are improved by -6.01 and $+6.15$, respectively, for the QE prediction condition and improved by -14.07 and $+20.13$, respectively, for the oracle QE condition. These results imply that post-editing based on translation suggestions can significantly improve the translation quality. Finally, the proposed model significantly outperforms XLM-R in all experimental settings, showing that fine-tuning XLM-R with the modified TLM objective is effective for the suggestion performance.

4.2 User Study

We conducted a user study to evaluate the effectiveness of IntelliCAT.

Tasks and Stimuli We asked participants to translate an English document to German using the given interface. As stimuli, we prepared three English documents, each with 12 sentences and 130, 160, and 164 words. The documents included 22, 18, and 20 styles, respectively (e.g., bold, italic, or a footnote), and participants were also asked to apply these styles in the target document.

Translation Interfaces We compared three translation interfaces: **MSWord**, **MT-Only**, and **Full**. In **MSWord**, the participants were asked to translate documents using a popular word processor, Microsoft Word. In this baseline condition, two Microsoft Word instances were shown side-by-side: one showing an English document (source) and the other showing an empty document where one could type the translated sentences (target). In **MT-Only**, participants started with a machine-translated document on IntelliCAT without QE, translation suggestion, and word alignment; they had to edit incorrect parts and transfer styles by themselves. In **Full**, the participants could use all the features of IntelliCAT.

Participants and Study Design We recruited nine participants (aged 23–31 years). All participants majored in German and were fluent in both English and German. We adopted a within-subject design; each participant tested all three interfaces and three documents. Thus, our study consisted of nine (participants) $\times$ 3 (conditions) = 27 trials in total. The order of interfaces and documents was counterbalanced using a 3×3 Latin square to alleviate the possible bias of learning effects or fatigue. For each trial, we measured the translation completion time.

Procedure Participants attended a training session for ten minutes, where they tried each interface with a short sample document. Subsequently, they performed three translation tasks with different interfaces. We allowed them to look up words for which they did not know the translation before

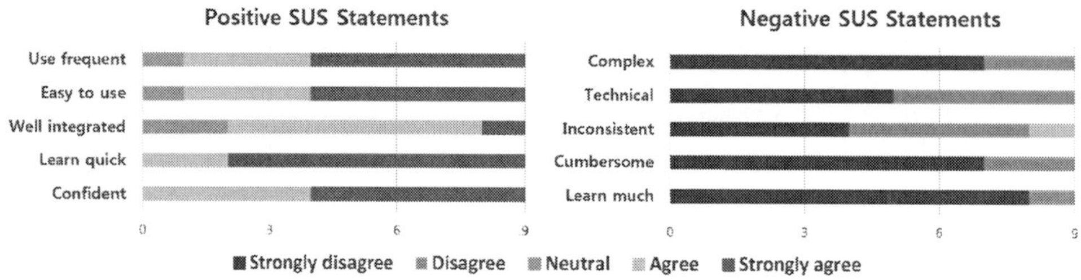

Figure 2: SUS Feedback. The usability of IntelliCAT was evaluated as an excellent level with a score of 88.61±7.82.

starting each translation task. Upon completing the three tasks, participants responded to a system usability scale (SUS) questionnaire (Brooke, 1996), and we gathered subjective feedback. The entire session took approximately 90 min per participant.

Interface	Avg. time (s)
MSWord	1178.78 ± 280.41
MT-Only	688.00 ± 175.02
Full	$\mathbf{555.66 \pm 200.81}$

Table 2: Translation completion time. The differences between the three interface conditions are statistically significant.

Result and Discussion Table 2 summarizes the result of the user study. A repeated measures ANOVA with a Greenhouse-Geisser correction found a significant difference in completion time between the three translation interfaces ($F(1.306, 10.449) = 56.398$, $p < 0.001$). Post hoc tests using the Bonferroni correction revealed that **Full** (555.66 ± 200.81 s) was significantly faster than **MT-Only** (688.00 ± 175.02 s) ($p = 0.013$) and **MT-Only** was significantly faster than **MSWord** (1,178.78 ± 280.41 s) ($p < 0.001$). These results suggest that our QE, translation suggestion, and word alignment features could further accelerate post-editing (a 19.2% speedup) (**Full** vs. **MT-Only**), and our system could reduce the translation time by more than half (52.9%) compared to translating from scratch (**Full** vs. **MSWord**).

We could not find a significant difference between documents ($F(1.964, 15.712) = 0.430$, ns) with the same statistical procedure, which suggests that the translation difficulties of the three English documents were not statistically different.

Our interface received a mean SUS score of 88.61 ($\sigma = 7.82$), which is slightly higher than the score for an "Excellent" adjective ratings (85.58, Bangor et al. (2008)). Eight out of nine participants reported that QE was useful for proofreading purposes; P2 stated, "With QE, I could double-check the words that are possibly wrong." All participants evaluated the translation suggestions to be useful; P7 mentioned "Translation suggestion was very convenient. It might significantly reduce the dependence on the dictionary."

Overall, the user study results demonstrated the effectiveness of IntelliCAT both quantitatively and qualitatively, and we found that human translators could streamline their post-editing process with the three features provided in IntelliCAT.

5 Conclusion and Future Work

In this paper, we introduce IntelliCAT, an intelligent MT post-editing interface for document translation. The interface provides three neural network-based features to assist post-editing: (1) sentence-level and word-level QEs, (2) alternative translation suggestions for words or phrases, and (3) automatic formatting of the translated document based on word alignments. The model evaluation shows that post-editing based on the proposed QE and translation suggestion models can significantly improve the quality of translation. Moreover, the user study shows that these features significantly accelerate post-editing, achieving a 52.9% speedup in translation time compared to translating from scratch. Finally, the usability of IntelliCAT was evaluated as an "excellent" level, with a SUS score of 88.61.

In future work, we will build a pipeline that continuously improves the performance of neural models based on automatically collected triplets consisting of source, MT, and post-edited sentences. We will implement an automatic post-editing (Chatterjee et al., 2020) model to continuously improve MT performance and apply online learning to QE models to continually enhance QE performance.

References

Vicent Alabau, Christian Buck, Michael Carl, Francisco Casacuberta, Mercedes García-Martínez, Ulrich Germann, Jesús González-Rubio, Robin Hill, Philipp Koehn, Luis A Leiva, et al. 2014. Casmacat: A computer-assisted translation workbench. In *Proceedings of the Demonstrations at the 14th Conference of the European Chapter of the Association for Computational Linguistics*, pages 25–28.

Nora Aranberri, Gorka Labaka, A Diaz de Ilarraza, and Kepa Sarasola. 2014. Comparison of post-editing productivity between professional translators and lay users. In *Proceeding of AMTA Third Workshop on Post-editing Technology and Practice (WPTP-3), Vancouver, Canada*, pages 20–33.

Aaron Bangor, Philip T Kortum, and James T Miller. 2008. An empirical evaluation of the system usability scale. *Intl. Journal of Human–Computer Interaction*, 24(6):574–594.

Loïc Barrault, Magdalena Biesialska, Ondřej Bojar, Marta R Costa-jussà, Christian Federmann, Yvette Graham, Roman Grundkiewicz, Barry Haddow, Matthias Huck, Eric Joanis, et al. 2020. Findings of the 2020 conference on machine translation (wmt20). In *Proceedings of the Fifth Conference on Machine Translation*, pages 1–55.

Jan Van den Bergh, Eva Geurts, Donald Degraen, Mieke Haesen, Iulianna Van der Lek-Ciudin, Karin Coninx, et al. 2015. Recommendations for translation environments to improve translators' workflows. *Translating and the Computer*, 37:106–119.

John Brooke. 1996. Sus: a "quick and dirty'usability. *Usability evaluation in industry*, 189.

Rajen Chatterjee, Markus Freitag, Matteo Negri, and Marco Turchi. 2020. Findings of the wmt 2020 shared task on automatic post-editing. In *Proceedings of the Fifth Conference on Machine Translation*, pages 646–659.

Alexis Conneau, Kartikay Khandelwal, Naman Goyal, Vishrav Chaudhary, Guillaume Wenzek, Francisco Guzmán, Édouard Grave, Myle Ott, Luke Zettlemoyer, and Veselin Stoyanov. 2020. Unsupervised cross-lingual representation learning at scale. In *Proceedings of the 58th Annual Meeting of the Association for Computational Linguistics*, pages 8440–8451.

Sven Coppers, Jan Van den Bergh, Kris Luyten, Karin Coninx, Iulianna Van der Lek-Ciudin, Tom Vanallemeersch, and Vincent Vandeghinste. 2018. Intellingo: An intelligible translation environment. In *Proceedings of the 2018 CHI Conference on Human Factors in Computing Systems*, pages 1–13.

Félix Do Carmo. 2020. Comparing post-editing based on four editing actions against translating with an auto-complete feature. In *Proceedings of the 22nd Annual Conference of the European Association for Machine Translation*, pages 421–430.

Marcello Federico, Nicola Bertoldi, Mauro Cettolo, Matteo Negri, Marco Turchi, Marco Trombetti, Alessandro Cattelan, Antonio Farina, Domenico Lupinetti, Andrea Martines, et al. 2014. The matecat tool. In *COLING (Demos)*, pages 129–132.

Erick Fonseca, Lisa Yankovskaya, André FT Martins, Mark Fishel, and Christian Federmann. 2019. Findings of the wmt 2019 shared tasks on quality estimation. In *Proceedings of the Fourth Conference on Machine Translation (Volume 3: Shared Task Papers, Day 2)*, pages 1–10.

Sarthak Garg, Stephan Peitz, Udhyakumar Nallasamy, and Matthias Paulik. 2019. Jointly learning to align and translate with transformer models. In *Proceedings of the 2019 Conference on Empirical Methods in Natural Language Processing and the 9th International Joint Conference on Natural Language Processing (EMNLP-IJCNLP)*, pages 4443–4452.

Spence Green, Jason Chuang, Jeffrey Heer, and Christopher D Manning. 2014a. Predictive translation memory: A mixed-initiative system for human language translation. In *Proceedings of the 27th annual ACM symposium on User interface software and technology*, pages 177–187.

Spence Green, Jeffrey Heer, and Christopher D Manning. 2013. The efficacy of human post-editing for language translation. In *Proceedings of the SIGCHI conference on human factors in computing systems*, pages 439–448.

Spence Green, Sida I Wang, Jason Chuang, Jeffrey Heer, Sebastian Schuster, and Christopher D Manning. 2014b. Human effort and machine learnability in computer aided translation. In *Proceedings of the 2014 Conference on Empirical Methods in Natural Language Processing (EMNLP)*, pages 1225–1236.

Nico Herbig, Tim Düwel, Santanu Pal, Kalliopi Meladaki, Mahsa Monshizadeh, Antonio Krüger, and Josef van Genabith. 2020. Mmpe: A multimodal interface for post-editing machine translation. In *Proceedings of the 58th Annual Meeting of the Association for Computational Linguistics*, pages 1691–1702.

Mandar Joshi, Danqi Chen, Yinhan Liu, Daniel S Weld, Luke Zettlemoyer, and Omer Levy. 2020. Spanbert: Improving pre-training by representing and predicting spans. *Transactions of the Association for Computational Linguistics*, 8:64–77.

Guillaume Klein, Yoon Kim, Yuntian Deng, Jean Senellart, and Alexander M. Rush. 2017. OpenNMT: Open-source toolkit for neural machine translation. In *Proc. ACL*.

Philipp Koehn. 2009. A process study of computer-aided translation. *Machine Translation*, 23(4):241–263.

Taku Kudo. 2018. Subword regularization: Improving neural network translation models with multiple subword candidates. In *Proceedings of the 56th Annual Meeting of the Association for Computational Linguistics (Volume 1: Long Papers)*, pages 66–75.

Guillaume Lample and Alexis Conneau. 2019. Cross-lingual language model pretraining. *arXiv preprint arXiv:1901.07291*.

Dongjun Lee. 2020. Two-phase cross-lingual language model fine-tuning for machine translation quality estimation. In *Proceedings of the Fifth Conference on Machine Translation*, pages 1024–1028, Online. Association for Computational Linguistics.

Jihyung Lee, WonKee Lee, Jaehun Shin, Baikjin Jung, Young-Gil Kim, and Jong-Hyeok Lee. 2020. Postech-etri's submission to the wmt2020 ape shared task: Automatic post-editing with cross-lingual language model. In *Proceedings of the Fifth Conference on Machine Translation*, pages 777–782.

Chi-kiu Lo and Eric Joanis. 2020. Improving parallel data identification using iteratively refined sentence alignments and bilingual mappings of pre-trained language models. In *Proceedings of the Fifth Conference on Machine Translation*, pages 972–978.

Joss Moorkens and Sharon O'Brien. 2017. Assessing user interface needs of post-editors of machine translation. *Human issues in translation technology*, pages 109–130.

Franz Josef Och and Hermann Ney. 2003. A systematic comparison of various statistical alignment models. *Computational Linguistics*, 29(1):19–51.

Santanu Pal, Marcos Zampieri, Sudip Kumar Naskar, Tapas Nayak, Mihaela Vela, and Josef van Genabith. 2016. Catalog online: Porting a post-editing tool to the web. In *Proceedings of the Tenth International Conference on Language Resources and Evaluation (LREC'16)*, pages 599–604.

Kishore Papineni, Salim Roukos, Todd Ward, and Wei-Jing Zhu. 2002. Bleu: a method for automatic evaluation of machine translation. In *Proceedings of the 40th Annual Meeting of the Association for Computational Linguistics*, pages 311–318, Philadelphia, Pennsylvania, USA. Association for Computational Linguistics.

Sebastin Santy, Sandipan Dandapat, Monojit Choudhury, and Kalika Bali. 2019. Inmt: Interactive neural machine translation prediction. In *Proceedings of the 2019 Conference on Empirical Methods in Natural Language Processing and the 9th International Joint Conference on Natural Language Processing (EMNLP-IJCNLP): System Demonstrations*, pages 103–108.

Rico Sennrich, Barry Haddow, and Alexandra Birch. 2016. Neural machine translation of rare words with subword units. In *Proceedings of the 54th Annual Meeting of the Association for Computational Linguistics (Volume 1: Long Papers)*, pages 1715–1725.

Matthew Snover, Bonnie Dorr, Richard Schwartz, Linnea Micciulla, and John Makhoul. 2006. A study of translation edit rate with targeted human annotation. In *Proceedings of association for machine translation in the Americas*, volume 200.

Lucia Specia, Frédéric Blain, Marina Fomicheva, Erick Fonseca, Vishrav Chaudhary, Francisco Guzmén, and André F. T. Martins. 2020. Findings of the wmt 2020 shared task on quality estimation. In *Proceedings of the Fifth Conference on Machine Translation*, pages 743–764, Online. Association for Computational Linguistics.

Antonio Toral, Martijn Wieling, and Andy Way. 2018. Post-editing effort of a novel with statistical and neural machine translation. *Frontiers in Digital Humanities*, 5:9.

Ashish Vaswani, Noam Shazeer, Niki Parmar, Jakob Uszkoreit, Llion Jones, Aidan N Gomez, Łukasz Kaiser, and Illia Polosukhin. 2017. Attention is all you need. In *Advances in neural information processing systems*, pages 5998–6008.

Jiayi Wang, Ke Wang, Kai Fan, Yuqi Zhang, Jun Lu, Xin Ge, Yangbin Shi, and Yu Zhao. 2020. Alibaba's submission for the wmt 2020 ape shared task: Improving automatic post-editing with pre-trained conditional cross-lingual bert. In *Proceedings of the Fifth Conference on Machine Translation*, pages 789–796.

A Sample Document Translation

Figure 3 shows a sample document and the translated document using IntelliCAT without human intervention.

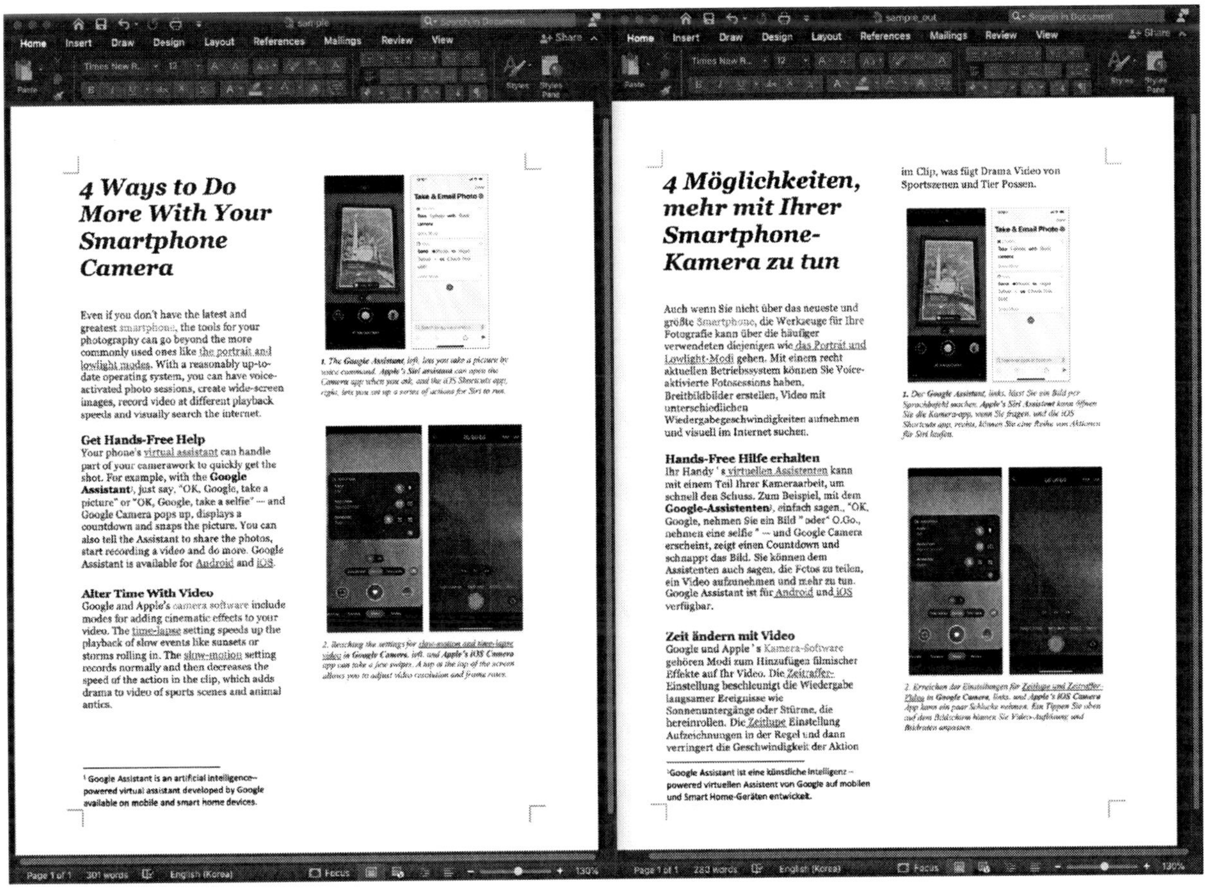

Figure 3: A sample document (left) and the translated document (right) without human intervention

The Classical Language Toolkit: An NLP Framework for Pre-Modern Languages

Kyle P. Johnson
Accenture
kyle@kyle-p-johnson.com

Patrick J. Burns
Department of Classics
University of Texas at Austin
patrick.burns@austin.utexas.edu

John Stewart
Amplify
johnstewart@aya.yale.edu

Todd G. Cook
Appen
todd.g.cook@gmail.com

Clément Besnier
clem@clementbesnier.fr

William J. B. Mattingly
Data Science Lab
Smithsonian Institution
wma229@g.uky.edu

Abstract

This paper announces version `1.0` of the Classical Language Toolkit (CLTK), an NLP framework for pre-modern languages. The vast majority of NLP, its algorithms and software, is created with assumptions particular to living languages, thus neglecting certain important characteristics of largely non-spoken historical languages. Further, scholars of pre-modern languages often have different goals than those of living-language researchers. To fill this void, the CLTK adapts ideas from several leading NLP frameworks to create a novel software architecture that satisfies the unique needs of pre-modern languages and their researchers. Its centerpiece is a modular processing pipeline that balances the competing demands of algorithmic diversity with pre-configured defaults. The CLTK currently provides pipelines, including models, for almost 20 languages.

1 Introduction

Pre-modern (or historical) languages are linguistically no different than those with speakers living today. Differences, however, manifest in how pre-modern languages are preserved, to what extent they are preserved, how they may be analyzed, and the ends to which they are studied. NLP is comprised of "computational techniques for the purpose of learning, understanding, and producing human language content" (Hirschberg and Manning, 2015, 261). In principle, such techniques may be applied to pre-modern languages. But because NLP, its algorithms and software, presumes living languages, there remains a significant void for NLP for pre-modern languages.

The Classical Language Toolkit (CLTK) is a Python library that borrows ideas from state-of-the-art NLP software, in order to cater to the particular needs of pre-modern languages and their researchers.[1] Its centerpiece is a modular processing pipeline that balances the competing demands of algorithmic diversity with pre-configured defaults. The CLTK currently provides pipelines, including models, for almost 20 languages. This architecture allows for relatively easy customization of currently available pipelines to new languages.

1.1 NLP for Pre-modern Languages

The authors adopt the term *pre-modern* to encompass the ISO 639-3 definitions of *ancient* (whose speakers died over 1,000 years ago), *extinct* (speakers who died within the last 200–300 years), and *historic* (distinct antecedents to living languages) (SIL International). The CLTK aims to treat all such languages, as they survive in written texts, from the 33rd century B.C. (Sumerian) up until the start of the A.D. 19th century.[2]

Pre-modern languages have traits distinguishing them from living languages, including:

- **A finite corpus**: Since native speakers no longer generate new texts, corpora may be too small for some machine learning algorithms, thus requiring rules-based or hybrid

[1] `http://cltk.org`. Begun in 2014, v. `0.1` was a collection of user-submitted NLP algorithms, plus models, for about a dozen pre-modern languages. In this `1.0` release, the CLTK offers a standard API and pre-configured processing pipelines. Burns et al. (2019) contains some earlier history and concepts behind v. `0.1`. The MIT-licensed code is available in version control (`https://github.com/cltk/cltk`) and packaged on PyPI (with `pip install cltk`).

[2] This cutoff date need not be absolute, as the date of introduction of the printing press may be taken into consideration. The press, which spread asynchronously, normalizes orthography and reduces copyist errors (Eisenstein, 1979, 181–225), thus obviating need for some of the CLTK's tools. As orthography stabilizes, coming closer to contemporary usage, living-language NLP becomes increasingly tractable. The Chinese movable type press (A.D. 11th century) could be considered an exception, though modern metal typefaces, with attendant productivity gains, were not applied to Chinese texts until the mid-19th century (Wilkinson, 2000, 451–453). The Sumerian date comes from (Michalowski, 2004, 19).

Proceedings of the Joint Conference of the 59th Annual Meeting of the Association for Computational Linguistics and the 11th International Joint Conference on Natural Language Processing: System Demonstrations, pages 20–29, August 1st - August 6th, 2021.

approaches. In some cases, a language's corpus may be small enough that it can be fully annotated.[3]

- **Variation**: Corpora of pre-modern languages are likely to demonstrate greater variation than living languages. This may include non-standardized orthography, regional dialects, and temporal language change (over spans of hundreds and even thousands of years).[4]
- **Limited resources**: Interest in pre-modern languages is largely scholarly or religious, meaning less funding from government and industry for the creation of resources such as text corpora, treebanks, and lexica.

These three differences spur the need for NLP specific to pre-modern languages.

1.2 Researchers of Pre-modern Languages

Researchers of pre-modern languages have concerns that are likely *philological*, *linguistic*, or *pedagogical*. Philology is an approach to pre-modern writing that focuses on the historical origins of texts; it is comparative as well as genealogical in nature (Turner, 2014, x). Historical linguists study diachronic change in a language itself, as opposed to philologists' focus upon written language.[5] Educators have unique concerns, too, including foremost that students generally do not learn by speaking and that they begin studying difficult, original texts within a year of study. In the classroom, a high premium is put upon sight translation, which is accomplished by the sub-tasks of identifying words' parts-of-speech, grammatical constructions, and lexical headwords.[6] These three objectives may find some representation among users of living-language NLP,[7] however they are not significant stimuli to industrial and governmental research.

1.3 Previous Work

Two software architectural patterns, the *framework* and the *pipeline*, are most relevant to the CLTK's design.

As NLP matured in the early 2000's, frameworks (or *toolkits*) emerged with the purpose of making the technology easier for non-specialists to use. To this end, these frameworks generally have documentation friendly for beginners, value diversity in algorithms, treat multiple languages, provide data sets, help with text preprocessing, and provide pre-trained models.[8] Of these characteristics, the CLTK especially values multilingual and multi-algorithmic NLP, the latter of which being necessary to accommodate the varying state of data sets of pre-modern languages. The CLTK shows some especial similarity to the quanteda library for the R language (Benoit et al., 2018), as it contains novel algorithms yet also "wraps" other NLP libraries.

Several NLP frameworks have popularized the pipeline processing architecture, in which default algorithms (tokenization, POS tagging, dependency parsing, etc.) are run in series upon input text. Algorithms may be added or removed from a default pipeline. Increasingly, frameworks use identical algorithms for every language, without special consideration for a language's nuances.

Aside from the CLTK, NLP tools for pre-modern languages have been uncommon,[9] despite a steady growth of language resources.[10] Pre-modern languages are often low-resource. Low-resource software applications, however, have tended toward transcription[11] and, in the case of en-

[3] As with Gothic, for which the only sizable evidence surviving is a 6th century manuscript containing a 4th century translation of the Bible (Miller, 2019, 1, 8–15), most of which the PROIEL project has annotated (Haug and Jøhndal, 2008).

[4] Sumerian, for example, survived 3,000 years (Michalowski, 2004, 19). Piotrowski (2012, 14–22) introduces the categories of difference (diachronic spelling variation), variance (synchronic spelling variation), and uncertainty (information loss during digital transcription).

[5] On linguists' focus on spoken language change: Hock (1991, 1–10) and Campbell (2013, 1–5); on contrast to philology: Hock (1991, 3–5) and Campbell (2013, 373, 391–392). Philology is fundamentally "intepretation of textual data" (Hock 1991, 5).

[6] See Adams (2016) on the origins of this pedagogy in the English-speaking world.

[7] E.g., for secondary language acquisition (Inniss et al., 2006)

[8] Prominent frameworks include the NLTK (Bird and Loper, 2004), OpenNLP (Apache Software Foundation, 2011), CoreNLP (Manning et al., 2014), spaCy (Honnibal and Johnson, 2015), and Stanza (Qi et al., 2020).

[9] For a previous discussion of NLP pipelines for the CLTK, see Burns (2019). There has been some noteworthy work on how generally pre-modern NLP should be done (Piotrowski, 2012; Köntges et al., 2019; McGillivray et al., 2019); also Zeldes and Schroeder (2016), a Python library for Coptic.

[10] Treebanks exist for twelve Indo-European languages according to the PROIEL annotation standards (Haug and Jøhndal, 2008; Eckhoff and Berdicevskis, 2015; Bech and Eide, 2014); texts also for Greek and Latin (Celano et al., 2014), Sanskrit (Hellwig et al., 2020), Cuneiform (Sumerian, Akkadian, etc.) (Englund, 2016), historical Arabic (Belinkov et al., 2016), and Classical Chinese (Lee and Kong, 2012; Yasuoka, 2019).

[11] E.g., Brugman et al. (2004); Ulinski et al. (2014).

dangered languages, language preservation.[12] An interesting exception may be UralicNLP (Hämäläinen, 2019), which provides algorithms intended for relatively small data sets in Finnish and related languages.

2 System Design

An NLP pipeline within a framework architecture standardizes I/O while preserving algorithmic diversity. The CLTK should provide:

- **Modular processing pipelines**: Each language should come with a pre-configured pipeline set to defaults expected by most users. A user should be able to modify, replace, and add processes to a pipeline. Pipelines may be adjusted for new languages.
- **Diversity of algorithms**: When there are several popular ways researchers perform a particular process (e.g., tagging entities with a word list or a neural network), the CLTK should support them both. Due to limited language resources, such as digitized texts and treebanks, machine learning at times may not be tractable (and if so, then only certain algorithms).[13] While rules-based approaches often do not adapt to the dynamism of living languages, they can perform well in restricted tasks within narrow domains.[14]
- **Standard I/O**: To optimize user productivity and facilitate scholarly communication, an API should accept standard input for all human languages. Likewise, when linguistically justified, outputs should be expressed using data structures and representations that are shared across languages.
- **Model management**: The project must provide models for every pipeline.

[12]E.g., Katinskaia et al. (2017); Buszard-Welcher (2018).

[13]For example, surviving literary Ancient Greek texts, from c. 800 B.C. to A.D. 1453, amount to only 65M words (Berkowitz and Squitier, 1990). By contrast, the original English-language BERT was trained on 3,300M tokens (Devlin et al., 2019, 5). (Nevertheless, a BERT model has been made for the Latin language with 643M tokens (Bamman and Burns, 2020, 2).) On small historical corpora, Hamilton et al. (2016) demonstrates benefits of SVD word embeddings over word2-vec.

[14]For example, the CLTK's meter scanners for Latin poetry (`cltk/prosody/lat/verse.py`).

```
>>> from cltk import NLP
>>> cltk_nlp = NLP(language="lat")
 ‎𐀀 CLTK version '1.0.14'.
Pipeline for language 'Latin' (ISO:
 ↪  'lat'): `LatinNormalizeProcess`,
 ↪  `LatinStanzaProcess`,
 ↪  `LatinEmbeddingsProcess`,
 ↪  `StopsProcess`,
 ↪  `LatinNERProcess`,
 ↪  `LatinLexiconProcess`.
>>> text = "Marcus Cato, ortus
 ↪  municipio Tusculo adulescentulus,
 ↪  priusquam honoribus operam daret,
 ↪  versatus est in Sabinis, quod
 ↪  ibi heredium a patre relict um
 ↪  habebat."
>>> cltk_doc =
 ↪  cltk_nlp.analyze(text=text)
>>> print(cltk_doc.tokens[:12])
['Marcus', 'Cato', ',', 'ortus',
 ↪  'municipio', 'Tusculo',
 ↪  'adulescentulus', ',',
 ↪  'priusquam', 'honoribus',
 ↪  'operam', 'daret']
>>> print(cltk_doc.pos[:12])
['PROPN', 'PROPN', 'PUNCT', 'NOUN',
 ↪  'NOUN', 'NOUN', 'ADJ', 'PUNCT',
 ↪  'ADV', 'NOUN', 'NOUN', 'VERB']
>>> print(cltk_doc.words[11].string)
daret
>>> print(cltk_doc.words[11].pos)
POS.verb
>>> print(cltk_
 ↪  doc.words[11].features)
{Aspect: [imperfective], Mood:
 ↪  [subjunctive], Number:
 ↪  [singular], Person: [third],
 ↪  Tense: [imperfect], VerbForm:
 ↪  [finite], Voice: [active]}
```

Code Block 1: Example of `NLP()` (3.1) processing the first sentence of Cornelius Nepos' *M. Porcius Cato*.

3 Architecture and Usage

The CLTK has one primary interface, `NLP()`, and five custom data types: When a user calls `NLP.analyze()`, it outputs a `Doc`, which contains all processed information. At `Doc.words` is a list of `Word` objects, each of which contains token-level information added by each `Process`. A `Pipeline` contains a list of `Process` objects for a given language.

3.1 NLP()

The CLTK's `NLP()` class offers a common interface for all languages, for which a pipeline of NLP algorithms is called. Calling `analyze()`, the class's only public method, triggers each `Process` in succession. The CLTK executes the algorithms and returns a `Doc` object. Code Block 1

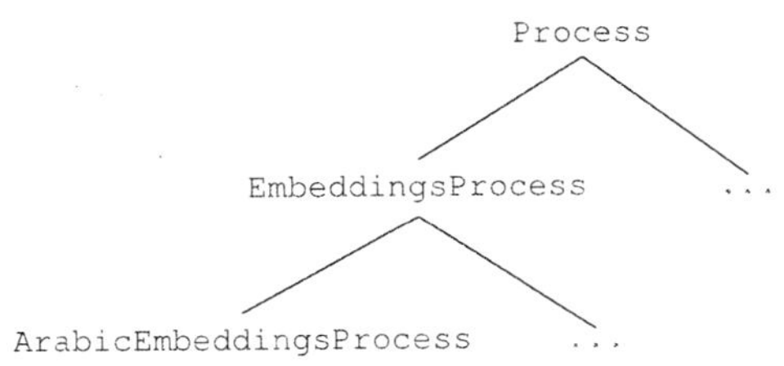

Figure 1: Illustration of the inheritance of `Process` (3.2) objects.

illustrates its use.[15]

3.2 `Process`

An algorithm in the CLTK may be called directly or wrapped in a `Process` that is incorporated into in a `Pipeline`. Each of the following classes, which inherit from `Process`, keep the project's algorithms organized according the kind of NLP they contain (Figure 1).[16]

- **`NormalizeProcess`**: Reads `Doc.raw`, then does Unicode normalization and other text transformation as required per language; outputs to `Doc.normalized_text`.
- **`TokenizationProcess`**: Normally the first `Process` run, splits input string into word tokens; sets string value at `Word.string`.
- **`SentenceProcess`**: Determines sentence boundaries and sets integer at `Word.index_sentence`.
- **`StopsProcess`**: Checks whether a token is contained within a stopword list; adds Boolean value at `Word.stop`.
- **`LemmatizationProcess`**: Reads `Word.string`, and perhaps other contextual information, then sets value at `Word.lemma`.[17]
- **`MorphologyProcess`**: Determines morphology and writes word class (noun, verb, etc.) and features (case, tense, etc.).[18] Values output by morphological taggers, before being set at `Word.pos` and `Word.features`, are normalized to custom CLTK data types that model the annotations of the Universal Dependencies project (see 3.4.3).
- **`DependencyProcess`**: Outputs results of a dependency grammar parser at `Word.dependency_relation` and `Word.governor`.[19]
- **`NERProcess`**: Determines whether a token is a named entity and, if so, what kind; sets string value at `Word.named_entity`.
- **`EmbeddingsProcess`**: Fetches word embedding from a language model; sets array at `Word.embedding`.[20]
- **`PhonologyProcess`**: Ascertains phonological properties of a word (specifically with the inheriting `PhonologicalTranscriptionProcess`) and then reconstructs a phonetic representation in IPA; sets output at `Word.phonetic_transcription`.[21]
- **`ProsodyProcess`**: Scans input strings and outputs scans of their poetic meter.[22]
- **`StemmingProcess`**: Writes a token's stem to `Word.stem`.[23]
- **`WordNetProcess`**: Queries WordNet and writes a word's synset to `Word.synsets`.[24]
- **`LexiconProcess`**: Matches `Word.lemma` to a dictionary's headword and writes to `Word.definition`.
- **`StanzaProcess`**: A `Process` has been created for Stanza because of its usefulness

[15] Text and translation from Rolfe (1984, 282–283): "Marcus Cato, born in the town of Tusculum, in his early youth, before entering on an official career, lived in the land of the Sabines, since he had there an hereditary property, left him by his father."

[16] See Appendix for how the actual code is organized.

[17] Previous work on CLTK lemmatization documented at Burns (2020).

[18] The CLTK relies on Stanza for morphological parsing for Chinese, Coptic, Gothic, Greek, Latin, Old Church Slavonic, and Old French. See also `StanzaProcess`. Other software, however, may be used, as in the case of Akkadian (`cltk/morphology/akk.py`).

[19] At time of publication, the CLTK uses the Stanza project's pretrained models with `StanzaProcess`. In the future, custom-trained models (e.g., with spaCy or Stanza) will be wrapped by `DependencyProcess`. See also section 3.4.4 for post-processing the flat `Doc.words` into a tree.

[20] Using fastText embeddings for Arabic, Aramaic, Gothic, Latin, Old English, Pali, and Sanskrit (Bojanowski et al., 2016); using NLPL for Ancient Greek and Old Church Slavonic (`http://vectors.nlpl.eu`).

[21] Subclassed `SyllabifierProcess` is also available for dividing words into a list of syllable strings; sets output at `Word.syllables`.

[22] Currently available for Greek, Latin, Middle High German, and Old Norse. Prose analysis of Latin clausulae also available (Keeline and Kirby, 2019).

[23] Akkadian, Latin, Middle English, Middle High German, and Old French.

[24] See Short for Latin WordNet API; Ancient Greek and Sanskrit WordNets are under development.

```
from dataclasses import dataclass,
↪  field
from typing import List, Type
from cltk.core.data_types import
↪  Language, Pipeline, Process
from cltk.languages.utils import
↪  get_lang

@dataclass
class LatinPipeline(Pipeline):
    """Default ``Pipeline`` for
    ↪  Latin."""
    description: str = "Pipeline for
    ↪  the Latin language"
    language: Language =
    ↪  get_lang("lat")
    processes: List[Type[Process]] =
    ↪  field(
        default_factory=lambda: [
            LatinNormalizeProcess,
            LatinStanzaProcess,
            LatinEmbeddingsProcess,
            StopsProcess,
            LatinNERProcess,
            LatinLexiconProcess,
        ]
    )
```

Code Block 2: Example of `LatinPipeline` (3.3) and the processes declared within it; defined at `cltk/languages/pipelines.py`.

```
>>> print(cltk_doc.words[11])
Word(index_char_start=None,
↪  index_char_stop=None,
↪  index_token=11, index_sentence=0,
↪  string='daret', pos=verb,
↪  lemma='do', stem=None,
↪  scansion=None,
↪  xpos='J3|modB|tem2|gen6',
↪  upos='VERB',
↪  dependency_relation='root',
↪  governor=-1, features={Aspect:
↪  [imperfective], Mood:
↪  [subjunctive], Number:
↪  [singular], Person: [third],
↪  Tense: [imperfect], VerbForm:
↪  [finite], Voice: [active]},
↪  category={F: [neg], N: [neg], V:
↪  [pos]}, stop=False,
↪  named_entity=False,
↪  syllables=None,
↪  phonetic_transcription=None,
↪  embedding=array([-1.2459e-01,
↪  ...], dtype=float32),
↪  definition="dō\n\n (old subj.
↪  duis, duit, duint, etc.), dedī,
↪  datus, are \n1 DA-, \nto hand
↪  over, deliver, give up, render,
↪  furnish, pay, surrender")
```

Code Block 3: Example of processed information contained within a `Word` (3.4.1) object. Continues from Code Block 1.

for seven languages (see ft. 18).

3.3 `Pipeline`

A language has one `Pipeline` defining a list of `Process` objects, as illustrated in Code Block 2. The objects within `Pipeline.processes` are looped over when called by `NLP.analyze()`. Each time, a `Doc` is sent into the `Process` and a new `Doc`, now with an updated `Doc.words`, is produced. These algorithms are invoked by default, though a user may override them by declaring his own `Pipeline` and passing it to `NLP()`. At time of publication, 19 languages have pre-configured pipelines.[25]

3.4 `Doc`

The `NLP.analyze()` method returns a `Doc` object that contains all information generated by the `Pipeline` (example at Code Block 1). Most of this information is stored within a list of `Word` objects at `Doc.words`, which may be accessed directly or by helper methods, such as `Doc.tokens` (returning a list of token strings) and `Doc.embeddings` (a list of arrays). When these access methods are not enough, a user may post-process the `Doc` and add attributes to it or the `Word` objects within.

3.4.1 `Word`

`Word` stores all token information. Code Block 3 shows some of what a `Word` object may contain.

3.4.2 `Language`

The module `cltk/languages/glottolog.py` contains 219 `Language` objects, each of which contains information about a pre-modern language that is, or should be, covered by the CLTK.[26] Code Block 4 shows how to retrieve a `Language` with a three-letter ISO code. Each

[25] Akkadian ("akk"), Arabic ("arb"), Aramaic ("arc"), Classical Chinese ("lzh"), Coptic ("cop"), Gothic ("grc"), Hindi ("hin"), Latin ("lat"), Middle High German ("gmh"), Old English ("ang"), Middle English ("enm"), Old French ("frm"), Old Church Slavonic ("chu"), Old Norse ("non"), Pali ("pli"), Panjabi ("pan"), and Sanskrit ("san").

[26] Language definitions and data provided by Glottolog, a database of the world's languages (Hammarström et al., 2021). These 219 languages are those falling within the definition of pre-modern (discussed at 1.1), plus some with significant continuity between pre-modern and contemporary written forms: Standard Arabic, nine South Asian languages (Bengali, Hindi, etc.), Western Farsi, and Coptic.

```
>>> from cltk.languages.utils import
↪   find_iso_name
>>> print(find_iso_name("Latin"))
['lat']
>>> from cltk.languages.utils import
↪   get_lang
>>> print(get_lang("lat"))
Language(name='Latin',
↪   glottolog_id='lati1261',
↪   latitude=41.9026,
↪   longitude=12.4502, dates=[],
↪   family_id='indo1319',
↪   parent_id='impe1234',
↪   level='language',
↪   iso_639_3_code='lat', type='a')
```

Code Block 4: Example of a `Language` (3.4.2) object for Latin (ISO code `"lat"`).

`Pipeline` references these classes (see Code Block 2).

3.4.3 `MorphosyntacticFeature` and `MorphosyntacticFeatureBundle`

Beyond the categorical information at `Word.pos`, a language's `Pipeline` adds complete morphology at the `Word.features` accessor (see Code Block 5). The sometimes arbitrary output strings of morphological taggers ("indicative," "Indic.," etc.) are mapped to these specific CLTK classes (inheriting from `MorphosyntacticFeature`) that represent all features defined by version 2 of the Universal Dependencies project.[27] Hence, different taggers resolve to a common annotation schema.

3.4.4 `DependencyTree`

The CLTK uses the "built-in" `xml` library to make trees for modeling dependency parses. A `Word` is mapped into a `Form`, then `ElementTree` is used to organize these into a `DependencyTree` (see Code Block 6).

3.5 `FetchCorpus`

Git repositories host models developed by CLTK contributors.[28] When the software cannot find a required model, `FetchCorpus` is invoked to download the required dependency and put it within the appropriate directory at `~/cltk_data/`.[29]

```
>>> print(cltk_doc.words[11].featur
↪   es)
{Aspect: [imperfective], Mood:
↪   [subjunctive], Number:
↪   [singular], Person: [third],
↪   Tense: [imperfect], VerbForm:
↪   [finite], Voice: [active]}
>>> print(type(cltk_doc.wor
↪   ds[11].features))
<class 'cltk.morphology.mor
↪   phosyntax.MorphosyntacticFeatur
↪   eBundle'>
>>> print(cltk_doc.words[11].featur
↪   es["Aspect"][0])
Aspect.imperfective
>>> print(cltk_doc.words[11].featur
↪   es["Mood"][0])
Mood.subjunctive
```

Code Block 5: Example of `MorphosyntacticFeature` and `MorphosyntacticFeatureBundle` (3.4.3). Continues from Code Block 3.

```
>>> from cltk.dependency.tree import
↪   DependencyTree
>>> a_tree = DependencyTree.to_tree
↪   (cltk_doc.sentences[0])
>>> print(a_tree.get_dependencie
↪   s()[:5])
[nsubj(daret_11, Marcus_0),
↪   nsubj(daret_11, Cato_1),
↪   nsubj(daret_11, ortus_3),
↪   nsubj(daret_11, Marcus_0),
↪   nsubj(daret_11, Cato_1)]
```

Code Block 6: Example of `DependencyTree` (3.4.4). Continues from Code Block 1.

4 Conclusion and Future Work

The architecture of the CLTK v. `1.0` has an engineering rigor necessary to model the world's several hundred pre-modern languages. Currently, it serves the basic, and several more advanced, needs of researchers for 19 languages.

Software alone, however, is not sufficient. The CLTK lacks formal evaluations of its models' accuracies. At time of publication, most `Process` definitions wrap models trained by upstream projects (e.g., Stanza). While these projects report accuracies respective to their training sets (i.e., with cross-validation), they do not provide evaluations against outside benchmarks. Unfortunately, such benchmarks do not yet exist for pre-modern languages, with the exception of the recent Sprugnoli et al.

[27] Annotation guidelines at Universal Dependencies (2016) and CLTK objects at `cltk/morphology/universal_dependencies_annotations.py`.

[28] All CLTK models are stored on GitHub at: `https://github.com/cltk/?q=model`.

[29] A language-specific Git repository is available for most languages, e.g., `"lat_models_cltk"` at the URI `https://github.com/cltk/lat_models_cltk.git`. Users may share private or non-official repositories by defining them at `~/cltk_data/distributed_corpora.yaml`.

(2020) for Latin. To remedy this problem, the authors will focus upon the following areas:

- to create evaluation benchmarks for each NLP task, for each language;
- to make a `TrainingPipeline`, similar to the inference `Pipeline`, that would standardize the training of new models;
- to normalize duplicative treebanks;[30]
- and to develop Internet infrastructure for training and hosting models;

These efforts will improve scientific procedure for pre-modern NLP.

Another initiative involves experimentation with transfer learning, along the lines of Multilingual BERT (Pires et al., 2019), training on all surviving pre-modern texts. Because languages are related and because texts, even in different languages, often share entities, information sharing may prove felicitous.[31]

The pre-modern world, its languages and peoples, was deeply networked.[32] The CLTK is a comprehensive collection of NLP technologies to support the study of this history.

Acknowledgments

The authors owe a special dept of gratitude to all of the CLTK's contributors.[33] They also thank early readers of this manuscript: Neil Coffee, Greg Crane, Jonathan Everett, Luke Hollis, Thomas Keeline, Leonard Muellner, Nigel Nicholson, Monica Park, Michael Piotrowski, Marco Romani, and William M. Short. The project's name is a play on the Natural Language Toolkit (NLTK), on which v. `0.1` heavily relied. The CLTK logo of a Phoenician *aleph* (or *ʾālep*, 𐤀), being the first letter of the first alphabet, was created by Pierre-Marie Pédrot.[34]

[30]For example, Universal Dependencies hosts five different, and to various degrees incompatible, Latin treebanks. The largest is 450,000 tokens, though adding the other four would bring the count close to 1,000,000. Ancient Greek also has duplicative treebanks (each at about 200,000 tokens).

[31]Considerations include use of original orthography versus normalizing to orthographic or phonetic transliteration.

[32]Several studies on trans-cultural diffusion across Eurasia: Beckwith (2009); Frankopan (2015).

[33]`https://github.com/cltk/cltk/graphs/contributors`.

[34]`https://commons.wikimedia.org/wiki/File:PhoenicianA-01.svg`.

References

M. Adams. 2016. *Teaching Classics in English Schools, 1500–1840*. Cambridge Scholars Publishing, Newcastle upon Tyne.

Apache Software Foundation. Apache OpenNLP [online]. 2011.

David Bamman and Patrick J. Burns. 2020. Latin BERT: A contextual language model for classical philology.

Kristin Bech and Kristine Eide. The ISWOC corpus [online]. 2014.

Christopher I. Beckwith. 2009. *Empires of the Silk Road: A History of Central Eurasia from the Bronze Age to the Present*. Princeton University Press, Princeton.

Yonatan Belinkov, Alexander Magidow, Maxim Romanov, Avi Shmidman, and Moshe Koppel. 2016. Shamela: A large-scale historical Arabic corpus. In *Proceedings of the Workshop on Language Technology Resources and Tools for Digital Humanities (LT4DH)*, pages 45–53, Osaka, Japan. The COLING 2016 Organizing Committee.

Kenneth Benoit, Kohei Watanabe, Haiyan Wang, Paul Nulty, Adam Obeng, Stefan Müller, and Akitaka Matsuo. 2018. quanteda: An R package for the quantitative analysis of textual data. *Journal of Open Source Software*, 3(30):774.

Luci Berkowitz and Karl A. Squitier. 1990. *Thesaurus Linguae Graecae: Canon of Greek Authors and Works*, 3rd edition. Thesaurus Linguae Graecae. Oxford University Press, New York.

Steven Bird and Edward Loper. 2004. NLTK: The Natural Language Toolkit. In *Proceedings of the ACL 2004 on Interactive Poster and Demonstration Sessions*, page 31. Association for Computational Linguistics.

Piotr Bojanowski, Edouard Grave, Armand Joulin, and Tomás Mikolov. 2016. Enriching word vectors with subword information. *CoRR*, abs/1607.04606.

Hennie Brugman, Albert Russel, and Xd Nijmegen. 2004. Annotating multi-media/multi-modal resources with ELAN. In *The Fourth International Conference on Language Resources and Evaluation*. European Language Resources Association (ELRA), Lisbon.

Patrick J. Burns. 2019. Building a text analysis pipeline for classical languages. In Monica Berti, editor, *Digital Classical Philology: Ancient Greek and Latin in the Digital Revolution*, number 10 in Age of Access? Grundfragen der Informationsgesellschaft, pages 159–176. de Gruyter, Berlin.

Patrick J. Burns. 2020. Ensemble lemmatization with the Classical Language Toolkit. *Studi e Saggi Linguistici*, 58(1):157–176.

Patrick J. Burns, Luke Hollis, and Kyle P. Johnson. 2019. The future of ancient literacy: Classical Language Toolkit and Google Summer of Code. *Classics@*, 17.

Laura Buszard-Welcher. 2018. New media for endangered languages. In Kenneth L. Rehg and Lyle Campbell, editors, *The Oxford Handbook of Endangered Languages*, Oxford Handbooks, chapter 22. Oxford University Press, Oxford.

Lyle Campbell. 2013. *Historical Linguistics*. Edinburgh University Press, Edinburgh.

Giuseppe G. A. Celano, Gregory Crane, and Bridget Almas. Ancient Greek and Latin dependency treebank v.2.1 [online]. 2014.

Jacob Devlin, Ming-Wei Chang, Kenton Lee, and Kristina Toutanova. 2019. BERT: Pre-training of deep bidirectional transformers for language understanding. In *Proceedings of the 2019 Conference of the North American Chapter of the Association for Computational Linguistics: Human Language Technologies, Volume 1 (Long and Short Papers)*, pages 4171–4186, Minneapolis, Minnesota. Association for Computational Linguistics.

Hanne Martine Eckhoff and Aleksandrs Berdicevskis. 2015. Linguistics vs. digital editions: The Tromsø Old Russian and OCS treebank. *Scripta & e-Scripta*, 14(15):9–25.

Elizabeth L. Eisenstein. 1979. *The Printing Press as an Agent of Change*. Cambridge University Press, Cambridge.

Robert K. Englund. 2016. The Cuneiform Digital Library Initiative: DL in DH. Microsoft PowerPoint.

Peter Frankopan. 2015. *The Silk Roads: A New History of the World*. Vintage Books, New York.

Mika Hämäläinen. 2019. UralicNLP: An NLP library for Uralic languages. *Journal of Open Source Software*, 4(37):1345.

William L. Hamilton, Jure Leskovec, and Dan Jurafsky 2016. Diachronic word embeddings reveal statistical laws of semantic change. In *Proceedings of the 54th Annual Meeting of the Association for Computational Linguistics (Volume 1: Long Papers)*, pages 1489–1501, Berlin, Germany. Association for Computational Linguistics.

Harald Hammarström, Robert Forkel, Martin Haspelmath, and Sebastian Bank. Glottolog 4.4 [online]. 2021.

Dag T. T. Haug and Marius L. Jøhndal. 2008. Creating a parallel treebank of the old Indo-European Bible translations. In Caroline Sporleder and Kiril Ribarov, editors, *Proceedings of the Second Workshop on Language Technology for Cultural Heritage Data (LaTeCH 2008)*, pages 27–34. European Language Resources Association (ELRA), Marrakech.

Oliver Hellwig, Salvatore Scarlata, Elia Ackermann, and Paul Widmer. 2020. The treebank of Vedic Sanskrit. In *Proceedings of the 12th Language Resources and Evaluation Conference*, pages 5137–5146, Marseille, France. European Language Resources Association.

Julia Hirschberg and Christopher D. Manning. 2015. Advances in natural language processing. *Science*, 349(6245):261–266.

Hans Henrich Hock. 1991. *Principles of Historical Linguistics*, 2nd edition. Mouton de Gruyter, Berlin.

Matthew Honnibal and Mark Johnson. 2015. An improved non-monotonic transition system for dependency parsing. In *Proceedings of the 2015 Conference on Empirical Methods in Natural Language Processing*, pages 1373–1378, Lisbon, Portugal. Association for Computational Linguistics.

Tasha R. Inniss, John R. Lee, Marc Light, Michael A Grassi, George Thomas, and Andrew B. Williams. 2006. Towards applying text mining and natural language processing for biomedical ontology acquisition. In *Proceedings of the 1st International Workshop on Text Mining in Bioinformatics*, pages 7–14.

Anisia Katinskaia, Javad Nouri, and Roman Yangarber. 2017. Revita: A system for language learning and supporting endangered languages. In *Proceedings of the joint workshop on NLP for Computer Assisted Language Learning and NLP for Language Acquisition*, pages 27–35, Gothenburg, Sweden. LiU Electronic Press.

Tom Keeline and Tyler Kirby. 2019. *Auceps syllabarum*: A digital analysis of Latin prose rhythm. *Journal of Roman Studies*, 109:161–204.

Thomas Köntges, Rhea Lesage, Bruce Robertson, Jeannie Sellick, and Lucie Wall Stylianopoulos. 2019. Open Greek and Latin: Digital humanities in an open collaboration with pedagogy. In *Libraries: Dialogue for Change*, Athens. IFLA WLIC.

John Lee and Yin Hei Kong. 2012. A dependency treebank of Classical Chinese poems. In *Proceedings of the 2012 Conference of the North American Chapter of the Association for Computational Linguistics: Human Language Technologies*, pages 191–199, Montréal, Canada. Association for Computational Linguistics.

Christopher Manning, Mihai Surdeanu, John Bauer, Jenny Finkel, Steven Bethard, and David McClosky. 2014. The Stanford CoreNLP natural language processing toolkit. In *Proceedings of 52nd Annual Meeting of the Association for Computational Linguistics: System Demonstrations*, pages 55–60.

Barbara McGillivray, Jon Wilson, and Tobias Blanke. 2019. Towards a quantitative research framework for historical disciplines. In *CEUR Workshop Proceedings*, volume 2314.

Piotr Michalowski. 2004. Sumerian. In Roger D. Woodard, editor, *The Cambridge Encyclopedia of the World's Ancient Languages*, pages 19–59. Cambridge University Press, Cambridge.

D. Gary Miller. 2019. *The Oxford Gothic Grammar*. Oxford Linguistics. Oxford University Press, Oxford.

Michael Piotrowski. 2012. *Natural Language Processing for Historical Texts*. Number 17 in Synthesis Lectures on Human Language Technologies. Morgan & Claypool Publishers, San Rafael.

Telmo Pires, Eva Schlinger, and Dan Garrette. 2019. How multilingual is Multilingual BERT? In *Proceedings of the 57th Annual Meeting of the Association for Computational Linguistics*, pages 4996–5001, Florence, Italy. Association for Computational Linguistics.

Peng Qi, Yuhao Zhang, Yuhui Zhang, Jason Bolton, and Christopher D. Manning. 2020. Stanza: A Python natural language processing toolkit for many human languages. In *Proceedings of the 58th Annual Meeting of the Association for Computational Linguistics: System Demonstrations*, pages 101–108, Online. Association for Computational Linguistics.

John C. Rolfe. 1984. *Cornelius Nepos*, volume 467 of *The Loeb Classical Library*. Harvard University Press, Cambridge, Mass.

William Michael Short. Latin WordNet [online].

SIL International. ISO 639-3 [online].

Rachele Sprugnoli, Marco Passarotti, Flavio Massimiliano Cecchini, and Matteo Pellegrini. 2020. Overview of the EvaLatin 2020 evaluation campaign. In *Proceedings of LT4HALA 2020 - 1st Workshop on Language Technologies for Historical and Ancient Languages*, pages 105–110, Marseille, France. European Language Resources Association (ELRA).

James Turner. 2014. *Philology: The Forgotten Origins of the Modern Humanities*. Princeton University Press, Princeton.

Morgan Ulinski, Anusha Balakrishnan, Daniel Bauer, Bob Coyne, Julia Hirschberg, and Owen Rambow. 2014. Documenting endangered languages with the WordsEye linguistics tool. In *Proceedings of the 2014 Workshop on the Use of Computational Methods in the Study of Endangered Languages*, pages 6–14, Baltimore, Maryland, USA. Association for Computational Linguistics.

Universal Dependencies. UD Guidelines V2 [online]. 2016.

Endymion Wilkinson. 2000. *Chinese History: A Manual*. Number 52 in Harvard-Yenching Institute Monograph Series. Harvard University Press, Cambridge, Mass.

Koichi Yasuoka. 2019. Universal dependencies treebank of the Four Books in Classical Chinese. In *DADH2019: 10th International Conference of Digital Archives and Digital Humanities*, pages 20–28. Digital Archives and Digital Humanities.

Amir Zeldes and Caroline T. Schroeder. 2016. An NLP pipeline for Coptic. In *Proceedings of the 10th SIGHUM Workshop on Language Technology for Cultural Heritage, Social Sciences, and Humanities*, pages 146–155, Berlin, Germany. Association for Computational Linguistics.

A Appendix

The following top-level directories are found at `src/cltk`, within the project's repository.

- **`nlp`**: The main module, contains class `NLP()`
- **`alphabet`**: Manipulate characters of a language's orthographic system
- **`core`**: Custom data types, error handling
- **`corpora`**: Metadata for and preprocessing of specific data sets
- **`data`**: Download CLTK-hosted data sets
- **`dependency`**: Dependency parsing
- **`embeddings`**: Making and loading word embeddings
- **`languages`**: Definition of all pre-modern languages, text snippets for demonstration
- **`lemmatize`**: Find lemma for an inflected form
- **`lexicon`**: Find a lemma's definition in a dictionary
- **`morphology`**: Model morphology and syntax with data types from Universal Dependencies
- **`ner`**: Tag named entities (i.e., proper nouns)
- **`phonology`**: Syllabifying and tagging phonemes
- **`prosody`**: Scanning poetic meter
- **`sentence`**: Splitting sentences
- **`stem`**: Create unique stem from inflected form
- **`stops`**: Identify if a token is a stopword
- **`tag`**: Part-of-speech tagging
- **`text`**: Language-specific, extensible text preprocessing

- `tokenizers`: Create tokens from an input string
- `utils`: Helpers for feature extraction and disk I/O
- `wordnet`: Lookup of lemma on available online WordNets

TextBox: A Unified, Modularized, and Extensible Framework for Text Generation

Junyi Li[1,3]†, **Tianyi Tang**[1]†, **Gaole He**[2], **Jinhao Jiang**[1], **Xiaoxuan Hu**[2], **Puzhao Xie**[2], **Zhipeng Chen**[2], **Zhuohao Yu**[2], **Wayne Xin Zhao**[1,3,4]* and **Ji-Rong Wen**[1,2,3]

[1]Gaoling School of Artificial Intelligence, Renmin University of China

[2]School of Information, Renmin University of China

[3]Beijing Key Laboratory of Big Data Management and Analysis Methods

[4]Beijing Academy of Artificial Intelligence, Beijing, 100084, China

`{lijunyi,steven_tang}@ruc.edu.cn` `batmanfly@gmail.com`

Abstract

In this paper, we release an open-source library, called `TextBox`, to provide a unified, modularized, and extensible text generation framework. TextBox aims to support a broad set of text generation tasks and models. In our library, we implement 21 text generation models on 9 benchmark datasets, covering the categories of VAE, GAN, and pretrained language models. Meanwhile, our library maintains sufficient modularity and extensibility by properly decomposing the model architecture, inference, and learning process into highly reusable modules, which allows users to easily incorporate new models into our framework. The above features make TextBox especially suitable for researchers and practitioners to quickly reproduce baseline models and develop new models. TextBox is implemented based on PyTorch, and released under Apache License 2.0 at the link `https://github.com/RUCAIBox/TextBox`.

1 Introduction

Text generation, which has emerged as an important branch of natural language processing (NLP), is often formally referred as natural language generation (NLG) (Li et al., 2021b). It aims to produce plausible and understandable text in human language from input data (*e.g.*, a sequence, keywords) or machine representation. Because of incredible performance of deep learning models, many classic text generation tasks have achieved rapid progress, such as machine translation (Vaswani et al., 2017), dialogue systems (Li et al., 2016b), text summarization (See et al., 2017), graph-to-text generation (Li et al., 2021a), and more.

To facilitate the development of text generation models, a few remarkable open-source libraries have been developed (Britz et al., 2017; Klein et al., 2017b; Miller et al., 2017b; Zhu et al., 2018; Hu et al., 2019). These frameworks are mainly designed for some or a small number of specific tasks, particularly machine translation and dialogue systems. They usually focus on a special kind of techniques for text generation such as generative adversarial networks (GAN), or have limitations in covering commonly-used baseline implementations. Even for an experienced researcher, it is difficult and time-consuming to implement all compared baselines under a unified framework. Therefore, it is highly desirable to re-consider the implementation of text generation algorithms in a unified and modularized framework.

In order to alleviate the above issues, we initiate a project to provide a unified framework for text generation algorithms. We implement an open-source text generation library, called `TextBox`, aiming to enhance the reproducibility of existing text generation models, standardize the implementation and evaluation protocol of text generation algorithms, and ease the development process of new algorithms. Our work is also useful to support several real-world applications in the field of text generation. We have extensively surveyed related text generation libraries and broadly fused their merits into TextBox. The key features and capabilities of our library are summarized in the following three aspects:

• Unified and modularized framework. TextBox is built upon PyTorch (Paszke et al., 2019), which is one of the most popular deep learning frameworks (especially in the research community). Moreover, it is designed to be highly modularized, by decoupling text generation models into a set of highly reusable modules, including data module, model module, evaluation module, and many common components and functionalities. In our library, it is convenient to compare different text generation

† Equal contribution.

* Corresponding author.

Proceedings of the Joint Conference of the 59th Annual Meeting of the Association for Computational Linguistics and the 11th International Joint Conference on Natural Language Processing: System Demonstrations, pages 30–39, August 1st - August 6th, 2021.

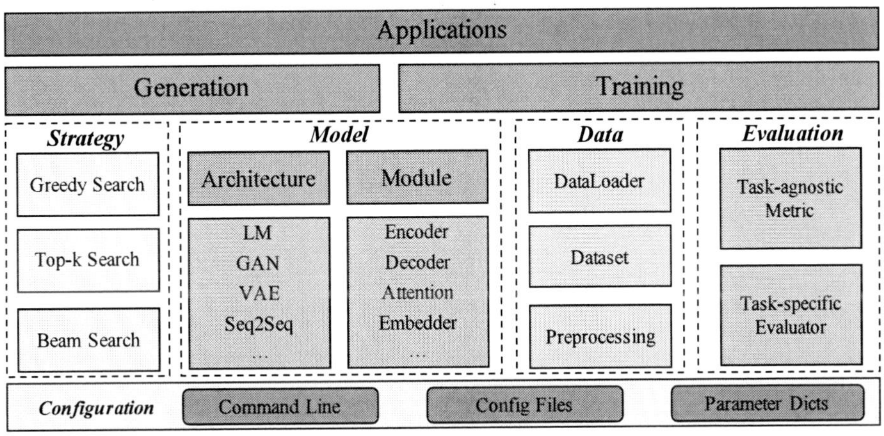

Figure 1: The illustration of the main functionalities and modules in our library TextBox.

algorithms with built-in evaluation protocols via simple yet flexible configurations, or develop new text generation models at a highly conceptual level by plugging in or swapping out modules.

• Comprehensive models, benchmark datasets and standardized evaluations. TextBox contains a wide range of text generation models, covering the categories of variational auto-encoder (VAE), generative adversarial networks (GAN), recurrent neural network (RNN) and pretrained language models (PLMs). We provide flexible supporting mechanisms via the configuration file or command line to run, compare and test these traditional and state-of-the-art algorithms. Based on these models, we implement two major text generation tasks, namely unconditional text generation tasks and conditional text generation tasks (*e.g.*, text summarization and machine translation). To construct a reusable benchmark, we incorporate 9 widely-used datasets with regards to different text generation tasks for evaluation. Our library supports a series of frequently adopted evaluation protocols for testing and comparing text generation algorithms, such as perplexity, BLEU, ROUGE, and Distinct.

• Extensible and flexible framework. TextBox provides convenient interfaces of various common functions or modules in text generation models, *e.g.*, RNN-based and Transformer-based encoders and decoders, pretrained language models, and attention mechanisms. Within our library, users are convenient to choose different API interfaces for building and evaluating their own models. Besides, the interfaces of our library are fully compatible with the PyTorch interface which allows seamless integration of user-customized modules and functions as needed.

2 Architecture and Design

Figure 1 presents the illustration of the main functionalities and modules in our library TextBox. The configuration module at the bottom helps users set up the experimental environment (*e.g.*, hyper-parameters and running details). Built upon the configuration module, the data, model, and evaluation modules form the core elements of our library. In the following, we describe the detailed structure of these three modules.

2.1 Data Module

A major design principle of our library is to support different text generation tasks. For this purpose, data module is the fundamental part to provide various data structures and functions adapting to different generation tasks.

For extensibility and reusability, our data module designs a unified data flow feeding input text into the models. The data flow can be described as: input text → `Dataset` → `DataLoader` → models. The class `Dataset` involves two special data structures, *i.e.*, single sequence and paired sequence, which are oriented to unconditional and conditional text generation tasks, respectively. The single sequence structure requires users to preprocess input text into one sequence per line in input files, while the paired sequence structure requires users to separate the source and target into two files with one sequence per line in each file. Specifically, for conditional text generation, TextBox supports several source formats corresponding to different tasks, *e.g.*, discrete attributes or tokens for attribute-to-text and keyword-to-text generation, a text sequence for machine translation or text summarization, and multiple text sequences for multi-turn dialogue systems. Furthermore, users can also provide additional information as inputs, *e.g.*, background text for agents in dialogues. The implementation of `Dataset` contains many common data preprocessing functionalities, such as converting text into lowercase, word tokenization, and building vocabulary. And the class `Dataloader` is based on the above two data structures, which is responsible for organizing the data stream.

In order to compare different generation models, we have collected 9 commonly-used benchmarks for text generation tasks, which makes it quite convenient for users to start with our library.

2.2 Model Module

To support a variety of models, we set up the model module by decoupling the algorithm implementation from other components and abstracting a set of widely-used modules, *e.g.*, `encoder` and `decoder`. These modules can be flexibly combined following the required interface and then connected with data and evaluation modules. Based on this abstract design, it is convenient to switch between different text generation tasks, and change from one modeling paradigm to another by simply plugging in or swapping out modules.

In addition to modularized design, our library also includes a large number of text generation baseline models for reproducibility. At the current released version, we have implemented 21 baseline models within four main categories of text generation models, namely VAE-based, GAN-based, pretrained language models, and sequence-to-sequence, corresponding to different generation architectures and tasks. For example, GAN-based models consist of `generator` and `discriminator`, and VAE-based models contain `encoder` and `decoder`. We summarize all the implemented models in Table 1. For all the implemented models, we test their performance for unconditional and conditional generation tasks on corresponding benchmarks, and invite a code reviewer to examine the correctness of the implementation. Overall, the extensible and comprehensive model modules can be beneficial for fast exploration of new algorithms for a specific task, and convenient comparison between different models.

In specific, for each model, we utilize two interface functions, *i.e.*, `forward` and `generate`, for training and testing, respectively. These functions are general to various text generation algorithms, so that we can implement various algorithms in a highly unified way. Such a design also enables quick development of new models.

Category	Models	Reference
VAE	LSTM-VAE	(Bowman et al., 2016)
	CNN-VAE	(Yang et al., 2017)
	Hybrid-VAE	(Semeniuta et al., 2017)
	CVAE	(Li et al., 2018)
GAN	SeqGAN	(Yu et al., 2017)
	TextGAN	(Zhang et al., 2017)
	RankGAN	(Lin et al., 2017)
	MaliGAN	(Che et al., 2017)
	LeakGAN	(Guo et al., 2018)
	MaskGAN	(Fedus et al., 2018)
Pretrained Language Model	GPT-2	(Radford et al., 2019)
	XLNet	(Yang et al., 2019)
	BERT2BERT	(Rothe et al., 2020)
	BART	(Lewis et al., 2020)
	ProphetNet	(Qi et al., 2020)
	T5	(Raffel et al., 2020)
Seq2Seq	RNN	(Sutskever et al., 2014)
	Transformer	(Vaswani et al., 2017)
	Context2Seq	(Tang et al., 2016)
	Attr2Seq	(Dong et al., 2017)
	HRED	(Serban et al., 2016)

Table 1: Implemented models in our library TextBox.

In order to improve the quality of generation results, we also implement a series of generation strategies when generating text, such as greedy search, top-k search and beam search. Users are allowed to switch between different generation strategies leading to better performance through setting a hyper-parameter, *i.e.*, `decoding_strategy`. Besides, we add the functions of model saving and loading to store and reuse the learned models, respectively. In the training process, one can print and monitor the change of the loss value and apply training tricks such as warm-up and early-stopping. These tiny tricks largely improve the usage experiences with our library.

2.3 Evaluation Module

It is important that different models should be compared under the unified evaluate protocols, which is useful to standardize the evaluation of text generation. To achieve this goal, we set up the evaluation module to implement commonly-used evaluation protocols for text generation models.

Our library supports both logit-based and word-based evaluation metrics. The logit-based metrics include perplexity (PPL) (Brown et al., 1992) and negative log-likelihood (NLL) (Huszar, 2015), measuring how well the probability distribution or a probability model predicts a sample compared with the ground-truth. The word-based metrics include the most widely-used generation metrics for evaluating lexical similarity, semantic equivalence and diversity. For example, BLEU-n (Papineni et al., 2002) and ROUGE-n (Lin, 2004) measure the ratios of the overlapping n-grams between the generated and real samples, METEOR (Banerjee and Lavie, 2005) measures the word-to-word matches based on WordNet, CIDEr (Vedantam et al., 2015) computes the TF-IDF weights for each n-gram in generated/real samples and CHRF++ (Popovic, 2015) computes F-score averaged on both character- and word-level n-grams. To evaluate the semantic equivalence between generated and real samples, we include BERTScore (Zhang et al., 2020), a metric based on the similarity of sentence embeddings relied on pretrained language model BERT (Devlin et al., 2019). Moreover, Distinct-n and Unique-n (Li et al., 2016a) measures the degree of diversity of generated text by calculating the number of distinct unigrams and bigrams in generated text. Besides, to evaluate the diversity of unconditionally generated samples, we also take into account the Self-BLEU (Zhu et al., 2018) metric. In summary, users can choose different evaluation protocols towards a specific generation task by setting the hyper-parameter, *i.e.*, `metrics`.

In practice, as the model may generate many text pieces, evaluation efficiency is an important concern. Hence, we integrate efficient computing package, `fastBLEU` (Alihosseini et al., 2019), to compute evaluation scores. Compared with other package, `fastBLEU` adopts the multi-threaded C++ implementation.

3 System Usage

In this section, we show a detailed guideline to use our system library. Users can run the existing models or add their own models as needed.

3.1 Running Existing Models

To run an existing model within TextBox, users only need to specify the dataset and model by setting hyper-parameters, *i.e.*, `dataset` and `model`. And then experiments can be run with a simple command-line interface:

```
python run_textbox.py \
  --model=GPT2 --dataset=COCO
```

The above case shows an example that runs GPT-2 (Radford et al., 2019) model on COCO dataset (Lin et al., 2015). In our system library, the generation task, such as `translation`, and `summarization`, is determined once users specify the dataset, thus the task is not necessary to be explicitly specified in hyper-parameters. To facilitate the modification of hyper-parameters, we provides two kinds of YAML configuration files, *i.e.*, dataset configuration and model configuration, which allow running many experiments without modifying source code. It also supports users to include hyper-parameters in the command line, which is useful for some specifically defined parameters. TextBox is designed to be run on different hardware devices. By default, CUDA devices will be used if users set the hyper-parameter `use_gpu` as `True`, or otherwise CPU will be used. Users can determine the ID of used CUDA devices by setting hyper-parameter `gpu_id`. We also support distributed model training in multiple GPUs by setting the hyper-parameter `DDP` as `True`.

Based on the configuration, we provide the auxiliary function to split the dataset into train, validation and test sets according to the provided hyper-parameter `split_ratio`, or load the pre-split dataset. Moreover, TextBox also allows users to load and re-train the saved model for speeding up reproduction, rather than training from scratch.

Figure 2 presents a general usage flow when running a model in our library. The running procedure relies on some experimental configuration, obtained from the files, command line or parameter dictionaries. The dataset and model are prepared and initialized according to the configured settings, and the execution module is responsible for training and evaluating models.

3.2 Implementing a New Model

With the unified `Data` and `Evaluation` modules, one needs to implement a specific `Model` class and three mandatory functions as follows:

• `__init__()` function. In this function, the user performs parameters initialization, global variable definition and so on. It is worth noting that, the imported new model should be a sub-class of the abstract model class defined in our library. One can

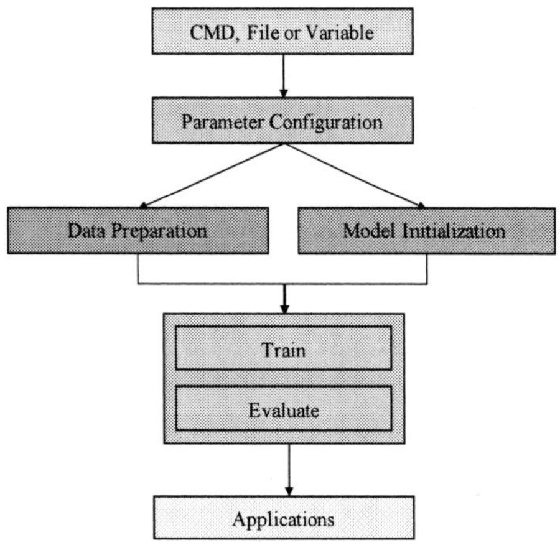

Figure 2: An illustrative usage flow of our library.

reuse the modules (*e.g.,* Transformer) and layers (*e.g.,* Highway net) already existing in our library for convenience. A configuration file is preferable to conduct further flexible adjustment.

• `forward()` function. This function calculates the training loss to be optimized and validation loss to avoid overfitting. Based on the returned training loss, our library will automatically invoke different optimization methods to learn the parameters according to pre-defined configuration.

• `generate()` function. This function is employed to generate output text based on input text or free text. Our library also provides several generation strategies, such as beam search and top-k search, for users to improve generation results.

In order to implement user-customized modules, one can reuse functions and classes inherited from our basic modules, or override original functions and add new functions.

4 Performance Evaluation

To evaluate the models in TextBox, we conduct extensive experiments to compare their performance on unconditional and conditional generation tasks.

4.1 Unconditional Text Generation

Following previous work, we adopt COCO (Lin et al., 2015), EMNLP2017 WMT News (Chatterjee et al., 2017) and IMDB Movie Reviews (Maas et al., 2011) datasets for comparing the performance of five traditional and state-of-the-art models, *i.e.,* LSTM-VAE, SeqGAN, RankGAN, MaliGAN, and GPT-2, in the unconditional text generation task.

In our experiments, we run models with the parameter configurations described in their original papers. Note that the BLEU-n metric employs the one-hot weights (*e.g.,* $(0, 0, 0, 1)$ for BLEU-4) instead of average weights, since we consider that one-hot weights can reflect the overlapping n-grams more realistically.

These results on COCO datasets are shown in Table 2, and other results on EMNLP2017 and IMDB datasets can be found in our GitHub page. We can see from Table 2, these models implemented in our library have the comparable performance compared with the results reported in the original papers. Moreover, the pretrained language model, *i.e.,* GPT-2, achieves consistent and remarkable performance, which is in line with our expectations.

4.2 Conditional Text Generation

In this section, we apply various models on four conditional text generation tasks, *i.e.,* attribute-to-text generation, dialogue systems, machine translation, and text summarization. The task of attribute-to-text generation is to generate text given several discrete attributes, such as user, item, and rating. We use the popular context-to-sequence (Context2Seq) and attribute-to-sequence (Attr2Seq) as base models, which utilize the multi-layer perceptron (MLP) and RNN as the encoder and decoder, respectively. Besides, dialogue systems aim to generate response given a conversation history. We consider two typical models, *i.e.,* attention-based RNN and Transformer, and one popular hierarchical recurrent encoder-decoder model (HRED) as base models. In RNN and Transformer, the multi-sequence conversation history is concatenated as one sequence feeding into the encoder, while in HERD the hierarchical structure of the conversation history is kept and modeled with a hierarchical encoder. Their results are shown in Table 2.

To showcase how our TextBox can support diverse techniques on several tasks with different decoding strategies, we compare the attention-based RNN model, Transformer, and four state-of-the-art pretrained language models, *i.e.,* BART, BERT2BERT, ProphetNet, and T5, for both machine translation and text summarization tasks. In Table 3, we adopt the IWSLT2014 German-to-English (Cettolo et al., 2014) translation dataset and utilize three generation strategies, *i.e.,* top-k, greedy, and beam search. The greedy strategy considers the most probable token at each generation step, the top-k search strategy means sorting by probability and zero-ing out the probabili-

Tasks	Datasets	Models	Distinct-1	Distinct-2	BLEU-1	BLEU-2	BLEU-3	BLEU-4
Unconditional Generation	COCO	LSTM-VAE	-	-	63.97	46.56	18.53	5.97
		SeqGAN	-	-	99.76	82.32	51.26	25.18
		RankGAN	-	-	99.76	82.92	52.46	26.40
		MailGAN	-	-	99.71	81.95	50.86	24.87
		GPT-2	-	-	88.15	78.13	55.81	31.88
Attribute-to-Text Generation	AMAZON	Context2Seq	0.07	0.39	17.21	2.80	0.83	0.43
		Attr2Seq	0.14	2.81	17.14	2.81	0.87	0.48
Dialogue Systems	Personal Chat	RNN+Attn	0.24	0.72	17.51	4.65	2.11	1.47
		Transformer	0.38	2.28	17.29	4.85	2.32	1.65
		HRED	0.22	0.63	17.29	4.72	2.20	1.60

Table 2: Performance comparisons of different methods for three tasks, *i.e.*, unconditional generation, attribute-to-text generation, and dialogue systems. Distinct-n is not applicable to the unconditional generation task. "-" denotes the metric Distinct-n is generally not applicable to unconditional text generation.

Model	Strategy	BLEU2	BLEU3	BLEU4
RNN+Attn	**Top-k**	26.68	16.95	10.85
	Greedy	33.74	23.03	15.79
	Beam	35.68	24.94	17.42
Transformer	**Top-k**	30.96	20.83	14.16
	Greedy	35.48	24.76	17.41
	Beam	36.88	26.10	18.54

Table 3: Performance comparison of different generation models with three strategies for machine translation from German to English.

Model	ROUGE-1	ROUGE-2	ROUGE-L
RNN+Attn	36.32	17.63	38.36
Transformer	36.21	17.64	38.10
BART	39.34	20.07	41.25
BERT2BERT	38.16	18.89	40.06
ProphetNet	38.49	18.41	39.84
T5	38.83	19.68	40.76

Table 4: Performance comparison of different generation models for text summarization. Specifically, we adopt the base version of BART, BERT2BERT, T5 and the large version of ProphetNet.

ties for anything below the k-th token, and beam search (Vijayakumar et al., 2018) strategy selects the top scoring B candidates from the set of all possible one token extensions of its beams, where B is the beam size ($B = 5$ in our experiments). From Table 3 we observe that the beam search strategy brings more improvement than the others. For text summarization, we compare RNN and Transformer with four pretrained models as shown in Table 4. These models are trained or fine-tuned in GigaWord (Graff et al., 2003) dataset. As observed in Table 4, pretrained models outperform the RNN model and Transformer by a clear margin.

The results of all implemented models in other tasks can be acquired from our GitHub page.

5 Related Work

Several toolkits have been released focusing on one or a few specific text generation tasks or techniques. For example, Tensor2Tensor (Vaswani et al., 2018), MarianNMT (Junczys-Dowmunt et al., 2018) and OpenNMT (Klein et al., 2017a) are designed for machine translation task, while ParlAI (Miller et al., 2017a) and Plato (Papangelis et al., 2020) specialized for dialog research in this field. There are two text generation libraries closely related to our library, including Texygen (Zhu et al., 2018) and Texar (Hu et al., 2019) focusing on GAN technique and high modularization, respectively. TextBox has drawn inspirations from these toolkits when designing relevant functions.

Compared with them, TextBox covers more text generation tasks and models, which is useful for reproducibility. Besides, we implement standardized evaluation to compare different models. Also, our library provides various common modules for convenience. It has a proper focus on text generation field, and provide a comprehensive set of modules and functionalities.

6 Conclusion

This paper presented a unified, modularized, and extensible text generation library, called `TextBox`. So far, we have implemented 21 text generation models, including VAE-based, GAN-based, pretrained language models, sequence-to-sequence and 9 benchmark datasets for unconditional and conditional text generation tasks. Moreover, Our library is modularized to easily plug in or swap out components, and extensible to support seamless incorporation of other external modules. In the future, features and functionalities will continue be added to our library, including more models and datasets, diverse inputs such as graph and table, and distributed training in multiple machines. We invite researchers and practitioners to join and enrich TextBox, and help push forward the research on text generation.

7 Broader Impacts

Text generation has a wide range of beneficial applications for society, including code auto-completion, game narrative generation, and answering questions. But it also has potentially harmful applications. For example, GPT-3 improves the quality of generated text over smaller models and increases the difficulty of distinguishing synthetic text from human-written text, such as fake news and reviews.

Here we focus on two potential issues: the potential for deliberate misuse of generation models and the issue of bias. Malicious uses of generation models can be somewhat difficult to anticipate because they often involve repurposing models in a very different environment or for a different purpose than researchers intended. To mitigate this, we can think in terms of traditional security risk assessment frameworks such as identifying threats. Biases present in training text may lead models to generate stereotyped or prejudiced content. This is concerning, since model bias could harm people in the relevant groups in different ways. In order to prevent bias, there is a need for building a common vocabulary tying together the normative, technical and empirical challenges of bias mitigation for generation models. We expect this to be an area of continuous research for us.

Acknowledgement

This work was partially supported by the National Natural Science Foundation of China under Grant No. 61872369 and 61832017, Beijing Academy of Artificial Intelligence (BAAI), Beijing Outstanding Young Scientist Program under Grant No. BJJWZYJH012019100020098, the Fundamental Research Funds for the Central Universities, and the Research Funds of Renmin University of China under Grant No. 18XNLG22 and 19XNQ047. Xin Zhao is the corresponding author.

References

Danial Alihosseini, Ehsan Montahaei, and Mahdieh Soleymani Baghshah. 2019. Jointly measuring diversity and quality in text generation models. In *Proceedings of the Workshop on Methods for Optimizing and Evaluating Neural Language Generation*, pages 90–98, Minneapolis, Minnesota. Association for Computational Linguistics.

Satanjeev Banerjee and Alon Lavie. 2005. METEOR: an automatic metric for MT evaluation with improved correlation with human judgments. In *IEEvaluation@ACL*, pages 65–72. Association for Computational Linguistics.

Samuel R. Bowman, Luke Vilnis, Oriol Vinyals, Andrew M. Dai, Rafal Józefowicz, and Samy Bengio. 2016. Generating sentences from a continuous space. In *Proceedings of the 20th SIGNLL Conference on Computational Natural Language Learning, CoNLL 2016, Berlin, Germany, August 11-12, 2016*, pages 10–21.

Denny Britz, Anna Goldie, Minh-Thang Luong, and Quoc Le. 2017. Massive exploration of neural machine translation architectures. In *Proceedings of the 2017 Conference on Empirical Methods in Natural Language Processing*, pages 1442–1451, Copenhagen, Denmark. Association for Computational Linguistics.

Peter F. Brown, Stephen Della Pietra, Vincent J. Della Pietra, Jennifer C. Lai, and Robert L. Mercer. 1992. An estimate of an upper bound for the entropy of english. *Comput. Linguistics*, 18(1):31–40.

Mauro Cettolo, Jan Niehues, Sebastian Stüker, Luisa Bentivogli, and Marcello Federico. 2014. Report on the 11th iwslt evaluation campaign, iwslt 2014. In *Proceedings of the International Workshop on Spoken Language Translation, Hanoi, Vietnam*, volume 57.

Rajen Chatterjee, Matteo Negri, Marco Turchi, Marcello Federico, Lucia Specia, and Frédéric Blain. 2017. Guiding neural machine translation decoding with external knowledge. In *Proceedings of the Second Conference on Machine Translation, Volume 1: Research Papers*, pages 157–168, Copenhagen, Denmark. Association for Computational Linguistics.

Tong Che, Yanran Li, Ruixiang Zhang, R. Devon Hjelm, Wenjie Li, Yangqiu Song, and Yoshua Bengio. 2017. Maximum-likelihood augmented discrete generative adversarial networks. *arXiv preprint arXiv:1702.07983*.

Jacob Devlin, Ming-Wei Chang, Kenton Lee, and Kristina Toutanova. 2019. BERT: pre-training of deep bidirectional transformers for language understanding. In *NAACL-HLT (1)*, pages 4171–4186. Association for Computational Linguistics.

Li Dong, Shaohan Huang, Furu Wei, Mirella Lapata, Ming Zhou, and Ke Xu. 2017. Learning to generate product reviews from attributes. In *Proceedings of the 15th Conference of the European Chapter of the Association for Computational Linguistics, EACL 2017, Valencia, Spain, April 3-7, 2017, Volume 1: Long Papers*, pages 623–632. Association for Computational Linguistics.

William Fedus, Ian J. Goodfellow, and Andrew M. Dai. 2018. Maskgan: Better text generation via filling in the ______. In *6th International Conference on Learning Representations, ICLR 2018, Vancouver, BC, Canada, April 30 - May 3, 2018, Conference Track Proceedings*.

David Graff, Junbo Kong, Ke Chen, and Kazuaki Maeda. 2003. English gigaword. *Linguistic Data Consortium, Philadelphia*, 4(1):34.

Jiaxian Guo, Sidi Lu, Han Cai, Weinan Zhang, Yong Yu, and Jun Wang. 2018. Long text generation via adversarial training with leaked information. In *Proceedings of the Thirty-Second AAAI Conference on Artificial Intelligence, (AAAI-18), the 30th innovative Applications of Artificial Intelligence (IAAI-18), and the 8th AAAI Symposium on Educational Advances in Artificial Intelligence (EAAI-18), New Orleans, Louisiana, USA, February 2-7, 2018*, pages 5141–5148.

Zhiting Hu, Haoran Shi, Bowen Tan, Wentao Wang, Zichao Yang, Tiancheng Zhao, Junxian He, Lianhui Qin, Di Wang, Xuezhe Ma, Zhengzhong Liu, Xiaodan Liang, Wanrong Zhu, Devendra Singh Sachan, and Eric P. Xing. 2019. Texar: A modularized, versatile, and extensible toolkit for text generation. In *Proceedings of the 57th Conference of the Association for Computational Linguistics, ACL 2019, Florence, Italy, July 28 - August 2, 2019, Volume 3: System Demonstrations*, pages 159–164. Association for Computational Linguistics.

Ferenc Huszar. 2015. How (not) to train your generative model: Scheduled sampling, likelihood, adversary? *arXiv preprint arXiv:1511.05101*.

Marcin Junczys-Dowmunt, Roman Grundkiewicz, Tomasz Dwojak, Hieu Hoang, Kenneth Heafield, Tom Neckermann, Frank Seide, Ulrich Germann, Alham Fikri Aji, Nikolay Bogoychev, André F. T. Martins, and Alexandra Birch. 2018. Marian: Fast neural machine translation in C++. In *Proceedings of ACL 2018, System Demonstrations*, pages 116–121, Melbourne, Australia. Association for Computational Linguistics.

Guillaume Klein, Yoon Kim, Yuntian Deng, Jean Senellart, and Alexander Rush. 2017a. OpenNMT: Open-source toolkit for neural machine translation. In *Proceedings of ACL 2017, System Demonstrations*, pages 67–72, Vancouver, Canada. Association for Computational Linguistics.

Guillaume Klein, Yoon Kim, Yuntian Deng, Jean Senellart, and Alexander M. Rush. 2017b. Opennmt: Open-source toolkit for neural machine translation. In *Proceedings of the 55th Annual Meeting of the Association for Computational Linguistics, ACL 2017, Vancouver, Canada, July 30 - August 4, System Demonstrations*, pages 67–72. Association for Computational Linguistics.

Mike Lewis, Yinhan Liu, Naman Goyal, Marjan Ghazvininejad, Abdelrahman Mohamed, Omer Levy, Veselin Stoyanov, and Luke Zettlemoyer. 2020. BART: denoising sequence-to-sequence pre-training for natural language generation, translation, and comprehension. In *Proceedings of the 58th Annual Meeting of the Association for Computational Linguistics, ACL 2020, Online, July 5-10, 2020*, pages 7871–7880.

Jiwei Li, Michel Galley, Chris Brockett, Jianfeng Gao, and Bill Dolan. 2016a. A diversity-promoting objective function for neural conversation models. In *NAACL HLT 2016, The 2016 Conference of the North American Chapter of the Association for Computational Linguistics: Human Language Technologies, San Diego California, USA, June 12-17, 2016*, pages 110–119. The Association for Computational Linguistics.

Jiwei Li, Will Monroe, Alan Ritter, Dan Jurafsky, Michel Galley, and Jianfeng Gao. 2016b. Deep reinforcement learning for dialogue generation. In *Proceedings of the 2016 Conference on Empirical Methods in Natural Language Processing, EMNLP 2016, Austin, Texas, USA, November 1-4, 2016*, pages 1192–1202. The Association for Computational Linguistics.

Juntao Li, Yan Song, Haisong Zhang, Dongmin Chen, Shuming Shi, Dongyan Zhao, and Rui Yan. 2018. Generating classical chinese poems via conditional variational autoencoder and adversarial training. In *Proceedings of the 2018 Conference on Empirical Methods in Natural Language Processing, Brussels, Belgium, October 31 - November 4, 2018*, pages 3890–3900. Association for Computational Linguistics.

Junyi Li, Tianyi Tang, Wayne Xin Zhao, Zhicheng Wei, Nicholas Jing Yuan, and Ji-Rong Wen. 2021a. Few-shot knowledge graph-to-text generation with pre-trained language models. In *Findings of ACL*.

Junyi Li, Tianyi Tang, Wayne Xin Zhao, and Ji-Rong Wen. 2021b. Pretrained language models for text generation: A survey. In *Proceedings of the 30th International Joint Conference on Artificial Intelligence, IJCAI 2021*.

Chin-Yew Lin. 2004. Rouge: A package for automatic evaluation of summaries. In *Text summarization branches out*, pages 74–81.

Kevin Lin, Dianqi Li, Xiaodong He, Ming-Ting Sun, and Zhengyou Zhang. 2017. Adversarial ranking for language generation. In *Advances in Neural Information Processing Systems 30: Annual Conference on Neural Information Processing Systems*

2017, December 4-9, 2017, Long Beach, CA, USA, pages 3155–3165.

Tsung-Yi Lin, Michael Maire, Serge Belongie, Lubomir Bourdev, Ross Girshick, James Hays, Pietro Perona, Deva Ramanan, C. Lawrence Zitnick, and Piotr Dollár. 2015. Microsoft coco: Common objects in context.

Andrew L. Maas, Raymond E. Daly, Peter T. Pham, Dan Huang, Andrew Y. Ng, and Christopher Potts. 2011. Learning word vectors for sentiment analysis. In *Proceedings of the 49th Annual Meeting of the Association for Computational Linguistics: Human Language Technologies*, pages 142–150, Portland, Oregon, USA. Association for Computational Linguistics.

Alexander Miller, Will Feng, Dhruv Batra, Antoine Bordes, Adam Fisch, Jiasen Lu, Devi Parikh, and Jason Weston. 2017a. ParlAI: A dialog research software platform. In *Proceedings of the 2017 Conference on Empirical Methods in Natural Language Processing: System Demonstrations*, pages 79–84, Copenhagen, Denmark. Association for Computational Linguistics.

Alexander H. Miller, Will Feng, Dhruv Batra, Antoine Bordes, Adam Fisch, Jiasen Lu, Devi Parikh, and Jason Weston. 2017b. Parlai: A dialog research software platform. In *Proceedings of the 2017 Conference on Empirical Methods in Natural Language Processing, EMNLP 2017, Copenhagen, Denmark, September 9-11, 2017 - System Demonstrations*, pages 79–84. Association for Computational Linguistics.

Alexandros Papangelis, Mahdi Namazifar, Chandra Khatri, Yi-Chia Wang, Piero Molino, and Gokhan Tur. 2020. Plato dialogue system: A flexible conversational ai research platform.

Kishore Papineni, Salim Roukos, Todd Ward, and Wei-Jing Zhu. 2002. Bleu: a method for automatic evaluation of machine translation. In *Proceedings of the 40th Annual Meeting of the Association for Computational Linguistics, July 6-12, 2002, Philadelphia, PA, USA*, pages 311–318. ACL.

Adam Paszke, Sam Gross, Francisco Massa, Adam Lerer, James Bradbury, Gregory Chanan, Trevor Killeen, Zeming Lin, Natalia Gimelshein, Luca Antiga, Alban Desmaison, Andreas Köpf, Edward Yang, Zachary DeVito, Martin Raison, Alykhan Tejani, Sasank Chilamkurthy, Benoit Steiner, Lu Fang, Junjie Bai, and Soumith Chintala. 2019. Pytorch: An imperative style, high-performance deep learning library. In *Advances in Neural Information Processing Systems 32: Annual Conference on Neural Information Processing Systems 2019, NeurIPS 2019, December 8-14, 2019, Vancouver, BC, Canada*, pages 8024–8035.

Maja Popovic. 2015. chrf: character n-gram f-score for automatic MT evaluation. In *WMT@EMNLP*, pages 392–395. The Association for Computer Linguistics.

Weizhen Qi, Yu Yan, Yeyun Gong, Dayiheng Liu, Nan Duan, Jiusheng Chen, Ruofei Zhang, and Ming Zhou. 2020. Prophetnet: Predicting future n-gram for sequence-to-sequence pre-training. In *Proceedings of the 2020 Conference on Empirical Methods in Natural Language Processing: Findings, EMNLP 2020, Online Event, 16-20 November 2020*, pages 2401–2410. Association for Computational Linguistics.

Alec Radford, Jeffrey Wu, Rewon Child, David Luan, Dario Amodei, and Ilya Sutskever. 2019. Language models are unsupervised multitask learners. *OpenAI blog*, 1(8):9.

Colin Raffel, Noam Shazeer, Adam Roberts, Katherine Lee, Sharan Narang, Michael Matena, Yanqi Zhou, Wei Li, and Peter J. Liu. 2020. Exploring the limits of transfer learning with a unified text-to-text transformer. *J. Mach. Learn. Res.*, 21:140:1–140:67.

Sascha Rothe, Shashi Narayan, and Aliaksei Severyn. 2020. Leveraging pre-trained checkpoints for sequence generation tasks. *Trans. Assoc. Comput. Linguistics*, 8:264–280.

Abigail See, Peter J. Liu, and Christopher D. Manning. 2017. Get to the point: Summarization with pointer-generator networks. In *Proceedings of the 55th Annual Meeting of the Association for Computational Linguistics, ACL 2017, Vancouver, Canada, July 30 - August 4, Volume 1: Long Papers*, pages 1073–1083. Association for Computational Linguistics.

Stanislau Semeniuta, Aliaksei Severyn, and Erhardt Barth. 2017. A hybrid convolutional variational autoencoder for text generation. In *Proceedings of the 2017 Conference on Empirical Methods in Natural Language Processing, EMNLP 2017, Copenhagen, Denmark, September 9-11, 2017*, pages 627–637.

Iulian Vlad Serban, Alessandro Sordoni, Yoshua Bengio, Aaron C. Courville, and Joelle Pineau. 2016. Building end-to-end dialogue systems using generative hierarchical neural network models. In *Proceedings of the Thirtieth AAAI Conference on Artificial Intelligence, February 12-17, 2016, Phoenix, Arizona, USA*, pages 3776–3784. AAAI Press.

Ilya Sutskever, Oriol Vinyals, and Quoc V. Le. 2014. Sequence to sequence learning with neural networks. In *Advances in Neural Information Processing Systems 27: Annual Conference on Neural Information Processing Systems 2014, December 8-13 2014, Montreal, Quebec, Canada*, pages 3104–3112.

Jian Tang, Yifan Yang, Samuel Carton, Ming Zhang, and Qiaozhu Mei. 2016. Context-aware natural language generation with recurrent neural networks. *arXiv preprint arXiv:1611.09900*.

Ashish Vaswani, Samy Bengio, Eugene Brevdo, Francois Chollet, Aidan Gomez, Stephan Gouws, Llion Jones, Łukasz Kaiser, Nal Kalchbrenner, Niki Parmar, Ryan Sepassi, Noam Shazeer, and Jakob Uszkoreit. 2018. Tensor2Tensor for neural machine translation. In *Proceedings of the 13th Conference of the Association for Machine Translation in the Americas (Volume 1: Research Track)*, pages 193–199, Boston, MA. Association for Machine Translation in the Americas.

Ashish Vaswani, Noam Shazeer, Niki Parmar, Jakob Uszkoreit, Llion Jones, Aidan N. Gomez, Lukasz Kaiser, and Illia Polosukhin. 2017. Attention is all you need. In *Advances in Neural Information Processing Systems 30: Annual Conference on Neural Information Processing Systems 2017, December 4-9, 2017, Long Beach, CA, USA*, pages 5998–6008.

Ramakrishna Vedantam, C. Lawrence Zitnick, and Devi Parikh. 2015. Cider: Consensus-based image description evaluation. In *CVPR*, pages 4566–4575. IEEE Computer Society.

Ashwin K. Vijayakumar, Michael Cogswell, Ramprasaath R. Selvaraju, Qing Sun, Stefan Lee, David J. Crandall, and Dhruv Batra. 2018. Diverse beam search for improved description of complex scenes. In *Proceedings of the Thirty-Second AAAI Conference on Artificial Intelligence, (AAAI-18), the 30th innovative Applications of Artificial Intelligence (IAAI-18), and the 8th AAAI Symposium on Educational Advances in Artificial Intelligence (EAAI-18), New Orleans, Louisiana, USA, February 2-7, 2018*, pages 7371–7379. AAAI Press.

Zhilin Yang, Zihang Dai, Yiming Yang, Jaime G. Carbonell, Ruslan Salakhutdinov, and Quoc V. Le. 2019. Xlnet: Generalized autoregressive pretraining for language understanding. In *Advances in Neural Information Processing Systems 32: Annual Conference on Neural Information Processing Systems 2019, NeurIPS 2019, December 8-14, 2019, Vancouver, BC, Canada*, pages 5754–5764.

Zichao Yang, Zhiting Hu, Ruslan Salakhutdinov, and Taylor Berg-Kirkpatrick. 2017. Improved variational autoencoders for text modeling using dilated convolutions. In *Proceedings of the 34th International Conference on Machine Learning, ICML 2017, Sydney, NSW, Australia, 6-11 August 2017*, pages 3881–3890.

Lantao Yu, Weinan Zhang, Jun Wang, and Yong Yu. 2017. Seqgan: Sequence generative adversarial nets with policy gradient. In *Proceedings of the Thirty-First AAAI Conference on Artificial Intelligence, February 4-9, 2017, San Francisco, California, USA*, pages 2852–2858.

Tianyi Zhang, Varsha Kishore, Felix Wu, Kilian Q. Weinberger, and Yoav Artzi. 2020. Bertscore: Evaluating text generation with BERT. In *ICLR*. OpenReview.net.

Yizhe Zhang, Zhe Gan, Kai Fan, Zhi Chen, Ricardo Henao, Dinghan Shen, and Lawrence Carin. 2017. Adversarial feature matching for text generation. In *Proceedings of the 34th International Conference on Machine Learning, ICML 2017, Sydney, NSW, Australia, 6-11 August 2017*, pages 4006–4015.

Yaoming Zhu, Sidi Lu, Lei Zheng, Jiaxian Guo, Weinan Zhang, Jun Wang, and Yong Yu. 2018. Texygen: A benchmarking platform for text generation models. In *The 41st International ACM SIGIR Conference on Research & Development in Information Retrieval, SIGIR 2018, Ann Arbor, MI, USA, July 08-12, 2018*, pages 1097–1100. ACM.

Inside ASCENT: Exploring a Deep Commonsense Knowledge Base and its Usage in Question Answering

Tuan-Phong Nguyen **Simon Razniewski** **Gerhard Weikum**
Max Planck Institute for Informatics
Saarbrücken, Germany
{tuanphong,srazniew,weikum}@mpi-inf.mpg.de

Abstract

ASCENT is a fully automated methodology for extracting and consolidating commonsense assertions from web contents (Nguyen et al., 2021). It advances traditional triple-based commonsense knowledge representation by capturing semantic facets like locations and purposes, and composite concepts, i.e., subgroups and related aspects of subjects. In this demo, we present a web portal that allows users to understand its construction process, explore its content, and observe its impact in the use case of question answering. The demo website[1] and an introductory video[2] are both available online.

1 Introduction

Commonsense knowledge (CSK) is an enduring theme of AI (McCarthy, 1960) that has been recently revived for the goal of building more robust and reliable applications (Monroe, 2020). Recent years have witnessed the emerging of large pretrained language models (LMs), notably BERT (Devlin et al., 2018), GPT (Brown et al., 2020) and their variants which significantly boosted the performance of tasks requiring natural language understanding such as question answering and dialogue systems (Clark et al., 2020). Although it has been shown that such LMs implicitly store some commonsense knowledge (Talmor et al., 2019), this comes with various caveats, for example regarding degree of truth, or negation, and their commercial development is inherently hampered by their low interpretability and explainability.

Structured knowledge bases (KBs), in contrast, give a great possibility of explaining and interpreting outputs of systems leveraging the resources. There have been great efforts towards building large-scale commonsense knowledge bases (CSKBs), including expert-annotated KBs (e.g., Cyc (Lenat, 1995)), crowdsourced KBs (e.g., ConceptNet (Speer and Havasi, 2012) and Atomic (Sap et al., 2019)) and KBs built by automatic acquisition methods such as WebChild (Tandon et al., 2014, 2017), TupleKB (Mishra et al., 2017), Quasimodo (Romero et al., 2019) and CSKG (Ilievski et al., 2020). Human-created KBs, although possessing high precision, usually suffer from low coverage. On the other hand, automatically-acquired KBs typically have better coverage, but also contain more noise. Nonetheless, despite different construction methods, these KBs are all based on a simple subject-predicate-object model, which has major limitations in validity and expressiveness.

We recently presented ASCENT (Nguyen et al., 2021), a methodology for automatically collecting and consolidating commonsense assertions from the general web. To overcome the limitations of prior works, ASCENT refines subjects with subgroups (e.g., *circus elephant* and *domesticated elephant*) and aspects (e.g., *elephant tusk* and *elephant habitat*), and captures semantic facets of assertions (e.g., ⟨*lawyer, represents, clients, LOCATION: in courts*⟩ or ⟨*elephant, uses, its trunk, PURPOSE: to suck up water*⟩).

For a given concept, ASCENT searches through the web with pattern-based search queries disambiguated using WordNet (Miller, 1995) hypernymy. Then, irrelevant documents are filtered out based on similarity comparison against the corresponding Wikipedia articles. We then use a series of judicious dependency-parse-based rules to collect faceted assertions from the retained texts. The semantic facets, which come from prepositional phrases and supporting adverbs are then labeled by a supervised classifier. Finally, assertions are clustered using similarity scores from word2vec (Mikolov et al., 2013) and a fine-tuned RoBERTa (Liu et al., 2019) model.

[1] https://ascent.mpi-inf.mpg.de
[2] https://youtu.be/qMkJXqu_Yd4

Proceedings of the Joint Conference of the 59th Annual Meeting of the Association for Computational Linguistics and the 11th International Joint Conference on Natural Language Processing: System Demonstrations, pages 40–47, August 1st - August 6th, 2021.

We executed the ASCENT pipeline for 10,000 prominent concepts (selected based on their respective number of assertions in ConceptNet) as primary subjects. In (Nguyen et al., 2021), we showed that the content of the resulting CSKB (hereinafter referred to as ASCENT KB) is a milestone in both salience and recall. As extrinsic evaluation, we conducted a comprehensive evaluation of the contribution of CSK to zero-shot question answering (QA) with pre-trained language models (Petroni et al., 2020; Guu et al., 2020).

This paper presents a companion web portal of the ASCENT KB, which enables the following interactions:

1. Exploration of the construction process of ASCENT, by inspecting word sense and Wikipedia disambiguation, web search queries, clustered statements, and source sentences and documents.

2. Inspection of the resulting KB, starting from subjects, predicates, objects, or examining specific subgroups or aspects.

3. Observation of the impact of structured knowledge on question answering with pretrained language models, comparing generated answers across various CSKBs and QA settings.

The web portal is available at `https://ascent.mpi-inf.mpg.de`, and a screencast demonstrating the system can be found at `https://youtu.be/qMkJXqu_Yd4`.

2 ASCENT

Two major contributions of ASCENT are its expressive knowledge model, and its state-of-the-art extraction methodology. Details are in the technical paper (Nguyen et al., 2021). In this section, we revisit the most important points.

2.1 Knowledge model

ASCENT extends the traditional triple-based data model in existing CSKBs in two ways.

Expressive subjects. Subjects in existing CSKBs are usually single nouns, which implies two shortcomings: (i) different meanings for the same word are conflated, and (ii) refinements and variants of word senses are missed out. ASCENT has addressed this problem with the following means:

1. When searching for source texts, ASCENT combines the target subject with an informative hypernym from WordNet to distinguish different senses of the word (e.g., "bus public transport" and "bus network topology" for the subject *bus*).

2. ASCENT refines subjects with multi-word phrases into *subgroups* and *aspects*. For example, subgroups for the subject *bus* would be *tourist bus* and *school bus*, while one of its aspects would be *bus driver*.

Semantic facets. The validity of commonsense assertions is usually non-binary (Zhang et al., 2017; Chalier et al., 2020), and depends on specific temporal and spatial circumstances (e.g., lions live for 10-14 years in the wild but for more than 15 years in captivity). Moreover, CSK triples often benefit from further context regarding causes/effects and instruments (e.g., elephants communicate with each other *by creating sounds*, beer is served *in bars*). In ASCENT's knowledge model, such information is added to SPO triples via semantic facets. ASCENT distinguished 8 types of facets: *cause, manner, purpose, transitive-object, degree, location, temporal* and *other-quality*.

2.2 Extraction pipeline

ASCENT is a pipeline operating in three phases: *source discovery, knowledge extraction* and *knowledge consolidation*. Fig. 1 illustrates the architecture of the pipeline.

Source discovery. We utilize the Bing Web Search API to obtain documents specific to each subject, with search queries refined by the subject's hypernyms in WordNet. We manually designed query templates for 35 prominent hypernyms (e.g., if subject s_0 has hypernym *animal.n.01*, we produce the search query "s_0 animal facts", similarly for the hypernym *professional.n.01*, the search query will be "s_0 job descriptions"). We then compute the cosine similarity between the bag-of-words representations of each obtained document and a respective Wikipedia article to determine the relevance of the documents. Low-ranked documents will be omitted in further steps.

Knowledge extraction. The extractors take in the relevant documents and their outputs include: open information extraction (OIE) tuples, list of subgroups and list of aspects. To obtain *OIE tuples*, we extend the STUFFIE approach (Prasojo et al.,

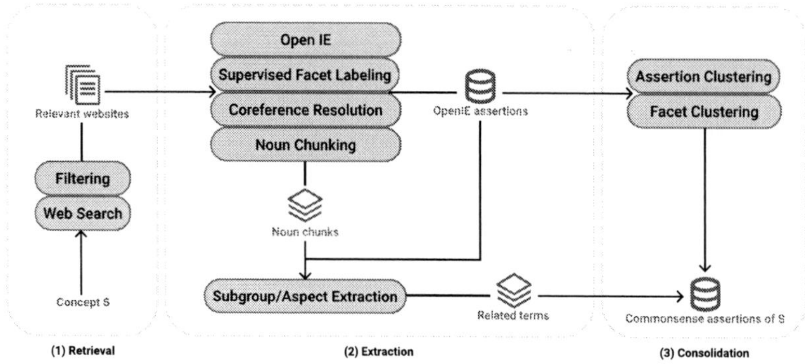

Figure 1: Architecture of the ASCENT extraction pipeline (Nguyen et al., 2021).

2018), a list of carefully crafted dependency-parse-based rules, to pull out faceted assertions from the texts. Then we classify each facet into one of the eight semantic labels using a fine-tuned RoBERTa model. For *subgroups*, noun phrases whose head word is the target subject are collected as candidates and then are clustered using the hierarchical agglomerative clustering (HAC) algorithm on average word2vec representations. Finally, we collect *aspects* from possessive noun chunks and SPO triples where P is either "have", "contain", "be assembled of" or "be composed of".

Knowledge consolidation. We perform clustering on SPO triples and facet values. As *SPO triples*, we first filter triple-pair candidates with fast word2vec similarity. After that, advanced similarity of triple pairs computed by another fine-tuned RoBERTa model is fed to the HAC algorithm to group the triples into semantically similar clusters. For *facet values*, we group phrases with the same head words together (e.g., "during evening" and "in the evening").

2.3 Web portal

The web portal (`https://ascent.mpi-inf.mpg.de`) is implemented in Python using Django, and hosted on an Nginx web server. The underlying structured CSK is stored in a PostgreSQL database, while for the QA part, statements of all CSKBs are indexed and queried via Apache Solr, for fast text-based querying. All components are deployed on a virtual machine with access to 4 virtual CPUs and 8 GB of RAM.

In the demonstration session, we show how users can interact with the portal for exploring the KB (Section 4.1), understanding the KB construction (Section 4.2), and observing its utility for question answering (Section 4.3).

3 Commonsense QA setups

One common extrinsic use case of KBs is question answering. Recently, it was observed that priming language models (LMs) with relevant context can considerably benefit their performance in QA-like tasks (Petroni et al., 2020; Guu et al., 2020). In (Nguyen et al., 2021), to evaluate the contribution of structured CSK to QA, we conducted a comprehensive evaluation consisting of four different setups, all based on the above idea.

1. In *masked prediction* (MP), LMs are asked to predict single masked tokens in generic sentences.

2. In *free generation* (FG), LMs arbitrarily generate answer sentences to given questions.

3. *Guided generation* (GG) extends free generation by answer prefixes that prevent the LMs from evading answering.

4. *Span prediction* (SP) is the task of locating the answer of a question in provided context.

Examples of the QA setups can be seen in Table 1. Generally, given a question, our system will retrieve from CSKBs assertions relevant to it, and then use the assertions as additional context to guide the LMs. In the ASCENT demonstrator, we provide a web interface for experimenting with all of those QA setups with context retrieved from several popular CSKBs.

4 Demonstration experience

In the demonstration session, attendees will experience three main functionalities of our demonstration system.

Setup	Input	Sample output
MP	Elephants eat [MASK]. [SEP] Elephants eat roots, grasses, fruit, and bark, and they eat a lot of these things.	everything (15.52%), trees (15.32%), plants (11.26%)
FG	C: Elephants eat roots, grasses, fruit, and bark, and they eat... Q: What do elephants eat? A:	They eat a lot of grasses, fruits, and...
GG	C: Elephants eat roots, grasses, fruit, and bark, and they eat... Q: What do elephants eat? A: Elephants eat	Elephants eat a lot of things.
SP	question="What do elephants eat?" context="Elephants eat roots, grasses, fruit, and bark, and they eat..."	start=14, end=46, answer="roots, grasses, fruit, and bark"

Table 1: Examples of QA setups (Nguyen et al., 2021).

4.1 Exploring the ASCENT KB

Concept page. Suppose a user wants to know which knowledge ASCENT stores for *elephants*. They can enter the concept into the search field in the top right of the start page, and select the first result from the autocompletion list, or press enter, to arrive at the intended concept. The resulting website (see Fig. 2) is divided into three main areas.

At the top left, they can inspect an image from `https://pixabay.com`, the WordNet synset used for disambiguation, the Wikipedia page used for result filtering, and a list of alternative lemmas, if existing.

At the top right, users can see subgroups and related aspects, which in our knowledge representation model, can carry their own statements. This way, they can learn that the most salient aspects of *elephants* are their *trunks, tusks* and *ears*, or that *elephant trunks have more than 40,000 muscles*.

The body of the page, presents the assertions, organized into groups of same-predicate assertions. In each group, assertions are sorted by their frequency displayed beside their objects. For example, the most commonly mentioned *foods* of *elephants* are *grasses, fruits,* and *plants*. Many assertions come with a red asterisk. This indicates that the assertion comes with semantic facets. When clicking on an assertion, it will show a small box displaying an SVG-based visualisation of the assertion in which we illustrate all elements of the assertion: its subject, predicate, object, facet labels and values, frequency of the assertion as well as frequency of each facet. For example, one can see that the purpose of *elephants using their trunks* is *to suck up water*.

Searching and downloading assertions. Alternatively to exploring statements starting from a subject, users can start from a search functionality under the *Browse* menu. This way, they can search, for instance, for all concepts that eat grass (*capybara, zebra, kangaroo, ...*).

The website also provides a JSON-formatted data dump (678MB) of all 8.9 million assertions extracted by the pipeline and their corresponding source sentences and documents. This dataset is also accessible via the HuggingFace Datasets package[3].

4.2 Inspecting the construction of assertions

For many downstream use cases, it is important to know about the provenance of information.

Users can inspect general properties of the construction process by observing the WordNet lemma and the Wikipedia page used for filtering, as well as inspect specific statistics about the number of retained websites, sentences, and assertions, in a panel at the bottom of subject pages (e.g., 435 websites were retained for *elephant*, from which 50k OpenIE assertions could be extracted).

Furthermore, users can look deeply into the construction process of each assertion on its own dedicated page, which displays the following:

1. *Clustered triples*: These are triples that were grouped together in the knowledge consolidation phase (cf. Section 2.2), where the most frequent triple was selected as cluster representative. For example, for the assertion ⟨*lion, eat, zebra, DEGREE: mostly*⟩ (14), the cluster contains: ⟨*lion, eat, zebra*⟩ (9), ⟨*lion, prey on, zebra*⟩ (2), ⟨*lion, feed on, zebra*⟩ (1), ⟨*lion, feed upon, zebra*⟩ (1), ⟨*lion, prey upon, zebra*⟩ (1). The numbers in parentheses indicate their corresponding frequency.

2. *Facets*: The assertion's facets are presented in a table whose columns are facet value, facet type and clustered facets. The frequency of each clustered facet is also indicated.

3. *Source sentences and documents*: Finally, we exhibit the sentences from which the assertions were extracted and their parent documents (in the form of URLs). Furthermore, in the extraction phase, we also recorded the position of assertion elements (i.e., subject, predicate, object, facet) in the source sentences.

[3]`https://huggingface.co/datasets/ascent_kb`

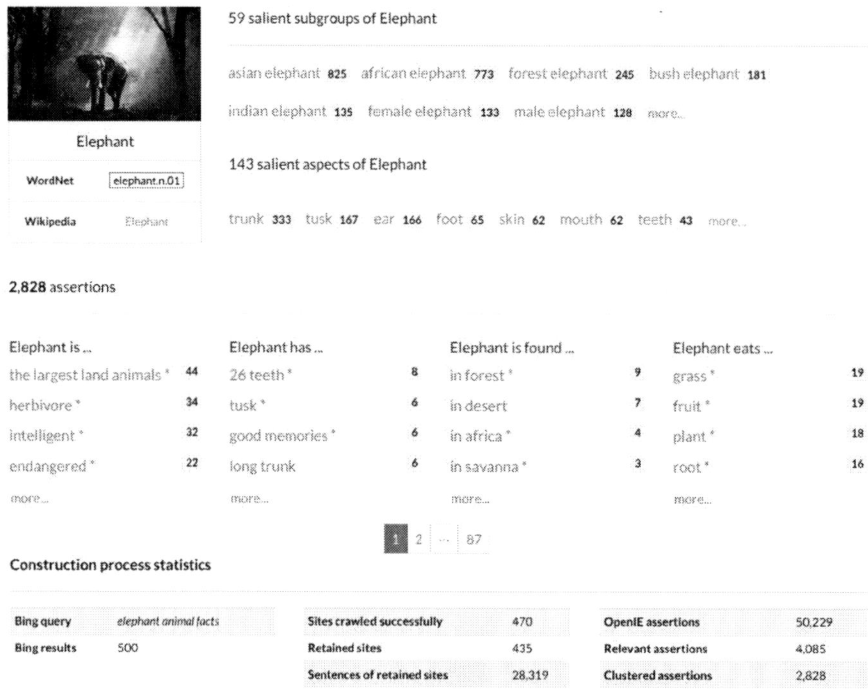

Figure 2: Example of ASCENT's page for the concept *elephant*.

We show that information to users by highlighting each kind of element with a different color in the source sentences.

4.3 Experimenting with commonsense QA

The third functionality experienced in the demo session is the utilization of commonsense knowledge for question answering (QA).

Input. There are four main parts in the input interface for the QA experiment:

1. *QA setup*: The user chooses one QA setup they want to experiment with. Available are *Masked Prediction*, *Span Prediction* and *Free/Guided Generation*. If *Masked Prediction* is selected, the user can choose how many answers the LM should produce. For the *Generation* settings, users can provide an answer prefix to avoid overly evasive answers.

2. *Input query*: The user enters the text question as input. The question can be in the form of a masked sentence (in the case of *Masked Prediction*), or a standard natural-language question (in other setups).

3. *Retrieval options*: The user can select one supported retrieval method and the number of assertions to be retrieved per CSKB for each question.

4. *Context sources*: The user selects the sources of context (i.e., "no context", CSKBs and "custom context"). If a CSKB is selected, the system will retrieve from that KB assertions relevant to the given input question. If "custom context" is selected, user must then enter their own content. The "no context" option is available for all setups but *Span Prediction*.

Output. The QA system presents its output in the form of a table which has three columns: *Source*, *Answer(s)* and *Context*. For *Masked Prediction* and *Span Prediction*, answers are printed with their respective confidence scores, meanwhile for *Free/Guided Generation*, only answers are printed. For *Span Prediction* in which answers come directly from given contexts, we also highlight the answers in the contexts.

An example of the QA demo's output for the question *"What do rabbits eat?"* under the *Free Generation* setting can be seen in Fig. 3. One can observe that language models' predictions are heavily influenced by given contexts. Without context, GPT-2 is only able to generate an evasive answer.

When being given context, it tends to re-generate the first sentence in the context first, (e.g., see the answers aligning with ASCENT, TupleKB and ConceptNet in Fig. 3). For the context retrieved from Quasimodo, GPT-2 is able to overlook the erroneous first sentence, however its generated answer is rather elusive despite the fact that subsequent statements in the context all contain direct answers to the question.

The question *"Bartenders work in [MASK]."* under the *Masked Prediction* setting is another example for the influence of context on LMs' output. Since *bartender* is a subject well covered by the ASCENT KB, the assertions pulled out are all relevant (i.e., *Bartenders work in bar. Bartenders work in restaurant...*) which help guide the LM to a good answer (*bar*). Meanwhile, because this subject is not present in TupleKB, its retrieved statements are rather unrelated (*Work capitals have firm. Work experiences include statement...*). Given that, the top-1 prediction for this KB was *tandem* which is obviously an evasive answer.

5 Related work

CSKB construction. Cyc (Lenat, 1995) is the first attempt to build a large-scale commonsense knowledge base. Since then, there have been a number of other CSKB construction projects, notably ConceptNet (Speer and Havasi, 2012), WebChild (Tandon et al., 2014, 2017), TupleKB (Mishra et al., 2017), and more recently Quasimodo (Romero et al., 2019), Dice (Chalier et al., 2020), Atomic (Sap et al., 2019), and CSKG (Ilievski et al., 2020). The early approach to building a CSKB is based on human annotation (e.g., Cyc with expert annotation and ConceptNet with crowdsourcing annotation). Later projects tend to use automated methods based on open information extraction to collect CSK from texts (e.g., WebChild, TupleKB and Quasimodo). Lately, CSKG is an attempt to combine various commonsense knowledge resources into a single KB. The common thread of these CSKB is that they are all based on SPO triples as knowledge representation, which has shortcomings (Nguyen et al., 2021). ASCENT is the first attempt to build a large-scale CSKB with assertions equipped with semantic facets built upon the ideas of semantic role labeling (Palmer et al., 2010).

KB visualization. Most CSKBs share their content via CSV files. Some, like ConceptNet[4], WebChild[5], Atomic[6] and Quasimodo[7], have a web portal to visualise their assertions. The most common way for CSKB visualisation is to use a single page for each subject and group assertions by predicate (e.g., in ConceptNet and WebChild). Quasimodo, on the other hand, implements a simple search interface to filter assertions and presents assertions in a tabular way (Romero and Razniewski, 2020). The ASCENT demo has both functionalities: exhibiting assertions of each concept in a separated page, and supporting assertion filtering. Our demo also uses an SVG-based visualisation of assertions with semantic facets, which are a distinctive feature of the ASCENT knowledge model.

Context in LM-based question answering. Priming large pretrained LMs with context in QA-like tasks is a relatively new line of research (Petroni et al., 2020; Guu et al., 2020). In our original paper, we made the first attempt to evaluate the contribution of CSKB assertions to QA via four different setups based on that idea. While others use commonsense knowledge for (re-)training language models (Hwang et al., 2021; Ilievski et al., 2021; Ma et al., 2021; Mitra et al., 2020), to the best of our knowledge, our demo system is the first to visualize the effect of priming vanilla language models, i.e., without task-specific retraining.

6 Conclusion

We presented a web portal for a state-of-the-art commonsense knowledge base—the ASCENT KB. It allows users to fully explore and search the CSKB, inspect the construction process of each assertion, and observe the impact of structured CSKBs on different QA tasks. We hope that the portal enables interesting interactions with the ASCENT methodology, and that the QA demo allows researchers to explore the potentials of combining structured data with pre-trained language models.

References

Tom B Brown et al. 2020. Language models are few-shot learners. In *NeurIPS*.

[4]http://conceptnet.io

[5]https://gate.d5.mpi-inf.mpg.de/webchild

[6]https://mosaickg.apps.allenai.org/kg-atomic2020

[7]https://quasimodo.r2.enst.fr

Output

Retriever: BM25 Retriever
Predictor: Free Generator `gpt2`

Source	Answer(s)	Context
No context	**They are very good at eating rabbits.**	
ASCENT^{triple}	**Rabbits eat grass.**	Rabbits eat grass. Rabbits eat plant. Rabbits eat vegetable. Rabbits eat food. Rabbits eat weed.
Quasimodo	**Rabbits eat the same things as humans.**	Eats can rabbit. Rabbits eat wires. Rabbits eat roses. Rabbits eat carpet. Rabbits eat mice.
TupleKB	**Rabbits eat rabbit.**	Rabbits eat rabbit. Rabbits eat food. Rabbits eat carrot. Rabbits eat leaf. Rabbits eat lettuce.
ConceptNet	**Rabbits are good to eat.**	Rabbits are good to eat. Eat vegetables need rabbit. Eating vegetables have pretend rabbit. Rabbits are cute. Rabbits are fast.

Figure 3: *Free Generation* output for question: *"What do rabbits eat?"*.

Yohan Chalier, Simon Razniewski, and Gerhard Weikum. 2020. Joint reasoning for multi-faceted commonsense knowledge. In *AKBC*.

Peter Clark et al. 2020. From 'F'to 'A' on the NY regents science exams: An overview of the Aristo project. *AI Magazine*.

Jacob Devlin, Ming-Wei Chang, Kenton Lee, and Kristina Toutanova. 2018. Bert: Pre-training of deep bidirectional transformers for language understanding. In *NAACL*.

Kelvin Guu, Kenton Lee, Zora Tung, Panupong Pasupat, and Ming-Wei Chang. 2020. Realm: Retrieval-augmented language model pre-training. In *ICML*.

Jena D Hwang, Chandra Bhagavatula, Ronan Le Bras, Jeff Da, Keisuke Sakaguchi, Antoine Bosselut, and Yejin Choi. 2021. Comet-atomic 2020: On symbolic and neural commonsense knowledge graphs. In *AAAI*.

Filip Ilievski, Alessandro Oltramari, Kaixin Ma, Bin Zhang, Deborah L McGuinness, and Pedro Szekely. 2021. Dimensions of commonsense knowledge. *arXiv preprint arXiv:2101.04640*.

Filip Ilievski, Pedro Szekely, and Bin Zhang. 2020. Cskg: The commonsense knowledge graph. *arXiv preprint arXiv:2012.11490*.

Douglas B Lenat. 1995. Cyc: A large-scale investment in knowledge infrastructure. *Communications of the ACM*.

Yinhan Liu, Myle Ott, Naman Goyal, Jingfei Du, Mandar Joshi, Danqi Chen, Omer Levy, Mike Lewis, Luke Zettlemoyer, and Veselin Stoyanov. 2019. Roberta: A robustly optimized BERT pretraining approach. *arXiv preprint arXiv:1907.11692*.

Kaixin Ma, Filip Ilievski, Jonathan Francis, Yonatan Bisk, Eric Nyberg, and Alessandro Oltramari. 2021. Knowledge-driven data construction for zero-shot evaluation in commonsense question answering. In *AAAI*.

John McCarthy. 1960. *Programs with common sense*. RLE and MIT computation center.

Tomas Mikolov, Kai Chen, Greg Corrado, and Jeffrey Dean. 2013. Efficient estimation of word representations in vector space. In *ICLR*.

George A Miller. 1995. Wordnet: a lexical database for English. *Communications of the ACM*.

Bhavana Dalvi Mishra, Niket Tandon, and Peter Clark. 2017. Domain-targeted, high precision knowledge extraction. *TACL*.

Arindam Mitra, Pratyay Banerjee, Kuntal Kumar Pal, Swaroop Mishra, and Chitta Baral. 2020. How additional knowledge can improve natural language commonsense question answering? *arXiv preprint arXiv:1909.08855*.

Don Monroe. 2020. Seeking artificial common sense. *Communications of the ACM*.

Tuan-Phong Nguyen, Simon Razniewski, and Gerhard Weikum. 2021. Advanced semantics for commonsense knowledge extraction. In *WWW*.

Martha Palmer, Daniel Gildea, and Nianwen Xue. 2010. Semantic role labeling. *Synthesis Lectures on Human Language Technologies*.

Fabio Petroni, Patrick Lewis, Aleksandra Piktus, Tim Rocktäschel, Yuxiang Wu, Alexander H Miller, and Sebastian Riedel. 2020. How context affects language models' factual predictions. In *AKBC*.

Radityo Eko Prasojo, Mouna Kacimi, and Werner Nutt. 2018. Stuffie: Semantic tagging of unlabeled facets using fine-grained information extraction. In *CIKM*.

Julien Romero and Simon Razniewski. 2020. Inside quasimodo: Exploring construction and usage of commonsense knowledge. In *CIKM*.

Julien Romero, Simon Razniewski, Koninika Pal, Jeff Z. Pan, Archit Sakhadeo, and Gerhard Weikum. 2019. Commonsense properties from query logs and question answering forums. In *CIKM*.

Maarten Sap et al. 2019. Atomic: An atlas of machine commonsense for if-then reasoning. In *AAAI*.

Robyn Speer and Catherine Havasi. 2012. Conceptnet 5: A large semantic network for relational knowledge. *Theory and Applications of Natural Language Processing*.

Alon Talmor, Yanai Elazar, Yoav Goldberg, and Jonathan Berant. 2019. olmpics - on what language model pre-training captures. *TACL*.

Niket Tandon, Gerard de Melo, Fabian M. Suchanek, and Gerhard Weikum. 2014. Webchild: harvesting and organizing commonsense knowledge from the web. In *WSDM*.

Niket Tandon, Gerard de Melo, and Gerhard Weikum. 2017. Webchild 2.0 : Fine-grained commonsense knowledge distillation. In *ACL*.

Sheng Zhang, Rachel Rudinger, Kevin Duh, and Benjamin Van Durme. 2017. Ordinal common-sense inference. *TACL*.

SciConceptMiner: A system for large-scale scientific concept discovery

Zhihong Shen **Chieh-Han Wu** **Li Ma** **Chien-Pang Chen** **Kuansan Wang**
Microsoft Research
Redmond, WA, USA
{zhihosh,chiewu,v-lima3,v-chienc,kuansanw}@microsoft.com

Abstract

Scientific knowledge is evolving at an unprecedented rate of speed, with new concepts constantly being introduced from millions of academic articles published every month. In this paper, we introduce a self-supervised end-to-end system, ***SciConceptMiner***, for the automatic capture of emerging scientific concepts from both independent knowledge sources (semi-structured data) and academic publications (unstructured documents). First, we adopt a BERT-based sequence labeling model to predict candidate concept phrases with self-supervision data. Then, we incorporate rich Web content for synonym detection and concept selection via a web search API. This two-stage approach achieves highly accurate (94.7%) concept identification with more than 740K scientific concepts. These concepts are deployed in the *Microsoft Academic*[1] production system and are the backbone for its semantic search capability.

1 Introduction

Scientific knowledge has been expanded at an exponential rate over the past decades and the fast-growing volume of academic literature accentuates a pressing need for automated capture of fine-grained emerging concepts. Statistical topic models (Blei, 2012), such as *latent Dirichlet allocation* (LDA) (Blei et al., 2003), have been well-recognized for automatically extracting the topic structure of large document collections for past decades. However, it has two main limitations to prevent it from being widely applied in a modern large-scale document collection.

First, it is the scalability issue on the number of topics an LDA can model. The latest development (Chen et al., 2018) can process 131M documents with 28B tokens efficiently, however, it only extracts 1,722 topics. With the fast-growing body

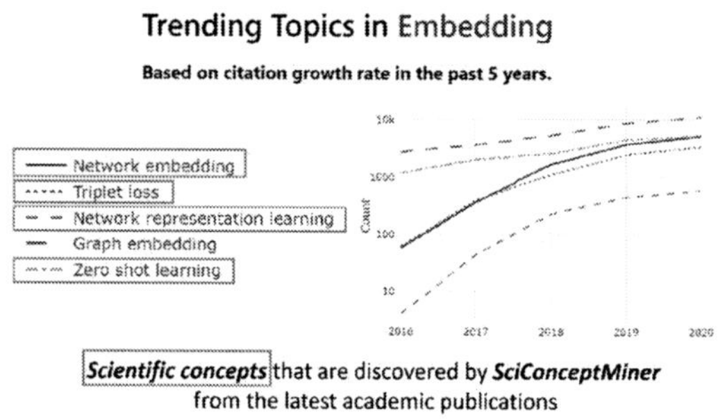

Figure 1: Trending Topics under concept *Embedding*.

of scholarly communications, a comprehensive manually controlled vocabulary like *Medical Subject Headings*(MeSH) (Lowe and Barnett, 1994) contains tens of thousands of subjects (concepts) mostly in the bio-med domain; and an automated scientific knowledge exploration system such as *Microsoft Academic Graph* (MAG) (Shen et al., 2018) has hundreds of thousands of topics across all academic disciplines. A topic modeling system that is scalable not only to the size of documents but also to the number of topics is imperative.

Second, the result of an LDA model is a list of frequency-based terms that form a topic. It requires manual efforts to annotate such lists to generate a human-readable theme or topic name. An automatic process of identifying topic themes with authoritative names and meaningful descriptions is desired to reduce costly human interventions.

In this paper, we introduce a self-supervised end-to-end system, ***SciConceptMiner***, for automatically discovering scientific concepts from both semi-structured independent knowledge sources and unstructured academic documents. It first obtains a list of concept candidates, either from external knowledge repositories such as *Wikipedia* (Völkel et al., 2006; Vrandečić and Krötzsch, 2014) and *Unified Medical Language System* (UMLS) (Bodenreider, 2004), or directly

[1] https://academic.microsoft.com/

Proceedings of the Joint Conference of the 59th Annual Meeting of the Association for Computational Linguistics and the 11th International Joint Conference on Natural Language Processing: System Demonstrations, pages 48–54, August 1st - August 6th, 2021.

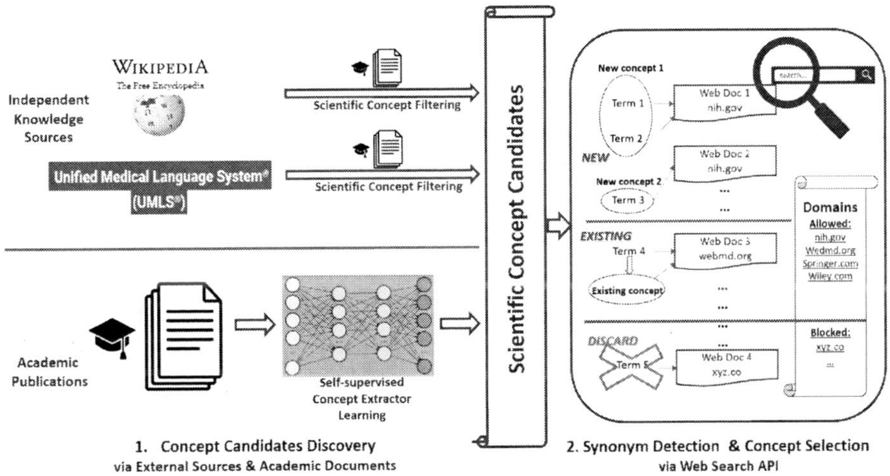

Figure 2: An overview of the ***SciConceptMiner*** system.

mining concepts from a collection of academic documents. Such concept lists are large and noisy. They are in the scale of millions and dominated by invalid or duplicate terms. We then send these candidates as queries to a search engine API and leverage rich Web content to identify legitimate concepts, cluster synonyms, and discard improper terms. The search API is also used to retrieve high-quality concept descriptions.

One example is shown in Figure 1.[2] Four out of five trending topics (*network embedding*, *triplet loss*, *network representation learning*, and *zero shot learning*) under *embedding* are extracted by our automatic concept extractor model trained on CS corpus. It demonstrates that our designed model can effectively capture the emerging trending topics from the latest scientific articles.

The **SciConceptMiner** has been deployed to identify concepts from millions of scholarly communications in *Microsoft Academic Graph* (MAG) (Sinha et al., 2015; Wang et al., 2019, 2020). The MAG with the full list of 740K scientific concepts can be freely accessed via the *Microsoft Academic*[3] search website and *MAG* data set[4].

2 System Description

As shown in Figure 2, the **SciConceptMiner** system has two stages: the first is the concept candidates discovery from various data sources; the second is synonym detection and concept clustering via a Web search API.

In the concept candidates discovery stage, we first integrate the semi-structured independent knowledge sources, *Wikipedia* and *UMLS*, into the system. Such an existing concept list in the system with associated documents enables us to train a concept extractor learning model with self-supervision. We design a BERT-based sequence labeling model to make a binary prediction on whether a word or phrase in a sentence is a scientific concept or not. This proposed model is trained on self-supervised data generated from existing concepts (from *Wikipedia* and *UMLS*) tagged to a collection of academic documents. We do the concept inference with the trained model to generate concept candidates for the next stage.

Concept candidates, as the input to the second stage, are either from external knowledge sources or inferred from academic documents. Both sources have high noisy ratios with different natures. The independent source such as *Wikipedia* has high-quality entities (well-defined names and descriptions, rare duplication, and rich links and relationships with each other) but type noisy (many other types of entities than academic concepts). The *UMLS* candidates and the inferred candidates from an unstructured corpus have more irrelevant phrases and concept synonyms. With the help of a search engine API to retrieve top N documents by using concept candidates as queries, we analyze the returning web pages and associated URL domain information collectively. This process would iden-

[2] This is a snapshot captured in March 2021 for *Embedding* concept at *Microsoft Academic* production system: https://academic.microsoft.com/topics/41608201.

[3] `https://academic.microsoft.com/`

[4] `https://docs.microsoft.com/en-us/academic-services/graph/`

tify around 3-5% of candidates from the first stage as proper scientific concepts with consistently high accuracy (94-95% based on sample results) across all data sources, with over 740K concepts in total.

2.1 Concept Candidate Discovery

2.1.1 Semi-structured Independent Knowledge Sources

There are many independent knowledge sources, either manually curated or automatically created or a hybrid of both. Among them, the most notable ones are Wikipedia, WikiData[5], DBpedia[6], and Yago[7] in general domains and MeSH[8], UMLS[9] in the bio-med fields. We have applied Wikipedia and UMLS as sources for *SciConceptMiner* system because of their data quality and comprehensive coverage on scientific terms and phrases. Other semi-structured sources can be integrated with the current system design seamlessly as long as they pass the quality and relevancy examination of their contents.

Wikipedia: Wikipedia[10] is the largest collaboratively edited online encyclopedic knowledge. It contains contents in more than 300 languages and has over 6 million English articles as of July 2020. It was the first external data source being integrated into MAG considering its comprehensive coverage on academic topics spanning from social sciences to natural sciences, as well as technology and applied sciences. Each topic in Wikipedia (as a separate article) is written in high quality and has rare duplication (Lewoniewski, 2018). The key challenge of mining quality academic concepts from Wikipedia is to identify the right type of entities, as most articles in Wikipedia are missing entity type information. We used graph link analysis (Milne and Witten, 2008) for type prediction and had expanded the concepts from an initial 3K to over 200K. The details are described in the *Concept Discovery* section in (Shen et al., 2018). For concepts from Wikipedia, we did not use the search engine API to further filter as the resulting concept list is already with high quality and rare duplication.

UMLS:

The Unified Medical Language System (UMLS) is a repository of biomedical vocabularies developed by the US National Library of Medicine (NLM) with sources from multiple datasets and standards. The latest 2020AA release contains approximately 4.28 million medical concepts and 15.5 million unique concept names from over 200 sources. A system with large, complex data sources typically has various inherent limitations on the data quality. For UMLS, these include structural inconsistencies such as cycles in graph hierarchy, semantic inconsistencies between different vocabularies, and missing hierarchical relationships (Bodenreider, 2004, 2007; Humphreys et al., 1998).

In the concept candidate discovery stage, we take the full list of the concept names from UMLS and first clean it with simple rules such as removing digit-only terms, two-char terms, too long terms (over 30 chars), etc. We further filter the remaining terms with a corpus consisting of titles and abstracts from 170 million English scientific articles in MAG and only keep terms that appeared at least N times in above academic corpus. The resulting list is ready to be sent to a search engine API for duplication detection and concept selection in the second stage.

2.1.2 Self-supervised Concept Extractor Learning

The volume of new research being published is rapidly increasing, with MAG adding over 1 million new papers every month. This creates a unique challenge to identify, describe, and categorize an ever-evolving set of emerging concepts in a timely fashion.

To tackle this challenge, we formulate the concept detection as a self-supervised sequence labeling problem that allows us to extract concept candidates directly from unstructured academic documents. This is motivated by the recent development of deep learning (DL) based *Named Entity Recognition (NER)* models, which become dominant and achieve state-of-the-art results (Lample et al., 2016; Chiu and Nichols, 2016; Yadav and Bethard, 2019). NER is the task of identifying named entities of a specific type, such as person or location, in text. A most recent survey (Li et al., 2020) proposed a new taxonomy of DL-based NER with three parts: *distributed representations for input*, *context encoder*, and *tag decoder*. We adopt this taxonomy to design our concept extractor learning model.

Instead of a typical NER model which would learn to identify several entity types at the same

[5] https://www.wikidata.org/
[6] https://wiki.dbpedia.org/
[7] https://yago-knowledge.org/
[8] https://www.nlm.nih.gov/mesh/meshhome.html
[9] https://www.nlm.nih.gov/research/umls/index.html
[10] https://www.wikipedia.org/

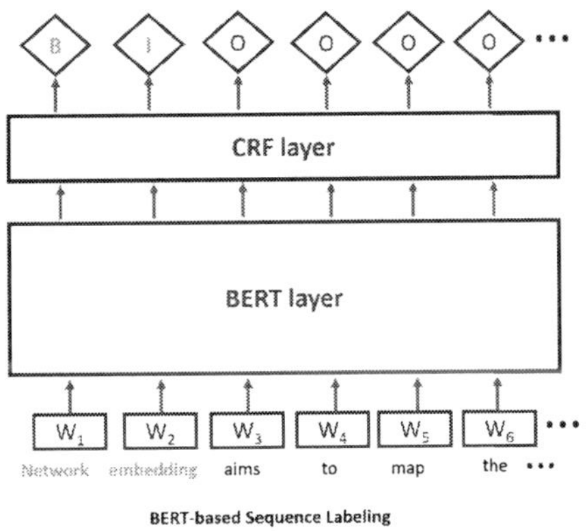

Figure 3: Concept extractor learning with a BERT-based sequence labeling model.

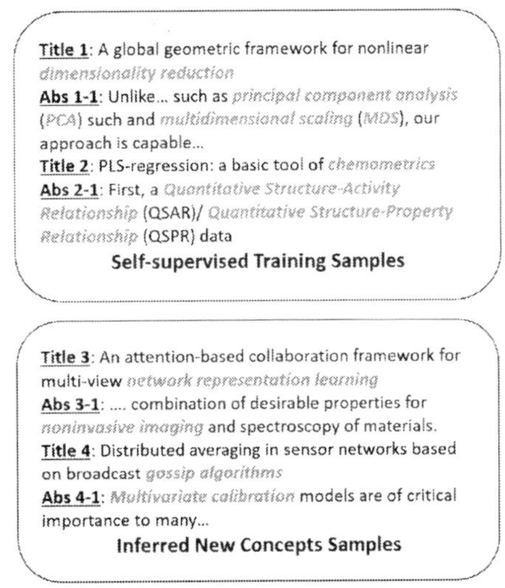

Figure 4: Self-supervised concept labeling samples.

time, we reduce our model design to identify a single entity type - scientific concept type. We propose to treat scientific concept extraction as a sequence labeling task. Tokens in the text are labeled with the BIO notation. 'B', 'I', and 'O' represent the beginning, inside, and outside of a scientific concept chunk respectively. On a sampled set of scientific articles in MAG, we do lexical matching using the synonyms of our existing concepts harvested from *Wikipedia* and *UMLS* as self-supervised labels. We fine-tune a transformer-based BERT model (Devlin et al., 2018) (e.g. BERT-Large) as a *context encoder* and use a Conditional Random Field (CRF) layer as a *tag decoder* to train a binary classifier on each word in a sentence to detect concept mentions.[11] Figure 3 illustrates the design of our concept extractor learning model. We infer scientific concept candidates using the trained model on a larger set of high-quality MAG documents, i.e. those published in prestigious journals/conferences. Figure 4 provides some self-supervised concept labeling samples as well as sample sentences with inferred new concepts. These new concept candidates are ready to be used in the next stage.

2.2 Synonym Detection and Concept Selection

In the second stage, we classify the scientific concept candidates detected in the first stage (either from UMLS or from automatic concept extractor models) into three broad categories: (1) synonyms of existing concepts, (2) new concepts, or (3) low-quality words/phrases we shall discard.

This is accomplished by searching for each concept candidate using the Bing Web Search API[12] and clustering candidates into scientific concept "identities" based on the URL relevance/reputation and the consistency of the mentions among top search results.

More specifically, if K out of top N URLs returned by two concept candidates is the same, we consider these two candidates are synonyms of a concept. We also curate the allowed-list and block-list of URL domains. The concept candidates whose top search results are from well-known domains of high-quality academic knowledge (in the allowed-list) would be accepted, and otherwise, they would be rejected. The block-list is used to reject terms that also have results from domains in the allowed list. That is usually the case for common words and phrases which returned with pages in online dictionary domains.

This simple yet effective approach can help trim around 92%-97% concept candidates as noisy terms and keep 3%-7% of high-quality concepts, synonyms, and well-written descriptions from domains containing credible academic knowledge and are in the allowed-list.

3 Evaluation and Analysis

3.1 Self-supervised concept extractor learning

We use the BERT-Large-Cased as the pre-trained language model and fine-tune the described con-

[11] We re-use the BERT vocabularies and their pre-trained embedding without regenerating and retraining on academic corpus.

[12] https://azure.microsoft.com/en-us/services/cognitive-services/bing-web-search-api/

cept extractor learner model with 4 epochs. We generate the training corpus from MAG from CS and Medicine domain respectively and split them in 8:1:1 for train/dev/test. Table 1 shows the corpus size used for training and inference.

Training Corpus	**CS**	**Med**
# of articles	500K	414K
# of sentences	3.4M	3.6M
# of tokens	72.8M	82.7M
# of concept tokens	8.9M	9.7M
Inference Corpus	**CS**	**Med**
# of articles	2.56M	2.07M
# of sentences	17.6M	18.1M
# of tokens	373.8M	413.4M
# of concept tokens	26.2M	91.2M
Inferred Concept Terms	**CS**	**Med**
# of distinct terms	1.06 M	4.66M
# of cur. concept terms	73,167	88,350
# of new concept terms	48,531	34,744
# of new distinct concepts	46,182	31,302
# of new terms for cur. concepts	16,021	11,389
# of discarded terms	921k	4.53K

Table 1: Training and Inference Corpus Stats.

To ensure that this model works for documents across various scientific domains, we conduct experiments training our model using documents in different top domains (e.g. *computer science* and *medicine*). We observe that higher-quality candidates are generated using models trained from the same domain corpus. For example, when we apply the model trained with a CS corpus to predict concepts in the medicine corpus, the F1 score drops from 0.942 to 0.682. Therefore, we train different models on the corpus from an individual top-level domain, and the F1 scores of inference results on in-domain and out-of-domain corpus are shown in Table 2.

	CS-Model	**Medicine-Model**
CS-Test	**0.942**	0.649
Medicine-Test	0.682	**0.912**

Table 2: F1 scores of test sets on different models.

We have only conducted model training and inference on CS and medicine corpus. Continued training on other discipline corpora as well as exploring more effective concept extractor learning models are among our ongoing efforts.

3.2 Concept Analysis Based on Data Sources

In this section, we conduct an evaluation of the concept quality in terms of accuracy and coverage. We estimate the coverage by evaluating potential missed opportunities on discarded terms. We also leverage MAG data to conduct the analysis of top domain distribution and topic age distribution conditioned on different data sources.

The stats in this section are collected on four groups of concepts by their data sources: *Wikipedia*, *UMLS*, automatically extracted concepts on *Computer Science* (*AutoCS* or *A-CS*) and *Medicine* (*AutoMed* or *A-Med*) corpus respectively. Since the concepts discovered in *SciConceptMiner* are already integrated into MAG, we use the paper-concept relationship, concept hierarchy, and paper metadata such as publication year in MAG to facilitate this analysis. The details on how to obtain these relationships and meta-data are out of the scope of this work and please refer to (Wang et al., 2019; Shen et al., 2018) for more information.

3.2.1 Size, Impact, and Accuracy

In Table 3, we report the number of concepts, average number of papers associated with a concept, average citation received of a paper tagged with a concept, as well as the accuracy of concepts. The independent knowledge sources (*Wikipedia* and *UMLS*) provide similar topic sizes on a scale of hundreds of thousands, while the automatic extraction models identify about one-tenth of the size from external sources. On average, the concepts from *Wikipedia* are broader (with more papers associated) and have a higher impact (with more citations received), while concepts from *UMLS* are more fine-grained with slightly smaller influence. We evaluate the accuracy with the same approach described in (Shen et al., 2018) and it achieves a similar accuracy level between 94% and 95% across all data sources.

Data Source	**Size**	**Paper**	**Cit.**	**Acc.**
Wiki	226,466	3,386	15.6	94.8%
UMLS	433,468	59	9.1	94.5%
AutoCS	46,182	1,462	10.1	94.8%
AutoMed	31,302	1,498	10.7	94.2%

Table 3: Concept size, impact, and accuracy.

3.2.2 Potential Opportunities on Discarded Contents

It is generally challenging to evaluate the coverage of such a large-scale concept discovery system since it is nearly impossible to identify the "ground truth" of full coverage, even in a narrowed subdomain. In order to estimate the coverage, we identify the potential opportunities that we may have missed by sampling and inspecting the discarded inferred terms from learned concept extractor models. We sample 300 discarded terms in *AutoCS* and *AutoMed* respectively and report the size and accuracy[13] in Table 4. In all terms with a positive label, roughly one quarter to one third are new concepts not in the current system, and the remaining 66% to 75% are synonyms. Hence, we estimate that we might have missed about 100K concepts and 200K synonyms from the inference results of our concept extractor models.

Source	Discarded Size	Accuracy
Auto-CS terms	4.53 M	3.3%
Auto-Med terms	921 K	12.7%

Table 4: Discarded term size and accuracy.

3.2.3 Topic Domain Distribution

About 75% of 740K concepts in MAG are organized into a six-level DAG (directed acyclic graph) structure taxonomy, with top two levels manually curated (19 domains and 270 sub-domains). We use this taxonomy to aggregate all concepts to top-level 19 domains and report the percentage distribution on top 5 domains per data source and for all concepts. As shown in Table 5, Bio-Med-Chem 3 domains dominate all concepts (67%),*Wikipedia* (51%), *UMLS* (90%), and auto-extracted *AutoMed* (73%). Technology and applied sciences such as *Computer Science* and *Material Science* are the second biggest categories for all concepts. These two applied sciences together with *Mathematics* and *Engineering* dominate the *AutoCS* data source (58%).

	ALL	Wiki	UMLS	AutoCS	AutoMed
Bio	**28.4%**	**28.3%**	35.4%	-	**41.3%**
Med	24.2%	11.0%	**35.9%**	7.5%	16.2%
Chem	14.7%	11.6%	18.6%	-	15.3%
ComSci	7.0%	9.3%	-	**25.8%**	4.9%
MatSci	5.1%	-	2.6%	13.8%	7.8%
Math	-	6.0%	-	8.5%	-
Engr	-	-	-	9.3%	-
Other	20.7%	33.9%	7.5%	35.0%	14.5%

Table 5: Top domain distribution of concepts.

3.2.4 Topic Age Distribution

In Table 6, we report the average age of the papers associated with a concept. The average publication year (rounded off to the floor), as well as 5%, 50% (the median), and 95% publication year of a concept are also reported. It shows that concepts from *UMLS* are generally discovered and used in earlier years, lasting longer (25 years for the middle 90%), while *AutoCS* and *AutoMed* contain newer concepts with shorter life span (17-18 years for the middle 90%).

[13] We split the sampled data of each category to 3 groups with 100 each and they are evaluated by 3 judges. We report the average of positive label ratios.

Source	Age	Avg Y	5% Y	50% Y	95% Y
Wiki	18.2	2002	1983	2003	2013
UMLS	21.0	1999	1982	1997	2007
A-CS	14.1	2006	1990	2008	2017
A-Med	15.7	2004	1989	2006	2016

Table 6: Age distribution of concepts.

Figure 5 provides a yearly distribution from 2010 to 2019. It represents the percentage of papers (associated with concepts in respective sources) over the past 10 years.[14] This is consistent with our expectation as one of our primary goals of leveraging the automatic concept extraction is to discover emerging concepts in the latest scientific documents.

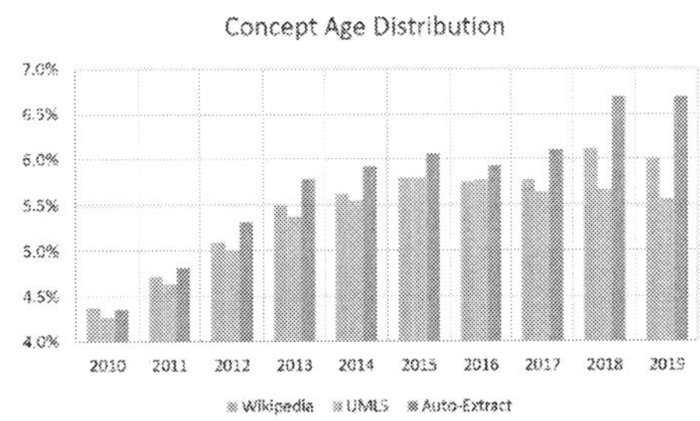

Figure 5: Concept Age Distribution 2010-2019.

4 Conclusion

In this work, we demonstrated a large-scale scientific concept discovery production system, *SciConceptMiner*, for automatically capturing academic concepts from both semi-structured data and unstructured documents. The system has two parts: the first is the concept candidate identification, and the second is synonym detection and concept selection. We used a BERT-based sequence labeling model to learn concept phrases with self-supervision and leverage a Web search API to cluster synonyms and identify valid concepts.

SciConceptMiner has discovered more than 740K scientific concepts across all research domains from *Wikipedia*, *UMLS*, and scholarly articles with high accuracy (94.7%). These concepts are integrated to build the *Microsoft Academic Graph*, which publishes one of the largest cross-domain scientific taxonomy. It enables easy exploration of scientific knowledge as well as facilitates many downstream applications like information retrieval, question answering, and recommendations.

[14] Please note that the percentage of papers of each year is calculated by dividing by all papers for a source. Since the earlier years' distributions are very close, we do not plot them. The sum of each source over the past 10 years is less than 1.

References

David M Blei. 2012. Probabilistic topic models. *Communications of the ACM*, 55(4):77–84.

David M Blei, Andrew Y Ng, and Michael I Jordan. 2003. Latent dirichlet allocation. *Journal of machine Learning research*, 3(Jan):993–1022.

Olivier Bodenreider. 2004. The unified medical language system (umls): integrating biomedical terminology. *Nucleic acids research*, 32(suppl_1):D267–D270.

Olivier Bodenreider. 2007. The unified medical language system what is it and how to use it? *Tutorial at Medinfo*.

Jianfei Chen, Jun Zhu, Jie Lu, and Shixia Liu. 2018. Scalable training of hierarchical topic models. *Proceedings of the VLDB Endowment*, 11(7):826–839.

Jason PC Chiu and Eric Nichols. 2016. Named entity recognition with bidirectional lstm-cnns. *Transactions of the Association for Computational Linguistics*, 4:357–370.

Jacob Devlin, Ming-Wei Chang, Kenton Lee, and Kristina Toutanova. 2018. Bert: Pre-training of deep bidirectional transformers for language understanding. *arXiv preprint arXiv:1810.04805*.

Betsy L Humphreys, Donald AB Lindberg, Harold M Schoolman, and G Octo Barnett. 1998. The unified medical language system: an informatics research collaboration. *Journal of the American Medical Informatics Association*, 5(1):1–11.

Guillaume Lample, Miguel Ballesteros, Sandeep Subramanian, Kazuya Kawakami, and Chris Dyer. 2016. Neural architectures for named entity recognition. *arXiv preprint arXiv:1603.01360*.

Włodzimierz Lewoniewski. 2018. Measures for quality assessment of articles and infoboxes in multilingual wikipedia. In *International Conference on Business Information Systems*, pages 619–633. Springer.

Jing Li, Aixin Sun, Jianglei Han, and Chenliang Li. 2020. A survey on deep learning for named entity recognition. *IEEE Transactions on Knowledge and Data Engineering*.

Henry J Lowe and G Octo Barnett. 1994. Understanding and using the medical subject headings (mesh) vocabulary to perform literature searches. *Jama*, 271(14):1103–1108.

David Milne and Ian H Witten. 2008. Learning to link with wikipedia. In *Proceedings of the 17th ACM conference on Information and knowledge management*, pages 509–518.

Zhihong Shen, Hao Ma, and Kuansan Wang. 2018. A web-scale system for scientific knowledge exploration. *arXiv preprint arXiv:1805.12216*.

Arnab Sinha, Zhihong Shen, Yang Song, Hao Ma, Darrin Eide, Bo-June Hsu, and Kuansan Wang. 2015. An overview of microsoft academic service (mas) and applications. In *Proceedings of the 24th international conference on world wide web*, pages 243–246.

Max Völkel, Markus Krötzsch, Denny Vrandecic, Heiko Haller, and Rudi Studer. 2006. Semantic wikipedia. In *Proceedings of the 15th international conference on World Wide Web*, pages 585–594.

Denny Vrandečić and Markus Krötzsch. 2014. Wikidata: a free collaborative knowledgebase. *Communications of the ACM*, 57(10):78–85.

Kuansan Wang, Zhihong Shen, Chi-Yuan Huang, Chieh-Han Wu, Darrin Eide, Yuxiao Dong, Junjie Qian, Anshul Kanakia, Alvin Chen, and Richard Rogahn. 2019. A review of microsoft academic services for science of science studies. *Frontiers in Big Data*, 2:45.

Kuansan Wang, Zhihong Shen, Chiyuan Huang, Chieh-Han Wu, Yuxiao Dong, and Anshul Kanakia. 2020. Microsoft academic graph: When experts are not enough. *Quantitative Science Studies*, 1(1):396–413.

Vikas Yadav and Steven Bethard. 2019. A survey on recent advances in named entity recognition from deep learning models. *arXiv preprint arXiv:1910.11470*.

NeurST: Neural Speech Translation Toolkit

Chengqi Zhao   Mingxuan Wang   Qianqian Dong   Rong Ye   Lei Li
ByteDance AI Lab, Shanghai, China
{zhaochengqi.d,wangmingxuan.89,dongqianqian,yerong,lileilab}@bytedance.com

Abstract

NeurST is an open-source toolkit for neural speech translation. The toolkit mainly focuses on end-to-end speech translation, which is easy to use, modify, and extend to advanced speech translation research and products. NeurST aims at facilitating the speech translation research for NLP researchers and building reliable benchmarks for this field. It provides step-by-step recipes for feature extraction, data preprocessing, distributed training, and evaluation. In this paper, we will introduce the framework design of NeurST and show experimental results for different benchmark datasets, which can be regarded as reliable baselines for future research. The toolkit is publicly available at https://github.com/bytedance/neurst and we will continuously update the performance of NeurST with other counterparts and studies at https://st-benchmark.github.io/.

1 Introduction

Speech translation (ST), which translates audio signals of speech in one language into text in a foreign language, is a hot research subject nowadays and has widespread applications, like cross-language videoconferencing or customer support chats.

Traditionally, researchers build a speech translation system via a cascading manner, including an automatic speech recognition (ASR) and a machine translation (MT) subsystem (Ney, 1999; Casacuberta et al., 2008; Kumar et al., 2014). Cascade systems, however, suffer from error propagation problems, where an inaccurate ASR output would theoretically cause translation errors. Owing to recent progress of sequence-to-sequence modeling for both neural machine translation (NMT) (Bahdanau et al., 2015; Luong et al., 2015; Vaswani et al., 2017) and end-to-end speech recognition (Chan et al., 2016; Chiu et al., 2018; Dong et al., 2018), it becomes feasible and efficient to train an end-to-end direct ST model (Berard et al., 2016; Duong et al., 2016; Weiss et al., 2017). This end-to-end fashion attracts much attention due to its appealing properties: *a*) modeling without intermediate ASR transcriptions obviously alleviates the propagation of errors; *b*) a single and unified ST model is beneficial to deployment with lower latency in contrast to cascade systems.

Recent studies show that end-to-end ST models achieve promising performance and are comparable with cascaded models (Ansari et al., 2020). The end-to-end solution has great potential to be the dominant technology for speech translation, however challenges remain. The first is about benchmarks. Many ST studies conduct experiments on different datasets. Liu et al. (2019) evaluate the method on TED English-Chinese; and Dong et al. (2021) use *libri-trans* English-French and IWSLT2018 English-German dataset; and Wu et al. (2020) show the results on CoVoST dataset and the FR/RO portions of MuST-C dataset. Different datasets make it difficult to compare the performance of their approaches. Further, even for the same dataset, the baseline results are not necessarily kept consistent. Take the *libri-trans* English-French dataset as an example. Dong et al. (2021) report the pre-trained baseline as 15.3 and the result of Liu et al. (2019) is 14.3 in terms of tokenized BLEU, while Inaguma et al. (2020) report 15.5 (detokenized BLEU). The mismatching baseline results in an unfair comparison on the improvements of their approaches. We think one of the primary reasons is that the preprocessing of audio data is complex, and the ST model training involves many tricks, such as pre-training and data augmentation.

Therefore a reproducible and reliable benchmark is required. In this work, we present NeurST, a toolkit for easily building and training end-to-end ST models, as well as end-to-end ASR and

Proceedings of the Joint Conference of the 59th Annual Meeting of the Association for Computational Linguistics and the 11th International Joint Conference on Natural Language Processing: System Demonstrations, pages 55–62, August 1st - August 6th, 2021.

NMT for cascade systems. We implement state-of-the-art Transformer-based models (Vaswani et al., 2017; Karita et al., 2019) and provide step-by-step recipes for feature extraction, data preprocessing, model training, and inference for researchers to reproduce the benchmarks. Though there exist several counterparts, such as *Lingvo* (Shen et al., 2019), *fairseq-ST* (Wang et al., 2020a) and *Kaldi* [1] style *ESPnet-ST* (Inaguma et al., 2020), NeurST is specially designed for speech translation tasks, which encapsulates the details of speech processing and frees the developers from data engineering. It is easy to use and extend. The contributions of this work are as follows:

- NeurST is designed specifically for end-to-end ST, with clean and simple code. It is lightweight and independent of *Kaldi*, which simplifies installation and usage, and is more compatible for NLP researchers.
- We report strong benchmarks with well-designed hyper-parameters and show best practice on several ST corpora. We provide a series of recipes to reproduce them, which serves as reliable baselines for the speech translation field.

2 Design and Features

NeurST is implemented with both TensorFlow2 and PyTorch backends. In this section, we will introduce the design components and features of this toolkit.

2.1 Design

NeurST divides one running job into four components: `Dataset`, `Model`, `Task` and `Executor`.

Dataset NeurST abstracts out a common interface `Dataset` for data input. For example, we can train a speech translation model from either a raw dataset tarball or pre-extracted record files. The `Dataset` iterates on the data files and standardizes the read records, e.g., ST tasks only accept key-value pairs storing audio signals/features and translations. One can implement their logic to accept the data of various modalities.

Model NeurST provides an optimal implementation of Transformer and its adaptation to speech-to-text tasks, which achieve state-of-the-art performance on standard benchmarks. Moreover, one can customize various models using TensorFlow2/PyTorch APIs or combine the encoders, decoders, and layers inside the NeurST .

Task NeurST abstracts out `Task` interface to bridge `Dataset` and `Model`. In detail, `Task` defines data pipelines to match the data samples from `Dataset` to the input formats of `Model`. For examples, ST task does tokenization on the text translations and transforms each token to index. In this way, user-defined `Dataset` and `Model` can be efficiently integrated into NeurST , as long as they share the same `Task`.

Executor NeurST provides the execution logic for handling basic workflows of training, validation, and inference. Researchers can either define their specific process of training and evaluation, or pay less attention to API details in `Executor` but reuse them by simply customizing `Dataset`, `Model` and `Task`.

2.2 Features

Computation NeurST has high computation efficiency and it can be further optimized by enabling mixed-precision (Micikevicius et al., 2018) and XLA (Accelerated Linear Algebra). Furthermore, NeurST supports fast distributed training using *Horovod* (Sergeev and Balso, 2018) and *Byteps* (Peng et al., 2019; Jiang et al., 2020) on large-scale scenarios.

Data Preprocessing NeurST supports on-the-fly data preprocessing via a number of lightweight python packages, like python_speech_features[2] for extracting audio features (e.g. mel-frequency cepstral coefficients and log-mel filterbank coefficients). And for text processing, NeurST integrates some effective tokenizers, including moses tokenizer[3], byte pair encoding (BPE) (Sennrich et al., 2016b) and SentencePiece[4]. Alternatively, the training data can be preprocessed and stored in binary files (e.g., TFRecord) beforehand, which is guaranteed to improve the I/O performance during training. Moreover, to simplify such operations, NeurST provides the command-line tool to create such record files, which automatically iterates on

[1] `https://kaldi-asr.org/`

[2] `https://github.com/jameslyons/python_speech_features`

[3] The python version: `https://github.com/alvations/sacremoses`

[4] `https://github.com/google/sentencepiece`

various data formats defined by `Dataset`, preprocesses data samples according to `Task` and writes to the disk.

Transfer Learning NeurST supports initializing the model variables from well-trained models as long as they have the same variable names. As for ST, we can initialize the ST encoder with a well-trained ASR encoder and initialize the ST decoder with a well-trained MT decoder, which facilitates to achieve promising improvements. Besides, NeurST also provides scripts for converting released models from other repositories, like wav2vec2.0 (Baevski et al., 2020) and BERT (Devlin et al., 2019). Researchers can conveniently integrate these pre-trained components to the customized models.

Simultaneous Translation NeurST keeps up with the recent progress of simultaneous translation. The models are extended to train with streaming audio or text input.

Validation while Training NeurST supports customizing validation process during training. By default, NeurST offers evaluation on development data during training and keeps track of the checkpoints with the best evaluation results.

Monitoring NeurST supports TensorBoard for monitoring metrics during training, such as training loss, training speed, and evaluation results.

Model Serving There is no gap between the research models and production models under NeurST , while they can be easily served with TensorFlow Serving. Moreover, for higher performance serving of standard transformer models, NeurST is able to integrate with other optimized inference libraries, like *lightseq* (Wang et al., 2021).

3 Speech Translation Benchmarks

We conducted experiments on several benchmark speech translation corpora using NeurST and compared the performance with other open-source codebases and studies. Though that would be an unfair comparison due to the different model structures and hyperparameters, the goal of NeurST is to provide strong and reproducible benchmarks for future research.

3.1 Datasets

We choose the following publicly available speech translation corpora that include speech in a source language aligned to text in a target language:

task	init scale	end scale	decay at	decay steps
MT	1.0	1.0	-	-
ASR	3.5	2.0	50k	50k
ST	3.5	1.5	50k	50k

Table 1: Hyperparameters of the learning rate schedule. Take the case of ST, the learning rate is scaled up by 3.5x for the first 50k steps. Then, we linearly decrease the scaling factor to 1.5 for 50k steps.

libri-trans (Kocabiyikoglu et al., 2018) [5] is a small EN→FR dataset which was originally started from the *LibriSpeech* corpus, the audiobook recordings for ASR (Panayotov et al., 2015). The English utterances were automatically aligned to the e-books in French, and 236 hours of English speech aligned to French translations at utterance level were finally extracted. It has been widely used in previous studies. As such, we use the clean 100-hour portion plus the augmented machine translation from Google Translate as the training data and follow its split of dev and test data.
MuST-C (Di Gangi et al., 2019)[6] is a multilingual speech translation corpus from English to 8 languages: Dutch (NL), French (FR), German (DE), Italian (IT), Portuguese (PT), Romanian (RO), Russian (RU) and Spanish (ES). MuST-C comprises at least 385 hours of audio recordings from English TED talks with their manual transcriptions and translations at sentence level for training, and we use the *dev* and *tst-COMMON* as our development and test data, respectively. To the best of our knowledge, MuST-C is currently the largest speech translation corpus available for each language pair.

3.2 Data Preprocessing

Beyond the officially released version, we performed no other audio to text alignment and data cleaning on *libri-trans* and MuST-C datasets.

For speech features, we extracted 80-channel logmel filterbank coefficients with windows of 25ms and steps of 10ms, resulting in 80-dimensional features per frame. The audio features of each sample were then normalized by the mean and the standard deviation. All texts were segmented into subword level by first applying Moses tokenizer and then BPE. In detail, we removed all punctuations and lowercased the sentences in the source side while

[5] `https://github.com/alicank/Translation-Augmented-LibriSpeech-Corpus`

[6] `https://ict.fbk.eu/must-c/`

	Model	tok	detok
Cascade	*ESPnet-ST* ASR *transf-s* + CTC → MT (Inaguma et al., 2020)†	-	17.0
	NeurST ASR *transf-s* → MT	18.2	16.8
End-to-End	ST BiLSTM (Bahar et al., 2019)	17.0	16.2
	ST *transf-s* (Liu et al., 2019)	14.3	-
	ST *transf-s* + KD (Liu et al., 2019)	17.0	-
	ESPnet-ST ST *transf-s* (Inaguma et al., 2020)†	-	16.7
	TCEN-LSTM (Wang et al., 2020b)♭	-	17.1
	ST *transf-s* (Wang et al., 2020c)	16.0	-
	ST *transf-s* + curriculum pre-training (Wang et al., 2020c)	17.7	-
	LUT (Dong et al., 2021)	17.8	-
	NeurST ST *transf-s*	18.7	17.2

Table 2: Case-insensitive BLEU scores on *libri-trans* test set under constrained setting (without additional ASR and MT data). †Notably, we refer to the results presented in `espnet/egs/libri_trans/st1` and consider them as detokenized BLEU according to the evaluation script in the repository[7]. ♭ The result of TCEN-LSTM is also marked as detokenized BLEU due to its implementation on *ESPnet-ST*.

	Model	DE	ES	FR	IT	NL	PT	RO	RU	avg.
Cascade	ESPnet-ST ASR *transf-s* + CTC → MT (Inaguma et al., 2020)	23.7	28.7	33.8	24.0	27.9	29.0	22.7	16.4	25.8
	NeurST ASR *transf-s* → MT	23.4	28.0	33.9	23.8	27.1	28.3	22.2	16.0	25.3
End-to-End	*ESPnet-ST* ST *transf-s* (Inaguma et al., 2020)	22.9	28.0	32.8	23.8	27.4	28.0	21.9	15.8	25.1
	fairseq-ST ST *transf-s* (Wang et al., 2020a)	22.7	27.2	32.9	22.7	27.3	28.1	21.9	15.3	24.8
	ST *transf-base* + AFS^{t,f} (Zhang et al., 2020)	22.4	26.9	31.6	23.0	24.9	26.3	21.0	14.7	23.9
	NeurST ST *transf-s*	22.8	27.4	33.3	22.9	27.2	28.7	22.2	15.1	24.9

Table 3: Case-sensitive detokenized BLEU scores on MuST-C *tst-COMMON*.

the cases and punctuations of target sentences were reserved. The BPE rules were jointly learned with 8,000 merge operations and shared across ASR, MT, and ST tasks.

3.3 Benchmark Models

We implemented Transformer (Vaswani et al., 2017), the state-of-the-art sequence-to-sequence model, for all our tasks.

In detail, for MT in cascade systems, the model included 6 layers for both encoder and decoders. The embedding dimension was 256, and the size of hidden units in feedforward layer was 2,048. The attention head for self-attention and cross-attention was set to 4. We used Adam optimizer (Kingma and Ba, 2015) with $\beta_1 = 0.9, \beta_2 = 0.98$ and applied the same schedule algorithm as Vaswani et al. (2017) for learning rate. We trained the MT models with a global batch size of 25,000 tokens.

As for ASR/ST, we referred to the recent progress of Transformer-based end-to-end ASR models (Dong et al., 2018; Karita et al., 2019) and extended the basic transformer model to be compatible with audio inputs. The audio frames were first compressed by two-layer CNN with 256 channels, 3×3 kernel and stride size 2, each of which was followed by a layer normalization. Then, we performed a linear transformation on the compressed audio representations to match the width of the transformer model. We used the same model structure as MT, except that we enlarged the number of encoder layers to 12 to obtain better performance. This configuration is labeled as *transf-s* (transformer small). For training, we used the same Adam optimizer as MT but set the warmup steps to 25,000, and we empirically scaled up the learning rate to accelerate the convergence. The hyperparameters of the learning rate schedule are listed in Table 1. Moreover, for GPU memory efficiency, we truncated the audio frames to 3,000 and removed training samples whose transcription length exceeded 120 and 150 for ASR and ST, respectively. The ASR models were trained with 120,000 frames per batch, while the batch size for ST was 80,000 frames. To further improve the performance of ST,

[7] `multi-bleu-detok.perl` in `https://github.com/espnet/espnet/blob/master/utils/score_bleu.sh`

Model	tok	detok
Cascade		
NeurST ASR *transf-s* → MT	17.4	16.0
End-to-End		
NeurST ST *transf-s*	17.8	16.3
ST *transf-base* + AFS$^{t,f\diamondsuit}$	18.6	17.2

Table 4: Case-sensitive BLEU scores on *libri-trans* test set under constrained setting. $^{\diamondsuit}$is from Zhang et al. (2020) with the proposed adaptive feature selection method, which uses the transformer base setting (embedding size=512).

we applied SpecAugment technique (Park et al., 2019) with frequency masking ($mF = 2, F = 27$) and time masking ($mT = 2, T = 70, p = 0.2$).

Additionally, we applied label smoothing of value 0.1 for training all three tasks. The encoder of the ST model is initialized by the ASR encoder by default unless noted.

3.4 Evaluation

For evaluation, we averaged the latest 10 checkpoints and used a beam width of 4 with no length penalty for all the above tasks.

We use word error rate (WER) to evaluate ASR models and report case-sensitive detokenized BLEU[8] for MT and ST models. In order to compare with existing works, we also report case-insensitive tokenized BLEU using `multi-bleu.perl` in Moses for *libri-trans* dataset.

3.5 Main Results

The overall results and comparisons with other studies are illustrated in Table 2 and 3. It is worth noting that all results are from single models rather than ensemble models.

To make a fair comparison on *libri-trans* corpus, we list both tokenized and detokenized BLEU scores in Table 2 and strive to distinguish the metric of existing literature. Our transformer-based ST model, which only applies ASR pre-training and SpecAugment, achieves superior results versus recent works about knowledge distillation (Liu et al., 2019), curriculum pre-training (Wang et al., 2020c), and LUT (Dong et al., 2021). Compared with the counterpart *ESPnet-ST*, we also outperform by 0.5 BLEU, even though Inaguma et al. (2020) apply additional techniques like speed perturbation, pre-trained MT decoder, and CTC loss for ASR pre-

[8]https://github.com/mjpost/sacrebleu

Model	NeurST	*ESPnet-ST*
ST + ASR enc init.	16.5	15.5
+ MT dec init.	16.6	16.2
+ SpecAug.	17.2	16.7
ST + ASR enc init. + SpecAug.	17.2	-

Table 5: Case-insensitive detokenized BLEU scores on *libri-trans* test set with difference setups.

Model	NeurST	*ESPnet-ST*
pure ST	18.6	-
+ ASR enc init.	21.9	21.8
+ MT dec init.	22.1	22.3
+ SpecAug.	23.3	22.9
ST + ASR enc init. + SpecAug.	22.8	-

Table 6: Case-sensitive detokenized BLEU scores on MuST-C EN-DE *tst-COMMON* with difference setups.

training. The cascade baseline is slightly worse than that of *ESPnet-ST* (-0.2 BLEU) because the ASR+CTC can achieve lower WER (6.4)[9] while our pure end-to-end ASR obtains 8.8. We surprisingly find that the end-to-end ST model exceeds the cascade system by 0.4~0.5 BLEU. We will discuss this in detail in section 3.7. And as a supplementary benchmark, we present case-sensitive BLEU scores in Table 4.

Table 3 illustrates the results on MuST-C *tst-COMMON*. The results of our end-to-end ST model are competitive with both *fairseq-ST* and *ESPnet-ST*.

3.6 Ablation Study

Training a direct ST model is more complicated than training an ASR or MT model. Our preliminary experiment based on a pure end-to-end ST model fails to converge on *libri-trans* corpus, which can be the result of the data scarcity. To alleviate this problem, pre-training some parts of the neural network is the most effective way and has been validated in all existing end-to-end ST studies. We show our results in Table 5 and 6 as a reference for future works. It turns out that we can obtain a reasonable or even better BLEU score by simply initializing the ST encoder with a pre-trained ASR encoder. The improvement by MT decoder initialization is relatively marginal in our setup. Furthermore, the SpecAugment technique can consistently boost ST models.

[9]from https://github.com/espnet/espnet/blob/master/egs/libri_trans/asr1/RESULTS.md

Model	BLEU
large MT (w/ punc. & cased)	36.2
large MT (w/o punc.& lc)	34.3
large cascade ST	31.4
large end-to-end ST	29.7

Table 7: Case-sensitive detokenized BLEU scores on MuST-C EN-DE *tst-COMMON*.

3.7 Cascade versus End-to-End

Previous experiments on *libri-trans* and MuST-C NL/PT show that the end-to-end systems have outperformed the cascade systems. Here we argue that the performance of the cascade systems above is hampered by a lack of quantitative data, and they should take advantage of large amounts of ASR and MT data separately. Hence, we further extended NeurST to large-scale scenarios and experimented on the allowed datasets for IWSLT 2021 evaluation campaign[10]. We followed the practice of Zhao et al. (2021) to build our large cascade and end-to-end ST systems, which contains large-scale back-translation (Sennrich et al., 2016a) and pseudo labeling (also known as knowledge distillation) technologies. The results are illustrated in Table 7. As seen, there is a significant loss of 1.7 BLEU between end-to-end ST and cascade ST. And the cascade system would have the potential to narrow the gap to the pure MT system by introducing extra punctuation restoration and true-case modules.

Though the cascade system is superior under large data conditions, we believe future researches on self-supervised learning, knowledge distillation, and dataset construction would realize the potential of end-to-end models.

4 Conclusion

We introduce NeurST toolkit for easily building and training end-to-end speech translation models. We provide straightforward recipes for audio data pre-processing, training, and inference, which we believe is friendly with NLP researchers. Moreover, we report strong and reproducible benchmarks and will continuously catch up on advanced progress using NeurST , which can be regarded as the reliable baselines for the ST field.

[10]https://iwslt.org/2021/offline

References

Ebrahim Ansari, Amittai Axelrod, Nguyen Bach, Ondřej Bojar, Roldano Cattoni, Fahim Dalvi, Nadir Durrani, Marcello Federico, Christian Federmann, Jiatao Gu, Fei Huang, Kevin Knight, Xutai Ma, Ajay Nagesh, Matteo Negri, Jan Niehues, Juan Pino, Elizabeth Salesky, Xing Shi, Sebastian Stüker, Marco Turchi, Alexander Waibel, and Changhan Wang. 2020. FINDINGS OF THE IWSLT 2020 EVALUATION CAMPAIGN. In *Proceedings of the 17th International Conference on Spoken Language Translation*, pages 1–34, Online. Association for Computational Linguistics.

Alexei Baevski, Yuhao Zhou, Abdelrahman Mohamed, and Michael Auli. 2020. wav2vec 2.0: A framework for self-supervised learning of speech representations. In *Advances in Neural Information Processing Systems 33: Annual Conference on Neural Information Processing Systems 2020, NeurIPS 2020, December 6-12, 2020, virtual*.

Parnia Bahar, Albert Zeyer, Ralf Schlüter, and Hermann Ney. 2019. On using specaugment for end-to-end speech translation. In *International Workshop on Spoken Language Translation (IWSLT) 2019*.

Dzmitry Bahdanau, Kyunghyun Cho, and Yoshua Bengio. 2015. Neural machine translation by jointly learning to align and translate. In *3rd International Conference on Learning Representations, ICLR 2015, San Diego, CA, USA, May 7-9, 2015, Conference Track Proceedings*.

Alexandre Berard, Olivier Pietquin, Christophe Servan, and Laurent Besacier. 2016. Listen and translate: A proof of concept for end-to-end speech-to-text translation. *NIPS workshop on End-to-end Learning for Speech and Audio Processing*.

Francisco Casacuberta, Marcello Federico, Hermann Ney, and Enrique Vidal. 2008. Recent efforts in spoken language translation. *IEEE Signal Process. Mag.*, 25(3):80–88.

William Chan, Navdeep Jaitly, Quoc V. Le, and Oriol Vinyals. 2016. Listen, attend and spell: A neural network for large vocabulary conversational speech recognition. In *2016 IEEE International Conference on Acoustics, Speech and Signal Processing, ICASSP 2016, Shanghai, China, March 20-25, 2016*, pages 4960–4964. IEEE.

Chung-Cheng Chiu, Tara N. Sainath, Yonghui Wu, Rohit Prabhavalkar, Patrick Nguyen, Zhifeng Chen, Anjuli Kannan, Ron J. Weiss, Kanishka Rao, Ekaterina Gonina, Navdeep Jaitly, Bo Li, Jan Chorowski, and Michiel Bacchiani. 2018. State-of-the-art speech recognition with sequence-to-sequence models. In *2018 IEEE International Conference on Acoustics, Speech and Signal Processing, ICASSP 2018, Calgary, AB, Canada, April 15-20, 2018*, pages 4774–4778. IEEE.

Jacob Devlin, Ming-Wei Chang, Kenton Lee, and Kristina Toutanova. 2019. BERT: Pre-training of deep bidirectional transformers for language understanding. In *Proceedings of the 2019 Conference of the North American Chapter of the Association for Computational Linguistics: Human Language Technologies, Volume 1 (Long and Short Papers)*, pages 4171–4186, Minneapolis, Minnesota. Association for Computational Linguistics.

Mattia A. Di Gangi, Roldano Cattoni, Luisa Bentivogli, Matteo Negri, and Marco Turchi. 2019. MuST-C: a Multilingual Speech Translation Corpus. In *Proceedings of the 2019 Conference of the North American Chapter of the Association for Computational Linguistics: Human Language Technologies, Volume 1 (Long and Short Papers)*, pages 2012–2017, Minneapolis, Minnesota. Association for Computational Linguistics.

Linhao Dong, Shuang Xu, and Bo Xu. 2018. Speech-transformer: A no-recurrence sequence-to-sequence model for speech recognition. In *2018 IEEE International Conference on Acoustics, Speech and Signal Processing, ICASSP 2018, Calgary, AB, Canada, April 15-20, 2018*, pages 5884–5888. IEEE.

Qianqian Dong, Rong Ye, Mingxuan Wang, Hao Zhou, Shuang Xu, Bo Xu, and Lei Li. 2021. Listen, understand and translate: Triple supervision decouples end-to-end speech-to-text translation. *Proceedings of the AAAI Conference on Artificial Intelligence.*

Long Duong, Antonios Anastasopoulos, David Chiang, Steven Bird, and Trevor Cohn. 2016. An attentional model for speech translation without transcription. In *Proceedings of the 2016 Conference of the North American Chapter of the Association for Computational Linguistics: Human Language Technologies*, pages 949–959, San Diego, California. Association for Computational Linguistics.

Hirofumi Inaguma, Shun Kiyono, Kevin Duh, Shigeki Karita, Nelson Yalta, Tomoki Hayashi, and Shinji Watanabe. 2020. ESPnet-ST: All-in-one speech translation toolkit. In *Proceedings of the 58th Annual Meeting of the Association for Computational Linguistics: System Demonstrations*, pages 302–311, Online. Association for Computational Linguistics.

Yimin Jiang, Yibo Zhu, Chang Lan, Bairen Yi, Yong Cui, and Chuanxiong Guo. 2020. A unified architecture for accelerating distributed DNN training in heterogeneous gpu/cpu clusters. In *14th USENIX Symposium on Operating Systems Design and Implementation (OSDI 20)*, pages 463–479.

Shigeki Karita, Xiaofei Wang, Shinji Watanabe, Takenori Yoshimura, Wangyou Zhang, Nanxin Chen, Tomoki Hayashi, Takaaki Hori, Hirofumi Inaguma, Ziyan Jiang, Masao Someki, Nelson Enrique Yalta Soplin, and Ryuichi Yamamoto. 2019. A comparative study on transformer vs RNN in speech applications. In *IEEE Automatic Speech Recognition and Understanding Workshop, ASRU 2019*, pages 449–456.

Diederik P. Kingma and Jimmy Ba. 2015. Adam: A method for stochastic optimization. In *3rd International Conference on Learning Representations, ICLR 2015, San Diego, CA, USA, May 7-9, 2015, Conference Track Proceedings.*

Ali Can Kocabiyikoglu, Laurent Besacier, and Olivier Kraif. 2018. Augmenting librispeech with French translations: A multimodal corpus for direct speech translation evaluation. In *Proceedings of the Eleventh International Conference on Language Resources and Evaluation (LREC 2018)*, Miyazaki, Japan. European Language Resources Association (ELRA).

Gaurav Kumar, Matt Post, Daniel Povey, and Sanjeev Khudanpur. 2014. Some insights from translating conversational telephone speech. In *IEEE International Conference on Acoustics, Speech and Signal Processing, ICASSP 2014*, pages 3231–3235.

Yuchen Liu, Hao Xiong, Jiajun Zhang, Zhongjun He, Hua Wu, Haifeng Wang, and Chengqing Zong. 2019. End-to-End Speech Translation with Knowledge Distillation. In *Proc. Interspeech 2019*, pages 1128–1132.

Thang Luong, Hieu Pham, and Christopher D. Manning. 2015. Effective approaches to attention-based neural machine translation. In *Proceedings of the 2015 Conference on Empirical Methods in Natural Language Processing*, pages 1412–1421, Lisbon, Portugal. Association for Computational Linguistics.

Paulius Micikevicius, Sharan Narang, Jonah Alben, Gregory F. Diamos, Erich Elsen, David García, Boris Ginsburg, Michael Houston, Oleksii Kuchaiev, Ganesh Venkatesh, and Hao Wu. 2018. Mixed precision training. In *6th International Conference on Learning Representations, ICLR 2018, Vancouver, BC, Canada, April 30 - May 3, 2018, Conference Track Proceedings*. OpenReview.net.

Hermann Ney. 1999. Speech translation: coupling of recognition and translation. In *Proceedings of the 1999 IEEE International Conference on Acoustics, Speech, and Signal Processing, ICASSP 1999*, pages 517–520.

Vassil Panayotov, Guoguo Chen, Daniel Povey, and Sanjeev Khudanpur. 2015. Librispeech: An ASR corpus based on public domain audio books. In *2015 IEEE International Conference on Acoustics, Speech and Signal Processing, ICASSP 2015, South Brisbane, Queensland, Australia, April 19-24, 2015*, pages 5206–5210. IEEE.

Daniel S. Park, William Chan, Yu Zhang, Chung-Cheng Chiu, Barret Zoph, Ekin D. Cubuk, and Quoc V. Le. 2019. Specaugment: A simple data augmentation method for automatic speech recognition. In *Interspeech 2019, 20th Annual Conference of the International Speech Communication Association, Graz, Austria, 15-19 September 2019*, pages 2613–2617.

Yanghua Peng, Yibo Zhu, Yangrui Chen, Yixin Bao, Bairen Yi, Chang Lan, Chuan Wu, and Chuanxiong Guo. 2019. A generic communication scheduler for distributed DNN training acceleration. In *Proceedings of the 27th ACM Symposium on Operating Systems Principles, SOSP 2019*, pages 16–29.

Rico Sennrich, Barry Haddow, and Alexandra Birch. 2016a. Improving neural machine translation models with monolingual data. In *Proceedings of the 54th Annual Meeting of the Association for Computational Linguistics (Volume 1: Long Papers)*, pages 86–96, Berlin, Germany. Association for Computational Linguistics.

Rico Sennrich, Barry Haddow, and Alexandra Birch. 2016b. Neural machine translation of rare words with subword units. In *Proceedings of the 54th Annual Meeting of the Association for Computational Linguistics (Volume 1: Long Papers)*, pages 1715–1725, Berlin, Germany. Association for Computational Linguistics.

Alexander Sergeev and Mike Del Balso. 2018. Horovod: fast and easy distributed deep learning in tensorflow. *CoRR*, abs/1802.05799.

Jonathan Shen, Patrick Nguyen, Yonghui Wu, Zhifeng Chen, Mia Xu Chen, Ye Jia, Anjuli Kannan, Tara N. Sainath, Yuan Cao, Chung-Cheng Chiu, Yanzhang He, Jan Chorowski, Smit Hinsu, Stella Laurenzo, James Qin, Orhan Firat, Wolfgang Macherey, Suyog Gupta, Ankur Bapna, Shuyuan Zhang, Ruoming Pang, Ron J. Weiss, Rohit Prabhavalkar, Qiao Liang, Benoit Jacob, Bowen Liang, HyoukJoong Lee, Ciprian Chelba, Sébastien Jean, Bo Li, Melvin Johnson, Rohan Anil, Rajat Tibrewal, Xiaobing Liu, Akiko Eriguchi, Navdeep Jaitly, Naveen Ari, Colin Cherry, Parisa Haghani, Otavio Good, Youlong Cheng, Raziel Alvarez, Isaac Caswell, Wei-Ning Hsu, Zongheng Yang, Kuan-Chieh Wang, Ekaterina Gonina, Katrin Tomanek, Ben Vanik, Zelin Wu, Llion Jones, Mike Schuster, Yanping Huang, Dehao Chen, Kazuki Irie, George F. Foster, John Richardson, and et al. 2019. Lingvo: a modular and scalable framework for sequence-to-sequence modeling. *CoRR*, abs/1902.08295.

Ashish Vaswani, Noam Shazeer, Niki Parmar, Jakob Uszkoreit, Llion Jones, Aidan N. Gomez, Lukasz Kaiser, and Illia Polosukhin. 2017. Attention is all you need. In *Advances in Neural Information Processing Systems 30: Annual Conference on Neural Information Processing Systems 2017, December 4-9, 2017, Long Beach, CA, USA*, pages 5998–6008.

Changhan Wang, Yun Tang, Xutai Ma, Anne Wu, Dmytro Okhonko, and Juan Pino. 2020a. Fairseq S2T: Fast speech-to-text modeling with fairseq. In *Proceedings of the 1st Conference of the Asia-Pacific Chapter of the Association for Computational Linguistics and the 10th International Joint Conference on Natural Language Processing: System Demonstrations*, pages 33–39, Suzhou, China. Association for Computational Linguistics.

Chengyi Wang, Yu Wu, Shujie Liu, Zhenglu Yang, and Ming Zhou. 2020b. Bridging the gap between pre-training and fine-tuning for end-to-end speech translation. In *AAAI*, pages 9161–9168. AAAI Press.

Chengyi Wang, Yu Wu, Shujie Liu, Ming Zhou, and Zhenglu Yang. 2020c. Curriculum pre-training for end-to-end speech translation. In *Proceedings of the 58th Annual Meeting of the Association for Computational Linguistics*, pages 3728–3738, Online. Association for Computational Linguistics.

Xiaohui Wang, Ying Xiong, Yang Wei, Mingxuan Wang, and Lei Li. 2021. LightSeq: A high performance inference library for transformers. In *Proceedings of the 2021 Conference of the North American Chapter of the Association for Computational Linguistics: Human Language Technologies: Industry Papers*, pages 113–120, Online. Association for Computational Linguistics.

Ron J. Weiss, Jan Chorowski, Navdeep Jaitly, Yonghui Wu, and Zhifeng Chen. 2017. Sequence-to-sequence models can directly translate foreign speech. In *Interspeech 2017, 18th Annual Conference of the International Speech Communication Association*, pages 2625–2629.

Anne Wu, Changhan Wang, Juan Pino, and Jiatao Gu. 2020. Self-supervised representations improve end-to-end speech translation. In *Interspeech 2020*.

Biao Zhang, Ivan Titov, Barry Haddow, and Rico Sennrich. 2020. Adaptive feature selection for end-to-end speech translation. In *Findings of the Association for Computational Linguistics: EMNLP 2020*, pages 2533–2544, Online. Association for Computational Linguistics.

Chengqi Zhao, Zhicheng Liu, Jian Tong, Tao Wang, Mingxuan Wang, Rong Ye, Qianqian Dong, Jun Cao, and Lei Li. 2021. The volctrans neural speech translation system for IWSLT 2021. *CoRR*, abs/2105.07319.

ParCourE: A Parallel Corpus Explorer for a Massively Multilingual Corpus

Ayyoob Imani[1], **Masoud Jalili Sabet**[1], **Philipp Dufter**[1], **Michael Cysouw**[2], **Hinrich Schütze**[1]

[1]Center for Information and Language Processing (CIS), LMU Munich, Germany

[2]Research Center Deutscher Sprachatlas, Philipps University Marburg, Germany.

{ayyoob, masoud, philipp}@cis.lmu.de

Abstract

With more than 7000 languages worldwide, multilingual natural language processing (NLP) is essential both from an academic and commercial perspective. Researching typological properties of languages is fundamental for progress in multilingual NLP. Examples include assessing language similarity for effective transfer learning, injecting inductive biases into machine learning models or creating resources such as dictionaries and inflection tables. We provide ParCourE, an online tool that allows to browse a word-aligned parallel corpus, covering 1334 languages. We give evidence that this is useful for typological research. ParCourE can be set up for any parallel corpus and can thus be used for typological research on other corpora as well as for exploring their quality and properties.

1 Introduction

While ≈7000 languages are spoken (Eberhard et al., 2020), the bulk of NLP research addresses English only. However, multilinguality is an essential element of NLP. It not only supports exploiting common structures across languages and eases maintenance for globally operating companies, but also helps save languages from digital extinction and fosters more diversity in NLP techniques.

There are extensive resources that can be used for massively multilingual typological research, such as WALS (Dryer and Haspelmath, 2013), Glottolog (Hammarstrm et al., 2020), BabelNet (Navigli and Ponzetto, 2012) or http://panlex.org. Many of them are manually created or crowdsourced, which guarantees high quality, but limits coverage, both in terms of content and languages.

We work on the Parallel Bible Corpus (PBC) (Mayer and Cysouw, 2014), covering 1334 languages. More specifically, we provide a word-aligned version of PBC, created using state-of-the-art word alignment tools. As word alignments

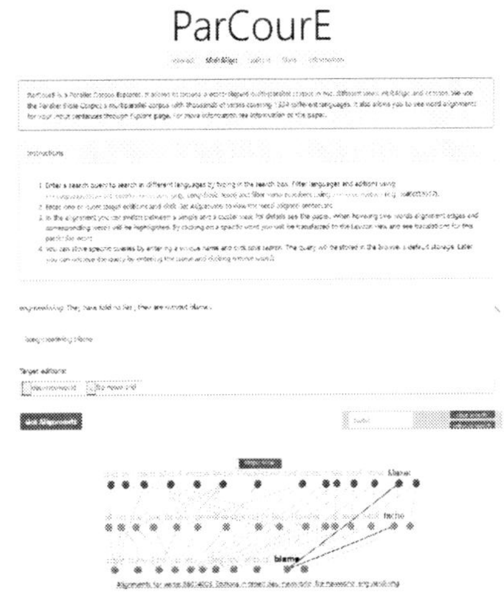

Figure 1: Screenshot of the ParCourE interface. It provides a word-aligned version of the Parallel Bible Corpus (PBC) spanning 1334 languages. Users can search for sentences in any language and see their alignments in other languages from MULTALIGN page. Alternatively they can feed their parallel sentences to INTERACTIVE view and see their word level alignments. They can look up translations of words in other languages, automatically induced from word alignments, from the LEXICON view (This page is interconnected with MULTALIGN). Statistics of the corpus is calculated and shown in the Stats view.

themselves are only of limited use, we provide an interactive online tool[1] that allows effective browsing of the alignments.

The main contributions of this work are: **i)** We provide a word-aligned version of the Parallel Bible Corpus (PBC) spanning 1334 languages and a total of 20M sentences ('verses'). For the alignment we use the state-of-the-art alignment methods SimAlign (Jalili Sabet et al., 2020) and Eflomal (Östling and Tiedemann, 2016a). **ii)** We release ParCourE,

[1]http://parcoure.cis.lmu.de/

Proceedings of the Joint Conference of the 59th Annual Meeting of the Association for Computational Linguistics and the 11th International Joint Conference on Natural Language Processing: System Demonstrations, pages 63–72, August 1st - August 6th, 2021.

a user interface for browsing word alignments, see the MULTALIGN view in Figure 1. We demonstrate the usefulness of ParCourE for typological research by presenting use cases in §6. **iii)** In addition to browsing word alignments, we provide an aggregated version in a LEXICON view and compute statistics that support assessing the quality of the word alignments. The two views (MULTALIGN and LEXICON views) are interlinked, resulting in a richer user experience. **iv)** ParCourE has a generic design and can be set up for any parallel corpus. This is useful for analyzing and managing parallel corpora; e.g., errors in an automatically mined parallel corpus can be inspected and flagged for correction.

2 Related Work

Word Alignment is an important tool for typological analysis (Lewis and Xia, 2008) and annotation projection (Yarowsky et al., 2001; Östling, 2015; Asgari and Schütze, 2017). Statistical models such as IBM models (Brown et al., 1993), Giza++ (Och and Ney, 2003), fast-align (Dyer et al., 2013) and Eflomal (Östling and Tiedemann, 2016b) are widely used. Recently, neural models were proposed, such as SimAlign (Jalili Sabet et al., 2020), Awesome-align (Dou and Neubig, 2021), and methods that are based on neural machine translation (Garg et al., 2019; Zenkel et al., 2020). We use Eflomal and SimAlign for generating alignments.

Resources. There are many online resources that enable typological research. WALS (Dryer and Haspelmath, 2013) provides manually created features for more than 2000 languages. We prepare a multiparallel corpus for investigating these features on real data. http://panlex.org is an online dictionary project with 2500 dictionaries covering 5700 languages and BabelNet (Navigli and Ponzetto, 2012) is a large semantic network covering 500 languages, but their information is generally on the type level, without access to example contexts. In contrast, ParCourE supports the exploration of word translations across 1334 languages in context.

Another line of work uses the **Parallel Bible Corpus (PBC)** for analysis. Asgari and Schütze (2017) investigate tense typology across PBC languages. Xia and Yarowsky (2017) created a multiway alignment based on fast-align (Dyer et al., 2013) and extracted resources such as paraphrases for 27 Bible editions. Wu et al. (2018) used alignments to extract names from the PBC.

One of the first attempts to index the Bible and align words in multiple languages were Strong's numbers (Strong, 2009[1890]); they tag words with similar meanings with the same ID. Mayer and Cysouw (2014) created an inverted index of word forms. Östling (2014) align massively parallel corpora simultaneously. We use the Eflomal word aligner by the same authorsostling2016efficient.

Finally, we review work on **Word Alignment Browsers.** Gilmanov et al. (2014)'s tool supports visualization and editing of word alignments. Akbik and Vollgraf (2017) use co-occurrence weights for word alignment and provide a tool for the inspection of annotation projection. Aulamo et al. (2020)'s filtering tool increases the quality of (mined) parallel corpora. Graën et al. (2017) rely on linguistic preprocessing, target corpus and word alignment exploration, do not show the graph of alignment edges and do not provide a dictionary view. While there is commonality with this prior work, ParCourE is distinguished by both its functionality and its motivating use cases: an important use case for us are typological searches; linguistic preprocessing is not available for many PBC languages; ParCourE can be used as an interactive explorer (but is not a fully-automated pipeline for a specific use case); our goal is not annotation; we use state-of-the-art word alignment methods. However, much of the complementary functionality in prior work would be useful additions to ParCourE. Another source of useful additional functionality would be work on embedding learning (Dufter et al., 2018; Kurfal and Östling, 2018) and machine translation (Tiedemann, 2018; Santy et al., 2019; Mueller et al., 2020) for PBC.

3 Features

ParCourE's user facing functionality can be divided into three main parts: MULTALIGN and LEXICON views and interconnections between the two.

3.1 Multiparallel Alignment Browser: MULTALIGN

ParCourE allows the user to search through the parallel corpus and check word alignments in a multiparallel corpus. An overview of MULTALIGN is shown in Figure 2.

In the **search field** (a(1)), the user can enter a text query and select (a(2)) multiple sentences for alignment. For narrowing the search scope, the

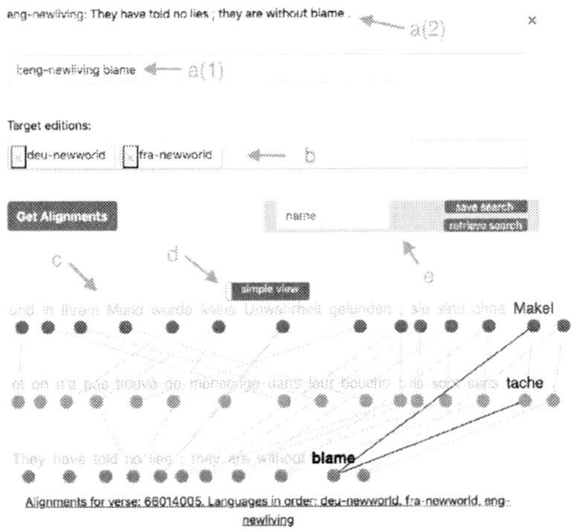

Figure 2: An overview of the MULTALIGN view. a) Search field for selecting sentences [a(1)] and the list of selected sentences [a(2)]. Any language can be used for the source sentence – in this case, it is English. b) Search bar for selecting the target languages. c) The alignment graph for the selected sentences in the source and the target languages. d) Switch button for simple view / cluster view. e) Save and retrieve search results

language and edition of the text segment can be specified in the beginning, e.g., by typing *l:eng-newworld2013*. Similarly, *v:40002017* specifies a verse ID.

PBC has 1334, so showing alignments for all translations of a sentence is difficult. We provide a drop-down (b) to select a subset of target languages for display.

For each sentence, a graph of alignment edges between selected languages is shown (c). By hovering over a word, the alignments of that word will be highlighted. Above each alignment graph, there is a button to switch between **Simple view** and **Cluster view** (d). In the simple view, when hovering over a word, only the alignment edges connected to that word are highlighted; in the cluster view, all words in a cluster (neighbors of neighbors) that are aligned together will be highlighted. We do not actually run any clustering algorithm on the alignment graph. Instead we simply highlight words that are up to two hops away from the hovered word. This helps spot a group of words across languages that have the same meaning.

Creating queries for typology research can take time. Thus, MULTALIGN allows the user to **save and retrieve** (e) queries.

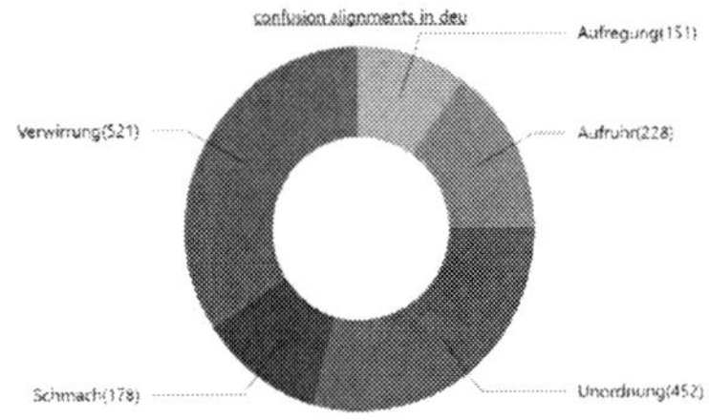

Figure 3: LEXICON view example: for the English word "confusion", there are five frequent translations in German. "Unordnung" literally means "disorder" and "Verwirrung" means "bewilderment".

3.2 Lexicon View: LEXICON

The MULTALIGN view allows the user to focus on word alignments on the sentence level and study the typological structure of languages in context. The LEXICON view focuses on word translations. The user can specify a source language by selecting the language code. This is to distinguish words with the same spelling in different languages. The user can search for one or multiple word(s) and specify target language(s). A pie chart for each target language depicting translations of the word is generated. Figure 3 shows German translations of "confusion" and the number of alignment edges for each. Word alignments are not perfect, so pie charts may also contain errors.

3.3 Interconnections

Both MULTALIGN and LEXICON views provide important features to the user for exploring the parallel corpus. For many use cases (cf. §6), the user may need to go back and forth between the views. For example, if she notices an error in the word alignment, she may want to check the LEXICON statistics to see if one of the typical translations of an incorrectly aligned word occurs in the sentence.

Thus, the two views are interconnected. In the MULTALIGN view, the user will be transferred to the LEXICON statistics of a word by clicking on it. This will open the LEXICON view, showing the search results for the selected word. Conversely, if the user clicks on one of the target translations in the LEXICON view, the MULTALIGN view will show sentences where this correspondence is part of the word alignment between source and target translation.

# editions	1758	# verses	20,470,892
# languages	1334	# verses / # editions	11,520
		# tokens / # verses	28.6

Table 1: PBC corpus statistics

3.4 Alignment Generation View: INTERACTIVE

The views mentioned so far provide the ability to search over the indexed corpus. This is useful when the main corpus of interest is fixed and the user has generated its alignments.

The INTERACTIVE view allows the user to study the alignments between arbitrary input sentences that are not necessarily in the corpus. Since the input sentences are not part of a corpus, INTERACTIVE uses SimAlign to generate alignments for all possible pairs of sentences. Similar to MULTALIGN, the INTERACTIVE view shows the alignment between the input sentences.

4 Experimental Setup

Corpus. We set up ParCourE on the PBC corpus provided by Mayer and Cysouw (2014). The version we use consists of 1758 editions (i.e., translations) of the Bible in 1334 languages (distinct ISO 639-3 codes). Table 1 shows corpus statistics. We use the PBC tokenization, which contains errors for a few languages (e.g., Thai). We extract word alignments for all possible language pairs. Since not all Bible verses are available in all languages, for each language pair we only consider mutually available verses.

PBC aligns Bible editions on the verse level by using verse-IDs that indicate book, chapter and verse (see below). Although one verse may contain multiple sentences, we do not split verses into individual sentences and consider each verse as one sentence.

Retrieval. Elasticsearch[2] is a fast and scalable open source search engine that provides distributed fulltext search. The setup is straightforward using an easy-to-use JSON web interface. We use it as the back-end for ParCourE's search requirement. We find that a single instance is capable of handling the whole PBC corpus efficiently, so we do not need a distributed setup. For bigger corpora, a distributed setup may be required. We created two types of inverted indices for our data: an edge-ngram index to support search-as-you-type capability and a standard index for normal queries.

Alignment Generation. SimAlign (Jalili Sabet et al., 2020) is a recent word alignment method that uses representations from pretrained language models to align sentences. It has achieved better results than statistical word aligners. For the languages that multilingual BERT (Devlin et al., 2019) supports, we use SimAlign to generate word alignments. For the remaining languages, we use Eflomal (Östling and Tiedemann, 2016a), an efficient word aligner using a Bayesian model with Markov Chain Monte Carlo (MCMC) inference. The alignments generated by SimAlign are symmetric. We use atools[3] and the grow-diag-final-and heuristic to symmetrize Eflomal alignments.

Lexicon Induction. We exploit the generated word alignments to induce lexicons for all 889,111 language pairs. To this end, we consider aligned words as translations of each other. For a given word from the source language, we count the number of times a word from the target language is aligned with it. The higher the number of alignments between two words, the higher the probability that the two have the same meaning. We filter out translations with frequency less than 5%.

5 Backend Design

An overview of our architecture can be found in Figure 4. The code is available online.[4]

Parallel Data Format. We use the PBC corpus format (Mayer and Cysouw, 2014): each verse has a unique ID across languages / editions, the *verse-ID*. The verse-ID is an 8-digit number, consisting of two digits for the book (e.g., 41 for the Gospel of Mark), three digits for the Chapter, and two digits for the verse itself. There are separate files for each edition. In each edition file, a line consists of the ID and the verse, separated by a tab.

Indexing. We identify a PBC verse using the following format: {verse-ID}@{language-code}-{edition-name}. We use this identifier to save and retrieve sentences with Elasticsearch. In addition, we store all metadata identifiers within Elasticsearch. Thus, we can search for a sentence by keyword, sentence number (= verse-ID), language code, or edition name.

ParCourE also supports the Corpus Alignment

[2] `https://www.elastic.co/`

[3] `https://github.com/clab/fast_align`

[4] `https://github.com/cisnlp/parcoure`

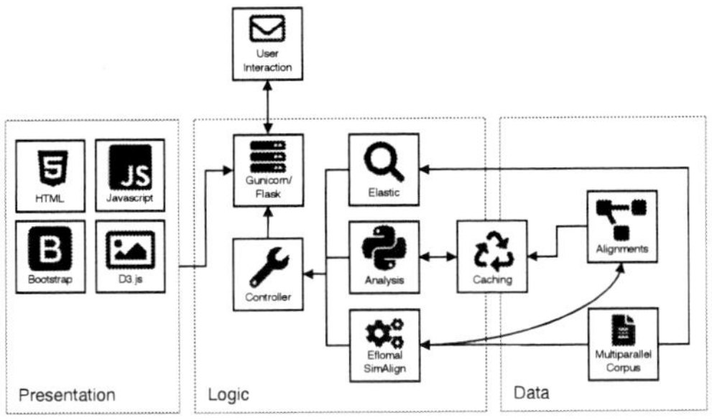

Figure 4: Overview of the system architecture. We use a standard front-end stack with d3.js for visualization. The backend is written in Python, which we use for computing alignments and performing analyses such as lexicon induction. We use Elasticsearch for search. The input is a multiparallel corpus for which all alignments are precomputed. For speeding up the system we use smart caching algorithms for our analyses. Icons taken without changes from https://fontawesome.com/license.

Encoding (CES)[5] format. One can download parallel corpora in CES format and use our tools to adapt them to ParCourE's input format.

Alignment Computation. Since Eflomal's performance depends on the amount of data it uses for training, we concatenate all editions to create a bigger training corpus for languages that have more than one edition. If language l_1 has two, and language l_2 three different editions, then the final training corpus for this language pair will contain six aligned edition pairs.

System Architecture. ParCourE is built on top of modern open source technologies, see Figure 4. The back-end uses the Flask web framework,[6] Gunicorn web server,[7] and Elasticsearch.[8] The front-end utilizes the Bootstrap CSS framework,[9] and the d3 visualization library.[10] Since all these tools are free and open-source, there is no restriction on setting up and releasing a new ParCourE instance. To extract word alignments, one can use any tool, such as Eflomal, fast_align or SimAlign.

Performance Improvements. For good runtime performance, we precompute the word alignments. Regarding LEXICON, given a query word and a target language, ParCourE first looks for a precomputed lexicon file; if it does not exist, ParCourE obtains the translations for the query word online. To accelerate the translation process, ParCourE employs Python's multiprocessing library. The number of CPU cores is decided online based on the number of editions available for source and target languages.

For a corpus with 1334 languages, we will end up with 890,445 alignment files and the same number of lexicon files. We cache alignment / lexicon files to speed up access. We use the Last Recently Used (LRU) cache replacement algorithm.

6 ParCourE Use Cases

Languages differ in how they encode meanings/functions. There are various aspects that make such differences an interesting problem when dealing with a dataset that has good coverage of the entire variation of the world's languages. (i) Many such differences between languages are not widely acknowledged in linguistic theory, so to document the extent of variation becomes a discovery of sorts. For example, the fact that interrogative words might distinguish between singular and plural (Figure 6) turns out to be a typologically salient differentiation (Mayer and Cysouw, 2012). (ii) The variation of linguistic marking is even stronger in the domain of grammatical function, like the differentiation between the interrogative and relative pronoun in Figure 6. (iii) In lexical semantics, ParCourE supports the investigation of how languages carve up the meaning space differently (cf. Figure 5), especially when it comes to the ≈1000 low-resource languages covered in PBC. Massively parallel texts are an ideal resource to investigate such variation (Haspelmath, 2003).

Grammatical differences between languages, like differences in word order, have a long history in research on worldwide linguistic variation (Greenberg, 1966; Dryer, 1992). However, being able to look at the usage of word order in specific contexts (and being able to directly compare exactly the same context across languages) is only possible by using parallel texts. For example, specific orders of more than two elements can be directly extracted from the parallel texts, like the order of demonstrative, numeral and noun "these two commandments" in Figure 7 (Cysouw, 2010).

For lack of space, we describe four more use cases only briefly: grammatical markers vs. morphology as devices to express grammatical features (Figure 8); differences in how languages use gram-

[5] https://www.cs.vassar.edu/CES/
[6] https://flask.palletsprojects.com
[7] https://gunicorn.org/
[8] https://www.elastic.co/
[9] https://getbootstrap.com/
[10] https://d3js.org/

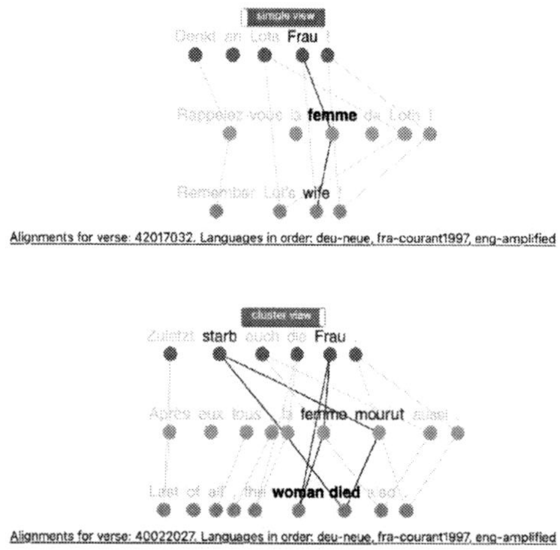

Figure 5: Use case 1, *lexical differentiation*. French "femme" has two different translations in English ("wife" and "woman") whereas German also conflates the two different meanings.

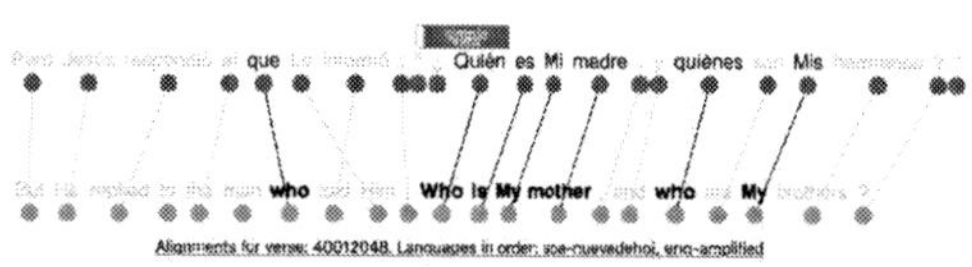

Figure 6: Use case 2, *grammatical differentiation*. English "who" has three different translations in this Spanish example: relative pronoun ("que"), and singular ("quién)" and plural ("quiénes") interrogative pronoun.

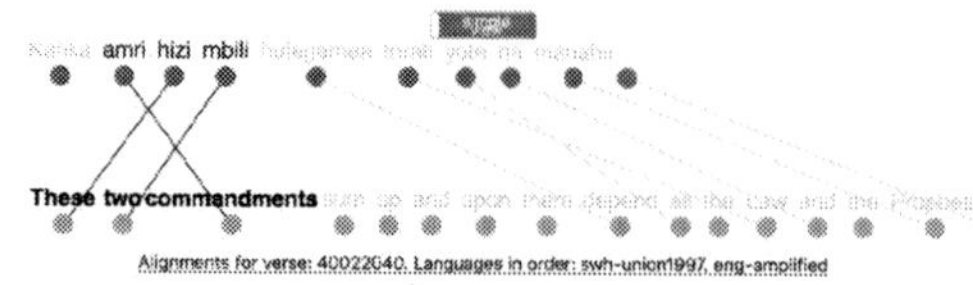

Figure 7: Use case 3, *word order variation*. The English order is demonstrative, numeral, noun whereas Swahili has noun, demonstrative, numeral.

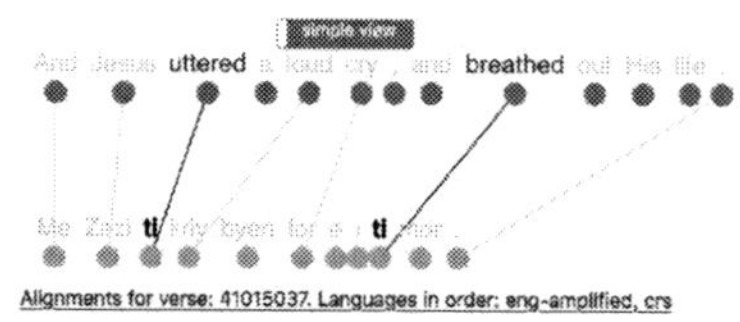

Figure 8: Use case 4, *grammatical markers*. In contrast to English, Seychelles Creole does not inflect verbs for tense and uses the past tense marker "ti" instead.

matical case (Figure 9, ablative/dative in Latin can correspond to five different cases in Croatian); and exploration of paraphrases (Figure 10). See the captions of the figures for more details.

7 Extension to Other Corpora

Our code is available on GitHub and can be generically applied: you can create a ParCourE instance for your own parallel corpus. Parallel corpora are essential for machine translation (MT); ParCourE's functionality is useful for analyzing the quality of a parallel corpus and the difficulty of the translation problem it poses. We give three examples **i)** Incorrect sentence alignments can be identified, e.g., cases in which a target sentence is matched with the merger of two sentences in the source: cf. Figure 11 where a short sentence in English is aligned with German and French sentences that also contain a second sentence that is missing in English. This functionality is particularly helpful for mined parallel corpora that tend to contain erroneous sentence pairs. **ii)** Suppose an MT system trained on the parallel corpus makes a lexical error in a particular context c by mistranslating source word w_s with target word w_t. The LEXICON view can be consulted for w_s and the user can then click on the erroneous target word w_t to get back to a MULTALIGN view of aligned sentence pairs containing w_s and w_t. She can then analyze why the MT system mismatched c with these contexts. Examples of the desired translation are easy to find and inspect to support the formation of hypotheses as to the source of the error. **iii)** For multi-source approaches to MT (Zoph and Knight, 2016; Firat et al., 2016; Libovický and Helcl, 2017; Crego et al., 2010), ParCourE supports the inspection of all input sentences together. The MT system output can also be loaded into ParCourE for a view that contains all input sentences and the output sentence. Since any of the input sentences can be responsible for an error in multi-source MT, this facilitates analysis and hypothesis formation as to what caused a specific error.

7.1 Computing Infrastructure and Runtime

We did all computations on a machine with 48 cores of Intel(R) Xeon(R) CPU E7-8857 v2 with 1TB memory. In this experiment only one core was used.

We created a corpus of 5 translations in 4 languages, with around 31k parallel sentences (overally 155k sentences) and applied the ParCourE pipeline to it. Runtimes for different parts of the

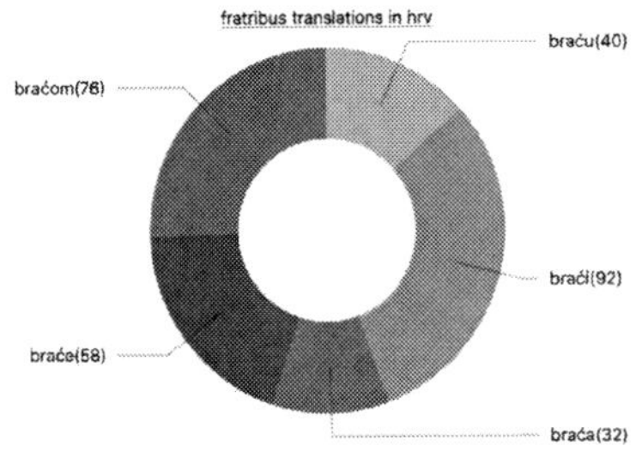

Figure 9: Use case 5, *morphology*. The Latin ending "ibus" in "fratribus" (dative/ablativ plural) corresponds to five different cases in Croatian: accusative, locative/dative, nominative, genitive, instrumental (clockwise starting from "braću").

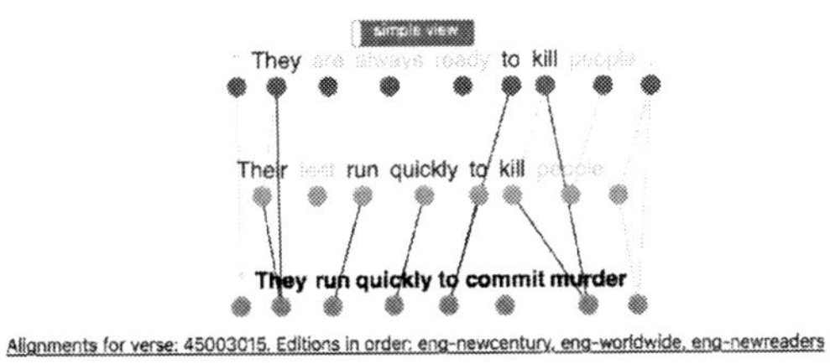

Figure 10: Use case 6, *paraphrases*. PBC is a rich source of paraphrases since high-resource languages have several translations (32 for English). ParCourE can be used to explore these paraphrases. Here, the paraphrases "kill" and "murder" are correctly aligned, "always ready" and "run quickly" are not.

pipeline are reported in Table 2. The installation of the package is straightforward and as shown in the table, it takes around 12 minutes to initiate ParCourE on a small corpus with 4 languages.

Method	Runtime
Conversion from CES to ParCourE format	153
Indexing with Elasticsearch	14
Alignment generation with Eflomal	537
Stats calculation	22
Overall	726

Table 2: Runtime in seconds for each part of the pipeline to initiate a ParCourE instance on a corpus with 4 languages and 31K parallel sentences.

8 Conclusion

Progress in multilingual NLP is an important goal of NLP and requires researching typological properties of languages. Examples include assessing language similarity for effective transfer learning, injecting inductive biases into machine learning models and creating resources such as dictionaries and inflection tables. To serve such use cases, we

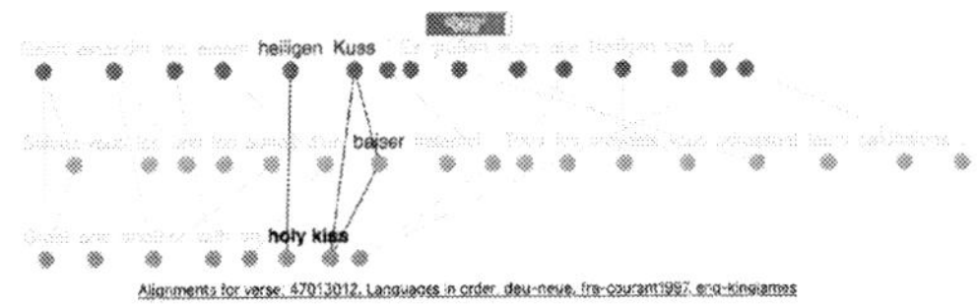

Figure 11: Use case 7, *quality analysis*. ParCourE makes it easy to analyze the quality of the parallel corpus. For this sentence, part of a Bible verse present in German and French is missing in English. Note that the alignment of *holy, heiligen* to French *fraternel* is not discovered.

have created ParCourE, an online tool for browsing a word-aligned parallel corpus of 1334 languages, and given evidence that it is useful for typological research. ParCourE can be set up for any other parallel corpus, e.g., for quality control and improvement of automatically mined parallel corpora.

Acknowledgments

This work was supported by the European Research Council (ERC, Grant No. 740516) and the German Federal Ministry of Education and Research (BMBF, Grant No. 01IS18036A). The third author was supported by the Bavarian research institute for digital transformation (bidt) through their fellowship program. We thank the anonymous reviewers for their constructive comments.

9 Ethical Considerations

Word alignments and lexicon induction as tasks themselves may not have ethical implications. However, working on a biblical corpus requires special consideration of the following issues.

i) The Bible is the central religious text of Christianity and the Hebrew Bible that of Judaism. It contains strong opinions and world views (e.g., on divorce and homosexuality) that are not generally shared. We would like to emphasize that we treat the PBC simply as a multiparallel corpus, and the corpus does not necessarily reflect the opinions of the authors nor of the institutions funding the authors. **ii)** In a similar vein, while the PBC has great language coverage and allows for typological analysis, we need to be aware that languages might not be accurately and completely reflected in the PBC. The language used in the PBC might be outdated and is restricted to a relatively small subset of topics and thus cannot be considered a balanced and complete view of the language. **iii)** We also need to be aware of selection bias. The PBC only covers a subset of the world's languages. The selection criteria are unknown and may be based on historical and cultural biases that we are not able to assess.

References

Alan Akbik and Roland Vollgraf. 2017. The projector: An interactive annotation projection visualization tool. In *Proceedings of the 2017 Conference on Empirical Methods in Natural Language Processing: System Demonstrations*, pages 43–48, Copenhagen, Denmark. Association for Computational Linguistics.

Ehsaneddin Asgari and Hinrich Schütze. 2017. Past, present, future: A computational investigation of the typology of tense in 1000 languages. In *Proceedings of the 2017 Conference on Empirical Methods in Natural Language Processing*, pages 113–124, Copenhagen, Denmark. Association for Computational Linguistics.

Mikko Aulamo, Sami Virpioja, and Jörg Tiedemann. 2020. OpusFilter: A configurable parallel corpus filtering toolbox. In *Proceedings of the 58th Annual Meeting of the Association for Computational Linguistics: System Demonstrations*, pages 150–156, Online. Association for Computational Linguistics.

Peter F. Brown, Stephen A. Della Pietra, Vincent J. Della Pietra, and Robert L. Mercer. 1993. The mathematics of statistical machine translation: Parameter estimation. *Computational Linguistics*, 19(2).

Josep Maria Crego, Aurélien Max, and François Yvon. 2010. Local lexical adaptation in machine translation through triangulation: SMT helping SMT. In *Proceedings of the 23rd International Conference on Computational Linguistics (Coling 2010)*, pages 232–240, Beijing, China. Coling 2010 Organizing Committee.

Michael Cysouw. 2010. Dealing with diversity: towards an explanation of NP word order frequencies. *Linguistic Typology*, 14(2):253–287.

Jacob Devlin, Ming-Wei Chang, Kenton Lee, and Kristina Toutanova. 2019. BERT: Pre-training of deep bidirectional transformers for language understanding. In *Proceedings of the 2019 Conference of the North American Chapter of the Association for Computational Linguistics: Human Language Technologies, Volume 1 (Long and Short Papers)*, pages 4171–4186, Minneapolis, Minnesota. Association for Computational Linguistics.

Zi-Yi Dou and Graham Neubig. 2021. Word alignment by fine-tuning embeddings on parallel corpora. *CoRR*, abs/2101.08231.

Matthew S. Dryer. 1992. The Greenbergian word order correlations. *Language*, 68(1):80–138.

Matthew S. Dryer and Martin Haspelmath, editors. 2013. *WALS Online*. Max Planck Institute for Evolutionary Anthropology, Leipzig.

Philipp Dufter, Mengjie Zhao, Martin Schmitt, Alexander Fraser, and Hinrich Schütze. 2018. Embedding learning through multilingual concept induction. In *Proceedings of the 56th Annual Meeting of the Association for Computational Linguistics (Volume 1: Long Papers)*, pages 1520–1530, Melbourne, Australia. Association for Computational Linguistics.

Chris Dyer, Victor Chahuneau, and Noah A. Smith. 2013. A simple, fast, and effective reparameterization of IBM model 2. In *Proceedings of the 2013 Conference of the North American Chapter of the Association for Computational Linguistics: Human Language Technologies*, pages 644–648, Atlanta, Georgia. Association for Computational Linguistics.

David M. Eberhard, F. Simons Gary, and D. Fennig (eds.) Charles. 2020. *Ethnologue: Languages of the World*, 23rd edition. SIL International.

Orhan Firat, Baskaran Sankaran, Yaser Al-onaizan, Fatos T. Yarman Vural, and Kyunghyun Cho. 2016. Zero-resource translation with multi-lingual neural machine translation. In *Proceedings of the 2016 Conference on Empirical Methods in Natural Language Processing*, pages 268–277, Austin, Texas. Association for Computational Linguistics.

Sarthak Garg, Stephan Peitz, Udhyakumar Nallasamy, and Matthias Paulik. 2019. Jointly learning to align and translate with transformer models. In *Proceedings of the 2019 Conference on Empirical Methods in Natural Language Processing and the 9th International Joint Conference on Natural Language Processing (EMNLP-IJCNLP)*, pages 4453–4462, Hong Kong, China. Association for Computational Linguistics.

Timur Gilmanov, Olga Scrivner, and Sandra Kübler. 2014. SWIFT aligner, a multifunctional tool for parallel corpora: Visualization, word alignment, and (morpho)-syntactic cross-language transfer. In *Proceedings of the Ninth International Conference on Language Resources and Evaluation (LREC'14)*, pages 2913–2919, Reykjavik, Iceland. European Language Resources Association (ELRA).

Johannes Graën, Dominique Sandoz, and Martin Volk. 2017. Multilingwis2 ėxtendash explore your parallel corpus. In *Proceedings of the 21st Nordic Conference on Computational Linguistics, NODALIDA 2017, Gothenburg, Sweden, May 22-24, 2017*, volume 131 of *Linköping Electronic Conference Proceedings*, pages 247–250. Linköping University Electronic Press / Association for Computational Linguistics.

Joseph H. Greenberg. 1966. *Language Universals: with special reference to feature hierarchies*. Janua Linguarum, Series Minor. Mouton, The Hague.

Harald Hammarstrm, Robert Forkel, Martin Haspelmath, and Sebastian Bank. 2020. Glottolog 4.3. Max Planck Institute for the Science of Human History.

Martin Haspelmath. 2003. The geometry of grammatical meaning: Semantic maps and cross-linguistic comparison. In Michael Tomasello, editor, *The New Psychology of Language: Cognitive and Functional Approaches to Language Structure (Volume 2)*, pages 211–242. Erlbaum, Mahwah, NJ.

Masoud Jalili Sabet, Philipp Dufter, François Yvon, and Hinrich Schütze. 2020. SimAlign: High quality word alignments without parallel training data using static and contextualized embeddings. In *Findings of the Association for Computational Linguistics: EMNLP 2020*, pages 1627–1643, Online. Association for Computational Linguistics.

Murathan Kurfal and Robert Östling. 2018. Word embeddings for 1250 languages through multi-source projection. In *Seventh Swedish Language Technology Conference*.

William D. Lewis and Fei Xia. 2008. Automatically identifying computationally relevant typological features. In *Proceedings of the Third International Joint Conference on Natural Language Processing: Volume-II*.

Jindrich Libovický and Jindrich Helcl. 2017. Attention strategies for multi-source sequence-to-sequence learning. In *Proceedings of the 55th Annual Meeting of the Association for Computational Linguistics, ACL 2017, Vancouver, Canada, July 30 - August 4, Volume 2: Short Papers*, pages 196–202. Association for Computational Linguistics.

Thomas Mayer and Michael Cysouw. 2012. Language comparison through sparse multilingual word alignment. In *Proceedings of the EACL 2012 Joint Workshop of LINGVIS & UNCLH*, pages 54–62, Avignon, France. Association for Computational Linguistics.

Thomas Mayer and Michael Cysouw. 2014. Creating a massively parallel Bible corpus. In *Proceedings of the Ninth International Conference on Language Resources and Evaluation (LREC'14)*, pages 3158–3163, Reykjavik, Iceland. European Language Resources Association (ELRA).

Aaron Mueller, Garrett Nicolai, Arya D. McCarthy, Dylan Lewis, Winston Wu, and David Yarowsky. 2020. An analysis of massively multilingual neural machine translation for low-resource languages. In *Proceedings of the 12th Language Resources and Evaluation Conference*, pages 3710–3718, Marseille, France. European Language Resources Association.

Roberto Navigli and Simone Paolo Ponzetto. 2012. BabelNet: The automatic construction, evaluation and application of a wide-coverage multilingual semantic network. *Artif. Intell.*, 193:217–250.

Franz Josef Och and Hermann Ney. 2003. A systematic comparison of various statistical alignment models. *Computational Linguistics*, 29(1).

Robert Östling. 2014. Bayesian word alignment for massively parallel texts. In *Proceedings of the 14th Conference of the European Chapter of the Association for Computational Linguistics, EACL 2014, April 26-30, 2014, Gothenburg, Sweden*, pages 123–127. The Association for Computer Linguistics.

Robert Östling. 2015. Word order typology through multilingual word alignment. In *Proceedings of the 53rd Annual Meeting of the Association for Computational Linguistics and the 7th International Joint Conference on Natural Language Processing (Volume 2: Short Papers)*, pages 205–211, Beijing, China. Association for Computational Linguistics.

Robert Östling and Jörg Tiedemann. 2016a. Efficient word alignment with Markov Chain Monte Carlo. *Prague Bulletin of Mathematical Linguistics*, 106:125–146.

Robert Östling and Jörg Tiedemann. 2016b. Efficient word alignment with Markov Chain Monte Carlo. *The Prague Bulletin of Mathematical Linguistics*, 106(1).

Sebastin Santy, Sandipan Dandapat, Monojit Choudhury, and Kalika Bali. 2019. INMT: Interactive neural machine translation prediction. In *Proceedings of the 2019 Conference on Empirical Methods in Natural Language Processing and the 9th International Joint Conference on Natural Language Processing (EMNLP-IJCNLP): System Demonstrations*, pages 103–108, Hong Kong, China. Association for Computational Linguistics.

James Strong. 2009[1890]. *Strong's exhaustive concordance of the Bible*. Hendrickson Publishers.

Jörg Tiedemann. 2018. Emerging language spaces learned from massively multilingual corpora. In *Proceedings of the Digital Humanities in the Nordic Countries 3rd Conference, DHN 2018, Helsinki, Finland, March 7-9, 2018*, volume 2084 of *CEUR Workshop Proceedings*, pages 188–197. CEUR-WS.org.

Winston Wu, Nidhi Vyas, and David Yarowsky. 2018. Creating a translation matrix of the Bible's names across 591 languages. In *Proceedings of the Eleventh International Conference on Language Resources and Evaluation (LREC 2018)*, Miyazaki, Japan. European Language Resources Association (ELRA).

Patrick Xia and David Yarowsky. 2017. Deriving consensus for multi-parallel corpora: an English Bible study. In *Proceedings of the Eighth International Joint Conference on Natural Language Processing (Volume 2: Short Papers)*, pages 448–453, Taipei, Taiwan. Asian Federation of Natural Language Processing.

David Yarowsky, Grace Ngai, and Richard Wicentowski. 2001. Inducing multilingual text analysis tools via robust projection across aligned corpora. In *Proceedings of the First International Conference on Human Language Technology Research*.

Thomas Zenkel, Joern Wuebker, and John DeNero. 2020. End-to-end neural word alignment outperforms GIZA++. In *Proceedings of the 58th Annual Meeting of the Association for Computational Linguistics*, pages 1605–1617, Online. Association for Computational Linguistics.

Barret Zoph and Kevin Knight. 2016. Multi-source neural translation. In *Proceedings of the 2016 Conference of the North American Chapter of the Association for Computational Linguistics: Human Language Technologies*, pages 30–34, San Diego, California. Association for Computational Linguistics.

MT-TELESCOPE
An interactive platform for contrastive evaluation of MT systems

Ricardo Rei[*†‡] **Ana C Farinha**[*] **Craig Stewart**[*]
Luisa Coheur[†‡] **Alon Lavie**[*]
[*]Unbabel Research
[‡]Instituto Superior Técnico, Universidade de Lisboa, Portugal
[†]INESC-ID, Lisboa, Portugal
[*]{firstname.lastname}@unbabel.com
luisa.coheur@inesc-id.pt

Abstract

We present MT-TELESCOPE, a visualization platform designed to facilitate comparative analysis of the output quality of two Machine Translation (MT) systems. While automated MT evaluation metrics are commonly used to evaluate MT systems at a corpus-level, our platform supports fine-grained segment-level analysis and interactive visualisations that expose the fundamental differences in the performance of the compared systems. MT-TELESCOPE also supports dynamic corpus filtering to enable focused analysis on specific phenomena such as; translation of named entities, handling of terminology, and the impact of input segment length on translation quality. Furthermore, the platform provides a bootstrapped t-test for statistical significance as a means of evaluating the rigor of the resulting system ranking. MT-TELESCOPE is open source[1], written in Python, and is built around a user friendly and dynamic web interface. Complementing other existing tools, our platform is designed to facilitate and promote the broader adoption of more rigorous analysis practices in the evaluation of MT quality.

1 Introduction

When developing MT systems or comparing experiments across papers, it has been common practice for researchers and developers to rely on automated metrics such as BLEU (Papineni et al., 2002) and METEOR (Banerjee and Lavie, 2005) as a means of quantifying the relative performance difference between two models. Commercial deployment of systems and the establishment of state-of-the-art in academia is often driven by these metrics alone. Automated metrics have long been an essential means for assessing quality improvements and driving progress in the field of MT. Recent state-of-the-art metrics such as COMET (Rei et al., 2020a), PRISM (Thompson and Post, 2020), and BLEURT (Sellam et al., 2020), show much higher levels of correlation with human judgement than their predecessors.

Notwithstanding the strength of available metrics, when applied and reported at corpus-level, they are only able to provide a general indication of whether one system is superior, based on a single score which in some cases is limited to an arithmetic mean of segment-level score predictions (Rei et al., 2020a). We contend that the broad definition of 'improvement' as an increase in a relevant corpus-level score is insufficient, especially when the relative difference between high-performing MT systems is negligible. Exposure of the changing distribution of performance at segment-level on targeted phenomena is fundamental to our understanding of translation quality. Manual inspection at this level is often too time-consuming and inefficient to be done rigorously and on a regular basis.

MT-TELESCOPE was inspired by other recent work on developing holistic approaches for fine-grained comparison of MT systems, such as COMPARE-MT (Neubig et al., 2019) and MT-COMPAREVAL (Klejch et al., 2015) and other more general comparative tools such as VIZSEQ (Wang et al., 2019). Despite the intention of such tools in addressing the above problem, none have been widely adopted as a standard method of evaluating MT. MT-TELESCOPE was specifically developed to leverage the best of existing approaches in a manner that is as user friendly as possible, with features specifically tailored to the MT use case. The platform supports fine-grained segment-level analysis and interactive visualisations that provide relevant and informative quality intelligence. In particular, the platform also supports focused anal-

[1]Code available at: https://github.com/Unbabel/MT-Telescope and Demo video at: https://youtu.be/MZOelyX8mII

Proceedings of the Joint Conference of the 59th Annual Meeting of the Association for Computational Linguistics and the 11th International Joint Conference on Natural Language Processing: System Demonstrations, pages 73–80, August 1st - August 6th, 2021.

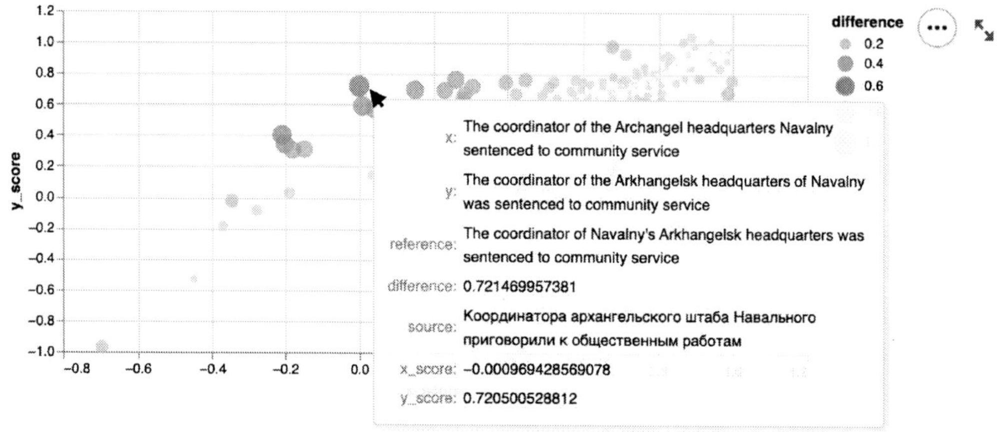

Figure 1: Segment comparison bubble plot.

ysis of MT-specific phenomena through interactive corpus filtering.

MT-TELESCOPE is differentiated from existing MT-specific tools by exposing features such as named entities and glossary handling which play a fundamental role in determining the suitability of an MT system for a production environment. Furthermore, the platform applies a bootstrapped t-test for statistical significance (Koehn, 2004) as a means of exposing the experimental rigor of system comparisons. These features are not widely available in other tools and provide a uniquely tailored solution to MT comparison that is highly informative and easy to use.

The fundamental goal of MT-TELESCOPE is to widen access to state-of-art, robust MT comparison, to the benefit of the MT community at large. MT-TELESCOPE is open source, written in Python and uses a dynamic web interface implemented in streamlit[2]. In this manner, MT-TELESCOPE provides a uniquely accessible framework that requires little technical skill to operate and exposes information about the critical differences between MT outputs that is interactive, informative and highly customizable.

2 MT-TELESCOPE: Features

In this section, we describe the main features and visualizations implemented in MT-TELESCOPE and illustrate the user experience with examples:

[2] https://streamlit.io/

2.1 User input and data

MT-TELESCOPE is opened in a web browser and takes four text (*.txt*) files as input; source and reference segments and one set of MT outputs for each of the compared systems. Users drag and drop these files directly onto the interface to begin evaluation. COMET (Rei et al., 2020a) is provided as a default metric given its proven value in the WMT Metrics Shared Task 2020 (Rei et al., 2020b; Mathur et al., 2020). Optionally the user can choose an alternate metric using a selection box. Currently available metrics include BLEU, METEOR and CHRF, and a selection of more recently proposed metrics such as PRISM, BLEURT, and BERTSCORE.

2.2 Visualizations

High-level results of the analysis are output in table format with the corresponding system scores. MT-TELESCOPE then exposes segment-level comparison in three primary visualizations:

First, a bubble plot (Figure 1) where the position of bubbles show how scores between the two systems differ for each segment, notable differences being highlighted with variations in bubble size and color. This method of visualization of MT is unique to MT-TELESCOPE in that it is fully interactive; by hovering the cursor over individual data points the user can preview the segments and output as well as relevant scores and the magnitude of the difference between them (as depicted in Figure 1). This plot allows for interactive exploration of the data which easily exposes differences in model

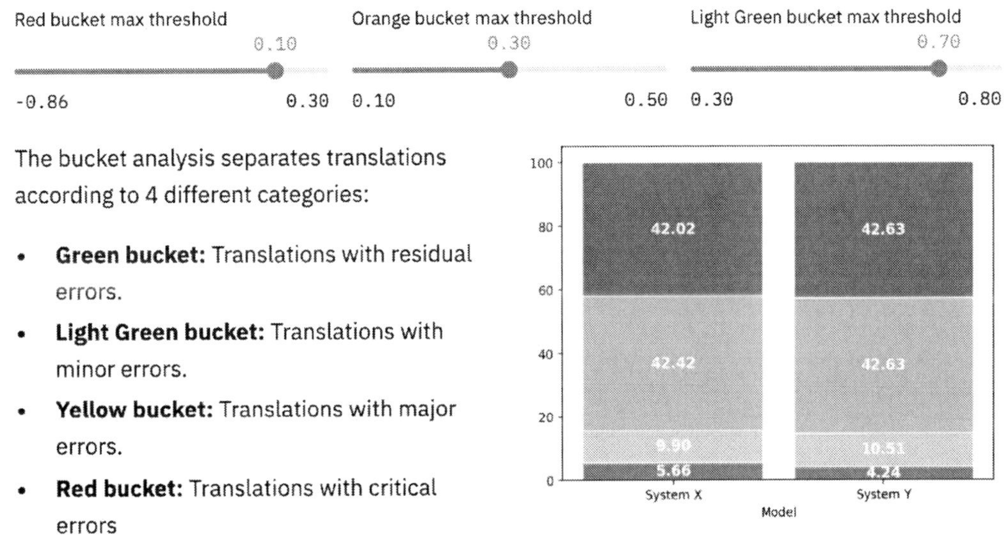

Figure 2: Segment-level error bucket analysis plot. In this plot, we can compare the two systems side by side according to the percentage of segments falling into 4 different category buckets: *residual errors*, *minor errors*, *major errors*, *critical errors*. The thresholds for defining these buckets can be dynamically adjusted using the sliders displayed above the plot.

behaviour at a glance. In particular, the distribution of points along the diagonal of this plot is highly informative; clustering along the diagonal indicates that the systems have minor differences whereas the contrary can indicate more dramatic change in behavior which can be hidden by the corpus-level mean.

Second, MT-TELESCOPE provides a bucketed error analysis in the form of a stacked bar plot (Figure 2). This plot serves to isolate specific bands of translation quality. These bands are highly customizable but can serve as a means of evaluating system utility; the plot can expose the extent to which either model outputs critical error for example. This is particularly useful in a commercial setting where the utility of a production system is inhibited by the presence of particular error types.

Segments are grouped into four buckets: *residual errors*, *minor errors*, *major errors*, and *critical errors*. The thresholds for each bucket can be dynamically adjusted by the user with appropriate sliders and (as with many of the features of MT-TELESCOPE) the plots are updated in real-time to reflect adjustments. Defaults were determined in line with suggestions outlined in the COMET GitHub documentation and with distributions of system-level scores from the WMT News Translation Shared Task 2020.

Residual Errors: The highest tier of quality by default reflects scores greater than 0.70, which generally equates to almost human-like translation with only minor, inconsequential error.

Minor Errors: By default this band reflects scores between 0.30 and 0.70 to reflect the division of quartiles from the distribution of system-level scores from the WMT News Translation Shared Task 2020. In general the band is associated with translation that is adequate but with minor flaws.

Major Errors: Translations scoring between 0.10 and 0.30 by default inhabit this band and are generally inadequate due to more serious error.

Critical Errors: Any translation scoring under 0.10 here is considered to contain critical error.

These bands are intended as a guide and utility of the default thresholds will vary according to use case. Translation quality and the difference between adequate and inadequate translation is highly subjective and language dependant; optimization of these thresholds is a critical direction for future work. Notwithstanding, we find that exposure of the general shift in distribution of inadequate translation in general is potentially informative, particularly given that corpus-level scores do not expose this type of analysis.

Finally, MT-TELESCOPE provides a histogram plot (Figure 3) for general evaluation of the distri-

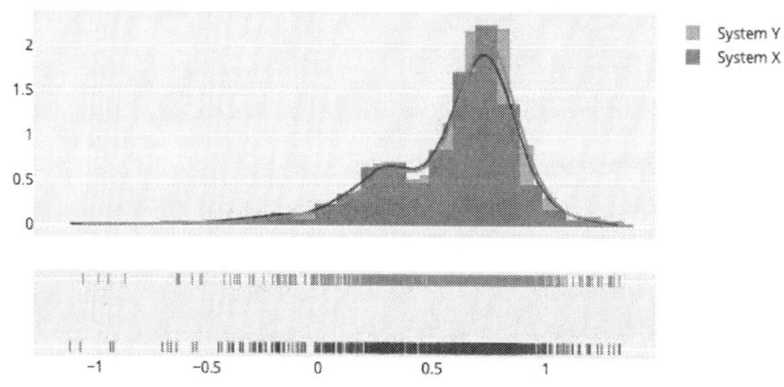

Figure 3: Segment-level histogram comparison.

bution of scores between models. We propose that this kind of plot can potentially provide a high-level overview of the shift in performance between models. A corpus-level score (particularly an arithmetic mean) can mask variance between distributions of scores.

2.3 Example evaluation

To demonstrate the utility of the MT-TELESCOPE evaluation we expose analyses for the *Online-G* and the *PROMT* (Molchanov, 2020) systems from the WMT News Translation Shared Task 2020 (Barrault et al., 2020) for Russian-English:

The *Online-G* system (System Y) achieves a COMET score of 0.6081, outperforming the *PROMT* system (System X) which only achieves 0.5972. We have isolated this example in particular as it represents a common occurrence of two systems achieving fairly comparable scores.

Figures 1, 2 and 3 above show the output of MT-TELESCOPE analysis on two sampled systems:

Figures 2 and 3 illustrate that the second system (System Y) in general exceeds performance of the first (System X). We can conclude from these plots that the systems perform comparably with System Y producing a higher percentage of adequate translations. In particular we note that System Y outputs fewer critical errors, consistent with its general performance gain.

Figure 1 illustrates isolation of an example where System Y makes substantial gain over System X. Here we note that both systems struggle to render the named entity and the corresponding possessive, but that System Y successfully produces the named entity as reflected in the reference and adds a pronoun to at least give possessive flavor.

3 MT-TELESCOPE: Dynamic Corpus Filtering

Given a test corpus, MT-TELESCOPE provides functionality to dynamically evaluate sub-samples of the system outputs as a means of focused analysis tailored to particular phenomena relevant to MT. On selection of any of the available filtering criteria, the MT-TELESCOPE Dynamic Corpus Filtering feature (DCF) updates the output evaluation in real-time to allow the user to 'zoom in' on relevant data points.

Currently, MT-TELESCOPE supports filtering by named entity, glossary and source segment length, as well as an option to remove duplicates. Whenever any of these options is selected, the interface will output the size of the sub-sample as a percentage of the original test corpus.

3.1 DCF: Named Entities

Successful rendering of named entities is a known challenge for even modern MT systems and can lead to distortion of locations, organization and other names (Koehn and Knowles, 2017; Modrzejewski et al., 2020). Recently, several methods have been proposed to improve the translation

Table 1: Example of named entity errors produced *Online-G* system in comparison to the *PROMT* system from the WMT20 shared task.

		COMET
Source	Маругов врезался на мотоцикле в такси, которым управлял Акбаров.	
Online-G	Murugov crashed into a motorcycle taxi, which was ruled by Akbar.	-0.1799
PROMT	Marugov crashed into a taxi driven by Akbarov on a motorcycle.	0.5154
Reference	Marugov crashed on a motorcyle into the taxi Akbarov was driving.	

of named entities in Neural Machine Translation (NMT) (Sennrich and Haddow, 2016; Ugawa et al., 2018; Modrzejewski et al., 2020), but precise measurement of translation quality improvements for these techniques is inhibited by the fact that not all sentences in traditional benchmark test sets (e.g. WMT test sets) contain named entities and that scores produced by automated evaluation metrics are not sufficiently fine-grained to reflect this type of variation. MT-TELESCOPE offers a potential solution to this by applying the following filter:

We initially run the Stanza Named Entity Recognition (NER) model (Stanza, Qi et al. 2020)[3] over the source test corpus to isolate segments that contain named entities. If the source language (as specified by the user) is not supported by Stanza, we run NER on the reference. MT-TELESCOPE will then update the output analysis allowing focused evaluation of the handling of segments containing named entities by either MT system.

To illustrate the utility of DCF analysis on named entities we again compare the outputs of the *Online-G* and the *PROMT* (Molchanov, 2020) systems from the Metrics Shared Task 2020 (Barrault et al., 2020) as above:

Applying DCF for named entities, the *Online-G* system COMET score drops to 0.5851 (previously 0.6081), while the *PROMT* system only drops to 0.5888 (previously 0.5972). We also observe that the percentage of critical segments from the *Online-G* system in our bucketed analysis jumps from 6.26% to 7.0%, while the corresponding percentage output by the *PROMT* system drops from 6.66% to 6.29%.

On the basis of the DCF analysis for named entities we can conclude that whilst in general the *Online-G* exhibits superior quality, it may be underperforming with regard to named entities. Interestingly, the system description paper for the *PROMT* system (Molchanov, 2020) specifically details a targeted approach to handling translation of named entities, which may explain its stronger performance on the isolated sub-sample.

In Table 1 we illustrate an example of a translation in which the *Online-G* system produces critical errors as a consequence of translating named entities incorrectly, specifically isolated by the DCF feature.

3.2 DCF: Terminology

Similarly to named entities, enforcing that MT systems use specific terminology during translation is a challenging task with particular relevance in commercial use cases. Measuring terminology adherence typically involves relying on automated metrics for MT as well as measuring the accuracy of terminology output (Dinu et al., 2019; Exel et al., 2020).

This approach presents two concrete problems: a) applying terminology constraints typically results in only minimal variance between translations, which limits the utility of using automated metrics at the corpus level; and b) measuring accuracy in terminology usage typically relies on exact string matching between a translation hypothesis and its respective reference, which implies that properly inflected translated terms often do not receive proper credit.

MT-TELESCOPE offers a DCF Terminology feature which allows a user to optionally upload a glossary by which to isolate a corresponding subsample of the test corpus. We apply string matching on the source and filter to only those segments which contain a corresponding glossary match.

3.3 DCF: Segment Length

Another common weakness of some MT systems is their inability to accurately translate long segments (Koehn and Knowles, 2017). In general, corpus level evaluation on a distribution that includes very short segments can artificially inflate performance, with substantial drops in scores being observed when these segments are specifically excluded (Koehn and Knowles, 2017). In the same manner, quality-based decisions regarding two systems can change when we consider segments of

[3]https://stanfordnlp.github.io/stanza/ner.html

different lengths.

Using our example systems outlined above in Section 3.1, when comparing the *Online-G* and the *PROMT* systems using only the top 50% longest segments, the *PROMT* system outperforms the *Online-G* system according to COMET and CHRF scores, changing the fundamental perception of which system is 'better'. With the above in mind, MT-TELESCOPE also offers an option to filter by segment length. This filter is adaptive to the distribution of segment lengths in the test corpus. We first build the distribution of the source segment lengths (measured in terms of characters) for the entire test set. Then, the user can select which part of the distribution to analyse by adjusting the a and b parameters of the density function $P(a \leq X \leq b)$; a and b being the minimum and maximum length allowed, respectively.

3.4 DCF: Duplication

The removal of duplicates can be particularly important in situations where the test corpus sample contains repetition. Repeated segments in a test sample can artificially inflate the corpus-level score, particularly where that score results from an average of segment-level scores. Whilst we acknowledge that removal of duplicate segments is fairly common in public data sets such as that used in the WMT Shared Tasks and consequently our example here, we propose that it is, nevertheless, a useful tool when evaluating on random samples.

4 Statistical Significance Testing

By default, MT-TELESCOPE implements the bootstrapped t-test for statistical significance promoted for use in comparison of MT systems by Koehn (2004). Specifically, we iteratively re-sample a portion of the test set (of size P) N times, compare corpus-level results of each sub-sample and record the comparative conclusions. The ratio of wins of a single system is a reasonable proxy to the probability that that system is better than the other. In other words, if one system outperforms the other system 95% of the time, we conclude that the former is better with a significance of $p = 0.05$ (Koehn, 2004).

This is particularly useful in cases where the relative difference between systems is minimal and acts as a measure of the robustness of any resulting decision. In our implementation P is an optional parameter which defaults to 0.5 (50%) or 500 segments, whichever is larger, to ensure reasonable stability in the output conclusion. N is also user defined and by default is set at 300 iterations.

5 Related Tools

MT-TELESCOPE is similar in spirit and largely inspired by recently proposed tools such as COMPARE-MT (Neubig et al., 2019), MT-COMPAREVAL (Klejch et al., 2015), and VIZSEQ (Wang et al., 2019). COMPARE-MT also provides a holistic analysis comparing two MT systems, although with different features. Using COMPARE-MT, the user can, for example, look at performance according to n-gram frequency and part-of-speech (POS) accuracy. MT-COMPAREVAL also provides comparative analysis of segment-level errors with highlighting of variant n-grams. The tool also provides some limited aggregate analysis. Both of the above tools also offer statistical significance testing in the form of a bootstrapped t-test.

VIZSEQ (Wang et al., 2019), whilst only tangentially related, is one of the only comparative tools that offers a web-based interface. Moreover, VIZSEQ has impressive coverage in terms of Natural Language Generation metrics. However, VIZSEQ was developed for multi-model comparison and is primarily focused at corpus-level. Other tools such as PET (Aziz et al., 2012) and APPRAISE (Federmann, 2012) are complementary to MT-TELESCOPE in that they offer features which leverage annotation and post-edition.

6 Conclusions and Future Work

MT-TELESCOPE is designed to provide robust and insightful comparative analysis specific to the MT use case with state-of-the-art metrics. Data visualizations are dynamic, interactive and highly customizable. The tools have been built specifically with ease of use in mind, in the hope of expanding access to high quality MT evaluation.

There is tremendous scope in the adaptation of the DCF framework to target many other phenomena and future work will be focused primarily in this area. We envisage for example adding filters for specific discourse phenomenon such as pronoun translation. Ideally such filter would allow researchers to measure context usage in NMT without having to rely only on contrastive evaluation (Müller et al., 2018; Lopes et al., 2020) and/or human evaluation.

We also plan to extend MT-TELESCOPE to handle a (possibly empty) set of references. This will bring more flexibility to the tool allowing more informed decision when multiple references are available while also supporting Quality Estimation (Specia et al., 2018) when references are not available. Finally we hope to implement exporting functionality to allow saving of analysis output in commonly used formats (e.g. json and PDF). Given that MT-TELESCOPE is an open source platform, we are excited to encourage other users to contribute to its growth with suggestions and new features.

Acknowledgments

We are grateful to the Unbabel MT team, specially Austin Matthews and João Alves, for their valuable feedback. This work was supported in part by the P2020 Program through projects MAIA and Unbabel4EU, supervised by ANI under contract numbers 045909 and 042671, respectively.

References

Wilker Aziz, Sheila Castilho, and Lucia Specia. 2012. PET: a tool for post-editing and assessing machine translation. In *Proceedings of the Eighth International Conference on Language Resources and Evaluation (LREC'12)*, pages 3982–3987, Istanbul, Turkey. European Language Resources Association (ELRA).

Satanjeev Banerjee and Alon Lavie. 2005. METEOR: An automatic metric for MT evaluation with improved correlation with human judgments. In *Proceedings of the ACL Workshop on Intrinsic and Extrinsic Evaluation Measures for Machine Translation and/or Summarization*, pages 65–72, Ann Arbor, Michigan. Association for Computational Linguistics.

Loïc Barrault, Magdalena Biesialska, Ondřej Bojar, Marta R. Costa-jussà, Christian Federmann, Yvette Graham, Roman Grundkiewicz, Barry Haddow, Matthias Huck, Eric Joanis, Tom Kocmi, Philipp Koehn, Chi-kiu Lo, Nikola Ljubešić, Christof Monz, Makoto Morishita, Masaaki Nagata, Toshiaki Nakazawa, Santanu Pal, Matt Post, and Marcos Zampieri. 2020. Findings of the 2020 conference on machine translation (WMT20). In *Proceedings of the Fifth Conference on Machine Translation*, pages 1–55, Online. Association for Computational Linguistics.

Georgiana Dinu, Prashant Mathur, Marcello Federico, and Yaser Al-Onaizan. 2019. Training neural machine translation to apply terminology constraints. In *Proceedings of the 57th Annual Meeting of the Association for Computational Linguistics*, pages 3063–3068, Florence, Italy. Association for Computational Linguistics.

Miriam Exel, Bianka Buschbeck, Lauritz Brandt, and Simona Doneva. 2020. Terminology-constrained neural machine translation at SAP. In *Proceedings of the 22nd Annual Conference of the European Association for Machine Translation*, pages 271–280, Lisboa, Portugal. European Association for Machine Translation.

Christian Federmann. 2012. Appraise: An open-source toolkit for manual evaluation of machine translation output. *The Prague Bulletin of Mathematical Linguistics*, 98:25–35.

Ondrej Klejch, Eleftherios Avramidis, Aljoscha Burchardt, and Martin Popel. 2015. MT-ComparEval: Graphical evaluation interface for Machine Translation development. *The Prague Bulletin of Mathematical Linguistics*, 104.

Philipp Koehn. 2004. Statistical significance tests for machine translation evaluation. In *Proceedings of the 2004 Conference on Empirical Methods in Natural Language Processing*, pages 388–395, Barcelona, Spain. Association for Computational Linguistics.

Philipp Koehn and Rebecca Knowles. 2017. Six challenges for neural machine translation. In *Proceedings of the First Workshop on Neural Machine Translation*, pages 28–39, Vancouver. Association for Computational Linguistics.

António Lopes, M. Amin Farajian, Rachel Bawden, Michael Zhang, and André F. T. Martins. 2020. Document-level neural MT: A systematic comparison. In *Proceedings of the 22nd Annual Conference of the European Association for Machine Translation*, pages 225–234, Lisboa, Portugal. European Association for Machine Translation.

Nitika Mathur, Johnny Wei, Markus Freitag, Qingsong Ma, and Ondřej Bojar. 2020. Results of the WMT20 metrics shared task. In *Proceedings of the Fifth Conference on Machine Translation*, pages 688–725, Online. Association for Computational Linguistics.

Maciej Modrzejewski, Miriam Exel, Bianka Buschbeck, Thanh-Le Ha, and Alexander Waibel. 2020. Incorporating external annotation to improve named entity translation in NMT. In *Proceedings of the 22nd Annual Conference of the European Association for Machine Translation*, pages 45–51, Lisboa, Portugal. European Association for Machine Translation.

Alexander Molchanov. 2020. PROMT systems for WMT 2020 shared news translation task. In *Proceedings of the Fifth Conference on Machine Translation*, pages 248–253, Online. Association for Computational Linguistics.

Mathias Müller, Annette Rios, Elena Voita, and Rico Sennrich. 2018. A large-scale test set for the evaluation of context-aware pronoun translation in neural machine translation. In *Proceedings of the Third Conference on Machine Translation: Research Papers*, pages 61–72, Brussels, Belgium. Association for Computational Linguistics.

Graham Neubig, Zi-Yi Dou, Junjie Hu, Paul Michel, Danish Pruthi, and Xinyi Wang. 2019. compare-mt: A tool for holistic comparison of language generation systems. In *Proceedings of the 2019 Conference of the North American Chapter of the Association for Computational Linguistics (Demonstrations)*, pages 35–41, Minneapolis, Minnesota. Association for Computational Linguistics.

Kishore Papineni, Salim Roukos, Todd Ward, and Wei-Jing Zhu. 2002. Bleu: a method for automatic evaluation of machine translation. In *Proceedings of the 40th Annual Meeting of the Association for Computational Linguistics*, pages 311–318, Philadelphia, Pennsylvania, USA. Association for Computational Linguistics.

Peng Qi, Yuhao Zhang, Yuhui Zhang, Jason Bolton, and Christopher D. Manning. 2020. Stanza: A python natural language processing toolkit for many human languages. In *Proceedings of the 58th Annual Meeting of the Association for Computational Linguistics: System Demonstrations*, pages 101–108, Online. Association for Computational Linguistics.

Ricardo Rei, Craig Stewart, Ana C Farinha, and Alon Lavie. 2020a. COMET: A neural framework for MT evaluation. In *Proceedings of the 2020 Conference on Empirical Methods in Natural Language Processing (EMNLP)*, pages 2685–2702, Online. Association for Computational Linguistics.

Ricardo Rei, Craig Stewart, Ana C Farinha, and Alon Lavie. 2020b. Unbabel's participation in the WMT20 metrics shared task. In *Proceedings of the Fifth Conference on Machine Translation*, pages 911–920, Online. Association for Computational Linguistics.

Thibault Sellam, Dipanjan Das, and Ankur Parikh. 2020. BLEURT: Learning robust metrics for text generation. In *Proceedings of the 58th Annual Meeting of the Association for Computational Linguistics*, pages 7881–7892, Online. Association for Computational Linguistics.

Rico Sennrich and Barry Haddow. 2016. Linguistic input features improve neural machine translation. In *Proceedings of the First Conference on Machine Translation: Volume 1, Research Papers*, pages 83–91, Berlin, Germany. Association for Computational Linguistics.

Lucia Specia, Carolina Scarton, and Gustavo Henrique Paetzold. 2018. Quality estimation for machine translation. *Synthesis Lectures on Human Language Technologies*, 11(1):1–162.

Brian Thompson and Matt Post. 2020. Automatic machine translation evaluation in many languages via zero-shot paraphrasing. In *Proceedings of the 2020 Conference on Empirical Methods in Natural Language Processing (EMNLP)*, pages 90–121, Online. Association for Computational Linguistics.

Arata Ugawa, Akihiro Tamura, Takashi Ninomiya, Hiroya Takamura, and Manabu Okumura. 2018. Neural machine translation incorporating named entity. In *Proceedings of the 27th International Conference on Computational Linguistics*, pages 3240–3250, Santa Fe, New Mexico, USA. Association for Computational Linguistics.

Changhan Wang, Anirudh Jain, Danlu Chen, and Jiatao Gu. 2019. VizSeq: a visual analysis toolkit for text generation tasks. In *Proceedings of the 2019 Conference on Empirical Methods in Natural Language Processing and the 9th International Joint Conference on Natural Language Processing (EMNLP-IJCNLP): System Demonstrations*, pages 253–258, Hong Kong, China. Association for Computational Linguistics.

Supporting Complaints Investigation for Nursing and Midwifery Regulatory Agencies

Piyawat Lertvittayakumjorn[*†], **Ivan Petej**[*], **Yang Gao**[*], **Yamuna Krishnamurthy**[*], **Anna van der Gaag**[*◇], **Robert Jago**[*], **Kostas Stathis**[*]

* Royal Holloway, University of London, United Kingdom
† Imperial College London, United Kingdom
◇ University of Surrey, United Kingdom

{piyawat.lertvittayakumjorn, i.petej, yang.gao}@rhul.ac.uk
yamuna.k.2018@live.rhul.ac.uk,
{anna.vandergaag, robert.jago, kostas.stathis}@rhul.ac.uk

Abstract

Health professional regulators aim to protect the health and well-being of patients and the public by setting standards for scrutinising and overseeing the training and conduct of health and care professionals. A major task of such regulators is the investigation of *complaints* against practitioners. However, processing a complaint often lasts several months and is particularly costly. Hence, we worked with international regulators from different countries (the UK, US and Australia), to develop the first decision support tool that aims to help such regulators process complaints more efficiently. Our system uses state-of-the-art machine learning and natural language processing techniques to process complaints and predict their risk level. Our tool also provides additional useful information including *explanations*, to help the regulatory staff interpret the prediction results, and similar past cases as well as non-compliance to regulations, to support the decision making.

1 Introduction

Nurses and midwives play important roles in the healthcare system as they provide highly skilled and often complex care in both hospitals and communities. To protect and prioritise the safety of the public from harmful practices, most countries have specific *health professional regulators* to set rules, monitor and shape the practice of nurses and midwives. When concerns over a nurse or midwife's practice are raised, a formal *complaint* can be submitted to the regulator, and investigations will be performed to decide further actions (e.g., warnings to the nurse/midwife in question, or even suspension of their practice). As the investigation results have significant impact on the practitioners' career and reputation, processing complaints is highly time-consuming and costly (see (NMC, 2020), p49), hence, the need for effective tools to support investigations is crucial.

In this paper, we present a decision support system to improve the *efficiency* of complaints investigation for nursing and midwifery regulators, by employing state-of-the-art machine learning and natural language processing (NLP) techniques with a human-in-the-loop. We worked closely with the UK Nursing and Midwifery Council (NMC[1]), the US Texas Board of Nursing (TBON[2]), and the Australian Health Practitioner Regulation Agency (AHPRA[3]), to understand their requirements for the system and collect data for training the machine learning models. Fig. 1 illustrates the major components and workflow of our proposed system. As new cases arrive, the system processes the corresponding complaints for each case and provides the following results: **(i)** *Risk level prediction*: each case is labelled as either *high* or *low* risk, along with a *confidence score*, which allows regulators to prioritise the new complaints. **(ii)** *Explanations* of the risk prediction results, by highlighting the most salient words in the complaint texts that led to the prediction. **(iii)** *Similar previous cases*, so that users can refer to relevant past cases to make decisions on the current case. **(iv)** *Entries in the regulation code* that a new complaint is most related to, that can help the regulators quickly link the allegations in the complaints to relevant requirements in the regulation code.

A major challenge in developing the system is *data sparsity*. Due to the sensitive nature of the healthcare data and the strict data-sharing policies of the regulators, we had access to a small amount of data (initially 1.2k complaints, later 5.7k complaints) to develop and test our system. To mitigate this problem, we use ensemble methods based

[1] https://www.nmc.org.uk/
[2] https://www.bon.texas.gov/
[3] https://www.ahpra.gov.au/

Proceedings of the Joint Conference of the 59th Annual Meeting of the Association for Computational Linguistics and the 11th International Joint Conference on Natural Language Processing: System Demonstrations, pages 81–91, August 1st - August 6th, 2021.

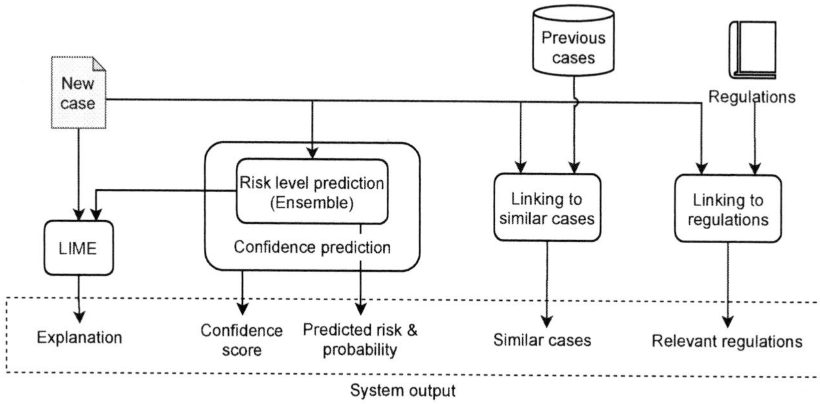

Figure 1: Workflow of the proposed system.

on both classical and neural models, including an adapted version of BERT (Devlin et al., 2019). In addition, to ensure that the predictions made by our system were *gender unbiased*, we pre-processed the text appropriately and experimented with several bias mitigation techniques. Experimental results show that the risk predictions made by the system achieved an accuracy of 0.71. An expert user evaluation, initially involving five regulatory staff at one regulator, suggests that the highlighted words and related regulation entries the system provides can not only help the regulators better understand how the predictions are made, but also allow them to provide better justifications for their decisions.

To the best of our knowledge, this is the first NLP system that supports complaints investigation for nursing and midwifery regulators.

2 Related Work

Decision Support Systems. Many NLP systems have been developed to process text data (such as records, reports, scientific papers, and social media posts) to assist in making highly critical decisions, in domains like healthcare (Bampa and Dalianis, 2020; Mascio et al., 2020; Feng et al., 2020; Proux et al., 2009), finance (Kogan et al., 2009; Wang et al., 2013), business and management (Dong and Wang, 2015; Assawinjaipetch et al., 2016; Filgueiras et al., 2019), and legislation (Rabelo et al., 2019; Soh et al., 2019; Shaffer and Mayhew, 2019). Our work proposes the first decision support system to process nursing/midwifery complaints.

Model Selection & Adaptation. *Data sparsity* is a common problem encountered by many NLP decision support systems, due to the sensitive nature of the data in certain domains and the high cost of labelling them. Hence, large neural network models do not always outperform classic feature-rich models and careful model selection is often necessary. For example, Filgueiras et al. (2019) found that, in an economic activity classification task, the SVM (Cortes and Vapnik, 1995) with TF-IDF (Salton and Buckley, 1988) representations performed better than an LSTM network (Hochreiter and Schmidhuber, 1997). On the other hand, Assawinjaipetch et al. (2016) and Mullenbach et al. (2018) showed that in complaint and clinical classification tasks, RNNs (Cho et al., 2014) or CNNs (Kim, 2014) with pre-trained word2vec embeddings (Mikolov et al., 2013) outperformed the classic machine learning models with bag-of-words representations. For each functionality in our system, we consider both classic and state-of-the-art neural network models and select the most appropriate one.

Another popular strategy to address data sparsity is to *adapt* large pre-trained models to an application domain. For example, BioBERT (Lee et al., 2019) and ClinicalBERT (Alsentzer et al., 2019) fine-tune BERT (Devlin et al., 2019) with biological and clinical trial data, to adapt BERT to their respective domains. Feng et al. (2020) performed sepsis and mortality prediction by deploying a hierarchical CNN-Transformer on top of BERT-based models. In our system, we fine-tune BERT with both nursing/midwifery complaints and other relevant data (e.g., MedSTS (Wang et al., 2020)) for downstream tasks (see §3).

Explainability is a highly desirable feature for decision support systems, especially in healthcare applications. Different types of information can be presented to users as explanations, including *attention distributions* (Mullenbach et al., 2018; Feng et al., 2020), *similar past cases* (Agirre et al., 2012; Rus et al., 2013; Cui et al., 2017; Tran et al., 2019), and *salient words* in the input text (Ribeiro et al., 2016; Lundberg and Lee, 2017). In the legal domain, to justify a verdict, relevant items in the law are often provided as explanations (Rabelo et al., 2020; Shaffer and Mayhew, 2019). Our method provides explanations in all the aforementioned forms except attention distributions, as it remains unclear whether attention distributions can be reliably used as explanations (Jain and Wallace, 2019; Wiegreffe and Pinter, 2019).

Gender Debiasing can help detect and reduce the decision support systems' biases against certain genders (Sun et al., 2019). Popular gender debiasing methods include gender swapping (Zhao et al., 2018), gender-debiased word embeddings (Bolukbasi et al., 2016; Manzini et al., 2019), adversarial training (Zhang et al., 2018), and fine-tuning (Park et al., 2018). To detect if there exists systematic biases against certain genders and reduce these biases, we test different gender debiasing methods in our system (see §5).

3 Our System

Initially, we used 1,241 real cases from one regulator to develop and test our system. Each case i consists of multiple fields, falling into three categories: the *complaint text* t_i, in which sensitive information is replaced with its corresponding entity type, e.g., all names are replaced with [PERSON]; *meta information of the case* $(c_{i1}, ..., c_{ik})$, e.g., status of the case, and who submitted the complaint; and the *investigation results*, including the *risk level* y_i of the case (high or low), and some additional assessment results $(a_{i1}, ..., a_{im})$, e.g., whether serious harm was caused to the patient or not. Table 1 presents some statistics of the dataset. Details of all fields are in the Appendix.

We understand from our collaborating regulatory agencies that the most essential functionality they need is to be able to *predict the risk level* of the case, as it allows them to prioritise the high-risk cases and better manage the workload. Hence, we formulated the problem as a binary classification task, which takes a complaint t_i and its meta-information $(c_{i1}, \cdots, c_{ik})$ as input and predicts the risk level y_i. We developed an ensemble model to predict the risk level (§3.1) and provided some additional information to further support the decision-making process of the regulator and help them interpret the prediction results (§3.2).

# High/low risk cases	766/475
# Words in each complaint	max/min/avg: 5922/5/280
# Serious harm to patient	185
# Maternity related cases	17
# Patient death	75
# Serious harm to nurse	5

Table 1: Statistics of the dataset, which has 1,241 cases received in 2019-20.

3.1 Risk Level Prediction

Due to the limited number of labelled examples, we decided to use *ensemble learning* for risk classification, exploiting the benefits of different models, both feature-rich and neural-based. In particular, we used *stacked generalisation* (Wolpert, 1992) with five base classifiers C1 – C5, detailed below.

(C1) Gradient boosting (Friedman, 2001), using the average of word2vec embeddings of words in the complaint text t_i as input. **(C2)** Adaptive boosting (AdaBoost) (Freund and Schapire, 1997) using the same input as C1. **(C3)** CNN (Kim, 2014) with t_i as input and GloVe (Pennington et al., 2014) as pre-trained word embeddings. We used the *multi-task learning* setup to train the CNN model: the model is trained to predict not only the risk levels y_i but also some additional assessment results $(a_{i1}, ..., a_{im})$. Preliminary results show that, compared to single-task learning (i.e., training the CNN for predicting only y_i), the multi-task learning setup improved the accuracy by about two percentage points. **(C4)** BERT-base (uncased), which was fine-tuned to predict the risk level. **(C5)** An ensemble which takes case meta information $(c_{i1}, ..., c_{ik})$ as input and uses three base classifiers (gradient boosting, AdaBoost, and linear SVM). Logistic regression is then used as a meta-classifier of C5.

For the main stacking model in the ensemble, we also used logistic regression, with the prediction probabilities returned by C1 – C5 as input.

3.2 Additional Information

Besides risk level predictions, our system outputs additional information to support the decision making and help users interpret the prediction results.

Confidence Scores are provided for each risk level prediction. We used a *conformal predictor* (Vovk et al., 2005) to produce the confidence scores. When the train and test data are i.i.d., the conformal predictor guarantees that the produced confidence scores are *valid*: for example, among all predictions with confidence score 0.6, the probability of the prediction being correct is 60%. We applied the conformal predictor to our ensemble model and used 40% of complaints as the *calibration set* to train the conformal predictor.

Explanations. To help regulators understand why the system labels a case as high or low risk, we used *LIME* (Ribeiro et al., 2016) to provide explanations for each prediction. LIME is a model-agnostic explanation method and does not need additional data for training. It is well suited to our system, which uses the ensemble classifier with different base models and only has access to a limited amount of data. For each case, LIME identifies the tokens that have the largest influence on the prediction probabilities and highlights these tokens as the *explanations*. Fig. 2 shows an example of the LIME explanation. If the highlighted words agree with the regulator's understanding of the key words in the text that could explain the risk prediction, then the regulator trusts the prediction results. If the regulator does not agree, then it is an indication that the prediction may not be reliable and hence the regulators need to investigate the case more carefully.

Similar Past Cases. In applications for legal decision-support, users often need to refer back to similar *past cases* to make decisions for new cases (see the *Explainability* paragraph in §2). To identify the similar past cases, we first computed the tfidf-cosine similarity scores of each of the past cases with the new case and selected the top 10 past cases with the highest similarity score. We then trained the BERT-base with 800 complaint texts (224k tokens) to create a new language model, fine-tuned the new model on two semantic similarity datasets, STSb (Cer et al., 2017) and MedSTS (Wang et al., 2020), and used the resulting model to further rank the selected past cases.

Initial results showed that the above method was very time-consuming, as, for the ranking, the fine-tuned BERT model needs to compare each sentence from the new case with each sentence from every past case. To reduce the computation time, we used *summarisation* models to generate a short summary for each case, so we could measure the similarity between cases by their summaries. We used an *extractive* summarisation model based on LSA (Ozsoy et al., 2011), which selects 1–3 representative sentences from each case to build the summary, and an *abstractive* summarisation model T5 (Raffel et al., 2020), which generates a few new sentences to summarise each case. We found that T5's summaries mostly focus on information from the first few sentences in each case. This strategy works well in summarising news articles but ignores much of the useful information in complaints. The LSA-based method, on the other hand, is not biased by the position of sentences and performs better and faster than T5, and hence we used it as the summarisation model.

Non-Compliance to Regulations. To assist regulators to check if the practice of the nurse/midwife, reported in the complaint complies with the regulations or not, our system exploits pre-trained *natural language inference* (NLI) models to detect non-compliance. Specifically, if we denote the entries in the regulation code as $R = \{r_1, r_2, \cdots, r_n\}$ and a complaint as a set of sentences $t = \{ts_1, ts_2, \cdots, ts_m\}$, then the task is to determine, for each (r_i, ts_j) pair, $i \in [1, n], j \in [1, m]$, if r_i contradicts ts_j or not. We used RoBERTa (Liu et al., 2019) fine-tuned on the MNLI dataset (Williams et al., 2018) as the NLI model. To reduce the computation time, we again used the LSA-based summarisation method to reduce the number of sentences in each complaint. The regulation entries R are from the latest NMC Code (NMC, 2015).

4 System Implementation

Backend. We used `Flask 1.0.2`, a Python based web development framework, to develop the backend of the system. We used `SQLite 3.34.0` to manage the database, `SQLAlchemy 1.2.6` for relational mapping, `Redis 3.5.3` for internal messaging and caching, `Nonconformist` for conformal prediction, and `Wtforms 2.1` to manage forms. The system receives new complaints in real time and can make predictions either in real time or batch so as to minimise the response time.

Frontend. The frontend of our web interface is implemented with `Bootstrap 4.1.3` and

Model	Accuracy	Macro F1
Majority Baseline	0.617 ± 0.032	NA
C1: Gradient Boost.	0.671 ± 0.025	0.629 ± 0.025
C2: AdaBoost	0.646 ± 0.028	0.611 ± 0.034
C3: CNNMultiTask	0.668 ± 0.029	0.623 ± 0.035
C4: BERT-base	0.680 ± 0.038	0.658 ± 0.028
C5: Meta info	0.662 ± 0.029	0.591 ± 0.056
Ensemble model	$\mathbf{0.708 \pm 0.036}$	$\mathbf{0.679 \pm 0.032}$

Table 2: Performance (mean ± standard deviation) of the risk classifiers, averaged over 10 random splits.

`Charts.js 2.5.4`. Functionalities like tool traversal, event handling, and animation are implemented using `JQuery 3.5.1`. Figure 2 shows a screenshot of a result page for a specific complaint using fictitious data. It depicts the complaint text on the left and the predicted risk as well as additional information on the right. The user can provide feedback for the predictions (accept or reject a prediction result, and provide reasons for the same). They can also provide feedback about the relevance of each similar case and regulation code, suggested by the system, to the selected case.

5 System Evaluation

Risk Level Classification results are presented in Table 2. All results were averaged over 10 runs with different random seeds, and in each run the data was randomly split into train, dev, and test sets with ratio 800:200:241. We found that all base models C1 – C5 significantly[4] outperform the majority baseline, in terms of both accuracy and macro F1, and the ensemble of the base models significantly outperforms all base models but BERT, which achieves comparable macro F1. Given the relatively small size of the data, we consider these results promising and believe that in real deployment the risk prediction performance can be further improved, as the model will have access to more labelled data.

Gender Debiasing. We aimed to answer two questions: (i) whether our risk prediction model is biased against certain genders (e.g., always associating some gender terms with the high risk class), and (ii) whether the gender biases can be reduced by using some debiasing methods. The study of ethnic biases will be conducted in the future, as most cases in our current dataset do not include any information about the ethnicity of the patients or the practitioners.

[4]Throughout this paper, p-values are computed with paired t-test and the significance level is 0.05.

Technique	Training data	Test data
Gender removing	he $\rightarrow \phi$	he $\rightarrow \phi$
Gender neutralising	he $\rightarrow$ they	he $\rightarrow$ they
Gender swapping	he $\rightarrow$ he, she	he $\rightarrow$ he

Table 3: Examples of three gender debias methods.

To measure to what extent a model is gender biased, two widely used metrics are *false positive equality difference* (FPED) and *false negative equality difference* (FNED) (Dixon et al., 2018). The lower the FPED (FNED, respectively) values, it means the gaps between the model's false positive (false negative, respectively) rates in the gender-specific and overall cases are smaller, hence suggesting lower gender bias of the model. The FPED and FNED values for our ensemble-based risk prediction model are 0.189 and 0.117, respectively (first row in Table 4). Since they are not zero, it suggests that the model does have gender biases.

To reduce the gender bias, we experimented with three methods to "clean" the data: *gender removing*, which removes all gender words from both training and test data; *gender neutralising*, which replaces each gender word with a neutral word (e.g., dad $\rightarrow$ parent) in both the training and test data; and *gender swapping*, which creates new training examples by swapping the genders (e.g., dad $\rightarrow$ mum), and train the model with both the original and the new gender-swapped data. Table 3 illustrates these gender debiasing methods. In addition to the above methods, we also tested the use of gender-debiased word embeddings (Bolukbasi et al., 2016), in base models C1 and C2, to further reduce biases. Note that, models C3 and C4 were not used as we did not debias embeddings of GloVe and BERT in C3 and C4; including them may obscure the effect of the debiased word2vec. Also, CNN and BERT are too time-consuming to train and run for ten times of the eight models.

Table 4 compares the performance of different debiasing methods. With standard word embeddings (the upper part in Table 4), all three gender debiasing methods managed to reduce gender biases, at the price of at most two percentage points loss in accuracy. However, when the gender debiasing methods are used together with the gender-debiased embeddings, the performance becomes even worse. This reminds us of existing work that questions the effectiveness of debiased embeddings (Gonen and Goldberg, 2019). Some also argue that it gets rid of more meanings beyond prejudice

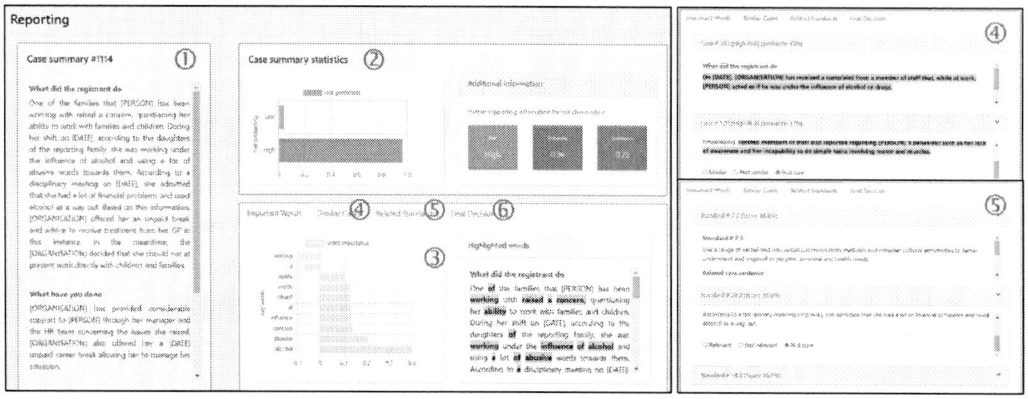

Figure 2: A screenshot of the result page for a fictitious complaint. The page consists of (1) the complaint text (2) the predicted risk level, probability, and confidence (3) word importance scores provided as the explanation by LIME (4) similar past cases (5) non-compliance to regulations (6) the final decision to be given by a case manager.

Debias Setting		Accuracy	Macro F1	FPED	FNED
O	unchanged	**0.718**	**0.688**	0.189	0.117
	remove	0.700	0.666	0.167	0.105
	neutralise	0.709	0.677	**0.129**	0.085
	swap	0.713	0.682	0.154	**0.080**
D	unchanged	0.705	0.674	0.186	0.117
	remove	0.699	0.664	0.191	0.082
	neutralise	0.707	0.675	0.190	0.101
	swap	0.708	0.676	0.186	0.117

Table 4: Performance of different gender debias methods. "O" and "D" in the leftmost column stand for original and gender-debiased embeddings, respectively.

rather than guiding the AI to act fairly (Caliskan et al., 2017). Hence, in real deployment, our system will only perform gender swapping and use the resulting data to train the ensemble model.

Human Evaluation. We invited five regulatory staff from NMC to use and evaluate our system. Each case maanager was provided with four complaints randomly sampled from our test set. They were asked to use our system to assist them in their investigation of the complaint. A questionnaire was provided to them after the test was completed, requesting their ratings (5-point Likert scores) and comments on different aspects of the system.

All participants found the usability and responsiveness of the system highly satisfactory, with average scores at 4.4 and 4.2, respectively. With respect to the quality of the risk predictions, explanations (i.e., the highlighted words), and the identified relevant regulations, participants provided moderate ratings at 2.8 for each of them. However, lower ratings (1.8) were given on the similar cases found by the system: for example, a complaint mentions that *the nurse has a strong odour of alcohol on her breath* and the experts want the system to find other cases about nurses who are inebriated or unfit to practice, but the system found cases with words like *alcohol* or *odour*, even though the words were used in very different contexts (e.g., *used alcohol as disinfectant*). We believe this is a highly challenging task as it requires not only domain knowledge but also *common sense knowledge* to capture the nuances in the complaints. We leave further investigation of this problem to future work.

As for the explanations (i.e, words highlighted by LIME), the participants reported that the highlighted words in the high-risk cases were often sensible and useful, while the words highlighted in the low-risk cases were sometimes stopwords and hence difficult to interpret. We believe the reason for this is that our models rely on the appearance of certain *keywords* (e.g., injured, died) to identify the high-risk cases, which are absent in the low-risk cases and hence the model picks up some spurious words to make the predictions. We note that, while highlighting the stopwords makes it difficult for the regulatory experts to interpret the explanations, it helps the system designers and machine learning experts better understand the problems with the system and hence allows them to improve the system accordingly. In the next version, we plan to hide stopwords highlighted by LIME from the regulatory experts to avoid confusion, but we will show them to system designers in order to help them improve the model.

6 Conclusion

In this work, we have presented the first system to support complaints investigation for nursing and midwifery regulators. The system exploits state-of-the-art text classification, summarisation, semantic similarity measurement and NLI techniques, and provides different types of information to assist the regulators, including risk level assessment, similar past cases, and non-compliance to regulations. In addition, explanations (in the form of highlighted words) are provided to improve the transparency of the system, and gender debiasing operations are performed to reduce systemic gender biases. Feedback received from domain experts confirmed the system's usefulness and potential.

We will continue our collaboration with the nursing and midwifery regulatory bodies and collect more labelled data, e.g., relevant case pairs and non-compliance to regulations; this data will help us develop domain-specific sentence similarity measurement and NLI models to further improve the performance of the system. We are considering extending the system with additional functionalities, for example, applying *active learning* (Klie et al., 2018) to allow the system learn more efficiently from human feedback and thus be constantly updated online. We also plan to perform additional experiments in control groups with domain experts to test the effectiveness of the system, e.g., by comparing the average time consumed to process a case with and without the use of our system.

Regulatory bodies in different jurisdictions face similar problems (e.g., long processing time, high cost, and an increase in the number of cases to investigate) and have similar requirements on the functionalities of the system (risk prediction, similar past cases, non-compliance to regulations). Hence, we hope this work will inspire more AI/NLP-based decision support systems across different jurisdictions, and encourage more collaborations between the NLP researchers and regulatory bodies in the legal, financial and healthcare sectors.

Acknowledgements

We thank our colleagues from the UK Nursing and Midwifery Council (NMC), the US Texas Board of Nursing (TBON), and the Australian Health Practitioner Regulation Agency (AHPRA), for their feedback to the development of the prototype. We also thank Francesco Fildani and Narinderpal Sehra from the CIM IT helpdesk at Royal Holloway, University of London, who helped us deploy the demonstration system. This project was funded by the US National Council of State Boards of Nursing (NCSBN).

Ethical Impact Statements

As our system processed highly sensitive data and its recommendations can have an impact on the person under investigation, we describe the system's potential ethical impact in different aspects below.

Data Collection. All data were collected, redacted and distributed by professionals from the regulatory agencies, strictly following all the related regulations in their respective countries.

Institutional Review. This project has been reviewed and approved by each participating institution, in line with their ethical approval process.

Expected Beneficiaries. The direct beneficiaries are the regulatory agencies, as the system improves the efficiency of their investigation and reduces the cost. The nursing/midwifery community and the patients will also benefit, as the waiting times will be reduced. Moreover, it will reduce costs which are often passed on to registrants via registration fees.

Failure Modes. Our system provides confidence scores and highlighted words to help users make sense of the predictions. Hence, even in the "failure cases" where the system provides imprecise predictions, the users can quickly identify the problems and reject the predictions (see §3). In terms of data security, our system does not edit or modify the original texts, and all texts have backup copies in secure servers; hence, the risk of data contamination or loss is minimised.

Biases. We inspected different types of potential biases and employed multiple techniques to minimise biases, as discussed in §5.

Misuse Potential. The system will be used by well-trained users from the regulatory bodies strictly inside their organisations, following all guidelines and requirements of the agencies. Hence, we believe that the potential for misuse is very low.

Potential Harm to Vulnerable Populations. Our system learns from past decisions to make new predictions. A potential risk is that, if the human decisions on the past cases have strong biases or systematic mistakes, the system may exploit those biases in its decision making. We believe the explanations produced by our system can be used to identify such systemic biases and mistakes. If users find that certain gender-related words are highlighted, it suggests that the model heavily relies on those words to make predictions, and the regulatory staff can perform further investigations accordingly.

References

Eneko Agirre, Daniel Cer, Mona Diab, and Aitor Gonzalez-Agirre. 2012. SemEval-2012 task 6: A pilot on semantic textual similarity. In **SEM 2012: The First Joint Conference on Lexical and Computational Semantics – Volume 1: Proceedings of the main conference and the shared task, and Volume 2: Proceedings of the Sixth International Workshop on Semantic Evaluation (SemEval 2012)*, pages 385–393, Montréal, Canada. Association for Computational Linguistics.

Emily Alsentzer, John Murphy, William Boag, Wei-Hung Weng, Di Jindi, Tristan Naumann, and Matthew McDermott. 2019. Publicly available clinical BERT embeddings. In *Proceedings of the 2nd Clinical Natural Language Processing Workshop*, pages 72–78, Minneapolis, Minnesota, USA. Association for Computational Linguistics.

Panuwat Assawinjaipetch, Kiyoaki Shirai, Virach Sornlertlamvanich, and Sanparith Marukata. 2016. Recurrent neural network with word embedding for complaint classification. In *Proceedings of the Third International Workshop on Worldwide Language Service Infrastructure and Second Workshop on Open Infrastructures and Analysis Frameworks for Human Language Technologies (WLSI/OIAF4HLT2016)*, pages 36–43, Osaka, Japan. The COLING 2016 Organizing Committee.

Maria Bampa and Hercules Dalianis. 2020. Detecting adverse drug events from Swedish electronic health records using text mining. In *Proceedings of the LREC 2020 Workshop on Multilingual Biomedical Text Processing (MultilingualBIO 2020)*, pages 1–8, Marseille, France. European Language Resources Association.

Tolga Bolukbasi, Kai-Wei Chang, James Zou, Venkatesh Saligrama, and Adam Kalai. 2016. Man is to computer programmer as woman is to homemaker? debiasing word embeddings. In *Proceedings of the 30th International Conference on Neural Information Processing Systems*, pages 4356–4364.

Aylin Caliskan, Joanna J Bryson, and Arvind Narayanan. 2017. Semantics derived automatically from language corpora contain human-like biases. *Science*, 356(6334):183–186.

Daniel Cer, Mona Diab, Eneko Agirre, Iñigo Lopez-Gazpio, and Lucia Specia. 2017. SemEval-2017 task 1: Semantic textual similarity multilingual and crosslingual focused evaluation. In *Proceedings of the 11th International Workshop on Semantic Evaluation (SemEval-2017)*, pages 1–14, Vancouver, Canada. Association for Computational Linguistics.

Kyunghyun Cho, Bart van Merriënboer, Caglar Gulcehre, Dzmitry Bahdanau, Fethi Bougares, Holger Schwenk, and Yoshua Bengio. 2014. Learning phrase representations using RNN encoder–decoder for statistical machine translation. In *Proceedings of the 2014 Conference on Empirical Methods in Natural Language Processing (EMNLP)*, pages 1724–1734, Doha, Qatar. Association for Computational Linguistics.

C. Cortes and V. Vapnik. 1995. Support vector networks. *Machine Learning*, 20:273–297.

Xiaolan Cui, Shuqin Cai, and Yuchu Qin. 2017. Similarity-based approach for accurately retrieving similar cases to intelligently handle online complaints. *Kybernetes*.

Jacob Devlin, Ming-Wei Chang, Kenton Lee, and Kristina Toutanova. 2019. BERT: Pre-training of deep bidirectional transformers for language understanding. In *Proceedings of the 2019 Conference of the North American Chapter of the Association for Computational Linguistics: Human Language Technologies, Volume 1 (Long and Short Papers)*, pages 4171–4186, Minneapolis, Minnesota. Association for Computational Linguistics.

Lucas Dixon, John Li, Jeffrey Sorensen, Nithum Thain, and Lucy Vasserman. 2018. Measuring and mitigating unintended bias in text classification. In *Proceedings of the 2018 AAAI/ACM Conference on AI, Ethics, and Society*, pages 67–73.

Shuang Dong and Zhihong Wang. 2015. Evaluating service quality in insurance customer complaint handling throught text categorization. In *2015 International Conference on Logistics, Informatics and Service Sciences (LISS)*, pages 1–5. IEEE.

Jinyue Feng, Chantal Shaib, and Frank Rudzicz. 2020. Explainable clinical decision support from text. In *Proceedings of the 2020 Conference on Empirical Methods in Natural Language Processing (EMNLP)*, pages 1478–1489, Online. Association for Computational Linguistics.

João Filgueiras, Luís Barbosa, Gil Rocha, Henrique Lopes Cardoso, Luís Paulo Reis, João Pedro Machado, and Ana Maria Oliveira. 2019. Complaint analysis and classification for economic and food safety. In *Proceedings of the Second Workshop on Economics and Natural Language Processing*, pages 51–60, Hong Kong. Association for Computational Linguistics.

Yoav Freund and Robert E Schapire. 1997. A decision-theoretic generalization of on-line learning and an application to boosting. *Journal of computer and system sciences*, 55(1):119–139.

Jerome H Friedman. 2001. Greedy function approximation: a gradient boosting machine. *Annals of statistics*, pages 1189–1232.

Hila Gonen and Yoav Goldberg. 2019. Lipstick on a pig: Debiasing methods cover up systematic gender biases in word embeddings but do not remove them. In *Proceedings of the 2019 Workshop on Widening NLP*, pages 60–63, Florence, Italy. Association for Computational Linguistics.

Sepp Hochreiter and Jürgen Schmidhuber. 1997. Long short-term memory. *Neural Computation*, 9(8):1735–1780.

Sarthak Jain and Byron C. Wallace. 2019. Attention is not Explanation. In *Proceedings of the 2019 Conference of the North American Chapter of the Association for Computational Linguistics: Human Language Technologies, Volume 1 (Long and Short Papers)*, pages 3543–3556, Minneapolis, Minnesota. Association for Computational Linguistics.

Yoon Kim. 2014. Convolutional neural networks for sentence classification. In *Proceedings of the 2014 Conference on Empirical Methods in Natural Language Processing (EMNLP)*, pages 1746–1751, Doha, Qatar. Association for Computational Linguistics.

Jan-Christoph Klie, Michael Bugert, Beto Boullosa, Richard Eckart de Castilho, and Iryna Gurevych. 2018. The inception platform: Machine-assisted and knowledge-oriented interactive annotation. In *COLING 2018, The 27th International Conference on Computational Linguistics: System Demonstrations, Santa Fe, New Mexico, August 20-26, 2018*, pages 5–9. Association for Computational Linguistics.

Shimon Kogan, Dimitry Levin, Bryan R. Routledge, Jacob S. Sagi, and Noah A. Smith. 2009. Predicting risk from financial reports with regression. In *Proceedings of Human Language Technologies: The 2009 Annual Conference of the North American Chapter of the Association for Computational Linguistics*, pages 272–280, Boulder, Colorado. Association for Computational Linguistics.

Jinhyuk Lee, Wonjin Yoon, Sungdong Kim, Donghyeon Kim, Sunkyu Kim, Chan Ho So, and Jaewoo Kang. 2019. BioBERT: a pre-trained biomedical language representation model for biomedical text mining. *Bioinformatics*, 36(4):1234–1240.

Yinhan Liu, Myle Ott, Naman Goyal, Jingfei Du, Mandar Joshi, Danqi Chen, Omer Levy, Mike Lewis, Luke Zettlemoyer, and Veselin Stoyanov. 2019. Roberta: A robustly optimized bert pretraining approach. *arXiv preprint arXiv:1907.11692*.

Scott M Lundberg and Su-In Lee. 2017. A unified approach to interpreting model predictions. *Advances in Neural Information Processing Systems*, 30:4765–4774.

Thomas Manzini, Yao Chong Lim, Yulia Tsvetkov, and Alan W Black. 2019. Black is to criminal as caucasian is to police: Detecting and removing multiclass bias in word embeddings. *arXiv preprint arXiv:1904.04047*.

Aurelie Mascio, Zeljko Kraljevic, Daniel Bean, Richard Dobson, Robert Stewart, Rebecca Bendayan, and Angus Roberts. 2020. Comparative analysis of text classification approaches in electronic health records. In *Proceedings of the 19th SIGBioMed Workshop on Biomedical Language Processing*, pages 86–94, Online. Association for Computational Linguistics.

Tomas Mikolov, Kai Chen, Greg Corrado, and Jeffrey Dean. 2013. Efficient estimation of word representations in vector space. *arXiv preprint arXiv:1301.3781*.

James Mullenbach, Sarah Wiegreffe, Jon Duke, Jimeng Sun, and Jacob Eisenstein. 2018. Explainable prediction of medical codes from clinical text. In *Proceedings of the 2018 Conference of the North American Chapter of the Association for Computational Linguistics: Human Language Technologies, Volume 1 (Long Papers)*, pages 1101–1111, New Orleans, Louisiana. Association for Computational Linguistics.

NMC. 2015. Professional standards of practice and behaviour for nurses, midwives and nursing associates.

NMC. 2020. Nursing and midwifery council annual report and accounts 2019–2020 and strategic plan 2020-2025.

Makbule Gulcin Ozsoy, Ferda Nur Alpaslan, and Ilyas Cicekli. 2011. Text summarization using latent semantic analysis. *Journal of Information Science*, 37(4):405–417.

Ji Ho Park, Jamin Shin, and Pascale Fung. 2018. Reducing gender bias in abusive language detection. In *Proceedings of the 2018 Conference on Empirical Methods in Natural Language Processing*, pages 2799–2804, Brussels, Belgium. Association for Computational Linguistics.

Jeffrey Pennington, Richard Socher, and Christopher Manning. 2014. Glove: Global vectors for word representation. In *Proceedings of the 2014 Conference on Empirical Methods in Natural Language Processing (EMNLP)*, pages 1532–1543, Doha, Qatar. Association for Computational Linguistics.

Denys Proux, Pierre Marchal, Frédérique Segond, Ivan Kergourlay, Stéfan Darmoni, Suzanne Pereira, Quentin Gicquel, and Marie-Hélène Metzger. 2009. Natural language processing to detect risk patterns related to hospital acquired infections. In *Proceedings of the Workshop on Biomedical Information Extraction*, pages 35–41, Borovets, Bulgaria. Association for Computational Linguistics.

Juliano Rabelo, Mi-Young Kim, and Randy Goebel. 2019. Combining similarity and transformer methods for case law entailment. In *Proceedings of the*

Seventeenth International Conference on Artificial Intelligence and Law, ICAIL 2019, Montreal, QC, Canada, June 17-21, 2019, pages 290–296. ACM.

Juliano Rabelo, Mi-Young Kim, Randy Goebel, Masaharu Yoshioka, Yoshinobu Kano, and Ken Satoh. 2020. A summary of the coliee 2019 competition. In *New Frontiers in Artificial Intelligence*, pages 34–49, Cham. Springer International Publishing.

Colin Raffel, Noam Shazeer, Adam Roberts, Katherine Lee, Sharan Narang, Michael Matena, Yanqi Zhou, Wei Li, and Peter J. Liu. 2020. Exploring the limits of transfer learning with a unified text-to-text transformer. *Journal of Machine Learning Research*, 21(140):1–67.

Marco Tulio Ribeiro, Sameer Singh, and Carlos Guestrin. 2016. " why should i trust you?" explaining the predictions of any classifier. In *Proceedings of the 22nd ACM SIGKDD international conference on knowledge discovery and data mining*, pages 1135–1144.

Vasile Rus, Mihai Lintean, Rajendra Banjade, Nobal Niraula, and Dan Stefanescu. 2013. SEMILAR: The semantic similarity toolkit. In *Proceedings of the 51st Annual Meeting of the Association for Computational Linguistics: System Demonstrations*, pages 163–168, Sofia, Bulgaria. Association for Computational Linguistics.

Gerard Salton and Chris Buckley. 1988. Term-weighting approaches in automatic text retrieval. *Inf. Process. Manag.*, 24(5):513–523.

Robert Shaffer and Stephen Mayhew. 2019. Legal linking: Citation resolution and suggestion in constitutional law. In *Proceedings of the Natural Legal Language Processing Workshop 2019*, pages 39–44, Minneapolis, Minnesota. Association for Computational Linguistics.

Jerrold Soh, How Khang Lim, and Ian Ernst Chai. 2019. Legal area classification: A comparative study of text classifiers on singapore supreme court judgments. In *Proceedings of the Natural Legal Language Processing Workshop 2019*, pages 67–77, Minneapolis, Minnesota. Association for Computational Linguistics.

Tony Sun, Andrew Gaut, Shirlyn Tang, Yuxin Huang, Mai ElSherief, Jieyu Zhao, Diba Mirza, Elizabeth Belding, Kai-Wei Chang, and William Yang Wang. 2019. Mitigating gender bias in natural language processing: Literature review. In *Proceedings of the 57th Annual Meeting of the Association for Computational Linguistics*, pages 1630–1640, Florence, Italy. Association for Computational Linguistics.

Vu Tran, Minh Le Nguyen, and Ken Satoh. 2019. Building legal case retrieval systems with lexical matching and summarization using a pre-trained phrase scoring model. In *Proceedings of the Seventeenth International Conference on Artificial Intelligence and Law*, pages 275–282.

Vladimir Vovk, Alex Gammerman, and Glenn Shafer. 2005. *Algorithmic learning in a random world*. Springer Science & Business Media.

Chuan-Ju Wang, Ming-Feng Tsai, Tse Liu, and Chin-Ting Chang. 2013. Financial sentiment analysis for risk prediction. In *Proceedings of the Sixth International Joint Conference on Natural Language Processing*, pages 802–808, Nagoya, Japan. Asian Federation of Natural Language Processing.

Yanshan Wang, Naveed Afzal, Sunyang Fu, Liwei Wang, Feichen Shen, Majid Rastegar-Mojarad, and Hongfang Liu. 2020. Medsts: a resource for clinical semantic textual similarity. *Lang. Resour. Evaluation*, 54(1):57–72.

Sarah Wiegreffe and Yuval Pinter. 2019. Attention is not not explanation. In *Proceedings of the 2019 Conference on Empirical Methods in Natural Language Processing and the 9th International Joint Conference on Natural Language Processing (EMNLP-IJCNLP)*, pages 11–20, Hong Kong, China. Association for Computational Linguistics.

Adina Williams, Nikita Nangia, and Samuel Bowman. 2018. A broad-coverage challenge corpus for sentence understanding through inference. In *Proceedings of the 2018 Conference of the North American Chapter of the Association for Computational Linguistics: Human Language Technologies, Volume 1 (Long Papers)*, pages 1112–1122, New Orleans, Louisiana. Association for Computational Linguistics.

David H Wolpert. 1992. Stacked generalization. *Neural networks*, 5(2):241–259.

Brian Hu Zhang, Blake Lemoine, and Margaret Mitchell. 2018. Mitigating unwanted biases with adversarial learning. In *Proceedings of the 2018 AAAI/ACM Conference on AI, Ethics, and Society*, AIES '18, page 335–340, New York, NY, USA. Association for Computing Machinery.

Jieyu Zhao, Tianlu Wang, Mark Yatskar, Vicente Ordonez, and Kai-Wei Chang. 2018. Gender bias in coreference resolution: Evaluation and debiasing methods. In *Proceedings of the 2018 Conference of the North American Chapter of the Association for Computational Linguistics: Human Language Technologies, Volume 2 (Short Papers)*, pages 15–20, New Orleans, Louisiana. Association for Computational Linguistics.

Appendix

Hyperparameters Selection

Hyperparameters of our models are selected using grid search on 250 randomly sampled cases; results are presented below. For the CNN model (base model C3 in the ensemble), we use three filter sizes (2,3 and 4) and 15 filters for each size. For the multi-task training (base model C3), the loss function we use is $L_y + 2L_A$, where L_y and L_A are the cross-entropy losses for predicting the risk level and additional assessment results, respectively. To fine-tune BERT (base model C4), we use Adam as the optimiser with fixed learning rate 2e-5, batch size 8 and perform the training for 10 epochs.

Data Fields

Fields in the dataset are summarised in Table 5.

Category	Data Fields
Meta Information ($c_{i1}, ..., c_{ik}$)	**CreateDate** (when the case was created), **CurrentStatus**(closed, in investigation, or await adjudication hearing), **Referrer** (who submitted the complaint)
Assessment Results ($a_{i1}, ..., a_{im}$)	**RiskLevel** (high or low), **RiskOfRepetition** (True or False), **SeriousHarmToRegistrant** (True of False), **SeriousHarmToPatient** (True of False) **BreachOfOngoingRegulatoryIntervention** (True or False), **MaternityRelated** (True or False), **PatientDeath** (True of False), **InvestigationResults** (free text)

Table 5: Fields in the complaints dataset.

CogIE: An Information Extraction Toolkit for Bridging Texts and CogNet

Zhuoran Jin[1,2], **Yubo Chen**[1,2], **Dianbo Sui**[1,2],
Chenhao Wang[1,2], **Zhipeng Xue**[1], **Jun Zhao**[1,2]
[1] National Laboratory of Pattern Recognition, Institute of Automation,
Chinese Academy of Sciences, Beijing, 100190, China
[2] School of Artificial Intelligence, University of Chinese Academy of Sciences,
Beijing, 100049, China
{zhuoran.jin, yubo.chen, dianbo.sui}@nlpr.ia.ac.cn
{chenhao.wang, zhipeng.xue, jzhao}@nlpr.ia.ac.cn

Abstract

CogNet is a knowledge base that integrates three types of knowledge: linguistic knowledge, world knowledge and commonsense knowledge. In this paper, we propose an information extraction toolkit, called CogIE, which is a bridge connecting raw texts and CogNet. CogIE has three features: **versatile**, **knowledge-grounded** and **extensible**. First, CogIE is a versatile toolkit with a rich set of functional modules, including named entity recognition, entity typing, entity linking, relation extraction, event extraction and frame-semantic parsing. Second, as a knowledge-grounded toolkit, CogIE can ground the extracted facts to CogNet and leverage different types of knowledge to enrich extracted results. Third, for extensibility, owing to the design of three-tier architecture, CogIE is not only a plug-and-play toolkit for developers but also an extensible programming framework for researchers. We release an open-access online system [1] to visually extract information from texts. Source code, datasets and pre-trained models are publicly available at GitHub [2], with a short instruction video [3].

1 Introduction

Knowledge bases (KBs) such as FrameNet (Baker et al., 1998), DBpedia (Lehmann et al., 2015), Wikidata (Vrandečić and Krötzsch, 2014), and ConceptNet (Liu and Singh, 2004) are becoming popular for a variety of downstream tasks including information retrieval, recommender system and dialog system. Wang et al. (2021) divide KBs into three categories according to the type of knowledge, respectively linguistic KBs (e.g., FrameNet), world KBs (e.g., DBpedia, Wikidata) and commonsense KBs (e.g., ConceptNet). Unlike most of the above KBs which focus on a single type of knowledge, CogNet (Wang et al., 2021) models linguistic, world and commonsense knowledge using a unified representation architecture for better knowledge integration.

To apply CogNet to downstream tasks, it is challenging to expand CogNet and ground raw texts to CogNet automatically. For this target, information extraction (IE) is an effective method, which aims to extract entity, relation, event, and other factual information from raw texts and link them to KBs.

With the rapid development of IE area, a few remarkable open-source toolkits have been developed in recent years. The mainstream toolkits can be classified into two categories: task-specific toolkits and task-agnostic toolkits. Task-specific toolkits focus on one or a few specific tasks, such as FLAIR (Akbik et al., 2019) for named entity recognition (NER), BLINK (Ledell Wu, 2020) for entity linking (EL), OpenNRE (Han et al., 2019) for relation extraction (RE) and Open-SESAME (Swayamdipta et al., 2017) for frame-semantic parsing. On the other end of the spectrum, AllenNLP (Gardner et al., 2017), OpenNMT (Klein et al., 2017) and other task-agnostic toolkits are designed to provide programming framework without the implementation of specific tasks.

As mentioned above, various toolkits have been widely used, but they also suffer from several limitations. First, most of the existing NLP toolkits only support one or a few IE functions, and there is a lack of an integrated and efficient IE toolkit. Second, very few IE toolkits can align the extracted facts to KBs, which may cause the extracted facts not to be applied directly to downstream tasks. Third, for an efficient and effective toolkit, providing application program interfaces (APIs) is as important as supporting the secondary development. Still, only a few toolkits can do both at the same time.

[1] http://cognet.top/cogie
[2] https://github.com/jinzhuoran/CogIE
[3] https://youtu.be/csgnjU_F3Qs

Proceedings of the Joint Conference of the 59th Annual Meeting of the Association for Computational Linguistics and the 11th International Joint Conference on Natural Language Processing: System Demonstrations, pages 92–98, August 1st - August 6th, 2021.

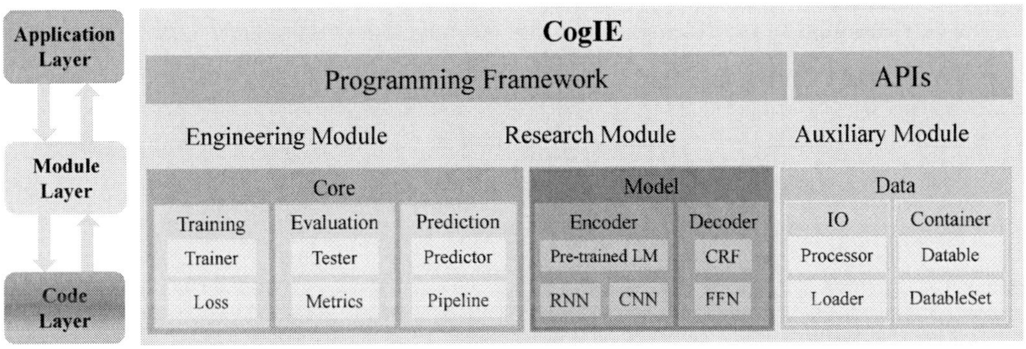

Figure 1: **Left:** The three-tier architecture of CogIE. **Right:** The internal structure of each layer.

Therefore, it is highly desirable to have an open-source toolkit that can implement and integrate various IE tasks and can take advantage of the knowledge resources in KBs to enrich the extracted facts. Such a toolkit should achieve the equilibrium among usability, extensibility and efficiency.

To this end, we propose **CogIE**, an **IE** toolkit that bridges raw texts and **Cog**Net, making it easy to extract facts from texts as well as ground the extracted facts to CogNet. The toolkit supports both English and Chinese, building upon PyTorch with the same uniform design. Moreover, CogIE can meet the requirements of function customizability and model extensibility for researchers. CogIE also provides APIs for developers to build applications rapidly. We release an online CogIE system to extract information from input texts with friendly interactive interfaces and fast response speed.

In summary, the main features and contributions are as follows:

- **Versatile.** We develop a professional and integrated IE toolkit. CogIE can support high-performance named entity recognition, entity typing, entity linking, relation extraction, event extraction and frame-semantic parsing.

- **Knowledge-grounded.** We build a bridge between raw texts and CogNet. CogIE can ground the extracted facts to CogNet and leverage different types of knowledge to enrich results.

- **Extensible.** We contribute not just user-friendly APIs, but an extensible programming framework. Our goal in designing CogIE is to provide a universal toolkit for all sorts of users.

2 System Design and Architecture

In this section, we introduce the design choice and system architecture of CogIE. Designing a powerful toolkit is challenging due to different types of IE tasks and fast-growing new models. As illustrated in Figure 1, we tackle the challenges by dividing the main modules and components of CogIE into three layers. Each layer in CogIE plays a unique role separately.

2.1 Application Layer

The application layer acts as a mediator between CogIE and users, including researchers and developers. Researchers pay more attention to internal details and prefer a programming framework to support function customization and model construction. On the contrary, developers are more likely to use the high-level functions provided by the toolkit directly without knowing too many low-level details. Considering the different requirements of both sides, we divide CogIE into two parts at the application layer: (1) a programming framework supporting NLP research; (2) APIs providing IE functions.

NLP Programming Framework. The primary design goal of CogIE is to make it easy to meet some individual requirements with our experiment paradigm. Specifically, we decouple NLP experiments, forming three consecutive parts of **Training - Evaluation - Prediction**. Thus, users can use the programming framework to train new models, validate performances and make predictions based on the trained models.

IE APIs. We also implement a series of typical models by the unified framework of CogIE. CogIE provides APIs with multilingual support (En-

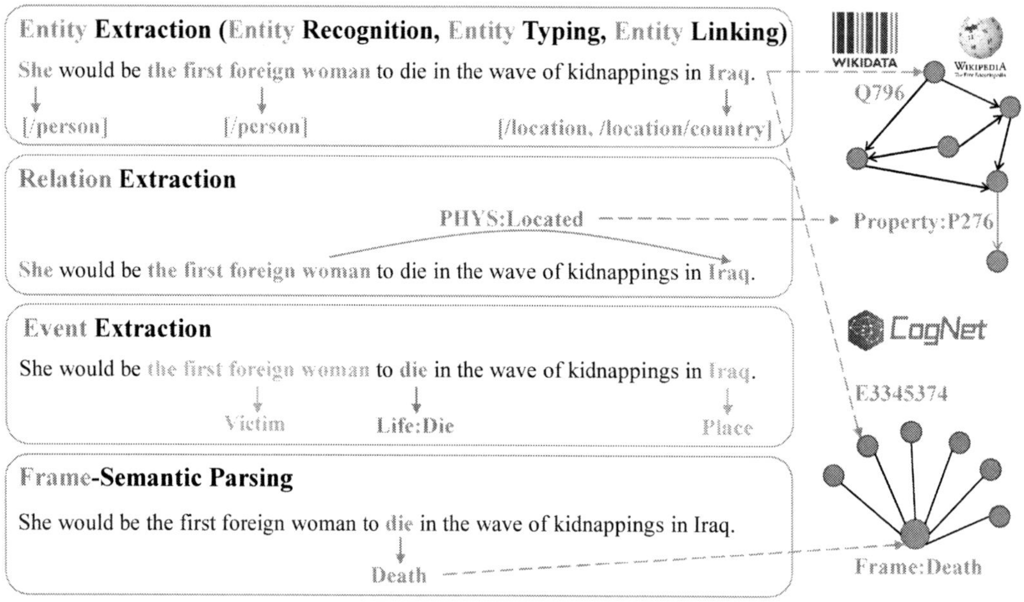

Figure 2: The examples of main functions in CogIE.

glish and Chinese), including word segmentation, named entity recognition, entity typing, entity linking, relation extraction, event extraction and frame-semantic parsing, etc. APIs take raw texts as input and produce structured extraction results accurately and quickly.

2.2 Module Layer

The module layer is based on the principle that each module has a single function and contacts with as few modules as possible. In this layer, CogIE consists of three independent modules, namely engineering module, research module and auxiliary module. In this way, users only need to focus on core neural network models without writing repetitive and complex engineering code, allowing experiments easier and faster. The following is the detailed design philosophy of each module.

Engineering Module. This module mainly integrates the code with high repeatability in different task scenarios. In this way, CogIE is less error-prone and more time-saving by automating most of the training loop and tricky engineering.

Research Module. To make code more concise and extensible, we decouple the research module from the engineering module. The research module mainly includes the user-defined neural network models, loss functions, etc., which are the core of research.

Auxiliary Module. The auxiliary module is designed to assist experiments by accelerating training, saving checkpoints, recording logs, and visualizing results. For example, CogIE can support 16-bit precision to cut memory footprint by half and use TensorBoard [4] to visualize experimental parameters.

2.3 Code Layer

The code layer relates to the underlying design of CogIE. This layer consists of three interdependent parts: core code, model code and data code.

Core Code. In the core code, we develop a variety of ready-to-use components for users. Because of the special **Training - Evaluation - Prediction** experiment paradigm, `Trainer`, `Tester` and `Predictor` class are the key components of core code. In the case of `Trainer` class, users just need to feed the expected components (e.g., model, dataset, loss function, evaluation metric, configuration file, etc.) into it, everything else is automatically done.

Model Code. `BaseModel` class is the base class of all models in CogIE. `BaseModel` class organizes code into four sections: (1) `forward`

[4] `https://github.com/lanpa/tensorboardX`

function for computation, (2) `loss` function for train, (3) `evaluate` function for validation, and (4) `predict` function for prediction. Model code consists of two parts: encoder module (e.g., Pretrained Language Model, RNN, CNN, etc.) and decoder module (e.g., CRF, FFN, etc.). By designing model code this way, it is convenient to change from one model to another by simply plugging in and swapping out a single or few modules.

Data Code. The data code is built around the notion of `Datable` which stores data in table form. CogIE includes built-in `Loader` and `Processor` class for lots of popular datasets and provides easy-to-use data containers to encapsulate all the steps needed to process data.

3 Core Functions

CogIE is designed for a series of IE functions, including named entity recognition, entity typing, entity linking, relation extraction, event extraction, and frame-semantic parsing, etc. CogIE can also align the extracted facts to CogNet via entity linking, relation matching and frame matching. As shown in Figure 2, we give some examples to illustrate these functions.

3.1 Named Entity Recognition

Named entity recognition (NER) is a task for locating and classifying certain occurrences of words or expressions in unstructured texts into predefined semantic categories. To achieve the function of entity recognition, we adopt BERT as the textual encoder and use CRF as the decoder. Up to now, CogIE can not only recognize the common four entity types: locations, persons, organizations, and miscellaneous entities, but also support the recognition of 54 entity types.

3.2 Entity Typing

Fine-grained entity typing aims to assign one or more types to each entity mention given a certain context and can provide valuable prior knowledge for a wide range of NLP tasks, such as relation extraction and question answering. To achieve the function of entity typing, we adopt a two-step mention-aware attention mechanism to enable the model to focus on important words like Lin and Ji (2019). Compared with NER, ET has finer and richer entity labels with internal correlations (e.g., /person, /person/artist, /person/artist/actor), there are 87 fine-grained entity lables in CogIE.

3.3 Entity Linking

Entity linking is the task to link entity mentions in texts with their corresponding entities in a knowledge base. To achieve the function of entity linking, we use BLINK which adopts a two-stage approach for entity linking based on fine-tuned BERT architectures. CogIE supports link entities to CogNet and Wikidata, users can leverage multiple types of knowledge obtained through EL to implement knowledge base population (KBP) and knowledge based question answering (KBQA).

3.4 Relation Extraction

Relation extraction aims at predicting semantic relations between pairs of entities. More specifically, after identifying entity mentions in texts, the main goal of RE is to classify relations. To achieve the function of relation extraction, we adopt BERT as the textual encoder and use FFN as the decoder. As CogIE implements relation extraction simultaneously, it also matches extracted relations to Wikidata in the form as shown in Figure 2. We train relation matching on T-REx (Elsahar et al., 2018), which is a large-scale alignment dataset between free text documents and KB triples, there are currently 500 relation classes in CogIE.

3.5 Event Extraction

Events are classified as things that happen or occur, and usually involve entities as their properties. Event extraction need to identify events that are composed of an event trigger, an event type, and a set of arguments with different roles. To achieve the function of event extraction, we realize DMCNN (Chen et al., 2015) and a joint model based on BERT.

3.6 Frame-Semantic Parsing

Frame semantic parsing is the task of automatically extracting semantic structures in plain texts according the framework of FrameNet. Each frame represents a kind of event, situation, or relationship, and consists of a frame name, a list of lexical units (LUs), and a set of frame elements (FEs). LU is a word that plays the role of evoking the corresponding frame. FE indicates different semantic roles associated with the frame.

Frame-semantic parsing is usually performed as a pipeline of tasks: target identification, frame identification and argument identification. To achieve the function of argument identification, we add tar-

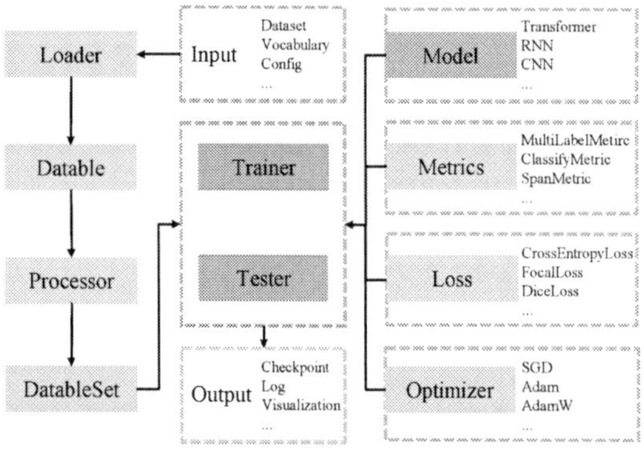


```
# load dataset
loader = Loader()
train_data, dev_data, test_data
    = loader.load_all('path of dataset')
# process dataset
processor = Processor()
train_datable = processor.process(train_data)
train_dataset = DataTableSet(train_datable)
dev_datable = processor.process(dev_data)
dev_dataset = DataTableSet(dev_datable)
test_datable = processor.process(test_data)
test_dataset = DataTableSet(test_datable)
# create model, loss, metric, optimizer for training
model = Model()
metric = Metric()
loss = Loss()
optimizer = Optimizer(model.parameters(), lr='learning rate')
# train and test the model
trainer = Trainer(model, train_dataset, dev_dataset, loss,
    optimizer, metric, model_path='path of checkpoint')
trainer.train()
tester = Tester(model, test_dataset, metric)
tester.test()
```

Figure 3: The sample code of model training in CogIE.

get representation and position representation to BERT encoder. CogIE currently supports to identify 749 frames and 816 FEs in FrameNet.

4 System Usage

Our goal of designing CogIE is to provide a user-friendly toolkit for users by achieving the equilibrium among usability, extensibility and efficiency.

4.1 Interface Calls

CogIE's APIs can be directly called by `Toolkit` class, where the previous output is pipelined to the following input. Considering APIs' flexibility, users need to specify different tasks, languages and datasets, while pre-trained models can be downloaded and loaded to `Toolkit` class automatically.

As shown in Figure 4, the code snippet shows a pipelined usage of CogIE for tokenizing a sentence into words, recognizing entities, and extracting relations between entities:

```
import cogie
# tokenize the text into words
token_toolkit =
    cogie.TokenizeToolkit(language='english')
words = token_toolkit.run('Ontario is the most
    populous province in Canada.')
# recognize the entities in the texts
ner_toolkit = cogie.NerToolkit(language='english')
ner_result = ner_toolkit.run(words)
# extract the relations between entities
re_toolkit = cogie.ReToolkit(language='english')
re_result = re_toolkit.run(words, ner_result)
print(re_result)
```

Figure 4: The sample code of interface calls in CogIE.

4.2 Model Training

The hallmark of any good toolkit is its extensibility. As a programming framework, CogIE supports users to train their customized models without modifying the CogIE codebase. Figure 3 shows the sample code of model training, and one can use only a tiny amount of code for data processing, component initializing, model training, and model evaluating.

To do this, users need to use `Loader` class to load the dataset and process it into `DatableSet` class by `Processor` class. Then, `Model`, `Loss`, `Metric`, `Optimizer` class should be initialized before added to `Trainer` class. And finally, `Trainer` and `Tester` class can train and validate the model while generating checkpoints, logs and visualization results.

4.3 Online System

Figure 5: An example of the online system.

In addition to this toolkit, we also release an open-access online system as shown in Figure 5.

Task		Corpus	Language	Types	Metric	Score
Word Segmentation		MSRA	Chinese	-	F_1	91.2
Named Entity Recognition		CoNLL2003	English	4	F_1	91.4
		OntoNotes5.0	English	18	F_1	85.6
		OntoNotes4.0	Chinese	4	F_1	80.0
Entity Typing		BBN	English	47	F_1	75.5
Relation Extraction		KBP37	English	37	F_1	69.9
		DuIE	Chinese	48	F_1	93.0
Event Extraction	Trigger	ACE2005	English	33	F_1	68.9
	Argument			35	F_1	46.4
	Trigger	ACE2005	Chinese	33	F_1	58.8
	Argument			35	F_1	52.8
Frame-Semantic Parsing	Frame	Frame 1.5	English	749	Acc	91.0
	Element			816	F_1	56.4

Table 1: Performance of each task. The datasets references are: MSRA (Emerson, 2005), CoNLL2003 (Sang and De Meulder, 2003), OntoNotes5.0 (Pradhan et al., 2013), OntoNotes4.0 (Weischedel et al., 2011), BBN (Weischedel and Brunstein, 2005), KBP37 (Zhang and Wang, 2015), DuIE (Li et al., 2019), ACE2005 (Walker et al., 2006), and Frame 1.5 (Kabbach et al., 2018).

We train models for different tasks and deploy pre-trained models for online access. The online system can be directly used for extracting entities, relations, events and frames from plain texts. Besides, the extracted results can be linked to CogNet, so users can further acquire external knowledge through CogNet. We also visualize the extracted results in the form of knowledge graphs to improve the availability of the online system. Meanwhile, open online APIs [5] can be called directly .

5 Experiment and Evaluation

In this section, we train and evaluate CogIE on several datasets in different tasks. Each task's performance is shown in Table 1, all pre-trained models are publicly downloadable.

For the NER component, we compare CogIE against Stanza (v1.0), FLAIR (v0.4.5) and spaCy (v2.2), we find that CogIE can achieve either higher or close F1 scores when compared against other toolkits. For the RE component, we compare CogIE with two baselines: RNN+PI (Zhang and Wang, 2015) and BERT_{EM} (Soares et al., 2019), we observe that CogIE can achieve comparable or even better performance than them. For the frame-semantic parsing component, we compare CogIE against SimpleFrameId (Hartmann et al., 2017), we find that CogIE can have better performance than SimpleFrameId. For the other components, we also compare CogIE with a series of baselines and toolkits, and the evaluation results show that CogIE can provide powerful IE functions.

[5] http://cognet.top/cogie/api.html

6 Conclusion and Future Work

In this paper, we propose CogIE, an information extraction toolkit for bridging texts and CogNet. We have shown that CogIE is a plug-and-play toolkit and an extensible programming framework due to its **Application - Module - Code** three-tier architecture design. Moreover, as an integrated and professional IE toolkit, CogIE can extract information from texts while aligning the extracted facts to CogNet and other KBs. We conduct experiments on several datasets in different tasks, and the evaluation results demonstrate the models implemented by CogIE are efficient.

In the future, we consider the following points during improvement: (1) To use CogIE on any device, we will further optimize model sizes and speed up computation in CogIE while striking a balance between accuracy and efficiency; (2) For making models robust to the texts of different domains and styles, we plan to utilize various sources of consistent data to train a universal model; (3) We will build an open-source community for CogIE so that all researchers can contribute their models and participate in long-term maintenance.

Acknowledgments

This work is supported by the National Key Research and Development Program of China (No. 2020AAA0106400), the National Natural Science Foundation of China (No.61806201).

References

Alan Akbik, Tanja Bergmann, Duncan Blythe, Kashif Rasul, Stefan Schweter, and Roland Vollgraf. 2019. Flair: An easy-to-use framework for state-of-the-art nlp. In *Proc. of NAACL-HLT*.

Collin F Baker, Charles J Fillmore, and John B Lowe. 1998. The berkeley framenet project. In *Proc. of ACL*.

Yubo Chen, Liheng Xu, Kang Liu, Daojian Zeng, and Jun Zhao. 2015. Event extraction via dynamic multi-pooling convolutional neural networks. In *Proc. of ACL*.

Hady Elsahar, Pavlos Vougiouklis, Arslen Remaci, Christophe Gravier, Jonathon Hare, Frederique Laforest, and Elena Simperl. 2018. T-rex: A large scale alignment of natural language with knowledge base triples. In *Proc. of LREC*.

Thomas Emerson. 2005. The second international chinese word segmentation bakeoff. In *Proc. of SIGHAN*.

Matt Gardner, Joel Grus, Mark Neumann, Oyvind Tafjord, Pradeep Dasigi, Nelson F. Liu, Matthew Peters, Michael Schmitz, and Luke S. Zettlemoyer. 2017. Allennlp: A deep semantic natural language processing platform. *ArXiv:1803.07640*.

Xu Han, Tianyu Gao, Yuan Yao, Demin Ye, Zhiyuan Liu, and Maosong Sun. 2019. Opennre: An open and extensible toolkit for neural relation extraction. In *Proc. of EMNLP*.

Silvana Hartmann, Ilia Kuznetsov, M Teresa Martín-Valdivia, and Iryna Gurevych. 2017. Out-of-domain framenet semantic role labeling. In *Proc. of ECAL*.

Alexandre Kabbach, Corentin Ribeyre, and Aurélie Herbelot. 2018. Butterfly effects in frame semantic parsing: impact of data processing on model ranking. In *Proc. of COLING*.

Guillaume Klein, Yoon Kim, Yuntian Deng, Jean Senellart, and Alexander M Rush. 2017. Opennmt: Open-source toolkit for neural machine translation. In *Proc. of ACL*.

Martin Josifoski Sebastian Riedel Luke Zettlemoyer Ledell Wu, Fabio Petroni. 2020. Zero-shot entity linking with dense entity retrieval. In *Proc. of EMNLP*.

Jens Lehmann, Robert Isele, Max Jakob, Anja Jentzsch, Dimitris Kontokostas, Pablo N Mendes, Sebastian Hellmann, Mohamed Morsey, Patrick Van Kleef, Sören Auer, et al. 2015. Dbpedia–a large-scale, multilingual knowledge base extracted from wikipedia. *Semantic web*.

Shuangjie Li, Wei He, Yabing Shi, Wenbin Jiang, Haijin Liang, Ye Jiang, Yang Zhang, Yajuan Lyu, and Yong Zhu. 2019. Duie: A large-scale chinese dataset for information extraction. In *Proc. of NLPCC*.

Ying Lin and Heng Ji. 2019. An attentive fine-grained entity typing model with latent type representation. In *Proc. of EMNLP*.

Hugo Liu and Push Singh. 2004. Conceptnet—a practical commonsense reasoning tool-kit. *BT technology journal*.

Sameer Pradhan, Alessandro Moschitti, Nianwen Xue, Hwee Tou Ng, Anders Björkelund, Olga Uryupina, Yuchen Zhang, and Zhi Zhong. 2013. Towards robust linguistic analysis using ontonotes. *Proc. of CoNLL*.

Erik Tjong Kim Sang and Fien De Meulder. 2003. Introduction to the conll-2003 shared task: Language-independent named entity recognition. In *Proc. of CoNLL*.

Livio Baldini Soares, Nicholas FitzGerald, Jeffrey Ling, and Tom Kwiatkowski. 2019. Matching the blanks: Distributional similarity for relation learning. In *Proc. of ACL*.

Swabha Swayamdipta, Sam Thomson, Chris Dyer, and Noah A. Smith. 2017. Frame-Semantic Parsing with Softmax-Margin Segmental RNNs and a Syntactic Scaffold. *ArXiv:1706.09528*.

Denny Vrandečić and Markus Krötzsch. 2014. Wikidata: a free collaborative knowledgebase. *Communications of the ACM*.

Christopher Walker, Stephanie Strassel, Julie Medero, and Kazuaki Maeda. 2006. Ace 2005 multilingual training corpus. *Linguistic Data Consortium*.

Chenhao Wang, Yubo Chen, Zhipeng Xue, Yang Zhou, and Jun Zhao. 2021. Cognet: Bridging linguistic knowledge, world knowledge and commonsense knowledge. In *Proc. of AAAI*.

Ralph Weischedel and Ada Brunstein. 2005. Bbn pronoun coreference and entity type corpus. *Linguistic Data Consortium*.

Ralph Weischedel, Sameer Pradhan, Lance Ramshaw, Martha Palmer, Nianwen Xue, Mitchell Marcus, Ann Taylor, Craig Greenberg, Eduard Hovy, Robert Belvin, et al. 2011. Ontonotes release 4.0. *Linguistic Data Consortium*.

Dongxu Zhang and Dong Wang. 2015. Relation classification via recurrent neural network. *ArXiv:1508.01006*.

fastHan: A BERT-based Multi-Task Toolkit for Chinese NLP

Zhichao Geng, Hang Yan, Xipeng Qiu*, Xuanjing Huang
School of Computer Science, Fudan University
Key Laboratory of Intelligent Information Processing, Fudan University
{zcgeng20,hyan19,xpqiu,xjhuang}@fudan.edu.cn

Abstract

We present fastHan, an open-source toolkit for four basic tasks in Chinese natural language processing: Chinese word segmentation (CWS), Part-of-Speech (POS) tagging, named entity recognition (NER), and dependency parsing. The backbone of fastHan is a multi-task model based on a pruned BERT, which uses the first 8 layers in BERT. We also provide a 4-layer base model compressed from the 8-layer model. The joint-model is trained and evaluated on 13 corpora of four tasks, yielding near state-of-the-art (SOTA) performance in dependency parsing and NER, achieving SOTA performance in CWS and POS. Besides, fastHan's transferability is also strong, performing much better than popular segmentation tools on a non-training corpus. To better meet the need of practical application, we allow users to use their own labeled data to further fine-tune fastHan. In addition to its small size and excellent performance, fastHan is user-friendly. Implemented as a python package, fastHan isolates users from the internal technical details and is convenient to use. The project is released on Github[1].

1 Introduction

Recently, the need for Chinese natural language processing (NLP) has a dramatic increase for many downstream applications. There are four basic tasks for Chinese NLP: Chinese word segmentation (CWS), Part-of-Speech (POS) tagging, named entity recognition (NER), and dependency parsing. CWS is a character-level task while others are word-level tasks. These basic tasks are usually the cornerstones or provide useful features for other downstream tasks.

However, the Chinese NLP community lacks an effective toolkit utilizing the correlation between the tasks. Tools developed for a single task cannot achieve the highest accuracy, and loading tools for each task will take up more memory. In practical, there is a strong correlation between these four basic Chinese NLP tasks. For example, the model will perform better in the other three word-level tasks if its word segmentation ability is stronger. Recently, Chen et al. (2017a) adopt cross-label to label the POS so that POS tagging and CWS can be trained jointly. Yan et al. (2020) propose a graph-based model for joint CWS and dependency parsing, in which a special "APP" dependency arc is used to indicate the word segmentation information. Thus, they can jointly train the word-level dependency parsing task and character-level CWS task with the biaffine parser (Dozat and Manning, 2016). Chen et al. (2017b) explore adversarial multi-criteria learning for CWS, proving more knowledge can be mined through training model on more corpora. As a result, there are many pieces of research on how to perform multi-corpus training on these tasks and how to conduct multi-task joint training. Zhang et al. (2020) show the joint training of POS tagging and dependency parsing can improve each other's performance and so on. Results of the CWS task are contained in the output of the POS tagging task.

Therefore, we developed fastHan, an efficient toolkit with the help of multi-task learning and pre-trained models (PTMs) (Qiu et al., 2020). FastHan adopts a BERT-based (Devlin et al., 2018) joint-model on 13 corpora to address the above four tasks. Through multi-task learning, fastHan shares knowledge among the different corpora. This shared information can improve fastHan's performance on these tasks. Besides, training on more corpora can obtain a larger vocabulary, which can reduce the number of times the model encounters characters outs of vocabulary. What's more, the joint-model can greatly reduce the occupied memory space. Compared with training a model for each task, the

*Corresponding author
[1] https://github.com/fastnlp/fastHan

Proceedings of the Joint Conference of the 59th Annual Meeting of the Association for Computational Linguistics and the 11th International Joint Conference on Natural Language Processing: System Demonstrations, pages 99–106, August 1st - August 6th, 2021.

joint-model can reduce the occupied memory space by *four* times.

FastHan has two versions of the backbone model, base and large. The large model uses the first eight layers of BERT, and the base model uses the Theseus strategy (Xu et al., 2020) to compress the large model to four layers. To improve the performance of the model, fastHan has done much optimization. For example, using the output of POS tagging to improve the performance of the dependency parsing task, using Theseus strategy to improve the performance of the base version model, and so on.

Overall, fastHan has the following advantages:

Small size: The total parameter of the base model is 151MB, and for the large model the number is 262MB.

High accuracy: The base version of the model achieved good results in all tasks, while the large version of the model approached SOTA in dependency parsing and NER, and achieved SOTA performance in CWS and POS.

Strong transferability: Multi-task learning allows fastHan to adapt to multiple criteria, and a large number of corpus allows fastHan to mine knowledge from rare samples. As a result, fastHan is robust to new samples. Our experiments in section 4.2 show fastHan outperforms popular segmentation tools on non-training dataset.

Easy to use: FastHan is implemented as a python package, and users can get started with its basic functions in one minute. Besides, all advanced features, such as user lexicon and fine-tuning, only need one line of code to use.

For developers of downstream applications, they do not need to do repetitive work for basic tasks and do not need to understand complex codes like BERT. Even if users have little knowledge of deep learning, by using fastHan they can get the results of SOTA performance conveniently. Also, the smaller size can reduce the need for hardware, so that fastHan can be deployed on more platforms.

For the Chinese NLP research community, the results of fastHan can be used as a unified preprocessing standard with high quality.

Besides, the idea of fastHan is not restricted to Chinese. Applying multi-task learning to enhance NLP toolkits also has practical value in other languages.

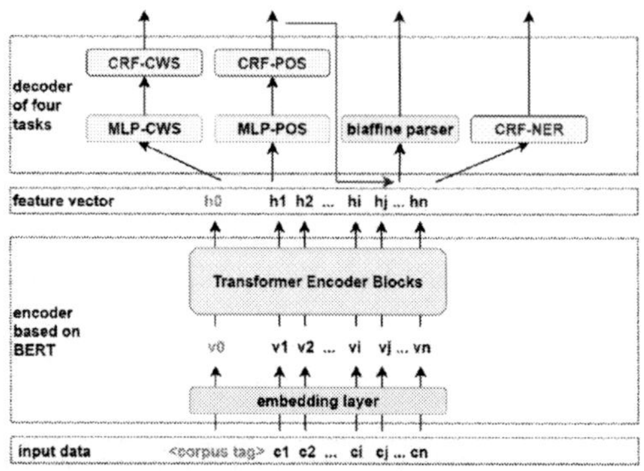

Figure 1: Architecture of the proposed model. The inputs are characters embeddings.

2 Backbone Model

The backbone of fastHan is a joint-model based on BERT, which performs multi-task learning on 13 corpora of the four tasks. The architecture of the model is shown in Figure 1. For this model, sentences of different tasks are first added with corpus tags at the beginning of the sentence. And then the sentences are input into the BERT-based encoder and the decoding layer. The decoding layer will use different decoders according to the current task: use conditional random field (CRF) to decode in the NER task; use MLP and CRF to decode in POS tagging and CWS task; use the output of POS tagging task combined with biaffine parser to decode in dependency parsing task.

Each task uses independent label sets here, CWS uses label set $Y = \{B, M, E, S\}$; POS tagging uses cross-labels set based on $\{B, M, E, S\}$; NER uses cross-labels set based on $\{B, M, E, S, O\}$; dependency parsing uses arc heads and arc labels to represent dependency grammar tree.

2.1 BERT-based feature extraction layer

BERT (Devlin et al., 2018) is a language model trained in large-scale corpus. The pre-trained BERT can be used to encode the input sequence. We take the output of the last layer of transformer blocks as the feature vector of the sequence. The attention (Vaswani et al., 2017) mechanism of BERT can extract rich and semantic information related to the context. In addition, the calculation of attention is parallel in the entire sequence, which is faster than the feature extraction layer based on LSTM. Different from vanilla BERT, we prune its layers and add corpus tags to input sequences.

Layer Pruning: The original BERT has 12 layers of transformer blocks, which will occupy a lot of memory space. The time cost of calculating for 12 layers is too much for these basic tasks even if data flows in parallel. Inspired by Huang et al. (2019), we only use 4 or 8 layers. Our experiment found that using the first eight layers performs well on all tasks, and after compressing, four layers are enough for CWS, POS tagging, and NER.

Corpus Tags: Instead of a linear projection layer, we use corpus tags to distinguish various tasks and corpora. Each corpus of each task corresponds to a specific corpus tag, and the embedding of these tags needs to be initialized and optimized during training. As shown in Figure 1, before inputting the sequence into BERT, we add the corpus tag to the head of the sequence. The attention mechanism will ensure that the vector of the corpus tag and the vector of each other position generate sufficiently complex calculations to bring the corpus and task information to each character.

2.2 CRF Decoder

We use the conditional random field (CRF) (Lafferty et al., 2001) to do the final decoding work in POS tagging, CWS, and NER tasks. In CRF, the conditional probability of a label sequence can be formalized as:

$$P(Y|X) = \frac{1}{Z(x;\theta)} exp(\sum_{t=1}^{T} \theta_1^\top f_1(X, y_t) + \sum_{t=1}^{T-1} \theta_2^\top f_2(X, y_t, y_{t+1})) \quad (1)$$

where θ are model parameters, $f_1(X, y_t)$ is the score for label y_t at position t, $f_2(X, y_t, y_{t+1})$ is the transition score from y_t to y_{t+1}, and $Z(x;\theta)$ is the normalization factor.

Compared with decoding using MLP only, CRF utilizes the neighbor information. When decoding using the Viterbi algorithm, CRF can get the global optimal solution instead of the label with the highest score for each position.

2.3 Biaffine Parser with Output of POS tagging

This task refers to the work of Yan et al. (2020). Yan's work uses the biaffine parser to address both CWS and dependency parsing tasks. Compared with the work of Yan et al. (2020), our model will use the output of POS tagging for two reasons. First, dependency parsing has a large semantic and formal gap with other tasks. As a result, sharing the parameter space with other tasks will reduce its performance. Our experimental results show that when the prediction of dependency parsing is independent of other tasks, the performance is worse than that of training dependency parsing only. And using the output of POS, dependency parsing can get more useful information, such as word segmentation and POS tagging labels. More importantly, users have the need to obtain all information in one sentence. If running POS tagging and dependency parsing separately, the word segmentation results of the two tasks may conflict, and this contradiction cannot be resolved by engineering methods. Even if there is error propagation in this way, our experiment shows the negative impact is acceptable with high POS tagging accuracy.

When predicting for dependency parsing, we first add the POS tagging corpus tag at the head of the original sentence to get the POS tagging output. Then we add the corpus tag of dependency parsing at the head of the original sentence to get the feature vector. Then, using the word segmentation results from POS tagging to split the feature vector of dependency parsing by token. The feature vectors of characters in a token are averaged to represent the token. In addition, embedding is established for POS tagging labels, with the same dimension as the feature vector. The feature vector of each token is added to the embedding vector by position, and the result is input into the biaffine parser. During the training phase, the model uses golden POS tagging labels. The premise of using POS tagging output is that the corpus contains both dependency parsing and POS tagging information.

2.4 Theseus Strategy

Theseus strategy (Xu et al., 2020) is a method to compress BERT, and we use it to train the base version of the model. As shown in Figure 2, after getting the large version of the model we use the module replacement strategy to train the four-layer base model. The base model is initialized with the first four layers of the large model, and its layer i is bound to the layer $2i-1$ and $2i$ of the large model. They are the corresponding modules. The training phase is divided into two parts. In the first part, we randomly choose whether to replace the module in the base model with its corresponding module in the large model. And we make the choice for

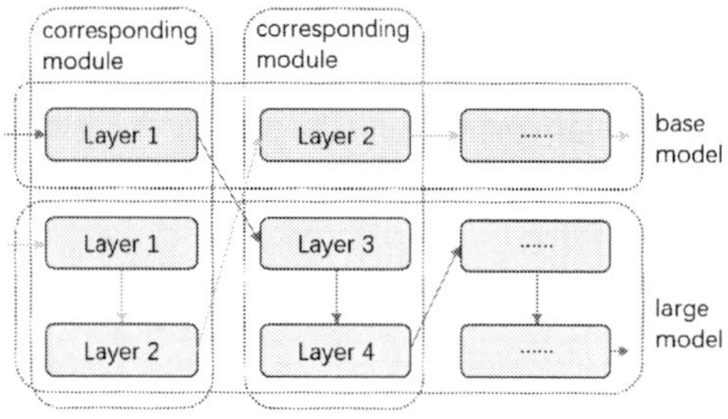

Figure 2: This diagram explains the replacement strategy when using Theseus method. When training the base model, we randomly replace the layer of base model with corresponding layers of large model. The red arrows and yellow arrows represent two possible data paths during training.

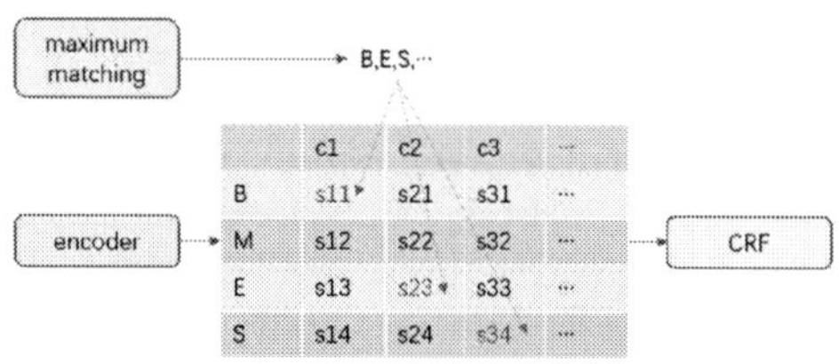

Figure 3: An example of segmentation of sequence $(c1, c2, c3, ...)$ combined with a user lexicon. According to the segmentation result of the maximum matching algorithm, a bias will be added to scores marked in red.

each module. We freeze the parameters of the large model when using gradients to update parameters. The replacement probability p is initialized to 0.5 and decreases linearly to 0. In the second part, We only fine-tune the base model and don't replace the modules anymore.

2.5 User Lexicon

In actual applications, users may process text of specific domains, such as technology, medical. There are proprietary vocabularies with high recall rates in such domains, and they rarely appear in ordinary corpus. It is intuitive to use a user lexicon to address this problem. Users can choose whether to add or use their lexicon. An example of combining a user lexicon is shown in Figure 3. When combined with a user lexicon, the maximum matching algorithm (Wong and Chan, 1996) is first performed to obtain a label sequence. After that, a bias will be added to the corresponding scores output by the encoder. And the result will be viewed as $f_1(X, y_t)$ in CRF in section 2.2. The bias is

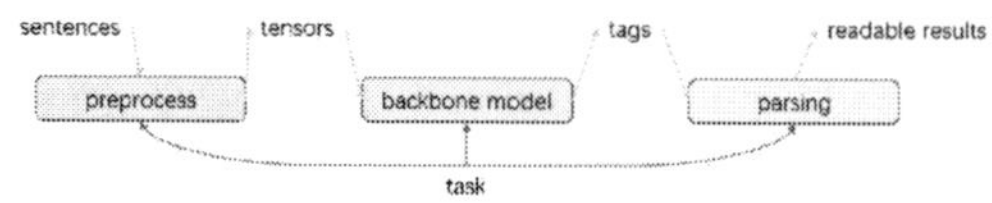

Figure 4: The workflow of fastHan. As indicated by the yellow arrows, data is converted between various formats in each stage. The blue arrows reveal that fastHan needs to act according to the task being performed currently.

calculated by the following equation:

$$b_t = (max(y_{1:n}) - average(y_{1:n})) * w \quad (2)$$

where b_t is the bias on position t, $y_{1:n}$ is the scores of each labels on position t output by the encoder, and w is the coefficient whose default value is 0.05. CRF decoder will generate the global optimal solution considering the bias. Users can set the coefficient value according to the recall rate of their lexicon. A development set can also be applied to get the optimal coefficient.

3 fastHan

FastHan is a Chinese NLP toolkit based on the above model, developed based on fastNLP[2] and PyTorch. We made a short video demonstrating fastHan and uploaded it to YouTube[3] and bilibili[4].

FastHan has been released on PYPI and users can install it by pip:

```
pip install fastHan
```

3.1 Workflow

When FastHan initializes, it first loads the pre-trained model parameters from the file system. Then, fastHan uses the pre-trained parameters to initialize the backbone model. FastHan will download parameters from our server automatically if it has not been initialized in the current environment before. After initialization, FastHan's workflow is shown in Figure 4.

In the preprocessing stage, fastHan first adds a corpus tag to the head of each sentence according to the current task and then uses the vocabulary to convert the sentence into a batch of vectors as well as padding. FastHan is robust and does not preprocess the original sentence redundantly, such

[2] https://github.com/fastnlp/fastnlp
[3] https://youtu.be/apM78cG06jY
[4] https://www.bilibili.com/video/BV1ho4y117H3

```
from fastHan import FastHan
model=FastHan('large')
sentence=["我爱踢足球","南京市长江大桥"]
print(model(sentence)
print(model(sentence,target="Parsing"))
print(model(sentence,target="NER"))
```

```
[['我', '爱', '踢', '足球'], ['南京市', '长江', '大桥']]
[[['我', 2, 'nsubj', 'PN'], ['爱', 0, 'root', 'VV'],
['踢', 2, 'ccomp', 'VV'], ['足球', 3, 'dobj', 'NN']],
[['南京市', 3, 'nn', 'NR'], ['长江', 3, 'nn', 'NR'],
['大桥', 0, 'root', 'NN']]]
[[], [['南京市', 'NS'], ['长江大桥', 'NS']]]
```

Figure 5: An example of using fastHan. On the left is the code entered by the user, and on the right is the corresponding output. The two sentences in the figure mean "I like playing football" and "Nanjing Yangtze River Bridge". The second sentence can be explained in a second way as "Daqiao Jiang, mayor of the Nanjing city", and it is quite easy to include a user lexicon to customize the output of the second sentence.

as removing stop words, processing numbers and English characters.

In the parsing phase, fastHan first converts the label sequence into character form and then parses it. FastHan will return the result in a form which is readable for users.

3.2 Usage

As shown in Figure 5, fastHan is easy to use. It only needs one line of code to initialize, where users can choose to use the base or large version of the model.

When calling fastHan, users need to select the task to be performed. The information of the three tasks of CWS, POS, and dependency parsing is in an inclusive relationship. And the information of the NER task is independent of other tasks. The input of FastHan can be a string or a list of strings. In the output of fastHan, words and their attributes are organized in the form of a list, which is convenient for subsequent processing. By setting parameters, users can also put their user lexicon into use. FastHan uses CTB label sets for POS tagging and dependency parsing tasks, and uses MSRA label set for NER.

Besides, users can call the set_device function to change the device utilized by the backbone model. Using GPU can greatly accelerate the prediction and fine-tuning of fastHan.

3.3 Advanced Features

In addition to using fastHan as a off the shelf model, users can utilize user lexicon and fine-tuning to enhance the performance of fastHan. As for user lexicon, users can call the add_user_dict function to add their lexicon, and call the $set\_user\_dict\_weight$ function to change the weight coefficient. As for fine-tuning, users can call the $finetune$ function to load the formatted data, make fine-tuning, and save the model parameters.

Users can change the segmentation style by calling the set_cws_style function. Each CWS corpus has different granularity and coverage. By changing the corpus tag, fastHan will segment words in the style of the corresponding corpus.

4 Evaluation

We evaluate fastHan in terms of accuracy, transferability, and execution speed.

4.1 Accuracy Test

The accuracy test is performed on the test set of training data. We refer to the CWS corpora used by (Chen et al., 2015; Huang et al., 2019), including PKU, MSR, AS, CITYU (Emerson, 2005), CTB-6 (Xue et al., 2005), SXU (Jin and Chen, 2008), UD, CNC, WTB (Wang et al., 2014) and ZX (Zhang et al., 2014). More details can be found in (Huang et al., 2019). For POS tagging and dependency parsing, we use the Penn Chinese Treebank 9.0 (CTB-9) (Xue et al., 2005). For NER, we use MSRA's NER dataset and OntoNotes.

We conduct an additional set of experiments to make the base version of fastHan trained on each task separately. The final results are shown in Table 1. Both base and large models perform satisfactorily. The result shows that multi-task learning greatly improves fastHan's performance on all tasks. The large version of fastHan outperforms the current best model in CWS and POS. Although fastHan's score on NER and dependency parsing is not the best, the parameters used by fastHan are reduced by one-third due to layer prune. FastHan's performance on NER can also be enhanced by a user lexicon with a high recall rate.

We also conduct an experiment about user lexicon on 10 CWS corpus respectively. With each corpus, a word is added to the lexicon once it has appeared in the training set. With such a low-quality lexicon, fastHan's score increases by an average of 0.127 percentage points. It is feasible to use

Model	CWS F	Dependency Parsing F_{udep}, F_{ldep}	POS F	NER MSRA F	NER OntoNotes F
SOTA models	97.1	**85.66, 81.71**	93.15	**96.09**	81.82
fastHan base trained separately	97.15	80.2, 75.12	94.27	92.2	80.3
fastHan base trained jointly	97.27	81.22, 76.71	94.88	94.33	82.86
fastHan large trained jointly	**97.41**	85.52, 81.38	**95.66**	95.50	**83.82**

Table 1: The results of fastHan's accuracy result. The score of CWS is the average of 10 corpora. When training dependency parsing separately, the biaffine parser use the same architecture as Yan et al. (2020). SOTA models are best-performing work we know for each task. They came from Huang et al. (2019), Yan et al. (2020), Meng et al. (2019), Li et al. (2020) in order. Li et al. (2020) uses lexicon to enhance the model.

user lexicon to enhance fastHan's performance in specific domains.

4.2 Transferability Test

Segmentation Tool	Weibo Test Set
`jieba`	83.58
`SnowNLP`	79.65
`THULAC`	86.65
`LTP-4.0`	92.05
`fastHan`	**93.38**
`fastHan(fine-tuned)`	**96.64**

Table 2: Transfer test for fastHan, using span F metric. We use the test set of Weibo, which has 8092 samples. For LTP-4.0, we use the base version, which has the best performance among their models.

For an NLP toolkit designed for the open domain, the ability of processing samples not in the training corpus is very important. We perform the transfer test on Weibo (Qiu et al., 2016), which has no overlap with our training data. Samples in Weibo[5] come from the Internet, and they are complex enough to test the model's transferability. We choose to test on CWS because nearly all Chinese NLP tools have this feature. We choose popular toolkits as the contrast, including Jieba[6], THULAC[7], SnowNLP[8] and LTP-4.0[9]. We also perform a test of fine-tuning using the training set of Weibo.

The results are shown in Table 2. As a off the shelf model, FastHan outperforms jieba, SnowNLP, and THULAC a lot. LTP-4.0 (Che et al., 2020) is another technical route for multi-task Chinese NLP, which is released after the first release of fastHan. However, FastHan still outperforms LTP with a much smaller model (262MB versus 492MB). The result proves fastHan is robust to new samples, and the fine-tuning feature allows fastHan to better be adapted to new criteria.

4.3 Speed Test

Models	Dependency Parsing CPU, GPU	Other Tasks CPU, GPU
`fastHan base`	25, 22	55, 111
`fastHan large`	14, 21	28, 97

Table 3: Speed test for fastHan. The numbers in the table represent the average number of sentences processed per second.

The speed test was performed on a personal computer configured with Intel Core i5-9400f + NVIDIA GeForce GTX 1660ti. The test was conducted on the first 800 sentences of the CTB CWS corpus, with an average of 45.2 characters per sentence and a batch size of 8.

The results are shown in Table 3. Dependency parsing runs slower, and the other tasks run at about the same speed. The base model with GPU performs poorly in dependency parsing because dependency parsing requires a lot of CPU calculations, and the acceleration effect of GPU is less than the burden of information transfer.

5 Conclusion

In this paper, we presented fastHan, a BERT-based toolkit for CWS, NER, POS, and dependency parsing in Chinese NLP. After our optimization, fastHan has the characteristics of high accuracy, small size, strong transferability, and ease of use.

In the future, we will continue to improve the fastHan with better performance, more features and more efficient learning methods, such as meta-learning (Ke et al., 2021).

[5]https://github.com/FudanNLP/NLPCC-WordSeg-Weibo

[6]https://github.com/fxsjy/jieba

[7]https://github.com/thunlp/THULAC

[8]https://github.com/isnowfy/snownlp

[9]https://github.com/HIT-SCIR/ltp

Acknowledgements

This work was supported by the National Key Research and Development Program of China (No. 2020AAA0106700), National Natural Science Foundation of China (No. 62022027) and Major Scientific Research Project of Zhejiang Lab (No. 2019KD0AD01).

References

Wanxiang Che, Yunlong Feng, Libo Qin, and Ting Liu. 2020. N-ltp: A open-source neural chinese language technology platform with pretrained models. *arXiv preprint arXiv:2009.11616*.

Xinchi Chen, Xipeng Qiu, and Xuanjing Huang. 2017a. A feature-enriched neural model for joint chinese word segmentation and part-of-speech tagging. In *Proceedings of the Twenty-Sixth International Joint Conference on Artificial Intelligence, IJCAI-17*, pages 3960–3966.

Xinchi Chen, Xipeng Qiu, Chenxi Zhu, Pengfei Liu, and Xuanjing Huang. 2015. Long short-term memory neural networks for chinese word segmentation. In *Proceedings of the Conference on Empirical Methods in Natural Language Processing*, pages 1197–1206.

Xinchi Chen, Zhan Shi, Xipeng Qiu, and XuanJing Huang. 2017b. Adversarial multi-criteria learning for chinese word segmentation. In *Proceedings of the 55th Annual Meeting of the Association for Computational Linguistics (Volume 1: Long Papers)*, pages 1193–1203.

Jacob Devlin, Ming-Wei Chang, Kenton Lee, and Kristina Toutanova. 2018. Bert: Pre-training of deep bidirectional transformers for language understanding. *arXiv preprint arXiv:1810.04805*.

Timothy Dozat and Christopher D Manning. 2016. Deep biaffine attention for neural dependency parsing. *arXiv preprint arXiv:1611.01734*.

Thomas Emerson. 2005. The second international chinese word segmentation bakeoff. In *Proceedings of the fourth SIGHAN workshop on Chinese language Processing*.

Weipeng Huang, Xingyi Cheng, Kunlong Chen, Taifeng Wang, and Wei Chu. 2019. Toward fast and accurate neural chinese word segmentation with multi-criteria learning. *arXiv preprint arXiv:1903.04190*.

Guangjin Jin and Xiao Chen. 2008. The fourth international chinese language processing bakeoff: Chinese word segmentation, named entity recognition and chinese pos tagging. In *Proceedings of the sixth SIGHAN workshop on Chinese language processing*.

Zhen Ke, Liang Shi, Songtao Sun, Erli Meng, Bin Wang, and Xipeng Qiu. 2021. Pre-training with meta learning for Chinese word segmentation. In *Proceedings of the 2021 Conference of the North American Chapter of the Association for Computational Linguistics: Human Language Technologies*, pages 5514–5523, Online. Association for Computational Linguistics.

John Lafferty, Andrew McCallum, and Fernando CN Pereira. 2001. Conditional random fields: Probabilistic models for segmenting and labeling sequence data. In *ICML*.

Xiaonan Li, Hang Yan, Xipeng Qiu, and Xuanjing Huang. 2020. FLAT: Chinese NER using flat-lattice transformer. In *Proceedings of the 58th Annual Meeting of the Association for Computational Linguistics*, pages 6836–6842, Online. Association for Computational Linguistics.

Yuxian Meng, Wei Wu, Fei Wang, Xiaoya Li, Ping Nie, Fan Yin, Muyu Li, Qinghong Han, Xiaofei Sun, and Jiwei Li. 2019. Glyce: Glyph-vectors for chinese character representations. In *Advances in Neural Information Processing Systems*, pages 2746–2757.

Xipeng Qiu, Peng Qian, and Zhan Shi. 2016. Overview of the NLPCC-ICCPOL 2016 shared task: Chinese word segmentation for micro-blog texts. In *Proceedings of The Fifth Conference on Natural Language Processing and Chinese Computing & The Twenty Fourth International Conference on Computer Processing of Oriental Languages*.

Xipeng Qiu, TianXiang Sun, Yige Xu, Yunfan Shao, Ning Dai, and Xuanjing Huang. 2020. Pre-trained models for natural language processing: A survey. *SCIENCE CHINA Technological Sciences*, 63(10):1872–1897.

Ashish Vaswani, Noam Shazeer, Niki Parmar, Jakob Uszkoreit, Llion Jones, Aidan N Gomez, Łukasz Kaiser, and Illia Polosukhin. 2017. Attention is all you need. In *Advances in neural information processing systems*, pages 5998–6008.

William Yang Wang, Lingpeng Kong, Kathryn Mazaitis, and William Cohen. 2014. Dependency parsing for weibo: An efficient probabilistic logic programming approach. In *Proceedings of the 2014 conference on empirical methods in natural language processing (EMNLP)*, pages 1152–1158.

Pak-kwong Wong and Chorkin Chan. 1996. Chinese word segmentation based on maximum matching and word binding force. In *Proceedings of the 16th Conference on Computational Linguistics - Volume 1*, COLING '96, page 200–203, USA. Association for Computational Linguistics.

Canwen Xu, Wangchunshu Zhou, Tao Ge, Furu Wei, and Ming Zhou. 2020. Bert-of-theseus: Compressing bert by progressive module replacing. *arXiv preprint arXiv:2002.02925*.

Naiwen Xue, Fei Xia, Fu-Dong Chiou, and Marta Palmer. 2005. The penn chinese treebank: Phrase structure annotation of a large corpus. *Natural language engineering*, 11(2):207.

Hang Yan, Xipeng Qiu, and Xuanjing Huang. 2020. A graph-based model for joint chinese word segmentation and dependency parsing. *Transactions of the Association for Computational Linguistics*, 8:78–92.

Meishan Zhang, Yue Zhang, Wanxiang Che, and Ting Liu. 2014. Type-supervised domain adaptation for joint segmentation and pos-tagging. In *Proceedings of the 14th Conference of the European Chapter of the Association for Computational Linguistics*, pages 588–597.

Yu Zhang, Zhenghua Li, Houquan Zhou, and Min Zhang. 2020. Is pos tagging necessary or even helpful for neural dependency parsing? *arXiv preprint arXiv:2003.03204*.

Erase and Rewind: Manual Correction of NLP Output through a Web Interface

Valentino Frasnelli, Lorenzo Bocchi
Dept. of Psychology and Cognitive Science
University of Trento
Rovereto (Trento), Italy
[name.surname]@studenti.unitn.it

Alessio Palmero Aprosio
Digital Humanities Unit
Fondazione Bruno Kessler
Trento, Italy
aprosio@fbk.eu

Abstract

In this paper, we present Tintful, an NLP annotation software that can be used both to manually annotate texts and to fix mistakes in NLP pipelines, such as Stanford CoreNLP. Using a paradigm similar to wiki-like systems, a user who notices some wrong annotation can easily fix it and submit the resulting (and right) entry back to the tool developers. Moreover, Tintful can be used to easily annotate data from scratch. The input documents do not need to be in a particular format: starting from the plain text, the sentences are first annotated with CoreNLP, then the user can edit the annotations and submit everything back through a user-friendly interface.

A video showing Tintful and its feature is available on YouTube.[1]

1 Introduction

In the last years, NLP tools are being more and more used in tasks such as textual inference, machine translation, hate speech detection (Socher et al., 2012). Most of these tasks rely on machine learning systems trained on large amounts of data, which have been manually labeled by annotators, often domain experts. In particular, recent deep learning algorithms are more accurate, but they need more data for training, making the data collection a major challenge for the NLP community.

When the annotation task does not require a specialised competence, one can use a platform such as Amazon Mechanical Turk (AMT),[2] that enables the distribution of low-skill but difficult-to-automate tasks to a network of humans, who could work in parallel, when and where they prefer.

However, not all NLP assignments can be solved by non-experts because they may require background knowledge or linguistic expertise. For these tasks, expert annotators should be hired and receive a specific training, which is time-consuming and can become costly.

A similar problem arises when a known task has to be ported to another domain, and existing tools turn out to have a poor accuracy, because the original training data does not include annotated instances from that domain (Ben-David et al., 2007). For example, the performance of standard NLP tools (part-of-speech taggers, dependency parsers, and so on) is severely degraded on tweets for this very reason (Ritter et al., 2011). One of the solutions to this set of problems would be to make NLP tools more similar to wiki-like systems, where a user who notices some wrong annotation can easily fix it and submit the resulting (and right) entry back to the tool developers, so that they can add the instance to the training examples and re-generate the model.

This is basically the paradigm already used for active learning (Settles, 2011) which uses "humans in the loop" to increase the accuracy of a system, by including in the workflow a targeted correction of instances that are misclassified (Fan et al., 2017). As someone said way back in 1969: "Computers are incredibly fast, accurate and stupid. On the other hand, a well trained operator as compared with a computer is incredibly slow, inaccurate and brilliant". (Various Authors, 1969)

To obtain a seamless integration between automatic classification and human correction, we need to develop NLP tools that are accessible through a user-friendly interface (Holzinger, 2013), easing the interaction between non-technical persons and the underlying technology.

In this paper, we present Tintful, a working example of the described paradigm, an interface that combines the output of Stanford CoreNLP (Manning et al., 2014) with a newly created annotation tool that allows the user to edit and fix the output

[1] https://youtu.be/iFDCbtfWdTg
[2] http://www.mturk.com/

Proceedings of the Joint Conference of the 59th Annual Meeting of the Association for Computational Linguistics and the 11th International Joint Conference on Natural Language Processing: System Demonstrations, pages 107–113, August 1st - August 6th, 2021.

data, in a wiki-like style. The user (registered or not) can edit the tokens, the lemmas, the parts of speech, the dependency trees and the named entities (persons, locations, organizations). Thanks to an API released with the web interface, the resulting annotation can be stored for later use (for example, the software retraining), so that users can contribute to improving the system performance on specific tasks or domains of interest.

Compared to other similar tools (see Section 2), Tintful has some main strengths:

- There is no need to pre-process the data one wants to annotate. The user can easily enter the raw text into the system and directly edit the output annotation.
- There is no need for an expert to setup the environment. Just install the tool and start to annotate.
- "Casual" users can contribute to the annotation by submitting their anonymous annotations to the system.
- The annotated data is immediately available just by querying the database, and can be used in an incremental learning framework (Schlimmer and Fisher, 1986).[3]

We believe that this paradigm may foster the adoption of NLP tools in domains and settings that so far have not taken full advantage of text processing. For example, social scientists or humanities scholars would have the possibility to correct the output of a parser or NER trained on news, which may perform poorly on other types of texts, directly through the tool interface, making it easier to adapt the model to new domains and genres.

Finally, the whole tool is released open source and available on Github (see Section 7).

2 Related work

Some of the available programs for the manual annotation of texts are generic and can be configured and used for a great variety of tasks. These are usually powerful but need some work for configuration. Some other, on the contrary, have been developed for a particular purpose, and usually are easier to launch and configure.

WebAnno[4] (Eckart de Castilho et al., 2016) is a general purpose web-based annotation tool for a wide range of linguistic annotations and belongs to the former category. It is multi-user and supports different roles to guarantee a quality check of the annotated data.

INCEpTION[5] (Klie et al., 2018) is an open-source and multi-user text annotation platform developed at the Technische Universität Darmstadt. It is general-purpose and can be configured to perform a number of annotation tasks.

Similarly, Doccano[6] (Nakayama et al., 2018) provides annotation features for text classification, sequence labeling and sequence to sequence tasks.

Regarding specifically the annotation of dependency graphs, there several tools that help researchers to manage complex output formats such as CoNLL-U.[7] For instance, ConlluEditor[8] (Heinecke, 2019) is an actively maintained tool which facilitates the editing of syntactic relations and morphological features of files in CoNLL-U format. Similarly, UD-Annotatrix[9] (Tyers et al., 2018) is a language-independent tool for editing dependency trees according to the guidelines established by the Universal Dependencies project. TrUDucer[10] (Hennig and Köhn, 2017) is a software for transforming dependency treebanks from one schema to another, especially to CoNLL-U.

Finally, Arborator[11] is an annotation tool for dependency trees that allows users to perform collaborative work. The tool has a specific focus on HCI aspects, since most of the actions can be done using mouse drag and drop.

In this paper, we propose a tool that is different from all the ones described above. With Tintful the user does not need the data to be in a particular format: starting from the plain text, the sentences are first annotated with Stanford CoreNLP, then the user can edit the annotations and submit everything back to the server.

[3]This part is not included in Tintful out-of-the-box, yet. For now, it can be done by external tool by a machine learning expert. We plan to add a feature to make it easy also for non-expert users in the future, see Section 8.

[4]https://webanno.github.io/

[5]https://inception-project.github.io/

[6]https://github.com/doccano/doccano

[7]https://universaldependencies.org/format.html

[8]https://github.com/Orange-OpenSource/conllueditor

[9]https://github.com/jonorthwash/ud-annotatrix

[10]http://nats.gitlab.io/truducer/

[11]https://arborator.ilpga.fr/

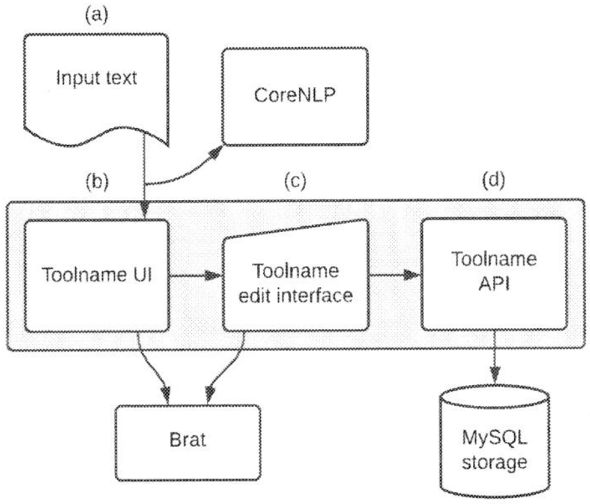

Figure 1: A graph representation of the Tintful architecture.

3 Existing components

Tintful is mainly based on two existing pieces of software: Stanford CoreNLP and Brat.

3.1 Stanford CoreNLP

Stanford CoreNLP (Manning et al., 2014) is an open-source framework written in Java that provides most of the common Natural Language Processing tasks out-of-the-box for several languages. The framework provides also an easy interface to extend the annotation to new tasks and/or languages.

Tintful is agnostic w.r.t. the language. One can use the plain Stanford CoreNLP software with Tintful if they need to annotate texts in English, German, Spanish, and so on. We processed Italian texts and therefore used TINT (Palmero Aprosio and Moretti, 2018), a language-specific extension whose output is compatible with CoreNLP.

3.2 BRAT

The BRAT Rapid Annotation Tool[12] (Stenetorp et al., 2012) is a web-based tool for text annotation and is developed at University of Manchester. Although its last version is quite old (November 2012), a large number of research organization still uses it, since it is very intuitive and can be used also for visualization-only (the official demo pages of Stanford Stanza[13] (Qi et al., 2020) and CoreNLP both use it). In Tintful, Brat is used for the graphical annotation of the syntactic dependencies. The main issue of this library is that it is not responsive, meaning that it is not optimized for mobile phones and tablets. Therefore, we slightly modified it to make Tintful usable on most devices.

4 Tintful architecture

The architecture of Tintful is represented in Figure 1.

1. First, the user inserts a text (a) in the Tintful interface (Figure 6).

2. The NLP pipeline (Stanford CoreNLP or compatible variants) is then launched, using the text as input.

3. The resulting JSON is parsed by Tintful and shown in the UI (b). In this screen, the user can browse through all the annotation layers (tokens, lemma, POS, dependency parsing, NER, and so on). See Figure 7. Additional modules not included in CoreNLP are shown, if the corresponding annotation is present in the JSON file. Among these modules, the Tint readability module (Palmero Aprosio and Moretti, 2018), that estimates the difficulty level of the document and calculates some indexes, such as lexical density, semantic richness, Flesch score (Gulpease for Italian), and so on.

4. If the annotation contains one or more mistakes, the user can enter the edit mode (c) to fix them; otherwise, the annotation can be saved as is (go to step 6). See, for example, Figure 2.

5. The edit screen shows the parsing results to the user sentence by sentence. One can edit every aspect of the annotation: tokens, lemma, POS, dependency labels, dependency tree hierarchy, NER).

6. Once the editing is finished, the user can save the resulting annotation, that is stored in the server (d).

7. If the user is logged in when submitting the edited data, they can recover the annotation and edit/delete it (Figure 8).

8. Finally, the annotated data can be exported and downloaded in CoNLL-U format.

[12]http://brat.nlplab.org/
[13]http://stanza.run/

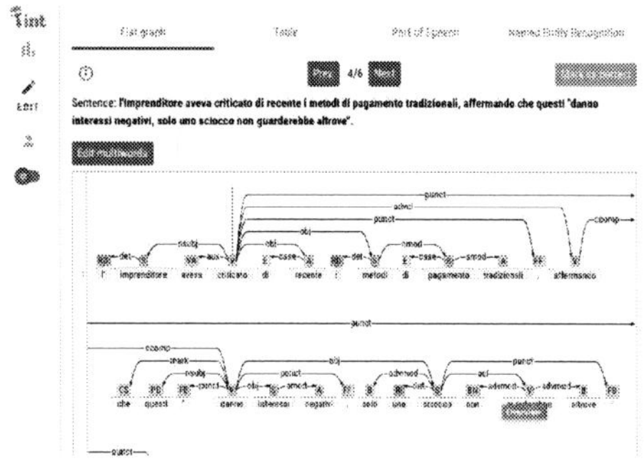

Figure 2: The syntactic dependency editing interface using Brat.

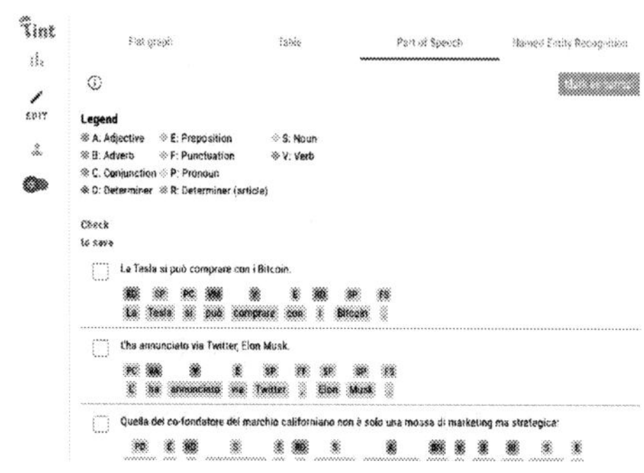

Figure 3: The editing interface for POS.

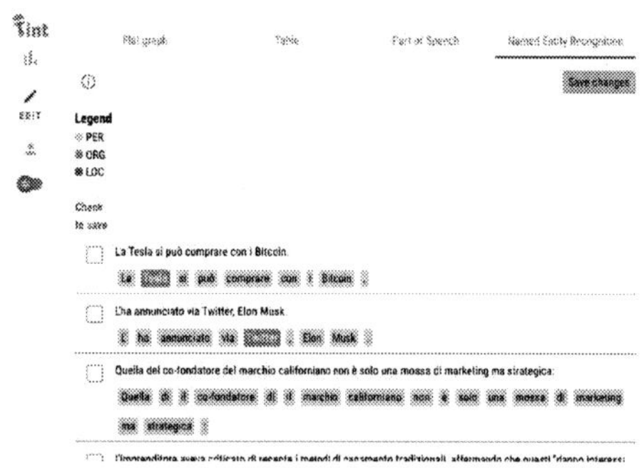

Figure 4: Interface for editing named entities.

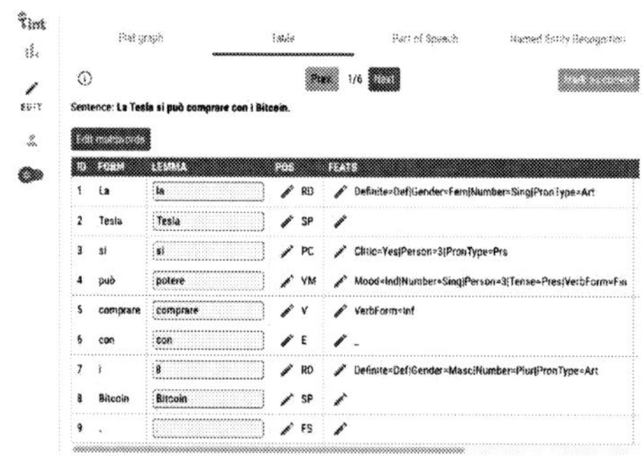

Figure 5: Editing the text information using a tabular view.

Figures 2, 3, 4, and 5 show some screenshots of the annotation interface. Manual annotations can be performed both by occasional and registered users, so that the administrator knows which data belongs to whom.

5 Additional features

5.1 Modular structure

When running Tintful, one can edit everything that normally is included in the CoNLL-U format (see Section 2): token, lemma, POS, morphological features, syntactic dependency hierarchy and labels. There is also room for the miscellaneous data (last field of the CoNLL-U file) and the named entities, that are not included in the format but can be added with our interface. It can happen that the casual user only edits some parts of the text (for example, the POS or the NER, without even touching the syntactic tree). When saving the data, Tintful select only the parts where the user did some edits. If a sentence is already correct and therefore is not edited by the user, no information is sent to the server. The user can manually force the sending, by clicking the "already correct" button (see, for instance, Figures 2, 3, and 5.

5.2 User management

The administrator can create users (with login and password), so that the data sent by that user can be identified. In addition, the registered user can retrieve the annotated sentences and edit them again. When multiple submissions occur, the server will merge the different parts in a smart way. For instance, if the user first edits the syntactic tree of sentence 5 and then it loads it again editing only the POS, the system will merge the edited POS into the syntactic structure. If the same user only edit POS for sentence 2, only the POS information is saved, ignoring the syntactic tree.

5.3 Contextual help

Since Tintful is meant to be used by non-expert users, every screen of the tool provides information buttons, where a quick documentation on how to use that screen is provided (see Figure 10).

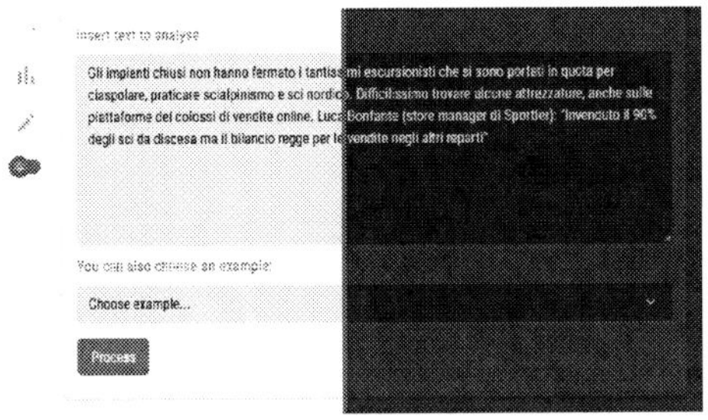

Figure 6: The input text screen of Tintful (light and dark).

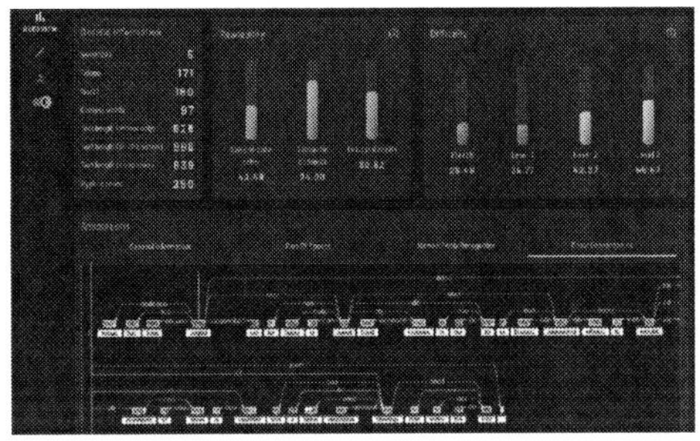

Figure 7: Visualization interface for an English text.

Figure 8: The edit history of Tintful.

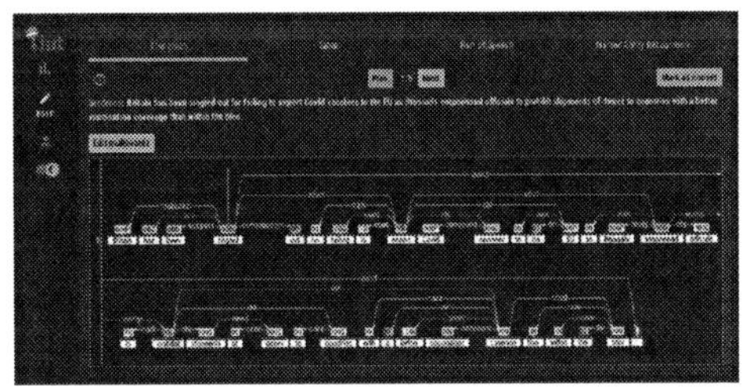

Figure 9: An example of the editing interface for an English text.

5.4 Language independence

Tintful is agnostic with respect to the language of the texts. The whole architecture is based (for now, see Section 8) on the Stanford CoreNLP json output. A developer can easily adapt the interface to work with any pipeline that work on top of CoreNLP or that can give the same format.

6 User experience

In developing Tintful, a particular attention has been paid to the interface, given that annotators performing linguistic tasks need to be focused and typically spend a lot of time interacting with the tool.

6.1 Human-Computer interaction

Some tools for linguistic annotations are very generic and can be configured for a potentially infinite set of guidelines. As a side effect of that flexibility, they sometime suffer from slowness in the practical use.

Tintful, instead, is optimized for a small list of possible annotations (syntactic tree, NER, part-of-speech), and therefore the interaction with the user is optimized, to spend as little time as possible for the annotation.

As an example, the NER annotation can be performed just by clicking on the word and looping between the different labels. Since there are only four possibility (PER, LOC, ORG, O), this action can be done very quickly.

On the contrary, the list of tags for part-of-speech is very long, therefore an intermediate modal screen with a dropdown menu is more practical.

6.2 Design and accessibility

The design is inspired by Material,[14] a set of guidelines, components, and tools developed by Google that support the best practices of user interface design.

The interface also satisfies the most common accessibility guidelines and it is responsive, therefore all the annotation steps can be performed on a tablet or a smartphone.

6.3 Dark mode vs. light mode

The high density of the data in the interface may lead to eyestrain, therefore we add a button that switches the interface between dark and light. The dark mode makes it more comfortable for users to use their devices outside the light hours or in environments with bad lighting conditions (Eisfeld and Kristallovich, 2020; Kim et al., 2019). In addition, reading white text from a black screen or tablet

[14]https://material.io/

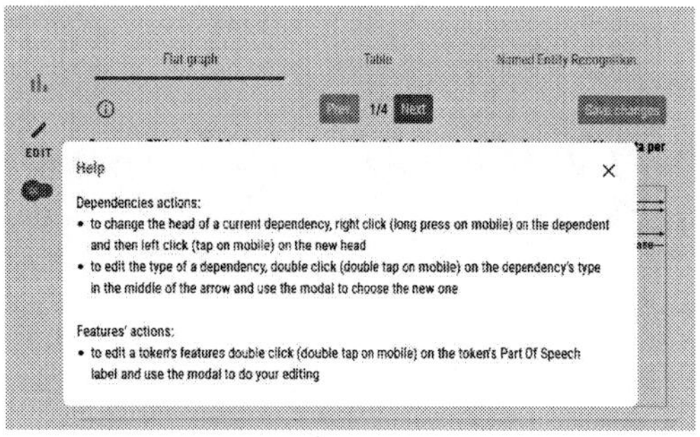

Figure 10: An example of contextual help.

may be a way to inhibit myopia (Aleman et al., 2018). When there is enough light, instead, one can have better reading performances on a white background (Piepenbrock et al., 2013). For all these reasons, users can switch independently between the two modes using the button in the Tintful interface. Figure 6 shows an example of the input screen of Tintful in light and dark mode.

6.4 Flat interface

Although in general there is criticism around using flat design for everything (Burmistrov et al., 2015), past studies showed that flat design allows expert users to execute their task faster (Spiliotopoulos et al., 2018). On the contrary, skeuomorphism[15] visually distracts users from intended targets. We therefore decide to use a flat design interface for Tintful: on one side, we want our interface to be as simple as possible; on the other side, NLP is a specialized discipline and we expect our users to have confidence with such tools.

7 Tintful release

The web interface of Tintful is written using VueJS.[16] and the structure of the website is built with Tailwind CSS.[17] The API is written in php and needs a machine with at least version 7 of the interpreter and MySQL server installed. It must be configured to work in a web server (such as Apache or Nginx).

The whole Tintful package is available on GitHub[18] and released under the Apache license.

[15] In graphical user interface design, skeuomorphism is the term describing interface objects that mimic their real-world counterparts in how they appear and how the user can interact with them.

[16] `https://vuejs.org/`

[17] `https://tailwindcss.com/`

[18] `https://github.com/dhfbk/tintful`

8 Conclusions and Future Work

In this paper, we present Tintful, an NLP annotation software that can be used both to annotate texts from scratch and to fix mistakes in NLP pipelines. Differently from other similar tools, data do not need to be in a particular format: starting from plain text, the sentences are first annotated with Stanford CoreNLP, then the user can edit the annotations and submit everything back to the server.

In the future, we will extend the tool to accept more input formats, so that Tintful can work with software different from CoreNLP, such as SpaCy (Honnibal et al., 2020) and UDPipe (Straka, 2018).

In addition, we want to improve the user management part, by creating an admin interface to simplify the user creation. We also want to add the login through external services, such as Google, Github, Facebook, and so on. For registered users, this means that they do not need to remember the password. For casual users, this allows them to review already submitted annotations.

Finally, we are integrating Tintful with the CoreNLP scripts that perform the training of the models (in particular for part-of-speech, dependency parsing and named-entities recognition), to obtain a fullly automatic incremental learning pipeline.

References

Andrea C. Aleman, Min Wang, and Frank Schaeffel. 2018. Reading and myopia: Contrast polarity matters. *Scientific Reports*, 8(1):10840.

Shai Ben-David, John Blitzer, Koby Crammer, Fernando Pereira, et al. 2007. Analysis of representations for domain adaptation. *Advances in neural information processing systems*, 19:137.

Ivan Burmistrov, Tatiana Zlokazova, Anna Izmalkova, and Anna Leonova. 2015. Flat design vs traditional design: Comparative experimental study. In *Human-Computer Interaction – INTERACT 2015*, pages 106–114, Cham. Springer International Publishing.

Richard Eckart de Castilho, Éva Mújdricza-Maydt, Seid Muhie Yimam, Silvana Hartmann, Iryna Gurevych, Anette Frank, and Chris Biemann. 2016. A web-based tool for the integrated annotation of semantic and syntactic structures. In *Proceedings of the Workshop on Language Technology Resources and Tools for Digital Humanities (LT4DH)*, pages 76–84, Osaka, Japan. The COLING 2016 Organizing Committee.

Henriette Eisfeld and Felix Kristallovich. 2020. The rise of dark mode: A qualitative study of an emerging user interface design trend.

Yang Fan, Fei Tian, Tao Qin, Jiang Bian, and Tie-Yan Liu. 2017. Learning what data to learn. *arXiv preprint arXiv:1702.08635*.

Johannes Heinecke. 2019. ConlluEditor: a fully graphical editor for Universal dependencies treebank files. In *Universal Dependencies Workshop 2019*, Paris.

Felix Hennig and Arne Köhn. 2017. Dependency schema transformation with tree transducers. In *Proceedings of the first Workshop on Universal Dependencies (22 May, Göteborg)*. Universität Hamburg.

Andreas Holzinger. 2013. Human-computer interaction and knowledge discovery (hci-kdd): What is the benefit of bringing those two fields to work together? In *Availability, Reliability, and Security in Information Systems and HCI*, pages 319–328, Berlin, Heidelberg. Springer Berlin Heidelberg.

Matthew Honnibal, Ines Montani, Sofie Van Landeghem, and Adriane Boyd. 2020. spaCy: Industrial-strength Natural Language Processing in Python.

Kangsoo Kim, Austin Erickson, Alexis Lambert, Gerd Bruder, and Greg Welch. 2019. Effects of dark mode on visual fatigue and acuity in optical see-through head-mounted displays. In *Symposium on Spatial User Interaction*, SUI '19, New York, NY, USA. Association for Computing Machinery.

Jan-Christoph Klie, Michael Bugert, Beto Boullosa, Richard Eckart de Castilho, and Iryna Gurevych. 2018. The inception platform: Machine-assisted and knowledge-oriented interactive annotation. In *Proceedings of the 27th International Conference on Computational Linguistics: System Demonstrations*, pages 5–9. Association for Computational Linguistics.

Christopher D. Manning, Mihai Surdeanu, John Bauer, Jenny Finkel, Steven J. Bethard, and David McClosky. 2014. The Stanford CoreNLP natural language processing toolkit. In *Association for Computational Linguistics (ACL) System Demonstrations*, pages 55–60.

Hiroki Nakayama, Takahiro Kubo, Junya Kamura, Yasufumi Taniguchi, and Xu Liang. 2018. doccano: Text annotation tool for human. Software available from https://github.com/doccano/doccano.

Alessio Palmero Aprosio and Giovanni Moretti. 2018. Tint 2.0: an all-inclusive suite for nlp in italian. In *Proceedings of the Fifth Italian Conference on Computational Linguistics CLiC-it*, volume 10, page 12.

C. Piepenbrock, S. Mayr, I. Mund, and A. Buchner. 2013. Positive display polarity is advantageous for both younger and older adults. *Ergonomics*, 56(7):1116–1124.

Peng Qi, Yuhao Zhang, Yuhui Zhang, Jason Bolton, and Christopher D. Manning. 2020. Stanza: A Python natural language processing toolkit for many human languages. In *Proceedings of the 58th Annual Meeting of the Association for Computational Linguistics: System Demonstrations*.

Alan Ritter, Sam Clark, Oren Etzioni, et al. 2011. Named entity recognition in tweets: an experimental study. In *Proceedings of the 2011 conference on empirical methods in natural language processing*, pages 1524–1534.

Jeffrey Schlimmer and Doug Fisher. 1986. A case study of incremental concept induction. pages 496–501.

Burr Settles. 2011. From theories to queries: Active learning in practice. In *Active Learning and Experimental Design workshop In conjunction with AISTATS 2010*, volume 16 of *Proceedings of Machine Learning Research*, pages 1–18, Sardinia, Italy. JMLR Workshop and Conference Proceedings.

Richard Socher, Yoshua Bengio, and Christopher D. Manning. 2012. Deep learning for nlp (without magic). In *Tutorial Abstracts of ACL 2012*, ACL '12, page 5, USA. Association for Computational Linguistics.

Konstantinos Spiliotopoulos, Maria Rigou, and Spiros Sirmakessis. 2018. A comparative study of skeuomorphic and flat design from a ux perspective. *Multimodal Technologies and Interaction*, 2(2):31.

Pontus Stenetorp, Sampo Pyysalo, Goran Topić, Tomoko Ohta, Sophia Ananiadou, and Jun'ichi Tsujii. 2012. brat: a web-based tool for NLP-assisted text annotation. In *Proceedings of the Demonstrations at the 13th Conference of the European Chapter of the Association for Computational Linguistics*, pages 102–107, Avignon, France. Association for Computational Linguistics.

Milan Straka. 2018. UDPipe 2.0 prototype at CoNLL 2018 UD shared task. In *Proceedings of the CoNLL 2018 Shared Task: Multilingual Parsing from Raw Text to Universal Dependencies*, pages 197–207, Brussels, Belgium. Association for Computational Linguistics.

Francis M. Tyers, Mariya Sheyanova, and Jonathan North Washington. 2018. Ud annotatrix: An annotation tool for universal dependencies. In *Proceedings of the 16th International Workshop on Treebanks and Linguistic Theories (TLT16)*, pages 10–17.

Various Authors. 1969. *Advances in Instrumentation, Vol. 24: Proceedings of the 24th Annual ISA Conference, Houston, Oktober 27-30, 1969*. pt. 4. Instrument Soc. of America.

ESRA: Explainable Scientific Research Assistant

Pollawat Hongwimol[1*], Peeranuth Kehasukcharoen[1*], Pasit Laohawarutchai[1*], Piyawat Lertvittayakumjorn[2], Aik Beng Ng[3], Zhangsheng Lai[3], Timothy Liu[3], Peerapon Vateekul[1†]

[1] Department of Computer Engineering, Faculty of Engineering, Chulalongkorn University, Thailand
[2] Department of Computing, Imperial College London, United Kingdom
[3] NVIDIA

{6030400021,6030416021,6031039321}@student.chula.ac.th
pl1515@ic.ac.uk, {aikbengn, zlai, timothyl}@nvidia.com
peerapon.v@chula.ac.th

Abstract

We introduce Explainable Scientific Research Assistant (ESRA), a literature discovery platform that augments search results with relevant details and explanations, aiding users in understanding more about their queries and the returned papers beyond existing literature search systems. Enabled by a knowledge graph we extracted from abstracts of 23k papers on the arXiv's cs.CL category, ESRA provides three main features: explanation (for why a paper is returned to the user), list of facts (that are relevant to the query), and graph visualization (drawing connections between the query and each paper with surrounding related entities). The experimental results with humans involved show that ESRA can accelerate the users' search process with paper explanations and helps them better explore the landscape of the topics of interest by exploiting the underlying knowledge graph. We provide the ESRA web application at http://esra.cp.eng.chula.ac.th/.[1]

1 Introduction

Existing literature search platforms mostly present metadata of papers as search results, and this requires users to read the entire abstracts to understand the brief contents of the returned papers. The users then need to reflect on the knowledge of the papers themselves so as to decide which keywords they should search next. Therefore, it is time-consuming to gradually expand their understanding of the field using existing platforms.

Meanwhile, research on analyzing scientific literature has been getting more attention due to the extremely large number of new papers published every day (Williams et al., 2014; Khan et al., 2017). Also, many of them are freely accessible online and the number is still rising (Munroe, 2013). These lead to several frameworks that aim for extracting knowledge (i.e., scientific concepts and their relations) from scientific documents and representing them as a Knowledge Graph (KG) (Luan et al., 2018; Eberts and Ulges, 2019). However, to the best of our knowledge, most of the existing literature platforms have not yet leveraged such extracted knowledge graphs, but only the graph of metadata and hierarchical topics (Ammar et al., 2018; Sinha et al., 2015). So, they are not aware of relations among scientific entities in the papers (e.g., methods, models, and materials) resulting in an inability to provide insightful knowledge beyond a list of papers and abstracts.

In this paper, we develop Explainable Scientific Research Assistant (ESRA) – a literature discovery platform that utilizes a knowledge graph and modern Natural Language Processing (NLP) models to augment user experience. ESRA has three main features built around our extracted knowledge graph as illustrated partly in Figure 1. First, "the explanation feature" explains how the query and each returned paper are related. Second, "the fact list feature" suggests top-related keywords with their relationships to the query supporting exploration of related scientific concepts. Third, "the graph visualization feature" provides a subgraph illustrating related knowledge around the query and the returned papers. These features aim to help researchers quickly discover and understand a collection of literature they are looking for.

The strengths of the main features are demonstrated through a use case in Figure 1. Suppose users want to know about "BERT", they initially enter "BERT" as the search query. On the top of the result page, there is a fact list displayed along with the graph visualization, showing facts (keywords) related to BERT such as "BERT is a subtype of

* Equal contributions
† Corresponding author

[1] A brief demo of ESRA is available at https://youtu.be/2RC6d4IFgIw

Proceedings of the Joint Conference of the 59th Annual Meeting of the Association for Computational Linguistics and the 11th International Joint Conference on Natural Language Processing: System Demonstrations, pages 114–121, August 1st - August 6th, 2021.

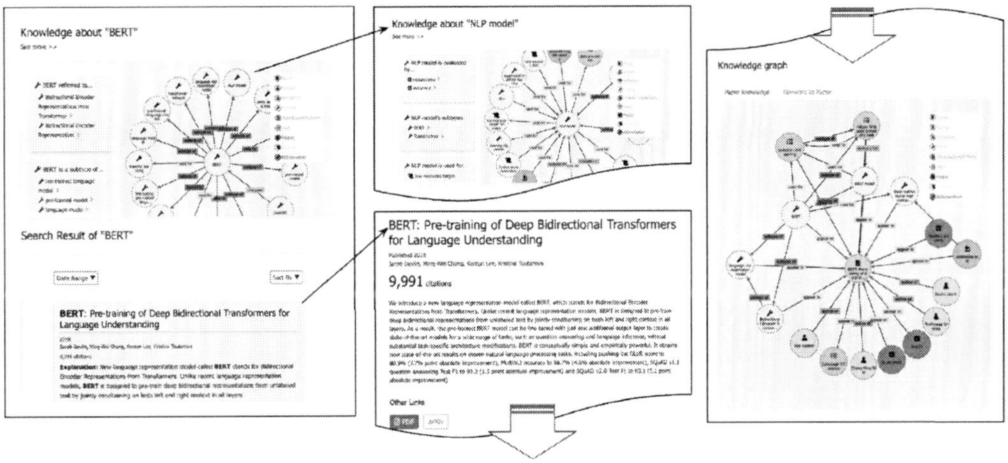

Figure 1: Searching scenario on the keyword "BERT" containing *(left)* the main result page, *(middle top)* routing to another keyword by clicking on the node, *(middle bottom)* meta data section of the paper page, *(right)* knowledge graph section of the paper page (continued from the middle bottom)

pre-trained language model" and "BERT is used for transfer learning". Users can navigate to pages of the related keywords conveniently by clicking the node names as shown in Figure 1 (middle-top). From the middle to the bottom of that page, there is a list of returned papers containing their metadata and explanations. For example, the explanation for the paper of RoBERTa (Liu et al., 2019) is "*We present a replication study of **BERT** pre-training (Devlin et al., 2019) that carefully measures the impact of many key hyperparameters and training data size. We find that **BERT** was significantly undertrained, and can match or exceed the performance of every model published after it.*" Users can click the paper title in order to redirect to the specific paper page which consists of all available metadata, knowledge graph visualization, references, and citations of the paper. With these features, users can quickly learn about the search query, check out related papers of their interest, and navigate to relevant concepts more conveniently.

2 Related Work

In this section, we present an overview of existing work related to ESRA along two topics, i.e., scientific knowledge extraction frameworks and scientific literature discovery platforms.

2.1 Scientific Knowledge Extraction Frameworks

In the past, research on information extraction (IE) for scientific texts focused mainly on citation relations (Sim et al., 2012; Kas, 2011) and unsupervised extraction (Gábor et al., 2016). With the arrival of the SemEval shared tasks 2017 and 2018 (Augenstein et al., 2017; Gábor et al., 2018), the associated datasets enabled the research on supervised and semi-supervised learning for entity and relation extraction task for scientific papers. Since then, many research papers on supervised scientific IE have emerged. For example, SpERT (Eberts and Ulges, 2019) performs entity extraction and relation extraction jointly using pre-trained Transformers. DyGIE++ (Wadden et al., 2019) also jointly addresses the two tasks with the event extraction task. Besides, Luan et al. (2018) added the coreference resolution task into their IE framework, called SciIE, and created the SciERC dataset to support coreference resolution between cross-sentence entities for more detailed relations. Our framework combines SpERT and SciIE to cover both entity/relation extraction and coreference resolution, i.e., using SpERT for the former task and SciIE for the latter task.

2.2 Scientific Literature Discovery Platforms

There are various modern literature discovery platforms such as ACM Digital Library[2], IEEE Xplore[3], Google Scholar[4], Microsoft Academic[5]

[2]https://dl.acm.org/
[3]https://ieeexplore.ieee.org/
[4]https://scholar.google.com/
[5]https://academic.microsoft.com/

Feature / Platform	Microsoft Academic	Semantic Scholar	ORKG	AceMap	ESRA (ours)
Scientific Knowledge Graph	✗	✓	✗	✗	✓
Metadata Graph	✓	✓	✓	✓	✓
Explanation	✗	✗	✗	✗	✓
Fact List	✗	✗	✗	✗	✓
Graph Visualization	✗	✗	✓	✓	✓

Table 1: A feature comparison of existing graph-based literature platforms and our ESRA system

(Sinha et al., 2015), AceMap[6] (Tan et al., 2016), ORKG[7] (Jaradeh et al., 2019), and Semantic Scholar[8] (Ammar et al., 2018). Most platforms are using the metadata of academic papers to rank and return results to their users. To the best of our knowledge, only Semantic Scholar uses scientific knowledge graph in their system. Table 1 compares prominent features of existing graph-based literature platforms to our ESRA system. We can see that the existing platforms focus on returning paper metadata as the search results without explaining why the papers are related to the query. In contrast, our ESRA system fills this gap by providing the explanations together with related scientific knowledge (via the fact list and the graph visualizations) to help the users better understand the query.

Besides the mentioned platforms, in the biomedical domain, there are many efforts to integrate knowledge bases into literature analysis systems. Similar to our fact list feature, Life-iNet (Ren et al., 2017) and BioTextQuest+ (Papanikolaou et al., 2014) are platforms that focus on exploring factual knowledge of a queried entity in the knowledge base and providing a list of supported documents. DeepLife (Ernst et al., 2016) and SetSearch+ (Shen et al., 2018) are entity-aware literature search engines that broaden results by expanding the query with related entities in the knowledge base. However, these platforms lack the ability to explain the relationship between the search query and the results. Our system uses the explanation and graph visualization feature to show the users how the query and the returned papers are related.

3 Explainable Scientific Research Assistant (ESRA)

Our goal is to create a scientific literature discovery platform that is explainable to users and helps them explore and expand knowledge more conveniently. This leads to the ESRA system with the following three main features, all of which leverage a knowledge graph we extracted from abstracts of the papers in our system.

Explanation: The explanation attached to each search result enables users to understand the reasons behind the recommendation of the system, i.e., why the paper is selected. The generated explanations for the same paper are dissimilar given different queries, making the explanations become specific to what the users want to know.

Fact list: For each query, ESRA displays related knowledge facts from the knowledge graph as a list for the users to explore. The goal of this feature is to aid users in having a better understanding of their search queries.

Graph visualization: Visualization gives users an understanding of the big picture of the relevant knowledge. In both the search result page and individual paper pages, the web application visualizes a subgraph of knowledge that is related to the search keyword and the papers, respectively.

To enable these three features, we implemented two main engines underlying ESRA as shown in Figure 2, including (1) a knowledge graph construction engine and (2) a web application engine. We will explain them and the overall system development in the next subsections.

3.1 Knowledge Graph Construction

Figure 2(a) shows the pipeline for extracting relations from scientific texts and constructing our knowledge graph. Given input texts (i.e., paper abstracts in our case), the pipeline works in three steps.

Step 1: Extraction The input abstracts are fed into an extractor which returns a list of extracted triples. The extractor consists of two models which

[6]https://www.acemap.info/
[7]https://www.orkg.org/
[8]https://www.semanticscholar.org/

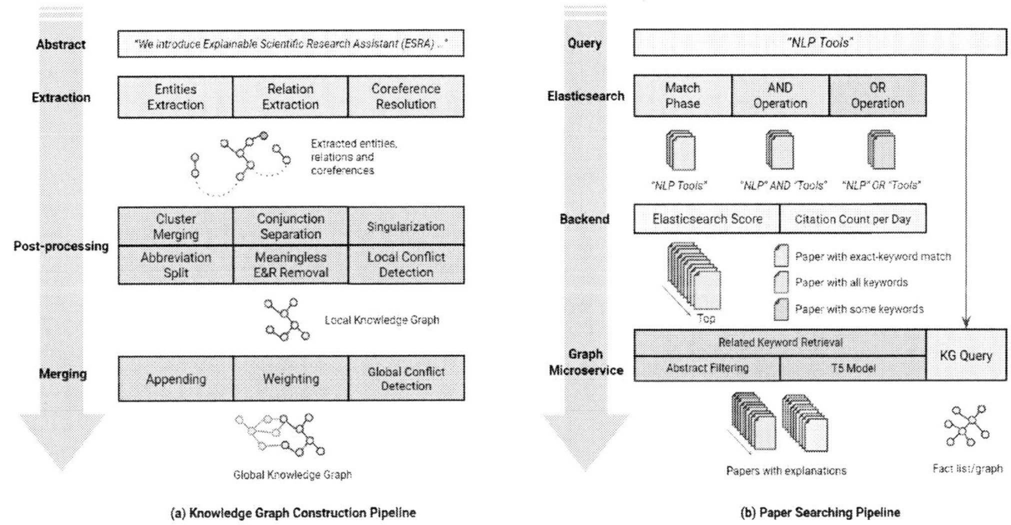

Figure 2: The two pipelines of ESRA: *(a)* Knowledge Graph Construction (section 3.1) and *(b)* Paper Searching for web application (section 3.2).

are SciIE (Luan et al., 2018) and SpERT (Eberts and Ulges, 2019). SciIE is a multi-task model that can perform named-entity recognition, relation extraction, and coreference resolution, whereas SpERT can only do the first two tasks but with better performance. Therefore, we combine the two models to be our extractor, using SciIE for coreference resolution and SpERT for entity and relation extraction, so as to achieve better performance across all the tasks.

Step 2: Post-processing The triples are then post-processed to clean duplicates and/or uninformative entities and relations to get the cleaned triples which form a local knowledge graph for each abstract. The post-processing includes *(i)* merging entities from the same coreference cluster, *(ii)* split entities with conjunction, *(iii)* converting plurals to singulars, *(iv)* relating abbreviations to the corresponding entities, *(v)* removing meaningless entities and relations and *(vi)* detecting conflicts against the knowledge graph ontology.

Step 3: Merging We insert the cleaned triples into the main knowledge graph and detect conflicts again to ensure that all comply with the ontology (e.g., no self-cycle or insensible relations). If the triple to be inserted already exists, its weight in the graph is then updated.

We use this pipeline to extract scientific knowledge from paper abstracts in the arXiv dataset (Clement et al., 2019), particularly in the Computation and Language category (cs.CL). At the end, our knowledge graph contains 242k entities and 1.67M relations. It consists of eight entity types and eleven relation types, the statistics of which are displayed in Table 2 and 3, respectively. Most of the entity types (excluding Abbreviation, Author, and Paper) and relation types (excluding appear_in, cite, related_to, and refer_to) are adopted from the SciERC dataset (Luan et al., 2018).

Note that this pipeline is optimized for a scenario with AI-related texts because the extraction models were initially trained on the SciERC dataset containing only AI-related documents (Luan et al., 2018). To extend this pipeline to other domains, we need to use an extractor that can effectively recognize entities and relations tailored for those domains. For example, to work on the life science domain, we should use an extractor that recognizes concepts of *drugs* and *diseases* rather than *tasks* and *methods* (Ren et al., 2017).

3.2 Web Application: Search, Rank, Explain, and Visualize

As shown in Figure 2(b), after receiving an input query from a user, we perform query expansion by using entity names from our knowledge graph that are similar to the user query according to the similarity score given by sentence-BERT embeddings (Reimers and Gurevych, 2019). Then, the system

Query Keyword	Related Keywords
machine translation	phrase-based system, neural network

Abstract

[1] Neural machine translation is a recently proposed approach to machine translation. **[2]** Unlike the traditional statistical machine translation, the neural machine translation aims at building a single neural network that can be jointly tuned to maximize the translation performance. **[3]** The models proposed recently for neural machine translation often belong to a family of encoder-decoders and consists of an encoder that encodes a source sentence into a fixed-length vector from which a decoder generates a translation. **[4]** In this paper, we conjecture that (...) . **[5]** With this new approach, we achieve a translation performance comparable to the existing state-of-the-art phrase-based system on the task of English-to-French translation. **[6]** Furthermore, qualitative analysis reveals that (...) .

Filtered Abstract

[1] [2] [2] [3] [5]

Explanation

The neural machine translation aims at building a single neural network that can be jointly tuned to maximize the translation performance. The models proposed recently belong to a family of encoder-decoders and consists of an encoder that encodes a source sentence into a fixed-length vector.

Figure 3: The process of the explanation generation using the conditional text summarization technique. The query keywords are highlighted as yellow and the related keywords are highlighted as green. Some sentences without important keywords are ignored by replacing them with '(...)'.

passes the query to Elasticsearch[9] for searching and ranking papers.

We retrieve the papers whose title or abstract contains an exact query, all of the keywords regardless of the orders, and some of the keywords. The results from each category will be sorted using a combination of *(i)* normalized Elasticsearch score and *(ii)* normalized citation count per day, before concatenated to be the final search results.

To provide a short explanation for why each paper is returned, we propose a technique called "Conditional text summarization", as illustrated in Figure 3. We start by collecting the related keywords, i.e., the entities along the knowledge graph paths (of length 1 or 2) from the query to the paper. Then, to form the input of the summarization, the query and those keywords are used to select important sentences in the paper abstract with the sentences containing more than one keyword being repeated twice. After that, we use T5 (Xiong et al., 2017), a pre-trained sequence-to-sequence model, to summarize the filtered abstract to be the explanation. With this method, ESRA can generate different explanations for the same paper given different queries. For example, Table 4 shows the three different explanations for the BERT paper (Devlin et al., 2019) in response to the three queries – *BERT*, *Transformer*, and *SQuAD*.

For the fact list feature, we choose a group of facts from our knowledge graph that is connected to the user's query nodes and show them along with the search results. In addition, ESRA provides visualizations of three subgraphs of our knowledge graph to the users. Firstly, the fact graph visualizes facts related to search keywords. In other words, it is the graphical view of the fact list. Secondly and thirdly, the paper graph and the keyword-to-paper graph visualize all nodes and relations that appear in the returned paper and relate the paper to the search keywords, respectively.

3.3 System Development

Users can interact with our platform, ESRA, via `http://esra.cp.eng.chula.ac.th/`. We developed the web application using React and Django frameworks for front-end and back-end services, respectively. The back-end also connects to (1) a knowledge graph manager which is responsible for searching and retrieving data from the graph database (Neo4j) and (2) a relational database (SQLite) that stores metadata. All the deep learning models used by ESRA are based on PyTorch.

4 Results and Evaluation

We evaluate ESRA in two ways. First, empirical evaluation concerns the effectiveness of knowledge graph extraction. Second, human evaluation targets the three main features of ESRA – explanation, fact list, and graph visualization.

4.1 Knowledge Graph Construction

According to section 3.1, our extractor combines SpERT (Eberts and Ulges, 2019) and SciIE (Luan et al., 2018) for achieving the three IE tasks in Table 5. Due to the lack of information extraction ground truth on the arXiv dataset, we decided to use the SciERC dataset (Luan et al., 2018) to evaluate the extractor instead. We compared our extractor to SpERT, SciIE, and DyGIE++ (Wadden et al., 2019). The results in Table 5 show that our extractor can retain the performance of SpERT on the first two tasks (entity and relation extraction), while it slightly sacrifices the performance of SciIE

[9] `https://www.elastic.co/elasticsearch/`

Statistics	Quantity
#Method	57,762
#OtherScientificTerm	56,553
#Author*	34,449
#Task	34,365
#Material	27,766
#Paper*	23,111
#Metric	4,992
#Abbreviation**	3,066
Total	**242,064**

* Obtained from arXiv metadata

** Obtained during post-processing

Table 2: Entity statistics

Statistics	Quantity
#appear_in**	715,948
#cite*	438,161
#used_for	190,386
#author_of	172,388
#hyponym_of	40,800
#evaluate_for	38,110
#compare	15,366
#related_to**	15,136
#feature_of	14,970
#part_of	14,398
#refer_to**	11,472
Total	**1,667,135**

* Obtained from arXiv metadata

** Obtained during post-processing

Table 3: Relation statistics

for coreference resolution due to the difference between recognized named entities of both models (SpERT and SciIE).

4.2 Human Evaluation

We recruited 32 human participants who have been studying or working in the area of Computer Science and Engineering to evaluate ESRA. 14 out of the 32 participants identified that they specialize in NLP. Each participant was asked to evaluate the three main features of ESRA along three main dimensions – usefulness, understandability, and visual appeal – using a scale from 1 to 5 where the numbers mean strongly disappointed, disappointed, neutral, satisfied, and strongly satisfied, respectively. The results are reported in Table 6. The average score from all participants on each dimension falls within the range between 3.6 and 4.2, meaning that our system could reasonably satisfy users with some room for further improvement. Apart from the satisfaction scores, we also collected users' opinions on feature-specific questions and let them give us free-text comments where the results are discussed next.

BERT: A language representation model called BERT is designed to pre-train deep bidirectional representations from unlabeled text. The pre-trained model can be fine-tuned with just one additional output layer to create state-of-the-art models for a wide range of tasks.

Transformer: We introduce a new language representation model called BERT, which stands for Bidirectional Encoder Representations from Transformers.

SQuAD: It obtains new state-of-the-art results on eleven natural language processing tasks. It includes pushing the GLUE score to 80.5% (7.7% point absolute improvement), MultiNLI accuracy to 86.7% (4.6% absolute improvement) and SQuAD v1.1 question answering Test F1 to 93.2.

Table 4: Explanations for the BERT paper (Devlin et al., 2019) given three different queries: *BERT*, *Transformer*, and *SQuAD*.

Model	F1 (on SciERC)		
	NER	RE	CR
SciIE	64.20	39.30	**48.20**
DyGIE++	67.50	48.40	-
SpERT	**70.33**	**50.84**	-
SpERT+SciIE (Ours)	**70.33**	**50.84**	45.87

Table 5: Evaluation of knowledge extraction models on three tasks: named-entity recognition (NER), relation extraction (RE), and coreference resolution (CR).

Explanation: Overall, the participants responded that the generated explanations have an appropriate length (score 4.44 / 5) and they are easy to understand (4.25 / 5). Moreover, the explanations help the participants screen papers faster (4.22 / 5). However, the score for usefulness of this feature is relatively low (3.94 / 5) because usually the output from T5 is not much different from the abstract. We believe that adding more contents apart from the filtered abstract to the summarizer's input would help mitigate this issue.

Fact list: The displayed facts are helpful for non-NLP-specialized users (4.07 / 5), probably because they can jump and explore related concepts in the list. However, NLP-specialized users gave a lower average score (3.78 / 5). Some comments suggested that the displayed facts are redundant. For example, "recall" and "recall value" should be

Dimension/Feature	Average score (1-5)		
	Explanation	Fact list	Graph viz.
Usefulness	3.94	3.91	3.88
Understandability	4.25	3.69	3.94
Visual appeal	3.81	3.81	3.81

Table 6: Human evaluation on the three main features

merged into one concept. This problem is a common weakness of automatic knowledge graph construction which could be alleviated by knowledge graph refinement (Paulheim, 2017).

Graph visualization: Some participants found that the graph visualization help them gather important points from the paper quickly such as evaluation metrics used in the paper. However, most of the comments noted that the graph is quite difficult to read, so they suggested the system show the full name of each graph node and adjust the layout for more readability.

5 Conclusion

Our literature discovery platform, ESRA, uses a scientific knowledge graph to enhance user's experience. Based on the human evaluation, ESRA can help users screen through papers faster using the generated explanations and capture important facts about the query and the papers using the fact list and the graph visualization. In the future, we aim to expand the coverage of our knowledge graph by extracting facts from the full documents to enhance the quality of ESRA results.

References

Waleed Ammar, Dirk Groeneveld, Chandra Bhagavatula, Iz Beltagy, Miles Crawford, Doug Downey, Jason Dunkelberger, Ahmed Elgohary, Sergey Feldman, Vu Ha, Rodney Kinney, Sebastian Kohlmeier, Kyle Lo, Tyler Murray, Hsu-Han Ooi, Matthew Peters, Joanna Power, Sam Skjonsberg, Lucy Wang, Chris Wilhelm, Zheng Yuan, Madeleine van Zuylen, and Oren Etzioni. 2018. Construction of the literature graph in semantic scholar. In *Proceedings of the 2018 Conference of the North American Chapter of the Association for Computational Linguistics: Human Language Technologies, Volume 3 (Industry Papers)*, pages 84–91, New Orleans - Louisiana. Association for Computational Linguistics.

Isabelle Augenstein, Mrinal Das, Sebastian Riedel, Lakshmi Vikraman, and Andrew McCallum. 2017. SemEval 2017 task 10: ScienceIE - extracting keyphrases and relations from scientific publications. In *Proceedings of the 11th International Workshop on Semantic Evaluation (SemEval-2017)*, pages 546–555, Vancouver, Canada. Association for Computational Linguistics.

Colin B. Clement, Matthew Bierbaum, Kevin P. O'Keeffe, and Alexander A. Alemi. 2019. On the use of arxiv as a dataset.

Jacob Devlin, Ming-Wei Chang, Kenton Lee, and Kristina Toutanova. 2019. BERT: Pre-training of deep bidirectional transformers for language understanding. In *Proceedings of the 2019 Conference of the North American Chapter of the Association for Computational Linguistics: Human Language Technologies, Volume 1 (Long and Short Papers)*, pages 4171–4186, Minneapolis, Minnesota. Association for Computational Linguistics.

Markus Eberts and Adrian Ulges. 2019. Span-based joint entity and relation extraction with transformer pre-training. *CoRR*, abs/1909.07755.

Patrick Ernst, Amy Siu, Dragan Milchevski, Johannes Hoffart, and Gerhard Weikum. 2016. DeepLife: An entity-aware search, analytics and exploration platform for health and life sciences. In *Proceedings of ACL-2016 System Demonstrations*, pages 19–24, Berlin, Germany. Association for Computational Linguistics.

K. Gábor, Haïfa Zargayouna, I. Tellier, D. Buscaldi, and Thierry Charnois. 2016. Unsupervised relation extraction in specialized corpora using sequence mining. In *IDA*.

Kata Gábor, Davide Buscaldi, Anne-Kathrin Schumann, Behrang QasemiZadeh, Haïfa Zargayouna, and Thierry Charnois. 2018. SemEval-2018 task 7: Semantic relation extraction and classification in scientific papers. In *Proceedings of The 12th International Workshop on Semantic Evaluation*, pages 679–688, New Orleans, Louisiana. Association for Computational Linguistics.

Mohamad Yaser Jaradeh, Allard Oelen, Kheir Eddine Farfar, Manuel Prinz, Jennifer D'Souza, Gábor Kismihók, Markus Stocker, and Sören Auer. 2019. Open research knowledge graph: Next generation infrastructure for semantic scholarly knowledge. In *Proceedings of the 10th International Conference on Knowledge Capture*, K-CAP '19, page 243–246, New York, NY, USA. Association for Computing Machinery.

M. Kas. 2011. Structures and statistics of citation networks.

Samiya Khan, Xiufeng Liu, Kashish A Shakil, and Mansaf Alam. 2017. A survey on scholarly data: From big data perspective. *Information Processing & Management*, 53(4):923–944.

Yinhan Liu, Myle Ott, Naman Goyal, Jingfei Du, Mandar Joshi, Danqi Chen, Omer Levy, Mike Lewis, Luke Zettlemoyer, and Veselin Stoyanov. 2019. Roberta: A robustly optimized bert pretraining approach. *arXiv preprint arXiv:1907.11692*.

Yi Luan, Luheng He, Mari Ostendorf, and Hannaneh Hajishirzi. 2018. Multi-task identification of entities, relations, and coreference for scientific knowledge graph construction. In *Proceedings of the 2018 Conference on Empirical Methods in Natural Language Processing*, pages 3219–3232, Brussels, Belgium. Association for Computational Linguistics.

Randall Munroe. 2013. The rise of open access. *Science*, 342(6154):58–59.

Nikolas Papanikolaou, G. Pavlopoulos, E. Pafilis, T. Theodosiou, Reinhard Schneider, V. Satagopam, C. Ouzounis, A. Eliopoulos, V. Promponas, and I. Iliopoulos. 2014. Biotextquest+: a knowledge integration platform for literature mining and concept discovery. *Bioinformatics*, 30 22:3249–56.

Heiko Paulheim. 2017. Knowledge graph refinement: A survey of approaches and evaluation methods. *Semantic web*, 8(3):489–508.

Nils Reimers and Iryna Gurevych. 2019. Sentence-BERT: Sentence embeddings using Siamese BERT-networks. In *Proceedings of the 2019 Conference on Empirical Methods in Natural Language Processing and the 9th International Joint Conference on Natural Language Processing (EMNLP-IJCNLP)*, pages 3982–3992, Hong Kong, China. Association for Computational Linguistics.

Xiang Ren, Jiaming Shen, Meng Qu, Xuan Wang, Zequi Wu, Qi Zhu, Meng Jiang, Fangbo Tao, Saurabh Sinha, David Liem, Peipei Ping, Richard Weinshilboum, and Jiawei Han. 2017. Life-iNet: A structured network-based knowledge exploration and analytics system for life sciences. In *Proceedings of ACL 2017, System Demonstrations*, pages 55–60, Vancouver, Canada. Association for Computational Linguistics.

J. Shen, Jinfeng Xiao, Yu Zhang, Carl Yang, Jingbo Shang, Jinda Han, Saurabh Sinha, P. Ping, R. Weinshilboum, Z. Lu, and Jiawei Han. 2018. Setsearch + : Entity-set-aware search and mining for scientific literature.

Yanchuan Sim, Noah A. Smith, and David A. Smith. 2012. Discovering factions in the computational linguistics community. In *Proceedings of the ACL-2012 Special Workshop on Rediscovering 50 Years of Discoveries*, pages 22–32, Jeju Island, Korea. Association for Computational Linguistics.

Arnab Sinha, Zhihong Shen, Yang Song, Hao Ma, Darrin Eide, Bo-June (Paul) Hsu, and Kuansan Wang. 2015. An overview of microsoft academic service (mas) and applications. In *Proceedings of the 24th International Conference on World Wide Web*, pages 243–246.

Zhaowei Tan, Changfeng Liu, Yuning Mao, Yunqi Guo, Jiaming Shen, and Xinbing Wang. 2016. Acemap: A novel approach towards displaying relationship among academic literatures. In *Proceedings of the 25th International Conference Companion on World Wide Web*, WWW '16 Companion, page 437–442, Republic and Canton of Geneva, CHE. International World Wide Web Conferences Steering Committee.

David Wadden, Ulme Wennberg, Yi Luan, and Hannaneh Hajishirzi. 2019. Entity, relation, and event extraction with contextualized span representations. In *Proceedings of the 2019 Conference on Empirical Methods in Natural Language Processing and the 9th International Joint Conference on Natural Language Processing (EMNLP-IJCNLP)*, pages 5784–5789, Hong Kong, China. Association for Computational Linguistics.

Kyle Williams, Jian Wu, Sagnik Ray Choudhury, Madian Khabsa, and C Lee Giles. 2014. Scholarly big data information extraction and integration in the citeseer χ digital library. In *2014 IEEE 30th international conference on data engineering workshops*, pages 68–73. IEEE.

Chenyan Xiong, Russell Power, and Jamie Callan. 2017. Explicit semantic ranking for academic search via knowledge graph embedding. In *WWW '17 Proceedings of the 26th International Conference on World Wide Web*, pages 1271–1279.

Trafilatura: A Web Scraping Library and Command-Line Tool for Text Discovery and Extraction

Adrien Barbaresi
Center for Digital Lexicography of German (ZDL)
Berlin-Brandenburg Academy of Sciences (BBAW)
Jgerstr. 22-23, 10117 Berlin, Germany
barbaresi@bbaw.de

Abstract

An essential operation in web corpus construction consists in retaining the desired content while discarding the rest. Another challenge finding one's way through websites. This article introduces a text discovery and extraction tool published under open-source license. Its installation and use is straightforward, notably from Python and on the command-line. The software allows for main text, comments and metadata extraction, while also providing building blocks for web crawling tasks. A comparative evaluation on real-world data also shows its interest as well as the performance of other available solutions.

The contributions of this paper are threefold: it references the software, features a benchmark, and provides a meaningful baseline for similar tasks. The tool performs significantly better than other open-source solutions in this evaluation and in external benchmarks.

1 Introduction

1.1 Gathering texts from the Web

As useful monolingual text corpora across languages are highly relevant for the NLP community (Caswell et al., 2020), web corpora seem to be a natural way to gather language data. Corpus construction usually involves "crawling, downloading, 'cleaning' and de-duplicating the data, then linguistically annotating it and loading it into a corpus query tool" (Kilgarriff, 2007). However, although text is ubiquitous on the Web, drawing accurate information from web pages can be difficult. In addition, the vastly increasing variety of corpora, text types and use cases makes it more and more difficult to assess the usefulness and appropriateness of certain web texts for given research objectives. As a result, content adequacy, focus and quality need to be evaluated after the downloads (Baroni et al., 2009).

A significant challenge lies in the ability to extract and pre-process web data to meet scientific expectations with respect to text quality. An essential operation in corpus construction consists in retaining the desired content while discarding the rest, a task carrying various names referring to specific subtasks or to pre-processing as a whole: web scraping, boilerplate removal, web page segmentation, web page cleaning, template extraction, or content extraction. This step is sometimes overlooked although it involves a series of design decisions and turning points in data processing. Depending on the purpose of data collection, adequate filtering and quality assessment can be crucial. It has a significant impact on a wide range of downstream applications like text analysis, information retrieval, link analysis, page adaptation to other terminals and screens, and especially natural language processing pipelines.

Another challenge is how to find one's way through the Web, notably as linguistic data are gathered by running targeted web crawlers (Scannell, 2007). As web crawling involves discarding much of the downloaded content (Olston and Najork, 2010), especially link filtering and prioritization can prove to be tricky for contexts in which data collection is just the first step of a project, so that time resources for this task are scarce. Data collection approaches using the CommonCrawl[1] have flourished as they allow for faster download and processing by skipping (or more precisely outsourcing) the crawling phase. Barring the fact that finding one's "own" way through the Web can be preferable, such data should not be used without forethought and exhaustive filtering. Beside the discovery of relevant websites, a major issue consists in selecting appropriate content after download and processing (Schäfer et al., 2013), which can be com-

[1] https://commoncrawl.org

Proceedings of the Joint Conference of the 59th Annual Meeting of the Association for Computational Linguistics and the 11th International Joint Conference on Natural Language Processing: System Demonstrations, pages 122–131, August 1st - August 6th, 2021.

plex due to unexpected machine-generated flaws and biases.

Finally, depending on the project's jurisdiction, legal aspects of retrieving and granting access to web documents can be unclear or restrictive. Boundaries of copyright law are not clear when it comes to corpus building (De Clercq and Perez, 2010) so that some corpus infrastructure projects leave it to users to decide what to do from a copyright standpoint (Benko, 2016). Copyright and intellectual property rights usually do not apply to resources such as language models or n-grams (Buck et al., 2014), so are shuffled sentences (Biemann et al., 2007). Web corpora focusing on manually selected sources under Creative Commons licenses have been built (Brunello, 2009; Lyding et al., 2014), although only a very small proportion of websites use them (Barbaresi and Würzner, 2014). Corpora based on machine-checked licenses have also been developed (Habernal et al., 2016), as well as systems to merge annotation with web parts from the CommonCrawl (Schäfer, 2016). Considering the progresses of annotation tools, is can be easier to retrieve documents directly from the Web or from archives and to process them to one's taste.

1.2 Research context

This effort is part of methods to derive information from web documents in order to build text databases for a lexicographic information platform (Geyken et al., 2017). Extracting and preprocessing web texts to the exacting standards of scientific research turned out to be a substantial challenge where existing open-source solutions were not entirely convincing in terms of accuracy, versatility, and ease of use. The current tool follows from earlier work on news and blog articles extraction (Barbaresi, 2015, 2016). Its packaging into a directly re-usable format generalizes the process and makes it available to the community, with thorough testing it has also become much more robust and versatile.

1.3 Contributions

Distinguishing between a whole page and the page's essential parts can help to alleviate many quality problems related to web text processing, notably by dealing with the noise caused by recurring elements (headers and footers, ads, links/blogroll, etc.). This can be particularly useful to de-duplicate recurring language samples. Tasks related to content extraction and language modeling also benefit from a cleaner text base. In the concrete case of linguistic and lexicographic research, it allows for content queries on meaningful parts of the documents.

The remainder of this article introduces a text extraction and web navigation tool published under open-source license. Its installation and use is straightforward, notably from Python and on the command-line. The software makes it easier to extract the main text, comments and metadata, while also providing building blocks for text discovery tasks such as web crawling. The following also entails a comparative evaluation of text extraction on real-world data. The contributions of this paper are thus threefold as it references the software, features a benchmark, and provides a fast, meaningful baseline for similar tasks.

2 State of the art

2.1 "A difficult IE problem"

Even before the "Web 2.0" paradigm with web pages assembling information from and for a variety of sources (notably the advertising industry), web pages have been known for their lack of focus on directly usable text content. Despite the quantity of pages following an article format where there is a main text to be found, web pages now accessible through archives cannot be expected to be easy to process: "Articles published on the WWW often contain extraneous clutter. Most articles consist of a main body which constitutes the relevant part of the particular page. [...] Identifying the main body of a web page in a general robust manner is a difficult information extraction problem." (Finn et al., 2001)

Web pages come in different shapes and sizes mostly because of the wide variety of platforms and content management systems, and not least because of varying reasons to publish and diverging goals followed during web publication. Web page structure is also constantly evolving from the perspective of standards. HTML 5 was first released in 2008 to provide support for multimedia and graphical elements. This standard streamlined syntax while retaining backward-compatibility. Web content extraction is also an active field of research in user experience, resulting from the need for higher download and rendering speeds as well as from a growing amount of "Web bloat" requiring the development of "reader modes" and "distillers"[2] for

[2]https://chromium.googlesource.com/chromium/dom-

web browsers (Ghasemisharif et al., 2019).

2.2 Wrappers

Data extraction has first been based on "wrappers" (now called "scrapers") which were mostly relying on manual design and tended to be brittle and hard to maintain (Crescenzi et al., 2001). These extraction procedures have also been used early on by blogs search engines (Glance et al., 2004). Since the genre of "web diaries" was established before the blogs in Japan, there have been attempts to target not only blog software but also regular pages (Nanno et al., 2004), in which the extraction of metadata also allows for a distinction based on heuristics. Regarding metadata extraction for pages in article form and blogs in particular, common targets include the title of the entry, the date, the author, the content, the number of comments, the archived link, and the trackback link (Glance et al., 2004); they can also aim at comments specifically (Mishne and Glance, 2006).

2.3 Generic web content extraction

Generic extraction techniques ground on Document Object Model (DOM) examination. An earlier, language-independent approach uses entropy measures applied to features, links, and content in order to discriminate among parts of a web page (Kao et al., 2004). Another notable technique, Visual Page Segmentation, applies heuristics to find visually grouped blocks (Cai et al., 2003). Other methods are based on style tree induction, that is detection of similarities of DOM trees on site-level (Yi et al., 2003; Vieira et al., 2006). Overall, efforts made to automatically generate wrappers have been centered on three different approaches (Guo et al., 2010): wrapper induction (e.g. building a grammar to parse a web page), sequence labeling (e.g. labeled examples or a schema of data in the page), and statistical analysis. This approach combined to the inspection of DOM tree characteristics (Wang et al., 2009; Guo et al., 2010) is a common ground to the information retrieval and computational linguistics communities, with the categorization of HTML elements and linguistic features (Ziegler and Skubacz, 2007) for the former and boilerplate removal for the latter.

The DOM considers a given HTML document as a tree structure whose nodes represent parts of the document to be operated on. Text, tag and/or link density have proven to be good indicators in order to select or discard content nodes, using the cumulative distribution of tags (Finn et al., 2001), or with approaches such as the content extraction via tag ratios (Weninger et al., 2010) and the content extraction via text density algorithms (Sun et al., 2011). Statistical selection of informative nodes through a combination of both methods proved more efficient on comparable datasets (Qureshi and Memon, 2012). The large majority of DOM-based approaches try to leverage semantic information conveyed by HTML tags, notably paragraphs (*p*) on which text-to-tag ratios are calculated (Carey and Manic, 2016), or tag ratios and semantic features from *id* and *class* attributes (Peters and Lecocq, 2013).

Machine learning approaches have also been used, whose interest generally consists in leveraging advances in classification tasks by treating a HTML document as a series of blocks to be classified. Relevant algorithms include conditional random fields learning header, text, and noisy blocks with markup-based, content-based, and document-related features (Spousta et al., 2008), support vector machines trained on linguistic, structural and visual features (Bauer et al., 2007), Naive Bayes (Pasternack and Roth, 2009), multi-layer perceptron based on paragraph-level features (Schäfer and Bildhauer, 2012), or logistic regressions (Peters and Lecocq, 2013). More recently, deep learning has also been used for similar classifications, e.g. the *Web2Text* system is based on convolutional neural networks learning combinations of DOM-based features (Vogels et al., 2018).

Despite the number of article on this topic, very few systems are open-source or freely available (Alarte et al., 2019).

2.4 Corpus linguistics and NLP

There are few comparable projects coming from the linguistics or natural language processing communities and focused on making software publicly available and usable. *Boilerpipe* uses shallow text features like word counts and link density with decision tree and SVM classifiers (Kohlschütter et al., 2010). *JusText* is based on length heuristics as well as link and stop word densities (Pomikálek, 2011). Both algorithms have been prevalent since their release and are now mostly used through their subsequent forks, as software needs to be kept up-to-date. More recent initiatives explicitly targeting

distiller

corpus creation feature the *Corpus Crawler*[3] or *Texrex*[4] (Schäfer, 2017), neither of which appears to be actively maintained.

An evaluation and discussion following from the Cleaneval initiative (Baroni et al., 2008) would put the topic back into focus, as content processing on the Web is affected by both time and geography. This benchmark could be elaborated on, results are not consistent in different languages and metrics sometime fail to capture the variable influence of extractors on downstream modules (Lejeune and Zhu, 2018). Often, tools are developed with particular page styles in mind, mostly from the English-speaking world (Barbaresi and Lejeune, 2020). For certain projects, customized scrapers which are adjusted to each website remain feasible (Krasselt et al., 2020). A generic approach can really save human time and resources, albeit at a certain cost in terms of accuracy depending on the context.

3 Introducing the Trafilatura tool

3.1 Features

Trafilatura is a web scraping tool for text discovery and retrieval which seamlessly downloads, parses, and scrapes web page data. It can crawl and discover texts within a website and process them accordingly. The extractor focuses on metadata, main body text and comments while preserving parts of the text formatting and page structure. It aims to be precise enough in order not to miss texts or to discard valid documents, as it must be robust but also reasonably fast. With these objectives in mind, Trafilatura is designed to run in production on millions of web documents.

The software features parallel online and offline processing: URLs, HTML files or parsed HTML trees can be used as input. Although straight output of Python variables is possible, conversion to various common output formats makes the software more versatile: plain text (minimal formatting), CSV (with metadata, tab-separated values), JSON (with metadata), XML and XML-TEI (for metadata and structure). The latter support for TEI format (following the recommendations of the Text Encoding Initiative) also includes a validator for Python which can be used apart from the extraction. The scraping and conversion parts also work with existing archives, Raw HTML documents can be retrieved from sources such as the CommonCrawl[5] or the Internet Archive[6].

In addition, download utilities are included, notably using a multi-threaded but "polite" processing of URL queues, i.e. time restrictions based on domain names. Persistent connections are managed by a connection pool, thus maintaining connections with websites to be scraped. The tool also entails web crawling capacities which provide accessible and fail-safe ways to gather data based on a series of target sites. First, support for sitemaps (XML and TXT formats) according to the sitemap protocol. Second, support for web feeds (ATOM, RDF and RSS formats) which make it possible to build a seamless news crawler. Third, crawling components to discover content. It can also manipulate URL lists, including filtering and prioritization based on site characteristics or language-aware heuristics based on internationalization.

The package provides a relatively light-weight and modular architecture, letting users choose the components they wish to include. It has been tested on Linux, MacOS and Windows, and can be used with Python, on the command-line, with R (using the *reticulate* adapter package), and through a graphical user interface. The package documentation also acts as a manual on web text collection.[7]

3.2 Extraction process

The extraction combines two acknowledged libraries, readability-lxml[8] and jusText[9], which are used as safety nets and fallbacks. Trafilatura's own extraction algorithm is based on a cascade of rule-based filters and content heuristics:
(1) Content delimitation is performed by XPath expressions targeting common HTML elements and attributes as well as idiosyncrasies of main content management systems, first in a negative perspective with the exclusion of unwanted parts of the HTML code (e.g. *<div class="nav">*) and next by centering on the desirable content (e.g. *<section id="entry-content">*). The same operations are performed for comments in case they are part of the extraction. The selected nodes of the HTML tree are then processed, i.e. checked for relevance (notably by element type, text length and link density) and simplified as to their HTML structure.

[3] https://github.com/google/corpuscrawler
[4] https://github.com/rsling/texrex
[5] https://commoncrawl.org/
[6] https://archive.org/
[7] https://trafilatura.readthedocs.io/
[8] https://github.com/buriy/python-readability
[9] https://github.com/miso-belica/jusText

(2) If fallbacks are selected and triggered by a possibly faulty extraction, the other algorithms are run as a backup. Since they proceed differently their approach is complementary. They notably apply heuristics based on line length, text-to-markup ratio, and position/depth of elements in the HTML tree. If applicable, the output of these generic algorithms is compared to the "homegrown" extraction and heuristics are applied to determine the most efficient extraction, mostly in terms of extraction length (all algorithms are fairly reliable, so much longer is better) and "impurities" (e.g. no media elements).
(3) In case nothing worked, a baseline extraction is run in order to look for "wild" text elements that most probably have been missed, which implies to discard unwanted parts and to look for any element which may contain useful text content (e.g. *div* elements without paragraphs).

The extraction is designed to be robust and modular and provides a trade-off between precision and recall in most settings. As a result, main texts and potential comments are returned, with optional preservation of structural elements (paragraphs, titles, lists, quotes, code, line breaks, in-line text formatting). Extraction of metadata is also included, that is by descending frequency title, site name, author, date, categories and tags. For date extraction the library acts like a wrapper around *htmldate* (Barbaresi, 2020), a module specifically developed for this task.

An optional language detection can be run on the extracted content, currently using the Compact Language Detector v3 (CLD3)[10], which can be subject to accuracy issues depending on text length and language modeling (Caswell et al., 2020).

4 Evaluation

4.1 Benchmark

The evaluation focuses on the ability to retain appropriate text spans and discarded unwanted clutter, a functionality shared by many tools. Text discovery and conversion utilities are not evaluated here as most solutions do not include them. The benchmark is run on a collection of 500 documents which are either typical for Internet articles (news outlets, blogs) or non-standard and thus harder to process. Some contain mixed content (lists, tables) and/or non-standard, not fully valid HTML code. They were selected from large collections of web pages in German, for the sake of completeness a few documents in other languages are added (notably English, French, other European languages, Chinese and Arabic). The evaluation is reproducible, the needed script and instructions are available from the project repository.[11]

Target of the extraction is the main content, which is usually the part displayed centrally, without the left or right bars, the header or the footer, but including potential titles and (optionally) comments. This task is also known as web scraping, boilerplate removal, DOM-based content extraction, main content identification, or web page cleaning.

Decisive document segments of a few words each are singled out, about three per webpage are manually annotated as being part of the main text or unwanted boilerplate. They represent parts of the documents which are of high significance in the perspective of working with the texts, most notably beginnings and endings, left/right columns, additional header, author or footer information such as imprints or addresses, as well as affiliated and social network links.

Raw text segments are expected as a way to evaluate extraction quality without markup, i.e. HTML to TXT in itself, which avoids indirectly factoring in how the systems deal with markup. The chosen segments are included in a single HTML element span and they do not imply trimming or normalizing spaces, which makes the output strings directly comparable. Due to the language diversity of the sample the documents entail different text encodings. Since not all packages deal with them in a similar way, the given input string is in Unicode format.

4.2 Tools

The benchmark focuses on the Python programming language, reportedly the most popular programming language in academia and one of the most popular overall.[12] A few algorithms have been ported from other languages such as Java and JavaScript, which contributes to giving an exhaustive yet incomplete panorama of available solutions overall. In case software packages are not actively maintained the most prominent usable fork is used.

First, these packages are provided for reference as they keep the structure intact but do not focus

[10]https://github.com/google/cld3

[11]https://github.com/adbar/trafilatura/

[12]https://spectrum.ieee.org/computing/software/the-top-programming-languages-2019

on main text extraction:

- *html2text*[13] converts HTML pages to Markup language
- *html_text*[14] converts HTML code to plain text
- *inscriptis*[15] converts HTML to text with a particular emphasis on nested tables

The following packages are strictly comparable as they focus on main text extraction:

- *boilerpy3*[16] is a Python version of the *boilerpipe* algorithm (Kohlschütter et al., 2010) for boilerplate removal and fulltext extraction
- *dragnet*[17] features machine-learning and combined approaches (Peters and Lecocq, 2013) but requires more dependencies and potentially fine-tuning: it is used with its default training data
- *goose3*[18] can extract information for embedded content but doesnt preserve markup
- *jusText*[19] is designed to preserve mainly text containing full sentences along with some markup, it has been explicitly developed to create linguistic resources (Pomikálek, 2011)
- *newspaper*[20] is mostly geared towards newspaper texts, provides additional functions but no structured text or comment extraction
- *news-please*[21] is a news crawler that extracts structured information (Hamborg et al., 2017)
- *readability-lxml*[22] cleans the page and preserves some markup

The tools are compared to the raw page source and to a meaningful baseline also provided by Trafilatura which consists in extracting all the text contained in JSON data or paragraph, code or quoting elements.

Two variants of Trafilatura are evaluated, first using its own algorithm and second including its fallback mechanisms based on external libraries.

[13]https://github.com/Alir3z4/html2text
[14]https://github.com/TeamHG-Memex/html-text
[15]https://github.com/weblyzard/inscriptis
[16]https://github.com/jmriebold/BoilerPy3
[17]https://github.com/dragnet-org/dragnet
[18]https://github.com/goose3/goose3
[19]https://github.com/miso-belica/jusText
[20]https://github.com/codelucas/newspaper
[21]https://github.com/fhamborg/news-please
[22]https://github.com/buriy/python-readability

4.3 Results

The results are listed in Table 1. Baseline extraction is simple and fast, it beats a few systems, showing its interest. JusText is highly configurable and tweaking its configuration leads to better performance than its generic settings, that is why it has been done here. The only solid conclusions which can be drawn for execution times are that goose3 and newspaper are slower than the rest while news-pleases execution time isn't comparable because of operations unrelated to text extraction. The *newspaper* and *boilerpy3* modules do not work without errors on every HTML file in the test set, probably because of malformed HTML, encoding or parsing bugs.

It turns out that rule-based approaches such as Trafilatura's own algorithm ("fast" option) obtain balanced results despite a lack of precision. Although the library in itself is already above the rest, it performs significantly better than the other tested solutions when combined with generic algorithmic approaches.

4.4 External evaluations

A few external evaluations are already available, they ground on early releases of the software during its development. A previous version of Trafilatura is the most efficient open-source library in ScrapingHub's article extraction benchmark.[23] Significantly better results are also reported in the case of French and Swedish for a previous version (Laippala et al., 2020), as well as the best overall macro-mean on the multilingual and manually-annotated DANIEL corpus comprising about 1,600 webpages in five different languages (Lejeune and Barbaresi, 2020). In a further context, the tool has proven to be efficient on main text extraction to create Russian-Turkic parallel corpora (Khusainov et al., 2020).

4.5 Discussion

In some cases, no text is returned, but there is no way to return text at all costs without impacting precision. Trafilatura as a whole is currently made for users aiming for better text quality. While rule-based approaches are both easier to use and to parameterize and could be more efficient in the long-run (Barbaresi and Lejeune, 2020), extraction presets would be useful in order to make the

[23]https://github.com/scrapinghub/article-extraction-benchmark

Python Package	Precision	Recall	Accuracy	F-Score	Diff.
naive baseline: raw HTML	0.527	0.878	0.547	0.659	0
html2text 2020.1.16	0.488	0.714	0.484	0.580	8.9x
html_text 0.5.2	0.526	**0.958**	0.548	0.679	1.9x
inscriptis 1.1	0.531	**0.958**	0.556	0.683	2.4x
justext 2.2.0 (custom)	0.870	0.584	0.749	0.699	6.1x
newspaper3k 0.2.8	0.921	0.574	0.763	0.708	12.9x
boilerpy3 1.0.2 (article mode)	0.851	0.696	0.788	0.766	4.8x
goose3 3.1.9	**0.950**	0.644	0.806	0.767	18.8x
trafilatura baseline	0.746	0.804	0.766	0.774	**1x**
dragnet 2.0.4	0.906	0.689	0.810	0.783	3.1x
readability-lxml 0.8.1	0.917	0.716	0.826	0.804	5.9x
news-please 1.5.21	0.924	0.718	0.830	0.808	60x
trafilatura 0.8.2 (fast)	0.925	0.868	0.899	0.896	3.9x
trafilatura 0.8.2	0.934	0.890	**0.914**	**0.912**	8.4x

Table 1: Benchmark on 500 documents, 1487 text and 1496 boilerplate segments.

tool more adaptable to research contexts, such as precision-based settings where discarding more elements is paramount or recall-based settings where empty or nearly empty documents are a concern (Gao et al., 2020).

Even if text encoding detection is performed at least as well and possibly better than the competition, a compromise has to be found between speed and accuracy. This issue impedes results to a variable extent, as character sequences are improperly recognized or completely skipped.

5 Conclusions and outlook

The variety of contexts and text genres leads to important design decisions impacting web corpora: could and should the tooling be adapted to particular sources that are targeted or should the extraction be as generic as possible to provide opportunistic ways of gathering information? Due to corpus size or limited resources, the second option is often best. The software package introduced here can help facilitate text data collection and enhance corpus quality. It can answer two research questions related to web corpus construction: How can an accessible generic extraction be run on web pages? And how can text content be found given a list of websites? In the evaluation, Trafilatura performs significantly better than other open-source solutions, which is corroborated by external benchmarks. The article also provided a fast and meaningful baseline which can be used in similar extraction tasks.

Most scraping tools are developed considering particular page styles, whereas linguistic and geographic factors are most probably reflected in HTML structure diversity. In addition, different eras of web development result in diverging "HTMLects". These discrepancies deeply affect extraction processes and can lead to diverging performances. Trafilatura tries to mitigate these biases but cannot bridge all potential gaps. While some large-scale natural language processing and language modeling algorithms can be expected to smooth out irregularities to a certain extent, uses requiring a low margin of error and close reading approaches can greatly benefit from refinements during construction and processing of corpora. As this tool has been released under an open-source license and field-tested by users, feedback loops and collaborative work will hopefully be carried on and foster further improvements.

Although the extraction parameters are configurable, recall- and precision-oriented settings will be made available to make major extraction settings more convenient. Presets corresponding to different usage scenarios could be developed. Comment extraction still has to be evaluated although most libraries do not offer this functionality. Forthcoming additions include refinements of navigation functions, notably further work on a spider in order to be able to derive links from websites which do not provide sitemaps or web feeds.

References

Julian Alarte, Josep Silva, and Salvador Tamarit. 2019. What Web Template Extractor Should I Use?A Benchmarking and Comparison for Five Template Extractors. *ACM Transactions on the Web (TWEB)*, 13(2):1–19.

Adrien Barbaresi. 2015. *Ad hoc and general-purpose corpus construction from web sources*. Ph.D. thesis, École Normale Supérieure de Lyon.

Adrien Barbaresi. 2016. Efficient construction of metadata-enhanced web corpora. In *Proceedings of the 10th Web as Corpus Workshop*, pages 7–16. Association for Computational Linguistics.

Adrien Barbaresi. 2020. htmldate: A Python package to extract publication dates from web pages. *Journal of Open Source Software*, 5(51):2439.

Adrien Barbaresi and Gaël Lejeune. 2020. Out-of-the-Box and Into the Ditch? Multilingual Evaluation of Generic Text Extraction Tools. In *Proceedings of the 12th Web as Corpus Workshop*, pages 5–13.

Adrien Barbaresi and Kay-Michael Würzner. 2014. For a fistful of blogs: Discovery and comparative benchmarking of republishable German content. In *Proceedings of KONVENS 2014, NLP4CMC workshop*, pages 2–10. Hildesheim University Press.

Marco Baroni, Silvia Bernardini, Adriano Ferraresi, and Eros Zanchetta. 2009. The WaCky Wide Web: a collection of very large linguistically processed web-crawled corpora. *Language Resources and Evaluation*, 43(3):209–226.

Marco Baroni, Francis Chantree, Adam Kilgarriff, and Serge Sharoff. 2008. Cleaneval: a Competition for Cleaning Web Pages. In *Proceedings of the 6th Conference on Language Resources and Evaluation (LREC'08)*, pages 638–643. ELRA.

Daniel Bauer, Judith Degen, Xiaoye Deng, Priska Herger, Jan Gasthaus, Eugenie Giesbrecht, Lina Jansen, Christin Kalina, Thorben Kräger, Robert Märtin, Martin Schmidt, Simon Scholler, Johannes Steger, Egon Stemle, and Stefan Evert. 2007. FIASCO: Filtering the internet by automatic subtree classification. In *Building and Exploring Web Corpora: Proceedings of the 3rd Web as Corpus Workshop (WAC-3)*, pages 111–121.

Vladimír Benko. 2016. wo Years of Aranea: Increasing Counts and Tuning the Pipeline. In *Proceedings of the 10th International Conference on Language Resources and Evaluation (LREC'16)*, pages 4245–4248. ELRA.

Chris Biemann, Gerhard Heyer, Uwe Quasthoff, and Matthias Richter. 2007. The Leipzig Corpora Collection: Monolingual Corpora of Standard Size. In *Proceedings of the Corpus Linguistics Conference*.

Marco Brunello. 2009. The creation of free linguistic corpora from the web. In *Proceedings of the Fifth Web as Corpus Workshop (WAC5)*, pages 9–16. Elhuyar Fundazioa.

Christian Buck, Kenneth Heafield, and Bas Van Ooyen. 2014. N-gram Counts and Language Models from the Common Crawl. In *Proceedings of the 9th International Conference on Language Resources and Evaluation (LREC'14)*. ELRA.

Deng Cai, Shipeng Yu, Ji-Rong Wen, and Wei-Ying Ma. 2003. VIPS: a Vision-based Page Segmentation Algorithm. Technical report, Microsoft Technical Report (MSR-TR-2003-79).

Howard J. Carey and Milos Manic. 2016. HTML web content extraction using paragraph tags. In *25th International Symposium on Industrial Electronics (ISIE)*, pages 1099–1105. IEEE.

Isaac Caswell, Theresa Breiner, Daan van Esch, and Ankur Bapna. 2020. Language ID in the wild: Unexpected challenges on the path to a thousand-language web text corpus. In *Proceedings of the 28th International Conference on Computational Linguistics*, pages 6588–6608. International Committee on Computational Linguistics.

Valter Crescenzi, Giansalvatore Mecca, and Paolo Merialdo. 2001. Roadrunner: Towards Automatic Data Extraction From Large Web Sites. In *Proceedings of the 27th VLDB Conference*, pages 109–118.

Orphée De Clercq and Maribel Montero Perez. 2010. Data Collection and IPR in Multilingual Parallel Corpora. Dutch Parallel Corpus. In *Proceedings of the 7th International Conference on Language Resources and Evaluation (LREC'10)*, pages 3383–3388. ELRA.

Aidan Finn, Nicholas Kushmerick, and Barry Smyth. 2001. Fact or Fiction: Content Classification for Digital Libraries. In *Joint DELOS-NSF Workshop: Personalization andRecommender Systems in Digital Libraries*.

Leo Gao, Stella Biderman, Sid Black, Laurence Golding, Travis Hoppe, Charles Foster, Jason Phang, Horace He, Anish Thite, Noa Nabeshima, et al. 2020. The Pile: An 800GB Dataset of Diverse Text for Language Modeling. *arXiv preprint arXiv:2101.00027*.

Alexander Geyken, Adrien Barbaresi, Jrg Didakowski, Bryan Jurish, Frank Wiegand, and Lothar Lemnitzer. 2017. Die Korpusplattform des "Digitalen Wrterbuchs der deutschen Sprache" (DWDS). *Zeitschrift fr germanistische Linguistik*, 45(2):327–344.

Mohammad Ghasemisharif, Peter Snyder, Andrius Aucinas, and Benjamin Livshits. 2019. SpeedReader: Reader Mode Made Fast and Private. In *Proceedings of the World Wide Web Conference*, pages 526–537.

Natalie Glance, Matthew Hurst, and Takashi Tomokiyo. 2004. Blogpulse: Automated Trend Discovery for Weblogs. In *WWW 2004 Workshop on the Weblogging Ecosystem: Aggregation, Analysis and Dynamics*.

Yan Guo, Huifeng Tang, Linhai Song, Yu Wang, and Guodong Ding. 2010. ECON: an Approach to Extract Content from Web News Page. In *Proceedings of 12th International Asia-Pacific Web Conference (APWEB)*, pages 314–320. IEEE.

Ivan Habernal, Omnia Zayed, and Iryna Gurevych. 2016. C4Corpus: Multilingual Web-size Corpus with Free License. In *Proceedings of the 10th Conference on Language Resources and Evaluation (LREC'16)*, pages 914–922.

Felix Hamborg, Norman Meuschke, Corinna Breitinger, and Bela Gipp. 2017. news-please: A Generic News Crawler and Extractor. In *Proceedings of the 15th International Symposium of Information Science*, pages 218–223.

Hung-Yu Kao, Shian-Hua Lin, Jan-Ming Ho, and Ming-Syan Chen. 2004. Mining web informative structures and contents based on entropy analysis. *IEEE Transactions on Knowledge and Data Engineering*, 16(1):41–55.

Aidar Khusainov, Dzhavdet Suleymanov, Rinat Gilmullin, Alina Minsafina, Lenara Kubedinova, and Nilufar Abdurakhmonova. 2020. First Results of the TurkLang-7 Project: Creating Russian-Turkic Parallel Corpora and MT Systems. In *Proceedings of the Computational Models in Language and Speech Workshop (CMLS 2020)*, pages 90–101. CEUR.

Adam Kilgarriff. 2007. Googleology is bad science. *Computational Linguistics*, 33(1):147–151.

Christian Kohlschütter, Peter Fankhauser, and Wolfgang Nejdl. 2010. Boilerplate detection using shallow text features. In *Proceedings of the Third ACM International Conference on Web Search and Data Mining, WSDM 10*, pages 441–450.

Julia Krasselt, Philipp Dressen, Matthias Fluor, Cerstin Mahlow, Klaus Rothenhäusler, and Maren Runte. 2020. Swiss-AL: A multilingual Swiss Web corpus for applied linguistics. In *Proceedings of the 12th Conference on Language Resources and Evaluation (LREC'20)*, pages 4145–4151. ELRA.

Veronika Laippala, Samuel Rönnqvist, Saara Hellström, Juhani Luotolahti, Liina Repo, Anna Salmela, Valtteri Skantsi, and Sampo Pyysalo. 2020. From Web Crawl to Clean Register-Annotated Corpora. In *Proceedings of the 12th Web as Corpus Workshop*, pages 14–22.

Gaël Lejeune and Adrien Barbaresi. 2020. Bien choisir son outil d'extraction de contenu à partir du Web (Choosing the appropriate tool for Web Content Extraction). In *Actes de la 6e conférence conjointe JEP, TALN, RÉCITAL. Volume 4: Démonstrations et résumés d'articles internationaux*, pages 46–49.

Gaël Lejeune and Lichao Zhu. 2018. A New Proposal for Evaluating Web Page Cleaning Tools. *Computación y Sistemas*, 22(4).

Verena Lyding, Egon Stemle, Claudia Borghetti, Marco Brunello, Sara Castagnoli, Felice Dell'Orletta, Henrik Dittmann, Alessandro Lenci, and Vito Pirrelli. 2014. The PAISÁ Corpus of Italian Web Texts. In *9th Web as Corpus Workshop (WaC-9) @ EACL 2014*, pages 36–43. European chapter of the Association for Computational Linguistics.

Gilad Mishne and Natalie Glance. 2006. Leave a Reply: An Analysis of Weblog Comments. In *Third Annual Workshop on the Weblogging Ecosystem, WWW 2006*.

Tomoyuki Nanno, Toshiaki Fujiki, Yasuhiro Suzuki, and Manabu Okumura. 2004. Automatically Collecting, Monitoring, and Mining Japanese Weblogs. In *Proceedings of the 13th international World Wide Web conference on Alternate track papers & posters*, pages 320–321. ACM.

Christopher Olston and Marc Najork. 2010. Web Crawling. *Foundations and Trends in Information Retrieval*, 4(3):175–246.

Jeff Pasternack and Dan Roth. 2009. Extracting article text from the web with maximum subsequence segmentation. In *Proceedings of the 18th international conference on World Wide Web*, pages 971–980.

Matthew E. Peters and Dan Lecocq. 2013. Content extraction using diverse feature sets. In *Proceedings of the 22nd International Conference on World Wide Web*, pages 89–90.

Jan Pomikálek. 2011. *Removing boilerplate and duplicate content from web corpora*. Ph.D. thesis, Masaryk University.

Pir Abdul Rasool Qureshi and Nasrullah Memon. 2012. Hybrid model of content extraction. *Journal of Computer and System Sciences*, 78(4):1248–1257.

Kevin P. Scannell. 2007. The Crúbadán Project: Corpus building for under-resourced languages. In *Proceedings of the 3rd Web as Corpus Workshop*, volume 4, pages 5–15, Louvain-la-Neuve.

Roland Schäfer. 2016. CommonCOW: massively huge web corpora from CommonCrawl data and a method to distribute them freely under restrictive EU copyright laws. In *Proceedings of the 10th International Conference on Language Resources and Evaluation (LREC'16)*, pages 4500–4504. ELRA.

Roland Schäfer. 2017. Accurate and efficient general-purpose boilerplate detection for crawled web corpora. *Language Resources and Evaluation*, 51(3):873–889.

Roland Schäfer, Adrien Barbaresi, and Felix Bildhauer. 2013. The Good, the Bad, and the Hazy: Design Decisions in Web Corpus Construction. In *Proceedings of the 8th Web as Corpus Workshop*, pages 7–15.

Roland Schäfer and Felix Bildhauer. 2012. Building Large Corpora from the Web Using a New Efficient Tool Chain. In *Proceedings of the 8th Conference on Language Resources and Evaluation (LREC'12)*, pages 486–493. ELRA.

Miroslav Spousta, Michal Marek, and Pavel Pecina. 2008. Victor: the Web-Page Cleaning Tool. In *4th Web as Corpus Workshop (WAC-4)*, pages 12–17.

Fei Sun, Dandan Song, and Lejian Liao. 2011. DOM-based content extraction via text density. In *Proceedings of the 34th international ACM SIGIR conference on Research and development in Information Retrieval*, pages 245–254.

Karane Vieira, Altigran S Da Silva, Nick Pinto, Edleno S De Moura, Joao MB Cavalcanti, and Juliana Freire. 2006. A Fast and Robust Method for Web Page TemplateDetection and Removal. In *Proceedings of the 15th ACM International Conference on Information and Knowledge Management*, pages 258–267.

Thijs Vogels, Octavian-Eugen Ganea, and Carsten Eickhoff. 2018. Web2text: Deep structured boilerplate removal. In *European Conference on Information Retrieval*, pages 167–179. Springer.

Junfeng Wang, Xiaofei He, Can Wang, Jian Pei, Jiajun Bu, Chun Chen, Ziyu Guan, and Gang Lu. 2009. News Article Extraction with Template-Independent Wrapper. In *Proceedings of the WWW 2009*, pages 1085–1086. ACM.

Tim Weninger, William H Hsu, and Jiawei Han. 2010. CETR: content extraction via tag ratios. In *Proceedings of the 19th international conference on World Wide Web*, pages 971–980.

Lan Yi, Bing Liu, and Xiaoli Li. 2003. Eliminating noisy information in web pages for data mining. In *Proceedings of the 9th ACM SIGKDD International Conference on Knowledge Discovery and Data Mining*, pages 296–305.

Cai-Nicolas Ziegler and Michal Skubacz. 2007. Content Extraction from News Pages using Particle Swarm Optimization on Linguistic and Structural Features. In *Proceedings of the IEEE/WIC/ACM International Conference on Web Intelligence*, pages 242–249. IEEE.

DODRIO: Exploring Transformer Models with Interactive Visualization

Zijie J. Wang **Robert Turko** **Duen Horng (Polo) Chau**
College of Computing, Georgia Tech
{jayw, rturko3, polo}@gatech.edu

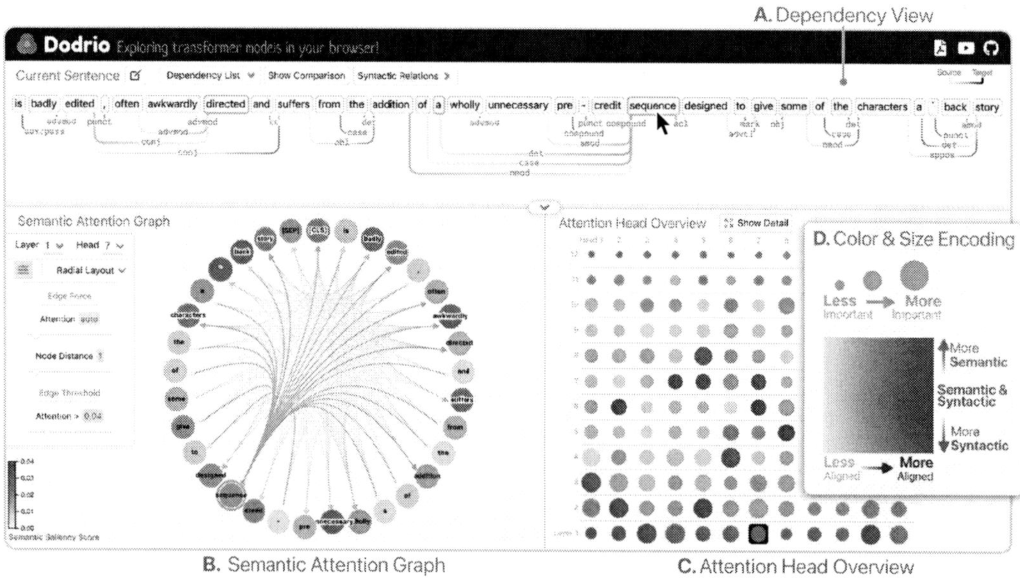

Figure 1: The DODRIO user interface showing user exploration of connections between attention weights from a fine-tuned BERT model and syntactic dependencies as well as semantic saliency scores on the SST2 dataset. **(A) Dependency View** enables users to hover over a word from the input sentence to highlight its associated dependency directed links as orange arcs (lighter is *source*; darker is *target*). **(B) Semantic Attention Graph** highlights the word's related tokens and their attentions; nodes are tokens (darker means more salient); a directed edge encodes attention weight between two tokens. **(C) Attention Head Overview** shows all attention heads in a multi-layer and multi-head model as a grid of circles, each head is **(D) colored** based on its linguistic knowledge in the model (more red→more semantic-aligned, more blue→more syntactic-aligned; darker→more aligned), and **sized** based on its importance score in the model (larger→more important).

Abstract

Why do large pre-trained transformer-based models perform so well across a wide variety of NLP tasks? Recent research suggests the key may lie in multi-headed attention mechanism's ability to learn and represent linguistic information. Understanding how these models represent both syntactic and semantic knowledge is vital to investigate why they succeed and fail, what they have learned, and how they can improve. We present DODRIO, an open-source interactive visualization tool to help NLP researchers and practitioners analyze attention mechanisms in transformer-based models with linguistic knowledge. DODRIO tightly integrates an overview that summarizes the roles of different attention heads, and detailed views that help users compare attention weights with the syntactic structure and semantic information in the input text. To facilitate the visual comparison of attention weights and linguistic knowledge, DODRIO applies different graph visualization techniques to represent attention weights scalable to longer input text. Case studies highlight how DODRIO provides insights into understanding the attention mechanism in transformer-based models. DODRIO is available at `https://poloclub.github.io/dodrio/`.

1 Introduction

The rise of transformer-based models have brought dramatic performance improvements across many NLP tasks (Wang et al., 2019). In particular,

Proceedings of the Joint Conference of the 59th Annual Meeting of the Association for Computational Linguistics and the 11th International Joint Conference on Natural Language Processing: System Demonstrations, pages 132–141, August 1st - August 6th, 2021.

BERT (Devlin et al., 2019) has demonstrated that transformer-based models pre-trained on large-scale corpora can be effectively fine-tuned for a wide variety of downstream tasks, such as sentiment analysis, question answering, and text summarization. However, how these language models generalize text representations learned from an unsupervised training process to downstream sentence understanding tasks remains unclear. There is a growing research body in interpreting transformer-based models, as understanding what these models have learned and why they succeed and fail is vital for NLP researchers to develop better models, and critical for decision makers to trust these models.

The current approach on interpreting transformer-based models focuses on probing and attention weight analysis (Hewitt and Liang, 2019). There is an active discussion on whether attention weights are explanations (Jain and Wallace, 2019), but more recent work has shown that they do provide insights on what the models have learned (Atanasova et al., 2020). In particular, research has shown that transformer-based models have learned to represent semantic knowledge and lexical structure in text (Rogers et al., 2020). Furthermore, interaction visualization systems have shown great potential in explaining complex deep learning models (Hohman et al., 2018; Wang et al., 2020). Some visualization tools have been developed for transformer-based models (Vig, 2019; Hoover et al., 2020; DeRose et al., 2021). However, these systems usually focus on visualizing and analyzing attention weights, instead of visually connecting them to linguistic knowledge that is crucial to investigate why transformer-based models work so well across different tasks (Rogers et al., 2020).

To address this research challenge, we present **DODRIO** (Figure 1), an interactive visualization tool to help NLP researchers and practitioners analyze and compare attention mechanisms with linguistic knowledge. For a demo video of DODRIO, visit `https://youtu.be/qB-T9j7UTgE`. In this work, our primary contributions are:

1. **DODRIO, a novel interactive visualization system** that helps users better understand the attention mechanisms in transformer-based models by linking attention weights to semantic and syntactic knowledge.
2. **Novel interactive visualization design** of DODRIO, which integrates overview + detail, linking + brushing, and graph visualizations that simultaneously summarizes a complex multi-layer and multi-head transformer model, and provides linguistic context for users to interpret attention weights at different levels of abstraction.
3. **An open-source**[1] and **web-based implementation** that broadens the public's access to modern deep learning techniques. We also provide thorough documentations to encourage users to extend DODRIO to their own models and datasets.

2 Background

Attention heads are comprised of weights incurred from words when calculating the next representation of the current word (Clark et al., 2019), which are known as attention weights. Easily interpretable, using attention to understand model predictions across domains is a very popular research area (Xu et al., 2015; Rocktäschel et al., 2016). In NLP, there has been a growing body of research on attention used as a tool for interpretability across many language tasks (Wiegreffe and Pinter, 2019; Vashishth et al., 2019; Kobayashi et al., 2020).

Existing visualization systems and techniques do not visually connect attention mechanisms to linguistic knowledge (Tenney et al., 2020; DeRose et al., 2021), we propose novel visualization approaches that foster exploration across semantically and syntactically significant attention heads in complex model architectures. For example, for every attention head in the 144 heads of BERT, the entry $A_{i,j}$ in the attention map A, represents the attention weight from token i to token j. With 144 $\times$ number of tokens $\times$ number of tokens attention weights in BERT for each input instance, it is challenging to systematically analyze these attention weights without abstraction and linguistic context. DODRIO aims to address this challenge by applying novel interactive visualization techniques.

3 Interface

3.1 Attention Head Overview

As a user explores the attention weights, the Attention Head Overview (Figure 1C) serves as a guide to effectively navigate the remaining views of the interface. With visual linking and brushing (McDonald, 1988), we unify attention head selection with the state of the remainder of the interface. This view of a grid of attention heads

[1] `https://github.com/poloclub/dodrio`

guides the user to inspect semantically and syntactically important heads. Attention heads are encoded as circles where color encodes the head's linguistic alignment (more red→more semantic-aligned, more blue→more syntactic-aligned; darker→more aligned), and sized represents its importance score in the model (larger→more important) (Figure 1B).

We calculate the **semantic score** m by computing the cosine similarity between the sum of attentions received for each token at a given head, and the sentiment score of each token. If the sentiment score is not available in a dataset, we use the saliency score for each token instead. The saliency score of a token measures how important that token contributes to the final model prediction (Barredo Arrieta et al., 2020), and it is shown to correlate with word semantics (Atanasova et al., 2020).

Following Clark et al. (2019)'s framework, we use the source token's most-attended token as its predicted dependency target. For each existing dependency relationship, we compute each head's average accuracy across all instances. Finally, we calculate the head's **syntactic score** n by taking the maximum of its average accuracy across all existing dependency relationships (ground truth or generated by a parser).

There are multiple metrics to measure the importance of a given attention head. By default, we calculate the **importance score** c of an attention head by the average of its maximum attention for all instances in the dataset (Voita et al., 2019). DODRIO also supports using the sum of absolute gradients of attention weights in an attention head as its importance score c (Clark et al., 2019).

After computing these three scores, we create a linear color scale and a linear size scale to encode them in the Attention Head Overview (Figure 1C, D). We use the Hue-chroma-luminance (HCL) color space to represent colors in DODRIO. The HCL color space is designed to better align with human perception of colors, so that interpolations in this space is smoother and more consistent (Zeileis et al., 2009). We use the hue value (H) in the HCL color space to encode $m - n$ with range [-1, 0, 1] as [**blue**, **purple**, **red**]; the luminance value (L) to encode $\max(m, n)$ (range [0, 1]); and the size of circles to encode c (range [0, 1]). With our color and size encoding, the Attention Head Overview (Figure 1C and Figure 2) provides an accurate and efficient summarization of attention heads.

In the Attention Head Overview, users can also

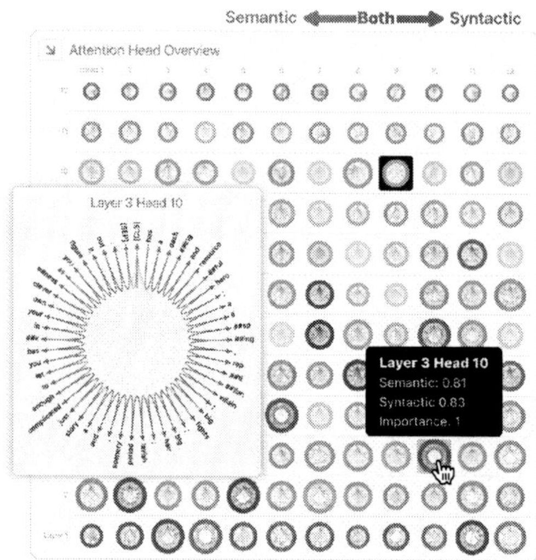

Figure 2: The expanded Attention Head Overview provides a preview of all attention heads for the input sentence. Attention heads are represented as a grid of rings (right) where their attention weights are shown in the middle. Each ring's color and size encode the attention head's linguistic knowledge alignment and importance score (**red**→semantic; **purple**→semantic and syntactic; **blue**→syntactic; larger→more important). Users can click an attention head to inspect its attention weights in detail in a radial layout window (left).

click a button to show the expanded Attention Head Overview (Figure 2) that additionally provides a preview of the attention pattern in each attention head through the *Radial Layout* visualization. Hovering over one attention head displays its linguistic and importance information.

3.2 Syntactic Dependencies

Word relations in a sentence are important features to understand the lexical makeup of a sentence, which can help users further deduce model decisions in the context of sentence structure. In DODRIO, a user can explore an attention head with input sentence's dependency relationships.

Dependency View (Figure 1A). We visualize true dependency relations, if available, or relations tagged by the CoreNLP pipeline (Manning et al., 2014) linked with the Semantic Attention Graph for users to investigate syntax-sensitive behavior at different attention heads. The user can further explore the dependency representation in a hierarchical structure by filtering dependency relations.

Comparison View (Figure 3). Understanding raw attention weights are best interpreted relative

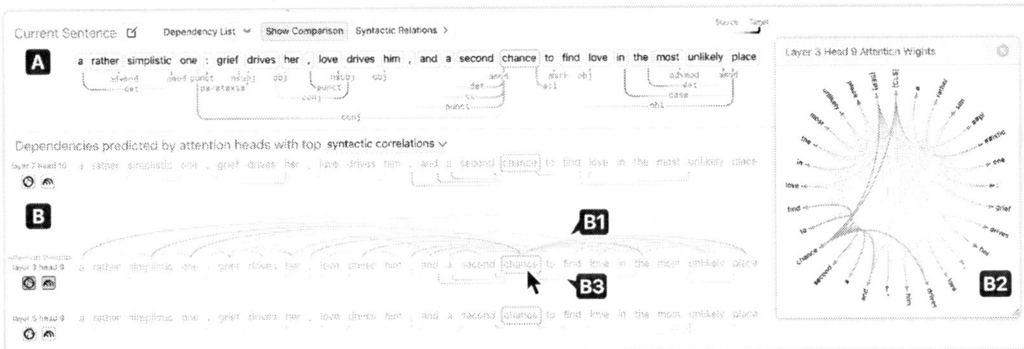

Figure 3: The Comparison View allows users to compare multiple attention heads and explore the connection between attention weights and the syntactic structure of the input sentence. (**A**) The top *rectangular arc diagram* visualizes dependencies generated by a parser (lighter is source; darker is target). (**B**) Each attention head is represented as a row of tokens where (**B1**) the top *curved arc diagram* and (**B2**) the *radial layout window* display the selected head's attention weights on demand. (**B3**) The *rectangular arc diagram* below the tokens shows the dependencies predicted using attentions. Hovering over one token highlights all associated attentions and dependency links.

to the attention weights at other attention heads in the model. The Comparison View enables users to examine the dependencies predicted by attention heads (Figure 3-B3). A user can select additional attention representations under each attention head label within this view to supplement their analysis of attention with respect to the grammatical structure of the sentences. By viewing the attention edges drawn above the tokens, which encode attention weight magnitude with opacity *in the Arc Layout* (Figure 3-B1), a user can maintain word-order context in the sentence, while the attention representation utilizing a *Radial Layout* (Figure 3-B2) of attention edges allows for a clearer interpretation the attention distribution. The edge linking with interaction between this view and the Dependency View further reinforces the syntax-sensitive behavior present in attention heads

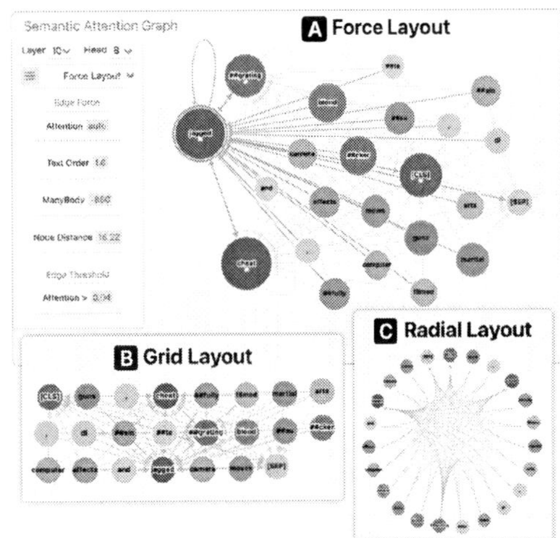

Figure 4: The Semantic Attention Graph employs three graph visualization techniques to show the attention weights. (**A**) The *force layout* allows users to flexibly change token positions; (**B**) the *grid layout* enhances the readability of input sentence; (**C**) the *radial layout* compactly highlights attention patterns.

3.3 Semantic Attention Graph

The attention map at each head can be interpreted as an adjacency matrix, which can be visualized using different graph visualization techniques (Figure 4). Users can primarily use this interactive graph view to inspect semantically significant attention heads, as defined the Attention Head Overview. Since the node color encodes the saliency score, linked to word's semantics (Li et al., 2016), the behavior of the attention mechanism in the model can be evaluated from a semantic perspective.

Similarly to representations in the Comparison View, the Semantic Attention Graph representations can be customized with interaction to allow for detailed attention inspection for selected tokens (Figure 4A), preserve token-order context in the *Grid Layout* (Figure 4B), or allow for clear attention analysis in the *Radial Layout* (Figure 4C). Adjusting graph parameters in the side panel of this view encourages the user to customize the graph representation to ease attention analysis (eg. adjusting the *edge threshold* parameter will only show attention weights with a greater magnitude) (Figure 4-A left). We utilize linking to allow the user to interpret tokens in the context of their attention weights and dependence relations simultaneously as both nodes and edges are highlighted when a user hovers over a node in either the Semantic Attention Graph or the Dependency View.

3.4 Instance Selection View

For a robust understanding of the attention mechanisms in Transformers, it is important to explore the behavior of attention across interesting components of a sentence (eg. coreferences, word sense, etc.) present in various instances in a dataset.

The **Embedding View** (Figure S1-A) uses UMAP (McInnes et al., 2018) to project text instance's model representation computed by concatenating the last four hidden state layers of BERT to a 2D space and visualizes it with a scatter plot.

The **Table View** (Figure S1-B) allows for instance selection while providing the user with instance's true and predicted labels. Users can hover over a dot in the Embedding View to view the sentence text, and click a dot or a row in the Table View to change DODRIO's input sentence.

4 Case Study

4.1 Understanding Sentiment in BERT

How does a Transformer handle conflicting sentiment in opinionated phrases when resolving coreferences? In DODRIO, we can explore the attention mechanism within a text instance from a movie review dataset, SST2 (Socher et al., 2013), such as *"A coming-of-age film that avoids the cartoonish clichés and sneering humor of the genre as it provides a fresh view of an old type."* Using this sentence, we can explore the concept of *sentiment consistency* as proposed by (Ding and Liu, 2010) in the context of coreference resolution.

When interpreting the sentence above, it is clear to us that "it" refers to the "film" because the first half of the sentence expresses positive sentiment towards the "film" and negative towards the "genre," while the second half of the sentence represents a positive opinion on the "film." We can deduce that "it" refers to the "film" as sentiment is expressed in a consistent manner as discussed by (Ding and Liu, 2010). By exploring the Attention Head Overview of DODRIO (Figure S3), we can select an attention head that conveys semantically significant information as indicated by the 2D color scale (eg. layer 1, head 7). As we begin to analyze the Semantic Attention Graph (Figure S3-left), we can hover over the node representing "it" to visualize the attention behavior. "It" attends highly to "film," which validates the coreference resolution policy that we discussed above (Figure S3-right). Users are encouraged to explore other attention heads as well to compare the behavior of the attention mechanism across various linguistic features.

4.2 Penn Treebank Analysis

Understanding attention across natural language tasks is pivotal for a systematic understanding of the attention mechanism as it relates to interpretability (Vashishth et al., 2019). If we visualize BERT on a text corpus with annotated syntactic sentence structure, like Penn Treebank (Marcus et al., 1993), can attention accurately predict syntactic heads, and what patterns will we observe?

To investigate these ideas, we navigate to the Dependency View within DODRIO. Beginning in the Dependency View, we observe edges of human annotated dependency relations connecting each token to its syntactic head, rather than part of speech (POS) tagging and dependency parsing annotations by the CoreNLP pipeline (Manning et al., 2014) when human annotations are not provided. To identify whether some attention heads more accurately attend to the syntactic heads of each token, we will enter the Comparison View (Figure 3) by clicking the *Show Comparison* button in the toolbar.

As we see in Figure 3-B3, DODRIO highlights correct syntactic head predictions by attention with a gradient edge, which is linked with the true dependencies in the Dependency View. After exploring various instances, we begin to understand patterns of certain attention heads. For example, we observe that attention head 9 in layer 3 attends to nominals (group of nouns and adjectives: `obj`, `nmod`, `obl`, etc.) across unique instances (Figure S2). This behavior highlights the syntax-aware attention that exists in BERT as discussed by (Clark et al., 2019). Visualizing consistent behavior by attention heads in Transformers outlines how the attention mechanism lends itself to model interpretability.

4.3 Exploring DistilBERT

The computational barrier to achieve state-of-the-art performance on natural language tasks with large pre-trained Transformers like BERT (Devlin et al., 2019) was lowered when DistilBERT (Sanh et al., 2019), a smaller version of BERT, was presented. DistilBERT is 40% smaller and retains up to 97% performance compared to BERT with half as many self-attention layers. With DODRIO,

A. DistilBERT

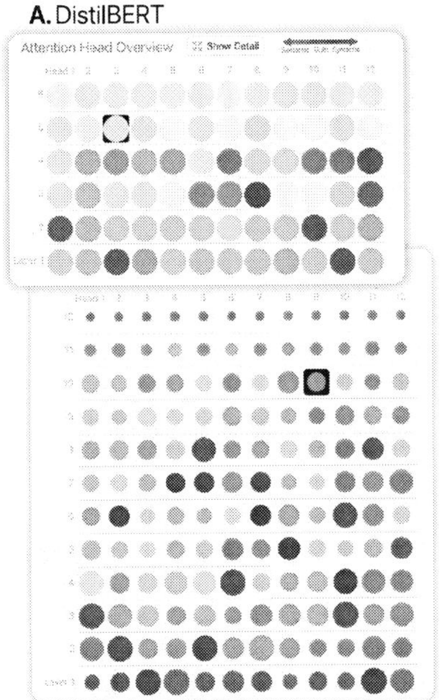

B. BERT-Base

Figure 5: The Attention Head Overview showing attention head roles for two transformer-based models. (**A**) All heads in DistilBERT are important and heads in early layers tend to have stronger linguistic alignment. (**B**) Attention heads in earlier layers tend to be more important and more semantic-aligned in BERT-Base.

we can analyze attention mechanisms at various attention heads in DistilBERT to understand how attention compares to its larger version, BERT.

Using the Attention Head Overview from DODRIO to visualize DistilBERT (Figure 5), we immediately notice that all radial attention head representations have the same diameter, unlike in the case of BERT. Upon further inspection, we see that all attention heads have a confidence score that is very close to one via the tooltip present when hovering over an attention head, which indicates that every attention head has highly attended to tokens on average. As we continue to explore the attention heads, we recognize a similar pattern of syntactic and semantic attention heads, but in the later layers the attention head rings have a much higher luminance in DistilBERT than they did in BERT. According to the 2D color scale (Figure 1D), this represents a lower overall score meaning that these attention heads neither attend to primarily text semantics of grammatical structure. It might imply that DistilBERT has learned some other linguistic knowledge beyond simple word semantics and syntactice dependencies. We can then conduct quantitative experiment to test this hypothesis formed by using DODRIO.

5 Discussion

DODRIO aims to help NLP researchers and practitioners to explore attention mechanisms in transformer-based models with linguistic knowledge. With overview + detail, linking + brushing, graph visualization techniques, DODRIO enables the users to investigate attention weights with different levels of abstraction in a context with both semantic and syntactic information. Through use cases, we demonstrate that DODRIO not only helps users validate existing research results regarding the connections between attention weights with linguistic information, but also inspires the users to form hypothesis regarding the behavior and roles of attention heads across different models.

We acknowledge that there is an active discussion on whether attention weights can help people interpret transformer-based models (Jain and Wallace, 2019) and whether the attentions can be directly linked to the corresponding tokens in interpretation tasks (Brunner et al., 2020). Our work joins the growing research body in NLP interpretability and human-centered NLP, highlighting novel visualization designs that can be generalized to other interactive NLP systems. Despite the increasing popularity of applying Human-computer Interaction techniques to help people from various fields interact with complex NLP systems, little work have been done to evaluate how effective these tools are (Wang et al., 2021). To fill this research gap, we plan to run a user study to evaluate the usability and usefulness of DODRIO.

6 Conclusion

We present DODRIO, an interactive visualization system that fosters the exploration of the attention mechanism in transformer-based models with linguistic knowledge. Through analysis from the model to the attention head level, users can explore how attention differs across a complex, state-of-the-art architecture over any instance within a dataset. Our tool runs in modern web browsers and is open-sourced, broadening the public's access to modern AI techniques. We hope our work will inspire further research in understanding attention mechanisms and development of visualization tools that help people interact with complex NLP models.

7 Broader Impact

We designed DODRIO with good intentions — to help researchers and practitioners more easily explore attention weights in transformer-based models and investigate why their models succeed and fail. However, bad actors could exploit this knowledge of whether and how the models may perform under different situations for malevolent purposes, such as manipulating the model prediction by injecting arbitrary keywords (Kurita et al., 2020). The potential vulnerability warrants further study.

Acknowledgments

We thank Haekyu Park, Rahul Duggal, and Nilaksh Das for their constructive feedback. This work was supported in part by NSF grants IIS-1563816, CNS-1704701, DARPA GARD, gifts from Intel, NVIDIA, Bosch, Google, Amazon. Use, duplication, or disclosure is subject to the restrictions as stated in Agreement number HR00112030001 between the Government and the Performer.

References

Pepa Atanasova, Jakob Grue Simonsen, Christina Lioma, and Isabelle Augenstein. 2020. A diagnostic study of explainability techniques for text classification. In *Proceedings of the 2020 Conference on Empirical Methods in Natural Language Processing (EMNLP)*, pages 3256–3274, Online. Association for Computational Linguistics.

Alejandro Barredo Arrieta, Natalia Díaz-Rodríguez, Javier Del Ser, Adrien Bennetot, Siham Tabik, Alberto Barbado, Salvador Garcia, Sergio Gil-Lopez, Daniel Molina, Richard Benjamins, Raja Chatila, and Francisco Herrera. 2020. Explainable artificial intelligence (xai): Concepts, taxonomies, opportunities and challenges toward responsible ai. *Information Fusion*, 58:82–115.

Gino Brunner, Yang Liu, Damián Pascual, Oliver Richter, Massimiliano Ciaramita, and Roger Wattenhofer. 2020. On identifiability in transformers.

Kevin Clark, Urvashi Khandelwal, Omer Levy, and Christopher D. Manning. 2019. What does BERT look at? an analysis of BERT's attention. In *Proceedings of the 2019 ACL Workshop BlackboxNLP: Analyzing and Interpreting Neural Networks for NLP*, pages 276–286, Florence, Italy. Association for Computational Linguistics.

J. F. DeRose, J. Wang, and M. Berger. 2021. Attention flows: Analyzing and comparing attention mechanisms in language models. *IEEE Transactions on Visualization and Computer Graphics*, 27(2):1160–1170.

Jacob Devlin, Ming-Wei Chang, Kenton Lee, and Kristina Toutanova. 2019. BERT: Pre-training of deep bidirectional transformers for language understanding. In *Proceedings of the 2019 Conference of the North American Chapter of the Association for Computational Linguistics: Human Language Technologies, Volume 1 (Long and Short Papers)*, pages 4171–4186, Minneapolis, Minnesota. Association for Computational Linguistics.

Xiaowen Ding and Bing Liu. 2010. Resolving object and attribute coreference in opinion mining. In *Proceedings of the 23rd International Conference on Computational Linguistics (Coling 2010)*, pages 268–276, Beijing, China. Coling 2010 Organizing Committee.

John Hewitt and Percy Liang. 2019. Designing and interpreting probes with control tasks. In *Proceedings of the 2019 Conference on Empirical Methods in Natural Language Processing and the 9th International Joint Conference on Natural Language Processing (EMNLP-IJCNLP)*, pages 2733–2743, Hong Kong, China. Association for Computational Linguistics.

Fred Hohman, Minsuk Kahng, Robert Pienta, and Duen Horng Chau. 2018. Visual analytics in deep learning: An interrogative survey for the next frontiers. *IEEE Transactions on Visualization and Computer Graphics (TVCG)*.

Benjamin Hoover, Hendrik Strobelt, and Sebastian Gehrmann. 2020. exBERT: A Visual Analysis Tool to Explore Learned Representations in Transformer Models. In *Proceedings of the 58th Annual Meeting of the Association for Computational Linguistics: System Demonstrations*, pages 187–196, Online. Association for Computational Linguistics.

Sarthak Jain and Byron C. Wallace. 2019. Attention is not Explanation. In *Proceedings of the 2019 Conference of the North American Chapter of the Association for Computational Linguistics: Human Language Technologies, Volume 1 (Long and Short Papers)*, pages 3543–3556, Minneapolis, Minnesota. Association for Computational Linguistics.

Goro Kobayashi, Tatsuki Kuribayashi, Sho Yokoi, and Kentaro Inui. 2020. Attention is not only a weight: Analyzing transformers with vector norms. In *Proceedings of the 2020 Conference on Empirical Methods in Natural Language Processing (EMNLP)*, pages 7057–7075, Online. Association for Computational Linguistics.

Keita Kurita, Paul Michel, and Graham Neubig. 2020. Weight poisoning attacks on pretrained models. In *Proceedings of the 58th Annual Meeting of the Association for Computational Linguistics*, pages 2793–2806, Online. Association for Computational Linguistics.

Jiwei Li, Xinlei Chen, Eduard Hovy, and Dan Jurafsky. 2016. Visualizing and understanding neural models in NLP. In *Proceedings of the 2016 Conference of the North American Chapter of the Association for Computational Linguistics: Human Language Technologies*, pages 681–691, San Diego, California. Association for Computational Linguistics.

Christopher Manning, Mihai Surdeanu, John Bauer, Jenny Finkel, Steven Bethard, and David McClosky. 2014. The Stanford CoreNLP natural language processing toolkit. In *Proceedings of 52nd Annual Meeting of the Association for Computational Linguistics: System Demonstrations*, pages 55–60, Baltimore, Maryland. Association for Computational Linguistics.

Mitchell P. Marcus, Mary Ann Marcinkiewicz, and Beatrice Santorini. 1993. Building a large annotated corpus of english: The penn treebank. *Comput. Linguist.*, 19(2):313–330.

John Alan McDonald. 1988. Orion i: Interactive graphics. *Dynamic Graphics Statistics*, page 179.

Leland McInnes, John Healy, Nathaniel Saul, and Lukas Grossberger. 2018. Umap: Uniform manifold approximation and projection. *The Journal of Open Source Software*, 3(29):861.

Tim Rocktäschel, Edward Grefenstette, Karl Moritz Hermann, Tomás Kociský, and Phil Blunsom. 2016. Reasoning about entailment with neural attention. In *4th International Conference on Learning Representations, ICLR 2016, San Juan, Puerto Rico, May 2-4, 2016, Conference Track Proceedings*.

Anna Rogers, Olga Kovaleva, and Anna Rumshisky. 2020. A primer in BERTology: What we know about how BERT works. *Transactions of the Association for Computational Linguistics*, 8:842–866.

Victor Sanh, Lysandre Debut, Julien Chaumond, and Thomas Wolf. 2019. Distilbert, a distilled version of bert: smaller, faster, cheaper and lighter. *arXiv preprint arXiv:1910.01108*.

Richard Socher, Alex Perelygin, Jean Wu, Jason Chuang, Christopher D. Manning, Andrew Ng, and Christopher Potts. 2013. Recursive deep models for semantic compositionality over a sentiment treebank. In *Proceedings of the 2013 Conference on Empirical Methods in Natural Language Processing*, pages 1631–1642, Seattle, Washington, USA. Association for Computational Linguistics.

Ian Tenney, James Wexler, Jasmijn Bastings, Tolga Bolukbasi, Andy Coenen, Sebastian Gehrmann, Ellen Jiang, Mahima Pushkarna, Carey Radebaugh, Emily Reif, and Ann Yuan. 2020. The language interpretability tool: Extensible, interactive visualizations and analysis for NLP models. In *Proceedings of the 2020 Conference on Empirical Methods in Natural Language Processing: System Demonstrations*, pages 107–118, Online. Association for Computational Linguistics.

Shikhar Vashishth, Shyam Upadhyay, Gaurav Singh Tomar, and Manaal Faruqui. 2019. Attention interpretability across NLP tasks.

Jesse Vig. 2019. A multiscale visualization of attention in the transformer model. In *Proceedings of the 57th Annual Meeting of the Association for Computational Linguistics: System Demonstrations*, pages 37–42, Florence, Italy. Association for Computational Linguistics.

Elena Voita, David Talbot, Fedor Moiseev, Rico Sennrich, and Ivan Titov. 2019. Analyzing multi-head self-attention: Specialized heads do the heavy lifting, the rest can be pruned. In *Proceedings of the 57th Annual Meeting of the Association for Computational Linguistics*, pages 5797–5808, Florence, Italy. Association for Computational Linguistics.

Alex Wang, Amanpreet Singh, Julian Michael, Felix Hill, Omer Levy, and Samuel R. Bowman. 2019. GLUE: A multi-task benchmark and analysis platform for natural language understanding. In *International Conference on Learning Representations*.

Zijie J. Wang, Dongjin Choi, Shenyu Xu, and Diyi Yang. 2021. Putting Humans in the Natural Language Processing Loop: A Survey. In *Proceedings of the First Workshop on Bridging Human–Computer Interaction and Natural Language Processing*. Association for Computational Linguistics.

Zijie J. Wang, Robert Turko, Omar Shaikh, Haekyu Park, Nilaksh Das, Fred Hohman, Minsuk Kahng, and Duen Horng Chau. 2020. CNN Explainer: Learning Convolutional Neural Networks with Interactive Visualization. *IEEE Transactions on Visualization and Computer Graphics (TVCG)*.

Sarah Wiegreffe and Yuval Pinter. 2019. Attention is not not Explanation. In *Proceedings of the 2019 Conference on Empirical Methods in Natural Language Processing and the 9th International Joint Conference on Natural Language Processing (EMNLP-IJCNLP)*, pages 11–20, Hong Kong, China. Association for Computational Linguistics.

Kelvin Xu, Jimmy Ba, Ryan Kiros, Kyunghyun Cho, Aaron Courville, Ruslan Salakhudinov, Rich Zemel, and Yoshua Bengio. 2015. Show, attend and tell: Neural image caption generation with visual attention. In *Proceedings of the 32nd International Conference on Machine Learning*, volume 37 of *Proceedings of Machine Learning Research*, pages 2048–2057, Lille, France. PMLR.

Achim Zeileis, Kurt Hornik, and Paul Murrell. 2009. Escaping rgbland: Selecting colors for statistical graphics. *Computational Statistics & Data Analysis*, 53(9):3259–3270.

8 Appendix

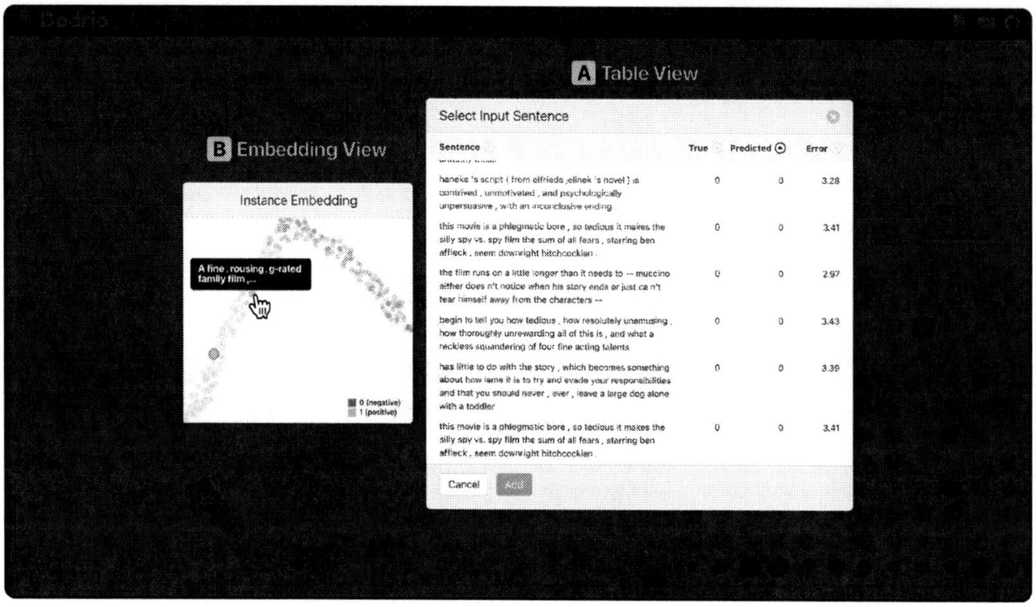

Figure S1: The Instance Selection View within DODRIO encourages users to explore sentences with interesting linguistic features to understand how various attention heads throughout a model attend to them. (A) **Table View** presents all text instances in a tabular format with other dataset and task-specific information as well with sortable columns for efficient instance browsing. (B) **Embedding View** motivates users to inspect text clustered by dataset label to explore semantically interesting phrases. These views are linked, so that clicking an instance in either view will update the state of the other view, while setting the instance will update the global state of the entire interface.

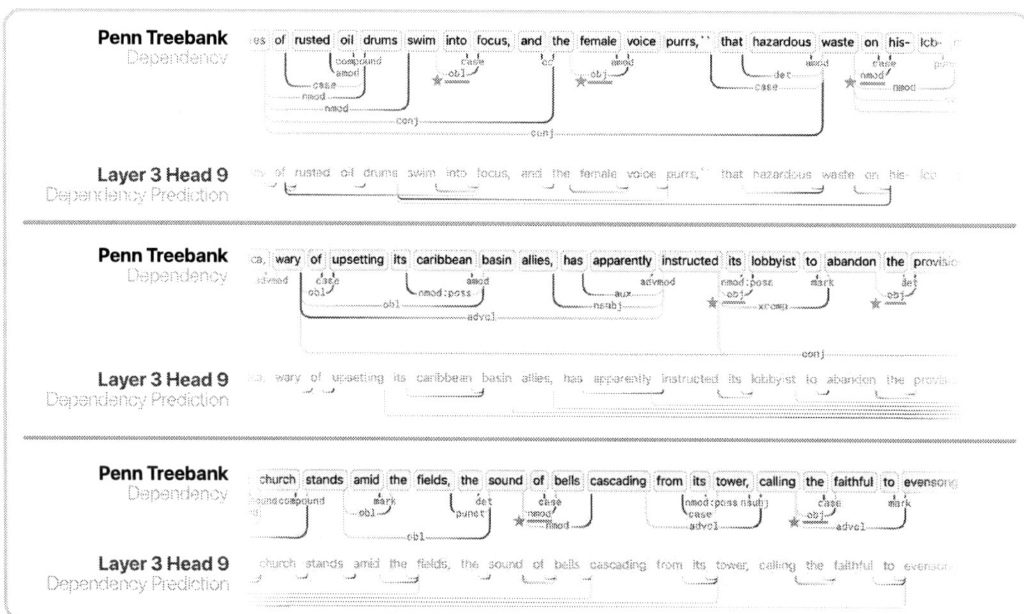

Figure S2: The Comparison View visualizes syntactic relationships on the Penn Treeback dataset. It highlights attention head (Layer 3 Head 9) that can accurately predict the nominal relationships (group of nouns and adjectives: `obj`, `nmod`, `obl`, etc.) across multiple unique instances.

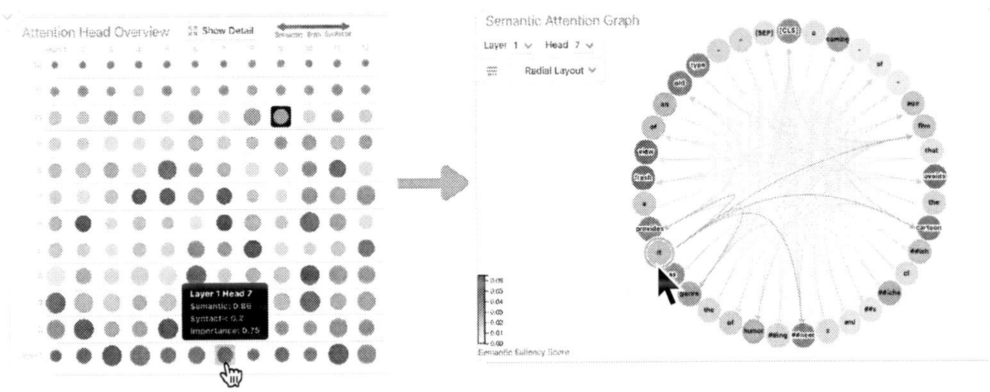

Figure S3: The **Attention Head Overview** (left) helps users identify interesting attention heads (e.g., more semantic-aligned and important heads), and then the **Semantic Attention Graph** (right) quickly visualizes the attention weight pattern of the selected head on the current input sentence, allowing users to rapidly validate their hypothesis regarding attention head's linguistic knowledge.

REM: Efficient Semi-Automated Real-Time Moderation of Online Forums

Jakob Smedegaard Andersen[1,2], **Olaf Zukunft**[1], and **Walid Maalej**[2]

[1]HAW Hamburg, Hamburg, Germany
jakob.andersen@haw-hamburg.de, olaf.zukunft@haw-hamburg.de
[2]University of Hamburg, Hamburg, Germany
maalej@informatik.uni-hamburg.de

Abstract

This paper presents REM, a novel tool for the semi-automated real-time moderation of large scale online forums. The growing demand for online participation and the increasing number of user comments raise challenges in filtering out harmful and undesirable content from public debates in online forums. Since a manual moderation does not scale well and pure automated approaches often lack the required level of accuracy, we suggest a semi-automated moderation approach. Our approach maximizes the efficiency of manual efforts by targeting only those comments for which human intervention is needed, e.g. due to high classification uncertainty. Our tool offers a rich visual interactive environment enabling the exploration of online debates. We conduct a preliminary evaluation experiment to demonstrate the suitability of our approach and publicly release the source code of REM.

1 Introduction

Online forums have become an integral part of many domains to facilitate participation and deliberation; particularly in online journalism (Manosevitch and Walker, 2009). More and more news sites enable users to participate in public debates around their reporting. Users regularly share their feedback, personal stories, and opinions about journalistic content (Häring et al., 2018). While online forums present a valuable space for deliberation and an information source for news organizations (Loosen et al., 2018), news sites are increasingly confronted with inappropriate and toxic content such as hate-speech (Davidson et al., 2017; Kolhatkar and Taboada, 2017) and spam (Chen and Chen, 2015; Martens and Maalej, 2019). Ethical and legal policies put pressure on news organizations to ensure lawful and netiquette compliant participation.

The expanding volume and velocity of user participation makes it increasingly difficult and expensive to rapidly detect and remove undesirable posts (Sood et al., 2012; Gillespie, 2020). Fully automated Machine Learning (ML) approaches for text classifications have shown remarkable improvements over the last years. However, ML models still lack user acceptance and applicability (Brunk et al., 2019; Gillespie, 2020). Fully automated approaches are known to be error-prone (Scharkow, 2013) and rarely reach the level of accuracy required to be applied in real-word settings.

We seek to overcome these limitations of fully automated approaches by letting humans manually correct and confirm artificial predictions. However, looping humans into supervised learning tasks is time consuming and cost intensive and does not scale well with larger workloads. The question arises which instances, i.e. forum posts, should better be assessed by humans. A common way to guide human moderation is to focus on instances where the ML model is unable to provide a reliable prediction (Pavlopoulos et al., 2017).

This paper introduces REM, a new user-centric tool for the semi-automated moderation of online forums, with a particular focus on online journalism. Our tool combines the fields of Human-in-the-Loop (HiL) (Holzinger, 2016) and Visual Analytics (Keim et al., 2008) to enable a more accurate, efficient, applicable, and transparent moderation process. Since the manual moderation of large datasets is tedious and cost intensive, we seek to minimize human efforts by focusing the manual moderation on instances which are most likely classified wrongly. We accomplish an efficient semi-automated moderation by relying on predictive uncertainty (Der Kiureghian and Ditlevsen, 2009).

Uncertainty estimates enable us to deal with instances a classifier can probably not infer correctly (known unknowns). However, classification

Proceedings of the Joint Conference of the 59th Annual Meeting of the Association for Computational Linguistics and the 11th International Joint Conference on Natural Language Processing: System Demonstrations, pages 142–149, August 1st - August 6th, 2021.

models can also provide misclassifications where a model does not know that its labelling might be wrong (unknown unknowns) (Attenberg et al., 2011). To deal with unknown unknowns, REM provides a rich visual-interactive interface to facilitate the exploratory analysis and labelling of forum discussions. We follow a user-centric moderation process, where moderators can correct arbitrary inferred labels. The uncertainty of predictions is visualized to support and guide moderation decisions. Further, we implement a novel moderation approach to reduce the amount of human effort required to reach a desired accuracy level. In a preliminary ML experiment, we evaluate the suitability and effectiveness of our moderation approach. The goal of REM is to:

- Support an efficient moderation of online forums.
- Facilitate overviewing online debates in news discussions.
- Plan of manual moderation efforts to reach a desired level of accuracy.

The remainder of the paper is structured as follows. Section 2 introduces our novel moderation approach implemented in REM. Section 3 describes the system design. Then, Section 4 presents our user-interface. In Section 5 we shortly describe the results of the preliminary ML experiment to demonstrate the suitability of our moderation approach as the core feature of our tool. Section 6 discusses related work, while Section 7 concludes the paper and outlines further work.

2 Content Moderation with Human-in-the-Loop

Content moderation in online forums is a typical labelling task. It refers to "the governance mechanisms that structure participation in a community to facilitate cooperation and prevent abuse" (Grimmelmann, 2015). Usually, ethical guidelines, moderation policies, or legal constraints are used to guide moderation decisions.

Our tool implements the Human-in-the-Loop (HiL) paradigm in order to achieve a more accurate and accepted moderation compared to fully automatic approaches. HiL describes a computational paradigm that is characterized by humans continually providing feedback, e.g. correcting artificial models in order to obtain a better predictive behaviour (Holzinger, 2016; Zanzotto, 2019). We aim to efficiently involve human moderators by only consulting them when artificial predictions are too unreliable to be trusted. For this, we use the predictive uncertainty (Der Kiureghian and Ditlevsen, 2009; Gal and Ghahramani, 2016) of an ML model to guide human involvement. Recent uncertainty quantification techniques are capable to identify likely-to-be-wrong predictions, which are worth being checked manually (Hendrycks and Gimpel, 2016).

Every moderation strategy is a trade-off between accuracy improvements and manual efforts. Generally, higher accuracy requires larger workloads. Since highly uncertain predictions are over-proportionally wrong (Hendrycks and Gimpel, 2016), the accuracy improvements are expected to saturate and get less rewarding. To the best of our knowledge, REM is the first tool to explicitly use the expected model behaviour evaluated on a representative dataset for providing guidelines about how much manual effort is needed to reach a desired level of accuracy. Section 5 reports on a preliminary evaluation of our moderation approach.

In addition, uncertainty quantification techniques are generally unable to detect all misclassifications, in particular those where the classifier is mistakenly assuming with a high certainty that they are correct (i.e. unknown unknown) (Attenberg et al., 2011). Therefore, our tool additionally relies on the exploratory visualization and analysis of the data (Keim et al., 2008). As in interactive-learning (Höferlin et al., 2012), we support the user-centred moderation of any instance. Using a visual-interactive interface, we assume that humans moderators are able to extract useful information to actively moderate model outcomes. Visual Analytics (Keim et al., 2008) enables moderators to better know and understand their data and thus to become capable to detect outliers, which are potentially misclassified by the model or are prone to a derailment, e.g., toxic users and topics which are prone to rudeness and require special care. Visual Analytics combines the strengths of humans' visual perception and reasoning along with the computational power of machines during the moderation process.

Figure 1 shows the HiL-workflow implemented in REM. New forum comments ① get immediately classified and enriched with uncertainty information ②. Our tool follows a holistic moderation approach, which builds on top of a binary classi-

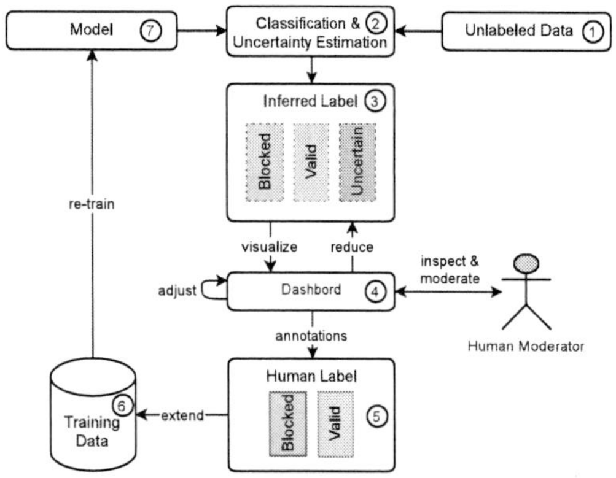

Figure 1: Human-in-the-Loop workflow of REM.

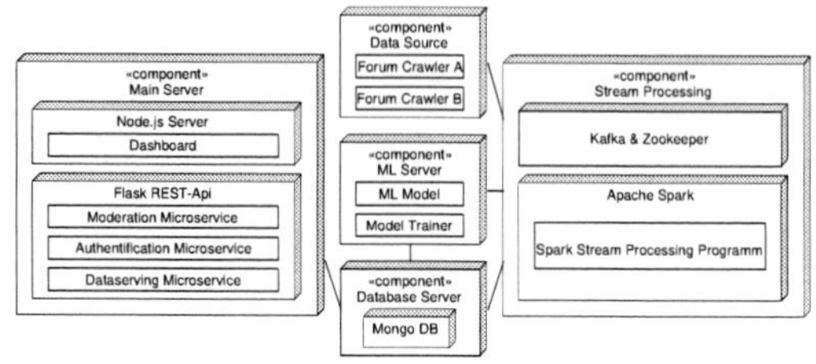

Figure 2: Main components of the semi-automated moderation tool REM.

fier. Each comment is either classified as *blocked* or *valid*. Comments can also be marked as *uncertain* ③ if their inferred labelling is too unreliable to reach a desired level of accuracy. Then, human moderators are asked to provide new and more reliable labels for uncertain comments ④. However, we also allow moderators to correct false-positives and false-negatives which are not marked as uncertain. Moreover, our approach integrates an active learning component (Lewis, 1995). Human labelled instances ⑤ are added to the training data ⑥ and used to continually re-train the model ⑦.

Previous studies indicate that such an active learning inspired approach is able to improve the accuracy of existing models (Arnt and Zilberstein, 2003). Since a continuous re-training is inefficient when moderators work in parallel, we implement active learning in batch mode (Hoi et al., 2009). The resulting incremental update of the model weights is particularly important since a model's accuracy is prone to decay over time due to data shifts (Moreno-Torres et al., 2012), i.e. statistical differences in training and operational data.

3 System Design

The components of our tool are depicted in the deployment diagram shown in Figure 2.

The access point of our tool is a web application served by a Node.js[1] server building on top of multiple micro-services. In our prototype, we obtain real-time data by frequently crawling the online forum of a large German news organization. We collect nearly 9,000 user comments daily, distributed across 20 news departments. To ensure a scalable processing of large volume and volatile real-time data, we implement an ML-pipeline based on the Kappa-Architecture (Kreps, 2014).

We use Apache Kafka (Kreps et al., 2011) as a message broker and the Structural Streaming API of Apache Spark (Zaharia et al., 2010) to implement the data stream processing. In the stream processing pipeline, we first check if comments are already classified with the current version of the model to save computational resources. For non-duplicates, we run text preprocessing steps such as stop word removal and lemmatization. We then apply a neural network based classification model. Then we use Monte Carlo Dropout (Gal and Ghahramani, 2016) to calculate uncertainty estimates. The ML model is built with Tensorflow (Abadi et al., 2016). Model training is performed offline. Finally, the data is persisted and served via MongoDB[2].

4 User Interface

Figure 3 shows the main page of our tool. The user interface consists of three views, which we describe in the following. We share the source code[3] of our prototype together with a video that showcases the tool's main features.[4]

4.1 Context-View

The *Context*-View provides an overview of the comments distribution according to the time-dimension and journalistic entities such as topics, articles, and users (comment writers). The upper bar chart displays the distribution of comments over time. The x-axis represents the time-dimension and the y-axis the total number of comments. Each bar represents a comment label with a three-colour scheme. Blocked comments (e.g. inappropriate, violating

[1] `https://nodejs.org/en/`

[2] `https://www.mongodb.com/`

[3] `https://github.com/jsandersen/REM`

[4] `https://youtu.be/cA92Io_xr6Q`

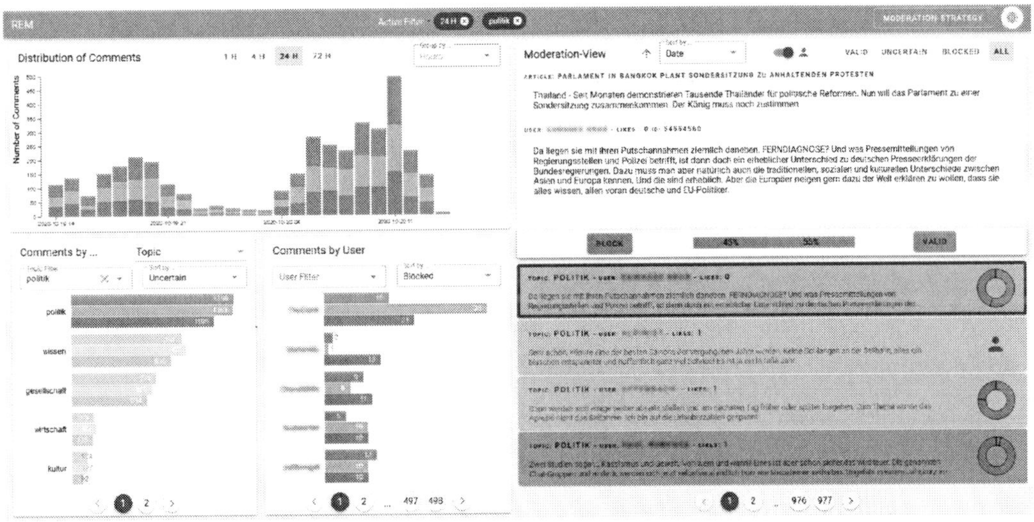

Figure 3: The main page of REM showing the Context-View (left) and the Moderation-View (right).

ect.) are marked as red, valid (none-blocked) comments are green, and uncertain comments are highlighted as grey.

Since the moderation of online forums is a real-time task, the tool focuses on recently added comments. The granularity of the time dimension can be changed through the button group on the top. Possible intervals are minutes, hours, and days. Moderators can select whether to show comments from the last 72 hours to only the last hour.

The lower part of the *Context*-View shows the distribution of comments with regard to journalistic entities, which are topics such as politics or economics and the articles identified by the titles. The second chart depicts the comment behaviour of the users. Each chart can be sorted according to the number of uncertain, blocked, valid, and all comments. All visualizations in the *Context*-View are responsive to filter operations. These can be triggered by clicking on the bars. Specific entities can also be searched over a text-field. Multiple filters can be chained to enable a flexible visual analysis.

4.2 Moderation-View

The *Moderation*-View shown in Figure 3 provides a detailed overview of the selected comments from the *Context*-View. All selected comments are listed here. Each entry on the list consists of the comment's text and additional meta information such as its corresponding topic, the posting user, and the number of recommendations given by other users. Similar to the colour scheme used in the *Context*-View, the colour of each cell represents the current label of the comment. The pie chart visualizes the model's conditional label probability for Blocked and Valid. In highly uncertain predictions, both class outcomes would be nearly equal. If a comment is already labelled by a human, a "human"-icon is shown instead of the pie chart. The list can be filtered to only show uncertain, valid, or blocked comments. Further, the entries can be sorted according to the timestamp or uncertainty. Most uncertain data must be moderated in our approach. Comments that are already manually moderated can also be hidden to enable a faster overview.

The detailed information about a selected comment is shown in the upper part of the view. Additional information about the corresponding article is also provided, followed by the text of the comment. The selected comment is highlighted with a blue box in the comments list. The actual moderation is performed via the buttons down below. An uncertain comment can be blocked or marked as valid. Predictions can also be corrected, e.g. a comment classified as valid can be manually blocked by the moderator. Additionally, the moderator can agree on artificial predictions to provide more training data for the active learning process. Corrections and additional labels are directly synchronized with the database of the training data.

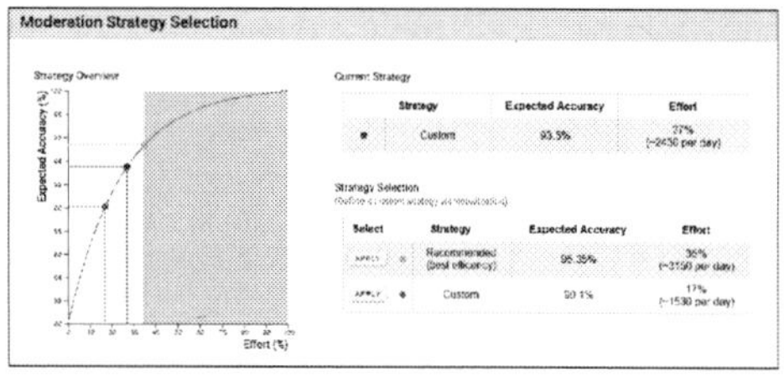

Figure 4: The *Control*-View of REM for managing the moderation strategy.

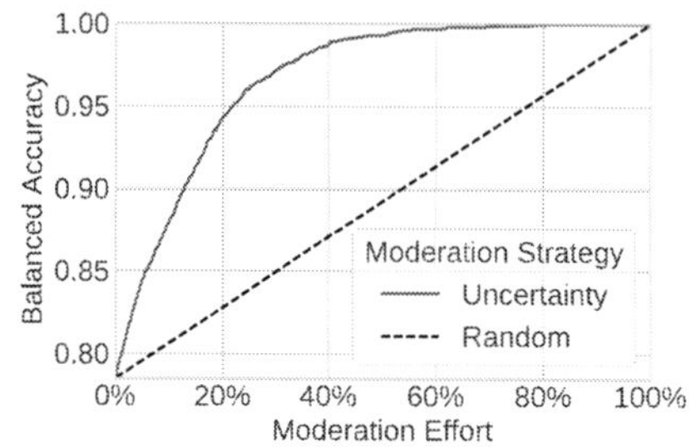

Figure 5: Balanced accuracy in term of moderation effort: uncertainty-based vs. randomly-sampled selection of instances to be moderated.

4.3 Control-View

The *Control*-View is dedicated to steer the moderation process. The view can be activated via the button *"Moderation-Strategy"* on the main page. As described in Section 2, we implement a novel approach to provide guidelines for how much manual effort is needed to efficiently reach a desired level of accuracy. The expected accuracy of the underlying classifier, when a certain amount of the most uncertain predictions are manually validated, is displayed by the line chart shown on Figure 4. On the right a user can select different moderation strategies which are also highlighted in the line chart. For each strategy the expected accuracy and the needed effort is depicted. A user can select a predefined moderation strategy or define a custom strategy by hovering and clicking on a point in the line chart. A moderation strategy affects the number of predictions, which are marked as uncertain. The currently applied strategy is shown above.

Since the efficiency of the moderation is expected to decrease with larger workloads, a point might be reached where further moderation efforts only lead to marginal accuracy improvements. To inform users of such inefficiencies, REM provides a recommended moderation strategy which seeks to optimize human moderation efforts with regard to the accuracy gain. We calculate the recommended moderation effort as the natural point of saturation (Satopaa et al., 2011). Inefficient workload is highlighted by the grey area in the line chart.

Usually, not every moderator should be able to change the moderation strategy and thus the target accuracy of forum moderation. Therefore, the *Control*-View can be secured by assigning specific roles like an administrator.

5 Preliminary ML Experiment

We conduct a preliminary experiment to demonstrate that our semi-automated ML approach is capable of efficiently improving the accuracy of a model during its operational use. For our experiment, we use the dataset provided by Davidson et al. (2017), which consists of 24.782 Twitter comments either labelled as offensive, hate-speech, or neither of them. In our experiment, we classify the comments into blocked (offensive and hate-speech) (83.2% of total) and valid comments (16.8% of total). Since the data is highly imbalanced, we use the balanced accuracy (Brodersen et al., 2010) to measure the performance of the classifier. We split the data into a training and validation set (7868 : 7868) for model training and a test set (9046) to evaluate our approach. The source-code of our experiment is part of our replication package.

We use Sentence-Bert (Reimers and Gurevych, 2019) to compute text encodings. These are used as the input for a feed forward neural network. Further, we apply Monte Carlo Dropout to estimate the uncertainty of the classifications. Our trained classifier reaches a balanced-accuracy of 78.48%. Figure 5 shows the balanced accuracy when a certain percentage of the most uncertain instances of the test data is moderated manually. In our experiment, we simulate manual moderation by selecting the ground truth labels. A workload of 100% corresponds to manually checking 9046 comments, which matches the daily amount of the expected comments in our application scenario. The balanced accuracy of a moderated classifier is computed based on the inferred and manually corrected labels. The results show that an uncertainty based moderation is more efficient than a random moderation strategy, where instances to be labelled are randomly sampled. For instance, moderating 25% of the data based on their uncertainty leads to a balanced accuracy of 96.08%. In comparison, a random moderation strategy requires a moderation effort of 81.8% to reach the same accuracy and is thus far less efficient.

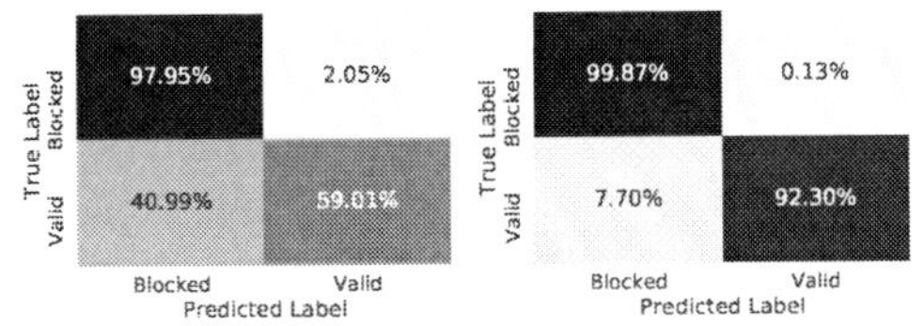

Figure 6: Normalized confusion matrix of the initial classifier (left) and the same classifier when 25% of the most uncertain predictions where moderated (right).

The confusion matrix of the initial and moderated classifier is depicted in Figure 6. The fully automated classifier obviously has difficulties to correctly detect valid comments. Only 59.01% of the valid comments were correctly identified. By moderating only 25% of the data, the detection of valid comments can be increased to 92.30%. As shown in Figure 5, the accuracy of the moderated classifier can be further improved by increasing the amount of human involvement. Thus, our approach is capable of improving the accuracy of a model with a reasonable manual effort.

6 Related Work

There have been previous attempts to efficiently coordinate human involvement to improve the accuracy of ML classifiers. Previous tools mainly focus on the task of interactive model building, also known as active learning (Settles, 2009) and heavily rely on multidimensional projections (Endert et al., 2012). Generally, HiL annotation tools provide a visual-interactive interface to guide human involvement (Höferlin et al., 2012; Bernard et al., 2018). However, tools based on point-visualization are limited in scalability, since data-points will overlap, causing visual clutter. Neves and Ševa (2019) presented a general review of annotation tools for documents.

HiL labelling tools: Seifert and Granitzer (2010) introduce a basic user-centered active learning tool, where humans sequentially select and label instances for the next training iteration. Similar to our approach, the authors utilize the predictive uncertainty to guide human involvement. However, they do not integrate a Visual Analytics component. Heimerl et al. (2012) present a user-centered visual-interactive active learning tool for text documents. Annotators can re-train models in batches and are able to inspect statistics about the model's performance. However, the authors do not consider uncertainty thresholds. The tool provided by Höferlin et al. (2012) enables annotators to manipulate the underlying model directly. This approach requires annotators to be Machine Learning experts, which does not hold for forum moderators e.g. in domains like online journalism. The HiL labelling tool proposed by Choi et al. (2019) facilitates an attention mechanism to explain predictions to annotators. They aim to reduce the time needed to perform annotation decisions and further increase the efficiency of labelling. Our tool might be improved by their findings. Link et al. (2016) introduce a similar semi-automated process for the moderation of social media content. Beside relying on the predictive uncertainty, they also define untrustworthy sources which need additional care. Similar to our approach, human moderation is requested when a prediction does not satisfy a certain confidence level. In contrast, they do not focus on optimizing the moderation in terms of reaching a desired level of accuracy and human efforts needed. Riehle et al. (2020) propose a platform for the semi-automated moderation of online discussions. Similar to our approach, comments are automatically pre-moderated and human moderators can correct or agree on the predicted labels. However, moderators are neither guided to identify comments that require manual attention nor do they assess the effect of the moderation process.

7 Conclusion and Future Work

We introduce a novel tool for the semi-automated moderation of large scale online forums to support content moderators during their daily work. Our tool combines methods from the field of Human in-the-Loop and Visual Analytics to enable an efficient and more accurate moderation process. We implement a unique approach to reduce and optimize human efforts, building on top of the predictive uncertainty of models. Further, we present a rich uncertainty aware visual-interactive interface to facilitate moderation via exploratory data analysis. Built on top of a big data architecture, our tool is designed to be highly scalable and to enable real-time moderation. A preliminary experiment indicates that our moderation approach is capable of improving the accuracy of a hate and offensive language classifier from 78.48% to 96.08% by only moderating 25% of a test dataset.

REM can be adapted to more generic use-cases, where annotators need to efficiently improve the accuracy of binary classifiers while also making use of active learning. Future work should focus on evaluating our approach regarding its usability, acceptance and usefulness in supporting the moderation of online forums.

Acknowledgments

This work was partly supported by the Hamburg's *ahoi.digital* program within the Forum 4.0 project.

References

Martín Abadi, Paul Barham, Jianmin Chen, Zhifeng Chen, Andy Davis, Jeffrey Dean, Matthieu Devin, Sanjay Ghemawat, Geoffrey Irving, Michael Isard, et al. 2016. Tensorflow: A system for large-scale machine learning. In *12th USENIX symposium on operating systems design and implementation (OSDI 16)*, pages 265–283.

Andrew Arnt and Shlomo Zilberstein. 2003. Learning to perform moderation in online forums. In *Proceedings IEEE/WIC International Conference on Web Intelligence (WI 2003)*, pages 637–641. IEEE.

Josh M Attenberg, Pagagiotis G Ipeirotis, and Foster Provost. 2011. Beat the machine: Challenging workers to find the unknown unknowns. In *Workshops at the Twenty-Fifth AAAI Conference on Artificial Intelligence*.

Jürgen Bernard, Matthias Zeppelzauer, Michael Sedlmair, and Wolfgang Aigner. 2018. Vial: a unified process for visual interactive labeling. *The Visual Computer*, 34(9):1189–1207.

Kay Henning Brodersen, Cheng Soon Ong, Klaas Enno Stephan, and Joachim M Buhmann. 2010. The balanced accuracy and its posterior distribution. In *2010 20th International Conference on Pattern Recognition*, pages 3121–3124. IEEE.

Jens Brunk, Jana Mattern, and Dennis M Riehle. 2019. Effect of transparency and trust on acceptance of automatic online comment moderation systems. In *2019 IEEE 21st Conference on Business Informatics (CBI)*, volume 1, pages 429–435. IEEE.

Yu-Ren Chen and Hsin-Hsi Chen. 2015. Opinion spam detection in web forum: a real case study. In *Proceedings of the 24th International Conference on World Wide Web*, pages 173–183.

Minsuk Choi, Cheonbok Park, Soyoung Yang, Yonggyu Kim, Jaegul Choo, and Sungsoo Ray Hong. 2019. Aila: Attentive interactive labeling assistant for document classification through attention-based deep neural networks. In *Proceedings of the 2019 CHI Conference on Human Factors in Computing Systems*, pages 1–12.

Thomas Davidson, Dana Warmsley, Michael Macy, and Ingmar Weber. 2017. Automated hate speech detection and the problem of offensive language. In *Proceedings of the 11th International AAAI Conference on Web and Social Media*, ICWSM '17, pages 512–515.

Armen Der Kiureghian and Ove Ditlevsen. 2009. Aleatory or epistemic? does it matter? *Structural safety*, 31(2):105–112.

Alex Endert, Patrick Fiaux, and Chris North. 2012. Semantic interaction for visual text analytics. In *Proceedings of the SIGCHI conference on Human factors in computing systems*, pages 473–482.

Yarin Gal and Zoubin Ghahramani. 2016. Dropout as a bayesian approximation: Representing model uncertainty in deep learning. In *international conference on machine learning*, pages 1050–1059.

Tarleton Gillespie. 2020. Content moderation, ai, and the question of scale. *Big Data & Society*, 7(2).

James Grimmelmann. 2015. The virtues of moderation. *Yale Journal of Law and Technology*, 17(1):2.

Marlo Häring, Wiebke Loosen, and Walid Maalej. 2018. Who is addressed in this comment? automatically classifying meta-comments in news comments. *Proceedings of the ACM on Human-Computer Interaction*, 2(CSCW):1–20.

Florian Heimerl, Steffen Koch, Harald Bosch, and Thomas Ertl. 2012. Visual classifier training for text document retrieval. *IEEE Transactions on Visualization and Computer Graphics*, 18(12):2839–2848.

Dan Hendrycks and Kevin Gimpel. 2016. A baseline for detecting misclassified and out-of-distribution examples in neural networks. *arXiv preprint arXiv:1610.02136*.

Benjamin Höferlin, Rudolf Netzel, Markus Höferlin, Daniel Weiskopf, and Gunther Heidemann. 2012. Inter-active learning of ad-hoc classifiers for video visual analytics. In *2012 IEEE Conference on Visual Analytics Science and Technology (VAST)*, pages 23–32. IEEE.

Steven CH Hoi, Rong Jin, and Michael R Lyu. 2009. Batch mode active learning with applications to text categorization and image retrieval. *IEEE Transactions on knowledge and data engineering*, 21(9):1233–1248.

Andreas Holzinger. 2016. Interactive machine learning for health informatics: when do we need the human-in-the-loop? *Brain Informatics*, 3(2):119–131.

Daniel A Keim, Florian Mansmann, Jörn Schneidewind, Jim Thomas, and Hartmut Ziegler. 2008. Visual analytics: Scope and challenges. In *Visual data mining*, pages 76–90. Springer.

Varada Kolhatkar and Maite Taboada. 2017. Constructive language in news comments. In *Proceedings of the First Workshop on Abusive Language Online*, pages 11–17.

Jay Kreps. 2014. Questioning the lambda architecture. *O'Reilly Media*. [accessed 2021-03-02].

Jay Kreps, Neha Narkhede, Jun Rao, et al. 2011. Kafka: A distributed messaging system for log processing. In *Proceedings of the NetDB*, volume 11, pages 1–7.

David D Lewis. 1995. A sequential algorithm for training text classifiers: Corrigendum and additional data. In *ACM SIGIR Forum*, volume 29, pages 13–19. ACM.

Daniel Link, Bernd Hellingrath, and Jie Ling. 2016. A human-is-the-loop approach for semi-automated content moderation. In *In Proceedings of the ISCRAM 2016 Conference*.

Wiebke Loosen, Marlo Häring, Zijad Kurtanović, Lisa Merten, Julius Reimer, Lies van Roessel, and Walid Maalej. 2018. Making sense of user comments: Identifying journalists' requirements for a comment analysis framework. *SCM Studies in Communication and Media*, 6(4):333–364.

Edith Manosevitch and Dana Walker. 2009. Reader comments to online opinion journalism: A space of public deliberation. In *International Symposium on Online Journalism*, volume 10, pages 1–30.

Daniel Martens and Walid Maalej. 2019. Towards understanding and detecting fake reviews in app stores. *Empirical Software Engineering*, 24(6):3316–3355.

Jose G Moreno-Torres, Troy Raeder, RocíO Alaiz-Rodríguez, Nitesh V Chawla, and Francisco Herrera. 2012. A unifying view on dataset shift in classification. *Pattern recognition*, 45(1):521–530.

Mariana Neves and Jurica Ševa. 2019. An extensive review of tools for manual annotation of documents. *Briefings in bioinformatics*, 22(1):146–163.

John Pavlopoulos, Prodromos Malakasiotis, and Ion Androutsopoulos. 2017. Deep learning for user comment moderation. In *Proceedings of the First Workshop on Abusive Language Online*, pages 25–35.

Nils Reimers and Iryna Gurevych. 2019. Sentence-bert: Sentence embeddings using siamese bert-networks. In *Proceedings of the 2019 Conference on Empirical Methods in Natural Language Processing and the 9th International Joint Conference on Natural Language Processing (EMNLP-IJCNLP)*, pages 3973–3983.

Dennis M Riehle, Marco Niemann, Jens Brunk, Dennis Assenmacher, Heike Trautmann, and Jörg Becker. 2020. Building an integrated comment moderation system–towards a semi-automatic moderation tool. In *International Conference on Human-Computer Interaction*, pages 71–86. Springer.

Ville Satopaa, Jeannie Albrecht, David Irwin, and Barath Raghavan. 2011. Finding a" kneedle" in a haystack: Detecting knee points in system behavior. In *2011 31st international conference on distributed computing systems workshops*, pages 166–171. IEEE.

Michael Scharkow. 2013. Thematic content analysis using supervised machine learning: An empirical evaluation using german online news. *Quality & Quantity*, 47(2):761–773.

Christin Seifert and Michael Granitzer. 2010. User-based active learning. In *2010 IEEE International Conference on Data Mining Workshops*, pages 418–425. IEEE.

Burr Settles. 2009. Active learning literature survey. Technical report, University of Wisconsin-Madison Department of Computer Sciences.

Sara Owsley Sood, Elizabeth F Churchill, and Judd Antin. 2012. Automatic identification of personal insults on social news sites. *Journal of the American Society for Information Science and Technology*, 63(2):270–285.

Matei Zaharia, Mosharaf Chowdhury, Michael J Franklin, Scott Shenker, Ion Stoica, et al. 2010. Spark: Cluster computing with working sets. *HotCloud*, 10(10-10):95.

Fabio Massimo Zanzotto. 2019. Human-in-the-loop artificial intelligence. *Journal of Artificial Intelligence Research*, 64:243–252.

SUMMVIS: Interactive Visual Analysis of Models, Data, and Evaluation for Text Summarization

Jesse Vig[‡] **Wojciech Kryściński**[‡] **Karan Goel**[†] **Nazneen Fatema Rajani**[‡]
[‡] Salesforce Research [†] Stanford University
{jvig, kryscinski, nazneen.rajani}@salesforce.com
kgoel@cs.stanford.edu

Abstract

Novel neural architectures, training strategies, and the availability of large-scale corpora haven been the driving force behind recent progress in abstractive text summarization. However, due to the black-box nature of neural models, uninformative evaluation metrics, and scarce tooling for model and data analysis, the true performance and failure modes of summarization models remain largely unknown. To address this limitation, we introduce SUMMVIS, an open-source tool for visualizing abstractive summaries that enables fine-grained analysis of the models, data, and evaluation metrics associated with text summarization. Through its lexical and semantic visualizations, the tools offers an easy entry point for in-depth model prediction exploration across important dimensions such as factual consistency or abstractiveness. The tool together with several pre-computed model outputs is available at `https://summvis.com`.

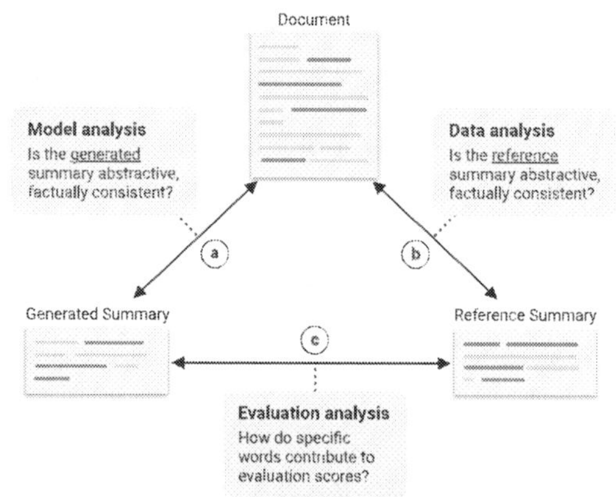

Figure 1: SUMMVIS supports fine-grained comparison between (a) source document and generated summary, (b) source document and reference summary, and (c) generated summary and reference summary, enabling analysis of models, data, and evaluation metrics.

1 Introduction

The field of Natural Language Processing has seen substantial progress in recent years driven by the availability of large-scale corpora (Brown et al., 2020; Raffel et al., 2020), developments in neural architectures (Vaswani et al., 2017; Zaheer et al., 2020) and training strategies (Devlin et al., 2019; Zhang et al., 2020a). Despite the promising results on benchmarks and recent findings in model analysis, the true performance, generalizability, and failure modes of modern neural models are not yet fully understood, due to the black-box nature of neural models and the unmanageable scale of recent datasets for manual analysis. Software tooling for NLP research provides a plethora of mature and easy-to-use libraries for model development, such as PyTorch (Paszke et al., 2019) or Transformers (Wolf et al., 2020a), but offers disproportionately fewer tools for visual analysis and debugging, which further hinders the understanding of model performance.

Within NLP, Automatic Text Summarization is a task that aims to convert long documents into short textual snippets that contain the most important information from the source document. To successfully summarize documents, models must first build an understanding of the source text that will allow them to evaluate the saliency of presented facts and then select only the most important details for the output summary. In case of abstractive approaches, the neural networks are also expected to paraphrase the selected content to generate novel sentences that fuse together the facts extracted from different sections of the document into coherent and factually consistent text.

Progress in the field is measured primarily using automatic metrics, such as ROUGE (Lin, 2004) or BERTScore (Zhang et al., 2020b), which quantify the lexical and semantic overlap between reference

Proceedings of the Joint Conference of the 59th Annual Meeting of the Association for Computational Linguistics and the 11th International Joint Conference on Natural Language Processing: System Demonstrations, pages 150–158, August 1st - August 6th, 2021.

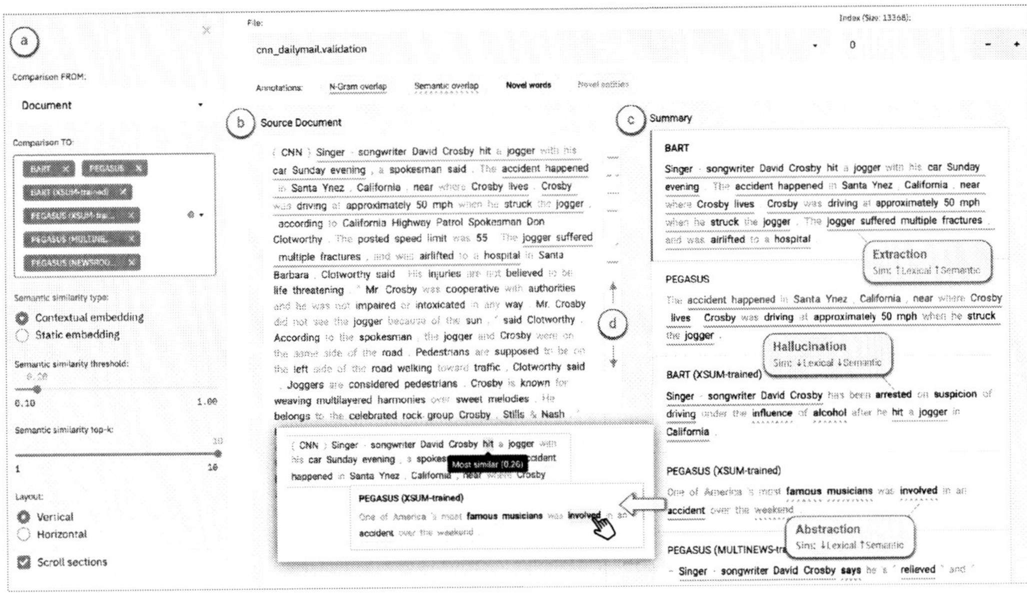

Figure 2: **Warning: Contains factually incorrect information.** SUMMVIS interface showing the first example from the CNN/DailyMail validation split. Interface components: (a) configuration panel, (b) source document (or reference summary, depending on configuration), (c) generated summaries (and/or reference summary, depending on configuration), (d) scroll bar with global view of annotations. Colored underlines align n-grams between source document and the selected summary (BART); colors are determined by the position of the containing sentence in the summary. Novel words in the summary that do not appear in the source document are **bolded**, while novel entities are bolded in red. Stopwords are grayed out and are not used in the matching algorithms. Dotted underlines indicate tokens that are semantically similar to a token in the source document (above the threshold specified in the configuration panel). The user may hover over a token to see the most semantically similar tokens in the source document (see inset image), or click on the token to auto-scroll the source document to the most similar token.

and generated summaries. While automatic metrics are convenient for model evaluation, they have been shown to be mismatched with human judgements (Fabbri et al., 2020) and only offer high-level insights while failing to pinpoint particular shortcomings of models. In-depth debugging across the different modes of analysis (Fig. 1) must be conducted through expensive and time-consuming human-based studies, where the substantial length of texts makes such efforts more labor-intensive.

Recent work in summarization analysis has looked at the problems of the field in isolation, focusing on: models (Kedzie et al., 2018; Kryściński et al., 2019, 2020), data (Zhong et al., 2019; Jung et al., 2019), and evaluation (Fabbri et al., 2020; Steen and Markert, 2021). However, these modes of analysis are strongly interconnected and isolating them could skew the broader view of the current state of the task and delay progress.

To address the mentioned challenges, we introduce SUMMVIS, an open-source interactive visualization tool for analyzing text summarization. SUMMVIS was designed to offer fine-grained insights into the models, data, and evaluation metrics, both in isolation and jointly, thus compensating for the shortcomings of automatic evaluation metrics and shortage of dedicated debugging tooling. SUMMVIS scaffolds human analysis by offering clear visual indicators of the semantic and lexical relationships between texts and intelligent navigation within text. The tool comes pre-loaded with a set of state-of-the-art model predictions for a quick starting point for model analysis and comparison and offers out-of-the-box integration with the HuggingFace Dataset API for custom use-cases. Through a case study of state-of-the-art summarization models we show how SUMMVIS can be used to quickly conduct non-trivial analysis, debugging, and comparison of model performance across important dimensions such as factual consistency or abstractiveness. A video demonstration of the tool is available at `https://vimeo.com/540429745`.

2 SUMMVIS

In this section, we present SUMMVIS, an interactive visualization tool that provides rich text comparison in summarization systems, enabling fine-grained analysis of models, data, and evaluation metrics. It comes pre-loaded with model outputs for state-of-the-art models over common benchmark datasets, as well as scripts for loading data for any dataset provided by the Datasets API (Wolf et al., 2020b) and any HuggingFace-compatible model.

2.1 Analysis Modes

SUMMVIS supports three modes of analysis, depending on the type of text being compared:

1. **Model Analysis** (Fig. 1a). By comparing the source document with *generated* summaries, SUMMVIS provides insights into a model's ability to abstract and faithfully retain information present in the document.
2. **Data Analysis** (Fig. 1b). By comparing the source document with the *reference* summary, SUMMVIS helps determine the degree to which the reference summary itself is abstractive and factually consistent with the source document.
3. **Evaluation Analysis** (Fig. 1c). By comparing the *reference* summary with the *generated* summary, SUMMVIS surfaces the word- and phrase-level relationships that form the basis of automated evaluation metrics such as ROUGE and BERTScore.

These analyses are interdependent with one another; for example, the behavior of a *model* depends on the *data* on which it was trained. By providing a unified interface for all modes of analyses, the user may also draw conclusions about the relationships between model, data, and evaluation, as we'll demonstrate in Section 3.

2.2 Text Comparison

Understanding abstractive summaries requires comparing not only surface similarities but also building a semantic understanding of the source document and summaries. Therefore SUMMVIS incorporates similarity measures based on both lexical and semantic overlap, as described below.

Lexical Overlap. The ability to quickly compare the lexical form of source document and summary is an important first step in analyzing a generated summary. For example, it is well known that many abstractive reference summaries are in fact largely extractive, copying long spans of text from the source document (Grusky et al., 2018). Other summaries might contain significant hallucinations, including words that are not found in the source document (Kryściński et al., 2020; Maynez et al., 2020). In order to identify these phenomena, SUMMVIS provides a lexical alignment based on shared n-grams between the two texts, which is also the basis for many automated metrics such as ROUGE.

Semantic Overlap. Lexical overlap is incomplete as a measure of similarity between texts since it only considers the surface form of words. For example, a summary that is highly abstractive may share few common words with the source article, despite having a similar meaning. To address such limitations, the tool also identifies semantically-related tokens by computing the cosine similarity between word embeddings, with the option of using static word embeddings provided by spaCy (Honnibal et al., 2020), or contextual embeddings from a pretrained RoBERTa (Liu et al., 2019) model. In the later case, we apply the same default embeddings[1] used in BERTScore, a common evaluation metric for abstractive summarization systems that correlates strongly with human evaluations (Zhang et al., 2020b). As we'll discuss in Section 3, the visualized semantic similarities can also help to interpret BERTScore values. We note that the BERTScore library[2] used in the tool also supports other models of semantic similarity, for example, models trained on scientific or non-English text.

Taxonomy. Considering both lexical and semantic measures of similarity provides a natural way to

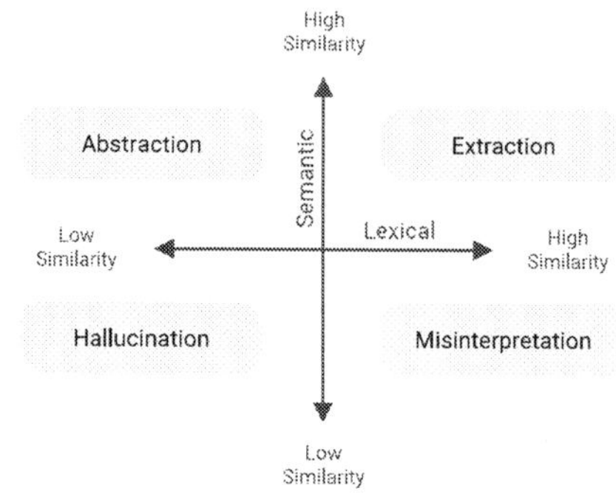

Figure 3: Taxonomy of textual relationships across lexical and semantic dimensions.

[1]RoBERTa-large layer 17

[2]https://github.com/Tiiiger/bert_score

chart out summarization datasets for further analysis. By comparing a source document to any summary along these two dimensions, four quadrants of behavior can be mapped out (Fig. 3):

1. **Extraction**: high lexical and high semantic similarity. The summary quotes text from the document verbatim.
2. **Abstraction**: low lexical and high semantic similarity. The summary consolidates and paraphrases information from the document.
3. **Hallucination**: low lexical and low semantic similarity. The summary is factually inconsistent, and includes information that is absent in the document.
4. **Misinterpretation**: high lexical and low semantic similarity. The summary misinterprets and uses information from the document, such as misunderstanding homonyms.

Examples of such cases will be discussed in the following sections.

2.3 Interface

The main components of the SUMMVIS interface are described in detail in Figure 2. The interface supports analysis of the model, data, and evaluation (Sec. 2.1) based on which types of text are selected by the user for comparison (Figs. 2b, 2c). The annotations provided by the tool highlight both lexical and semantic relations between the text (Sec. 2.2) and are designed to be lightweight, allowing users to quickly grasp the relationship between texts while still being able to clearly read the text.

The joint lexical and semantic annotations enable the user to understand the summaries according to the taxonomy in Figure 3. Examples of extraction, abstraction, and hallucination are highlighted in Figure 2. Since measures of semantic similarity may be unreliable, the tool also enables users to hover over tokens for additional details on the semantically matched tokens in the source document, which are highlighted based on their semantic similarity scores (Fig. 2, inset image). Additionally the score of the closest match is displayed, following the BERTScore algorithm, which computes the maximum semantic similarity score for each token before averaging the results over the full text. These features enable users to manually assess whether the tokens are in fact semantically similar.

The tool supports two additional features to accommodate long source documents: a global view and auto-scrolling functionality. The global view, embedded in the scroll bar region of the source document (Fig. 2d), displays a compressed view of the full document's annotations that is visible even when the document exceeds the viewable region. The user may also directly navigate to matched portions of the source documents not currently visible by clicking on related annotations in the summary.

2.4 System Architecture

The interface is implemented as a Streamlit[3] application with a highly customized HTML/JavaScript component that handles most interactions in the tool. The custom component enables a much richer interaction than a vanilla Streamlit app, while the Streamlit infrastructure allows for adapting or extending some components in the tool without necessarily writing additional HTML or JavaScript.

We provide pre-processing scripts to generate and cache all data required by SUMMVIS to ensure fast response times in the interface. These scripts are implemented using Robustness Gym (Goel et al., 2021) and integrate with the HuggingFace Datasets API (Wolf et al., 2020b) so that any summarization dataset available in the dataset repository or provided by the user as a `jsonl` file may be viewed in the tool. We additionally include scripts for caching outputs for any HuggingFace summarization model, and share pre-computed outputs of state-of-the-art summarization models: PEGASUS (Zhang et al., 2020a) and BART (Lewis et al., 2020). To increase the variaty of outputs, we chose model checkpoints fine-tuned on multiple popular summarization datasets: CNN/DailyMail (Hermann et al., 2015), XSum (Narayan et al., 2018), Newsroom (Grusky et al., 2018), and MultiNews (Fabbri et al., 2019), and decoded on the validation splits of two benchmark datasets: CNN/DailyMail and XSum.

3 Case Study: Debugging Hallucination

As discussed earlier, SUMMVIS supports joint analysis of the model, data, and evaluation metrics. We now demonstrate how we can draw from all three modes of analysis to study the problem of hallucination in summarization systems. Through the unified view of SUMMVIS, we analyze the example shown in Figure 4 and demonstrate the existence of hallucination, suggest a possible cause, and show

[3]https://github.com/streamlit/streamlit

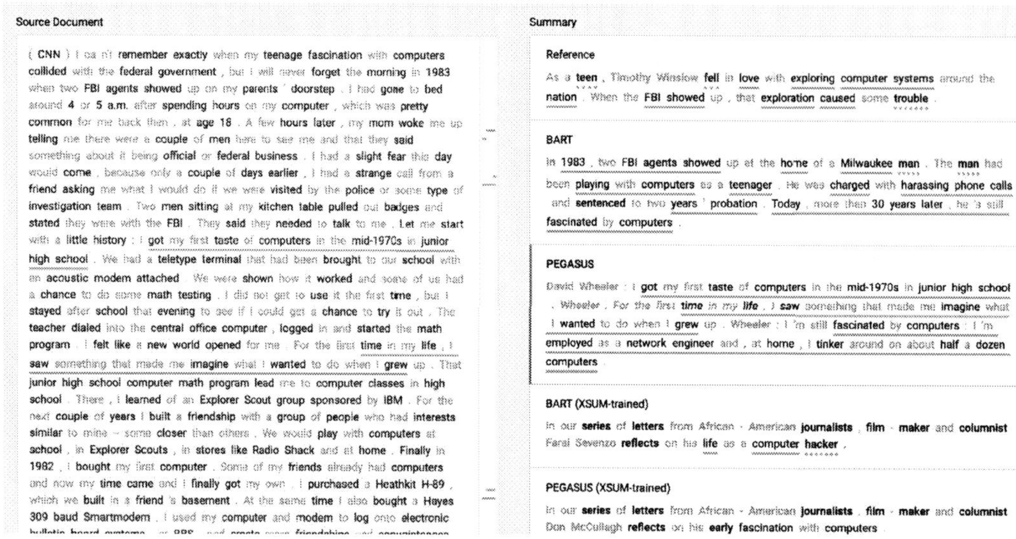

Figure 4: SUMMVIS snapshot of an example from CNN/DailyMail, showing the source document (left) and the reference summary along with generated summaries from four different models (right). The first two models are trained on CNN/DailyMail, while the last two are trained on XSum. Red text highlights entities in the summaries that are not present in the source document.

how a common evaluation metric prefers hallucinated entities over faithful descriptors in this case.

Model Analysis. SUMMVIS supports analysis of the model by visualizing the relationship between each generated summary and the source document. For the example in question (Fig. 4), this visualization reveals that three of the four models generate names of people that are absent from the source document. The XSum-trained models generate the names in the context of the phrase *"In our series of letters from African-American journalists, filmmaker and columnist <person_name> reflects on ..."*. suggesting that the hallucinations for these two models may be related to artifacts in the shared XSum training set that both models have memorized. On the other hand, the summary generated by the version of PEGASUS that was trained on CNN/DailyMail is largely extractive, copying several sentences, but then also inserting the name "*David Wheeler*", which is absent from the source document. We now show how artifacts in the *reference* summaries may explain this hallucination.

Data Analysis. We now turn to the visualization comparing source document and *reference* summary (Fig. 4, top right). We see that the reference summary also contains an entity that is missing from the source document ("*Timothy Winslow*"). This may be due to the name appearing in metadata such as author name that was available to the person writing the summary, but was not included in the dataset. If this pattern occurs in similar types of examples in the training set (e.g., first-person written articles), then it may effectively teach the model to hallucinate, providing a possible explanation for the model behavior described earlier.

Evaluation Analysis. One remaining question is how state-of-the-art models can hallucinate but still perform well on benchmark datasets according to standard evaluation metrics. Of course, one reason is that the models only hallucinate on some fraction of examples in the dataset. However, there is also the question of how the evaluation metrics score hallucinated content. While lexical overlap metrics such as ROUGE are well-defined, semantic similarity metrics like BERTScore are less well understood as they depend on embeddings from black-box neural network models.

SUMMVIS supports fine-grained analysis of evaluation metrics through its comparison of *generated* and *reference* summaries. In particular, the token-level semantic similarity scores visualized in the tool use the same similarity measure as BERTScore (Sec. 2.2). By inspecting these token-level relationships, we can better understand how hallucinated tokens contribute to the overall BERTScore, which is computed by aggregating token-level scores.

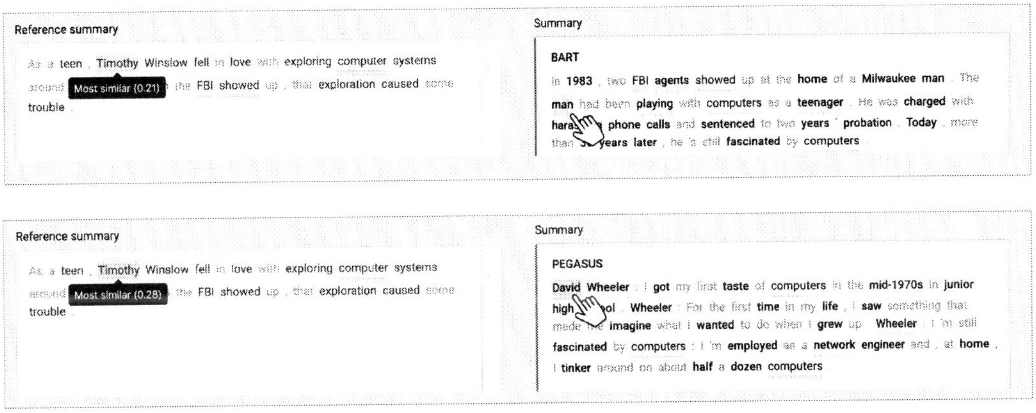

Figure 5: Snapshot from SUMMVIS showing the reference summary on the left and two of the generated summaries on the right. In the first example, the user has hovered over "*man*" in the generated summary, which causes the tool to highlight the most semantically similar word in the reference summary, "*Timothy*", with a similarity score of 0.21. A second occurrence of "*man*" has an even lower semantic similarity score of just 0.02 (not shown). In the second example, the user hovers over "*David*", revealing that this word is also most semantically similar to "*Timothy*", but with a higher similarity score (0.28).

Figure 5 shows the comparison between the reference summary and two of the generated summaries, revealing that the factually correct "*man*" has a lower maximum semantic similarity score compared to the hallucinated "*David*". The same is true for the corresponding hallucinated last name "*Wheeler*" (similarity: 0.28), and this disparity with "man" is even more pronounced for the hallucinated name "*Don McCullagh*" (Similarity: 0.34, 0.31) generated by the last model shown in Figure 4. Thus BERTScore does not discriminate factual consistency of proper names in this example, consistent with anecdotal evidence for other types of entities (Zhang et al., 2020b). Note that the hallucinated name "*Farai Sevenzo*" (Fig. 4, 4th row) has maximum similarity scores that are negative (-0.43, -0.12). This disparity may relate to name biases in word embeddings (Caliskan et al., 2017).

4 Related Work

Text Summarization requires models to be adept at both natural language understanding (NLU) and natural language generation (NLG). A gap in either of these areas has consequences on the progress of summarization as a whole. An example of this is the lack of meaningful metrics in NLG for high entropy tasks (Steen and Markert, 2021). Several recent works have realized the need for evolving benchmarks and evaluations (Goel et al., 2021; Gehrmann et al., 2021; Khashabi et al., 2021).

Existing tools support some forms of text comparison for summarization models. The Newsroom dataset visualization tool (Grusky et al., 2018) highlights n-grams in the summary that overlap with the source article. The LIT tool (Tenney et al., 2020) highlights words or characters that differ between reference and generated texts. However neither tool aligns (Yousef and Janicke, 2021) the matched text. The CSI framework (Gehrmann et al., 2019) and the Seq2SeqVis (Strobelt et al., 2019) tool align the source document and summary, but use model-specific attention mechanisms. SUMMVIS on the other hand supports a model-agnostic comparison between source document, reference summary, and generated summary, and aligns text along lexical and semantic dimensions.

5 Conclusion

In this work we introduced SUMMVIS, an interactive visualization tool for analyzing text summarization models, datasets, and evaluation metrics. Through a case study we showed that our tool can be used to efficiently identify the shortcomings and failure modes of state-of-the-art summarization models and datasets. Together with the tool we released a set of pre-computed model outputs to enable easy, out-of-the-box use. We hope this work will positively contribute to the ongoing efforts in building tools for model evaluation and analysis and enable a deeper understanding of the performance of summarization models and the intricacies of datasets and metrics.

6 Ethics Statement

To the best of our knowledge, there is no work on ethical bias in automated text summarization. The news summarization datasets currently used by the NLP community are mainly crawled from Western news outlets and therefore are not representative of a majority of geographies. There are also biases in news reporting that can distill into parameters of models trained on such biased datasets and may even be further amplified in the generated model outputs. All datasets are in English, and all models are trained on English datasets.

SUMMVIS uses spaCy for entity detection and because we did not stress test the detector, there might be biases in the system that have percolated into our tool. Similarly, the text similarity metrics used in our tool including the BERTScore and the word-embeddings carry biases of the data they were trained on. For example, they have been known to have bias associating professions with a particular gender. We request our users to be aware of these ethical issues that might affect their analyses.

Acknowledgments

We would like to thank Michael Correll for his insightful feedback.

References

Tom B. Brown, Benjamin Mann, Nick Ryder, Melanie Subbiah, Jared Kaplan, Prafulla Dhariwal, Arvind Neelakantan, Pranav Shyam, Girish Sastry, Amanda Askell, Sandhini Agarwal, Ariel Herbert-Voss, Gretchen Krueger, Tom Henighan, Rewon Child, Aditya Ramesh, Daniel M. Ziegler, Jeffrey Wu, Clemens Winter, Christopher Hesse, Mark Chen, Eric Sigler, Mateusz Litwin, Scott Gray, Benjamin Chess, Jack Clark, Christopher Berner, Sam McCandlish, Alec Radford, Ilya Sutskever, and Dario Amodei. 2020. Language models are few-shot learners. In *Advances in Neural Information Processing Systems 33: Annual Conference on Neural Information Processing Systems 2020, NeurIPS 2020, December 6-12, 2020, virtual.*

Aylin Caliskan, Joanna J. Bryson, and Arvind Narayanan. 2017. Semantics derived automatically from language corpora contain human-like biases. *Science*, 356(6334):183–186.

Jacob Devlin, Ming-Wei Chang, Kenton Lee, and Kristina Toutanova. 2019. BERT: pre-training of deep bidirectional transformers for language understanding. In *Proceedings of the 2019 Conference of the North American Chapter of the Association for Computational Linguistics: Human Language Technologies, NAACL-HLT 2019, Minneapolis, MN, USA, June 2-7, 2019, Volume 1 (Long and Short Papers)*, pages 4171–4186. Association for Computational Linguistics.

Alexander Fabbri, Irene Li, Tianwei She, Suyi Li, and Dragomir Radev. 2019. Multi-news: A large-scale multi-document summarization dataset and abstractive hierarchical model. In *Proceedings of the 57th Annual Meeting of the Association for Computational Linguistics*, pages 1074–1084, Florence, Italy. Association for Computational Linguistics.

Alexander R. Fabbri, Wojciech Kryściński, Bryan McCann, Caiming Xiong, Richard Socher, and Dragomir R. Radev. 2020. Summeval: Re-evaluating summarization evaluation. *CoRR*, abs/2007.12626.

Sebastian Gehrmann, Tosin Adewumi, Karmanya Aggarwal, Pawan Sasanka Ammanamanchi, Aremu Anuoluwapo, Antoine Bosselut, Khyathi Raghavi Chandu, Miruna Clinciu, Dipanjan Das, Kaustubh D Dhole, et al. 2021. The gem benchmark: Natural language generation, its evaluation and metrics. *arXiv preprint arXiv:2102.01672.*

Sebastian Gehrmann, Hendrik Strobelt, Robert Krüger, Hanspeter Pfister, and Alexander M Rush. 2019. Visual interaction with deep learning models through collaborative semantic inference. *IEEE transactions on visualization and computer graphics*, 26(1):884–894.

Karan Goel, Nazneen Rajani, Jesse Vig, Zachary Taschdjian, Mohit Bansal, and Christopher Ré. 2021. Robustness Gym: Unifying the NLP evaluation landscape. In *Proceedings of the 2021 Conference of the North American Chapter of the Association for Computational Linguistics: System Demonstrations.*

Max Grusky, Mor Naaman, and Yoav Artzi. 2018. Newsroom: A dataset of 1.3 million summaries with diverse extractive strategies. In *Proceedings of the 2018 Conference of the North American Chapter of the Association for Computational Linguistics: Human Language Technologies, Volume 1 (Long Papers)*, pages 708–719, New Orleans, Louisiana. Association for Computational Linguistics.

Karl Moritz Hermann, Tomas Kocisky, Edward Grefenstette, Lasse Espeholt, Will Kay, Mustafa Suleyman, and Phil Blunsom. 2015. Teaching machines to read and comprehend. In *Advances in neural information processing systems*, pages 1693–1701.

Matthew Honnibal, Ines Montani, Sofie Van Landeghem, and Adriane Boyd. 2020. spaCy: Industrial-strength Natural Language Processing in Python.

Taehee Jung, Dongyeop Kang, Lucas Mentch, and Eduard Hovy. 2019. Earlier isn't always better: Subaspect analysis on corpus and system biases in summarization. In *Proceedings of the 2019 Conference on Empirical Methods in Natural Language Processing and the 9th International Joint Conference on Natural Language Processing (EMNLP-IJCNLP)*, pages 3324–3335, Hong Kong, China. Association for Computational Linguistics.

Chris Kedzie, Kathleen R. McKeown, and Hal Daumé III. 2018. Content selection in deep learning models of summarization. In *Proceedings of the 2018 Conference on Empirical Methods in Natural Language Processing, Brussels, Belgium, October 31 - November 4, 2018*, pages 1818–1828. Association for Computational Linguistics.

Daniel Khashabi, Gabriel Stanovsky, Jonathan Bragg, Nicholas Lourie, Jungo Kasai, Yejin Choi, Noah A Smith, and Daniel S Weld. 2021. Genie: A leaderboard for human-in-the-loop evaluation of text generation. *arXiv preprint arXiv:2101.06561*.

Wojciech Kryściński, Nitish Shirish Keskar, Bryan McCann, Caiming Xiong, and Richard Socher. 2019. Neural text summarization: A critical evaluation. In *Proceedings of the 2019 Conference on Empirical Methods in Natural Language Processing and the 9th International Joint Conference on Natural Language Processing, EMNLP-IJCNLP 2019, Hong Kong, China, November 3-7, 2019*, pages 540–551. Association for Computational Linguistics.

Wojciech Kryściński, Bryan McCann, Caiming Xiong, and Richard Socher. 2020. Evaluating the factual consistency of abstractive text summarization. In *Proceedings of the 2020 Conference on Empirical Methods in Natural Language Processing, EMNLP 2020, Online, November 16-20, 2020*, pages 9332–9346. Association for Computational Linguistics.

Mike Lewis, Yinhan Liu, Naman Goyal, Marjan Ghazvininejad, Abdelrahman Mohamed, Omer Levy, Veselin Stoyanov, and Luke Zettlemoyer. 2020. BART: Denoising sequence-to-sequence pretraining for natural language generation, translation, and comprehension. In *Proceedings of the 58th Annual Meeting of the Association for Computational Linguistics*, pages 7871–7880, Online. Association for Computational Linguistics.

Chin-Yew Lin. 2004. ROUGE: A package for automatic evaluation of summaries. In *Text Summarization Branches Out*, pages 74–81, Barcelona, Spain. Association for Computational Linguistics.

Yinhan Liu, Myle Ott, Naman Goyal, Jingfei Du, Mandar Joshi, Danqi Chen, Omer Levy, Mike Lewis, Luke Zettlemoyer, and Veselin Stoyanov. 2019. Roberta: A robustly optimized bert pretraining approach.

Joshua Maynez, Shashi Narayan, Bernd Bohnet, and Ryan McDonald. 2020. On faithfulness and factuality in abstractive summarization. In *Proceedings of the 58th Annual Meeting of the Association for Computational Linguistics*, pages 1906–1919, Online. Association for Computational Linguistics.

Shashi Narayan, Shay B. Cohen, and Mirella Lapata. 2018. Don't give me the details, just the summary! Topic-aware convolutional neural networks for extreme summarization. In *Proceedings of the 2018 Conference on Empirical Methods in Natural Language Processing*, Brussels, Belgium.

Adam Paszke, Sam Gross, Francisco Massa, Adam Lerer, James Bradbury, Gregory Chanan, Trevor Killeen, Zeming Lin, Natalia Gimelshein, Luca Antiga, Alban Desmaison, Andreas Köpf, Edward Yang, Zachary DeVito, Martin Raison, Alykhan Tejani, Sasank Chilamkurthy, Benoit Steiner, Lu Fang, Junjie Bai, and Soumith Chintala. 2019. Pytorch: An imperative style, high-performance deep learning library. In *Advances in Neural Information Processing Systems 32: Annual Conference on Neural Information Processing Systems 2019, NeurIPS 2019, December 8-14, 2019, Vancouver, BC, Canada*, pages 8024–8035.

Colin Raffel, Noam Shazeer, Adam Roberts, Katherine Lee, Sharan Narang, Michael Matena, Yanqi Zhou, Wei Li, and Peter J. Liu. 2020. Exploring the limits of transfer learning with a unified text-to-text transformer. *J. Mach. Learn. Res.*, 21:140:1–140:67.

Julius Steen and Katja Markert. 2021. How to evaluate a summarizer: Study design and statistical analysis for manual linguistic quality evaluation. In *Proceedings of the 16th Conference of the European Chapter of the Association for Computational Linguistics: Main Volume*, pages 1861–1875, Online. Association for Computational Linguistics.

Hendrik Strobelt, Sebastian Gehrmann, Michael Behrisch, Adam Perer, Hanspeter Pfister, and Alexander M. Rush. 2019. Seq2seq-vis: A visual debugging tool for sequence-to-sequence models. *IEEE Transactions on Visualization and Computer Graphics*, 25(1):353–363.

Ian Tenney, James Wexler, Jasmijn Bastings, Tolga Bolukbasi, Andy Coenen, Sebastian Gehrmann, Ellen Jiang, Mahima Pushkarna, Carey Radebaugh, Emily Reif, and Ann Yuan. 2020. The language interpretability tool: Extensible, interactive visualizations and analysis for NLP models. In *Proceedings of the 2020 Conference on Empirical Methods in Natural Language Processing: System Demonstrations*, pages 107–118, Online. Association for Computational Linguistics.

Ashish Vaswani, Noam Shazeer, Niki Parmar, Jakob Uszkoreit, Llion Jones, Aidan N. Gomez, Lukasz Kaiser, and Illia Polosukhin. 2017. Attention is all you need. In *Advances in Neural Information Processing Systems 30: Annual Conference on Neural Information Processing Systems 2017, December 4-9, 2017, Long Beach, CA, USA*, pages 5998–6008.

Thomas Wolf, Lysandre Debut, Victor Sanh, Julien Chaumond, Clement Delangue, Anthony Moi, Pierric Cistac, Tim Rault, Rémi Louf, Morgan Funtowicz, Joe Davison, Sam Shleifer, Patrick von Platen,

Clara Ma, Yacine Jernite, Julien Plu, Canwen Xu, Teven Le Scao, Sylvain Gugger, Mariama Drame, Quentin Lhoest, and Alexander M. Rush. 2020a. Transformers: State-of-the-art natural language processing. In *Proceedings of the 2020 Conference on Empirical Methods in Natural Language Processing: System Demonstrations, EMNLP 2020 - Demos, Online, November 16-20, 2020*, pages 38–45. Association for Computational Linguistics.

Thomas Wolf, Quentin Lhoest, Patrick von Platen, Yacine Jernite, Mariama Drame, Julien Plu, Julien Chaumond, Clement Delangue, Clara Ma, Abhishek Thakur, Suraj Patil, Joe Davison, Teven Le Scao, Victor Sanh, Canwen Xu, Nicolas Patry, Angie McMillan-Major, Simon Brandeis, Sylvain Gugger, François Lagunas, Lysandre Debut, Morgan Funtowicz, Anthony Moi, Sasha Rush, Philipp Schmidd, Pierric Cistac, Victor Muštar, Jeff Boudier, and Anna Tordjmann. 2020b. Datasets. *GitHub. Note: https://github.com/huggingface/datasets*, 1.

T. Yousef and S. Janicke. 2021. A survey of text alignment visualization. *IEEE Transactions on Visualization and Computer Graphics*, 27(2):1149–1159.

Manzil Zaheer, Guru Guruganesh, Kumar Avinava Dubey, Joshua Ainslie, Chris Alberti, Santiago Ontañón, Philip Pham, Anirudh Ravula, Qifan Wang, Li Yang, and Amr Ahmed. 2020. Big bird: Transformers for longer sequences. In *Advances in Neural Information Processing Systems 33: Annual Conference on Neural Information Processing Systems 2020, NeurIPS 2020, December 6-12, 2020, virtual.*

Jingqing Zhang, Yao Zhao, Mohammad Saleh, and Peter J. Liu. 2020a. PEGASUS: pre-training with extracted gap-sentences for abstractive summarization. In *Proceedings of the 37th International Conference on Machine Learning, ICML 2020, 13-18 July 2020, Virtual Event*, volume 119 of *Proceedings of Machine Learning Research*, pages 11328–11339. PMLR.

Tianyi Zhang, Varsha Kishore, Felix Wu, Kilian Q. Weinberger, and Yoav Artzi. 2020b. Bertscore: Evaluating text generation with BERT. In *8th International Conference on Learning Representations, ICLR 2020, Addis Ababa, Ethiopia, April 26-30, 2020*. OpenReview.net.

Ming Zhong, Danqing Wang, Pengfei Liu, Xipeng Qiu, and Xuanjing Huang. 2019. A closer look at data bias in neural extractive summarization models. In *Proceedings of the 2nd Workshop on New Frontiers in Summarization*, pages 80–89, Hong Kong, China. Association for Computational Linguistics.

A Graphical Interface for Curating Schemas

Piyush Mishra[1,2] **Akanksha Malhotra**[1,2] **Susan W. Brown**[1,2]

Martha Palmer[1,2] **Ghazaleh Kazeminejad**[1,2]

[1]: University of Colorado Boulder
[2]: firstname.lastname@colorado.edu

Abstract

Much past work has focused on extracting information like events, entities, and relations from documents. Very little work has focused on analyzing these results for better model understanding. In this paper, we introduce a curation interface that takes an Information Extraction (IE) system's output in a pre-defined format and generates a graphical representation of its elements. The interface supports editing while curating schemas for complex events like Improvised Explosive Device (IED) based scenarios. We identify various schemas that either have linear event chains or contain parallel events with complicated temporal ordering. We iteratively update an induced schema to uniquely identify events specific to it, add optional events around them, and prune unnecessary events. The resulting schemas are improved and enriched versions of the machine-induced versions.

1 Introduction

Understanding events, how they progress, and who is involved in them is fundamental to our knowledge of the world and our ability to anticipate future events. Human beings have mental representations of typical scenarios at various levels of granularity. Defining such scenarios or templates for use in information extraction, knowledge base construction, and narrative prediction has a long history. As these fields have progressed, the complexity of the events and sequences being represented has increased. Any machine-readable format capable of representing multiple events, tracking their participants across the events, and delineating the temporal and causal relations between the events will be extremely difficult for a person to read and review. Because the extraction and construction of such complex schemas has accelerated in recent years (Li et al., 2020; Zhang et al., 2020), the need for a way for people to easily review them has increased. In this paper we will describe a tool designed to take complex event schemas in a json format and render them graphically for human review and revision.

The complex schemas handled by our tool include multiple levels of intersecting information. For example, imagine a typical emergency medical intervention. We know this includes a Victim who is injured or ill and usually begins with communication by the Victim or a Bystander to an emergency Dispatcher, then progresses to communication from the Dispatcher to Medical Personnel, travel by Medical Personnel to the Victim, immediate medical assessment of the Victim, and, finally, possible transportation of the Victim to a Medical facility. A more complete schema would include some alternative or parallel events, such as the possibility of Medical personnel already being on site or the death of the Victim at any point in the sequence of subevents. As we will describe in more detail, the tool uses distinctive nodes and edges to represent these subevents and participants and their relationships to each other. Left to right progression of subevents across the visual field represents temporal progression, and types of edges further indicate specific temporal and causal relations. Users can zoom in to specific subevents to see participants and their relations. In addition, our tool allows for simultaneous visualization of a complex schema and direct revision of the underlying json file.

Our paper begins by describing the background and motivation for our schema editing tool in Section 2. Section 3 gives detailed description of the tool implementation, while Sections 4 and 5 provide examples of its use, and discuss general issues with respect to editing schemas. We conclude in Section 6.

Proceedings of the Joint Conference of the 59th Annual Meeting of the Association for Computational Linguistics and the 11th International Joint Conference on Natural Language Processing: System Demonstrations, pages 159–166, August 1st - August 6th, 2021.

2 Background

The idea of typical event scenarios being stored by people as abstract mental frames or schemas with slots for particular participants has a long history in psychology (Bobrow and Norman, 1975), linguistics (Fillmore, 1976) and artificial intelligence (Schank and Abelson, 2013). Prototypical sequences of events, such as the medical intervention sequence described above, can be made explicit in scripts that detail the usual subevents, their typical sequence, the people and objects generally involved in those events, and the progression of those participants through the subevents.

Proving useful for both linguistic analysis and natural language processing, repositories of defined schemas and event representations were manually developed, such as FrameNet (Fillmore et al., 2002), PropBank (Kingsbury and Palmer, 2002) and VerbNet (Kipper et al., 2008). Most longstanding repositories of such frames or scripts were built at the level of single events and their participants, although some have made sparse connections between these simple event descriptions (e.g., FrameNet's Uses and Precedes relations). The desire to extend these event representations to include more complex relations led to the development of systems of temporal, causal and other semantic relations, such as TimeML (Pustejovsky et al., 2005), Richer Event Descriptions (O'Gorman et al., 2016), Reference Event Ontology (Brown et al., 2017), and Abstract Meaning Representations (Banarescu et al., 2013).

Because of the substantial effort involved in manually creating schemas, automatically inducing schemas from textual and visual data has become a priority. Automatically generated schemas have advanced from schemas for single events (Balasubramanian et al., 2013; Chambers and Jurafsky, 2009; Chambers, 2013; Cheung et al., 2013; Huang et al., 2016; Nguyen et al., 2015) to complex, multi-step schemas (Li et al., 2020; Zhang et al., 2020) However, for optimal usefulness, these generated schemas still benefit from human revision. To our knowledge, no open-source interface for complex schema visualization and editing has previously been developed.

One large-scale effort to create a repository of complex event schemas is the DARPA Knowlege-directed Artificial Intelligence Reasoning Over Schemas (KAIROS) program. KAIROS relies on the assumption discussed above, that humans make sense of events by organizing them into frequently occurring narrative structures that in this context are called schemas. The goal of the program is to develop schema-based AI systems that can identify, link and temporally sequence complex events and their subsidiary elements and participants. The program is set up with separate tasks. Task 1 involves inducing schemas from large amounts of text, followed by careful hand curation, with the goal of creating a schema library. Task 2 is aimed at finding schema instances that match schemas from the schema library in streaming news feeds. In order to evaluate system performance for both of these tasks, a common, agreed upon KAIROS Schema Format is needed. This also allows one DARPA team to try to instantiate schemas from another team's Schema Library and vice versa. The KAIROS Schema Format (KSF) stores representations of real-world complex events in a systematic JSON-LD format containing primitive events, their participants, possible entities acting as the participants, and the relations between these events and entities. Our tool takes these JSON files as input and assumes that all the schemas are validated and tested for format consistency before use. An additional complexity in this beginning phase of the program is a restriction against hierarchical schemas, in which subschemas could be collapsed into a single parent node. The schemas are orderings of all individual events, that can therefore get quite lengthy.

3 Schema Curation Interface

The Schema Curation Interface[1 2] is a web application designed for interpreting induced schemas. It provides a visual representation of the schema to understand the underlying structure, reflects relations between events and entities, and allows correction of potential flaws. The interface accepts KSF-validated schemas as input, extracts the events and participants as nodes and relations as edges, and visualizes them as a graph on a canvas. These graphs, in turn, can be corrected at the discretion of the curators. The interface is an open-source project that is accessible from *'cu-clear'* GitHub repository.

We use React.js and Flask for designing the web application. React.js is a JavaScript library to build interactive user interfaces (UI). It allows

[1]GitHub: https://github.com/cu-clear/schema-interface
[2]Demo: https://youtu.be/J9yox50gZUU

encapsulated component building and easy debugging, which makes new features easy to integrate. Flask is a micro web framework written in Python that acts as the web server for receiving requests from the user and sending a response. React passes the schema, uploaded by a user, to the Flask web server, which in turn extracts the possible nodes and edges between them and returns them to the UI for rendering. Cytoscape.js (Franz et al., 2015) uses these nodes and links to generate the graph on a canvas. Cytoscape.js is a fully featured graph library written in JavaScript that allows users to display and manipulate rich, interactive graphs. In the curation interface, it controls the positioning and layout. Explicit configuration constrains Cytoscape.js to orient the representation from left to right within the canvas, which preserves any possible temporal ordering and parallel events. It also has standard gestures like dragging and zooming on desktops as well as touch devices. Besides the canvas, a JSON-viewer provides a JSON view of the uploaded schema. It allows the user to edit the schema and dynamically update the graph structure. Add, edit, and delete are the three operations the "react-json-view" library allows for manipulating schemas. "react-json-view" is a React component for displaying and editing JavaScript arrays and JSON objects.

The interface is currently accessible from the web using Google Cloud Platform (GCP). We use Docker and Kubernetes in this process. Docker enables the packing, shipping, and running of our application as a portable and self-sufficient container, which can run virtually anywhere. Kubernetes runs and coordinates these containerized applications across a cluster of machines, automating the deployment, scaling, and management process. Kubernetes' load balancing configuration keeps at least one instance always available to a user. Since the user count is small, six replicas serve the purpose. But as the users increase, we can scale it up. A separate log server keeps track of any issue or error that occurs while parsing the schemas using RabbitMQ. It helps in debugging and analyzing the usage of the interface.

The representation consists of nodes and edges. The nodes signify an event (referred to in the schema as "step"), entity (as "participant" or "slot"), or filler (as "value" for the mentioned "participant"). Shapes like ellipse, round-rectangle, and round-pentagon distinguish one node type from another. The edges signify temporal relations between any two events, an entity's participation in an event, or co-reference between two entities.

The current implementation allows a dual-layer view. The first (default) view (Figure 2) shows only the representation of events and their temporal relations. Selecting an event opens the second view (Figure 3), consisting of entities and values for that event. As a result, all the entities and fillers remain hidden in the default view and reduce the clutter in the visualization, increasing readability.

While the dual-layer view allows a cleaner visualization of schemas, having many events in a schema (currently constrained to not make use of hierarchical structure) can still clutter the representation. Since the layout is from left to right, a complex event with a long sequential chain of events becomes partially hidden on reaching the screen width. Cytoscape.js reacts by zooming out the canvas to keep the graph in view as much as possible. However, in doing so, the schema graph becomes illegible. The only solution is manually arranging the nodes so they are in the scope and are using an appropriate zoom setting.

4 Interface Use

Approximately 10 people collaborating across three institutions used the interface heavily to induce schemas and manually curate them. The schemas were induced from shared data using information extraction systems. After evaluating a system's output, the inducers shared the schema draft with the human curators for editing. The interface facilitated the interpretation of the schemas and simplified the identification of needed changes to events, entities, values, or relations between them. We then created a new set of visualizations for comparison with the pre-curated version. The schema library inducers, after discussion, used these curated sets of schemas for improved inductions, which were passed back for further curation. We repeated this process until we reached a version where the schema had the highest coverage over the data for each complex event.

The human curators worked with two sets of automatically induced schemas, from two different institutions. One set of schemas consisted of events in a linear chain, lacking parallel events. The other set contained parallel events with more complex temporal ordering. By comparing the visualizations of these schemas, curators were able to identify which schemas covered similar events and could select the best parts of each to create a single, comprehensive schema. In addition, we aimed to include all possible events in a scenario from planning stages to results. Every induced schema was missing events or had extraneous events, which were easy to identify and fix with the curation interface. However, the greatest improvement to curation came from the ease of visualizing parallel and optional events and of tracking entities across multiple subevents, all of which are obscured in the necessarily linear presentation of a JSON file.

Label	Life.Die
Description	The death of a person
Slot Role	**Slot Argument Constraints**
Victim	per
Place	loc, gpe, fac
Temporal	
Start and End	(times specific to event)
Duration	1 minute through 1 day expected

Figure 1: Life.Die Event Primitive

KAIROS Event Primitives are the backbone of the schemas. KAIROS has defined event primitives to be elemental single events that are unlikely to be decomposed into subevents, but could themselves form crucial elements of more complex events. The event primitives are comprised of the event definition, the roles associated with the event and their corresponding constraints, as well as temporal information about the event. Figure 1 provides an example of a Life.Die Event Primitive.

Events in the schema are automatically generated in temporal order from left to right in the curation interface. Parallel events originate from the same source and can occur simultaneously or independently of the sibling events. A gray rectangle labeled START indicates the beginning of the schema. Individual events are green ellipses. The general attack schema (Figure 2) can be used to represent any attack. We include a demonstration event as an instigating event that could motivate an attack. Alternative instigating events will be added in future work. After the instigating event, the attack event happens, leading to three simultaneously occurring parallel events - death, injury, and damages due to the attack, and one independently occurring parallel event - an investigation. Events related to medical intervention, an arrest, a trial, and sentencing follow.

By clicking on individual events, the event's arguments are revealed, along with various relationships between them. The entity nodes are peach-colored pentagons. Coreference relationships are indicated using the relation "Same as." In Figure 3, these coreference relations indicate that the attacker is the same as the agent of the Death event and of the Damage event. On the right side of the schema, the interface shows the schema in the JSON format (see Figure 2), which is directly editable. Therefore, if one sees that the order of events is wrong, or deletion or addition of events is necessary, these changes can be made within the interface.

We can also see details of the events and participant entities more legibly on the screen's left side by right-clicking on any specific event or entity, as shown in Figure 3.

The Drone IED (Figure 4) is an expansion of the general attack schema. We added more events specific to Drone IED's, such as buying drones, buying parts to make an IED, moving both to a common place, and assembling them. We added options like a drone crash, and a detonate event in place of the attack event from the general attack schema. We also added more event primitives related to damage and destruction. All other events are similar to the general attack schema.

5 Iterative Schema Updates

As mentioned above, there were several rounds of schema curation. One of our goals was identifying distinctive schema events. For example, in a drone-based IED schema, acquiring a drone is an essential step; and in a vehicle-based IED schema, acquiring a vehicle is an essential step. The final step was checking the proper temporal ordering between the events. We went through several wiki articles about various IED attacks to determine generic event types and the correct temporal ordering for all the steps. The visualization in the interface facilitated these tasks by allowing us to see generalities across schemas and to easily spot gaps in the temporal ordering.

In the subsequent rounds, we focused on robustness. We introduced new optional events to schemas, such as an acquittal event, which better encompassed the possible outcomes of a trial. We also introduced additional phases to the schemas, such as instigating events like conflict between the terrorist organization and a government. We also introduced retaliatory events to describe what ac-

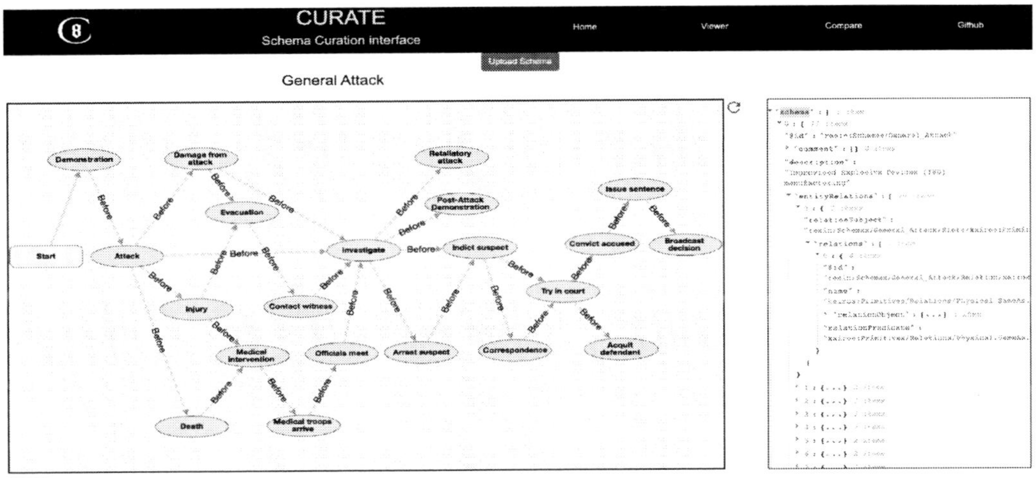

Figure 2: Editable JSON for schema curation

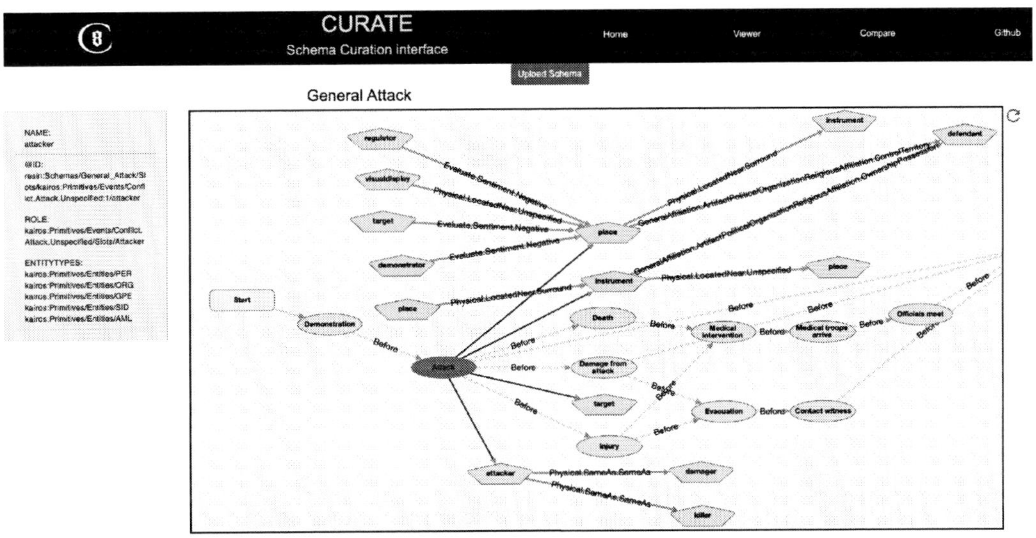

Figure 3: Entity associated to event Attack

tions were taken after the attack happened, such as demonstrations against the IED attacks or retaliatory actions taken by the army.

To demonstrate a typical editing task, the following example walks through the steps needed to make a new temporal connection between events. This example is also illustrated in our demo video.

In Figure 5a, there is a missing link between the events Injury and Medical Intervention. To add the link, we get the IDs of the Injury and Medical Intervention events by right-clicking on these events, and then create a new entry in the order key provided in the JSON editor on the right side of the screen by clicking on the plus sign next to the order key. This creates a new order step with NULL value. As shown in Figure 5b, within this box, we write the ID of the Injury event as the value to the "before" key, and the ID of the Medical Intervention event as the value to the "after" key. This signifies that an injury event needs to happen before medical intervention. We can also add flags like optional or precondition. The flag name is displayed on the arrow connecting the events. If no flags are given, "Before" is displayed on the arrow. We also need to provide a unique ID to this order step. After saving the JSON, the changes are automatically reflected in the visualization. Figure 5c shows the curated schema, with a link present between the

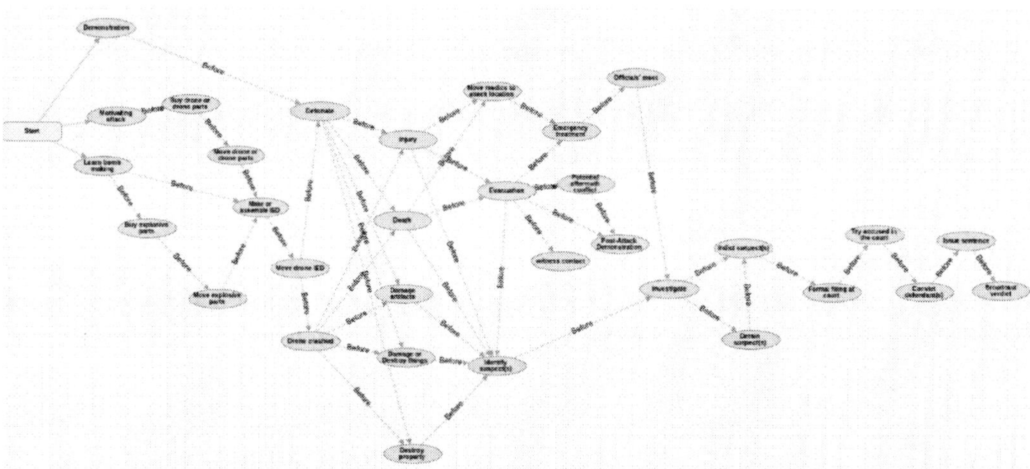

Figure 4: Drone IED

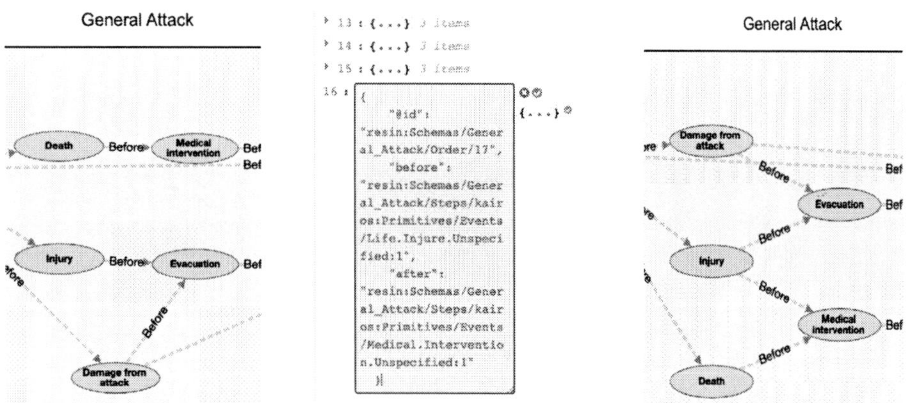

(a) No temporal link between Injury and Medical Intervention

(b) Editing JSON

(c) Temporal Link Added

Figure 5: Schema Curation Demo

Injury and Medical Intervention Event. Similarly, we can delete the events or link them. An event can be deleted by removing it from the step key in the JSON, and links can be deleted by deleting the order ID containing the mentioned events.

6 Conclusion and Future Work

In this paper, we introduced an interface that assists human curators in refining induced schemas. These schemas contain events, entities, and the relations between them. The curation interface extracts these elements in the form of nodes and edges and represents them in a graphical structure. The visualization enables the curators to better understand the ordering of events and the relations between entities, resulting in an improved and enriched schema. We also discussed leveraging the attributes of two structurally different induced schemas to design a single unified schema. This schema captures the salient events from its parents while reducing the schema size. We explored various IED-based schemas, General Attack, Medical Intervention, and Disease outbreak schemas using the curation interface.

The schemas currently include a small set of primitive events, limiting the scope of an induced complex event. In the future, a schema can have a hierarchical composition, meaning a combination of complex and primitive events within a single schema. Future work will focus on improving the handling of hierarchical schemas, provide dynamicity to the visualization, and comparison of two schemas. It will also allow changes, like editing or deleting nodes and edges, on the graph beside the JSON editor.

Acknowledgements

We gratefully acknowledge the support of the DARPA KAIROS Program (contract FA8750-19-2-1004-A20-0047-S005, sub from RPI) for RESIN: Reasoning about Event Schemas for Induction of kNowledge, Approved for Public Release, Distribution Unlimited. The views and conclusions contained herein are those of the authors and should not be interpreted as necessarily representing the official policies, either expressed or implied, of DARPA or the U.S. Government.

References

Niranjan Balasubramanian, Stephen Soderland, Mausam, and Oren Etzioni. 2013. Generating coherent event schemas at scale. In *Proceedings of the 2013 Conference on Empirical Methods in Natural Language Processing*, pages 1721–1731, Seattle, Washington, USA. Association for Computational Linguistics.

Laura Banarescu, Claire Bonial, Shu Cai, Madalina Georgescu, Kira Griffitt, Ulf Hermjakob, Kevin Knight, Philipp Koehn, Martha Palmer, and Nathan Schneider. 2013. Abstract meaning representation for sembanking. In *Proceedings of the 7th linguistic annotation workshop and interoperability with discourse*, pages 178–186.

Daniel G Bobrow and Donald A Norman. 1975. Some principles of memory schemata. In *Representation and understanding*, pages 131–149. Elsevier.

Susan Brown, Claire Bonial, Leo Obrst, and Martha Palmer. 2017. The rich event ontology. In *Proceedings of the Events and Stories in the News Workshop*, pages 87–97.

Nathanael Chambers. 2013. Event schema induction with a probabilistic entity-driven model. In *Proceedings of the 2013 Conference on Empirical Methods in Natural Language Processing*, pages 1797–1807.

Nathanael Chambers and Dan Jurafsky. 2009. Unsupervised learning of narrative schemas and their participants. In *Proceedings of the Joint Conference of the 47th Annual Meeting of the ACL and the 4th International Joint Conference on Natural Language Processing of the AFNLP*, pages 602–610.

Jackie Chi Kit Cheung, Hoifung Poon, and Lucy Vanderwende. 2013. Probabilistic frame induction. *arXiv preprint arXiv:1302.4813*.

Charles J. Fillmore. 1976. Frame semantics and the nature of language*. *Annals of the New York Academy of Sciences*, 280(1):20–32.

Charles J Fillmore, Collin F Baker, and Hiroaki Sato. 2002. The framenet database and software tools. In *LREC*.

Max Franz, Christian T. Lopes, Gerardo Huck, Yue Dong, Onur Sumer, and Gary D. Bader. 2015. Cytoscape.js: a graph theory library for visualisation and analysis. *Bioinformatics*, 32(2):309–311.

Lifu Huang, Taylor Cassidy, Xiaocheng Feng, Heng Ji, Clare R. Voss, Jiawei Han, and Avirup Sil. 2016. Liberal event extraction and event schema induction. In *Proceedings of the 54th Annual Meeting of the Association for Computational Linguistics (Volume 1: Long Papers)*, pages 258–268, Berlin, Germany. Association for Computational Linguistics.

Paul R Kingsbury and Martha Palmer. 2002. From treebank to propbank. In *LREC*, pages 1989–1993. Citeseer.

Karin Kipper, Anna Korhonen, Neville Ryant, and Martha Palmer. 2008. A large-scale classification of english verbs. *Language Resources and Evaluation*, 42(1):21–40.

Manling Li, Qi Zeng, Ying Lin, Kyunghyun Cho, Heng Ji, Jonathan May, Nathanael Chambers, and Clare Voss. 2020. Connecting the dots: Event graph schema induction with path language modeling. In *Proceedings of the 2020 Conference on Empirical Methods in Natural Language Processing (EMNLP)*, pages 684–695.

Kiem-Hieu Nguyen, Xavier Tannier, Olivier Ferret, and Romaric Besançon. 2015. Generative event schema induction with entity disambiguation. In *Proceedings of the 53rd Annual Meeting of the Association for Computational Linguistics and the 7th International Joint Conference on Natural Language Processing (Volume 1: Long Papers)*, pages 188–197.

Tim O'Gorman, Kristin Wright-Bettner, and Martha Palmer. 2016. Richer event description: Integrating event coreference with temporal, causal and bridging annotation. In *Proceedings of the 2nd Workshop on Computing News Storylines (CNS 2016)*, pages 47–56.

James Pustejovsky, Robert Ingria, Roser Sauri, José M Castaño, Jessica Littman, Robert J Gaizauskas, Andrea Setzer, Graham Katz, and Inderjeet Mani. 2005. The specification language timeml.

Roger C Schank and Robert P Abelson. 2013. *Scripts, plans, goals, and understanding: An inquiry into human knowledge structures*. Artificial Intelligence Series. Psychology Press.

Hongming Zhang, Muhao Chen, Haoyu Wang, Yangqiu Song, and Dan Roth. 2020. Analogous process structure induction for sub-event sequence prediction. *arXiv preprint arXiv:2010.08525*.

TEXTOIR: An Integrated and Visualized Platform for Text Open Intent Recognition

Hanlei Zhang[1]*, **Xiaoteng Li**[1,2]*, **Hua Xu**[1]*†, **Panpan Zhang**[1,2], **Kang Zhao**[1,2], **Kai Gao**[2]
[1]State Key Laboratory of Intelligent Technology and Systems,
Department of Computer Science and Technology, Tsinghua University,
[2]School of Information Science and Engineering, Hebei University of Science and Technology
zhang-hl20@mails.tsinghua.edu.cn, xuhua@tsinghua.edu.cn

Abstract

TEXTOIR is the first integrated and visualized platform for text open intent recognition. It is composed of two main modules: open intent detection and open intent discovery. Each module integrates most of the state-of-the-art algorithms and benchmark intent datasets. It also contains an overall framework connecting the two modules in a pipeline scheme. In addition, this platform has visualized tools for data and model management, training, evaluation and analysis of the performance from different aspects. TEXTOIR provides useful toolkits and convenient visualized interfaces for each sub-module[1], and designs a framework to implement a complete process to both identify known intents and discover open intents[2].

1 Introduction

Analyzing user intents plays a critical role in human-machine interaction services (e.g., dialogue systems). However, many current dialogue systems are confined to recognizing user intents in closed-world scenarios, and they are limited to handle the uncertain open intents. As shown in figure 1, it is easy to identify specific purposes, such as Flight Booking and Restaurant Reservation. Nevertheless, as the user intents are varied and uncertain, predefined categories may be insufficient to cover all user needs. That is, there may exist some unrelated user utterances with open intents. It is valuable to distinguish these open intents from known intents, which is helpful to improve service qualities, and further discover fine-grained classes for mining potential user needs.

We divide open intent recognition (OIR) into two modules: open intent detection and open intent discovery. The first module aims to identify n-class known intents and detect one-class open intent (Yan et al., 2020; Lin and Xu, 2019; Shu et al., 2017). It can identify known classes but fail to discover specific open classes. The second module further groups the one-class open intent into multiple fine-grained intent-wise clusters (Vedula et al., 2020; Lin et al., 2020; Perkins and Yang, 2019). Nevertheless, the adopted clustering techniques are not able to identify known categories.

User utterances	Intent Label
Book a flight from LA to Madrid.	Flight Booking
Can you get me a table at Steve's?	Restaurant reservation
Book Delta ticket Madison to Atlanta.	Flight Booking
Schedule me a table at Red Lobster.	Restaurant reservation
...	...
Can you tell me the name of this song?	**Open Intent$_1$**
What is the calorie of this food?	**Open Intent$_2$**

Figure 1: An example for Open Intent Recognition.

The two modules have achieved huge progress with various advanced methods on benchmark datasets. However, there still exist some issues, which bring difficulties for future research. Firstly, there are no unified and extensible interfaces to integrate various algorithms for two modules, bringing challenges for further model development. Secondly, the current methods of the two modules lack convenient visualized tools for model management, training, evaluation and result analysis. Thirdly, the two modules both have some limitations for OIR. That is, neither of them can identify known intents and discover open intents simultaneously. Therefore, OIR remains at the theoretical level, and it needs an overall framework to connect the two modules for finishing the whole process.

To address these issues, we propose TEXTOIR, the first integrated and visualized text open intent recognition platform. The platform has the follow-

* These authors contributed equally to this work.

† Hua Xu is the corresponding author.

[1]Toolkit code: https://github.com/thuiar/TEXTOIR

[2]Demo code: https://github.com/thuiar/TEXTOIR-DEMO

Proceedings of the Joint Conference of the 59th Annual Meeting of the Association for Computational Linguistics and the 11th International Joint Conference on Natural Language Processing: System Demonstrations, pages 167–174, August 1st - August 6th, 2021.

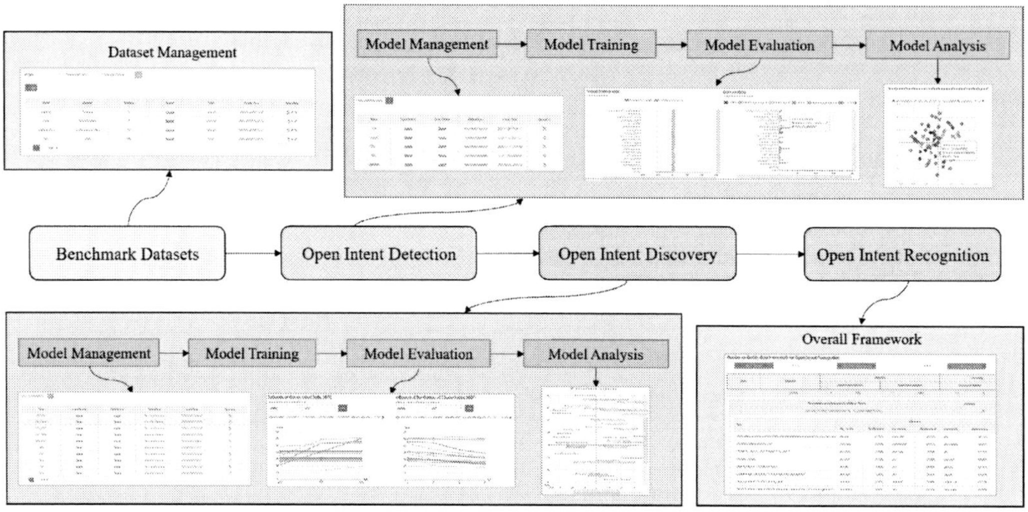

Figure 2: The architecture of the TEXTOIR platform.

ing features:

(1) It provides toolkits for open intent detection and open intent discovery, respectively. The toolkits contain flexible interfaces for data, configuration, backbone and method integration. Specifically, it integrates a series of advanced models for two modules. Each module supports a complete workflow, including data and backbone preparation with different assigned parameters, training, and evaluation. It provides standard and convenient modules to add new methods. More detailed information can be found on `https://github.com/thuiar/TEXTOIR`.

(2) It designs an overall framework combining two sub-modules naturally, achieving a complete OIR process. The overall framework integrates the advantages of two modules, which can automatically identify known intents and discover open intent clusters with recommended keywords.

(3) It provides a visualized surface for utilization. Users can leverage the provided methods or add their datasets and models for open intent recognition. We provide the front end interface for the two modules and the pipeline module. Each of the two modules supports model training, evaluation and detailed result analysis of different methods. The pipeline module leverages both the two modules and shows the complete text OIR results. More detailed information can be found on `https://github.com/thuiar/TEXTOIR-DEMO`.

2 Open Intent Recognition Platform

Figure 2 shows the architecture of the proposed TEXTOIR platform, which contains four main modules. The first module integrates a series of standard benchmark datasets. The second and third modules have toolkits for both open intent detection and open intent discovery. Besides, it visualizes the whole process (including model management, training, evaluation and result analysis) of two modules. The last module leverages the two modules in a pipeline framework to finish open intent recognition.

2.1 Data Management

Our platform supports standard benchmark datasets for intent recognition, including CLINC (Larson et al., 2019), BANKING (Casanueva et al., 2020), SNIPS (Coucke et al., 2018), and StackOverflow (Xu et al., 2015). They are all split into training, evaluation and test sets.

As shown in Figure 3, we provide unified data-processing interfaces. It supports preparing data in the format of two modules. For example, it samples known intents and labeled data with the assigned parameters for training and evaluation. Besides these labeled data, the remaining unlabeled data are also leveraged for open intent discovery. Users can see detailed statistics information from the front-end webpage and manage their datasets.

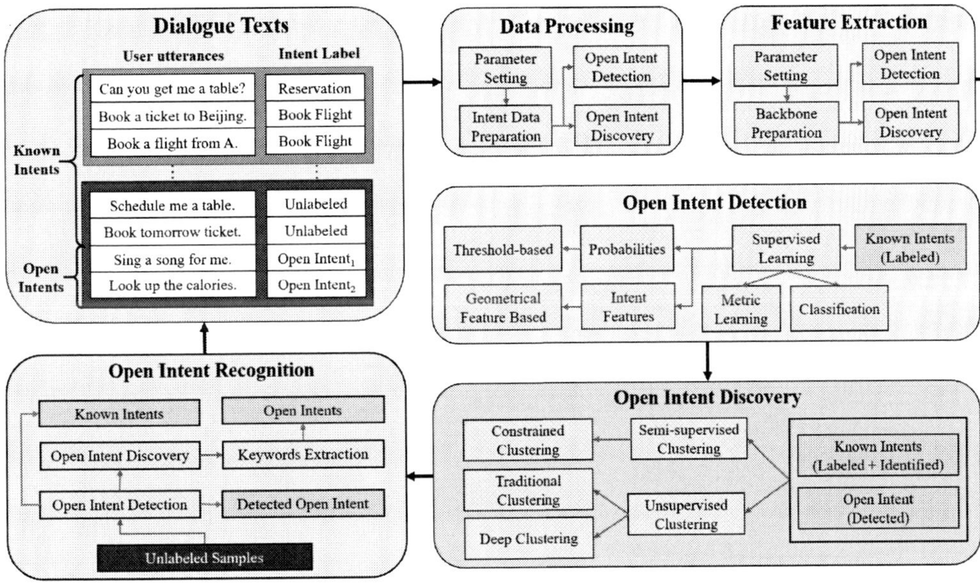

Figure 3: The architecture of Open Intent Recognition.

2.2 Models

Our platform integrates a series of advanced and competitive models for two modules, and provides toolkits with standard and flexible interfaces.

2.2.1 Open Intent Detection

This module leverages partial labeled known intent data for training. It aims to identify known intents and detect samples that do not belong to known intents. These detected samples are grouped into a single open intent class during testing. We divide the integrated methods into two categories: threshold-based and geometrical feature-based methods.

The threshold-based methods consist of MSP (Hendrycks and Gimpel, 2017), DOC (Shu et al., 2017), and OpenMax (Bendale and Boult, 2016). These methods are first pre-trained under the supervision of the known intent classification task. Then, they leverage the probability threshold for detecting the low-confidence open intent samples. The geometrical feature-based methods include DeepUnk (Lin and Xu, 2019) and ADB (Zhang et al., 2021a). DeepUnk adopts the metric-learning method to learn discriminative intent features, and the density-based methods to detect the open intent samples as anomalies. ADB further uses the boundary loss to learn adaptive decision boundaries.

2.2.2 Open Intent Discovery

This module uses both known and open intent samples as inputs, and aims to obtain intent-wise clusters by learning from similarity properties with clustering technologies. As suggested in (Zhang et al., 2021b; Lin et al., 2020), the integrated methods are divided into two parts, including unsupervised and semi-supervised methods.

The unsupervised methods include K-Means (KM) (MacQueen et al., 1967), agglomerative clustering (AG) (Gowda and Krishna, 1978), SAE-KM, DEC (Xie et al., 2016), and DCN (Yang et al., 2017). The first two methods adopt the Glove (Pennington et al., 2014) embedding, and the last three methods leverage stacked auto-encoder to extract representations. These methods do not need any labeled data as prior knowledge and learn structured semantic-similar knowledge from unlabeled data.

The semi-supervised methods include KCL (Hsu et al., 2018), MCL (Hsu et al., 2019), DTC (Han et al., 2019), CDAC+ (Lin et al., 2020) and DeepAligned (Zhang et al., 2021b). These methods can further leverage labeled known intent data for discovering fine-grained open intents.

2.2.3 Interfaces

We provide a series of interfaces for the two modules. Firstly, the backbones are flexible and unified. For example, the primary backbone is the pre-trained BERT (Devlin et al., 2019) model, and

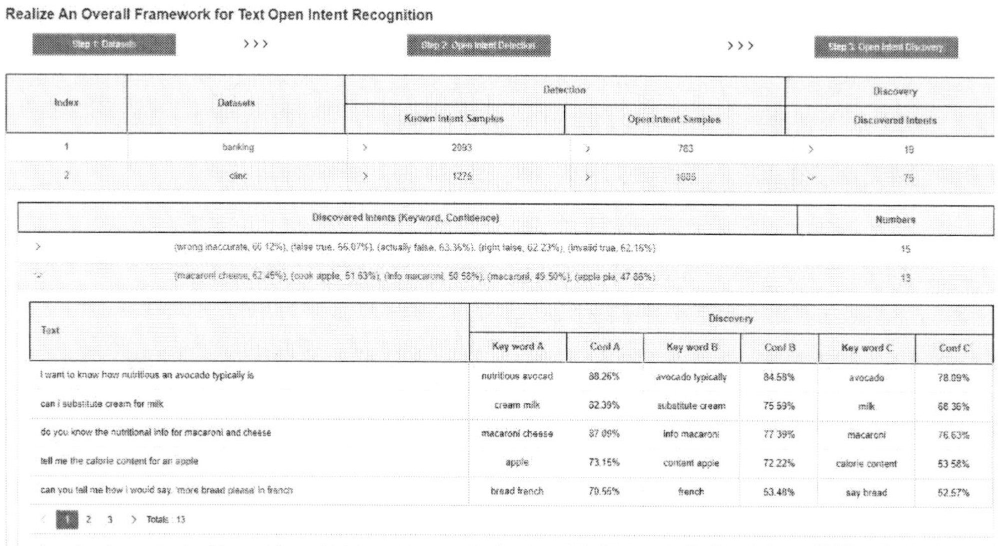

Figure 4: The pipeline framework of open intent recognition.

it supports adding new bert-based models with different downstream tasks. The open intent discovery module also supports other backbones for unsupervised clustering. Secondly, each module has the common data-loaders following the needed formats of the adopted backbones. They encode unified data vectors from the prepared data as mentioned in section 2.1. Thirdly, the parameter configurations are convenient. We extract common parameters (e.g., known intent ratio, dataset, etc.) for each module and support adding different sets of hyper-parameters for tuning each method. Finally, each approach integrates standard components of training, evaluation, and other specific functions.

3 Pipeline Framework

The two modules of open intent detection and discovery are closely related. However, there lacks an overall framework to successively invoke the two modules for both identifying known intents and discovering open intents. TEXTOIR addresses this issue with a proposed pipeline framework, as shown in Figure 3 and Figure 4.

The pipeline framework first processes the original data for two modules. Then, it feeds the labeled known intent data to the open intent detection module and trains the selected model by the users. As there is still a mass of unlabeled data containing both known and open intents, it leverages the well-trained open intent detection model to predict the unlabeled training data. The evaluated results on training data contain identified known intents and the detected open intent. We use the predicted known intent data, detected open intent and original labeled data as the inputs of the open intent discovery module. In this case, the discovery module benefits from the detection module to obtain the augmented inputs for training. Next, the preferred clustering method selected by the users is trained to obtain the open intent clusters.

After training the two modules, they are used to perform open intent recognition on unlabeled data. Specifically, the well-trained open intent detection method is first used to predict the identified known intents and detected open intent. Then, the open intent discovery method is utilized to predict the detected open intent data to obtain the fine-grained open intent clusters. Finally, the KeyBERT toolkit (mentioned in section 4.2.2) is leveraged to extract keywords for each open intent cluster with similar-intent sentences. Therefore, our framework identifies known intents and discovers open intent samples in group with keywords as recommended labels.

4 Visualization

4.1 Training and Evaluation

Our platform provides visualized surfaces for model training and evaluation. For each method, users can change the main hyper-parameters to tune the model. When training starts, it automatically creates a record for the training process, which state

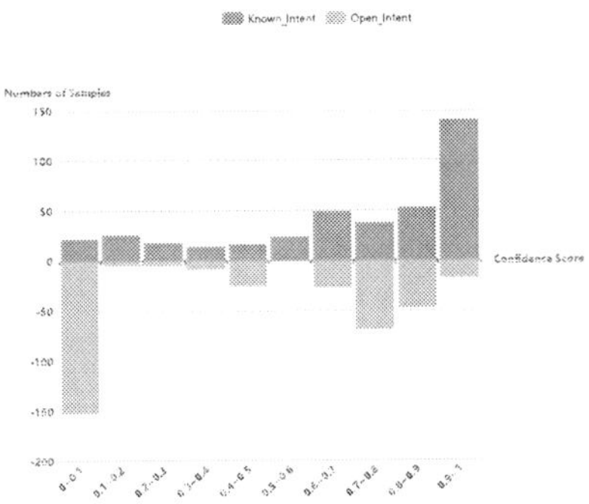

Figure 5: Known and Open intent distributions with different confidence scores.

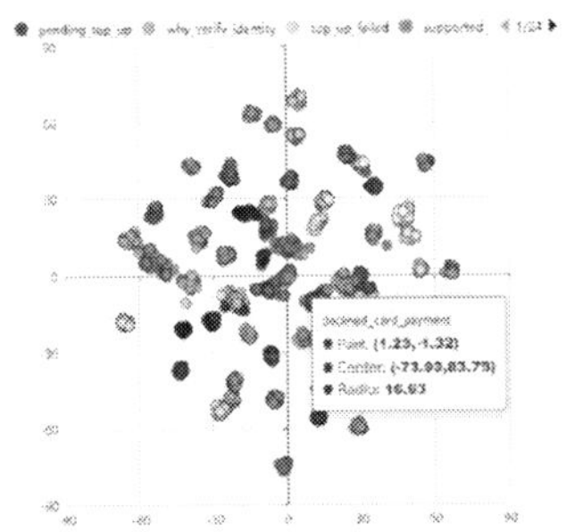

Figure 6: Visualization of the intent representations.

can be monitored by the users. When the training process finishes successfully, the trained model and related parameters are saved for further utilization.

For model evaluation, the predicted results are observed from different views. Firstly, the overall performance is shown with the number of correct and false samples for each intent class. On this basis, the number of fine-grained false-predicted classes is further shown to analyze the easily-confused intents regarding the ground truth. Secondly, the influences of the known intent ratio and labeled ratio are correspondingly shown with line charts. Users can observe the results on different selected datasets and evaluation metrics.

4.2 Result Analysis

4.2.1 Open Intent Detection

This module shows the results of identified known intent samples and detected open intent samples. For threshold-based methods, it visualizes the distribution of known and open intents with different confidence scores, which may be helpful for selecting suitable probability threshold, as shown in Figure 5.

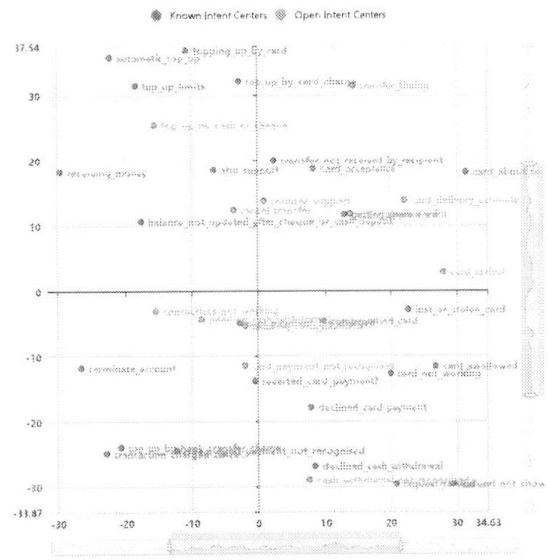

Figure 7: Intent center distribution.

For geometrical-based methods, it visualizes the intent representations on the two-dimension plane. Specifically, t-SNE (Maaten and Hinton, 2008) is applied to the high-dimension features to achieve the dimensionality reduction. Moreover, we show some auxiliary information of each point (e.g., the centre and radius of ADB), as shown in Figure 6.

4.2.2 Open Intent Discovery

For unsupervised and semi-supervised clustering methods, it shows the geometric positions of each produced cluster center with corresponding labels. These centers are categorized into the known and open classes, as shown in Figure 7. Users can mine the similarity relations of both known and open intents from observation of center distribution.

As the labels of clusters are not applicable in real scenarios, we adopt the KeyBERT [3] toolkit to extract keywords for open intents in the sentence-level and cluster-level. Furthermore, it calculates the confidence scores of the keywords in the cosine similarity space. The top-3 keywords are recommended for each discovered open intent with respective confidence scores, as shown in Figure 4.

5 Experiments

We use four intent benchmark datasets mentioned in section 2.1 to verify the performance of our TEXTOIR platform. The known intent ratios are varied between 25%, 50% and 75%. The labeled proportions are varied between 50% and 100%. To evalu-

[3]https://github.com/MaartenGr/keyBERT/

ADB + DeepAligned		CLINC		BANKING		SNIPS		StackOverflow	
KIR	LR	Known	Open	Known	Open	Known	Open	Known	Open
25%	50%	89.65	86.53	84.61	63.50	87.68	32.05	82.60	45.48
25%	100%	90.88	87.71	89.08	63.67	94.79	48.89	84.13	38.87
50%	50%	91.56	87.03	84.08	69.25	94.60	61.23	80.40	55.00
50%	100%	93.42	87.80	87.50	70.61	93.83	65.84	81.73	52.37
75%	50%	91.31	86.90	83.23	68.73	95.13	63.47	79.93	48.44
75%	100%	92.80	89.21	87.89	69.83	96.10	69.11	81.24	49.78

Table 1: The open intent recognition results of ADB+DeepAligned on four datasets. "KIR" and "LR" mean the known intent ratio and labeled ratio respectively. "Known" denotes the accuracy score on known intents, and "Open" denotes the NMI score on open intents.

ate the fine-grained performance, we calculate the accuracy score (ACC) on known intents and the Normalized Mutual Information (NMI) score on open intents. We use two state-of-the-art methods of open intent detection and discovery (ADB and DeepAligned) as the components of the pipeline framework. The results are shown in Table 1.

The pipeline framework successfully connects two modules, and achieves competitive and robust results in different settings. It essentially overcomes the shortcoming of two modules, and uses the first module to identify known intents, the second module to discover open intents.

6 Related Work

6.1 Open Intent Detection

Open intent detection has attracted much attention in recent years. It aims to identify known intents while detecting the open intent. The threshold-based methods use an assigned threshold to detect the open intent. For example, MSP (Hendrycks and Gimpel, 2017) computes the softmax confidence score of each known class and regards the low-confidence samples as open. OpenMax (Bendale and Boult, 2016) uses the Weibull distribution to produce the open class probability. (Shu et al., 2017) replaces the softmax with the sigmoid activation function and fits Gaussian distribution to the outputs for each known class. ODIN (Liang et al., 2018) adopts temperature scaling and input preprocessing technologies to obtain further discriminative probabilities for detecting open intent. The geometrical feature-based methods use the characteristics of intent features to solve this task. For example, DeepUnk (Lin and Xu, 2019) first uses the margin loss to learn the discriminative features. Then, it adopts a density-based algorithm, LOF (Breunig et al., 2000) to discover the anomaly data as the unknown intent. ADB (Zhang et al., 2021a) learns the adaptive decision boundary for each known class among Euclidean space. However, all these methods mentioned above fail to discover fine-grained open classes.

6.2 Open Intent Discovery

Open intent discovery leverages clustering methods to help find fine-grained clusters as open intents. Unsupervised clustering methods include traditional partition-based method K-Means (MacQueen et al., 1967), hierarchical method Agglomerative Clustering (Gowda and Krishna, 1978), and density-based method (Ester et al., 1996). There are also clustering methods based on deep neural networks, such as Deep Embedded Clustering (DEC) (Xie et al., 2016), joint unsupervised learning (JULE) (Yang et al., 2016), and Deep Clustering Network (DCN) (Yang et al., 2017).

As unsupervised methods may not work well on open settings (Lin et al., 2020), researchers try to leverage some prior knowledge to improve the performance. Some methods use pairwise constraints to guide the clustering process, such as KCL (Hsu et al., 2018), MCL (Hsu et al., 2019) and CDAC+ (Lin et al., 2020). DTC (Han et al., 2019) extends DEC with temporal and ensemble information. DeepAligned (Zhang et al., 2021b) leverages clustering information to obtain aligned targets for self-supervised feature learning. However, all these clustering methods fail to identify the specific known intent classes.

7 Conclusion

We propose the first open intent recognition platform TEXTOIR, which integrates two complete modules: open intent detection and open intent discovery. It provides toolkits for each module with common interfaces and integrates multiple advanced models and benchmark datasets for the convenience of further research. Additionally, it realizes a pipeline framework to combine the advantages of two modules. The overall framework achieves both identifying known intents and discovering open intents. A series of visualized surfaces help users to manage, train, evaluate, and analyze the performance of different methods.

Acknowledgments

This work is founded by National Key R&D Program Projects of China (Grant No: 2018YFC1707605). This work is also supported by seed fund of Tsinghua University (Department of Computer Science and Technology)-Siemens Ltd., China Joint Research Center for Industrial Intelligence and Internet of Things. We would like to thank the help from Xin Wang and Huisheng Mao, and constructive feedback from Ting-En Lin on this work.

References

Abhijit Bendale and Terrance E Boult. 2016. Towards open set deep networks. In *Proceedings of CVPR*, pages 1563–1572.

Markus M Breunig, Hans-Peter Kriegel, Raymond T Ng, and Jörg Sander. 2000. Lof: identifying density-based local outliers. In *ACM sigmod record*, volume 29, pages 93–104. ACM.

Iñigo Casanueva, Tadas Temcinas, Daniela Gerz, Matthew Henderson, and Ivan Vulic. 2020. Efficient intent detection with dual sentence encoders. In *Proceedings of the 2nd Workshop on NLP for ConvAI - ACL 2020*.

Alice Coucke, Alaa Saade, Adrien Ball, Théodore Bluche, Alexandre Caulier, David Leroy, Clément Doumouro, Thibault Gisselbrecht, Francesco Caltagirone, Thibaut Lavril, Maël Primet, and Joseph Dureau. 2018. Snips voice platform: an embedded spoken language understanding system for private-by-design voice interfaces. *arXiv preprint arXiv:1805.10190*.

Jacob Devlin, Ming-Wei Chang, Kenton Lee, and Kristina Toutanova. 2019. Bert: Pre-training of deep bidirectional transformers for language understanding. In *Proceedings of NAACL-HLT 2019*.

Martin Ester, Hans-Peter Kriegel, Jörg Sander, Xiaowei Xu, et al. 1996. A density-based algorithm for discovering clusters in large spatial databases with noise. In *Kdd*, volume 96, pages 226–231.

K Chidananda Gowda and G Krishna. 1978. Agglomerative clustering using the concept of mutual nearest neighbourhood. *Pattern recognition*, 10(2):105–112.

Kai Han, Andrea Vedaldi, and Andrew Zisserman. 2019. Learning to discover novel visual categories via deep transfer clustering. In *International Conference on Computer Vision (ICCV)*.

Dan Hendrycks and Kevin Gimpel. 2017. A baseline for detecting misclassified and out-of-distribution examples in neural networks. In *Proceedings of ICLR*.

Yen-Chang Hsu, Zhaoyang Lv, and Zsolt Kira. 2018. Learning to cluster in order to transfer across domains and tasks. In *International Conference on Learning Representations*.

Yen-Chang Hsu, Zhaoyang Lv, Joel Schlosser, Phillip Odom, and Zsolt Kira. 2019. Multi-class classification without multi-class labels. In *International Conference on Learning Representations*.

Stefan Larson, Anish Mahendran, Joseph J. Peper, Christopher Clarke, Andrew Lee, Parker Hill, Jonathan K. Kummerfeld, Kevin Leach, Michael A. Laurenzano, Lingjia Tang, and Jason Mars. 2019. An evaluation dataset for intent classification and out-of-scope prediction. In *Proceedings of the 2019 Conference on Empirical Methods in Natural Language Processing and the 9th International Joint Conference on Natural Language Processing (EMNLP-IJCNLP)*, pages 1311–1316, Hong Kong, China. Association for Computational Linguistics.

Shiyu Liang, Yixuan Li, and R. Srikant. 2018. Enhancing the reliability of out-of-distribution image detection in neural networks. In *ICLR*.

Ting-En Lin and Hua Xu. 2019. Deep unknown intent detection with margin loss. In *Proceedings of the 57th Annual Meeting of the Association for Computational Linguistics*, pages 5491–5496, Florence, Italy. Association for Computational Linguistics.

Ting-En Lin, Hua Xu, and Hanlei Zhang. 2020. Discovering new intents via constrained deep adaptive clustering with cluster refinement. In *Thirty-Fourth AAAI Conference on Artificial Intelligence*.

Laurens van der Maaten and Geoffrey Hinton. 2008. Visualizing data using t-sne. *Journal of machine learning research*, 9(Nov):2579–2605.

James MacQueen et al. 1967. Some methods for classification and analysis of multivariate observations. In *Proceedings of the fifth Berkeley symposium on mathematical statistics and probability*, volume 1, pages 281–297. Oakland, CA, USA.

Jeffrey Pennington, Richard Socher, and Christopher D Manning. 2014. Glove: Global vectors for word representation. In *Proceedings of EMNLP 2014*, volume 14, pages 1532–1543.

Hugh Perkins and Yi Yang. 2019. Dialog intent induction with deep multi-view clustering. In *Proceedings of the 2019 Conference on Empirical Methods in Natural Language Processing and the 9th International Joint Conference on Natural Language Processing (EMNLP-IJCNLP)*, pages 4016–4025, Hong Kong, China. Association for Computational Linguistics.

Lei Shu, Hu Xu, and Bing Liu. 2017. Doc: Deep open classification of text documents. In *Proceedings of EMNLP*, pages 2911–2916.

Nikhita Vedula, Nedim Lipka, Pranav Maneriker, and Srinivasan Parthasarathy. 2020. Open intent extraction from natural language interactions. In *Proceedings of The WWW*, page 2009–2020.

Junyuan Xie, Ross Girshick, and Ali Farhadi. 2016. Unsupervised deep embedding for clustering analysis. In *International conference on machine learning*, pages 478–487.

Jiaming Xu, Peng Wang, Guanhua Tian, Bo Xu, Jun Zhao, Fangyuan Wang, and Hongwei Hao. 2015. Short text clustering via convolutional neural networks. In *Proceedings of the 1st Workshop on Vector Space Modeling for Natural Language Processing*, pages 62–69, Denver, Colorado. Association for Computational Linguistics.

Guangfeng Yan, Lu Fan, Qimai Li, Han Liu, Xiaotong Zhang, Xiao-Ming Wu, and Albert Y.S. Lam. 2020. Unknown intent detection using Gaussian mixture model with an application to zero-shot intent classification. In *Proceedings of the 58th Annual Meeting of the Association for Computational Linguistics*, pages 1050–1060, Online. Association for Computational Linguistics.

Bo Yang, Xiao Fu, Nicholas D Sidiropoulos, and Mingyi Hong. 2017. Towards k-means-friendly spaces: Simultaneous deep learning and clustering. In *Proceedings of the 34th International Conference on Machine Learning-Volume 70*, pages 3861–3870.

Jianwei Yang, Devi Parikh, and Dhruv Batra. 2016. Joint unsupervised learning of deep representations and image clusters. In *Proceedings of the IEEE Conference on Computer Vision and Pattern Recognition*, pages 5147–5156.

Hanlei Zhang, Hua Xu, and Ting-En Lin. 2021a. Deep open intent classification with adaptive decision boundary. In *Proceedings of the AAAI Conference on Artificial Intelligence*, volume 35, pages 14374–14382.

Hanlei Zhang, Hua Xu, Ting-En Lin, and Rui Lyu. 2021b. Discovering new intents with deep aligned clustering. In *Proceedings of the AAAI Conference on Artificial Intelligence*, volume 35, pages 14365–14373.

KuiLeiXi: a Chinese Open-Ended Text Adventure Game

Yadong Xi[1]*, Xiaoxi Mao[1†]*, Le Li[1], Lei Lin[1], Yanjiang Chen[1], Shuhan Yang[1], Xuhan Chen[1], Kailun Tao[1], Zhi Li[1], Gongzheng Li[1] Lin Jiang[1], Siyan Liu[1], Zeng Zhao[1], Minlie Huang[2], Changjie Fan[1], Zhipeng Hu[1]

[1] Fuxi AI Lab, NetEase Inc., Hangzhou, China

[2] Department of Computer Science and Technology, Institute for Artifical Intelligence, State Key Lab of Intelligent Technology and Systems, Beijing National Research Center for Information Science and Technology, Tsinghua University, Beijing, China.

{xiyadong, maoxiaoxi, lile, lin_lei}@corp.netease.com, aihuang@tsinghua.edu.cn

Abstract

There is a long history of research related to automated story generation, dating back as far as the 1970s. Recently, the rapid development of pre-trained language models has spurred great progresses in this field. Equipped with GPT-2 and the latest GPT-3, AI Dungeon has been seen as a famous example of the powerful text generation capabilities of large-scale pre-trained language models, and a possibility for future games. However, as a game, AI Dungeon lacks incentives to players and relies entirely on players to explore on their own. This makes players' enthusiasm decline rapidly. In this paper, we present an open-ended text adventure game in Chinese, named as *KuiLeiXi*[1]. In *KuiLeiXi*, players need to interact with the AI until the pre-determined plot goals are reached. By introducing the plot goals, players have a stronger incentive to explore ways to reach plot goals, while the AI's abilities are not abused to generate harmful contents. This limited freedom allows this game to be integrated as a part of a romance simulation mobile game, *Yu Jian Love*[2]. Since *KuiLeiXi* was launched, it has received a lot of positive feedbacks from more than 100,000 players. A demo video is available at https://youtu.be/DyYZhxMRrkk.

1 Introduction

The past few years have seen a significant improvement in the capabilities of neural networks for text generation(Radford et al., 2019; Brown et al., 2020; Zhang et al., 2020b). Large-scale pre-trained language models with tens of billions of parameters are capable of producing human-like text. This capability has spawned a range of revolutionary applications(Roller et al., 2020; Zhang et al., 2020a; Guan et al., 2020). AI Dungeon is a typical example of them. It is an open-ended text adventure game, where players are allowed to create their own adventures in any way they like. The original AI Dungeon is based on GPT-2 large, fintuned on a dataset of text adventures collected online[3]. Since the launch of its Colab version, AI Dungeon has gained a lot of attention on social networks.

However, from the point of view of game developers, AI Dungeon suffers from several problems, hindering it from becoming mainstream gaming. The first problem is that it relies entirely on players to explore on their own. The lack of incentives may lead to a rapid decline of players' enthusiasm. The second problem is the boundaryless nature of generated contents. Every game is associated with a certain series of world settings where the stories take place. To integrate AI Dungeon-like technology in a game, considerable adaptation works are necessary. On the other hand, in the absence of necessary guidance and restraints, players tend to abuse AI Dungeon to create malicious or offensive contents[4]. In areas with more conservative values, it is of high risk to launch an AI Dungeon-like feature in a commercial product.

Considering the problems described above, we extended the original AI Dungeon so that it could be accommodated in a commercial game. When playing AI Dungeon, depending on the player's choice of different topics, the AI will generate a story beginning, and then the player is free to explore the development of the story. Unlike AI Dungeon, in our game, players need to play a fixed character of their choice and interact with the AI to develop the story according to the pre-defined story background until they reach the specified plot goal to obtain the mission rewards. Multiple plot

* Equal contribution

† Corresponding Author

[1] http://yujian.163.com/klx-silk/redirect.html

[2] https://yujian.163.com

[3] https://chooseyourstory.com/

[4] https://www.wired.com/story/ai-fueled-dungeon-game-got-much-darker/

Proceedings of the Joint Conference of the 59th Annual Meeting of the Association for Computational Linguistics and the 11th International Joint Conference on Natural Language Processing: System Demonstrations, pages 175–184, August 1st - August 6th, 2021.

goals are contained in a story script. By elaborately design the plot goals, the difficulty of game and the freedom of players to create could be manipulated. The game supports multiplayer, scripts are created both by the game developers and by the players themselves. Because in the gaming process, the player seems to be maninulating the puppet of the character, we figuratively call this game KuiLeiXi, which refers to the puppetry in the Song Dynasty.

Deploying a neural text generation model for many players is quite expensive. So we adopted a range of methods to reduce the cost, including layer drop and knowledge distillation. In addition, we implemented a highly optimized transformer in CUDA for inference. After applying these methods, the inference speed of the model is increased by 10 times, the throughput is increased by 20 times, greatly reducing the deployment cost.

KuiLeiXi has been launched as a part of *Yu Jian Love*. *Yu Jian Love* is a mobile romance simulation game where players can role play as a girl that lives in the era of Northern Song Dynasty and develop romantic relationship with different handsome male characters. Since launched, it received a lot of positive feedbacks from players and industry. We hope KuiLeiXi could inspire fellow game developers and NLP researchers to bring more NLP capabilities into games and make game content more dynamic and personalized.

2 Architecture

In this section, we will describe the implementation and optimization of *KuiLeiXi* in detail. As seen in Figure 1, the system consists of three components: **Input Processor**, **Story Generator** and **Candidates Ranker**. As both the **Story Generator** and **Candidates Ranker** are based on our in-house pre-trained language model, we will firstly describe the pre-training details. Then we will present the implementation details of the three components in order. Finally, we will introduce the optimization details for deployment.

2.1 Pre-training

Our in-house pre-trained language model for story generation is based on GPT-2 large. It has 36 layers, 1280 hidden size, 20 self-attention heads, and 725 million parameters. It is pre-trained on a dataset consisted of around 30 gigabytes of Chinese web-novels collected online. The vocabulary size is 13762 and the context length is 1024. In addition, we pre-trained a Roberta-large(Liu et al., 2019) based bidirectional transformer model(Vaswani et al., 2017) on the same dataset. It has 24 layers, 1024 hidden size, 16 self-attention heads and 317 million parameters. We used *fairseq*[5] for training of the models.

2.2 Input Processor

The input text of a player will firstly be checked by a toxicity detection service[6] to avoid potential risks. It is then processed by a semantic similarity detection model to determine if it is too semantically close to the plot goal. This is to avoid making it too easy for players to reach the plot goal. The semantic similarity detection model is based on Sentence-Bert(Reimers and Gurevych, 2019), trained on the combination of several Chinese NLI datasets(Bowman et al., 2015; Williams et al., 2018; Hu et al., 2020). The virtual adversarial training(Zhu et al., 2020) is also adopted. This approach improves the generalization of the model by adding small perturbations to the input embeddings. For every plot goal, at least three textual descriptions of that goal should be prepared. The input text will be compared with all the textual descriptions of current plot goal. If any of the similarity scores is above a certain threshold, the player will receive a message telling the player to input again. After the input text has passed the toxicity detection and semantic similarity detection, it will be concatenated to the context to form the input for story generation.

2.3 Story Generator

The story generator is in charge of generating consistent and fluent story contents based on the context and player input. In below we will describe in detail how the story generator is implemented.

2.3.1 Finetuning

Because KuiLeiXi is supposed to be launched as a part of *Yujian Love*, the generated text needs to be consistent with the original stories of the game in terms of language style and backdrop. Therefore, the game's existing story scripts are critical for finetuning. However, these scripts only contain approximately 2 million tokens, barely enough for effective finetuning. So we carefully selected 10 online novels with similar language styles and backdrops to form an augmented dataset along with

[5]https://github.com/pytorch/fairseq

[6]https://dun.163.com/locale/en

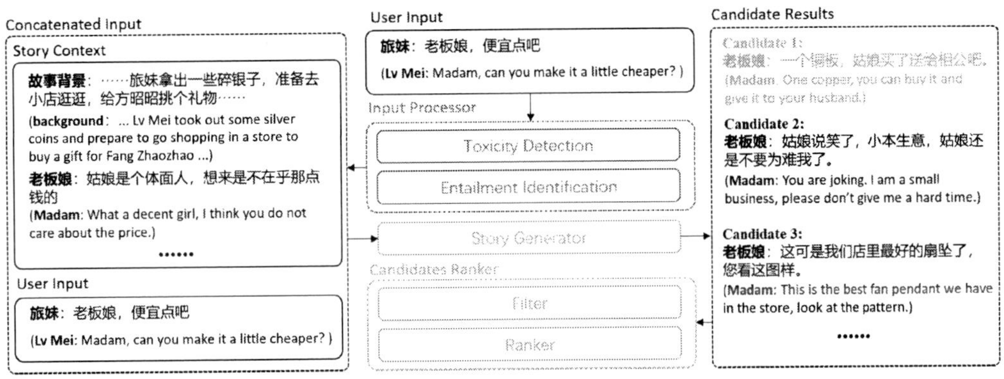

Figure 1: Architecture of *KuiLeiXi*. The user input is first passed through the input processor module, which detects whether it contains toxic content and whether it is too semantically similar to the current plot goal; after the processing, the user input is concatenated to the existing context and truncated to ensure that the length is within the context length of the story generation model; the story generation model generates a series of candidate stories that are then sent to the candidate ranker for ranking; the ranker contains a filter that removes inappropriate stories based on multiple rules, and the remaining candidate stories are ranked based on their overlapping with the context and how smoothly they connect to the plot goal, with the highest ranked being output to the player as the final result.

in-game story scripts. For scripts from the game, we assign every line a label indicating if it is dialogue or narrative content, as seen in Figure 2. It is easy because the dialogues and narratives are naturally separated in different lines in the scripts and the dialogues are with double quotation marks. This allows the finetuned model to control the generate subsequent story contents to be dialogue or narrative content. In addition, the label can guide the model to generate more consistent content with the story's background similar to (Keskar et al., 2019).

2.3.2 Inference

Input Truncation: At inference, the generation model receives a concatenation of the player input and the previous context as the input. As game continues, the input length will easily exceed the context length 1024. So we need to design a truncation strategy. Naively keeping the latest story context is not feasible in this application, as the pre-written story beginning corresponding to the current plot goal is neccessary to keep the story unfold without straying too far from the current plot goal. Therefore, we keep the pre-written story beginning corresponding to the current plot goal along with the latest story context as the input.

Decoding Strategy: We use the top-k sampling(Fan et al., 2018) for decoding. Sampling temperature and k are set to 0.8 and 8 respectively. We observed that the model tend to copy from the input. To alleviate this issue, we adopt the penalized sampling technique(Keskar et al., 2019; See et al., 2019). In general, penalty sampling penalizes words that occur throughout the context by default, reducing their sampling probability. However, we argue that this is inappropriate, especially for penalizing words that are far from the decoding position. The reasons are twofold. Firstly we observed that, the model tends to copy from words closer to the decoding position, rather than a very distant context, like contents with more than 200 words away from the decoding position. Secondly, we conducted statistics in the webnovel corpus, and the probability of the next word appearing in the previous 800 words reached 75%, indicating that copying from context is also common in real world texts. In summary, if the probability of words occurring in very distant contexts is also penalized at inference, the distribution of the generated text will be significantly different from the real world text distribution, which may reduce the generation performance. Therefore, we only penalize the probability of words that have appeared in previous 200 words prior to the decoding position.

Given the input tokens $G[1, 2, .., t]$ and the context window size c, the probability distribution p_i for the next token is defined as:

$$p_i = \frac{exp(x_i/(I(i \in g[(t-c):t]))}{\sum_j (exp(x_j/(I(j \in g[(t-c):t])))} \quad (1)$$

$$I(e) = \theta \quad if\ e\ is\ True\ else\ 1 \quad (2)$$

描述：宋朝的中秋和现代一样热闹，不，是有过之而无不及。未到傍晚，街上就已经人头攒动，大家都忙着为节日置办物什。这时节正是桂花盛开，甜香阵阵，不少店家都将桂花加进了吃食中，让人食指大动。	Description: The Mid-Autumn Festival in the Song Dynasty was as lively as in modern times, no, it was even more. Before evening, the streets were already crowded with people who were busy buying things for the festival. This is the time of the year when the osmanthus flowers are in full bloom and the sweet fragrance is so strong that many stores have added them to their food, making people's appetites tingle.
旅妹："大娘，来一碗玩月羹！"	Lv Mei: "Auntie, a bowl of wanyuegeng!"
大娘："好嘞，姑娘慢用啊！"	Auntie: "Okay, enjoy your meal!"
描述：玩月羹还未端上，就已经闻到了清甜的香味。旅妹忍不住大吸了几口，赞叹道。	Description: Before the wanyuegeng was served, the sweet aroma could already be smelled. Lv Mei couldn't help but took a few big sips and praised.
旅妹："好香！"	Lv Mei: "It smells so good!"
方昭昭："神侯府是看你太能吃，把你扫地出门了吗？怎么这个时候还在街上乱晃？"	Fang Zhaozhao: "Did the people in Divine Constabulary think you eat too much every meal and drive you out? Why are you still wandering the streets at this time?"
描述：光听声音旅妹都能想象出方昭昭挑眉带笑的样子，于是大大方方地回头和他打招呼。	Description: By the sound of her voice, Lv Mei could imagine Fang Zhaozhao raising his eyebrows and smiling, so she turned around and greeted him graciously.

Figure 2: A story fragment from the preprocessed story dataset.

We set θ to 1.2, which makes a balance between generated text quality and elimination of duplication.

2.4 Candidates Ranker

For each player input, we generate 5 candidate stories for re-ranking. The candidate stories are then sent to the ranker to select the best one to return to the user.

To ensure the quality, we developed a series of filtering rules to remove inappropriate candidates in the stories. Firstly, if a candidate story contains a character name that does not appear in *Yujian Love*, the story will be moved out of the candidates. Secondly, candidate stories that contain a lot of content copied from context will be removed. Thirdly, stories with inappropriate content detected by toxicity detection service will be removed. Fourthly, if a character described in a story behaves inconsistently with his or her gender, that story will also be removed. We trained a discriminator model to detect whether a character in the story behaves inconsistently with his/her gender. The training data is generated automatically. We use the original text as a positive sample and the text after the character name replacement as a negative sample. When replacing character names, a character is replaced with the name of a character having the other gender.

For the remaining stories, we rank them based on the weighted sum of two metrics. The first is the overlapping score, which is calculated based on the overlapping of tokens in the generated story and context. Generally, when the overlapping score is higher, repetition is heavier and will hurt the text quality. The second is the goal matching score, which measures how likely a story entails the current plot goal. Given the list of context tokens C, the list of generated story tokens G and the length l of G, the overlapping score is defined below:

$$Score_{overlap} = \frac{\sum_i I(i \in G)}{l} \tag{3}$$

$$I(i) = 1 \; if \; i \; in \; G \; else \; 0 \tag{4}$$

Determining whether a story contains a specified plot is a typical textual entailment problem. However. because players can create story scripts and submit them to the game community, it is intractable to create a dataset dealing with numerous possible plot goals. So we had to approach the problem from a different angle. We argue that it is easier to solve this problem by transforming it into a problem similar to Next Sentence Prediction (NSP), i.e., determining whether a plot goal can be coherently connected to a generated story. It is well known that the original NSP task proposed in BERT(Devlin et al., 2019) is too easy, many latest pre-trained language models have abandoned it(Liu et al., 2019; Lan et al., 2019). We argue that discriminating the randomly sampled negative examples is relatively easy so we adopt a novel strategy to enhance the difficulty of NSP. When generating the training dataset, in addition to the randomly sampled sentences, we also take the next sentence of next sentence as a negative sample with a certain probability. We finetuned the pre-trained Roberta-large based model as described in Section 2.1 on this generated dataset. The finetuned model is then used as a discriminator to detect whether the plot goal can be smoothly connected to the generated story.

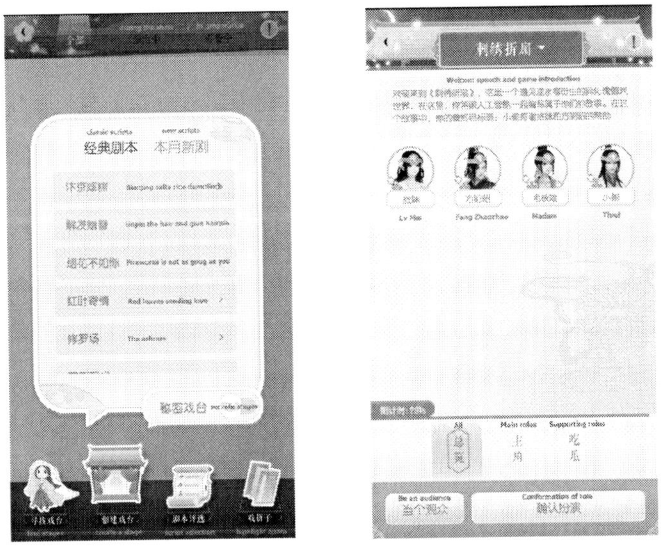

(a) Script selection interface (b) Character selection interface

Figure 3: The script and character selection interfaces

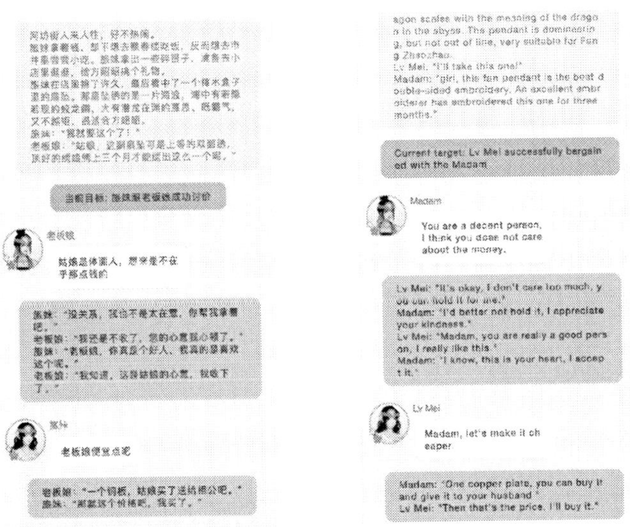

(a) (b)

Figure 4: The screenshot at the beginning of the game. The right figure is the English translation of the left figure. Text in the orange box shows the story background. Text in red box shows the current plot goal. Text in the white boxes are the players' inputs. Text in the purple boxes are the generated stories.

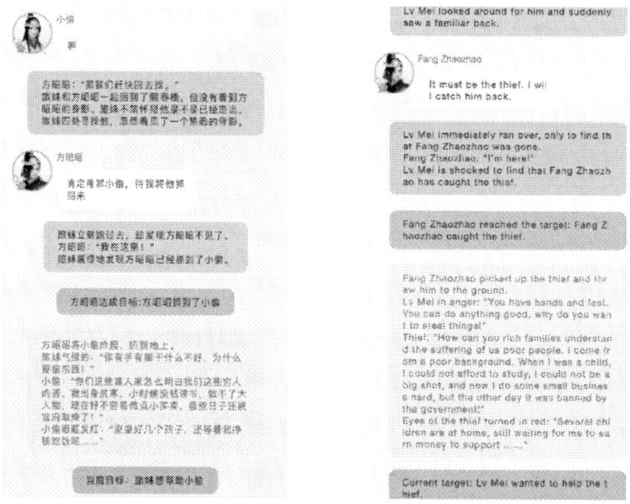

(a) (b)

Figure 5: The screenshot when a plot goal is reached. The right figure is the English translation of the left figure.

2.5 Optimization

Our original story generation model is of 36 layers and 725 millions of parameters. It takes around 10 seconds to generate a piece of story with one RTX 2080ti, which is totally unacceptable. To improve the inference speed, we need to compress the original model. We firstly adopted the *layerdrop* technique(Fan et al., 2020), reducing the number of layers to 20. We then used the knowledge distillation technique(Hinton et al., 2015) to distill this 20-layer model. Finally, we finetuned the distilled model over the story dataset.Our experiments showed that combining *layerdrop* and knowledge distillation performs better than directly performing knowledge distillation.

In addition, we optimized the incremental decoding implementation in *fairseq* to reduce computation overhead. We developed custom CUDA kernels for better support of long sequence and large hidden size. We also developed an inference server supporting dynamic batching and variable input length. After applying these methods, the inference speed is increased by 10 times, the throughput is increased by 20 times. We have integrated these optimization techniques into a python library named as *Easy and Efficient Transformer*(**?**). It has been opensourced at https://github.com/NetEase-FuXi/EET.

3 Demonstration

In this section, we demonstrate how to play *KuiLeiXi*.

First, we demonstrate how to start a game. After entering the game, if there is no ready game for joining, you can click the *create stage* button to start a new game. You then need to pick a story script from the candidates, as demonstrated in Figure 3a. The scripts are both created by game developers and players. Scripts submitted by players will be voted by all players and the winners become playable. After picking the script, you need to choose the character you want to play, as demonstrated in Figure 3b. The playable characters in each script are different. Wait for other players joining your game until the number of players exceeds the minimum player limit. Then you could either start the game or wait for other players joining as additional characters or audience.

After the game starts, all players can see the story background as well as the first plot goal. Players will play in order. The order is randomly decided at the start of the game and does not change during the game. When it is your turn to play, you can choose to write a dialogue with your character or describe a narration. Figure 4a shows the situation at the beginning of the game. Overall, you need to consider the development of the current story, the persona of the character you play and the plot goal. After completing the input, the AI will generate the corresponding story to unfold based on the input, so on and so forth until the current plot goal is reached. Once the current plot goal is reached, the AI will show a pre-written storyline, as well as a new plot goal, as seen in the Figure 5a. Usually a script has multiple plot goals. When the final plot goal is reached, players win and are rewarded with game props. The whole process of playing will be saved in the database, and players can share it with their friends or make it public on social networks.

4 Conclusion

In this paper, we demonstrate *KuiLeiXi*, an open-ended text adventure game in Chinese. In order for it to be released as part of a commercial game, we have made many innovations based on AI Dungeon. We believe that the current advances in NLP technology can not only reduce the cost of game content development to a certain extent, but also make the game world more dynamic and personalized. We hope our work will be of interest to fellow game developers and NLP researchers. In future work, we will further explore the generation of game quests and ambient dialogues with up-to-date NLP techniques.

References

Samuel R. Bowman, Gabor Angeli, Christopher Potts, and Christopher D. Manning. 2015. A large annotated corpus for learning natural language inference. In *Proceedings of the 2015 Conference on Empirical Methods in Natural Language Processing*, pages 632–642, Lisbon, Portugal. Association for Computational Linguistics.

Tom B. Brown, Benjamin Mann, Nick Ryder, Melanie Subbiah, Jared Kaplan, Prafulla Dhariwal, Arvind Neelakantan, Pranav Shyam, Girish Sastry, Amanda Askell, Sandhini Agarwal, Ariel Herbert-Voss, Gretchen Krueger, Tom Henighan, Rewon Child, Aditya Ramesh, Daniel M. Ziegler, Jeffrey Wu, Clemens Winter, Christopher Hesse, Mark Chen, Eric Sigler, Mateusz Litwin, Scott Gray, Benjamin Chess, Jack Clark, Christopher Berner, Sam McCandlish, Alec Radford, Ilya Sutskever, and Dario Amodei. 2020. Language models are few-shot learners. In *Advances in Neural Information Processing Systems 33: Annual Conference on Neural Information Processing Systems 2020, NeurIPS 2020, December 6-12, 2020, virtual*.

Jacob Devlin, Ming-Wei Chang, Kenton Lee, and Kristina Toutanova. 2019. BERT: Pre-training of deep bidirectional transformers for language understanding. In *Proceedings of the 2019 Conference of the North American Chapter of the Association for Computational Linguistics: Human Language Technologies, Volume 1 (Long and Short Papers)*, pages 4171–4186, Minneapolis, Minnesota. Association for Computational Linguistics.

Angela Fan, Edouard Grave, and Armand Joulin. 2020. Reducing transformer depth on demand with structured dropout. In *8th International Conference on Learning Representations, ICLR 2020, Addis Ababa, Ethiopia, April 26-30, 2020*. OpenReview.net.

Angela Fan, Mike Lewis, and Yann Dauphin. 2018. Hierarchical neural story generation. In *Proceedings of the 56th Annual Meeting of the Association for Computational Linguistics (Volume 1: Long Papers)*, pages 889–898, Melbourne, Australia. Association for Computational Linguistics.

Jian Guan, Fei Huang, Zhihao Zhao, Xiaoyan Zhu, and Minlie Huang. 2020. A Knowledge-Enhanced Pretraining Model for Commonsense Story Generation. *Transactions of the Association for Computational Linguistics*, 8:93–108.

Geoffrey Hinton, Oriol Vinyals, and Jeff Dean. 2015. Distilling the knowledge in a neural network. *arXiv preprint arXiv:1503.02531*.

Hai Hu, Kyle Richardson, Liang Xu, Lu Li, Sandra Kübler, and Lawrence Moss. 2020. OCNLI: Original Chinese Natural Language Inference. In *Findings of the Association for Computational Linguistics: EMNLP 2020*, pages 3512–3526, Online. Association for Computational Linguistics.

Nitish Shirish Keskar, Bryan McCann, Lav R Varshney, Caiming Xiong, and Richard Socher. 2019. Ctrl: A conditional transformer language model for controllable generation. *arXiv preprint arXiv:1909.05858*.

Zhenzhong Lan, Mingda Chen, Sebastian Goodman, Kevin Gimpel, Piyush Sharma, and Radu Soricut. 2019. ALBERT: A lite BERT for self-supervised learning of language representations. *CoRR*, abs/1909.11942.

Yinhan Liu, Myle Ott, Naman Goyal, Jingfei Du, Mandar Joshi, Danqi Chen, Omer Levy, Mike Lewis, Luke Zettlemoyer, and Veselin Stoyanov. 2019. Roberta: A robustly optimized bert pretraining approach. *arXiv preprint arXiv:1907.11692*.

Alec Radford, Jeffrey Wu, Rewon Child, David Luan, Dario Amodei, and Ilya Sutskever. 2019. Language models are unsupervised multitask learners. *OpenAI blog*, 1(8):9.

Nils Reimers and Iryna Gurevych. 2019. Sentence-BERT: Sentence embeddings using Siamese BERT-networks. In *Proceedings of the 2019 Conference on Empirical Methods in Natural Language Processing and the 9th International Joint Conference on Natural Language Processing (EMNLP-IJCNLP)*, pages 3982–3992, Hong Kong, China. Association for Computational Linguistics.

Stephen Roller, Emily Dinan, Naman Goyal, Da Ju, Mary Williamson, Yinhan Liu, Jing Xu, Myle Ott, Kurt Shuster, Eric M Smith, et al. 2020. Recipes for building an open-domain chatbot. *arXiv preprint arXiv:2004.13637*.

Abigail See, Aneesh Pappu, Rohun Saxena, Akhila Yerukola, and Christopher D. Manning. 2019. Do massively pretrained language models make better storytellers? In *Proceedings of the 23rd Conference on Computational Natural Language Learning (CoNLL)*, pages 843–861, Hong Kong, China. Association for Computational Linguistics.

Ashish Vaswani, Noam Shazeer, Niki Parmar, Jakob Uszkoreit, Llion Jones, Aidan N. Gomez, Lukasz Kaiser, and Illia Polosukhin. 2017. Attention is all you need. In *Advances in Neural Information Processing Systems 30: Annual Conference on Neural Information Processing Systems 2017, December 4-9, 2017, Long Beach, CA, USA*, pages 5998–6008.

Adina Williams, Nikita Nangia, and Samuel Bowman. 2018. A broad-coverage challenge corpus for sentence understanding through inference. In *Proceedings of the 2018 Conference of the North American Chapter of the Association for Computational Linguistics: Human Language Technologies, Volume 1 (Long Papers)*, pages 1112–1122, New Orleans, Louisiana. Association for Computational Linguistics.

Rongsheng Zhang, Xiaoxi Mao, Le Li, Lin Jiang, Lin Chen, Zhiwei Hu, Yadong Xi, Changjie Fan, and Minlie Huang. 2020a. Youling: an AI-assisted lyrics creation system. In *Proceedings of the 2020 Conference on Empirical Methods in Natural Language Processing: System Demonstrations*, pages 85–91, Online. Association for Computational Linguistics.

Zhengyan Zhang, Xu Han, Hao Zhou, Pei Ke, Yuxian Gu, Deming Ye, Yujia Qin, Yusheng Su, Haozhe Ji, Jian Guan, Fanchao Qi, Xiaozhi Wang, Yanan Zheng, Guoyang Zeng, Huanqi Cao, Shengqi Chen, Daixuan Li, Zhenbo Sun, Zhiyuan Liu, Minlie Huang, Wentao Han, Jie Tang, Juanzi Li, Xiaoyan Zhu, and Maosong Sun. 2020b. Cpm: A large-scale generative chinese pre-trained language model.

Chen Zhu, Yu Cheng, Zhe Gan, Siqi Sun, Tom Goldstein, and Jingjing Liu. 2020. Freelb: Enhanced adversarial training for natural language understanding. In *8th International Conference on Learning Representations, ICLR 2020, Addis Ababa, Ethiopia, April 26-30, 2020*. OpenReview.net.

5 Appendices

In the figures below, we present a complete gameplay record of KuiLeiXi.

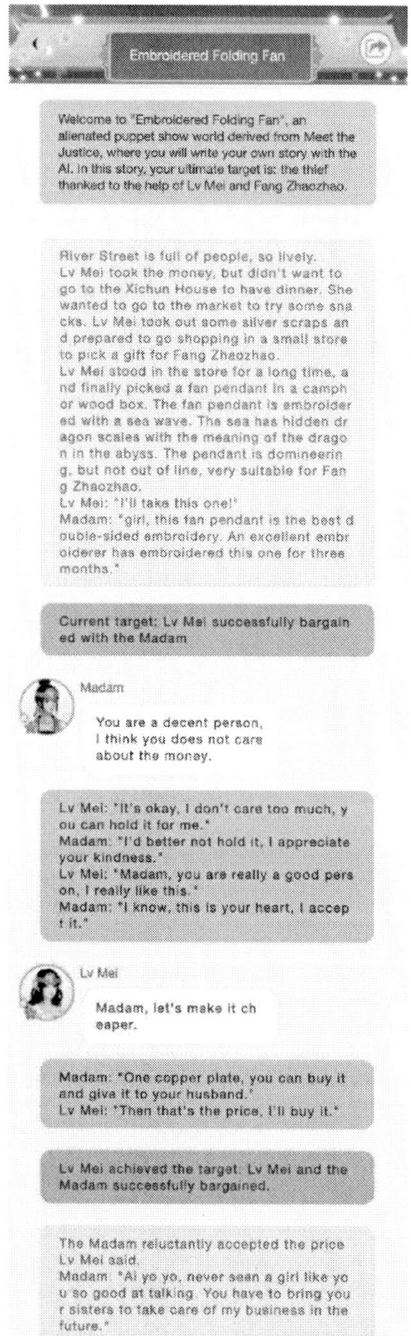

Figure 6: The first part of the game play.

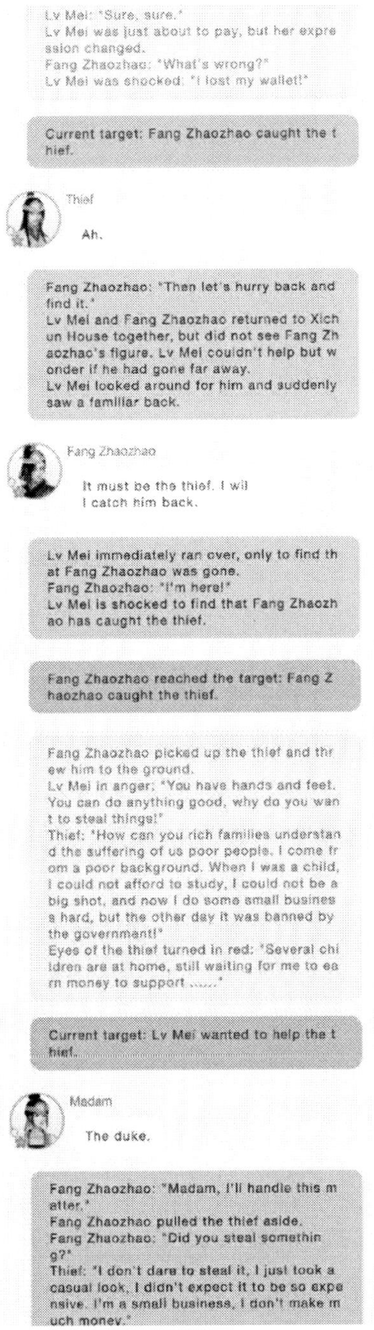

Figure 7: The second part of the game play.

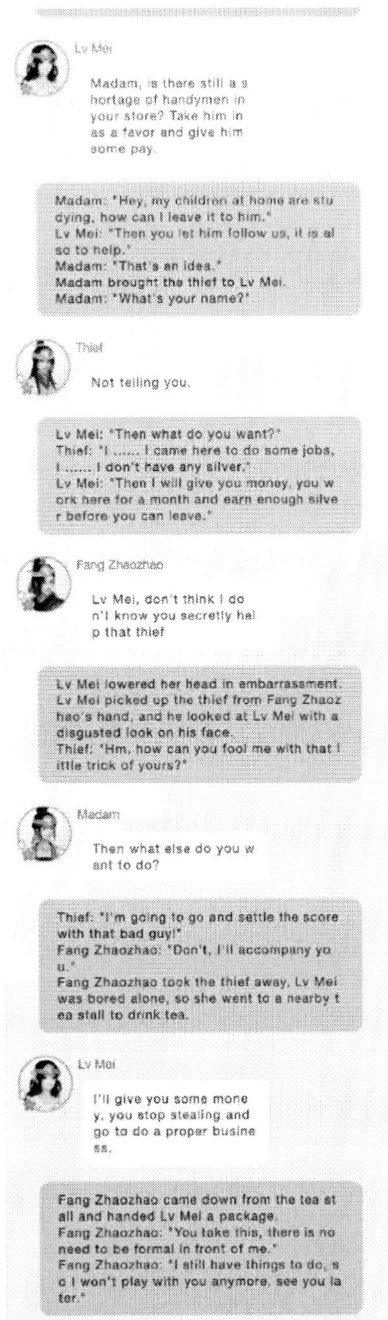

Figure 8: The third part of the game play.

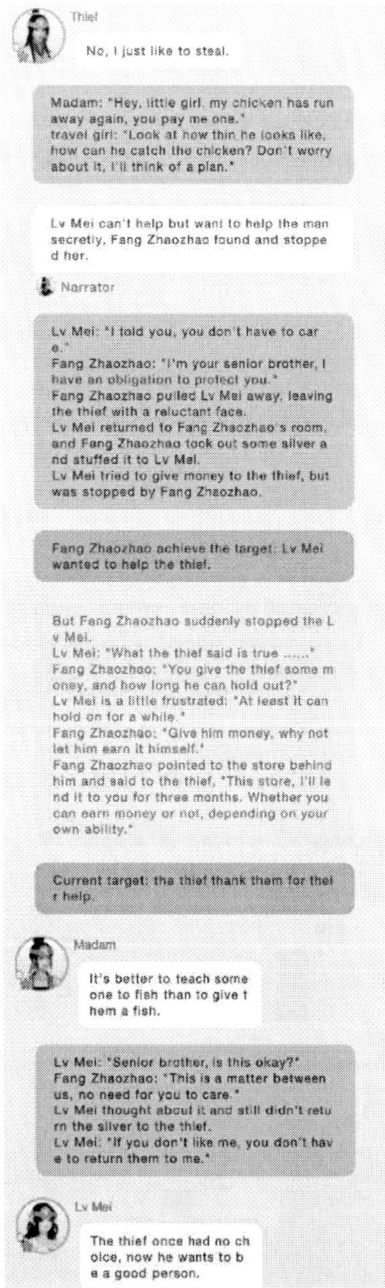

Figure 9: The fourth part of the game play.

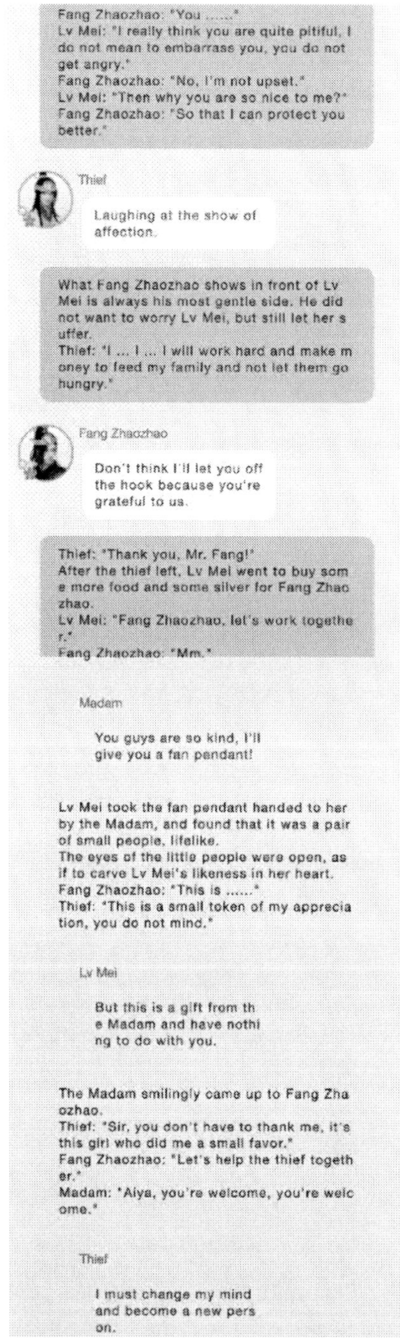

Figure 10: The fifth part of the game play.

CRSLab: An Open-Source Toolkit for Building Conversational Recommender System

Kun Zhou[1,3] [†], **Xiaolei Wang**[2] [†], **Yuanhang Zhou**[1,3], **Chenzhan Shang**[1], **Yuan Cheng**[4], **Wayne Xin Zhao**[2,3] [*], **Yaliang Li**[5], and **Ji-Rong Wen**[1,2,3]
[1]School of Information, Renmin University of China
[2]Gaoling School of Artificial Intelligence, Renmin University of China
[3]Beijing Key Laboratory of Big Data Management and Analysis Methods
[4]School of Statistics, Renmin University of China
[5]Alibaba Group

Abstract

In recent years, conversational recommender systems (CRSs) have drawn a wide attention in the research community, which focus on providing high-quality recommendations to users via natural language conversations. However, due to diverse scenarios and data formats, existing studies on CRSs lack unified and standardized implementation or comparison. To tackle this challenge, we release an open-source toolkit **CRSLab**, which provides a unified and extensible framework with highly-decoupled modules to develop CRSs. Based on this framework, we collect 6 commonly used human-annotated CRS datasets and implement 19 models that include advanced techniques such as graph neural networks and pre-training models. Besides, our toolkit provides a series of automatic evaluation protocols and a human-machine interaction interface to evaluate and compare different CRS methods. The project and documents are released at `https://github.com/RUCAIBox/CRSLab`.

1 Introduction

Recent years have witnessed remarkable progress in recommender systems, which aim to present items (*e.g.*, products or movies) of potential interests to users based on their preferences (Sarwar et al., 2001; Rendle et al., 2012). Traditional recommender systems mainly leverage the user historical behavior data (*e.g.*, click or purchase) to estimate user preferences implicitly. Recently, with the rapid development of human-machine conversation techniques (Shang et al., 2015; Zhang et al., 2018a; Lee et al., 2019), conversational recommender systems (CRSs) (Christakopoulou et al., 2016; Sun and Zhang, 2018; Gao et al., 2021) is gaining increasing attention in recent years. It relies on multi-turn natural language conversations to clarify explicit user preferences and generate more appropriate recommendations.

To build an effective CRS, researchers have proposed several datasets (Li et al., 2018; Kang et al., 2019; Liu et al., 2020) and models (Liao et al., 2020; Lei et al., 2020; Xu et al., 2020). However, due to their diverse scenarios (*e.g.*, E-commerce or movie recommendation) and data formats (*e.g.*, historical utterances or interacted items), it is challenging for users to quickly set up reasonable baseline systems and compare their performances.

To alleviate the above issues, we have developed **CRSLab**, an open-source CRS toolkit for research purpose. In CRSLab, we offer a unified and extensible framework to develop CRSs. Based on this toolkit, users are able to quickly train and evaluate CRS models via a few lines of code, and easily design new CRS models using the provided interfaces. To implement the overall framework, we design six highly-decoupled modules (*e.g.*, data module and model module), each module provides clear interfaces for specific functions. Besides, we encapsulate useful procedures and common functions shared by different modules for users to add new datasets or develop new models using our toolkit.

Based on the framework, we integrate comprehensive benchmark datasets and models in CRSLab. So far, we have incorporated 6 commonly used human-annotated datasets and implemented 19 models, including advanced techniques such as graph neural networks (GNN) (Schlichtkrull et al., 2018; Chen et al., 2019) and pre-training models (Devlin et al., 2019; Zhou et al., 2020b). To support these models, we perform necessary preprocessing (*e.g.*, entity linking and word segmentation) on included datasets, and release the processed version. Be-

[†] Equal contribution.
[*] Corresponding author, Email: batmanfly@gmail.com.

Proceedings of the Joint Conference of the 59th Annual Meeting of the Association for Computational Linguistics and the 11th International Joint Conference on Natural Language Processing: System Demonstrations, pages 185–193, August 1st - August 6th, 2021.

sides, CRSLab supports both configuration files and command-line instructions, which facilitate running, comparing and testing models on different datasets.

Furthermore, CRSLab provides a series of automatic evaluation protocols for testing and comparing different methods, covering commonly used metrics in existing works. It makes our work useful for the standardization of evaluation protocols for conversational recommendations. In addition, CRSLab provides a human-machine interactive interface to perform quantitative analysis, which is helpful for users to deploy their systems and converse with the systems via graphical interfaces.

Our contributions are as follows:

• To the best of our knowledge, CRSLab is the first open-source CRS toolkit covering 6 human-annotated datasets and 19 models.

• CRSLab provides a unified and extensible framework consisting of highly-decoupled modules, which helps users run and develop different CRS models.

• CRSLab contains commonly used automatic evaluation metrics and a human-machine interactive interface for users to test CRS performance from different perspectives.

2 Background

As aforementioned, the various scenarios and input formats in earlier works lead to inconvenience when applying existing CRS models on different datasets. By surveying previous CRS works (Sun and Zhang, 2018; Li et al., 2018; Lei et al., 2020), we summarize two basic tasks and an auxiliary task, namely recommendation task, conversation task and policy task.

Given the dialog context (*i.e.,* historical utterances) and other useful side information (*e.g.,* user historical behaviors and knowledge graphs), the recommendation sub-task is defined as predicting user-preferred items (*e.g.,* movies or products), and the conversation sub-task is to generate a proper response for conversing with the user. In existing works, the recommendation and the conversation sub-tasks are considered as the primary objective of the CRS. As a complementary sub-task, policy sub-tasks are proposed by recent works (Sun and Zhang, 2018; Lei et al., 2020; Liu et al., 2020) to better control the overall CRS. It usually focuses on selecting appropriate system actions (*e.g.,* recommendation or conversation) or tracking dialog states (topic prediction or goal tracking) to proactively guide the conversation.

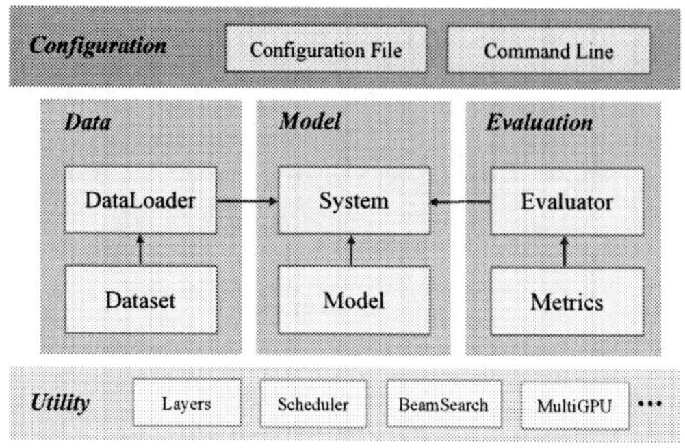

Figure 1: The overall framework of CRSLab.

3 CRSLab

The overall framework of our toolkit CRSLab is presented in Figure 1. The configuration module provides a flexible interface for users to easily set up the experiment environment (*e.g.,* datasets, models and hyperparameters). The data, model and evaluation modules are built upon the configuration module, which forms the core part of our toolkit. The bottom part is the utility module, providing auxiliary functions and interfaces for reuse in other modules (*e.g.,* Layers and Scheduler). In the following part, we briefly present the design of the above modules. More details can be found in the toolkit documents.

3.1 Configuration Module

In CRSLab, we design the configuration module for users to conveniently select or modify the experiment settings (*e.g.,* training data and hyperparameters). Specifically, we design the class Config to store all the configuration settings, which specify the data, model, hyperparameters and other necessary settings of a given experiment. To avoid complicated command line parameters, we transfer most of them into YAML configuration files, while other commonly used ones (*i.e.,* file path and debug mode) are provided as command line instructions. In this way, users can build and evaluate a variety of CRSs with only a few modifications in the configuration files.

3.2 Data Module

For extensibility and reusability, we design an elegant data flow that transforms raw dataset

Dataset	Dialog	Utterance	Domain	Policy Task	Entity KG	Word KG
ReDial (Li et al., 2018)	10,006	182,150	Movie	–	DB	CNet
OpenDialKG (Moon et al., 2019)	13,802	91,209	Movie, Book	Path Generation	DB	CNet
GoRecDial (Kang et al., 2019)	9,125	170,904	Movie	Action Prediction	DB	CNet
DuRecDial (Liu et al., 2020)	10,200	156,000	Movie, Music	Goal Planning	CN-DB	HNet
INSPIRED (Hayati et al., 2020)	1,001	35,811	Movie	Strategy Prediction	DB	CNet
TG-ReDial (Zhou et al., 2020c)	10,000	129,392	Movie	Topic Prediction	CN-DB	HNet

Table 1: The collected datasets in CRSLab. DB and CN-DB stand for the entity-oriented knowledge graph DBpedia and CN-DBpedia, respectively. CNet and HNet stand for the word-oriented knowledge graph ConceptNet and HowNet, respectively.

into the model input as follows: raw public dataset ⟶ preprocessed dataset ⟶ Dataset ⟶ DataLoader ⟶ System. Next, we detail the design of each component.

Data Preprocessing Since raw datasets vary in formats and features, we preprocess them to support unified interfaces in data modules. Based on the task description in Section 2, we first preprocess CRS datasets to match the input and output formats. Exactly, we organize the dialog contexts and side information as the input, and extract the recommended items, dialog actions and responses as the output of recommendation, policy and conversation tasks, respectively. To support some advanced models (*e.g.*, graph neural networks and pre-training models), we incorporate useful side data (*e.g.*, knowledge graph) and conduct specific data preprocessing (*e.g.*, entity linking and BPE segmentation).

As shown in Table 1, we collect 6 commonly used human-annotated datasets and release the preprocessed version with side data in CRSLab. Besides, we also release the pre-trained word embeddings and other associated files, which ease the use of integrated datasets and reduce the time cost.

Dataset Class To decouple the implementation of data preparation in CRSLab, we design the class Dataset for integrating the model-agnostic data processing functions, while the rest functions are implemented within the class DataLoader. In this way, Dataset only focuses on processing the input data into a unified format (*i.e.*, a list of python.dict), without considering specific models. In CRSLab, we design the class BaseDataset which includes some common attributes (*e.g.*, configurations and data paths) and basic functions (*e.g.*, data loading) of Dataset. Users can inherit BaseDataset with very few modifications to introduce new datasets.

DataLoader Class To support different input formats, DataLoader further transforms data from the Dataset module to support various models. It focuses on selecting input data from the processed data to form tensor data (*i.e.*, torch.Tensor) in a batch or mini-batch, which can be directly used for training or testing. To implement it, we design the class BaseDataLoader to integrate commonly used attributes and functions, and inherit it to produce new DataLoader for corresponding models.

3.3 Model Module

Based on the task descriptions and the above data modules, we reorganize the implementations of different CRSs in the model module. Existing works either integrate specific models to accomplish the recommendation, conversation and policy task, respectively (Chen et al., 2019; Zhou et al., 2020a), or only focus on one of the above tasks (Kang and McAuley, 2018; Hayati et al., 2020). Therefore, we divide commonly used models into four categories, namely CRS models (containing several sub-models to complete the corresponding tasks), recommendation models, conversation models and policy models. Besides, we also consider some classic heuristic methods (*e.g.*, Popularity and PMI) and several popular models which can be utilized to solve one of the above tasks, such as TextCNN (Kim, 2014) and BERT (Devlin et al., 2019). As illustrated in Table 2, we have implemented 19 models in the first released version, including some advanced models such as graph neural networks and pre-training models.

For implementation of these models, we develop the model class to provide functions and interfaces of specific models for corresponding tasks. In the model class, we focus on providing a basic structure and highly-decoupled useful functions or procedures for further development. In detail, we unify the basic attributes and func-

Category	Model	GNN	PTM	Reference
CRS model	ReDial	×	×	(Li et al., 2018)
	KBRD	√	×	(Chen et al., 2019)
	KGSF	√	×	(Zhou et al., 2020a)
	TG-ReDial	×	√	(Zhou et al., 2020c)
Recommendation model	Popularity	×	×	–
	GRU4Rec	×	×	(Hidasi et al., 2016)
	SASRec	×	×	(Kang and McAuley, 2018)
	TextCNN	×	×	(Kim, 2014)
	R-GCN	√	×	(Schlichtkrull et al., 2018)
	BERT	×	√	(Devlin et al., 2019)
Conversation model	HERD	×	×	(Serban et al., 2016)
	Transformer	×	×	(Vaswani et al., 2017)
	GPT-2	×	√	(Radford et al., 2019)
	INSPIRED	×	√	(Hayati et al., 2020)
Policy model	PMI	×	×	–
	MGCG	×	×	(Liu et al., 2020)
	Conv-BERT	×	√	(Zhou et al., 2020c)
	Topic-BERT	×	√	(Zhou et al., 2020c)
	Profile-BERT	×	√	(Zhou et al., 2020c)

Table 2: The implemented models in CRSLab. The CRS models integrate several sub-models to complete the overall conversational recommendation process, while recommendation, policy and conversation models only focus on one individual task. GNN and PTM stand for the graph neural networks and pre-training models, respectively.

tions of various models (*e.g.,* parameter initialization and model loading) into the class BaseModel. A user can inherit BaseModel and implement a few functions to design and develop new models. In this way, we re-implement the above models in our toolkit and unify the implementation of commonly used layers and components into the Utility Module for future usage. For all the implemented models, we have tested their performance on several datasets, and invited a code reviewer to examine the correctness of implementation. In the future, more methods will be incorporated along with regular updates.

3.4 System Module

In the system module, we build, train and evaluate contained models for accomplishing the overall conversational recommendation task. We aim to integrate the dataloader, model and evaluator modules into a complete system. To support flexible architectures for CRSs at the system level, we devise the system class with several functions for various usage. In detail, we design the class BaseSystem to unify the structures and interfaces, where we develop basic attributes and functions in the process. Among them, we develop the __init__() function to set up the required dataloader, contained models and evaluation protocols, which can be implemented by users for building new systems. Besides, we also implement a series of useful functions, such as optimizer initialization, learning ratio adjustment and early stop strategy. These functions and tiny tricks ease the developing process of a new system and greatly improve the user experience with our toolkit.

Based on the above settings, we design the fit() and step() functions in BaseSystem. The fit() function is used to train the whole system and then conduct evaluation, in which users need to devise the overall training process of all the models in the system, including data distribution, training orders and so on. In the step() function, users implement the detailed learning process for specific models, and functions within the corresponding models can be utilized to optimize model parameters.

3.5 Evaluation Module

The evaluation module implements the evaluation protocols for CRSs. In CRSLab, we implement some commonly used automatic evaluation metrics, and design a human-machine interactive interface for users to perform an end-to-end qualitative analysis.

Automatic Evaluation Since the CRS task is divided into three sub-tasks, we develop automatic evaluation metrics for each one. All the supported metrics are summarized in Table 3.

For the recommendation task, following exist-

Category	Metrics
Recommendation Metrics	Hit@{1,10,50}, MRR@{1,10,50}, NDCG@{1,10,50}
Conversation Metrics	Perplexity, BLEU-{1,2,3,4}, Embedding Average/Extreme/Greedy, Distinct-{1,2,3,4}
Policy Metrics	Accuracy, Hit@{1,3,5}

Table 3: The implemented automatic evaluation metrics in CRSLab.

ing CRSs (Sun and Zhang, 2018; Zhang et al., 2018b), we develop ranking-based metrics (*i.e.*, Hit, MRR and NDCG) to measure the ranking performance of the generated recommendation lists. For the conversation task, CRSLab supports both relevance-based (*i.e.*, BLEU (Papineni et al., 2002) and embedding-based metrics (Liu et al., 2016)) and diversity-based evaluation metrics (*i.e.*, Distinct-{1,2,3,4} (Li et al., 2016)). For the policy task, we implement commonly used metrics (*i.e.*, Accuracy and Hit@K) for evaluation.

Similarly, we design the class BaseEvaluator with common attributes and functions. Then, we inherit this class to implement RecEvaluator, ConvEvaluator and PolicyEvaluator for evaluating recommendation, conversation and policy tasks, respectively. Note that we implement the report() function in these classes. With this, users can print and monitor the performance of models evaluating on validation or test set.

Human-Machine Interaction Interface To evaluate CRSs qualitatively, CRSLab offers a human-machine interaction interface to help perform an end-to-end evaluation. The human-machine interaction interface is implemented within the system module, where the interaction strategy can be easily adapted to a specific policy model. In this way, a user can converse with a CRS or diagnose the system, which provides a direct approach to evaluating the overall performance of a CRS. Besides, the interaction interface enables users to correct errors by modifying intermediate results.

For end-to-end evaluation, users first need to set up the background of a simulated user (*e.g.*, interaction history and user profile), then freely chat with the CRS through the interface. During a conversation, the dialog history and the output of each component (*e.g.*, the recommended items and generated responses) are stored within a dictionary (*i.e.*, python.dict), helping users get a better understanding of how the system works.

3.6 Utility Module

To facilitate the usage of our toolkit, we design the utility module to include a series of useful functions (*e.g.*, layers() and scheduler()). We collect commonly used functions in various models (*e.g.*, CNN, RNN and Transformer layers) to constitute Layers, which can be easily used to develop new CRSs. Besides, we also decouple commonly used functions or procedures in other modules to form the utility file (*i.e.*, utils.py) for reuse.

Another particularly useful function is scheduler(), which provides a set of strategies for training large-scale models, such as warming-up strategy and weight decay. In addition, we also implement other functions to enhance user experiences, such as BeamSearch() to improve the inference performance, MultiGPU() for parallel training, logger() to print and monitor the running process, save_model() and load_model() to store and reuse the pre-trained models.

4 System Demonstration

In this section, we show how to use our CRSLab with code examples. We detail the usage descriptions in two parts, namely running an existing CRSs in our toolkit and implementing a new CRS based on the interfaces provided in our toolkit.

4.1 Running an Existing CRS

Our CRSLab enables quickly building a CRS with a few lines of code. Figure 2 presents a general procedure for running an existing CRS in our toolkit. To begin with, the whole procedure relies on the configurations to prepare the dataset and build the system. In the configurations, the user selects a dataset to use and specifies the tokenizer. Then, the Dataset class will automatically download the dataset and perform necessary processesing steps (*e.g.*, tokenization and converting tokens to IDs) based on the configurations. This procedure is executed by the function get_dataset(). Based on the processed datasets, users can use the function get_dataloader() to generate training, validation and test sets, in which the configurations specify the batch size and other necessary parameters for data processing. After that, the function get_system() can be adopted to leverage the prepared data for building a CRS. Similarly, the configurations specify the hyperparameters of

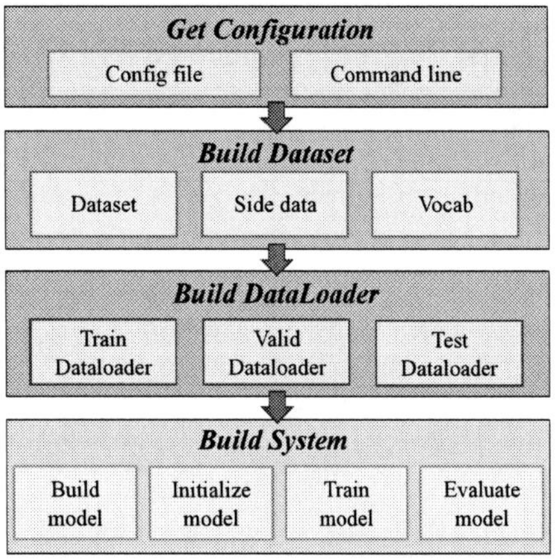


```
import ... #import necessary modules

#Get configs from file and command line
args, _ = parser.parse_known_args()
config = Config(args.config)

#Build dataset, get processed side data and vocab
Dataset = get_dataset(config, config['tokenize'])
side_data = Dataset.side_data
vocab = Dataset.vocab

#Build train/valid/test dataloader
train_loader = get_dataloader(config, Dataset.train_data, vocab)
valid_loader = get_dataloader(config, Dataset.valid_data, vocab)
test_loader = get_dataloader(config, Dataset.test_data, vocab)

#Build CRS system
CRS = get_system(config, train_loader, valid_loader,
                 test_loader, vocab, side_data)

#Train and evaluate CRS system
CRS.fit()
```

Figure 2: An illustrative usage flow of our CRSLab.

models and set up the training and evaluation procedures. Finally, users can start the running process by the function System.fit().

4.2 Developing a New CRS

Based on our toolkit, it is convenient to implement a new CRS with the provided interfaces. Users only need to inherit a few basic classes and implement some interface functions. In this part, we will introduce the detailed implementation process of adding a new dataset and model, respectively.

4.2.1 New Dataset

To add a new dataset, users need to inherit BaseDataset to design a new Dataset class for preparing the dataset into a unified format. In Dataset, the following functions are required to be implemented: __init__(), _load_data() and _data_preprocess().

In __init__(), users set up parameters and links for downloading data. In _load_data(), the training, validation, test data and other side data are loaded from corresponding files. If users follow our naming protocol, all they need is to reuse the functions from the Dataset class. The function _data_preprocess() is to prepare the loaded data, and we have integrated useful functions in the utility module to ease the implementation.

4.2.2 New Model

To add a new model, users should inherit BaseModel to design a new Model class, in which they need to implement the build_model() and forward() functions. In build_model(), users build the model, initialize the parameters and set up the loss function, while in forward() users use the model to predict the result or calculate the loss given the input data. Indeed, users can leverage the encapsulated layers and functions from Layers or the utility files to implement these two functions.

4.3 Performance Evaluation

To evaluate CRSLab, we train and test various implemented models on the TG-ReDial dataset (Zhou et al., 2020c), and compare their performance on recommendation, conversation and policy tasks. In our experiments, we have tuned the hyperparameters of these models to achieve their best performance on this dataset. Due to the space limit, we present the results in our GitHub page [1]. As we can see, our toolkit provides a possibility to compare the performance of various CRS models under different evaluation protocols. Among them, GNN-based models and pretraining methods achieve consistent and remarkable performance on the above tasks. These results are compatible with our expectations.

5 Conclusion

In this paper, we released a toolkit called **CRSLab**, which is the first open-source conversational recommender systems (CRSs) toolkit for research purpose. In CRSLab, we offered a unified and extensible framework with highly-decoupled modules to develop CRSs. Based on this framework, we have incorporated 6 datasets and implemented 19 models in our toolkit. Besides, we also provided extensive automatic evaluation pro-

[1] https://github.com/RUCAIBox/CRSLab

tocols and a human-machine interactive interface in CRSLab, to help evaluate and compare different CRSs. For demonstration, we illustrated how to run or implement a CRS using our toolkit.

With this toolkit, we expect to help users quickly run existing CRSs, ease the development of new CRSs, and set up a benchmark framework for the research of CRSs. In the future, we will make continuous efforts to add more datasets and models. We will also consider adding more utilities for improving the usage of our toolkit, such as result visualization and algorithm debugging.

Acknowledgement

This work was partially supported by the National Natural Science Foundation of China under Grant No. 61872369 and 61832017, Beijing Academy of Artificial Intelligence (BAAI) under Grant No. BAAI2020ZJ0301, Beijing Outstanding Young Scientist Program under Grant No. BJJWZYJH012019100020098, the Fundamental Research Funds for the Central Universities, and the Research Funds of Renmin University of China under Grant No.18XNLG22 and 19XNQ047. Xin Zhao is the corresponding author.

References

Qibin Chen, Junyang Lin, Yichang Zhang, Ming Ding, Yukuo Cen, Hongxia Yang, and Jie Tang. 2019. Towards knowledge-based recommender dialog system. In *Proceedings of the 2019 Conference on Empirical Methods in Natural Language Processing and the 9th International Joint Conference on Natural Language Processing, EMNLP-IJCNLP 2019, Hong Kong, China, November 3-7, 2019*, pages 1803–1813.

Konstantina Christakopoulou, Filip Radlinski, and Katja Hofmann. 2016. Towards conversational recommender systems. In *Proceedings of the 22nd ACM SIGKDD International Conference on Knowledge Discovery and Data Mining, San Francisco, CA, USA, August 13-17, 2016*, pages 815–824.

Jacob Devlin, Ming-Wei Chang, Kenton Lee, and Kristina Toutanova. 2019. BERT: pre-training of deep bidirectional transformers for language understanding. In *Proceedings of the 2019 Conference of the North American Chapter of the Association for Computational Linguistics: Human Language Technologies, NAACL-HLT 2019, Minneapolis, MN, USA, June 2-7, 2019, Volume 1 (Long and Short Papers)*, pages 4171–4186.

Chongming Gao, Wenqiang Lei, Xiangnan He, Maarten de Rijke, and Tat-Seng Chua. 2021. Advances and challenges in conversational recommender systems: A survey. *CoRR*, abs/2101.09459.

Shirley Anugrah Hayati, Dongyeop Kang, Qingxiaoyang Zhu, Weiyan Shi, and Zhou Yu. 2020. INSPIRED: toward sociable recommendation dialog systems. In *Proceedings of the 2020 Conference on Empirical Methods in Natural Language Processing, EMNLP 2020, Online, November 16-20, 2020*, pages 8142–8152.

Balázs Hidasi, Alexandros Karatzoglou, Linas Baltrunas, and Domonkos Tikk. 2016. Session-based recommendations with recurrent neural networks. In *4th International Conference on Learning Representations, ICLR 2016, San Juan, Puerto Rico, May 2-4, 2016, Conference Track Proceedings*.

Dongyeop Kang, Anusha Balakrishnan, Pararth Shah, Paul Crook, Y-Lan Boureau, and Jason Weston. 2019. Recommendation as a communication game: Self-supervised bot-play for goal-oriented dialogue. In *Proceedings of the 2019 Conference on Empirical Methods in Natural Language Processing and the 9th International Joint Conference on Natural Language Processing, EMNLP-IJCNLP 2019, Hong Kong, China, November 3-7, 2019*, pages 1951–1961.

Wang-Cheng Kang and Julian J. McAuley. 2018. Self-attentive sequential recommendation. In *IEEE International Conference on Data Mining, ICDM 2018, Singapore, November 17-20, 2018*, pages 197–206.

Yoon Kim. 2014. Convolutional neural networks for sentence classification. In *Proceedings of the 2014 Conference on Empirical Methods in Natural Language Processing, EMNLP 2014, October 25-29, 2014, Doha, Qatar, A meeting of SIGDAT, a Special Interest Group of the ACL*, pages 1746–1751.

Sungjin Lee, Qi Zhu, Ryuichi Takanobu, Zheng Zhang, Yaoqin Zhang, Xiang Li, Jinchao Li, Baolin Peng, Xiujun Li, Minlie Huang, and Jianfeng Gao. 2019. Convlab: Multi-domain end-to-end dialog system platform. In *Proceedings of the 57th Conference of the Association for Computational Linguistics, ACL 2019, Florence, Italy, July 28 - August 2, 2019, Volume 3: System Demonstrations*, pages 64–69.

Wenqiang Lei, Xiangnan He, Yisong Miao, Qingyun Wu, Richang Hong, Min-Yen Kan, and Tat-Seng Chua. 2020. Estimation-action-reflection: Towards deep interaction between conversational and recommender systems. In *WSDM '20: The Thirteenth ACM International Conference on Web Search and Data Mining, Houston, TX, USA, February 3-7, 2020*, pages 304–312.

Jiwei Li, Michel Galley, Chris Brockett, Jianfeng Gao, and Bill Dolan. 2016. A diversity-promoting objective function for neural conversation models. In

NAACL HLT 2016, The 2016 Conference of the North American Chapter of the Association for Computational Linguistics: Human Language Technologies, San Diego California, USA, June 12-17, 2016, pages 110–119.

Raymond Li, Samira Ebrahimi Kahou, Hannes Schulz, Vincent Michalski, Laurent Charlin, and Chris Pal. 2018. Towards deep conversational recommendations. In *Advances in Neural Information Processing Systems 31: Annual Conference on Neural Information Processing Systems 2018, NeurIPS 2018, 3-8 December 2018, Montréal, Canada*, pages 9748–9758.

Lizi Liao, Ryuichi Takanobu, Yunshan Ma, Xun Yang, Minlie Huang, and Tat-Seng Chua. 2020. Topic-guided relational conversational recommender in multi-domain. *IEEE Transactions on Knowledge and Data Engineering*.

Chia-Wei Liu, Ryan Lowe, Iulian Serban, Michael Noseworthy, Laurent Charlin, and Joelle Pineau. 2016. How NOT to evaluate your dialogue system: An empirical study of unsupervised evaluation metrics for dialogue response generation. In *Proceedings of the 2016 Conference on Empirical Methods in Natural Language Processing, EMNLP 2016, Austin, Texas, USA, November 1-4, 2016*, pages 2122–2132.

Zeming Liu, Haifeng Wang, Zheng-Yu Niu, Hua Wu, Wanxiang Che, and Ting Liu. 2020. Towards conversational recommendation over multi-type dialogs. In *Proceedings of the 58th Annual Meeting of the Association for Computational Linguistics, ACL 2020, Online, July 5-10, 2020*, pages 1036–1049.

Seungwhan Moon, Pararth Shah, Anuj Kumar, and Rajen Subba. 2019. Opendialkg: Explainable conversational reasoning with attention-based walks over knowledge graphs. In *Proceedings of the 57th Conference of the Association for Computational Linguistics, ACL 2019, Florence, Italy, July 28- August 2, 2019, Volume 1: Long Papers*, pages 845–854.

Kishore Papineni, Salim Roukos, Todd Ward, and Wei-Jing Zhu. 2002. Bleu: a method for automatic evaluation of machine translation. In *Proceedings of the 40th Annual Meeting of the Association for Computational Linguistics, July 6-12, 2002, Philadelphia, PA, USA*, pages 311–318.

Alec Radford, Jeffrey Wu, Rewon Child, David Luan, Dario Amodei, and Ilya Sutskever. 2019. Language models are unsupervised multitask learners. *OpenAI Blog*, 1(8):9.

Steffen Rendle, Christoph Freudenthaler, Zeno Gantner, and Lars Schmidt-Thieme. 2012. Bpr: Bayesian personalized ranking from implicit feedback. *arXiv preprint arXiv:1205.2618*.

Badrul Sarwar, George Karypis, Joseph Konstan, and John Riedl. 2001. Item-based collaborative filtering recommendation algorithms. In *Proceedings of the 10th international conference on World Wide Web*, pages 285–295.

Michael Sejr Schlichtkrull, Thomas N. Kipf, Peter Bloem, Rianne van den Berg, Ivan Titov, and Max Welling. 2018. Modeling relational data with graph convolutional networks. In *The Semantic Web - 15th International Conference, ESWC 2018, Heraklion, Crete, Greece, June 3-7, 2018, Proceedings*, pages 593–607.

Iulian Vlad Serban, Alessandro Sordoni, Yoshua Bengio, Aaron C. Courville, and Joelle Pineau. 2016. Building end-to-end dialogue systems using generative hierarchical neural network models. In *Proceedings of the Thirtieth AAAI Conference on Artificial Intelligence, February 12-17, 2016, Phoenix, Arizona, USA*, pages 3776–3784.

Lifeng Shang, Zhengdong Lu, and Hang Li. 2015. Neural responding machine for short-text conversation. In *Proceedings of the 53rd Annual Meeting of the Association for Computational Linguistics and the 7th International Joint Conference on Natural Language Processing of the Asian Federation of Natural Language Processing, ACL 2015, July 26-31, 2015, Beijing, China, Volume 1: Long Papers*, pages 1577–1586.

Yueming Sun and Yi Zhang. 2018. Conversational recommender system. In *The 41st International ACM SIGIR Conference on Research & Development in Information Retrieval, SIGIR 2018, Ann Arbor, MI, USA, July 08-12, 2018*, pages 235–244.

Ashish Vaswani, Noam Shazeer, Niki Parmar, Jakob Uszkoreit, Llion Jones, Aidan N. Gomez, Lukasz Kaiser, and Illia Polosukhin. 2017. Attention is all you need. In *Advances in Neural Information Processing Systems 30: Annual Conference on Neural Information Processing Systems 2017, 4-9 December 2017, Long Beach, CA, USA*, pages 5998–6008.

Hu Xu, Seungwhan Moon, Honglei Liu, Bing Liu, Pararth Shah, and Philip S. Yu. 2020. User memory reasoning for conversational recommendation. In *Proceedings of the 28th International Conference on Computational Linguistics, COLING 2020, Barcelona, Spain (Online), December 8-13, 2020*, pages 5288–5308.

Saizheng Zhang, Emily Dinan, Jack Urbanek, Arthur Szlam, Douwe Kiela, and Jason Weston. 2018a. Personalizing dialogue agents: I have a dog, do you have pets too? In *Proceedings of the 56th Annual Meeting of the Association for Computational Linguistics, ACL 2018, Melbourne, Australia, July 15-20, 2018, Volume 1: Long Papers*, pages 2204–2213.

Yongfeng Zhang, Xu Chen, Qingyao Ai, Liu Yang, and W. Bruce Croft. 2018b. Towards conversational search and recommendation: System ask, user respond. In *Proceedings of the 27th ACM International Conference on Information and Knowledge*

Management, CIKM 2018, Torino, Italy, October 22-26, 2018, pages 177–186.

Kun Zhou, Wayne Xin Zhao, Shuqing Bian, Yuanhang Zhou, Ji-Rong Wen, and Jingsong Yu. 2020a. Improving conversational recommender systems via knowledge graph based semantic fusion. In *KDD '20: The 26th ACM SIGKDD Conference on Knowledge Discovery and Data Mining, Virtual Event, CA, USA, August 23-27, 2020*, pages 1006–1014.

Kun Zhou, Wayne Xin Zhao, Hui Wang, Sirui Wang, Fuzheng Zhang, Zhongyuan Wang, and Ji-Rong Wen. 2020b. Leveraging historical interaction data for improving conversational recommender system. In *CIKM '20: The 29th ACM International Conference on Information and Knowledge Management, Virtual Event, Ireland, October 19-23, 2020*, pages 2349–2352.

Kun Zhou, Yuanhang Zhou, Wayne Xin Zhao, Xiaoke Wang, and Ji-Rong Wen. 2020c. Towards topic-guided conversational recommender system. In *Proceedings of the 28th International Conference on Computational Linguistics, COLING 2020, Barcelona, Spain (Online), December 8-13, 2020*, pages 4128–4139.

Does My Representation Capture X? Probe-Ably

Deborah Ferreira[*], **Julia Rozanova**[*], **Mokanarangan Thayaparan**[*], **Marco Valentino**[*], **André Freitas**

Department of Computer Science, University of Manchester, United Kingdom

Idiap Research Institute, Switzerland

{firstname.surname}@manchester.ac.uk

Abstract

Probing (or *diagnostic classification*) has become a popular strategy for investigating whether a given set of intermediate features is present in the representations of neural models. Probing studies may have misleading results, but various recent works have suggested more reliable methodologies that compensate for the possible pitfalls of probing. However, these best practices are numerous and fast-evolving. To simplify the process of running a set of probing experiments in line with suggested methodologies, we introduce **Probe-Ably:** an extendable probing framework which supports and automates the application of probing methods to the user's inputs.

1 Introduction

Recent interest in investigating the intermediate features present in neural models' representations has led to the use of structural analysis methods such as *probing*.

At its simplest, **probing**[1] is the training of an external classifier model (a "probe") to determine the extent to which a set of auxiliary target feature labels can be predicted from the internal model representations. For example, probing studies have been carried out to determine whether word and sentence representations generated by models such as BERT (Devlin et al., 2019) capture intermediate syntactic and semantic features such as parts of speech and dependency labels (Hewitt and Manning, 2019b; Tenney et al., 2019b) and lexical relations (Vulić et al., 2020).

Various problems can arise when performing probing experiments (Hewitt and Liang, 2019), such as achieving a high probing accuracy without being due to a high mutual information between the representation and the auxiliary task labels. This has prompted much recent work on establishing more reliable methodologies for probing (Hewitt and Liang, 2019; Voita and Titov, 2020; Pimentel et al., 2020b,a).

These approaches introduce various steps such as controlling and varying model complexity and structure, including randomized control tasks and incorporating more informative metrics such as selectivity (Hewitt and Liang, 2019) and minimum description length (Voita and Titov, 2020).

To make these methods more accessible and quick to implement for any user wishing to probe the representations of their neural models in line with the evolving suggested methodologies, we introduce **Probe-Ably:** an extendable probing framework which supports and automates the application of suggested best practices for probing studies.

2 Probe-Ably

Probe-Ably[2] is a framework designed for PyTorch[3] to support researchers in the implementation of probes for neural representations in a flexible and extendable way.

The core facility provided by Probe-Ably is the encapsulation of the end-to-end experimental probing pipeline. Specifically, Probe-Ably provides a complete implementation of the core tasks necessary for probing neural representations, starting from the configuration and training of heterogeneous probe models, to the calculation and visualization of metrics for the evaluation.

The probing pipeline and the core tasks operate on a set of abstract classes, making the whole

[*] Equal contribution, presented in alphabetical order.

[1] The term "probing" has also been used describe stress-test style analyses, but we mean "probing" in the sense of *diagnostic classification* as in (Alain and Bengio, 2018; Pimentel et al., 2020b).

[2] Video demonstration: https://youtu.be/1E30_BENBxk

[3] https://pytorch.org/

Proceedings of the Joint Conference of the 59th Annual Meeting of the Association for Computational Linguistics and the 11th International Joint Conference on Natural Language Processing: System Demonstrations, pages 194–201, August 1st - August 6th, 2021.

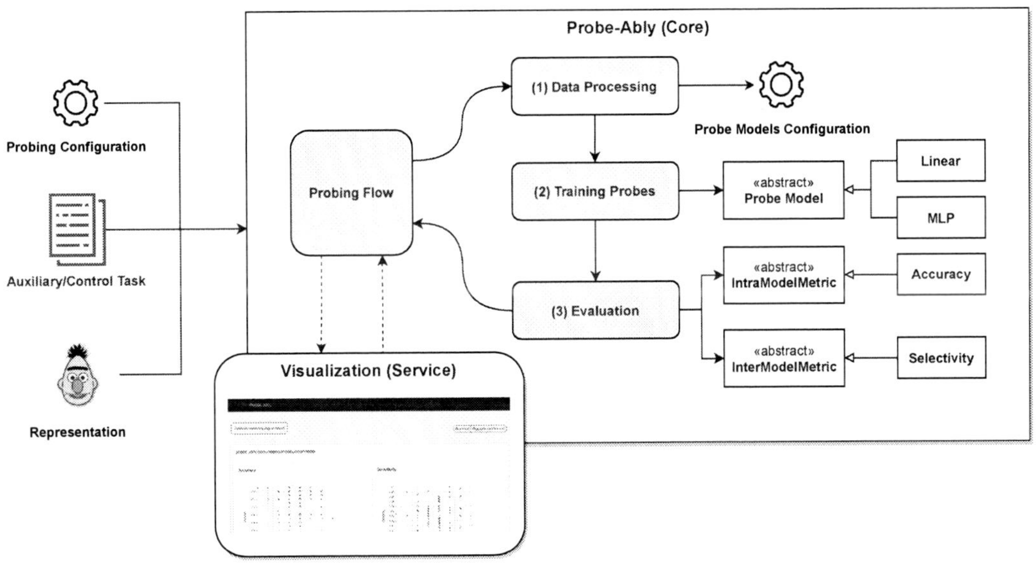

Figure 1: An overview of Probe-Ably. The core facility provided by Probe-Ably is the encapsulation of an end-to-end experimental probing pipeline. The framework offers a complete implementation and orchestration of the main tasks required for probing, together with a suite of standard probe models and evaluation metrics.

framework agnostic to the specific representation, auxiliary task, probe model, and metrics used in the concrete experiments (see Fig 1). This architectural design allows the user to:

1. Configure and run probing experiments on different representations and auxiliary tasks in parallel;
2. Automatically generate control tasks for the probing, allowing the computation of inter-model metrics such as *selectivity*;
3. Extend the suite of probes with new models without the need to change the core probing pipeline;
4. Customize, implement and adopt novel evaluation metrics for the experiments.

2.1 Probing Pipeline

In this section we describe the core components implemented in Probe-Ably.

A probing pipeline is typically composed of the following sub-tasks:

1. **Data Processing:** This task consists in data preparation and configuration of the probe models for the subsequent training task. For each representation to be probed and each auxiliary task, a requirement in this stage is the generation of a *control task* (Hewitt and Liang, 2019), along with the selection of distinct hyperparameter configurations for the probe models. Generally, the control task can be either designed by researchers or automatically constructed by randomly assigning labels to the examples in the auxiliary task. On the other hand, the hyperparameter selection is crucial for the interpretation of the probing results, and has to guarantee a large coverage of the configuration space to allow for a significant comparison of the representations under investigation. Common methods for hyperparameter selection adopt a combination of grid search and random sampling techniques.

2. **Training Probes:** This task consists in training a set Φ of probe models. In particular, for each representation and each auxiliary task, researchers need to train probe models of different types (e.g., *linear models*, *multi-layer perceptrons*) and distinct hyperparameter configurations (e.g., hidden size, number of layers). Therefore, the number of probe models to be trained can rapidly increase with the number of representations, auxiliary tasks, and possible configurations. Let n be the number of representations to be probed, m the number of auxiliary tasks, z the number of probe models, and k the number of selected

hyperparameter configurations for each probe. The total cardinality of Φ is generally equal to $|\Phi| = n \times m \times z \times k$. Thus, because of the potentially large space of models and configurations, the training task typically represents the most demanding and time-consuming stage in the overall probing pipeline.

3. **Evaluation:** The evaluation stage consists in calculating a set of metrics for assessing the performance and quality of the probes on the auxiliary tasks. The most common metrics adopted for probing evaluation are *accuracy* and *selectivity*. Generally, these quantities are plotted against the complexity of the probe models and are used to compare the trend in the performance of different neural representations on a given auxiliary task.

Probe-Ably provides a complete implementation and orchestration of the aforementioned tasks, which are integrated by a component named *Probing Flow* (see Fig. 1).

The Probing Flow is ready to use for configuring and running standard probing experiments including hyperparameters selection via grid search. Moreover, the flow can be flexibly adapted to new models and metrics if necessary by extending the appropriate abstract classes and configuration files (additional details are described in section 3). We provide a pre-implemented suite of probe models and metrics whose details are described in sections 2.2 and 2.3.

In order to configure and run a new probing experiment, the user has to provide the following input:

- **Probing Configuration:** a JSON file describing the components and parameters for the probing experiments. This file allows specifying the concrete probe models to train on each auxiliary task, along with pre-defined training parameters such as batch-size, number of epochs and number of different hyperparameter configurations to test. Additionally, the probing configuration file can be used to indicate the metrics to use for the final evaluation.
- **Auxiliary Task:** a TSV file containing the data and labels composing the auxiliary task. Probe-Ably allows the user to configure experiments that run on more than one auxiliary task in parallel.
- **Control Task (Optional):** a TSV file containing the labels composing a control task. The control tasks are automatically generated for each auxiliary task during the data processing stage. If not provided, we assign random labels to the example in the auxiliary tasksfor.
- **Representation:** a TSV file containing the pre-trained embeddings for each example in the auxiliary task (e.g. BERT (Devlin et al., 2019), RoBERTa (Liu et al., 2019)). Similarly to the auxiliary tasks, Probe-Ably can run experiments on more than one representation in parallel.

2.2 Available Models

A common theme in probing studies is the use of structurally *simple* classifiers: two common choices are *linear* models and *multi layer perceptrons*[4].

Following works such as (Hewitt and Manning, 2019a) and (Pimentel et al., 2020a), each instantiated model comes with some approximate appropriate *complexity*. This is varied in a controlled way in order to include results for a range of model complexities: this mitigates the possible confounding effect of *overly expressive probes* which might be "memorizing" the task (Hewitt and Liang, 2019; Pimentel et al., 2020a).

For linear models $\hat{y} = W\mathbf{x} + \mathbf{b}$, we mimic (Pimentel et al., 2020a) in using the nuclear norm

$$||\mathbf{W}||_* = \sum_{i=1}^{min(|T|,d)} \sigma_i(\mathbf{W}).$$

of the matrix W as the approximate measure of complexity. The rationale here is that the nuclear norm approximates the rank of the transformation matrix. The rank may be used instead in situations where there is a large number of class labels, but as it is limited by this number the nuclear norm presents a wider range of values. The nuclear norm is included in the loss (weighted by a parameter λ)

$$-\sum_{i=1}^{n} \log p(t^{(i)} \mid \mathbf{h}^{(i)}) + \lambda \cdot ||\mathbf{W}||_*$$

and is thus regulated in the training loop.

Multi-layer perceptrons are the only non-linear models currently included. Their flexibility and

[4]The hyperparameters of all implemented models are configurable, but we use the same default hyperparameter ranges as (Pimentel et al., 2020b).

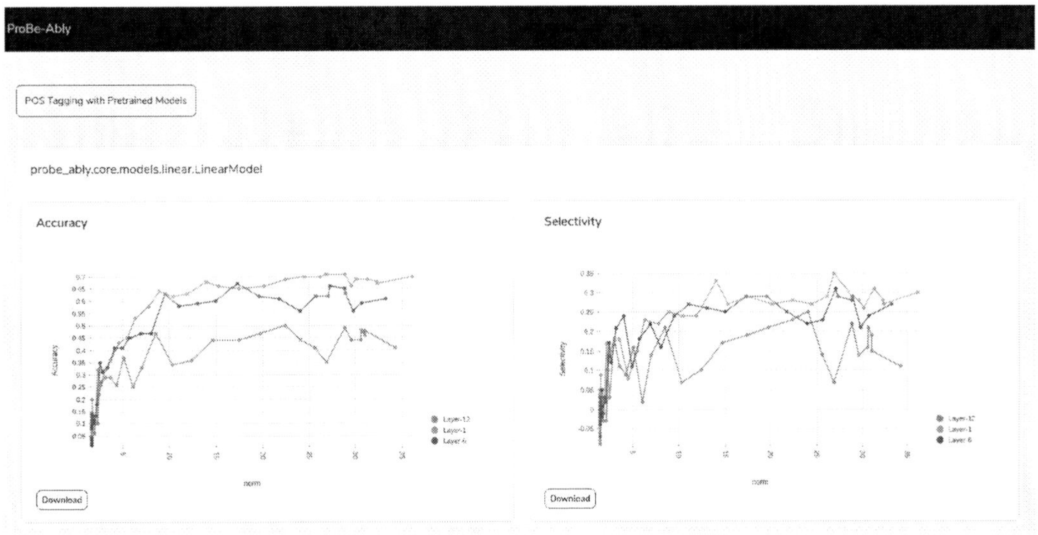

Figure 2: Probe-Ably is integrated with a front-end visualization service, which supports researchers in consulting and plotting the results of their experiments.

simplicity has made them popular choices in probing studies. We use the *number of parameters* as an estimation of model complexity. Since sufficiently large MLP models could be prone to "fitting" noise in the data, it is especially important to monitor the *selectivity* when using this class of probes.

2.3 Available Metrics

Certain probing metrics are not tied to the output of a specific probe, but to two or more probes or training runs. As such, we have chosen to distinguish between *intra-model* and *inter-model* metrics.

Intra-Model Metrics. Individual model results and losses fall into this category. This includes the usual suspects such as *cross-entropy loss* and *accuracy*. Intra-model metrics can be used for training, model-selection and reporting purposes.

Inter-Model Metrics. An important component of assessing the reliability of a probe's result is the *selectivity* metric (Hewitt and Liang, 2019): for a fixed probe architecture and hyperparameter configuration, the auxiliary task accuracy is compared to the accuracy on a *control task*, hence incorporating the results of two trained models. This is our primary example of an inter-model metric, but this format could be useful for other probing metrics such as minimum description length (online code version) (Voita and Titov, 2020) or pareto hypervolume (Pimentel et al., 2020a), which incorporate the results of multiple models or training runs. These are only used for *reporting* purposes, as they are external to each model's training loop.

2.4 Front-end Visualization

Probe-Ably is integrated with a front-end visualization service. The front-end is used to plot the results of each probing experiment in a user-friendly way. The service is designed to be accessible via standard web browsers, and support researchers in analysing and comparing the probing performance of each representation on different auxiliary tasks.

An example of plots included in the front-end visualization is shown in Figure 2. Each plot can be downloaded in a pdf format to be stored locally or integrated in a LaTeX project.

3 Customized Probing Experiments

Probe-Ably can be flexibly adapted and extended to run experiments on different representations, novel probe models and evaluation metrics. The following sections provide an overview of how researchers and users can customize their experiments via configuration files or implementation of new concrete classes.

For a complete guide on how to extend and customize Probe-Ably, please consult the documentation[5][6].

[5]Documentation: `https://ai-systems.github.io/Probe-Ably/`

[6]Repository: `https://github.com/ai-systems/Probe-Ably/`

3.1 Configuration

Although default configurations are ready to use to run a basic set of experiments, the details of the latter can be customized according to specific needs, using the apposite probing configuration file. This pertains to aspects such as probe model choice, number of experiments, auxiliary tasks labels, input representations and custom control labels.

Therefore, the settings can be modified by providing or editing the values of the attributes in the configuration file which specifies details about auxiliary tasks, probing model/s and training regime, including paths to any custom metrics or models.

The structure of the probing configuration file is as follows:

- tasks (list)
  - task_name (attr)
  - representations (list)
    - representation_name (attr)
    - file_location (attr)
    - control_location (attr)
- probing_setup (dict)
  - train_size (attr)
  - dev_size (attr)
  - test_size (attr)
  - intra_metric (attr)
  - inter_metric (attr)
  - probing_models (list)
    - probing_model_name (attr)
    - batch_size (attr)
    - epochs (attr)
    - number_of_models (attr)

3.2 Adding a Probe Model

Custom probe models can be introduced by extending the abstract `ProbeModel` class (Fig. 1). This class inherits the methods and attributes of a `nn.Module` in PyTorch. To extend Probe-Ably with a new probe model, the user needs to implement two methods, namely `forward` and `get_complexity`.

The `forward` method is inherited from PyTorch and is adopted to compute the predictions of the probe models along with their loss function. On the other hand, the `get_complexity` method has to return a complexity measure for the model (e.g., nuclear norm, number of parameters). This method is internally used by the Probing Flow for setting up and executing the probing pipeline, and creating the right visualization for the results.

In order to make a customized probe model available for new experiments, the user needs to specify a model configuration file (JSON format) containing the path to the concrete class, together with the parameters required for its instantiation. The model configuration file is organized as follows:

- model_class (attr)
- params (list)
  - name (attr)
  - type (attr)
  - options (attr)

3.3 Adding an Evaluation Metric

Similarly to probe models, it is possible to extend Probe-Ably with new evaluation metrics. In order to add a new metric, the user can extend one of the available abstract classes (i.e., `IntraModelMetric` or `InterModelMetric`).

In this case, it is not necessary to specify a configuration file for the metrics, and the user only needs to implement the apposite function, `calculate_metrics`, that performs the appropriate computation. Subsequently, the user can adopt the new metric in a probing experiment by editing the apposite attribute in the probing configuration file.

4 Interpreting Results

We provide the following list of guidelines for interpreting results:

- Regions of low selectivity indicates a less trustworthy auxiliary task accuracy result. As accuracy increases with model complexity, keep an eye on the selectivity value: if it starts to drop again, this indicates that the probe is expressive enough to fit the randomized control task (and thus high expressivity and overfitting may be responsible for a high auxiliary task accuracy).
- We recommend a focus on *comparison of trends* between models/representations rather than probe performance on any fixed set of representations.
- These comparisons are more convincing if they are consistent across a range of probe complexities.

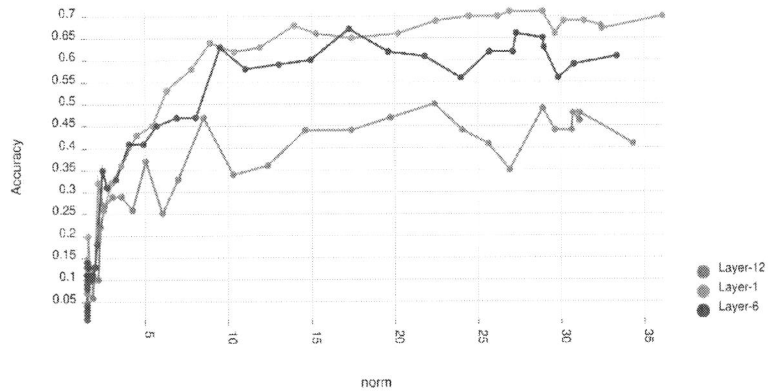

(a) Linear Model Accuracy.

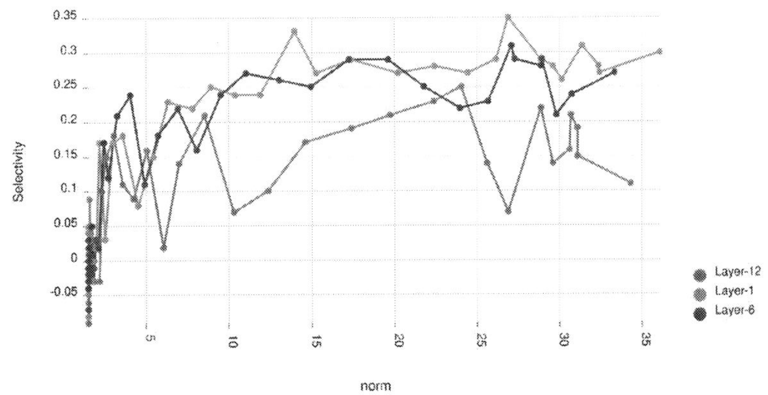

(b) Linear Model Selectivity.

Figure 3: Probing results for different layers of BERT on the *Part-Of-Speech* task using the control task presented in (Hewitt and Liang, 2019), implemented and executed through Probe-Ably (see Section 5). The results are consistent with observations in (Tenney et al., 2019a), which note that syntactic features (such as part of speech tags) are more prevalent in earlier layers of BERT.

- Note that any given probe architecture imposes a structural assumption. For example, *linear* probes may only attain a high accuracy if the representation-target relationship is linear. We recommend that these assumptions/probe model choices be guided by prior visualizations and hypothesized relationships.
- As far as possible, stick to comparing representations of the same sizes. Lower-dimensional representations may reach their maximum accuracy at lower probe complexity values; as such they may give the "appearance" of superior probe accuracy scores to larger representations. For this reason, it is also important that you investigate a sufficiently large range of model complexities.

5 Case Study

To demonstrate the Probe-Ably system, we include an implementation of a Part-Of-Speech tagging auxiliary task based on the Penn Treebank corpus (Marcus et al., 1993). It has been used multiple times in works on probing methodology (Hewitt and Liang, 2019; Voita and Titov, 2020; Pimentel et al., 2020b). We use the custom control task from (Hewitt and Liang, 2019). Using linear models as probes, we compare the probing results for different layers of BERT (`bert-base-uncased`) pre-trained on the masked language modelling task (Devlin et al., 2019), across 50 probing runs. The results are consistent with observations in (Tenney et al., 2019a), which note that syntactic features (such as part of speech tags) are more prevalent in earlier layers of BERT. This case study is available as a ready-to-run example.

6 Related Work

Previous interpretability tools for neural models have focused on gradient-based methods (Wallace et al., 2019), the visualization of attention weights (Vig, 2019) and other tools focusing on NLP model explainability and interpretability (Wexler et al., 2020; Tenney et al., 2020).

The ongoing discussion on probing, auxiliary tasks and the surrounding best practices can be traced back to the early definitions in (Alain and Bengio, 2018), where it was first described as *diagnostic classification*. Early probing studies in NLP include (Zhang and Bowman, 2018) and (Tenney et al., 2019c), the former being an early example of the importance of comparing with randomized representations or labels. Further discussion has introduced control tasks and the selectivity metric (Hewitt and Liang, 2019), formalized notions of *ease of extraction* (Voita and Titov, 2020) and described other strategies for taking model complexity into account (Pimentel et al., 2020a).

7 Conclusion

While probing can be used to explore hypotheses about linguistic (or general) features present in model representations, there are various pitfalls that can lead to premature or incorrect claims. Much progress has been made in establishing better practices for probing studies, but these involve running large systematic sets of experiments employing recently-developed metrics and correctly interpreting results. **Probe-Ably** is designed to simplify and encourage the use of emerging methodological developments in probing studies, serving as a task-agnostic and model-agnostic platform for auxiliary diagnostic classification for high-dimensional vector representations.

Acknowledgements

The authors would like to thank the anonymous reviewers for the constructive feedback. Additionally, we would like to thank the Computational Shared Facility of the University of Manchester for providing the infrastructure to run our experiments. Thanks to Alber Santos for the helpful discussions.

References

Guillaume Alain and Yoshua Bengio. 2018. Understanding intermediate layers using linear classifier probes.

Jacob Devlin, Ming-Wei Chang, Kenton Lee, and Kristina Toutanova. 2019. Bert: Pre-training of deep bidirectional transformers for language understanding. In *Proceedings of the 2019 Conference of the North American Chapter of the Association for Computational Linguistics: Human Language Technologies, Volume 1 (Long and Short Papers)*, pages 4171–4186.

John Hewitt and Percy Liang. 2019. Designing and interpreting probes with control tasks. In *Proceedings of the 2019 Conference on Empirical Methods in Natural Language Processing and the 9th International Joint Conference on Natural Language Processing (EMNLP-IJCNLP)*, pages 2733–2743, Hong Kong, China. Association for Computational Linguistics.

John Hewitt and Christopher D. Manning. 2019a. A structural probe for finding syntax in word representations. In *Proceedings of the 2019 Conference of the North American Chapter of the Association for Computational Linguistics: Human Language Technologies, Volume 1 (Long and Short Papers)*, pages 4129–4138, Minneapolis, Minnesota. Association for Computational Linguistics.

John Hewitt and Christopher D Manning. 2019b. A structural probe for finding syntax in word representations. In *Proceedings of the 2019 Conference of the North American Chapter of the Association for Computational Linguistics: Human Language Technologies, Volume 1 (Long and Short Papers)*, pages 4129–4138.

Yinhan Liu, Myle Ott, Naman Goyal, Jingfei Du, Mandar Joshi, Danqi Chen, Omer Levy, Mike Lewis, Luke Zettlemoyer, and Veselin Stoyanov. 2019. Roberta: A robustly optimized bert pretraining approach. *arXiv preprint arXiv:1907.11692*.

Mitchell P. Marcus, Beatrice Santorini, and Mary Ann Marcinkiewicz. 1993. Building a large annotated corpus of English: The Penn Treebank. *Computational Linguistics*, 19(2):313–330.

Tiago Pimentel, Naomi Saphra, Adina Williams, and Ryan Cotterell. 2020a. Pareto probing: Trading-off accuracy and complexity. In *Proceedings of the 2020 Conference on Empirical Methods in Natural Language Processing (EMNLP)*, pages 3138–3153.

Tiago Pimentel, Josef Valvoda, Rowan Hall Maudslay, Ran Zmigrod, Adina Williams, and Ryan Cotterell. 2020b. Information-theoretic probing for linguistic structure. In *Proceedings of the 58th Annual Meeting of the Association for Computational Linguistics*, pages 4609–4622.

Ian Tenney, Dipanjan Das, and Ellie Pavlick. 2019a. Bert rediscovers the classical nlp pipeline. In *Proceedings of the 57th Annual Meeting of the Association for Computational Linguistics*, pages 4593–4601.

Ian Tenney, James Wexler, Jasmijn Bastings, Tolga Bolukbasi, Andy Coenen, Sebastian Gehrmann, Ellen Jiang, Mahima Pushkarna, Carey Radebaugh, Emily Reif, and Ann Yuan. 2020. The language interpretability tool: Extensible, interactive visualizations and analysis for NLP models.

Ian Tenney, Patrick Xia, Berlin Chen, Alex Wang, Adam Poliak, R Thomas McCoy, Najoung Kim, Benjamin Van Durme, Sam Bowman, Dipanjan Das, and Ellie Pavlick. 2019b. What do you learn from context? probing for sentence structure in contextualized word representations. In *International Conference on Learning Representations*.

Ian Tenney, Patrick Xia, Berlin Chen, Alex Wang, Adam Poliak, R. Thomas McCoy, Najoung Kim, Benjamin Van Durme, Samuel R. Bowman, Dipanjan Das, and Ellie Pavlick. 2019c. What do you learn from context? probing for sentence structure in contextualized word representations. In *International Conference on Learning Representations*.

Jesse Vig. 2019. Visualizing attention in transformer-based language representation models. *CoRR*, abs/1904.02679.

Elena Voita and Ivan Titov. 2020. Information-theoretic probing with minimum description length. In *Proceedings of the 2020 Conference on Empirical Methods in Natural Language Processing (EMNLP)*, pages 183–196.

Ivan Vulić, Edoardo Maria Ponti, Robert Litschko, Goran Glavaš, and Anna Korhonen. 2020. Probing pretrained language models for lexical semantics. In *Proceedings of the 2020 Conference on Empirical Methods in Natural Language Processing (EMNLP)*, pages 7222–7240.

Eric Wallace, Jens Tuyls, Junlin Wang, Sanjay Subramanian, Matt Gardner, and Sameer Singh. 2019. AllenNLP Interpret: A framework for explaining predictions of NLP models. In *Empirical Methods in Natural Language Processing*.

J. Wexler, M. Pushkarna, T. Bolukbasi, M. Wattenberg, F. Viégas, and J. Wilson. 2020. The what-if tool: Interactive probing of machine learning models. *IEEE Transactions on Visualization and Computer Graphics*, 26(1):56–65.

Kelly Zhang and Samuel Bowman. 2018. Language modeling teaches you more than translation does: Lessons learned through auxiliary syntactic task analysis. In *Proceedings of the 2018 EMNLP Workshop BlackboxNLP: Analyzing and Interpreting Neural Networks for NLP*, pages 359–361, Brussels, Belgium. Association for Computational Linguistics.

CLTR: An End-to-End, Transformer-Based System for Cell Level Table Retrieval and Table Question Answering

Feifei Pan[1], **Mustafa Canim** [2], **Michael Glass** [2], **Alfio Gliozzo**[2], **Peter Fox**[1]
panf2@rpi.edu, mustafa@us.ibm.com,
mrglass@us.ibm.com, gliozzo@us.ibm.com
pfox@cs.rpi.edu
[1] Rensselaer Polytechnic Institute
[2] IBM TJ Watson Research Center

Abstract

We present the first end-to-end, transformer-based table question answering (QA) system that takes natural language questions and massive table corpus as inputs to retrieve the most relevant tables and locate the correct table cells to answer the question [1]. Our system, CLTR, extends the current state-of-the-art QA over tables model to build an end-to-end table QA architecture. This system has successfully tackled many real-world table QA problems with a simple, unified pipeline. Our proposed system can also generate a heatmap of candidate columns and rows over complex tables and allow users to quickly identify the correct cells to answer questions. In addition, we introduce two new open-domain benchmarks, E2E_WTQ and E2E_GNQ, consisting of 2,005 natural language questions over 76,242 tables. The benchmarks are designed to validate CLTR as well as accommodate future table retrieval and end-to-end table QA research and experiments. Our experiments demonstrate that our system is the current state-of-the-art model on the table retrieval task and produces promising results for end-to-end table QA.

1 Introduction

Tables are widely used in digital documents across many domains, ranging from open-domain knowledge bases to domain-specific scientific journals, enterprise reports, to store structured information in tabular format. Many algorithms have been developed to retrieve tables based on given queries (Cafarella et al., 2008, 2009; Sun et al., 2019; Bhagavatula et al., 2013; Shraga et al., 2020a; Chen et al., 2021). The majority of these solutions exploit traditional information retrieval (IR) techniques where tables are treated as documents without considering the tabular structure. However, these retrieval methods often result in an inferior quality due to a major limitation that most of these approaches highly rely on lexical matching between keyword queries and table contents. Recently, there is a growing demand to support natural language questions (NLQs) over tables and answer the NLQs directly, rather than simply retrieving top-k relevant tables for keyword-based queries. Shraga et al. (2020c) introduce the first NLQ-based table retrieval system, which leverages an advanced deep learning model. Although it is a practical approach to better understand the structure of NLQs and table content, it only focuses on table retrieval rather than answering NLQs. Lately, transformer-based pre-training approaches have been introduced in TaBert (Yin et al., 2020), TaPas (Herzig et al., 2020), and the Row-Column Intersection model (RCI) (Glass et al., 2020). These algorithms are very powerful at answering questions on given tables; however, one cannot apply them over all tables in a corpus due to the computationally expensive nature of transformers. An end-to-end table QA system that accomplishes both tasks is in need as it has the following advantages over separated systems: (1) It reduces error accumulations caused by inconsistent, separated models; (2) It is easier to fine-tune, optimize, and perform error analysis and reasoning on an end-to-end system; and (3) It better accommodates user needs with a single, unified pipeline. Hence, we propose a table retrieval and QA over tables system in this paper, called **C**ell **L**evel **T**able **R**etrieval (*CLTR*). It first retrieves a pool of tables from a large table corpus with a coarse-grained but inexpensive IR method. It then applies a transformer-based QA over tables model to re-rank the table pool and finally finds the table cells as answers. To the best of our knowledge, this is the first end-to-end framework where a transformer-based, fine-grained QA model is used along with efficient coarse-grained IR methods to

[1]System page: https://github.com/IBM/row-column-intersection

Proceedings of the Joint Conference of the 59th Annual Meeting of the Association for Computational Linguistics and the 11th International Joint Conference on Natural Language Processing: System Demonstrations, pages 202–209, August 1st - August 6th, 2021.

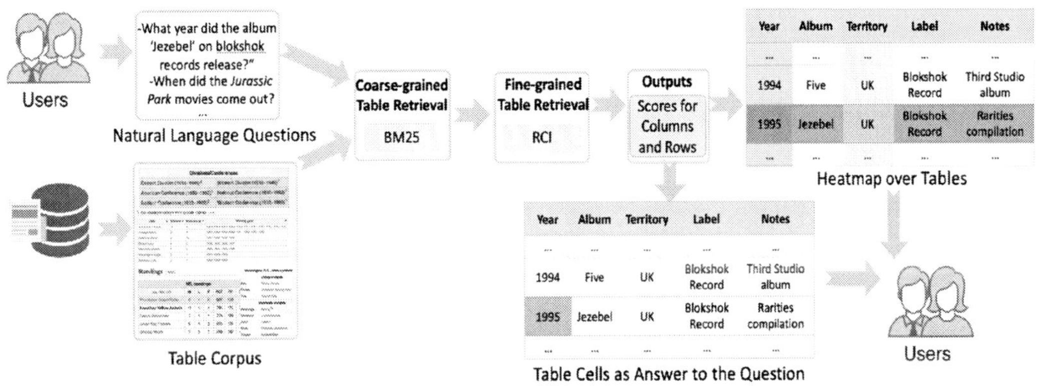

Figure 1: The overview of the end-to-end table QA architecture of CLTR.

retrieve tables and answer questions over them. Our experiments demonstrate that CLTR outperforms current state-of-the-art models on the table retrieval task while further helping customers find answers over returned tables.

To build such a Table QA system, an end-to-end benchmark is needed to evaluate alternative approaches. Current benchmarks, however, are not designed for such tasks, as they either focus on the retrieval task over multiple tables or QA task on a single table. To address the problems, we propose two new benchmarks: E2E_WTQ and E2E_GNQ. The details of these benchmarks and more discussions are provided in Section 4.1.

The specific contributions of this paper are summarized as follows:

- **A transformer-based end-to-end table QA system:** We build a novel end-to-end table QA pipeline by utilizing a transfer learning approach to retrieve tables from a massive table corpus and answer questions over them. The end system outperforms the state-of-the-art approaches on the table retrieval task.
- **Creating heatmaps over complex tables:** To highlight all relevant table columns, rows, and cells, CLTR generates heatmaps on tables. Following a pre-defined color code, the highlighted columns, rows, and cells are ranked according to their relevance to the questions. Using the heatmap, users can efficiently glance through complex tables and accurately locate the answers to the questions.
- **Two new benchmarks for the end-to-end table QA evaluation:** We propose and release two new benchmarks, E2E_WTQ and E2E_GNQ, extending two existing benchmarks, *WikiTableQuestions* and *GNQtables*, respectively. The benchmarks can be used to evaluate systems for table retrieval and end-to-end table QA.

2 Overview

The Architecture The architecture of our end-to-end table QA system, CLTR, is illustrated in Figure 1. This system aims to solve the end-to-end table QA task by generating a reasonable-sized subset of relevant tables from a massive table corpus, and employs the transformer-based approach to re-rank them based on their relevance to the user given NLQs, and finally answer the given NLQs with cells from these tables.

CLTR possess an abundant number of tables generated from documents of various knowledge sources to form a large table corpus. The system has two components: an inexpensive *tf-idf* (Salton and McGill, 1986) based coarse-grained table retrieval component and a fine-grained RCI-based table QA component. CLTR first takes as input any user given NLQs and processes the questions and the table corpus with the inexpensive BM25 algorithm to generate a set of relevant tables, which is relatively large and contains noise (i.e., irrelevant tables). Here we use BM25 to efficiently narrow down the table candidates from a massive table corpus and highly reduce the execution time and computational cost for CLTR. The output of this coarse-grained table retrieval component is later fed into the more expensive but accurate, transformer-based RCI to learn probability scores for table columns and rows, respectively. The scores produced by RCI indicate how likely the given question's final answer exists within a table column or row.

With the probability scores, CLTR re-ranks the tables and produces two outputs to the users: (1) a heatmap over top-ranked tables that highlights the most relevant columns and rows with a color code; (2) the table cells that contain the answers to the NLQs.

The applications Figure 2 presents the user interface of an application of the CLTR system. In this example, we apply the system to table QA over an aviation-related dataset, a domain-specific dataset on tables in aviation companies' annual reports. This user interface consists of two major sections, with *Tag A* and *Tag B* point to the user input and the system output sections, respectively. Under *Tag A* and *B*, the CLTR pipeline is employed to support multiple functionalities. Users can input any NLQs, such as "When is the purchase agreement signed between Airbus and Virgin America?" in this example, into the text box at *Tag D* and click the *Search* button at *Tag C* to query the preloaded table corpus. Users may select to reset the system for new queries or re-train a new model with a new corpus. In the system output sections, a list of tables similar to the table at *Tag F* is generated and presented to users. For each table, the system output includes: (a) the surrounding text of the table from the original PDF (*Tag E*); (b) the pre-processed table in a clean, human-readable format with a heatmap on it, indicating the most relevant rows, columns, and cells (*Tag F*); (c) an annotation option, where the users can contribute to refining the system with feedback (*Tag G*). In addition, the CLTR architecture has been widely applied to datasets from many other domains, varying from finance to medical. The system is also validated with open-domain benchmarks, with more details discussed in Section 4.

3 The RCI-based Table QA

Traditional approaches solve the table QA problem with two consecutive steps: retrieval of the most relevant tables for a given NLQ and locating the correct answers out of the cells with the help of a QA over tables model. These steps are usually studied separately. Our proposed system, CLTR, unifies the two-step table QA with a single pipeline by leveraging the novel RCI model. RCI is the state-of-the-art approach for locating answers over tables (Glass et al., 2020); however, it is not designed to retrieve tables out of large table corpus. In this section, we describe how we build an end-to-end table QA system combining the strength of inexpensive IR methods and the RCI model.

3.1 The Row-Column Intersection Model

We first briefly introduce the Row-Column Intersection model (RCI), which supports the fine-grained table retrieval component of our system. The RCI model decomposes table QA into its two components: projection, corresponding to identifying columns, and selection, identifying rows. Every row and column identification is a binary sequence-pair classification. The first sequence is the question and the second sequence is the row or column textual sequence representation. We use the interaction model of RCI that concatenates the two sequences, with standard separator tokens, as the input to a transformer.

The RCI interaction model uses the sequence representation which is later appended to the question with standard $[CLS]$ and $[SEP]$ tokens to delimit the two sequences. This sequence pair is fed into a transformer encoder, ALBERT (Lan et al., 2020). The final hidden state for the $[CLS]$ token is used in a linear layer followed by a softmax to classify if the column or row containing the answer or not. Each row and column is assigned with a probability of containing the answer. The RCI model outputs the top-ranked cell as the intersection of the most probable row and the most probable column.

Figure 3 gives a sample question fed into the transformer architecture along with the column and row representation of a table.

3.2 The End-to-End Table QA with RCI

To tackle the table retrieval problem, we exploit an inexpensive IR method together with the state-of-the-art RCI model. Unlike the traditional methods treating tables as free text, a set of features, or multi-modal objects, CLTR treats tables as a set of columns and rows and re-rank the tables based on cell-level RCI scores.

As we previously mentioned in Section 2, CLTR first processes the question and table corpus with the inexpensive BM25 algorithm to generate a pool of highly relevant tables. Later, the RCI model is used to produce probability scores for every column and row for tables in the pool. Therefore, for every table t with n columns and m rows in the table pool T, we have two set of scores, $P_{column} = \{p_{c_1}, p_{c_2}, p_{c_3}, ..., p_{c_n}\}$ for columns and $P_{row} = \{p_{r_1}, p_{r_2}, p_{r_2}, ..., p_{r_m}\}$ for rows. We calculate the overall probability score for each ta-

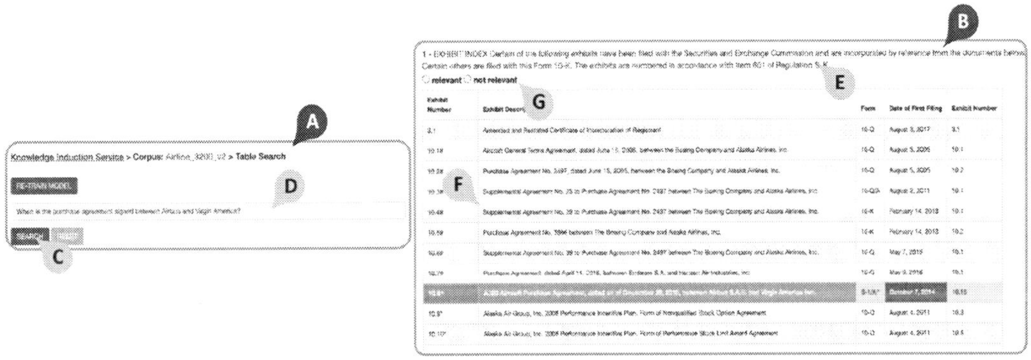

Figure 2: The application of CLTR on an aviation corpus

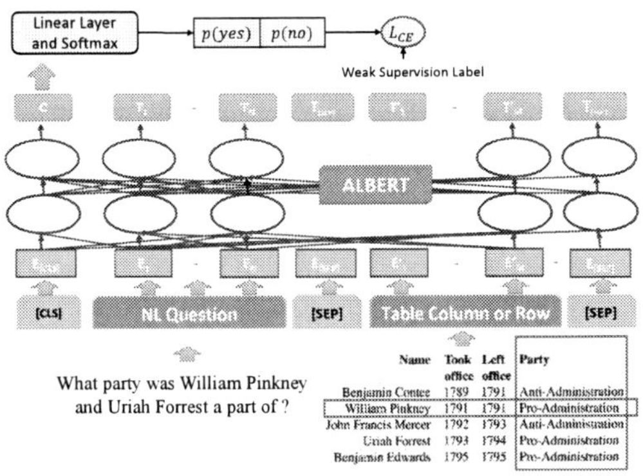

Figure 3: The RCI Table QA Model

ble by taking the maximum cell-level score, using $P_t = max(P_{col}) + max(P_{row})$. Our experiments prove the advantages of this method over the other algorithms (e.g., taking the averaged cell-level scores).

CLTR re-ranks the tables within the table pool T using the maximum cell-level scores. Once the re-ranking is done, the top-k tables out of T are returned to the users. The correct cells on the top-k tables are later identified by locating the intersection of the most relevant columns and rows discovered by the RCI model.

4 Experiments

4.1 Data

Proposed Benchmarks: Existing table retrieval and QA benchmarks focus on either answering NLQs on a single table or the retrieval of multiple tables for a keyword query. A comprehensive comparison of existing benchmarks with their limitations is listed in Table 1. WikiSQL (Zhong et al., 2017) and WikiTableQuestions (Pasupat and Liang, 2015) are widely used to evaluate table QA systems. More recently, they have been used by TAPAS (Herzig et al., 2020) and TABERT (Yin et al., 2020) where transformer-based models for QA over tables have been introduced. However, these benchmarks are not created to be used as part of an end-to-end table retrieval and QA pipeline. On the other hand, WikiTables was created based on the corpus introduced by Bhagavatula et al. (2015) and used in many recent table retrieval studies (Zhang and Balog, 2018a; Deng et al., 2019; Shraga et al., 2020b,c). Despite its popularity, the WikiTables benchmark has two major limitations. First, the query set is fairly limited, containing only 100 keyword-based queries. Many recent studies use this small set of queries for a learning-to-rank (LTR) task with 5-fold cross-validation, potentially causing overfitting issues for the proposed table retrieval models. Second, the query set includes only keyword-based queries, which do not represent the NLQs customers are expected to ask to get answers over tables. To solve the aforementioned issues and create an end-to-end table QA benchmark with NLQs, we introduce two new benchmarks, E2E_WTQ and E2E_GNQ, inspired by *WikiTableQuestions* and *GNQtables*.

The *WikiTableQuestions* (Pasupat and Liang, 2015) benchmark is originally designed for finding answer to questions from given tables. It consists of complex NLQs and tables extracted from Wikipedia. We filter the benchmark following Glass et al. (2020) to generate a subset of 1,216 questions with 2,108 tables.

The *GNQtables* dataset, introduced in Shraga et al. (2020c), extends the Google Natural Questions (NQ) benchmark (Kwiatkowski et al., 2019). It contains 789 NLQs and a large table corpus of 74,224 tables. For each question, the ground truth

	# of tables	# of queries	Retrieval task	QA task	Reference
WikiSQL	24,241	80,654	✗	✓	(Zhong et al., 2017)
TabMCQ	68	9,092	✗	✓	(Jauhar et al., 2016)
WikiTableQuestions	2,108	22,033	✗	✓	(Pasupat and Liang, 2015)
WikiTables	1.6M	100	✓	✗	(Bhagavatula et al., 2015)
GNQtables	74,224	789	✓	✗	(Shraga et al., 2020c)
E2E_WTQ	2,108	1,216	✓	✓	
E2E_GNQ	74,224	789	✓	✓	

Table 1: Comparison of table QA and retrieval benchmarks

only points to the most relevant table (with a binary grade 1 indicates *relevant*), while all other tables in the table corpus are considered *irrelevant* (grade 0). *GNQtables* is the only table retrieval benchmark using NLQs, which makes it possible to adapt it to end-to-end table QA. To create the E2E_GNQ, we manually annotate and enhance *GNQtables* with additional ground truth data for each question: (1) the table cells containing the correct answers; (2) the index of the target columns; (3) the index of the target rows.

Experimental Data: We experiment with E2E_WTQ to test the portability of CLTR, in which we fine-tune the RCI model with two other table QA benchmarks. We utilize an open-domain benchmark, WikiSQL (Zhong et al., 2017), and a domain-specific benchmark, TabMCQ (Jauhar et al., 2016). The WikiSQL dataset has 80,654 questions on 24,241 Wikipedia tables, while the TabMCQ is a much smaller dataset, with only 68 hand-crafted tables and 9,092 multiple-choice questions.

4.2 Experimental Setup

Overall Setup: We test our system under two experimental settings for table retrieval: (1) We test CLTR without task-specific training on E2E_WTQ and fine-tune the RCI model with WikiSQL and TabMCQ; (2) To fairly compare against the state-of-the-art, we follow the experimental setup in Shraga et al. (2020c) and fine-tune CLTR with E2E_GNQ. We implement 5-fold cross-validation on E2E_GNQ, where 80% of data is used for fine-tuning and 20% is used for validation. For both E2E_GNQ and E2E_WTQ, we use BM25 as our baseline model, which is widely used in industry-scale IR systems. We test the end-to-end table QA capability of CLTR with our newly proposed benchmarks. Since we are the first publicly accessible end-to-end table QA system, we do not have a baseline to fairly compare to for our end-to-end table QA experiments.

We implement the coarse-grained table retrieval with the BM25 algorithm embedded in the ElasticSearch python API for all of our experiments. This API can be accessed at *https://elasticsearch-py.readthedocs.io/en/master/*. Each table is indexed as a single text document with the embedded English analyzer. For each question, we generate a pool of 300 tables with the highest BM25 similarity scores. Following the current state-of-the-art model in Shraga et al. (2020c), we set $k1 = 1.2$ and $b = 0.7$. The tables in the pool are later processed with the RCI model.

Our experiments employ the RCI model with ALBERT XXL version (Lan et al., 2020). The RCI model is fine-tuned for different benchmarks with the following configurations: (1) training batch size = 128; (2) Number of epochs = 2; (3) Learning rate = 2.5e-5; and (4) maximum sequence length = 512.

The model and data for the experiments with CLTR are available at *https://github.com/IBM/row-column-intersection*.

Evaluation metrics: For table retrieval evaluation, we use the three metrics from previous work (Zhang and Balog, 2018b; Shraga et al., 2020c) for the top-k retrieved tables, namely precision (P) with $k \in \{5, 10\}$, normalized discounted gain (NDCG) with $k \in \{5, 10, 20\}$, and the mean average precision (MAP). For the end-to-end table QA tasks, we evaluate our proposed model following Glass et al. (2020) with two commonly used metrics in the IR community, accuracy at top 1 retrieved answer (Hit@1) and the mean reciprocal rank (MRR).

All experimental results are evaluated with the TREC standard evaluation tool (Voorhees and Harman, 2005). The source code of the TREC evaluation tool can be found at *https://trec.nist.gov/trec_eval/*.

4.3 Experimental Results

We experimentally compare CLTR against the BM25 baseline and the current state-of-the-art model on table retrieval in this section. Furthermore, we test CLTR with our proposed benchmarks on the end-to-end table QA task.

	P@5	P@10	N@5	N@10	N@20	MAP
BM25	0.5938	0.6587	0.5228	0.5356	0.5359	0.4704
CLTR	**0.7437**	**0.8735**	**0.6915**	**0.7119**	**0.7321**	**0.5971**

(a) E2E_WTQ

	P@5	P@10	N@5	N@10	N@20	MAP
BM25	0.0413	0.0242	0.1650	0.1764	0.1852	0.1601
MTR_{point}	0.1460	0.0767	0.6227	0.6349	0.6359	0.5920
MTR_{pair}	0.1826*	0.0990*	0.6945*	0.7198*	0.7220*	0.6328*
CLTR	**0.2203**	**0.1660**	**0.7235**	**0.7402**	**0.7458**	**0.7176**

(b) E2E_GNQ

Table 2: A comparison of CLTR and the baselines (* indicates the current state-of-the-art numbers).

Table Retrieval: We present the experimental results for table retrieval without task specific training on E2E_WTQ in Table 2a. Since the MTR model (Shraga et al., 2020c) is not available to us and this dataset has never been used in any published table retrieval work, we only compare our results to the coarse-grained BM25 baseline. The results indicate our proposed model outperforms the BM25 baseline with average improvements of 29.12%, 33.94% and 26.93% on precision, NDCG, and MAP, respectively. The results on E2E_WTQ also indicate that pre-trained CLTR can be adapted to new datasets without task-specific training.

The experimental results for E2E_GNQ are shown in Table 2b, comparing against BM25 and the current state-of-the-art, the two MTR models, MTR_{point} (with point-wise training) and MTR_{pair} (with pair-wise training) in Shraga et al. (2020c). The comparison shows that our proposed model outperforms the current best MTR_{pair} model on all metrics, with an average improvement of 28.73% on precision, 3.43% on NDCG, and 13.40% on MAP. The experimental results indicates CLTR is the new state-of-the-art system for table retrieval. Moreover, CLTR can further locate cell values to answer NLQs after table retrieval.

	MRR	Hit@1
E2E_WTQ	0.5503	0.4675
E2E_GNQ	0.4067	0.2699

Table 3: Model evaluation for end-to-end table QA

End-to-End Table QA: To further validate CLTR, we implement the end-to-end Table QA evaluation with E2E_WTQ and E2E_GNQ. The only existing end-to-end table QA model, Sun et al. (2016), and its dataset are not publicly available. Therefore, we do not have any baseline models to compare to. Our experimental results are reported in Table 3. As the first attempt for an end-to-end table QA system with transformer-based architecture on complex table benchmarks, we show that our approach is able to achieve promising and consistent performance. Our results indicate CLTR performs better for the first benchmark, E2E_WTQ, where the table corpus mainly contains well-structured tables. On the other hand, we expect the results for E2E_GNQ to be worse due to the amount of poorly formatted tables in the table corpus.

Qualitative Analysis: The experiments indicate CLTR outperforms all baselines, as well as the current state-of-the-art models on table retrieval. It also produces promising results for the end-to-end table QA task. We further demonstrate the high-portability of CLTR with pre-trained models using unseen benchmarks.

The system performance is much better for E2E_WTQ based on the experimental results. After a thorough investigation, we notice that the original *GNQtables* contains a large amount of noisy tables which do not have tabular structures. A considerable amount of tables in *GNQtables* are Wikipedia *InfoBoxes*, which may have multiple column/row headers and are difficult to process by machines accurately. Although table quality is crucial for table QA models, CLTR proves its advantageous by producing state-of-the-art results with noisy table corpus. Furthermore, the example shown in Figure 2 demonstrates the effectiveness of CLTR when applied to real-world data.

5 Related Work

Table Retrieval A majority of the table retrieval methods proposed in the literature treat tables as individual documents without taking the tabular structure into consideration (Pyreddy and Croft, 1997; Wang and Hu, 2002; Liu et al., 2007; Cafarella et al., 2008, 2009). More recent approaches utilize features generated from queries, tables, or query-table pairs. For example, Zhang and Balog (2018b) introduces an ad-hoc table retrieval method, retrieving tables with features such as #query_term, #columns, #null_values, etc. Similar work includes

Sun et al. (2019), Bhagavatula et al. (2013), and Shraga et al. (2020a). The current state-of-the-art model is introduced in Shraga et al. (2020c), where tables are treated as multi-modal objects and retrieved with a neural ranking model. We compare CLTR with this approach in Section 4.

Table QA Models Early table QA systems typically convert natural language questions into SQL format to answer questions over tables (Yu et al., 2018; Guo and Gao, 2020; Lin et al., 2019; Xu et al., 2018). In Jiménez-Ruiz et al. (2020), the authors promote the idea of matching tabular data to knowledge graphs and create the Semantic Web Challenge on Tabular Data to Knowledge Graph Matching (SemTab), which provide a new solution for table understanding and QA related tasks. Recently, TAPAS (Herzig et al., 2020) and TABERT (Yin et al., 2020) introduce the transformer-based approaches for this task. The RCI (Glass et al., 2020) model is the state-of-the-art model for QA over tables. It utilizes a transfer learning based framework to independently classify the most relevant columns and rows for a given question and further identify the most relevant cells as the intersections of top-ranked columns and rows.

End-to-End Table QA Models To the best of our knowledge, the table cell search framework published in Sun et al. (2016) is the only existing end-to-end Table QA system. This work leverages the semantic relations between table cells and uses relational chains to connect queries to table cells. However, the proposed model only works for well-formatted questions containing at least one highly relevant entity to link tables to the questions. In addition, the model and the data are not publicly available for comparison.

6 Conclusion

This paper proposes an end-to-end solution for table retrieval and finding answers for NLQs over tables. To the best of our knowledge, this is the first system built where a transformer-based QA model is used for locating answers over tables while improving the ranking of tables out of a table pool formed by inexpensive IR methods. To evaluate the efficacy of this system, we introduce two benchmarks, namely E2E_WTQ and E2E_GNQ.

The experimental results indicates that the proposed system, CLTR, outperforms the baselines and the current state-of-the-art model on the table retrieval task. Furthermore, CLTR produces promising results on the end-to-end table QA task. In real-world applications, CLTR can be applied to create a heatmap over tables to assist users in quickly identifying the correct cells on tables.

References

Chandra Bhagavatula, Thanapon Noraset, and Doug Downey. 2013. Methods for exploring and mining tables on wikipedia. *Proceedings of the ACM SIGKDD Workshop on Interactive Data Exploration and Analytics.*

Chandra Sekhar Bhagavatula, Thanapon Noraset, and Douglas C Downey. 2015. Tabel: Entity linking in web tables. In *The Semantic Web – ISWC 2015 - 14th International Semantic Web Conference, Proceedings*, Lecture Notes in Computer Science (including subseries Lecture Notes in Artificial Intelligence and Lecture Notes in Bioinformatics), pages 425–441. Springer Verlag.

Michael J Cafarella, Alon Halevy, and Nodira Khoussainova. 2009. Data integration for the relational web. *Proceedings of the VLDB Endowment*, 2(1):1090–1101.

Michael J Cafarella, Alon Halevy, Daisy Zhe Wang, Eugene Wu, and Yang Zhang. 2008. Webtables: exploring the power of tables on the web. *Proceedings of the VLDB Endowment*, 1(1):538–549.

Wenhu Chen, Ming-Wei Chang, Eva Schlinger, William Yang Wang, and William W. Cohen. 2021. Open question answering over tables and text. In *International Conference on Learning Representations.*

L. Deng, Shuo Zhang, and K. Balog. 2019. Table2vec: Neural word and entity embeddings for table population and retrieval. *Proceedings of the 42nd International ACM SIGIR Conference on Research and Development in Information Retrieval.*

Michael Glass, Mustafa Canim, Alfio Gliozzo, Saneem Chemmengath, Rishav Chakravarti, Avi Sil, Feifei Pan, Samarth Bharadwaj, and Nicolas Rodolfo Fauceglia. 2020. Capturing row and column semantics in transformer based question answering over tables. *Proceedings of the Annual Conference of the North American Chapter of the Association for Computational Linguistics (NAACL-HLT2020).*

Tong Guo and Huilin Gao. 2020. Content enhanced bert-based text-to-sql generation.

Jonathan Herzig, Pawel Krzysztof Nowak, Thomas Müller, Francesco Piccinno, and Julian Eisenschlos. 2020. TaPas: Weakly supervised table parsing via pre-training. In *Proceedings of the 58th Annual Meeting of the Association for Computational*

Linguistics, pages 4320–4333, Seattle, Washington, United States. Association for Computational Linguistics.

Sujay Kumar Jauhar, Peter Turney, and Eduard Hovy. 2016. Tabmcq: A dataset of general knowledge tables and multiple-choice questions.

Ernesto Jiménez-Ruiz, Oktie Hassanzadeh, Vasilis Efthymiou, Jiaoyan Chen, and Kavitha Srinivas. 2020. Semtab 2019: Resources to benchmark tabular data to knowledge graph matching systems. In *ESWC*, pages 514–530.

Tom Kwiatkowski, Jennimaria Palomaki, Olivia Redfield, Michael Collins, Ankur Parikh, Chris Alberti, Danielle Epstein, Illia Polosukhin, Matthew Kelcey, Jacob Devlin, Kenton Lee, Kristina N. Toutanova, Llion Jones, Ming-Wei Chang, Andrew Dai, Jakob Uszkoreit, Quoc Le, and Slav Petrov. 2019. Natural questions: a benchmark for question answering research. *Transactions of the Association of Computational Linguistics*.

Zhenzhong Lan, Mingda Chen, Sebastian Goodman, Kevin Gimpel, Piyush Sharma, and Radu Soricut. 2020. Albert: A lite bert for self-supervised learning of language representations. In *International Conference on Learning Representations*.

Kevin Lin, Ben Bogin, Mark Neumann, Jonathan Berant, and Matt Gardner. 2019. Grammar-based neural text-to-sql generation.

Ying Liu, Kun Bai, Prasenjit Mitra, and C Lee Giles. 2007. Tableseer: automatic table metadata extraction and searching in digital libraries. In *Proceedings of the 7th ACM/IEEE-CS joint conference on Digital libraries*, pages 91–100.

Panupong Pasupat and Percy Liang. 2015. Compositional semantic parsing on semi-structured tables.

Pallavi Pyreddy and W Bruce Croft. 1997. Tintin: A system for retrieval in text tables. In *Proceedings of the second ACM international conference on Digital libraries*, pages 193–200.

Gerard Salton and Michael J McGill. 1986. Introduction to modern information retrieval.

Roee Shraga, Haggai Roitman, Guy Feigenblat, and Mustafa Canim. 2020a. Ad hoc table retrieval using intrinsic and extrinsic similarities. In *Proceedings of The Web Conference 2020*, pages 2479–2485.

Roee Shraga, Haggai Roitman, Guy Feigenblat, and Mustafa Canim. 2020b. Ad hoc table retrieval using intrinsic and extrinsic similarities. In *WWW '20: The Web Conference 2020, Taipei, Taiwan, April 20-24, 2020*, pages 2479–2485. ACM / IW3C2.

Roee Shraga, Haggai Roitman, Guy Feigenblat, and Mustafa Cannim. 2020c. Web table retrieval using multimodal deep learning. In *Proceedings of the 43rd International ACM SIGIR Conference on Research and Development in Information Retrieval*, SIGIR '20, page 1399–1408, New York, NY, USA. Association for Computing Machinery.

Huan Sun, Hao Ma, Xiaodong He, Wen-tau Yih, Yu Su, and Xifeng Yan. 2016. Table cell search for question answering. In *Proceedings of the 25th International Conference on World Wide Web*, pages 771–782.

Yibo Sun, Zhao Yan, Duyu Tang, Nan Duan, and Bing Qin. 2019. Content-based table retrieval for web queries. *Neurocomputing*, 349:183–189.

Ellen M. Voorhees and Donna K. Harman. 2005. *TREC: Experiment and Evaluation in Information Retrieval (Digital Libraries and Electronic Publishing)*. The MIT Press.

Yalin Wang and Jianying Hu. 2002. A machine learning based approach for table detection on the web. In *Proceedings of the 11th International Conference on World Wide Web*, WWW '02, page 242–250, New York, NY, USA. Association for Computing Machinery.

Xiaojun Xu, Chang Liu, and Dawn Song. 2018. SQLNet: Generating structured queries from natural language without reinforcement learning.

Pengcheng Yin, Graham Neubig, Wen-tau Yih, and Sebastian Riedel. 2020. TaBERT: Pretraining for joint understanding of textual and tabular data. In *Proceedings of the 58th Annual Meeting of the Association for Computational Linguistics*, pages 8413–8426, Online. Association for Computational Linguistics.

Tao Yu, Rui Zhang, Kai Yang, Michihiro Yasunaga, Dongxu Wang, Zifan Li, James Ma, Irene Li, Qingning Yao, Shanelle Roman, Zilin Zhang, and Dragomir Radev. 2018. Spider: A large-scale human-labeled dataset for complex and cross-domain semantic parsing and text-to-SQL task. In *Proceedings of the 2018 Conference on Empirical Methods in Natural Language Processing*, pages 3911–3921, Brussels, Belgium. Association for Computational Linguistics.

Shuo Zhang and K. Balog. 2018a. Ad hoc table retrieval using semantic similarity. *Proceedings of the 2018 World Wide Web Conference*.

Shuo Zhang and Krisztian Balog. 2018b. Ad hoc table retrieval using semantic similarity. In *Proceedings of the 2018 World Wide Web Conference*, pages 1553–1562.

Victor Zhong, Caiming Xiong, and Richard Socher. 2017. Seq2sql: Generating structured queries from natural language using reinforcement learning. *CoRR*, abs/1709.00103.

Neural Extractive Search

Shauli Ravfogel[1,2] **Hillel Taub-Tabib**[2] **Yoav Goldberg**[1,2]
[1]Computer Science Department, Bar Ilan University
[2]Allen Institute for Artificial Intelligence
{shauli.ravfogel, yoav.goldberg}@gmail.com
hillelt@allenai.org

Abstract

Domain experts often need to extract structured information from large corpora. We advocate for a search paradigm called "extractive search", in which a search query is enriched with capture-slots, to allow for such rapid extraction. Such an extractive search system can be built around syntactic structures, resulting in high-precision, low-recall results. We show how the recall can be improved using neural retrieval and alignment. The goals of this paper are to concisely introduce the extractive-search paradigm; and to demonstrate a prototype neural retrieval system for extractive search and its benefits and potential. Our prototype is available at `https://spike.neural-sim.apps.allenai.org/` and a video demonstration is available at `https://vimeo.com/559586687`.

1 Introduction

In this paper we demonstrate how to extend a search paradigm we call "extractive search" with neural similarity techniques.

The increasing availability of large datasets calls for search tools which support different types of information needs. Search engines like Google Search or Microsoft Bing are optimized for surfacing documents addressing information needs that can be satisfied by reviewing a handful of top results. Academic search engines (Semantic Scholar, Google Scholar, Pubmed Search, etc) address also information needs targeting more than a handful of documents, yet still require the user to read through the returned documents.

However, some information needs require *extracting* and *aggregating* sub-sentence information (words, phrases, or entities) from multiple documents (e.g. a list of all the risk factors for a specific disease and their number of mentions, or a comprehensive table of startups and CEOs). These typically fall outside the scope of search engines and instead are classified as Information Extraction (IE), entailing a research project and a dedicated team per use-case, putting them well beyond the abilities of the typical information seeker.

In contrast, we advocate for a complementary search paradigm: *extractive search*, which combines document selection with information extraction. The query is extended with *capture slots*: these are search terms that act as variables, whose values should be *extracted* ("captured").[1] The user is then presented with the matched documents, each annotated with the corresponding captured spans, as well as aggregate information over the captured spans (e.g., a count-ranked list of the values that were captured in the different slots). The extractive search paradigm is currently implemented in our SPIKE system.[2] Aspects of its earlier versions are presented in Shlain et al. (2020); Taub-Tabib et al. (2020). One way of specifying which slots to capture is by their roles with respect to some predicate, semantic-frame, or a sentence. In particular, the SPIKE system features syntax-based *symbolic extractive search*—described further in section 2—where the capture slots correspond to specific positions in a syntactic-configuration (i.e., "capture the subject of the predicate *founded* in the first capture slot, and the object of the predicate in the second capture slot"). These are specified using a "by-example" syntax (Shlain et al., 2020), in which the user marks the predicate and capture slots on a provided example sentence, and the syntactic configuration is inferred.

While such parse-based matching can be very effective, it also suffers from the known limitations of symbolic systems: it excels in precision and control, but often lacks in recall. In this work,

[1]Capture-slots can be thought of as being analogous to captures in regular-expressions.

[2]`https://allenai.github.io/spike/`

Proceedings of the Joint Conference of the 59th Annual Meeting of the Association for Computational Linguistics and the 11th International Joint Conference on Natural Language Processing: System Demonstrations, pages 210–217, August 1st - August 6th, 2021.

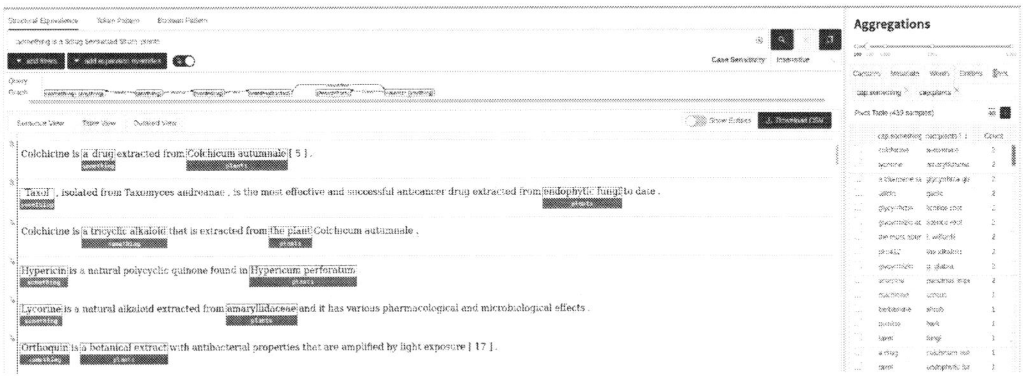

Figure 1: Results of neural extractive search. The neural results are based on the syntactic query: $\underline{Something}_{ARG_1}$ *is a* ***drug extracted from*** $\underline{plants}_{ARG_2}$ (underlines denote named capture slots, and bold text denotes an exact lexical match). The results show linguistic and lexical diversity w.r.t to the initial query, and highlight also spans corresponding to ARG_1 and ARG_2 (in light blue and yellow). The right box contains an aggregate view of the captured spans over many results.

we demonstrate how the symbolic system can be combined with the flexibility of *neural* semantic similarity as induced by large pre-trained language models. Figure 1 presents an overview of the system, containing a query with capture slots, the derived syntactic query, the returned (neural) results with marked spans, and an aggregate summary of the extracted pairs.

By allowing fuzzy matches based on neural similarity search, we substantially improve recall, at the expense of some of the precision and control.

The incorporation of neural similarity search requires two stages: retrieval of relevant sentences, and locating the roles corresponding to the capture-spans on each sentence. We use standard dense passage retrieval methods for the first part (section 3), and present a neural alignment model for the second part (section 4). The alignment model is generic: it is designed to be pre-trained once, and then applied to every query in real time. This allows to provide an *interactive* search system which returns an initial response in near real-time, and continues to stream additional responses.

The purpose of this paper then is twofold: first, it serves as a concise introduction of the extractive-search paradigm. Second, and more importantly, it demonstrates an incorporation of neural similarity techniques into this paradigm.

2 Symbolic Extractive Search

We introduce the extractive search paradigm through usage examples.

Boolean Extractive Search. Consider a researcher who would like to compile a list of treatments to Bacteremia (bloodstream infection). Searching Google for "Bacteremia treatment" might lead to a Healthline article discussing a handful of treatments.[3], which is not a great outcome. A similar query in PubMed Search leads to over 30,000 matching papers, not all are relevant and each including only nuggets of relevant information. Compare this with the extractive boolean query:

Bacteremia treatment :entity=CHEMICAL

in SPIKE-PubMed (Taub-Tabib et al., 2020), a search system over PubMed abstracts. "entity=CHEMICAL" indicates that we are interested in spans that correspond to chemicals, and the preceding colon (":") designate this term as a *capture*. The query retrieves 1822 sentences which include the word *Bactermia*, the word *treatment* (added to establish a therapeutic context) and a CHEMICAL entity. The user interface also displays the ranked list of 406 different chemicals captured by the query variable. The researcher can click each one to inspect evidence for its association with Bacteremia, quickly arriving at a clean list of the common therapeutic compounds.

Syntactic Extractive Search ("by example"). In the previous example, the capture slot was based on pre-annotated span level information ("named entities"). While very effective, it requires the entity type of interest to be pre-annotated, which

[3]https://www.healthline.com/health/bacteremia

will likely not be the case for most entity types. Additionally, the search is rather loose: it identifies any *chemical* in the same sentence of the terms "Bactermia" and "treatment", but without establishing a semantic connection between them. What can we do when the entity type is not pre-annotated, or when we want to be more specific in our extraction target? One option is to define the capture slots using their syntactic sentential context. For example, consider a researcher interested in risk factors of stroke. An example of this relation is given in the syntactic configuration:

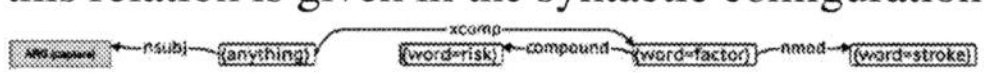

We can search for sentences that match this pattern,[4] and extract the information which aligns with the capture node.[5] However, such syntactic patterns require expertise to specify and are challenging to master. To counter this, Shlain et al. (2020) introduced to SPIKE the notion of query by example: the user enters a sentence which demonstrates the configuration: "*something is a risk factor of stroke*", marks which words are essential and should match exactly (*risk, factor, stroke*), and which correspond to capture slots (*something*), resulting in the query:[6]

$\underline{something}_{ARG}$ *is a* ***risk factor*** *for* ***stroke***

The system then derives the corresponding syntactic query (see (Shlain et al., 2020) for the details), returning results like: "*These cases illustrate that* *<u>PXE</u>* *is a rare but significant* ***risk factor*** *for small vessel disease and* ***stroke*** *in patients of all age groups.*", with the top aggregate terms being *Hypertension, Artial fibrillation, AF, Diabetes, Obesity* while less frequent terms include *VZV reactivation* and *palmitic acid*. By modifying the query such that stroke is also marked as a capture slot:

$\underline{something}_{ARG_1}$ *is a* ***risk factor*** *for* $\underline{stroke}_{ARG_2}$

one could easily obtain a table of risk factors for various conditions.

[4]Potentially with additional restrictions such as the occurrence of other words, phrases or patterns in the document

[5]This mode of operation is facilitated also by, e.g., the open-source toolkit Odinson (Valenzuela-Escárcega et al., 2020), and similar workflows are discussed by Akbik et al. (2013); Hoffmann et al. (2015).

[6]In this paper, we avoid the exact SPIKE syntax, and use underlines to indicate named capture slots, and bolded words to indicate exact matches. The corresponding SPIKE query would be "⟨⟩ARG:something is a $risk $factor for $stroke".

3 Neural Extractive Search

The syntactic search by example lowers the barriers for IE: it easy to specify, accurate and effective. However, it is also limited in its recall: it considers only a specific configuration (both in terms of syntax and lexical items), and will not allow for alternations unless these are explicitly expressed by the user. Neural models, and in particular large pre-trained language models (Devlin et al., 2019; Beltagy et al., 2019), excel at this kind of fuzzier, less-rigid similarity matching. We show how to incorporate them in the extractive search paradigm. This requires two stages: first, we need to match relevant sentences for a given query. Second, we need to identify the relevant capture spans in the returned sentences. Crucially, this needs to be done in a reasonable time: we do not have the luxury of re-training a model for each query, nor can we afford to run a large neural model on the entire corpus for every query. We *can* afford to run a pre-trained model on the query sentence(s), as well as over each of the sentences in the result set (similar to neural-reranking retrieval models (Guo et al., 2020)). We operate under these constraints.

The final system enables the user to search for specified information with minimal technical expertise. We demonstrate this approach on the CORD corpus (Wang et al., 2020), a collection of research papers concerning the COVID-19 pandemic.

3.1 'By-example" neural queries

The core of the system is a "by-example" query, where the user enters a simple sentence expressing the relation of interest, and marks the desired capture roles on the sentence. To facilitate effective neural search based on the short example, we perform symbolic (syntactic) search that retrieves many real-world sentences following the syntactic pattern. The result is a list of sentences that all satisfy the same relation, which are then combined and used as query to the neural retrieval system. At neural alignment model is then used to align the role marking on the syntactically-retrieved sentences, to corresponding roles on the neurally-retrieved sentences.

3.2 Pipeline

Our system pipeline is summarized in Figure 2. It includes the following steps.

Index Construction. Given a corpus $D = \{s_1, s_2, \ldots, s_n\}$ of n sentences, we calculate a vec-

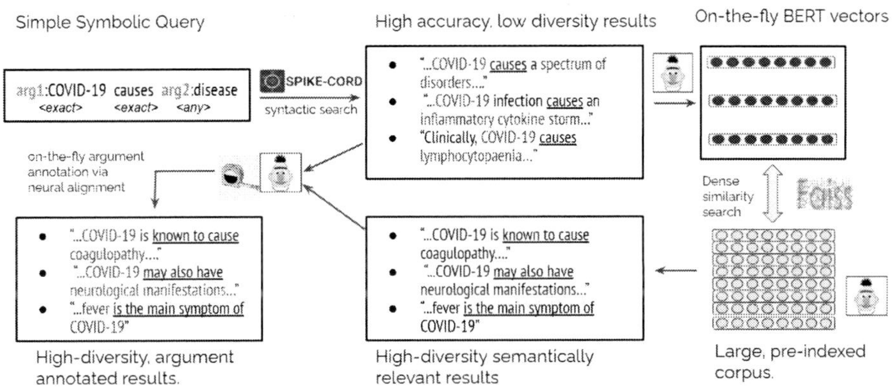

Figure 2: The proposed pipeline, presented from top left clockwise. Top: A simple symbolic query with two argument marks is provided. The query is executed, yielding accurate results that suffer from low recall. Those are encoded by BERT and used for k-NN query over a large set of pre-indexed vectors. Bottom: The k-NN neural similarity search results in a diverse set of relevant sentences. An alignment model then predicts and annotates argument spans over the retrieved sentences, based on the symbolic query results.

tor representation $M(s_i)$ for each sentence using a neural model M, and index them to allow efficient search.[7]

Symbolic Query Encoding. We use the syntactic-query capabilities of the SPIKE system to retrieve examples of natural sentences that convey the meaning the user aims to capture: we collect the first 75 results of a simple "by-example" syntactic query as described in §2—which often contain lexically-diverse, but semantically coherent, sentences—and average their BERT representations in order to get a single dense query vector $\vec{h^q}$. The averaging helps focus the model on the desired semantic relation.

Neural retrieval and ranking. We perform dense retrieval for the query h^q, with a k-NN search over the pre-indexed sentence representations. These results are substantially more diverse than the initial set returned by the syntactic query.

Argument Identification. We encode each retrieved sentence using (Sci)BERT, and use the alignment model described in Section 4 to align spans over the retrieved sentences to the captured spans in the symbolic result set. The alignment process operates over contextualized span representations, hopefully capturing both entity type and semantic frame information.

The system returns a syntactically and lexically diverse set of results, with marked capture spans.

4 Argument-identification via Alignment

The dense neural retrieval over the averaged query vector results in topically-related sentences. To obtain the full benefit of extractive search, we need to provide span annotations over the sentences. This is achieved via a span alignment model which is trained to align semantically corresponding spans across sentences. At query time, we apply this model to align the marked spans over the first syntactic-query result, to spans over the neurally-retrieved sentences.

The alignment model is pre-trained over a diverse set of relation, with the intent of making it a general-purpose alignment model. We describe the model architecture, training data, and training procedure.

The argument-alignment task. The user marked in the query q a two spans, denoted as ARG_1 and ARG_2. Given a sentence (a dense retrieval result) with n tokens $s = w_1, ..., w_n$, we seek a consecutive sequence of tokens $w_{i:j}$ corresponding to ARG_1, and another consecutive sequence of tokens $w_{k:\ell}$ corresponding to ARG_2. For example, consider the query:

virus$_{ARG_1}$ ***infection causes*** *a* *condition*$_{ARG_2}$

[7] Concretely, we encode each sentence in the CORD-19 corpus using the pre-trained SciBERT model (Beltagy et al., 2019), a BERT-based model (Devlin et al., 2019) trained on scientific text. We do not finetune the pre-trained model. We represent each sentence by the *[CLS]* representation on layer-12 of the model, and perform PCA to retain 99% of the variance, resulting in 601-dimensional vectors. To allow efficient search over the approximately 14M resulting dense vectors, we index them with FAISS (Johnson et al., 2017).

In which the span ARG_1 corresponds to a kind of infection, and ARG_2 corresponds to the outcome of the infection.
The syntactic query may return a result such as:
The infection of <u>*SARS-CoV-2*</u>$_{ARG_1}$ *causes* <u>*fever*</u>$_{ARG_2}$.
While a neural result might be:

It has been noted that headaches are one side effect of Flu infection.

We would like to align *Flu* to ARG_1 (SARS-COV-2) and *headaches* to ARG_2 (fever).

Training and evaluation data creation. To train an alignment model in a supervised setting, we need a training set that consists of pairs of sentences, both corresponding to the same relation, with arguments marked only on the first sentence. We use SPIKE for the generation of this dataset. We introduce a resource that contains 440 manually-curated SPIKE queries in the biomedical domain, divided into 67 unique relations, s.t. each relation is expressed via at least 2 syntactically-distinct queries. For instance, for the relation *molecules and their chemical derivatives*, we include the following patterns, among others:

- <u>Something</u>$_{ARG_1}$, a <u>Purine</u>$_{ARG_2}$ **derivative**.
- <u>Something</u>$_{ARG_1}$, a **derivative** of <u>Purine</u>$_{ARG_2}$.
- <u>Purine</u>$_{ARG_1}$ **derivative such as** <u>something</u>$_{ARG_2}$.

We ran each SPIKE query, collect the results, and then construct a dataset that consists of randomly-sampled pair of results (s_1^R, s_2^R) for each relation R of the 62 relations. This process resulted in a training set of 95,000 pairs of sentences, and a development set of 15,000 pairs of sentences, where each sentence has marked argument spans.[8]

Model architecture and training. We adopt a contrastive finetuning approach for the argument alignment task (Figure 3). In training, the model is fed with two sentences s_1 and s_2, belonging to the same relation. On one of the sentences, we mark the argument spans using special ARG tokens. We derive contextualized representations of all consecutive spans of tokens, and contrastively train the matching spans to be more similar to each other than to any other span.

[8]We focused our efforts on maintaining high syntactic diversity alongside high topical relevance for each relation, and aimed for the patterns to cover a large set of biomedical relations. The relations in the development set are randomly chosen subset of all relations, and are *disjoint* from the relations included in the training set.

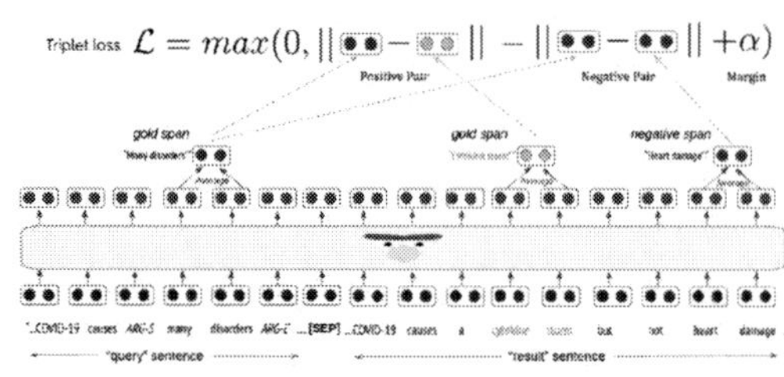

Figure 3: Illustration of the argument-alignment model. We choose corresponding arguments ("many disorders" and "cytokine storm") from the two sentences. We represent all possible spans of words, and choose the negative example to be the closest wrong span under euclidean distance (here, "heart damage"). The triplet objective encourages the corresponding argument to be closer to each other than to the wrong span.

We begin with the pretrained SciBERT model, with an additional linear layer that maps the representations to dimensionality of 64. On each training iteration we feed to the model the two sentences with arguments marked on one of them, and collect the last-hidden-layer-representations of all tokens.

Then, we construct the representations of the two arguments in the first sentence, $\vec{h}^{s_1}_{arg_1}$ and $\vec{h}^{s_1}_{arg_2}$, by averaging the BERT representations of the tokens included in those spans. We similarly construct representations of all possible consecutive spans of tokens up to length 9 in the second sentence. The "hardest" negative spans are identified: those are the two representations $\vec{h}^{s_2,-}_{arg_1}$ and $\vec{h}^{s_2,-}_{arg_2}$, which do not correspond to the captures in the first sentence, yet are most similar to them by euclidean distance. Those are pushed away using a triplet loss objective (Schultz and Joachims, 2003; Chechik et al., 2010):

$$\mathcal{L} = max(0, ||\vec{h}^{s_1}_{arg1} - \vec{h}^{s_2}_{arg1}|| - ||\vec{h}^{s_1}_{arg1} - \vec{h}^{s_2,-}_{arg1}|| + \alpha)$$

And similarly for arg_2. This objective encourages the gold span in s_1 to be closer to the gold span s_2 than to any other span, with a margin of at least α; we take $\alpha = 1$ and train for 50 epochs with the Adam optimizer (Kingma and Ba, 2015).

In inference time, we take s_1 to be an arbitrary (single) result of the syntactic query, and take s_2 to be any of the neural search results. For each s_2, we collect the spans having the least distance to the spans in s_1 (as provided by the SPIKE system).

5 Evaluation

Retrieval quality. To simulate a real-world extraction scenarios, we randomly chose 11 types

Relation	% Relevant
Disease-duration	25.000
Lacunas in knowledge	100.000
Conditions without risk	77.273
Isolation place	100.000
Percentage asymptomatic	9.091
Symptoms	85.000
Potential treatment	95.455
Immunutherapies and diseases	86.364
Persistence-place	82.609
Pretreatments	54.545
Involved organs	77.273

Table 1: Relevance scores (manual) by relation type.

of relation not included in the training set, with one randomly-selected syntactic pattern per relation. We augmented those patterns, and collected the 10 top-ranked augmented results, as well the 10 results ranked in places 90-100. We manually evaluated the relevancy of the 20 results per relation, resulting in 240 test sentences in total. In case they were relevant, we also marked the capture spans.

Results. Overall, 72.2% of the results were relevant to the relation, with 75.0% relevant in the top-10 group and 69.5% relevancy in the sentences ranked 90-100. In Table 1 with provide the results per relation. Relevancy is not uniform across relations: certain relations focusing on numerical information – such as *duration of a disease* and *percentage of asympotatmic cases in a disease* had very low accuracy: the results often focused on similar but different numerical information such as *"The median time to the onset of the infection was 95 days"* for *duration of a disease*, and *"Between 10 % and 20 % of the world population is infected each year by the influenza virus"* for *percentage of asympotatmic cases*. In contrast, for the others relations, many of the results are relevant, and are characterized by high syntactic diversity, generalizing beyond the syntactic structure of the original symbolic query.

Alignment quality. To evaluate the quality of the alignment, we generate a test set from the 240 manually-annotated sentences mentioned above, by randomly sampling 1,240 pairs of sentences that belong to the same relation, and are both relevant. We keep the gold argument marking on the first sentence, omit it from the second, and have the model predict the corresponding captures. As evaluation measure, we calculate the percentage of cases where the gold argument are a subset of the predicted arguments, or vice verca.

	SPIKE		Neural Extractive Search	
	#Caputres	%Accuracy	#Caputres	%Accuracy
spreads by	5	83%	40	96%
potential treatment	14	80%	55	67.6%
risk factor	57	89%	44	83%

Table 2: Comparing result count and accuracy between symbolic and neural extractive search

Results. In total, 73.8% of the arguments are aligned correctly. When considering only cases where both arguments were correctly aligned as a success, accuracy drops to 58%. Note, however, that the captures are often multi-word expressions, and the choice of span boundaries is somewhat arbitrary, and does not take into account conjunctions or cases where possible distinct spans can be regarded as corresponding to a capture in the first sentence, and multiple valid captures that often exist within a single sentence.

Comparison with symbolic extractive search. How do the results of the neural extractive search differ from the results of directly applying a symbolic rule based solution? To compare the systems we choose another 3 development relations, "is a risk factor for COVID-19", "COVID-19 spreading mechanisms" and "potential treatment for COVID-19". For each of these relations we try out 2-3 syntactic SPIKE queries and choose the best one as a representative query. We then use the query as input for both SPIKE and for neural search .

As shown in Table 2, for two of the three relations, *spread* by and *potential treatment*, neural search has been effective in significantly improving recall while maintaining relatively high precision. For the third relation, *risk-factor*, neural search did not show benefit but did not lag far behind. We hypothesize that this is due to this relation appearing many times in the data and in less diverse ways compared to the other relations, allowing a symbolic pattern to accurately extract it. Importantly, these data suggest that the neural search system is less sensitive to the exact relation and query used and that in some cases it also significantly improves performance.

6 Example Search

We demonstrate the system via an example where one aims to find sentences containing information on compounds and their origin (e.g. plant-derived, isolated from soil, etc.). We start with the query:

$\underline{Something}_{A_1}$ *is a* ***drug extracted*** *from* $\underline{plants}_{A_2}$.

The syntactic yields only few results, all of them are relevant. Among the results:

-Colchicine *is a drug extracted from* Colchicum autumnale.

-Berbamine *is an experimental drug extracted from* a shrub *native to Japan, Korea, and parts of China*

-Taxol*, isolated from* Taxomyces andreanae *, is the most effective and successful anticancer drug extracted from endophytic fungi to date .* Figure 1 shows the output (top results) of the neural system. The neural results are notably more diverse. While the syntactic results follow the pattern "X extracted from Y", the neural results are both lexically and syntactically diverse: the explicit descriptor "a drug" is absent at times; the verbal phrase "extracted from [a plant]" is sometimes replaced with the paraphrases "found in [a plant]" and "[is a] botanical extract"; and the third result contains an unreduced relative clause structure.

Several additional results are presented below:

- *Allicin is the major biologically active component of garlic.*
- *Berberine is an isoquinoline alkaloid that has been isolated from Berberis aquifolium.*
- *Phillyrin (Phil), the main pharmacological component of Forsythia suspensa, possesses a wide range of pharmacological activities .*
- *Dimethyl cardamonin (DMC) is the active compound isolated from the leaves of Syzygium samarangense.*
- *Triostin is a well-known natural product with antibiotic , antiviral, and antitumor activities .*

Note that the last two examples demonstrate *failure modes*: in the the fourth example, the model failed to identify *Dimethyl cardamonin* as an argument; and in the last sentence there is no clear capture corresponding to the second argument.

Finally, we perform an aggregation over the predicted captures (Fig 1, right-pane), allowing the user to quickly get a high-level overview of the interactions. From our experience, users are mostly interested in this table, and turn to the text as support for validating interesting findings.

7 Limitations of the neural approach

While we find the neural approach to be very effective, we would also like to discuss some of its limitations. First, speed and scalability are still lagging behind that of symbolic search systems: dense retrieval systems do not yet scale as well as symbolic ones, and running the (Sci)BERT-base argument-aligner for each candidate sentence is significantly slower than performing the corresponding similarity search. While the user can see the first results almost immediately, getting extractions from thousands of sentences may take several minutes. We hope to improve this speed in future work.

In terms of accuracy, we find the system to be hit-or-miss. For many symbolic queries we get fantastic resutls, while for others we observe failures of the dense retrieval model, or frequent failures of the alignment model, or both. For effective incorporation in a user-facing system, we should—beyond improvements in retrieval and alignment accuracy—be able to predict which queries are likely to yield poor results, and not extend them with fuzzy neural matches.

8 Conclusions

We presented a system for neural extractive search. While we found our system to be useful for scientific search, it also has clear limitations and areas for improvement, both in terms of accuracy (only 72.2% of the returned results are relevant, both the alignment and similarity models generalize well to some relations but not to others), and in terms of scale. We see this paper as a beginning rather than an end: we hope that this demonstration will inspire others to consider the usefulness of the neural extractive search paradigm, and develop it further.

Acknowledgements

This project received funding from the Europoean Research Council (ERC) under the Europoean Union's Horizon 2020 research and innovation programme, grant agreement No. 802774 (iEXTRACT).

References

Alan Akbik, Oresti Konomi, and Michail Melnikov. 2013. Propminer: A workflow for interactive information extraction and exploration using dependency trees. In *Proceedings of the 51st Annual Meeting of the Association for Computational Linguistics: System Demonstrations*, pages 157–162.

Iz Beltagy, Kyle Lo, and Arman Cohan. 2019. Scibert: A pretrained language model for scientific text. In *Proceedings of the 2019 Conference on Empirical Methods in Natural Language Processing and the 9th International Joint Conference on Natural Language Processing, EMNLP-IJCNLP 2019, Hong Kong, China, November 3-7, 2019*, pages 3613–3618. Association for Computational Linguistics.

Gal Chechik, Varun Sharma, Uri Shalit, and Samy Bengio. 2010. Large scale online learning of image similarity through ranking. *J. Mach. Learn. Res.*, 11:1109–1135.

Jacob Devlin, Ming-Wei Chang, Kenton Lee, and Kristina Toutanova. 2019. BERT: pre-training of deep bidirectional transformers for language understanding. In *Proceedings of the 2019 Conference of the North American Chapter of the Association for Computational Linguistics: Human Language Technologies, NAACL-HLT 2019, Minneapolis, MN, USA, June 2-7, 2019, Volume 1 (Long and Short Papers)*, pages 4171–4186. Association for Computational Linguistics.

Jiafeng Guo, Yixing Fan, Liang Pang, Liu Yang, Qingyao Ai, Hamed Zamani, Chen Wu, W Bruce Croft, and Xueqi Cheng. 2020. A deep look into neural ranking models for information retrieval. *Information Processing & Management*, 57(6):102067.

R. Hoffmann, Luke Zettlemoyer, and Daniel S. Weld. 2015. Extreme extraction: Only one hour per relation. *ArXiv*, abs/1506.06418.

Jeff Johnson, Matthijs Douze, and Hervé Jégou. 2017. Billion-scale similarity search with gpus. *CoRR*, abs/1702.08734.

Diederik P. Kingma and Jimmy Ba. 2015. Adam: A method for stochastic optimization. In *3rd International Conference on Learning Representations, ICLR 2015, San Diego, CA, USA, May 7-9, 2015, Conference Track Proceedings*.

Matthew Schultz and Thorsten Joachims. 2003. Learning a distance metric from relative comparisons. In *Advances in Neural Information Processing Systems 16 [Neural Information Processing Systems, NIPS 2003, December 8-13, 2003, Vancouver and Whistler, British Columbia, Canada]*, pages 41–48. MIT Press.

Micah Shlain, Hillel Taub-Tabib, Shoval Sadde, and Yoav Goldberg. 2020. Syntactic search by example. In *Proceedings of the 58th Annual Meeting of the Association for Computational Linguistics: System Demonstrations, ACL 2020, Online, July 5-10, 2020*, pages 17–23. Association for Computational Linguistics.

Hillel Taub-Tabib, Micah Shlain, Shoval Sadde, Dan Lahav, Matan Eyal, Yaara Cohen, and Yoav Goldberg. 2020. Interactive extractive search over biomedical corpora. In *Proceedings of the 19th SIGBioMed Workshop on Biomedical Language Processing, BioNLP 2020, Online, July 9, 2020*, pages 28–37. Association for Computational Linguistics.

Marco A Valenzuela-Escárcega, Gus Hahn-Powell, and Dane Bell. 2020. Odinson: A fast rule-based information extraction framework. In *Proceedings of the 12th Language Resources and Evaluation Conference*, pages 2183–2191.

Lucy Lu Wang, Kyle Lo, Yoganand Chandrasekhar, Russell Reas, Jiangjiang Yang, Darrin Eide, Kathryn Funk, Rodney Kinney, Ziyang Liu, William Merrill, Paul Mooney, Dewey Murdick, Devvret Rishi, Jerry Sheehan, Zhihong Shen, Brandon Stilson, Alex D. Wade, Kuansan Wang, Chris Wilhelm, Boya Xie, Douglas Raymond, Daniel S. Weld, Oren Etzioni, and Sebastian Kohlmeier. 2020. CORD-19: the covid-19 open research dataset. *CoRR*, abs/2004.10706.

FastSeq: Make Sequence Generation Faster

Yu Yan[1] *, Fei Hu[1] *, Jiusheng Chen[1] *†, Nikhil Bhendawade[1] *, Ting Ye[1], Yeyun Gong[2], Nan Duan[2], Desheng Cui[1], Bingyu Chi[1] and **Ruifei Zhang[1]**
[1]Microsoft, [2] Microsoft Research Asia
{yyua, fhu, jiuchen, nibhenda, tiy, yegong, nanduan, decu, bingychi, bzhang}@microsoft.com

Abstract

Transformer-based models have made tremendous impacts in natural language generation. However the inference speed is a bottleneck due to large model size and intensive computing involved in auto-regressive decoding process. We develop FastSeq framework to accelerate sequence generation without accuracy loss. The proposed optimization techniques include an attention cache optimization, an efficient algorithm for detecting repeated n-grams, and an asynchronous generation pipeline with parallel I/O. These optimizations are general enough to be applicable to Transformer-based models (e.g., T5, GPT2, and UniLM). Our benchmark results on a set of widely used and diverse models demonstrate 4-9x inference speed gain. Additionally, FastSeq is easy to use with a simple one-line code change. The source code is available at `https://github.com/microsoft/fastseq`.

1 Introduction

Transformer-based model architectures have made tremendous impact in multiple domains. However, due to large model size and intensive computing involved in the decoding process, the inference speed is still a bottleneck for long sequences applications (Wu et al., 2016; Tay et al., 2020). A variety of model architectural innovations have been proposed to increase the generation speed from different perspectives. One trend is to change the model architectures, like model distillation (Shleifer and Rush, 2020) and sparse attention (Beltagy et al., 2020). Although these techniques can alleviate the performance issue, there may be still some tradeoff between model accuracy and speed. On the other hand, efficient infrastructures have been developed to accelerate the inference speed, e.g., TensorRT (Vanholder, 2016) and FasterTransformers[1].

In this paper, we present FastSeq framework to make sequence generation faster. FastSeq can accelerate the sequence generation by 4x to 9x with a simple one-line code change for models in FairSeq (Ott et al., 2019) and Huggingface-Transformers (Wolf et al., 2020). The design principle of FastSeq is to improve the inference speed without losing model accuracy and usability.

Our optimization approaches include an attention cache optimization, an efficient algorithm for detecting repeated n-grams, and an asynchronous generation pipeline with parallel I/O. These optimizations are general enough for a wide range of Transformer-based model (Vaswani et al., 2017) architectures, including the encoder-decoder architecture (e.g., T5 Raffel et al. 2020, BART Lewis et al. 2020, ProphetNet Qi et al. 2020), the decoder-only architecture (e.g., GPT2 Radford et al. 2019), and the encoder-only architecture (e.g., UniLM Dong et al. 2019). FastSeq is also designed to be flexible for extension on supporting other models and frameworks. Our technologies are partially adopted by FairSeq[2]. A demo video can be found at `https://www.youtube.com/watch?v=jrdsEUxhSEE`.

2 Preliminary Analysis

For models with similar size, the sequence generation is much slower than classification, regression or language score computation. Why is the generation so time-consuming? Before analyzing the reasons, let's recap the generation algorithms first.

2.1 Generation Algorithms

Encoder-decoder structure is used in the most competitive models for sequence-to-sequence genera-

* Equal contribution
† Corresponding author

[1]FasterTransformer Github
[2]See pull requests FastSeq n-gram Blocking and Beam Search Perf Improvement

Proceedings of the Joint Conference of the 59th Annual Meeting of the Association for Computational Linguistics and the 11th International Joint Conference on Natural Language Processing: System Demonstrations, pages 218–226, August 1st - August 6th, 2021.

tion. The encoder side takes an input sequence of symbol representations $(x_1, ..., x_n)$ and outputs a sequence of continuous representations $\mathbf{z} = (z_1, ..., z_n)$. Then the decoder side generates an output sequence $(y_1, ..., y_t)$ with one element at a time. At each step, the model is auto-regressive by consuming the previously generated symbols and then computing the probability scores to select the next element. Greedy search and beam search are two popular algorithms used for the selection of next element. The difference between them is that at each step, greedy search only selects one candidate with maximum score, but beam search selects the top k candidates as beams. As beam search maintains multiple beams during the generation, it usually outputs a better result than greedy search.

To avoid repeated computation in the attention layer, the key (K) and value (V) from previous and current steps are usually cached to compute the next token. Equation (1) describes how the self-attention with the cache mechanism is implemented at step t.

$$\begin{aligned}
\underset{[B\times M,1,D]}{Q_t} &= \underset{[B\times M,1,D]}{y_{t-1}} \cdot \underset{[D\times D]}{W_q} \\
\underset{[B\times M,t,D]}{K_t} &= concat(\underset{[B\times M,t-1,D]}{Cache_K_{t-1}}, y_{t-1} \cdot \underset{[D\times D]}{W_k}) \\
\underset{[B\times M,t,D]}{V_t} &= concat(\underset{[B\times M,t-1,D]}{Cache_V_{t-1}}, y_{t-1} \cdot \underset{[D\times D]}{W_v}) \\
\underset{[B\times M,1,D]}{attn_t} &= softmax(\frac{Q_t K_t^T}{\sqrt{d_{k_t}}})V_t
\end{aligned} \tag{1}$$

where B is the batch size; M is the beam size; D is the embedding dimension; Q_t, K_t, V_t represent **query**, **key**, **value** respectively, and are in the shape of $\mathbb{R}^{B\times M} \times \mathbb{R}^T \times \mathbb{R}^D$; W_q, W_k, W_v are the weights for the query, key, and value in the shape of $\mathbb{R}^{D\times D}$; $attn_t$ is in the shape of $\mathbb{R}^{B\times M} \times \mathbb{R}^1 \times \mathbb{R}^D$.

To simplify the equations, we do not consider multi-heads here, but these equations can be adjusted to be of multi-head style.

2.2 Bottlenecks in Generation

Figure 1a shows the profiling results of running the official BART model implemented by FairSeq. It indicates that maintaining cache, blocking n-gram repeats, and post-process individually take longer time than decoding itself. Profiling is done by running the official BART implemented by FairSeq v0.0.9 on CNN DM dataset with default parameters (batch size 32, beam size 4, and no-repeat n-gram 3). Non-computation parts, like maintain cache, blocking n-gram repeats and post-process, cost more than 80% of the generation time. We analyze these time-consuming components below.

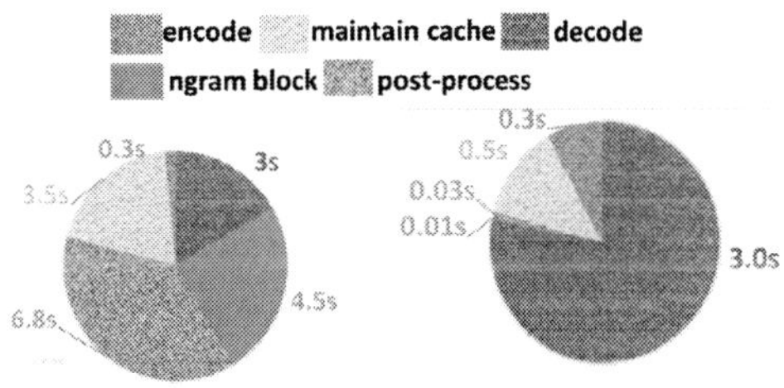

(a) Before optimizations (b) After optimizations

Figure 1: (a) Before optimizations: non-computation operations, e.g, maintain cache, n-gram blocking and post-process cost most of the time. (b) After optimizations: majority of time is spent on encode and decode.

Cache Maintenance Along with better generation results, beam search introduces significant additional computational and memory cost. As Equation (1) indicates, the size of X_t, Q_t, K_t, V_t, and $attn_t$ in beam search is M times larger than those in greedy search. It results in more memory consumption, larger matrix operations (e.g., $concat$), and more expensive cache maintenance (e.g., re-ordering the top-k beams and the cached key and value at each step). Moreover, the batch size is constrained by large occupied memory, which results in a low GPU utilization.

Block N-Gram Repeats Blocking N-Gram Repeats is a widely used operation to avoid an n-gram appears more than once in natural language model (Paulus et al., 2018; Klein et al., 2017). It prohibits the repetitive generation of n-grams by setting their probability scores to zero. However, conventional implementation often needs to scan text sequentially and move data between GPU and CPU frequently. Its time complexity is quadratic in terms of sequence length. When processing long sequences, this operation becomes another bottleneck.

Post-process It deals with detokenization and final result output. Post-process performance is largely restricted by two parts: frequent exchange of small data between GPU and CPU and the detokenization efficiency. In addition, for a synchronized pipeline, post-process will block the generation for the next batch of samples, while there is no required dependency between these two components.

3 Design

In order to address above bottlenecks, optimizations need to be done at multiple levels, including operations, models, and pipelines, which basically touch every component of a sequence generation framework. It is a non-trivial burden for researchers and practitioners. As a result, we develop this FastSeq library to address these barriers and speed up end-to-end inference in sequence generation. FastSeq is designed with following features: (i) speed up the inference of sequence models without any accuracy loss; (ii) easy to use and compatible Python APIs with FairSeq and HuggingFace-Transformers; (iii) flexible to be extended to support new models and frameworks.

FastSeq is written in PyTorch (Paszke et al., 2019) and composed of (1) **ops** module: provide efficient implementations of kernels (e.g., block n-gram repeats); (2) **optimizer** module: optimize model implementations in run-time, where more efficient implementations will be automatically patched to replace the ones in existing NLP toolkits (e.g., FairSeq and HuggingFace-Transformers) or the deep learning libraries (e.g., PyTorch); (3) **models** module: define the model architectures (e.g., ProphetNet, UniLM). It is noteworthy that the models in FairSeq and HuggingFace-Transformers are natively supported as well. Only one-line code change is needed to make them work with FastSeq; (4) **command line interfaces (CLIs)** module: run the inference via commands with an asynchronous pipeline, including preprocess (e.g., tokenization), generation process, and post-process (e.g., detokenization). These CLIs are compatible with FairSeq and HuggingFace-Transformers as well. Users can use the same parameters to run their end-to-end inferences.

FastSeq is designed to be easy to use. Existing model usages (e.g., model content and parameter settings) in FairSeq and Huggingface-Transformers do not need to be changed. The example code can be found in below:

- Python API

```
# simply add the import of FastSeq

import fastseq
import torch

bart = torch.hub.load(
    'pytorch/fairseq',
    'bart.large.cnn')
bart.cuda().eval().half()
slines = [
    "Welcome to FastSeq. "
    "Hope you enjoy it."]
hypotheses = bart.sample(
    slines,
    beam=4,
    lenpen=2.0,
    max_len_b=140,
    min_len=55,
    no_repeat_ngram_size=3)
print(hypotheses)
```

- Command Line Interface

```
fastseq-generate-for-fairseq \
      DATA \
      --path MODEL \
      --fp16 \
      --task translation \
      --batch-size BATCH_SIZE \
      --gen-subset valid \
      --bpe gpt2 \
      --beam 4 \
      ...
```

4 Optimizations

To address the bottlenecks discovered in Section 2.2, we develop following optimizations.

4.1 Attention Cache Optimization

This section introduces how the cache for the key and value in self-attention and encoder-decoder attention can be optimized to further speed up the inference. We describe the cache deduplication below, see more comprehensive analysis and a new attention method with faster speed in our work EL-Attention (Yan et al., 2021)

4.1.1 Cache Optimization in Self-Attention

For the decoder-only or encoder-only Transformer models (e.g., GPT2, UniLM), X is the prefix of the generated hypothesis. In conventional implementations, X is replicated along beam dimension, and the corresponding partial in the key (K) and value (V) is same for each beam. This means, assuming K_t and V_t to be of dimension $[B, M, N + T, D]$, $K_0(b, i, n, d) = \cdots = K_t(b, j, n, d)$ and $V_0(b, i, n, d) = \cdots = V_t(b, j, n, d)$, for $\forall b \in [0, B)$, $\forall i, j \in [0, M)$, $\forall n \in [0, N)$, $\forall d \in [0, D)$, where N is the length of X, B is the batch size, M is the beam size, D is the embedding dimension.

To optimize the cache in self-attention, we can split the cached key and value in Equation (1) in two parts: $Cache\_K'$ and $Cache\_V'$ for the prefix; $Cache\_K_t$ and $Cache\_V_t$ for the generated sequence up till the time step t. With this split, the size of $Cache\_K'$ and $Cache\_V'$ can be reduced from $B \times M \times N \times D$ to $B \times 1 \times N \times D$. This also helps decrease cache reorder complexity by a factor of M.

However, the above split operation results in incompatible shapes between $Cache\_K'$ and $Cache\_K_t$, and between $Cache\_V'$ and $Cache\_V_t$. Instead of reshaping these cached keys and values, $einsum$ is utilized to compute $attn_t$. This way, the expensive $concat$ operations on large tensors can be avoided.

With the above changes, the matrix operations will be conducted on the tensors with much smaller size, so the peak memory can be smaller, the operations can run faster, and then a larger batch size can be leveraged. For example, at the step t, the sizes of $Cache\_K_{t-1}$ and $Cache\_V_{t-1}$ decrease from $B \times M \times (N+t-1) \times D$ to $B \times M \times (t-1) \times D$ by $\frac{N+t-1}{t-1}$ times. Then $concat(Cache\_K_{t-1}, x_t \cdot W_k)$ and $concat(Cache\_V_{t-1}, x_t \cdot W_V)$ can be much quicker than before due to less GPU memory allocation, copy, and deallocation. The peak memory during $concat$ is largely reduced as well. Meanwhile, this implementation will save the same amount of data movement when reordering the beams in $Cache\_K_{t-1}$ and $Cache\_V_{t-1}$ because $Cache\_K'$ and $Cache\_V'$ do not need to be frequently reordered since they are de-duplicated along beam dimension.

4.1.2 Cache Optimization in Encoder-Decoder Attention

The cached key and value in the encoder-decoder attention also have duplication. The reason is that the key and value in the encoder-decoder attention are calculated based on the final output hidden state (S) from the encoder side. Accordingly, the elements of cached key and value at the beam dimension are the same. Therefore, the size of $Cache\_K$ and $Cache\_V$ can be reduced by M times, from $B \times M \times N \times D$ to $B \times 1 \times N \times D$. Then the optimization benefits mentioned in Section 4.1.1 can be achieved here as well, including peak memory reduction and larger batch size. Additionally, the cached key and value are not needed to be frequently reordered since the elements at the beam dimension are exactly the same.

Notably, the above proposed optimizations are general and can be applied to a variety of models with different architectures if they share following features: 1) attention-based architectures, including self-attention or encoder-decoder attention; 2) auto-regressive decoding based on beam search. These models could be classic Transformer-based encoder-decoder architectures (e.g., BART, ProphetNet, T5), Transformer-based decoder-only architectures (e.g, GPT2), or Transformer-based encoder-only architectures (e.g., UniLM).

The detailed implementations of the optimized self-attention and encoder-decoder attention is provided in the Appendix.

Algorithm 1 GPU version no-repeat-ngram algorithm with arguments - ngram length n, previously generated tokens $tokens$, current step token probability distribution $probs$.

```
function BLOCK(tokens, probs, n)
    nBlk = tokens.rows
    nThr = tokens.columns + 1 - n
    shMem = sizeof(tokens.row(0))
    BAN <<< nBlk, nThr, shMem >>>
    (tokens, probs, n)

function BAN(tokens, probs, n)
    row = blockIdx.x
    copy row-th row of tokens from global
    mem to shared mem shm
    col = threadIdx.x
    start = tokens.columns + 1 - n
    for i = 0 to n - 1 do
        if shm[col + i] ≠ shm[start + i] then
            return
    tokenToBan = shm[col + n - 1]
    probs[row, tokenToBan] = 0
```

4.2 GPU-based Block N-Gram Repeats Algorithm

As observed in Figure 1a, the cost of block n-gram repeats algorithm is as high as 25% of generation time. To reduce the cost, a new GPU-based kernel (see Algorithm 1) is developed to leverage the power of parallel compute and achieves the following benefits: 1) avoiding data movement between GPU and CPU to alleviate the throughput bottleneck of PCIe bus interface. 2) scanning n-grams in parallel. Instead of sequentially scanning tokens for detecting repeated n-grams, they can be scanned in parallel using threads equal to the number of n-grams generated till the time step t. Furthermore, each sample in a batch can be processed in parallel using multiple thread-blocks. 3) using GPU shared memory for faster memory access.

Since each token needs to be read multiple times

Model	Architecture	Task	Baseline	FastSeq	Speedup
encoder-decoder architecture					
BART (Lewis et al., 2020)	12L-12L-1024	CNN/DailyMail	2.4	18.4	7.7x
DistilBART (Wolf et al.)	12L-6L-1024	CNN/DailyMail	3.4	18.5	5.4x
ProphetNet (Qi et al., 2020)	12L-12L-1024	CNN/DailyMail	2.8	10.7	3.8x
T5 (Raffel et al., 2020)	12L-12L-768	WMT16 EN-RO	8.7	31.3	4.3x
Transformer (Ott et al., 2018)	6L-6L-1024	WMT16 EN-DE	96.0	417.0	4.3x
decoder-only architecture					
GPT2 (Radford et al., 2019)	0L-12L-768	CNN/DailyMail	3.0	16.7	5.5x
encoder-only architecture					
UniLM (Dong et al., 2019)	12L-0L-768	CNN/DailyMail	1.7	16.4	9.6x

Table 1: Benchmark results on models of different architectures. Speed is measured by samples/s.

(equal to token length of n-gram), they are stored in shared memory instead of global memory for faster access. Jia et al. (2018) reports shared memory bandwidth for Volta V100 is 16x of global memory bandwidth. Although there are multiple ways to organize CUDA thread blocks, our approach is to assign each n-gram to a thread and each thread-block to handle a sequence stream. In this way, Block N-gram repeats is parallelized along horizontal and vertical dimensions of a batch.

4.3 Asynchronous Pipeline with Parallel I/O

As shown in Figure 1a, post-process takes significant time (6.8s) in the generation process. It is under-optimized in many existing seq2seq frameworks. One reason is that post-process is not a part of the training process, many efforts are spent on optimizing the training pipeline and the model structure rather than the generation speed. Another reason is, despite of works focusing on generation speed, like distilling model, the speed metric only covers the computation time but does not include the post-process part. For example, FairSeq does not consider the post-process time when it measures the speed. These biases result in a big overlooked speed-up opportunity.

To improve the efficiency of the pipeline, we develop an asynchronous pipeline with parallel I/O. Similar to pre-fetch technology which loads next batch of data to GPU while running inference on the current batch, we post-process the current batch in a background thread while running generation on the next batch.

5 Evaluation

In the benchmarks, FairSeq and HuggingFace-Transformers are used as the baseline to evaluate the performance. The selected models cover different kinds of architectures, including the encoder-decoder models (e.g., BART, DistilBART, T5, ProphetNet), the decoder-only models (e.g., GPT2), and the encoder-only models (e.g., UniLM). CNN / Daily Mail dataset (Hermann et al., 2015) and WMT'16 (Bojar et al., 2016) are used as the benchmark datasets. The benchmark experiments are split into two groups 1) HuggingFace-Transformers with/without FastSeq; 2) FairSeq with/without FastSeq. If both FairSeq and HuggingFace-Transformers have implemented the model, we choose the faster result as the baseline.

Hardware The experiments are conducted on a node with 1 GPU (NVIDIA Tesla V100 PCIe 16GB) and 24 cores CPU (Intel(R) Xeon(R) CPU E5-2690 v4 @ 2.60GHz).

5.1 End-to-end Performance

The end-to-end benchmarks (including model loading, preprocess, model inference, and post-process) have been conducted to evaluate the performance. For each model, we use the same configuration except batch size. We search the largest batch size for each framework by doubling it per search run. Each experiment is executed 10 times and the average running time is computed as the final result. The speed number is measured in samples per second.

With the optimizations of FastSeq, the end-to-end performance yields a roughly 4x to 9x speedup, see Table 1 for more details[3]. In the baseline, for summarization dataset CNN/DailyMail, the speed of all models (e.g., BART, DistilBART, ProphetNet, GPT2, UniLM) is between 1.7 and 3.4 samples per second. Enabling FastSeq boosts the speed to

[3]The baseline for BART is FairSeq and the baseline for DistilBART is Huggingface Transformers.

Model	Batch size	Cache GB	Throughput samples/s
$BART_{large}$ no cache	32	0.0	1.8 (0.7x)
$BART_{large}$	32	6.3	2.4 (1.0x)
+Asynchronous pipeline	32	6.3	3.6 (1.5x)
+GPU n-gram block	32	6.3	5.6 (2.3x)
+Attention cache optimize	32	1.8	8.1 (3.3x)
+Larger batch	128	7.2	18.4 (7.7x)

Table 2: $BART_{large}$ is the official version from FairSeq. No cache: disable cache on FairSeq. Generation parameters: beam size = 4, no-repeat n-gram = 3. Data: CNN DM validation dataset. Cache size is estimated according to max input length 1024, output length 50.

more than 10 samples per second for all models studied here, and the BART model achieves 18.4 samples per second, which is 7.7 times speedup. On the two WMT16 translation datasets, FastSeq improves throughput by 4.3 times.

In following sections, we will present analyses on the three optimizations used in FastSeq.

5.2 Analysis of the Cache Optimization

To evaluate effect of the cache optimizations introduced in Section 4.1, Table 2 compares the results of not using cache, using conventional cache, and using the proposed optimized cache. Although the computing complexity is the same for both cache-based approaches, the proposed cache optimization approach reduces the usage of GPU memory by 3.5 times. Such smaller cache memory can speed up *concat* operations and reduce the data movement during the beam reordering, and also allow a larger batch size. These advantages together increase generation throughput from 5.6 to 18.4 samples/s.

5.3 Analysis of Block N-Gram Repeats

To demonstrate the effectiveness of GPU kernel described in Section 4.2, the new method is compared with two other methods in Table 3: 1) the one implemented by FairSeq (called baseline). 2) a revised CPU-based kernel, which improves baseline by moving data from GPU to CPU before computing to avoid multiple data transfers (called CPU kernel). The time difference (4477.1 ms vs 584.9 ms) between baseline and CPU kernel indicates that data transfer optimization alone can speedup about 8x. Furthermore, the proposed GPU kernel, which avoids data transfer and uses parallel computation has about 75x speed gain compared to CPU kernel. As shown in Figure 1b, the computing time after optimization becomes quite small, from about 25% to 1% of the overall time.

Method	Time (ms)
baseline	4477.1
CPU kernel	584.9
GPU kernel	7.8

Table 3: Compare three implementations of no-repeat n-gram.

Model	With fp16	Baseline R-1/R-2/R-L	FastSeq R-1/R-2/R-L
$UniLM_{large}$[4]	✗	43.08/20.43/40.34	43.09/20.29/40.32
$UniLM_{large}$	✓	43.06/20.42/40.32	43.08/20.29/40.32
$BART_{large}$	✗	44.21/21.20/41.03	44.21/21.20/41.03
$BART_{large}$	✓	44.22/21.20/41.04	44.22/21.21/41.03
$ProphetNet_{large}$	✗	44.20/21.17/41.30	44.20/21.17/41.30
$ProphetNet_{large}$	✓	44.17/21.17/41.28	44.17/21.17/41.28

Table 4: Metrics (ROUGE-1, ROUGE-2, and ROUGE-L) on CNN/DailyMail test set.

5.4 Analysis of Asynchronous Pipeline with Parallel I/O

Table 2 measures the performances of the synchronized pipeline with single process implemented by FairSeq and the proposed asynchronous pipeline with parallel I/O in FastSeq. The throughput is increased from 2.4 samples/s to 3.6 samples/s (around 1.5x). The speedup comes from the better resource scheduling, where the asynchronous pipeline allows post-process to run in the background when running the model inference, and the support of multi-thread detokenization. As shown in Figure 1b, the post-process unique time is reduced from about 38% to 1% of the overall time.

5.5 Analysis of Generation Quality

All optimizations in FastSeq do not affect the model generation quality. As discussed in Section 4, the logic for detecting the repeated n-gram blocks is the same for the CPU-based and GPU-based kernels, and the asynchronous pipeline with Parallel I/O only optimizes the I/O efficiency, so these two optimizations do not change the model outputs in any fashion. For the attention cache optimization, it does not affect model outputs in theory. However, in practice, if using mix precision (e.g., floating point 16) for inference, there may be a few trivial differences in the outputs due to the numerical stability issue in GPU. Similar differences can be observed when changing batch size during floating point 16 inference. But if using floating point 32, the generated results are exactly

[4] The differences between the ROUGE scores for UniLM are due to the differences in the data preprocess and the implementations of length-penalty.

the same. That means the minor differences are not caused by the proposed cache optimization itself. In FastSeq, the unit tests have been developed to make sure the inference outputs are the same with and without FastSeq when using floating point 32. We also compare the output quality based on the CNN/DailyMail dataset (Table 4). The quite similar ROUGE scores demonstrate that FastSeq does not impact the model quality.

6 Related Work

A variety of efforts have been developed to improve the efficiency of Transformer models. From the perspective of model architectures, there are efforts on reducing attention matrix size by chunking input sequences into blocks (Beltagy et al., 2020), or using strided convolution over the keys and queries to compress memory (Liu* et al., 2018). Another kind of approaches focus on reducing model size and memory consumption by weight quantization (Zafrir et al., 2019), weight sharing (Dehghani et al., 2019), and weight pruning (Michel et al., 2019). Knowledge distillation is another popular approach (Hinton et al., 2015).

On the other hand, a dozen of innovations on infrastructure side have been conducted to speed up serving of Transformer models. The fused chains of basic operators in the attention layers have been widely adopted in many frameworks (e.g., Onnx Runtime [5], Deep Speed[6]). It is also performance critical to optimize data layout and movement among the connected operations (Ivanov et al., 2020). In situation of varied input lengths, TurboTransformers (Fang et al., 2021) is developed to better serve online models by using dynamic batch scheduler, more efficient memory allocation and deallocation algorithms. FasterTransformers[7] deeply optimizes kernels of encoder, decoder and beam search to better utilize computer power of Tensor Core.

7 Conclusion

In this work, we present FastSeq, which provides general solutions for speeding up the sequence generation without accuracy loss. The proposed optimizations include an attention cache optimization, an GPU-based n-grams blocking algorithm, and an asynchronous generation pipeline. In the future, we will support more models and explore more techniques to accelerate the generation speed.

[5]`https://github.com/microsoft/onnxruntime`

[6]`https://www.deepspeed.ai`

[7]FasterTransformer Github

References

Iz Beltagy, Matthew E Peters, and Arman Cohan. 2020. Longformer: The long-document transformer. *arXiv preprint arXiv:2004.05150*.

Ondřej Bojar, Rajen Chatterjee, Christian Federmann, Yvette Graham, Barry Haddow, Matthias Huck, Antonio Jimeno Yepes, Philipp Koehn, Varvara Logacheva, Christof Monz, Matteo Negri, Aurélie Névéol, Mariana Neves, Martin Popel, Matt Post, Raphael Rubino, Carolina Scarton, Lucia Specia, Marco Turchi, Karin Verspoor, and Marcos Zampieri. 2016. Findings of the 2016 conference on machine translation. In *Proceedings of the First Conference on Machine Translation: Volume 2, Shared Task Papers*, pages 131–198, Berlin, Germany. Association for Computational Linguistics.

Mostafa Dehghani, Stephan Gouws, Oriol Vinyals, Jakob Uszkoreit, and Lukasz Kaiser. 2019. Universal transformers. In *International Conference on Learning Representations*.

Li Dong, Nan Yang, Wenhui Wang, Furu Wei, Xiaodong Liu, Yu Wang, Jianfeng Gao, Ming Zhou, and Hsiao-Wuen Hon. 2019. Unified language model pre-training for natural language understanding and generation. In *Advances in Neural Information Processing Systems*, volume 32. Curran Associates, Inc.

Jiarui Fang, Yang Yu, Chengduo Zhao, and Jie Zhou. 2021. Turbotransformers: an efficient gpu serving system for transformer models. In *Proceedings of the 26th ACM SIGPLAN Symposium on Principles and Practice of Parallel Programming*, pages 389–402.

Karl Moritz Hermann, Tomas Kocisky, Edward Grefenstette, Lasse Espeholt, Will Kay, Mustafa Suleyman, and Phil Blunsom. 2015. Teaching machines to read and comprehend. In *Advances in Neural Information Processing Systems*, volume 28. Curran Associates, Inc.

Geoffrey Hinton, Oriol Vinyals, and Jeff Dean. 2015. Distilling the knowledge in a neural network. *arXiv preprint arXiv:1503.02531*.

Andrei Ivanov, Nikoli Dryden, Tal Ben-Nun, Shigang Li, and Torsten Hoefler. 2020. Data movement is all you need: A case study on optimizing transformers. *arXiv e-prints*, pages arXiv–2007.

Zhe Jia, Marco Maggioni, Benjamin Staiger, and Daniele P Scarpazza. 2018. Dissecting the nvidia volta gpu architecture via microbenchmarking. *arXiv preprint arXiv:1804.06826*.

Guillaume Klein, Yoon Kim, Yuntian Deng, Jean Senellart, and Alexander Rush. 2017. OpenNMT: Open-source toolkit for neural machine translation. In *Proceedings of ACL 2017, System Demonstrations*, pages 67–72, Vancouver, Canada. Association for Computational Linguistics.

Mike Lewis, Yinhan Liu, Naman Goyal, Marjan Ghazvininejad, Abdelrahman Mohamed, Omer Levy, Veselin Stoyanov, and Luke Zettlemoyer. 2020. BART: Denoising sequence-to-sequence pre-training for natural language generation, translation, and comprehension. In *Proceedings of the 58th Annual Meeting of the Association for Computational Linguistics*, pages 7871–7880, Online. Association for Computational Linguistics.

Peter J. Liu*, Mohammad Saleh*, Etienne Pot, Ben Goodrich, Ryan Sepassi, Lukasz Kaiser, and Noam Shazeer. 2018. Generating wikipedia by summarizing long sequences. In *International Conference on Learning Representations*.

Paul Michel, Omer Levy, and Graham Neubig. 2019. Are sixteen heads really better than one? In *Advances in Neural Information Processing Systems*, volume 32. Curran Associates, Inc.

Myle Ott, Sergey Edunov, Alexei Baevski, Angela Fan, Sam Gross, Nathan Ng, David Grangier, and Michael Auli. 2019. fairseq: A fast, extensible toolkit for sequence modeling. In *Proceedings of the 2019 Conference of the North American Chapter of the Association for Computational Linguistics (Demonstrations)*, pages 48–53, Minneapolis, Minnesota. Association for Computational Linguistics.

Myle Ott, Sergey Edunov, David Grangier, and Michael Auli. 2018. Scaling neural machine translation. In *Proceedings of the Third Conference on Machine Translation: Research Papers*, pages 1–9, Brussels, Belgium. Association for Computational Linguistics.

Adam Paszke, Sam Gross, Francisco Massa, Adam Lerer, James Bradbury, Gregory Chanan, Trevor Killeen, Zeming Lin, Natalia Gimelshein, Luca Antiga, Alban Desmaison, Andreas Kopf, Edward Yang, Zachary DeVito, Martin Raison, Alykhan Tejani, Sasank Chilamkurthy, Benoit Steiner, Lu Fang, Junjie Bai, and Soumith Chintala. 2019. Pytorch: An imperative style, high-performance deep learning library. In *Advances in Neural Information Processing Systems*, volume 32. Curran Associates, Inc.

Romain Paulus, Caiming Xiong, and Richard Socher. 2018. A deep reinforced model for abstractive summarization. In *International Conference on Learning Representations*.

Weizhen Qi, Yu Yan, Yeyun Gong, Dayiheng Liu, Nan Duan, Jiusheng Chen, Ruofei Zhang, and Ming Zhou. 2020. ProphetNet: Predicting future n-gram for sequence-to-SequencePre-training. In *Findings of the Association for Computational Linguistics: EMNLP 2020*, pages 2401–2410, Online. Association for Computational Linguistics.

Alec Radford, Jeff Wu, Rewon Child, David Luan, Dario Amodei, and Ilya Sutskever. 2019. Language models are unsupervised multitask learners.

Colin Raffel, Noam Shazeer, Adam Roberts, Katherine Lee, Sharan Narang, Michael Matena, Yanqi Zhou, Wei Li, and Peter J. Liu. 2020. Exploring the limits of transfer learning with a unified text-to-text transformer. *Journal of Machine Learning Research*, 21(140):1–67.

Sam Shleifer and Alexander M Rush. 2020. Pre-trained summarization distillation. *arXiv preprint arXiv:2010.13002*.

Yi Tay, Mostafa Dehghani, Dara Bahri, and Donald Metzler. 2020. Efficient transformers: A survey. *arXiv preprint arXiv:2009.06732*.

Han Vanholder. 2016. Efficient inference with tensorrt.

Ashish Vaswani, Noam Shazeer, Niki Parmar, Jakob Uszkoreit, Llion Jones, Aidan N Gomez, Ł ukasz Kaiser, and Illia Polosukhin. 2017. Attention is all you need. In *Advances in Neural Information Processing Systems*, volume 30. Curran Associates, Inc.

Thomas Wolf, Lysandre Debut, Victor Sanh, Julien Chaumond, Clement Delangue, Anthony Moi, Pierric Cistac, Tim Rault, Remi Louf, Morgan Funtowicz, Joe Davison, Sam Shleifer, Patrick von Platen, Clara Ma, Yacine Jernite, Julien Plu, Canwen Xu, Teven Le Scao, Sylvain Gugger, Mariama Drame, Quentin Lhoest, and Alexander Rush. 2020. Transformers: State-of-the-art natural language processing. In *Proceedings of the 2020 Conference on Empirical Methods in Natural Language Processing: System Demonstrations*, pages 38–45, Online. Association for Computational Linguistics.

Yonghui Wu, Mike Schuster, Zhifeng Chen, Quoc V. Le, Mohammad Norouzi, Wolfgang Macherey, Maxim Krikun, Yuan Cao, Qin Gao, Klaus Macherey, Jeff Klingner, Apurva Shah, Melvin Johnson, Xiaobing Liu, Łukasz Kaiser, Stephan Gouws, Yoshikiyo Kato, Taku Kudo, Hideto Kazawa, Keith Stevens, George Kurian, Nishant Patil, Wei Wang, Cliff Young, Jason Smith, Jason Riesa, Alex Rudnick, Oriol Vinyals, Greg Corrado, Macduff Hughes, and Jeffrey Dean. 2016. Google's neural machine translation system: Bridging the gap between human and machine translation.

Yu Yan, Jiusheng Chen, Weizhen Qi, Nikhil Bhendawade, Yeyun Gong, Nan Duan, and Ruofei Zhang. 2021. El-attention: Memory efficient lossless attention for generation. *arXiv preprint arXiv:2105.04779*.

Ofir Zafrir, Guy Boudoukh, Peter Izsak, and Moshe Wasserblat. 2019. Q8bert: Quantized 8bit bert. *arXiv preprint arXiv:1910.06188*.

A Cache Optimization in Self-Attention

First, we can split the cached key and value to two parts: $Cache\_K'$ and $Cache\_V'$ are for the prefix; $Cache\_K_t$ and $Cache\_V_t$ are for the generated sequence at the t step as below:

$$
\begin{aligned}
\underset{[B,1,N,D]}{Cache\_K'} &= \underset{[B\times 1,N,D]}{X} W_k \\
\underset{[B,1,N,D]}{Cache\_V'} &= XW_v \\
\underset{[B\times M,t,D]}{K_t} &= concat(\underset{[B\times M,t-1,D]}{Cache\_K_{t-1}}, y_{t-1} \cdot \underset{[D,D]}{W_k}) \\
\underset{[B\times M,t,D]}{V_t} &= concat(\underset{[B\times M,t-1,D]}{Cache\_V_{t-1}}, y_{t-1} \cdot \underset{[D,D]}{W_v})
\end{aligned} \tag{2}
$$

The above split operation results in incompatible shapes between $Cache\_K'$ and $Cache\_K_t$, and between $Cache\_V'$ and $Cache\_V_t$. Instead of reorganizing these cached keys and values, Equation (3) is leveraged to compute $attn_t$. By this way, the expensive $concat$ operations on large tensors can be avoided.

$$
\begin{aligned}
\underset{[B\times M,1,N]}{attn\_w_0} &= einsum(Q_t, Cache\_K') \\
\underset{[B\times M,1,t]}{attn\_w_1} &= Q_t \cdot K_t^T \\
\underset{[B\times M,1,N+t]}{attn\_w} &= concat(attn\_w_0, attn\_w_1) \\
\underset{[B\times M,1,N+t]}{attn\_prob} &= softmax(\frac{attn\_w}{\sqrt{d_{k_t}}}) \\
\underset{[B\times M,1,N]}{attn\_prob_0}, \underset{[B,M,1,t]}{attn\_prob_1} &= split(attn\_prob) \\
\underset{[B\times M,1,D]}{attn_{t0}} &= einsum(attn\_prob_0, Cache\_V') \\
\underset{[B\times M,1,D]}{attn_{t1}} &= attn\_prob_1 \cdot V_t \\
\underset{[B\times M,1,D]}{attn_t} &= attn_{t0} + attn_{t1}
\end{aligned} \tag{3}
$$

B Cache Optimization in Encoder-Decoder Attention

The first step is to remove the duplication in Cache_K and Cache_V. For the incompatible shape between Q and Cache_K, $einsum$ is leveraged to avoid the reshape.

$$
\begin{aligned}
\underset{[B,1,N,D]}{Cache\_K} &= \underset{[B,1,N,D]}{S} \cdot W_k \\
\underset{[B,1,N,D]}{Cache\_V} &= S \cdot W_v \\
\underset{[B\times M,1,N]}{attn\_w} &= einsum(Q_t, Cache\_K) \\
\underset{[B\times M,1,N]}{attn\_prob_t} &= softmax(\frac{attn\_w}{\sqrt{d_{k_t}}}) \\
\underset{[B\times M,1,D]}{attn_t} &= einsum(attn\_prob_t, Cache\_V)
\end{aligned} \tag{4}
$$

As such, the size of $Cache\_K$ and $Cache\_V$ can be reduced by M times from $B \times M \times N \times D$ to $B \times 1 \times N \times D$. Then the optimization benefits in self-attention can be achieved here as well, including peak memory reduction and larger batch size. Additionally, the cached key and value are not needed to be reordered since the elements at the beam dimension are exactly the same.

LOA: Logical Optimal Actions for Text-based Interaction Games

Daiki Kimura* **Subhajit Chaudhury*** **Masaki Ono** **Michiaki Tatsubori**
Don Joven Agravante **Asim Munawar** **Akifumi Wachi** **Ryosuke Kohita** **Alexander Gray**
IBM Research AI
{daiki, subhajit, moono, mich}@jp.ibm.com,
{don.joven.r.agravante, asim, akifumi.wachi, kohi, alexander.gray}@ibm.com

Abstract

We present Logical Optimal Actions (LOA), an action decision architecture of reinforcement learning applications with a neuro-symbolic framework which is a combination of neural network and symbolic knowledge acquisition approach for natural language interaction games. The demonstration for LOA experiments consists of a web-based interactive platform for text-based games and visualization for acquired knowledge for improving interpretability for trained rules. This demonstration also provides a comparison module with other neuro-symbolic approaches as well as non-symbolic state-of-the-art agent models on the same text-based games. Our LOA also provides open-sourced implementation in Python for the reinforcement learning environment to facilitate an experiment for studying neuro-symbolic agents. Demo site: https://ibm.biz/acl21-loa, Code: https://github.com/ibm/loa

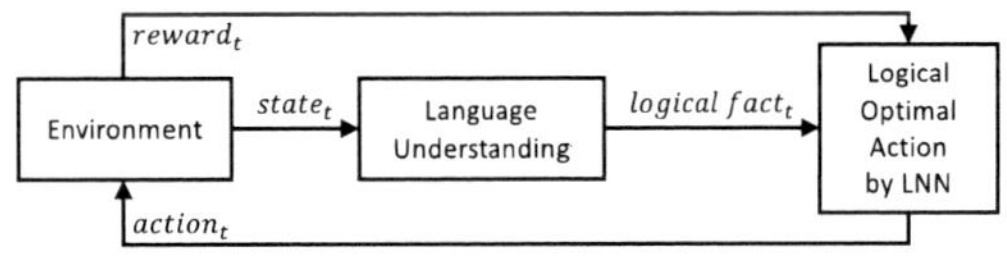

Figure 1: An architecture overview for LOA.

1 Introduction

Neuro-symbolic (NS) hybrid approaches have been proposed for overcoming the weakness of deep reinforcement learning (Dong et al., 2019; Jiang and Luo, 2019; Kimura, 2018; Kimura et al., 2018), including less training data with generalization, external knowledge utilization, and direct explainability of what is learned. Study of reinforcement learning (RL) in non-symbolic environments, such as those with natural language and visionary observations, would be an important step towards the real-world application of the approaches beyond classic and symbolic environments.

Under certain controls necessary for studying RL, text-based games provide complex, interactive, and a variety of simulated environments where the environmental game state observation is obtained through the text description, and the agent is expected to make progress by entering text commands. In addition to language understanding (Ammanabrolu and Riedl, 2019; Adhikari et al., 2020), successful play requires skills such as long-term memory (Narasimhan et al., 2015), exploration (Yuan et al., 2018), observation pruning (Chaudhury et al., 2020), and common sense reasoning (Keerthiram Murugesan and Campbell, 2021). However, these studies are not using the neuro-symbolic approach which is a combination of the neural network and the symbolic framework.

A recent neuro-symbolic framework called the Logical Neural Networks (LNN) (Riegel et al., 2020) simultaneously provides key properties of both neural networks (learning) and symbolic logic (reasoning). The LNN can train the constraints and rules with logical functions in the neural networks, and since every neuron in the network has a component for a formula of weighted real-valued logics, it can calculate the probability and contradiction loss for each of the propositions. At the same time, trained LNN follow symbolic rules, which means they yield a highly interpretable disentangled representation. Using this benefit of LNN, we proposed a neuro-symbolic RL method that uses pre-defined external knowledge in logical networks, and the method successfully plays on the text-based games (Kimura et al., 2021).

In this demonstration (demo site: https://ibm.biz/acl21-loa), we present a Logical Optimal Actions (LOA) architecture for neuro-symbolic RL applications with LNN (Riegel

* denotes equal contribution

Proceedings of the Joint Conference of the 59th Annual Meeting of the Association for Computational Linguistics and the 11th International Joint Conference on Natural Language Processing: System Demonstrations, pages 227–231, August 1st - August 6th, 2021.

et al., 2020) for text-based interaction games. While natural language-based interactive agents are the ambitious but attractive target as real-world applications of neuro-symbolic, it is not easy to provide an environment for the agent. The proposed demonstration uses text-based games learning environment, called TextWorld (Côté et al., 2018), as a miniature of a natural language-based interactive environment. The demonstration provides a web-based user interface for visualizing the game interaction, which is including displaying the natural text observation from the environment, typing the action sentence, and showing the reward value from the taken action. The LOA in this demonstration also visualizes trained and pre-defined logical rules in LNN via the same interface, and this will help the human user understand the benefits of introducing the logical rules via neuro-symbolic frameworks. We also supply an open-sourced implementation for demo environment and some RL methods. This implementation contains our logical approaches and other state-of-the-art agents.

2 Logical Optimal Action

Our proposing LOA is an RL framework which is combining logical reasoning and neural network training. These training and reasoning are provided from functionalities of LNN (Riegel et al., 2020) that is simultaneously providing key properties of both neural networks and symbolic logic. Figure 1 shows the overview architecture for LOA. The LOA model receives the logical state value as logical fact from the language understanding component which receives raw natural language state value from the environment. The model forwards into LNN for the input to get the optimal action for it, the action goes into the environment to execute the action command, then reward is input to LOA agent. The LOA will be trained the action decision network in LNN by using the acquired reward value and chosen action from the network.

3 LOA Demo

The proposing web-based LOA demonstration supports two functionalities: 1) play the text-based game by human interactions, 2) visualize the trained and pre-defined LNN to increase interpretability for acquired rules.

For playing the games by web interface, Fig. 2 shows an initial view for the LOA demonstration.

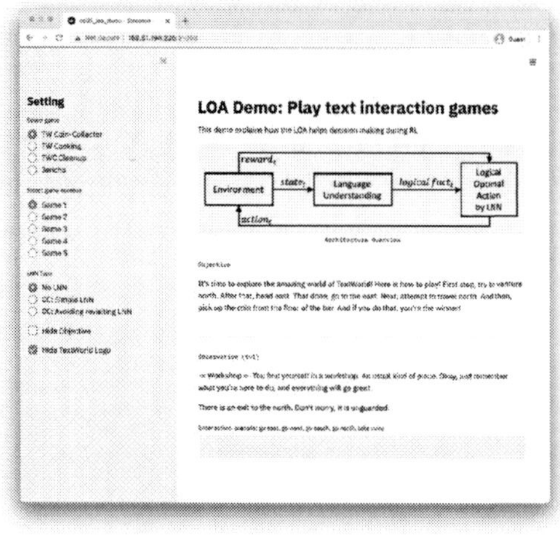

Figure 2: Initial view for LOA demo.

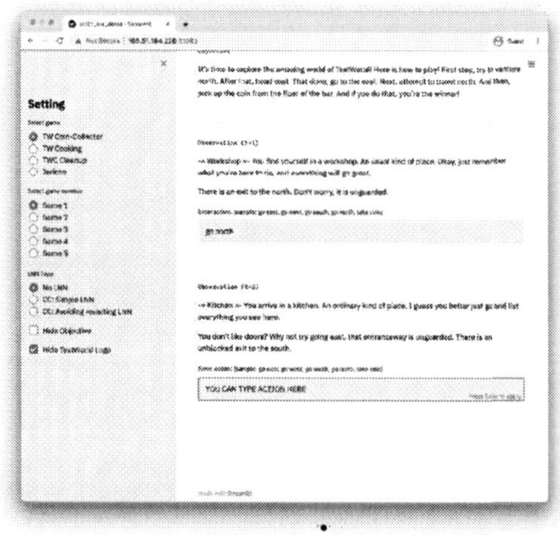

Figure 3: View for playing the game.

On the left-hand side, we can choose the game from some existing text-based interaction games [1], such as TextWorld Coin-Collector game (Côté et al., 2018), TextWorld Cooking game (Côté et al., 2018), TextWorld Commonsense Cleanup game (Keerthiram Murugesan and Campbell, 2021), and Jericho game (Hausknecht et al., 2019). Figure 3 shows the view for playing the TextWorld game, and Fig. 4 shows the view for another game (cleanup task). The human player can input any action by natural language then the demonstration system displays the raw observation output from the environment.

For visualizing the trained and pre-defined neuro-symbolic network in LNN, Fig. 5 and Fig. 6 show the example of the LNN output. In these

[1] We are planning to add other games.

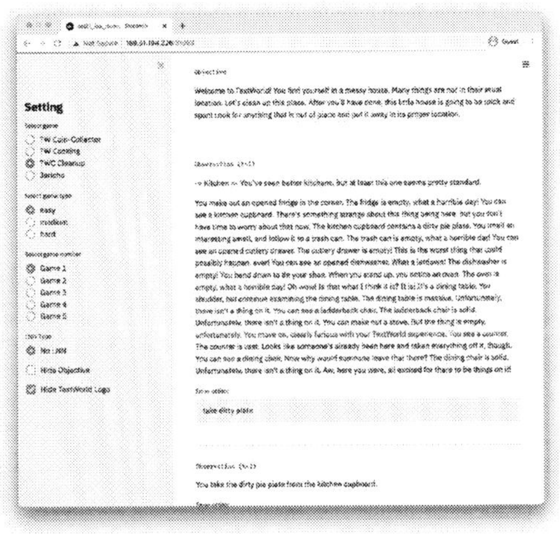

Figure 4: View for playing the cleanup game.

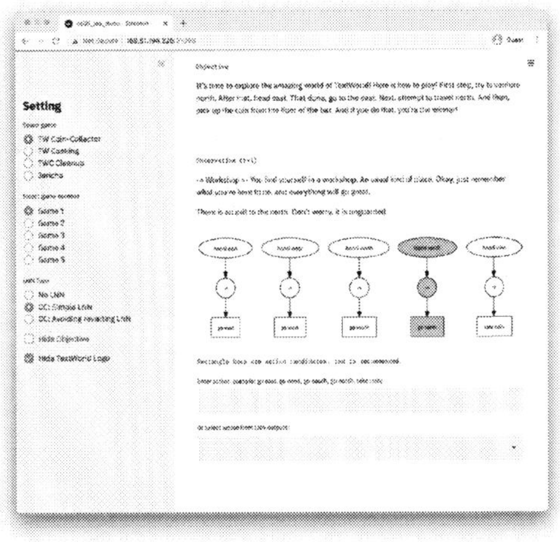

Figure 5: Displaying the simple LNN with given state.

figures, the LNN contains simple rules for the TextWorld Coin-Collector game; for example, the rule is the agent takes 'go east' action, when the agent finds the east room ("`found west`" → "`go west`"). The round box explains the proposition from the given observation inputs, the circle with a logical function means a logical function node of LNN, and the rectangle box explains an action candidate for the agent. The highlighted nodes (red node) have 'true' value, and non-highlighted nodes (white node) have 'false' value. In Fig. 5, the agent found the north exit from the given observation ("`Observation (t=1)`") by using semantic parser [2], then the going north room action ("`go north`") are activated. In Fig. 6, if the user clicks the selectable box, the LOA recommends only one action which is 'go north'. In this demonstration, we show the benefit of introducing the LNN into an RL agent, we don't prepare to automatically choose the action by LOA framework. However, if we execute the RL with LOA framework, the RL agent can converge faster than other non-symbolic and neuro-symbolic methods.

After selecting "`go north`" action at $t = 1$, next observation sentence and LNN output for next step are shown in Fig 7. In this step, the agent found two doors, which are east and south; however, the south door is connected to the previous room because the agent took going north action at the previous step. Since this LNN is simple LNN, the "`go south`" action is also recommended in

[2] This parser is out of our current research topic, we prepare a simple semantic parser.

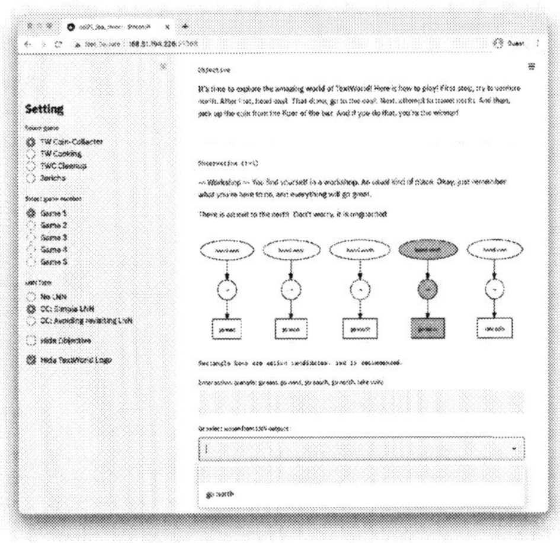

Figure 6: User can choose the recommended action.

Fig 7. Figure 8 shows the output of the complicated LNN which has functionality for avoiding revisiting the visited room. By using such the LNN, LOA can output only "`go east`" action by having contradiction loss in LNN. This is a benefit of introducing the neuro-symbolic framework, and the human user can easily understand the reason for the taken action by the agent with this interpretability by LOA.

4 Conclusion

We propose a novel demonstration (URL: https://ibm.biz/acl21-loa) which provides to play the text-based games on the web interface and visualize the benefit of the neuro-symbolic algorithm. This application helps the human user understand

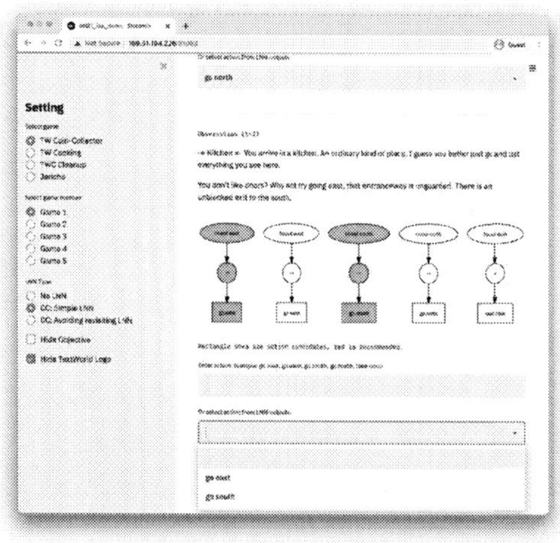

Figure 7: Result for simple LNN.

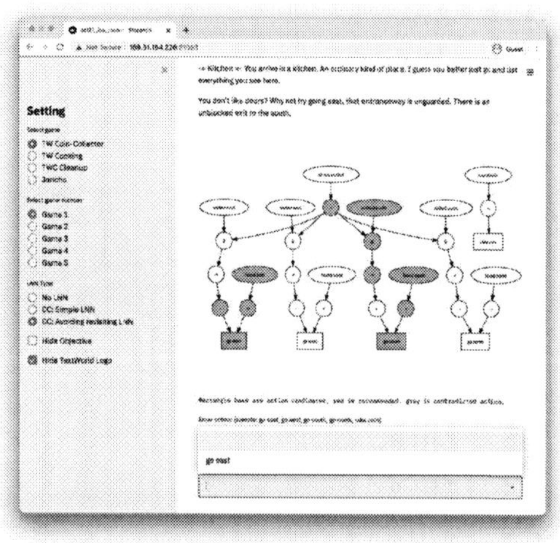

Figure 8: Result for avoiding revisiting LNN.

the trained network and the reason for taken action by the agent. We also extend more complicated LNN for other difficult games on the demo site. At the same time, we open the source code for the demonstration (URL: https://github.com/ibm/loa).

References

Ashutosh Adhikari, Xingdi Yuan, Marc-Alexandre Côté, Mikuláš Zelinka, Marc-Antoine Rondeau, Romain Laroche, Pascal Poupart, Jian Tang, Adam Trischler, and William L. Hamilton. 2020. Learning dynamic belief graphs to generalize on text-based games. In *Advances in Neural Information Processing Systems 33: Annual Conference on Neural Information Processing Systems 2020, NeurIPS 2020, December 6-12, 2020, virtual.*

Prithviraj Ammanabrolu and Mark Riedl. 2019. Playing text-adventure games with graph-based deep reinforcement learning. In *Proceedings of the 2019 Conference of the North American Chapter of the Association for Computational Linguistics: Human Language Technologies, NAACL-HLT 2019, Minneapolis, MN, USA, June 2-7, 2019, Volume 1 (Long and Short Papers)*, pages 3557–3565.

Subhajit Chaudhury, Daiki Kimura, Kartik Talamadupula, Michiaki Tatsubori, Asim Munawar, and Ryuki Tachibana. 2020. Bootstrapped q-learning with context relevant observation pruning to generalize in text-based games. In *Proceedings of the 2020 Conference on Empirical Methods in Natural Language Processing, EMNLP 2020, Online, November 16-20, 2020*, pages 3002–3008.

Marc-Alexandre Côté, Ákos Kádár, Xingdi Yuan, Ben Kybartas, Tavian Barnes, Emery Fine, James Moore, Matthew J. Hausknecht, Layla El Asri, Mahmoud Adada, Wendy Tay, and Adam Trischler. 2018. Textworld: A learning environment for text-based games. In *Computer Games - 7th Workshop, CGW 2018, Held in Conjunction with the 27th International Conference on Artificial Intelligence, IJCAI 2018, Stockholm, Sweden, July 13, 2018, Revised Selected Papers*, pages 41–75.

Honghua Dong, Jiayuan Mao, Tian Lin, Chong Wang, Lihong Li, and Denny Zhou. 2019. Neural logic machines. In *7th International Conference on Learning Representations, ICLR 2019, New Orleans, LA, USA, May 6-9, 2019.*

Matthew Hausknecht, Prithviraj Ammanabrolu, Côté Marc-Alexandre, and Yuan Xingdi. 2019. Interactive fiction games: A colossal adventure. *CoRR*, abs/1909.05398.

Zhengyao Jiang and Shan Luo. 2019. Neural logic reinforcement learning. In *Proceedings of the 36th International Conference on Machine Learning, ICML 2019, 9-15 June 2019, Long Beach, California, USA*, pages 3110–3119.

Pavan Kapanipathi Pushkar Shukla Sadhana Kumaravel Gerald Tesauro Kartik Talamadupula Mrinmaya Sachan Keerthiram Murugesan, Mattia Atzeni and Murray Campbell. 2021. Text-based RL Agents with Commonsense Knowledge: New Challenges, Environments and Baselines. In *Thirty Fifth AAAI Conference on Artificial Intelligence.*

Daiki Kimura. 2018. Daqn: Deep auto-encoder and q-network. *arXiv preprint arXiv:1806.00630.*

Daiki Kimura, Subhajit Chaudhury, Ryuki Tachibana, and Sakyasingha Dasgupta. 2018. Internal model from observations for reward shaping.

Daiki Kimura, Subhajit Chaudhury, Akifumi Wachi, Ryosuke Kohita, Asim Munawar, Michiaki Tatsubori, and Alexander Gray. 2021. Reinforcement learning with external knowledge by using logical neural networks. *arXiv preprint arXiv:2103.02363.*

Karthik Narasimhan, Tejas D. Kulkarni, and Regina Barzilay. 2015. Language understanding for text-based games using deep reinforcement learning. In *Proceedings of the 2015 Conference on Empirical Methods in Natural Language Processing, EMNLP 2015, Lisbon, Portugal, September 17-21, 2015*, pages 1–11.

Ryan Riegel, Alexander G. Gray, Francois P. S. Luus, Naweed Khan, Ndivhuwo Makondo, Ismail Yunus Akhalwaya, Haifeng Qian, Ronald Fagin, Francisco Barahona, Udit Sharma, Shajith Ikbal, Hima Karanam, Sumit Neelam, Ankita Likhyani, and Santosh K. Srivastava. 2020. Logical neural networks. *CoRR*, abs/2006.13155.

Xingdi Yuan, Marc-Alexandre Côté, Alessandro Sordoni, Romain Laroche, Remi Tachet des Combes, Matthew J. Hausknecht, and Adam Trischler. 2018. Counting to explore and generalize in text-based games. *CoRR*, abs/1806.11525.

ProphetNet-X: Large-Scale Pre-training Models for English, Chinese, Multi-lingual, Dialog, and Code Generation

Weizhen Qi[1]*, Yeyun Gong[2]†, Yu Yan[3], Can Xu[3], Bolun Yao[4], Bartuer Zhou[2]
Biao Cheng[2], Daxin Jiang[3], Jiusheng Chen[3], Ruofei Zhang[3], Houqiang Li[1], Nan Duan[2]
[1]University of Science and Technology of China, [2]Microsoft Research Asia,
[3]Microsoft, [4] Nanjing University of Science and Technology
[1]weizhen@mail.ustc.edu.com, lihq@ustc.edu.com,
[2]{yegong,bazhou,bicheng,nanduan}@microsoft.com,
[3]{yyua,caxu,djiang,jiuchen,bzhang}@microsoft.com [4]yaobl001@njust.edu.cn

Abstract

Now, the pre-training technique is ubiquitous in natural language processing field. ProphetNet is a pre-training based natural language generation method which shows powerful performance on English text summarization and question generation tasks. In this paper, we extend ProphetNet into other domains and languages, and present the ProphetNet family pre-training models, named ProphetNet-X, where X can be English, Chinese, Multi-lingual, and so on. We pre-train a cross-lingual generation model ProphetNet-Multi, a Chinese generation model ProphetNet-Zh, two open-domain dialog generation models ProphetNet-Dialog-En and ProphetNet-Dialog-Zh. And also, we provide a PLG (Programming Language Generation) model ProphetNet-Code to show the generation performance besides NLG (Natural Language Generation) tasks. In our experiments, ProphetNet-X models achieve new state-of-the-art performance on 10 benchmarks. All the models of ProphetNet-X share the same model structure, which allows users to easily switch between different models. We make the code and models publicly available[1], and we will keep updating more pre-training models and finetuning scripts.

1 Introduction

In recent years, quite a few natural language generation pre-training models are proposed (Qi et al., 2020; Lewis et al., 2019; Song et al., 2019; Brown et al., 2020). Downstream generation tasks benefit from these large scale pre-training models greatly in fluency and accuracy. Researchers also extend these general pre-training works into specific domains such as DialoGPT (Zhang et al., 2019) is extended from GPT (Brown et al., 2020) for dialog system, mBART (Liu et al., 2020b) is extended from BART (Lewis et al., 2019) for multi-lingual generation, CodeBERT (Feng et al., 2020) is extended from BERT (Devlin et al., 2018) for programming language modeling, etc.

Although there are pre-trained models for some specific domains, it is not convenient for users to find them and set them up. Besides, even some models in the same pre-training family with the same model structure and pre-training tasks, their codes and details vary a lot because of different implementation and backends selection.

ProphetNet (Qi et al., 2020) is firstly proposed as an English text pre-training model with future tokens' prediction, and successfully improves the performance on different downstream NLG tasks. In this work, we pre-train the ProphetNet on different corpus, respectively. The corpus covers different languages and domains. All the pre-trained models share the same model structure with different vocabularies. We provide six pre-trained models with downstream task finetuning scripts, including ProphetNet-En pre-trained with 160GB English raw text, ProphetNet-Zh pre-trained with 160GB Chinese raw text, ProphetNet-Multi with 101GB Wiki-100 corpus and 1.5TB Common Crawl[2] data, ProphetNet-Dialog-En with 60 million sessions Reddit open-domain dialog corpus, ProphetNet-Dialog-Zh with collected Chinese dialog corpus over 30 million sessions, and ProphetNet-Code pre-trained with 10 million codes and documents. ProphetNet-X achieves new state-of-the-art results on 10 benchmarks, including Chinese summarization (MATINF-SUMM (Xu et al., 2020a) and LCSTS (Hu et al., 2015)), Chinese question answering (MATINF-QA (Xu et al., 2020a)), cross-lingual generation (XGLUE NTG (Liang et al., 2020) and

---

* Work is done during internship at Microsoft Research Asia.

† Corresponding Author.

[1]https://github.com/microsoft/ProphetNet

[2]https://commoncrawl.org/

Proceedings of the Joint Conference of the 59th Annual Meeting of the Association for Computational Linguistics and the 11th International Joint Conference on Natural Language Processing: System Demonstrations, pages 232–239, August 1st - August 6th, 2021.

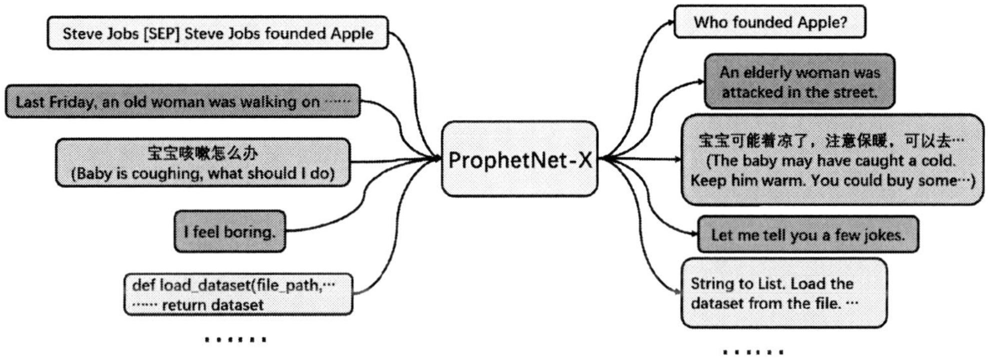

Figure 1: A diagram of ProphetNet-X framework. ProphetNet-X models share the same model structure and cover various languages and domains.

XGLUE QG (Liang et al., 2020)), English summarization (MSNews (Liu et al., 2020a)), English dialog generation (DailyDialog (Li et al., 2017), PersonaChat (Zhang et al., 2018), and DSTC7-AVSD (Alamri et al., 2019)), and code summarization (CodeXGLUE (Lu et al., 2021)). Users can simply download the ProphetNet-X repository and find corresponding pre-trained model with downstream task finetuning scripts.

The main contributions of ProphetNet-X can be described as follows:

- We provide a family of pre-trained models named ProphetNet-X, with six models including English and Chinese natural language generation in open-domain and dialog, multilingual generation, and code generation.
- All the pre-trained ProphetNet-X models share the same model structure. Users only need to simply modify one model file to use it in different language or domain tasks.
- We conduct extensive experiments, the results show that ProphetNet-X models achieve new state-of-the-art performance on 10 publicly available benchmarks.

2 ProphetNet-X

2.1 Architecture

We train different ProphetNet-X models based on ProphetNet. ProphetNet is an encoder-decoder natural language generation model with future n-gram prediction. ProphetNet leverages stacked Transformer encoder layers and stacked multi-stream self-attention Transformer decoder layers. ProphetNet aims to prevent overfitting on strong local correlations such as 2-gram combinations, and deploy future tokens' prediction to enhance auto-regressive generation ability.

Given the input sequence $x = (x_1, \dots, x_M)$ and output sequence $y = (y_1, \dots, y_T)$, n-gram ProphetNet-X replaces the auto-regressive predicting dependency relationship $p(y_t|y_{<t}, x)$ with $p(y_{t:t+n-1}|y_{<t}, x)$. Firstly, ProphetNet-X gets the encoded hidden states with stacked Transformer encoder layers $H_{\text{enc}} = \textbf{Encoder}(x_1, \dots, x_M)$. Then, decoder with n-stream self-attention predicts next n tokens at each time step, as: $p(y_t|y_{<t}, x), \dots, p(y_{t+n-1}|y_{<t}, x) = \textbf{Decoder}(y_{<t}, H_{\text{enc}})$. The optimization target of ProphetNet-X can be described as:

$$
\begin{aligned}
\mathcal{L} &= -\sum_{j=0}^{n-1} \alpha_j \cdot \left(\sum_{t=1}^{T-j} \log p_\theta(y_{t+j}|y_{<t}, x) \right) \\
&= \underbrace{-\alpha_0 \cdot \left(\sum_{t=1}^{T} \log p_\theta(y_t|y_{<t}, x) \right)}_{\text{language modeling loss}} \\
&\quad \underbrace{-\sum_{j=1}^{n-1} \alpha_j \cdot \left(\sum_{t=1}^{T-j} \log p_\theta(y_{t+j}|y_{<t}, x) \right)}_{\text{future n-gram loss}}
\end{aligned}
$$

The details of ProphetNet and multi-stream self-attention can be found in Qi et al. (2020).

2.2 Pre-training Corpus

In this section, we introduce the pre-training corpus for ProphetNet-X.

language	Fr	It	Es	De	Nl	Pt	En	Sv	Pl	Vi	Ar	Ru	Tr
size(GB)	77.25	74.01	72.97	71.48	71.19	71.05	68.34	67.48	67.44	67.43	65.18	64.09	62.96
language	Ja	Zh	Cs	El	Ko	Ro	Th	Da	Bg	Fi	Hu	No	Hi
size(GB)	61.49	58.70	56.62	55.15	45.28	44.05	35.65	32.43	28.44	27.85	27.04	25.24	17.18
language	Sk	Id	Ca	Uk	Lt	Sr	Sl	Hr	Et	Lv	Ka	Az	Ur
size(GB)	14.78	13.68	13.08	10.80	9.20	8.59	6.86	6.51	6.47	5.48	4.16	3.38	3.13
language	Kk	Ne	Gl	My	Eu	Gu	Si	Ms	Sq	Af	Cy	Sw	Bs
size(GB)	3.09	2.18	1.95	1.83	1.37	1.23	1.20	1.03	1.03	0.93	0.51	0.34	0.15

Table 1: Statistics of our multi-lingual pre-training corpus. The total pre-training corpus size is 1.54 TB. ISO codes are used to represent each language.

For ProphetNet-Zh, we collect Chinese Wikipedia, CLUE (Xu et al., 2020b) and Chinese Common Crawl data to reach 160GB. For traditional Chinese data, we firstly use OpenCC [3] to convert them to simplified Chinese. The pre-training corpus includes common webs, online forums, comments websites, Q&A websites, Chinese Wikipedia, and other encyclopedia websites. We build a simplified Chinese char vocabulary. The char vocabulary size is 9,360.

For ProphetNet-Multi, besides Wiki-100 corpus, we select 52 common languages to collect and clean multi-lingual data from Common Crawl. After cleaning and tokenizing, the Common Crawl corpus size we use is described in Table 1. The ProphetNet-Multi vocabulary is same as XLM-R (Conneau et al., 2019) 250k sentencepiece[4] model.

For ProphetNet-Dialog-En, we utilize Reddit comments dataset (Zhou et al., 2018; Galley et al., 2019). We firstly load the weights of ProphetNet-En then clean 60 million sessions for pre-training.

For ProphetNet-Dialog-Zh, we use the pre-training corpus from Wang et al. (2020) and we crawled 18.2 million dyadic dialogues (conversation between two persons) longer than or equal to 2 turns (one turn denotes one utterance from one person) from the Douban group[5] which is a popular social networking service in China. The pre-training corpus size comparison between Wang et al. (2020) and ProphetNet-Dialog-Zh is shown in Table 2. We also load the pre-trained model from ProphetNet-Zh before pre-training, which already contains external knowledge from open-domain Chinese corpus.

For ProphetNet-Code, we conduct pre-training on both PLs (Programming Languages) and their describing NL (Natural Language). We use the pre-training corpus provided by CodeSearchNet (Husain et al., 2019). It covers 6 programming languages, including Go, Java, Javascript, PHP, Python, and Ruby. We employ the same sentencepiece tokenizer as CodeBERT (Feng et al., 2020). The tokenizer is used for both PL and NL, with a vocabulary size 50,365.

Corpus Size	Single-turn	Multi-turn
LCCC-base	3,354,382	3,466,607
LCCC-large	7,273,804	4,733,955
ProphetNet-Dialog-Zh	23,309,502	6,985,425

Table 2: Statistics of Chinese Dialog pre-training corpus

For ProphetNet-En, we directly take the model pre-trained in ProphetNet (Qi et al., 2020). It is pre-trained with 160GB English raw texts, including Wikipedia, books, stories, news, and web texts. The vocabulary of ProphetNet-En is same as BERT sub-words vocabulary. The vocabulary is based on bpe subwords with a max length matching algorithm. Its vocabulary size is 30,522.

3 Experiments

3.1 Pre-training Settings

We carry out pre-training with 12-layer encoder, 12-layer decoder ProphetNet models. The hidden size is 1,024, feed forward size is 4,096, future tokens' prediction length is 2. Both the max sequence lengths of the input and output are set to 512.

For ProphetNet-En, ProphetNet-Zh, ProphetNet-Multi, ProphetNet-Dialog-En, and ProphetNet-Code, we carry out un-supervised pre-training with masked span prediction task. Spans of continuous tokens are masked out from the encoder input sentences and predicted from the decoder side. We masked continuous 9 tokens in every 64 tokens from the encoder side, and predict the 9 tokens on the decoder side. In other words, for maximum 512 encoder sequence length, totally $8(spans) \times 9(tokens\ per\ span) = 72$ tokens

[3]https://github.com/BYVoid/OpenCC

[4]https://github.com/google/sentencepiece

[5]https://www.douban.com/group

Method	MATINF-QA			MATINF-SUMM			LCSTS		
	R-1	R-2	R-L	R-1	R-2	R-L	R-1	R-2	R-L
TextRank (Mihalcea and Tarau, 2004)	-	-	-	35.53	25.78	36.84	24.38	11.97	16.76
LexRank (Erkan and Radev, 2004)	-	-	-	33.08	23.31	34.96	22.15	10.14	14.65
Seq2Seq (Sutskever et al., 2014)	16.62	4.53	10.37	23.05	11.44	19.55	-	-	-
Seq2Seq+Att (Luong et al., 2015)	19.62	5.87	13.34	43.05	28.03	38.58	33.80	23.10	32.50
WEAN (Ma et al., 2018)	-	-	-	34.63	22.56	28.92	37.80	25.60	35.20
Global Encoding (Lin et al., 2018)	-	-	-	49.28	34.14	47.64	39.40	26.90	36.50
BertAbs (Liu and Lapata, 2019)	-	-	-	57.31	44.05	**55.93**	-	-	-
MTF-S2S$_{single}$ (Xu et al., 2020a)	20.28	5.94	13.52	43.02	28.05	38.55	33.75	23.20	32.51
MTF-S2S$_{multi}$ (Xu et al., 2020a)	21.66	6.58	14.26	48.59	35.69	43.28	-	-	-
ProphetNet-Zh	**24.18**	**6.38**	**15.47**	**58.82**	**44.96**	54.26	**42.32**	**27.33**	**37.08**

Table 3: Results of ProphetNet-Zh on MATINF-QA, MATINF-SUMM, and LCSTS. "R-1", "R-2", and "R-L" represent "ROUGE-1", "ROUGE-2", and "ROUGE-L", respectively.

Task	Model	De	En	Es	Fr	It	Pt	Ru	AVG
QG	M-BERT (Devlin et al., 2018)	0.1	7.8	0.1	0.1	0.2	0.1	-	1.4
	XLM-R$_{base}$ (Conneau et al., 2019)	0.1	6.0	0.0	0.0	0.1	0.0	-	1.0
	Unicoder$_{DAE}$ (Liang et al., 2020)	3.0	14.0	12.4	4.2	15.8	8.3	-	9.6
	Unicoder$_{FNP}$ (Liang et al., 2020)	3.7	13.9	14.8	4.9	17.0	9.5	-	10.6
	ProphetNet-Multi	**4.9**	**14.9**	**17.0**	**6.0**	**19.2**	**11.3**	-	**12.2**
NTG	M-BERT (Devlin et al., 2018)	0.7	9.0	0.4	0.4	-	-	0.0	2.1
	XLM-R$_{base}$ (Conneau et al., 2019)	0.6	8.1	0.4	0.3	-	-	0.0	1.9
	Unicoder$_{DAE}$ (Liang et al., 2020)	6.8	15.6	9.0	8.7	-	-	7.7	9.6
	Unicoder$_{FNP}$ (Liang et al., 2020)	7.5	15.8	11.9	9.9	-	-	8.4	10.7
	ProphetNet-Multi	**8.7**	**16.7**	**12.7**	**11.4**	-	-	**8.5**	**11.6**

Table 4: Results of ProphetNet-Multi on XGLUE zero-shot cross-lingual generation task. Task QG and NTG represent Question Generation and News Title Generation. Numbers in this table are BLEU-4 scores.

are masked and predicted. If the last part does not reach a maximum length of 64, 15% continuous tokens are masked. ProphetNet-Dialog-En has special tokens [X_SEP] to separate turns in a session and [SEP] to separate different sessions. For ProphetNet-Dialog-Zh, we conduct supervised pre-training. Previous turns of dialogs are fed into the encoder, and the response is predicted from the decoder. It means that for a multi-turn session with n sentences, $n-1$ samples are created for pre-training. The pre-trained ProphetNet-Dialog-Zh can be used to directly generate dialogs without finetuning.

We carry out pre-training on NVIDIA Tesla V100 GPUs, and the total cost exceeds 30,000 GPU hours.

3.2 Finetuning Benchmarks

For different ProphetNet-X models, we select different benchmarks to evaluate them, respectively.

For ProphetNet-Zh, we evaluate our pre-trained model with MATINF-QA (Xu et al., 2020a) for generative question answering task, MATINF-SUMM (Xu et al., 2020a) and LCSTS (Hu et al., 2015) for summarization task.

For ProphetNet-Multi, we follow Unicoder$_{FNP}$ to evaluate on XGLUE (Liang et al., 2020) for cross-lingual zero-shot generation tasks. The pre-trained multi-lingual model is finetuned with English supervised data and inference with English and other un-seen languages data. There are NTG (News Title Generation) and QG (Question Generation) tasks.

For ProphetNet-Dialog-En, we carry out finetuning on DailyDialog (Li et al., 2017) for chit-chat generation, Persona-Chat (Zhang et al., 2018) for knowledge grounded conversation generation and DSTC7-AVSD (Alamri et al., 2019) for conversational question answering.

For ProphetNet-Dialog-Zh, we use the STC (Shang et al., 2015) single-turn open-domain dialog dataset cleaned by Wang et al. (2020), and real-world Xiaoice Chinese dialog dataset for evaluation.

For ProphetNet-Code, we evaluate the performance on code summarization task from CodeXGLUE (Lu et al., 2021).

For ProphetNet-En, we reports the results on summarization tasks CNN/DM (Hermann et al., 2015), Gigaword (Rush et al., 2015), and MSNews (Liu et al., 2020a); question generation tasks SQuAD 1.1 (Rajpurkar et al., 2016) and MSQG (Liu et al., 2020a).

Model	BLEU-1	BLEU-2	BLEU-3	BLEU-4	METEOR	ROUGE-L	CIDEr
AVSD Baseline (Alamri et al., 2019)	0.629	0485	0.383	0.309	0.215	0.487	0.746
CMU Sinbad's (Sanabria et al., 2019)	0.718	0.584	0.478	0.394	0.267	0.563	1.094
PLATO (Bao et al., 2020)	0.784	0.637	0.525	0.435	0.286	0.596	1.209
ProphetNet-Dialog-En	**0.823**	**0.688**	**0.578**	**0.482**	**0.309**	**0.631**	**1.354**

Table 5: Results of ProphetNet-Dialog-En on DSTC7-AVSD.

Model	DailyDialog					PersonaChat				
	B-1	B-2	D-1	D-2	AVG	B-1	B-2	D-1	D-2	AVG
Seq2Seq (Vinyals and Le, 2015)	0.336	0.238	0.03	0.128	0.183	0.448	0.353	0.004	0.016	0.205
iVAE_MI (Fang et al., 2019)	0.309	0.249	0.029	0.25	0.209	-	-	-	-	-
LIC (Golovanov et al., 2019)	-	-	-	-	-	0.405	0.320	0.019	0.113	0.214
PLATO w/o latent (Bao et al., 2020)	0.405	0.322	0.046	0.246	0.255	0.458	0.357	0.012	0.064	0.223
PLATO (Bao et al., 2020)	0.397	0.311	**0.053**	**0.291**	0.263	0.406	0.315	**0.021**	**0.121**	0.216
ProphetNet-Dialog-En	**0.461**	**0.402**	0.038	0.208	**0.277**	**0.459**	**0.382**	0.010	0.060	**0.228**

Table 6: Results of ProphetNet-Dialog-En on DailyDialog and PersonaChat. "B-1", "B-2", "D-1" and "D-2" represent "BLEU-1", "BLEU-2", "Distinct-1" and " Distinct-2", respectively.

3.3 Results

For ProphetNet-Zh, we see significant improvements in Table 3. TextRank (Mihalcea and Tarau, 2004) and LexRank (Erkan and Radev, 2004) are extractive baselines and others are abstractive baselines. MTF-S2S$_{single}$ (Xu et al., 2020a) and MTF-S2S$_{multi}$ denote single task finetuning and multi-task finetuning on MATINF dataset. We see consistent gains on both Chinese question answering task and summarization tasks.

For ProphetNet-Multi, we show the results in Table 4, Unicoder$_{DAE}$ and Unicoder$_{FNP}$ are pre-trained on Wiki-100 with denoising auto encoder task and ProphetNet, respectively. Comparing the results between the Unicoder$_{FNP}$ and ProphetNet-Multi, we see that more pre-training corpus improves supervised English inference results and other zero-shot languages inference performance. And compared with other baseline methods, ProphetNet-Multi achieves new state-of-the-art results on both NTG and QG tasks.

For English open-domain dialog generation, we show the results in Table 5 and Table 6, compared with strong new proposed PLATO (Bao et al., 2020), we see that ProphetNet-Dialog achieves performance improvements.

Results for ProphetNet-Dialog-Zh on STC can be seen in Table 7. In addition, Table 8 shows the results on real-world Xiaoice dialog dataset with human evaluation. Results in Table 7 hint that for dialog generation, the auto-evaluation metrics (BLEU-2 and BLEU-4) may fail because open-domain dialog outputs could be very different from the given golden targets but still good responses. We observe that ProphetNet-Dialog-Zh without finetuning can

Models	B-2	B-4
Seq2Seq-Attn (Luong et al., 2015)	3.93	0.9
Transformer (Vaswani et al., 2017)	6.72	3.14
GPT$_{Novel}$ (Wang et al., 2020)	5.96	2.71
CDialGPT$_{LCCC-base}$ (Wang et al., 2020)	6.48	3.08
CDialGPT2$_{LCCC-base}$ (Wang et al., 2020)	5.69	2.50
CDialGPT$_{LCCC-large}$ (Wang et al., 2020)	6.63	**3.20**
ProphetNet-Dialog-Zh w/o finetuning	2.54	0.75
ProphetNet-Dialog-Zh w/ finetuning	**6.78**	3.05

Table 7: Results of ProphetNet-Dialog-Zh on STC dataset. "B-2", and "B-4" represent "BLEU-2" and "BLEU-4", respectively.

Setting	Win	Lose	Tie	Kappa
Ours-C vs Xiaoice-C	68%	26%	6%	0.73
Ours-C vs Xiaoice-S	76%	24%	0%	0.65
Ours-S vs Xiaoice-S	81%	19%	0%	0.67

Table 8: Human evaluated results for ProphetNet-Dialog-Zh on real-world Xiaoice dataset. Here, Ours means ProphetNet-Dialog-Zh, Xiaoice means old Xiaoice retrieval based dialog system. -S(single-turn) denotes only the last turn is fed to our model or Xiaoice traditional single-turn retrieval model. -C(context) denotes feeding dialog history into our model or Xiaoice traditional multi-turn retrieval model.

generate fluent and meaningful responses but have lower BLEU scores because of the writing style difference. Thus, we conduct a human evaluation as in (Zhao et al., 2020). We randomly collect 500 single-turn and 500 multi-turn context-response pairs from the online logs of the real-word dialog system Xiaoice. Then, we recruit 3 native speakers as human annotators. The annotators have to judge which response is better, based on informativeness, consistency, and fluency of the responses. If an annotator cannot tell which response is better, he/she is required to label a "Tie". With the

Models	Ruby	Javascript	Go	Python	Java	PHP	overall
Seq2Seq (Vinyals and Le, 2015)	9.64	10.21	13.98	15.93	15.09	21.08	14.32
Transformer (Vaswani et al., 2017)	11.18	11.59	16.38	15.81	16.26	22.12	15.56
RoBERTa (Liu et al., 2019)	11.17	11.90	17.72	18.14	16.47	24.02	16.57
CodeBERT (Feng et al., 2020)	12.16	14.90	18.07	19.06	17.65	25.16	17.83
PLBART (Ahmad et al., 2021)	14.11	15.56	**18.91**	**19.30**	18.45	23.58	18.32
Prophetnet-Code	**14.37**	**16.60**	18.43	17.87	**19.39**	**24.57**	**18.54**

Table 9: Results of ProphetNet-Code on CodeXGLUE for code-to-text summarization task. Numbers in this table are smoothed BLEU-4 scores.

Method	CNN/DM			Gigaword			MSNews		
	R-1	R-2	R-L	R-1	R-2	R-L	R-1	R-2	R-L
LSTM (Bahdanau et al., 2014)	37.3	15.7	34.4	33.6	15.4	31.2	30.0	14.6	27.7
Transformer (Vaswani et al., 2017)	39.5	16.7	36.7	36.4	17.7	33.8	33.0	15.4	30.0
MASS (Song et al., 2019)	42.9	19.8	39.8	38.9	20.2	36.2	40.4	21.5	36.8
BART (Lewis et al., 2019)	44.1	**21.2**	40.9	37.5	17.6	34.3	43.8	24.0	39.2
ProphetNet-En	**44.2**	21.1	**41.3**	**39.5**	**20.4**	**36.6**	**44.1**	**24.4**	**40.2**

Table 10: Results of ProphetNet-En for text summarization. "R-1", "R-2", and "R-L" represent "ROUGE-1", "ROUGE-2", and "ROUGE-L", respectively.

experts' annotation, we see that ProphetNet-Dialog-Zh obviously outperforms Xiaoice retrieval based old system. Kappa (Fleiss and Cohen, 1973) values of all models exceed 0.6, indicating substantial agreement overall annotators.

For ProphetNet-Code, the code summarization results are shown in Table 9. We can see new state-of-the-art results are obtained with ProphetNet-Code. It shows that ProphetNet-X models not only benefit from pre-training on natural language generation tasks but also perform well in programming language tasks.

Model	SQuAD 1.1			MSQG		
	R-L	B-4	MTR	R-L	B-4	MTR
LSTM	27.2	3.8	8.9	25.3	3.5	14.1
Transformer	30.7	4.8	10.9	29.3	5.1	16.6
MASS	49.9	21.3	25.2	**38.9**	9.5	23.5
BART	50.3	22.0	**26.4**	38.8	9.2	**24.3**
ProphetNet-En	**51.5**	**22.5**	26.0	38.3	**9.6**	23.3

Table 11: Results of ProphetNet-En for question generation on SQuAD1.1 and MSQG. "R-L", "B-4", and "MTR" represent "ROUGE-L", "BLEU-4", and "METEOR", respectively.

For ProphetNet-En, we report the results for ProphetNet in Table 10 and Table 11. We also report the results for two new tasks MSNTG and MSQG introduced from GLGE (Liu et al., 2020a).

4 Related Work

ProphetNet (Qi et al., 2020) is the most related to our work since we carry out pre-training based on it. Other related works involve pre-training works in different domains. For English generation pre-training, MASS (Song et al., 2019) proposes an unsupervised pre-training task with span masked and recover. BART (Lewis et al., 2019) feeds corrupted sentences into the encoder and reconstructs the original sentences. GPT (Radford et al., 2019) models perform language modeling pre-training with Transformer decoder. For multilingual pre-training, mBART (Liu et al., 2020b) introduces language labels to adopt BART denoising pre-training. Based on GPT (Radford et al., 2019), DialoGPT (Zhang et al., 2019) and CDial-GPT (Wang et al., 2020) adopts language model pre-training with English and Chinese dialog corpus respectively. CodeBERT (Feng et al., 2020) and GraphCodeBERT (Guo et al., 2020) are two pre-training models for programming languages. PLBART (Ahmad et al., 2021) is similar to multilingual BART with language tags to perform denoising pre-training on programming languages.

5 Conclusion

In this paper, we pre-train ProphetNet-X on various languages and domains, including open-domain (for English, Chinese, and Multi-lingual), dialog (for English and Chinese), and programming (for Ruby, Javascript, Go, Python, Java, and PHP). All the models share the same model structure and are easy to use. Extensive experiments show that ProphetNet-X achieves new state-of-the-art performance on 10 benchmarks. In the future, we will extend ProphetNet-X to support more domains such as biomedical text and protein pre-training.

References

Wasi Uddin Ahmad, Saikat Chakraborty, Baishakhi Ray, and Kai-Wei Chang. 2021. Unified pre-training for program understanding and generation. *arXiv preprint arXiv:2103.06333*.

Huda Alamri, Vincent Cartillier, Abhishek Das, Jue Wang, Anoop Cherian, Irfan Essa, Dhruv Batra, Tim K Marks, Chiori Hori, Peter Anderson, et al. 2019. Audio visual scene-aware dialog. In *Proceedings of the IEEE/CVF Conference on Computer Vision and Pattern Recognition*, pages 7558–7567.

Dzmitry Bahdanau, Kyunghyun Cho, and Yoshua Bengio. 2014. Neural machine translation by jointly learning to align and translate. *arXiv preprint arXiv:1409.0473*.

Siqi Bao, Huang He, Fan Wang, Hua Wu, and Haifeng Wang. 2020. PLATO: Pre-trained dialogue generation model with discrete latent variable. In *Proceedings of the 58th Annual Meeting of the Association for Computational Linguistics*, pages 85–96, Online. Association for Computational Linguistics.

Tom B Brown, Benjamin Mann, Nick Ryder, Melanie Subbiah, Jared Kaplan, Prafulla Dhariwal, Arvind Neelakantan, Pranav Shyam, Girish Sastry, Amanda Askell, et al. 2020. Language models are few-shot learners. *arXiv preprint arXiv:2005.14165*.

Alexis Conneau, Kartikay Khandelwal, Naman Goyal, Vishrav Chaudhary, Guillaume Wenzek, Francisco Guzmán, Edouard Grave, Myle Ott, Luke Zettlemoyer, and Veselin Stoyanov. 2019. Unsupervised cross-lingual representation learning at scale. *arXiv preprint arXiv:1911.02116*.

Jacob Devlin, Ming-Wei Chang, Kenton Lee, and Kristina Toutanova. 2018. Bert: Pre-training of deep bidirectional transformers for language understanding. *arXiv preprint arXiv:1810.04805*.

Günes Erkan and Dragomir R Radev. 2004. Lexrank: Graph-based lexical centrality as salience in text summarization. *Journal of artificial intelligence research*, 22:457–479.

Le Fang, Chunyuan Li, Jianfeng Gao, Wen Dong, and Changyou Chen. 2019. Implicit deep latent variable models for text generation. In *Proceedings of the 2019 Conference on Empirical Methods in Natural Language Processing and the 9th International Joint Conference on Natural Language Processing (EMNLP-IJCNLP)*, pages 3937–3947.

Zhangyin Feng, Daya Guo, Duyu Tang, Nan Duan, Xiaocheng Feng, Ming Gong, Linjun Shou, Bing Qin, Ting Liu, Daxin Jiang, et al. 2020. Codebert: A pre-trained model for programming and natural languages. *arXiv preprint arXiv:2002.08155*.

Joseph L Fleiss and Jacob Cohen. 1973. The equivalence of weighted kappa and the intraclass correlation coefficient as measures of reliability. *Educational and psychological measurement*, 33(3):613–619.

Michel Galley, Chris Brockett, Xiang Gao, Jianfeng Gao, and Bill Dolan. 2019. Grounded response generation task at dstc7. In *AAAI Dialog System Technology Challenges Workshop*.

Sergey Golovanov, Rauf Kurbanov, Sergey Nikolenko, Kyryl Truskovskyi, Alexander Tselousov, and Thomas Wolf. 2019. Large-scale transfer learning for natural language generation. In *Proceedings of the 57th Annual Meeting of the Association for Computational Linguistics*, pages 6053–6058.

Daya Guo, Shuo Ren, Shuai Lu, Zhangyin Feng, Duyu Tang, Shujie Liu, Long Zhou, Nan Duan, Jian Yin, Daxin Jiang, et al. 2020. Graphcodebert: Pre-training code representations with data flow. *arXiv preprint arXiv:2009.08366*.

Karl Moritz Hermann, Tomas Kocisky, Edward Grefenstette, Lasse Espeholt, Will Kay, Mustafa Suleyman, and Phil Blunsom. 2015. Teaching machines to read and comprehend. In *NIPS*, pages 1693–1701.

Baotian Hu, Qingcai Chen, and Fangze Zhu. 2015. Lcsts: A large scale chinese short text summarization dataset. *arXiv preprint arXiv:1506.05865*.

Hamel Husain, Ho-Hsiang Wu, Tiferet Gazit, Miltiadis Allamanis, and Marc Brockschmidt. 2019. Codesearchnet challenge: Evaluating the state of semantic code search. *arXiv preprint arXiv:1909.09436*.

Mike Lewis, Yinhan Liu, Naman Goyal, Marjan Ghazvininejad, Abdelrahman Mohamed, Omer Levy, Ves Stoyanov, and Luke Zettlemoyer. 2019. Bart: Denoising sequence-to-sequence pre-training for natural language generation, translation, and comprehension. *arXiv preprint arXiv:1910.13461*.

Yanran Li, Hui Su, Xiaoyu Shen, Wenjie Li, Ziqiang Cao, and Shuzi Niu. 2017. Dailydialog: A manually labelled multi-turn dialogue dataset. In *Proceedings of the Eighth International Joint Conference on Natural Language Processing (Volume 1: Long Papers)*, pages 986–995.

Yaobo Liang, Nan Duan, Yeyun Gong, Ning Wu, Fenfei Guo, Weizhen Qi, Ming Gong, Linjun Shou, Daxin Jiang, Guihong Cao, et al. 2020. Xglue: A new benchmark dataset for cross-lingual pre-training, understanding and generation. *arXiv preprint arXiv:2004.01401*.

Junyang Lin, Xu Sun, Shuming Ma, and Qi Su. 2018. Global encoding for abstractive summarization. *arXiv preprint arXiv:1805.03989*.

Dayiheng Liu, Yu Yan, Yeyun Gong, Weizhen Qi, Hang Zhang, Jian Jiao, Weizhu Chen, Jie Fu, Linjun Shou, Ming Gong, et al. 2020a. Glge: A new general language generation evaluation benchmark. *arXiv preprint arXiv:2011.11928*.

Yang Liu and Mirella Lapata. 2019. Text summarization with pretrained encoders. *arXiv preprint arXiv:1908.08345*.

Yinhan Liu, Jiatao Gu, Naman Goyal, Xian Li, Sergey Edunov, Marjan Ghazvininejad, Mike Lewis, and Luke Zettlemoyer. 2020b. Multilingual denoising pre-training for neural machine translation. *Transactions of the Association for Computational Linguistics*, 8:726–742.

Yinhan Liu, Myle Ott, Naman Goyal, Jingfei Du, Mandar Joshi, Danqi Chen, Omer Levy, Mike Lewis, Luke Zettlemoyer, and Veselin Stoyanov. 2019. Roberta: A robustly optimized bert pretraining approach. *arXiv preprint arXiv:1907.11692*.

Shuai Lu, Daya Guo, Shuo Ren, Junjie Huang, Alexey Svyatkovskiy, Ambrosio Blanco, Colin Clement, Dawn Drain, Daxin Jiang, Duyu Tang, et al. 2021. Codexglue: A machine learning benchmark dataset for code understanding and generation. *arXiv preprint arXiv:2102.04664*.

Minh-Thang Luong, Hieu Pham, and Christopher D Manning. 2015. Effective approaches to attention-based neural machine translation. *arXiv preprint arXiv:1508.04025*.

Shuming Ma, Xu Sun, Wei Li, Sujian Li, Wenjie Li, and Xuancheng Ren. 2018. Query and output: Generating words by querying distributed word representations for paraphrase generation. *arXiv preprint arXiv:1803.01465*.

Rada Mihalcea and Paul Tarau. 2004. Textrank: Bringing order into text. In *Proceedings of the 2004 conference on empirical methods in natural language processing*, pages 404–411.

Weizhen Qi, Yu Yan, Yeyun Gong, Dayiheng Liu, Nan Duan, Jiusheng Chen, Ruofei Zhang, and Ming Zhou. 2020. Prophetnet: Predicting future n-gram for sequence-to-sequence pre-training. In *Proceedings of the 2020 Conference on Empirical Methods in Natural Language Processing: Findings*, pages 2401–2410.

Alec Radford, Jeffrey Wu, Rewon Child, David Luan, Dario Amodei, and Ilya Sutskever. 2019. Language models are unsupervised multitask learners. *OpenAI blog*, 1(8):9.

Pranav Rajpurkar, Jian Zhang, Konstantin Lopyrev, and Percy Liang. 2016. Squad: 100,000+ questions for machine comprehension of text. In *EMNLP*, pages 2383–2392.

Alexander M Rush, Sumit Chopra, and Jason Weston. 2015. A neural attention model for abstractive sentence summarization. In *EMNLP*, pages 379–389.

Ramon Sanabria, Shruti Palaskar, and Florian Metze. 2019. Cmu sinbad's submission for the dstc7 avsd challenge.

Lifeng Shang, Zhengdong Lu, and Hang Li. 2015. Neural responding machine for short-text conversation. *arXiv preprint arXiv:1503.02364*.

Kaitao Song, Xu Tan, Tao Qin, Jianfeng Lu, and Tie-Yan Liu. 2019. Mass: Masked sequence to sequence pre-training for language generation. *arXiv preprint arXiv:1905.02450*.

Ilya Sutskever, Oriol Vinyals, and Quoc V Le. 2014. Sequence to sequence learning with neural networks. *arXiv preprint arXiv:1409.3215*.

Ashish Vaswani, Noam Shazeer, Niki Parmar, Jakob Uszkoreit, Llion Jones, Aidan N Gomez, Lukasz Kaiser, and Illia Polosukhin. 2017. Attention is all you need. *arXiv preprint arXiv:1706.03762*.

Oriol Vinyals and Quoc Le. 2015. A neural conversational model. *arXiv preprint arXiv:1506.05869*.

Yida Wang, Pei Ke, Yinhe Zheng, Kaili Huang, Yong Jiang, Xiaoyan Zhu, and Minlie Huang. 2020. A large-scale chinese short-text conversation dataset. In *CCF International Conference on Natural Language Processing and Chinese Computing*, pages 91–103. Springer.

Canwen Xu, Jiaxin Pei, Hongtao Wu, Yiyu Liu, and Chenliang Li. 2020a. Matinf: A jointly labeled large-scale dataset for classification, question answering and summarization. *arXiv preprint arXiv:2004.12302*.

Liang Xu, Xuanwei Zhang, Lu Li, Hai Hu, Chenjie Cao, Weitang Liu, Junyi Li, Yudong Li, Kai Sun, Yechen Xu, et al. 2020b. Clue: A chinese language understanding evaluation benchmark. *arXiv preprint arXiv:2004.05986*.

Saizheng Zhang, Emily Dinan, Jack Urbanek, Arthur Szlam, Douwe Kiela, and Jason Weston. 2018. Personalizing dialogue agents: I have a dog, do you have pets too? In *ACL*, pages 2204–2213.

Yizhe Zhang, Siqi Sun, Michel Galley, Yen-Chun Chen, Chris Brockett, Xiang Gao, Jianfeng Gao, Jingjing Liu, and Bill Dolan. 2019. Dialogpt: Large-scale generative pre-training for conversational response generation. *arXiv preprint arXiv:1911.00536*.

Yufan Zhao, Can Xu, Wei Wu, and Lei Yu. 2020. Learning a simple and effective model for multi-turn response generation with auxiliary tasks. *arXiv preprint arXiv:2004.01972*.

Hao Zhou, Tom Young, Minlie Huang, Haizhou Zhao, Jingfang Xu, and Xiaoyan Zhu. 2018. Commonsense knowledge aware conversation generation with graph attention. In *IJCAI*, pages 4623–4629.

IFlyEA: A Chinese Essay Assessment System with Automated Rating, Review Generation, and Recommendation

Jiefu Gong[†], **Xiao Hu**[†], **Wei Song**[‡], **Ruiji Fu**[†], **Zhichao Sheng**[¶],

Bo Zhu[¶], **Shijin Wang**[†¶£], **Ting Liu**[§]

[†]State Key Laboratory of Cognitive Intelligence, iFLYTEK Research, Beijing, China
[‡]Academy for Multidisciplinary Studies, Capital Normal University, Beijing, China
[¶]iFLYTEK AI Research (Hefei), China [£]iFLYTEK AI Research (Hebei), LangFang, China
[§]Research Center for SCIR, Harbin Institute of Technology, Harbin, China
{jfgong, xiaohu2, rjfu, zcsheng, bozhu, sjwang3}@iflytek.com,
wsong@cnu.edu.cn, tliu@ir.hit.edu.cn

Abstract

Automated Essay Assessment (AEA) aims to judge students' writing proficiency in an automatic way. This paper presents a Chinese AEA system IFlyEssayAssess (IFlyEA), targeting on evaluating essays written by native Chinese students from primary and junior schools. IFlyEA provides multi-level and multi-dimension analytical modules for essay assessment. It has state-of-the-art grammar level analysis techniques, and also integrates components for rhetoric and discourse level analysis, which are important for evaluating native speakers' writing ability, but still challenging and less studied in previous work. Based on the comprehensive analysis, IFlyEA provides application services for essay scoring, review generation, recommendation, and explainable analytical visualization. These services can benefit both teachers and students during the process of writing teaching and learning.

1 Introduction

Automated essay assessment (AEA) is an important educational application (Page, 1968; Rudner et al., 2006). It aims to reduce the burden of teachers for scoring student essays and give students direct instructions to improve their writing ability.

Automated essay scoring (AES) is one of the most important modules for AEA, which is usually formulated as a supervised learning problem. The early approaches utilized hand-crafted features to predict essay scores (Yannakoudakis et al., 2011; Chen and He, 2013; Phandi et al., 2015). Recently, deep learning has been applied to AES as well (Taghipour and Ng, 2016; Dong et al., 2017; Song et al., 2020c).

One issue about AES is that its prediction lacks explainability since a single score gives very limited information. Many efforts have been paid to expand the boundary of AES, and try to analyze detailed linguistic properties, such as grammatical errors (Ng et al., 2014), coherence (Somasundaran et al., 2014), organization (Burstein et al., 2003; Persing et al., 2010) and so on.

Several AES systems, such as E-Rater (Attali and Burstein, 2006) and Lingglewrite (Tsai et al., 2020), have been successfully applied in the education scenario. However, many of them focus on evaluating second-language learners' writing ability or evaluating basic language usages depending on shallow features, which may be not sufficient for evaluating essays written by native speakers. Moreover, most existing platforms mainly target on English, while there are significantly fewer systems working on other languages, such as Chinese.

In this paper, we introduce the IFlyEssayAssess (IFlyEA) system, which is a Chinese automated essay assessment system, focusing on assessing the quality of essays written by native Chinese students from primary and junior schools.

IFlyEA has the following highlights:

- IFlyEA has comprehensive multi-level and multi-dimension analytical modules. It provides state-of-the-art Chinese spelling error correction and grammatical error diagnosis at grammar level. More specially, it also provides rich rhetoric and discourse level analysis, which are less studied but important for evaluating native speakers' writing ability.

- Based on the information provided by the analytical modules, IFlyEA provides a complete set of application services, including rating, review generation and recommendation.

- IFlyEA has an easy-to-use visualization and interactive interface, which can clearly show the detailed analytical results of an essay, and

Proceedings of the Joint Conference of the 59th Annual Meeting of the Association for Computational Linguistics and the 11th International Joint Conference on Natural Language Processing: System Demonstrations, pages 240–248, August 1st - August 6th, 2021.

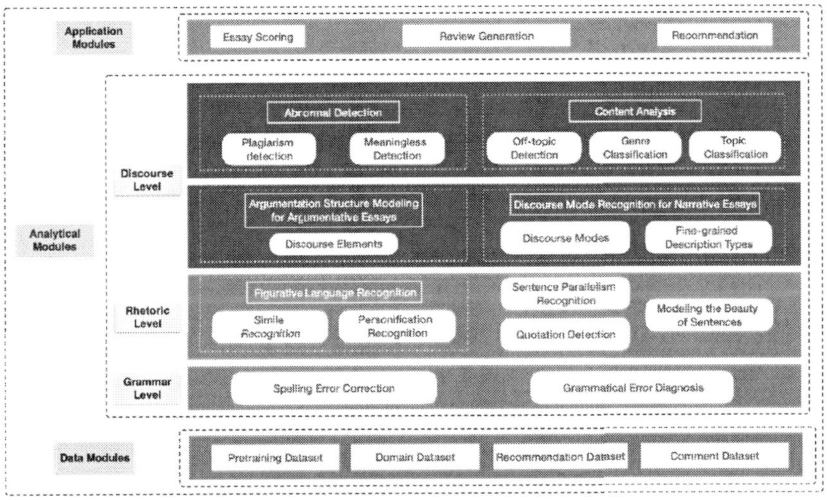

Figure 1: The architecture of IFlyEA.

improve the explainability of predictions at the application level.

The target users of IFlyEA is students from primary and junior schools, in other hands, it is also helpful for teachers to reduce their heavy work. IFlyEA has been applied in practice and it is being continually improved by learning from user feedback.

2 System Architecture

The main modules of IFlyEA can be categorized into two types: **analytical modules** and **application modules**, as shown in Figure 1. These modules are integrated with visualization and interactive interfaces.

The analytical modules involve multi-level and multi-dimension analysis of essay quality, which mainly cover three levels:

- **Grammar level**: This level aims to judge whether students can *correctly* use words to communicate. IFlyEA applies several technical approaches such as spelling correction and grammatical error diagnosis.
- **Rhetoric level**: This level aims to judge whether students can *gracefully* and *skillfully* convey their ideas. IFlyEA can recognize rhetorical devices and *beautiful* sentences in essays.
- **Discourse level**: This level aims to judge whether students can *logically* connect basic discourse units to construct a coherent whole. The system identifies discourse elements for representing and evaluating essay organization, and also has other discourse level analysis such as topic classification and genre classification.

The techniques at grammar level are widely used for essay scoring, especially for evaluating second-language learners. The rhetoric and discourse levels are more important for evaluating essays written by native speakers, especially for distinguishing well-written essays from moderate ones.

The application modules include:

- **Essay scoring**: This module gives scores to indicate the general quality of an essay and the quality of specific aspects.
- **Review generation**: This module provides readable reviews on multiple writing dimensions.
- **Recommendation**: This module suggests relevant and potentially helpful materials to students.

The review generation and recommendation modules depend on the results from the analytical modules and the essay scoring module.

In general, the analytical modules are the basis of the application modules, providing evidence and diagnosis, and also improving the explainability for the predictions of application modules. As illustrated in Figure 2, through web page visualization

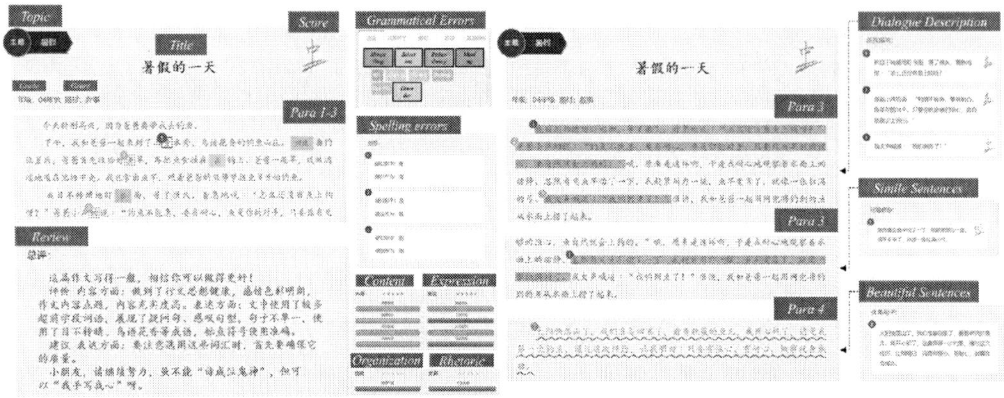

Figure 2: The visualization and interactive interfaces of IFlyEA.

and interfaces, students or teachers can receive rich information and interact with the analytical results.

3 Analytical Modules

IFlyEA has multi-level and multi-dimension quality evaluation to provide comprehensive analytical results. This section will introduce the main analytical modules, which can be roughly categorized into 3 levels: grammar, rhetoric and discourse levels.

3.1 Grammar-level Analysis

Correctly using words is a fundamental requirement for effective writing. Grammar-level analysis would try to detect spelling and grammatical errors in essays, and highlight detected errors as a reminder.

3.1.1 Spelling Error Correction

Given a sentence, our spelling checker would locate spelling errors if there is any, and provide a list of corrected candidates (Tseng et al., 2015).

Inspired by Liu et al. (2013); Yu and Li (2014), we establish a confusion-set based unsupervised two-stage method to detect and correct spelling errors.

Confusion set: A confusion set is built to group characters with similar pronunciation or graphemic into clusters. We implement it with an inverted indexing structure so that given a target character, we can quickly get a list of *confusion characters* from the same cluster.

Stage 1: Correction candidate detection with local context: We train a 5-gram language model `LM` on a large-scale corpus. For each character in a sentence, we substitute it with its corresponding confusion characters one by one, and use `LM` to compute perplexity. If any confusion character leads to a lower perplexity than the original one by a pre-defined threshold, it would be retained as a *correction candidate*. After state 1, we obtain a small list of correction candidates. This stage can be processed very fast.

Stage 2: Correction candidate reranking with global context: We further use the masked language model `MLM` from BERT (Devlin et al., 2019) to take advantage of the pre-trained transformer based language model and exploit the whole sentence as context to rerank the correction candidates at different positions, respectively.

Model	P	R	F_1
Wang et al. (2019)	0.715	0.595	0.649
Zhang et al. (2020)	0.667	0.662	0.664
Ours	0.662	0.641	0.651

Table 1: Chinese spelling error correction performance on SIGHAN 2015 dataset.

We evaluate our system on the SIGHAN 2015 benchmark. As shown in Table 1, the results demonstrate that our system can obtain competitive results to state-of-the-art methods, although it is unsupervised.

3.1.2 Grammatical Error Diagnosis

We focus on 4 types of grammatical errors: *redundant word, missing word, word selection*, and *word ordering* (Rao et al., 2018). We concentrate on detecting whether a sentence has any grammatical error (detection level), and show the positions of possible grammatical errors (position level).

In line with (Bell et al., 2019; Fu et al., 2018),

Dataset	Detection level	Position level
CGED 2020 data (Rao et al., 2020)	0.894	0.404
Domain data	0.797	0.631

Table 2: Comparison of best F_1 results reported in the CGED 2020 dataset and the domain dataset of primary students' essays.

we formulate grammatical error diagnosis as a sequence labeling problem. Specifically, we build our model based on (Wang et al., 2020), where a ResNet enhanced multi-layer bidirectional transformer encoder (ResELECTRA) is used to encode sentences. This solution ranked 1st in the NLPTEA-2020 CGED shared task at identification and position level.

Since we target on student essays, we continue to train ResELECTRA on a sample of primary students' essays annotated with grammatical error types. The performance on primary students' essays can reach 63% F1-score at position level. The score is higher at position level but lower at detection level than on the CGED 2020 test set. This is because that the label distributions of both levels are different.

3.2 Rhetoric-level Analysis

Grammar-level analysis is important but is not enough for sufficiently evaluating the quality of native speakers' writing. For example, grammatical errors already become much less in junior students' essays compared with that in second-language learners' essays.

This section will introduce rhetoric-level analytical modules, which aim to identify excellent sentences and rhetorical devices, to explore whether language is used in a graceful way.

3.2.1 Modeling the Beauty of Sentences

We define *beautiful sentences* as the ones that can induce aesthetic feelings in us. This definition is vague and the criterion is subjective. Therefore, we construct a classifier to identify beautiful sentences in a data-driven way.

We collect more than $20k$ sentences with beautiful or not labels through crowd-sourcing. Each sentence is at least labeled by two annotators. For training, we only keep the sentences that are labeled with the same tags by two annotators. We train a simple attention based BiLSTM model (Bahdanau et al., 2014) to classify whether a sentence should be annotated as beautiful. The classifier can get an accuracy of 81% through cross-validation evaluation.

3.2.2 Figurative Language Recognition

Figurative language refers to the use of words in a way that deviates from the literal meaning to convey a complicated meaning to amplify our writing. Figurative language recognition in essays enables monitoring students' ability in using figurative language and providing clues for evaluating quality of essays. Currently, we focus on identifying simile and personification.

Simile Recognition Simile leads a comparison between concepts using explicit comparators such as *like, as* in English and *Xiang, Si, Ru* in Chinese. But a sentence with a comparator does not always trigger a simile, unless the two arguments of the comparator form a cross-domain mapping (Lakoff and Johnson, 2008). So simile recognition is not a trivial task.

We adopt a multi-task learning framework for simile recognition (Liu et al., 2018). The framework jointly optimizes two subtasks: *simile sentence classification* and *simile component extraction*. The model is trained on $12k$ annotated sentences that contain a comparator. The simile sentence classifier can obtain a 86% F_1 score in 5-fold cross-validation evaluation on the dataset.

Personification Recognition Personification is another special case of figurative language, borrowing human's actions, expressions, or other characteristics to ascribes specific attributes of non-human objects, such as, "*Life has cheated me*" (Lakoff and Johnson, 2008).

This task is cast as a typical classification problem. We adopt an attention based BiLSTM (Bahdanau et al., 2014) to encode a sentence into a dense feature vector. This vector is then fed into a nonlinear layer and a softmax layer to generate the classification result. Considering the characteristics of this task, we introduce an external knowledge base Chinese CiLin (A Synonymy Thesaurus of Chinese Words) (Mei, 1984) to group words into clusters according to word senses, and assign a learnable embedding vector for each cluster. Each word is represented by the concatenation of its word embedding and cluster embedding, which is fed into the encoder for learning. The personification recognizer can achieve a 80% F_1 score. This task shows to be more difficult than simile recognition.

3.2.3 Sentence Parallelism Recognition

Sentence parallelism is also a widely used rhetorical device in writing. It can be defined as two or more coherent text spans (phrases or sentences), which have similar syntactic structures and related semantics, and express relevant content or emotion together (Song et al., 2016). Parallelism adds balance and rhythm to make speeches and writings more vivid and powerful.

We adopt a feature-based method for this task. The features contain a set of alignment measures at position, word, syntactic and semantic levels. We find that sentence parallelism can be recognized with accepted performance (82% F1-score at pairwise level and 72% F1-score at parallelism block level) using a random forest classifier trained on hundreds of training samples. We also observe that sentence parallelism has a positive correlation to the quality of essays, especially in argumentative essays.

3.2.4 Quotation Detection

Quotation is a figure-of-speech that intentionally referring to some predecessor's words, like poems, maxims, and proverbs, to explain one's own idea, which is aim to amplify the writing or enhance the persuasiveness of argument. We collect a large-scale quotation corpus from the Internet, ranging from poetry to proverbs, and exploit information retrieval (IR) techniques and semantic matching for quotation detection.

3.3 Discourse-level Analysis

Discourse analysis aims to build connections between discourse units to form a whole (Song and Liu, 2020). For essay scoring, we mainly focus on analyzing the organization of essays. One important issue is how to represent essay organization. Our solution is to use discourse elements, which are defined as the function of discourse units in building a coherent discourse. The discourse elements of an essay are dependent on its genre. For example, narrative and argumentative essays usually have different organizational strategies and have different discourse elements.

3.3.1 Argumentation Structure Modeling for Argumentative Essays

For argumentative essays, we define a set of discourse elements following previous work (Attali and Burstein, 2006; Persing et al., 2010), including *prompt*, *thesis*, *main idea*, *support* and *conclusion*. These discourse elements can be used for both sentences and paragraphs (Song et al., 2020a,b).

IFlyEA currently maintains a hybrid organization module. A discourse element is represented by combining its distributed semantic vector and a manually constructed feature vector (Song et al., 2015). The learning framework is based on hierarchical multi-task learning (Song et al., 2020b), which jointly optimizes sentence and paragraph level discourse element identification and organization evaluation. Evaluation shows that some minority discourse elements, such as *thesis* and *ideas*, are more difficult to recognize, and organization evaluation of argumentative essays is still challenging due to the lack of large-scale training data. However, visualizing recognized discourse elements helps teachers quickly see the organization structure of an essay, and helps us collect user feedback through interactions to accumulate more training data.

3.3.2 Discourse Mode Recognition for Narrative Essays

Evaluating organization of narrative essays is even more difficult, since narrative text understanding is still very challenging and open in both theory and practice.

IFlyEA uses discourse modes as discourse elements influenced by (Smith, 2003). The main reasons are: (1) discourse modes can represent the essay organization by segmenting an essay into discourse mode zones; (2) discourse modes are closely related to rhetoric (Connors, 1981; Brooks and Warren, 1958) so that discourse modes can reflect writing proficiency in a degree.

Discourse modes are categorized into *narration*, *description*, *exposition*, *argument* and *emotion*, following (Song et al., 2017). Moreover, we further identify fine-grained description types, such as *appearance, facial expression, action, natural scene, psychology, dialogue* and so on. How to accurately and vividly describe details of a character, a scene or an object is an important lesson to be learned for writing. Identifying and visualizing fine-grained description types let people quickly find some highlights in writing descriptions.

Technically, we adopt a two-stage approach. In the first stage, we use a discourse-level hierarchical encoder to encode an essay and identify 5 discourse modes (Song et al., 2017). The hidden state of each sentence is used as a sentence representation for classification. In the second stage, we further classify descriptive sentences into fine-grained description types, which is formulated as a typical classification problem.

3.3.3 Discourse-level Abnormal Detection and Content Analysis

Abnormal detection is important for building a robust system. For example, intentional plagiarism is a terrible behavior and should be detected. We build a large-scale corpus covering common plagiarism resource, and exploit IR techniques and semantic matching to detect plagiarism. We also filter out malicious input, such as non-Chinese essays or meaningless character sequences, utilizing a pre-trained language model.

Other content analysis, including off-topic detection, genre classification, and topic classification, are also required to support the comprehensive assessment of essays. We formulate these tasks as a classification problem. The genre and topic classification can be well solved, while off-topic detection is very challenging at present.

4 Application Modules

4.1 Essay Scoring

Essay scoring is a main module for AES. Instead of giving a single general score only, we consider scoring from multiple aspects additionally, including *content*, *expression*, *rhetoric* and *organization*, to provide a comprehensive assessment.

We formulate these scoring tasks as an essay classification problem, classifying a given essay into four grades: *bad, moderate, good* and *excellent*. We construct a feature-based model for each task, and use different feature templates for different aspects. The feature templates can be divided into three types: *basic features*, such as length, vocabulary, syntax and distributed dense representations; *common analytical features*, which are based on the output of our analytical modules, such as the counts of spelling and grammatical errors, and the use of rhetorical devices; and *genre related features*, for example, we use different strategies for modeling the organization of narrative and argumentative essays so that the features would be extracted accordingly.

4.2 Review Generation

Generating a review based on the multi-level evaluation can benefit students for getting direct instructions, and also benefit teachers for getting scoring reports fast and automatically. Currently, our system generates reviews based on a series of predefined templates. The scores of multiple aspects and the whole essay are generated by essay scoring module. According to these scores, the system would manage template selection and integration to generate a coherent review, revealing both the advantages and the shortcomings of an essay.

4.3 Recommendation

In addition to rate and review essays, it is also important to help students learn from feedback to overcome existing weaknesses. To tackle this, We build a module to recommend relevant materials according to diagnosis results at three levels.

We trigger the grammar-level recommendation if spelling errors are detected. In addition to recommending the correct characters, IFlyEA will automatically generate a set of cloze test questions. We first retrieve sentences containing the correct character from an existing corpus of this module, then mask the character in each sentence, and mix it with characters from its confusion set, and finally let students choose the best character to fill the blank. We expect students can better master correct usage of characters and distinguish confusion characters through exercises. As a supplement, the meaning and example usage of both the correct character and its confusion set are prepared previously, which will be displayed after the exercises.

At rhetoric level, we recommend some well-written rhetorical sentences that describe similar objects or scenes as in the target essay, while at discourse level, we show more well-written essays or passages related to similar topics. To achieve this, we have constructed a high quality resource bank of high scoring essays, proses and novels written by famous writers. We use the analytical modules to analyze the resource to support recommendations according to different demands.

5 Conclusion and Future Work

This paper presented IFlyEA, a Chinese automated essay assessment system. IFlyEA demonstrates the techniques, that we have developed, could tackle with evaluating the quality of essays written by native Chinese students. A demonstrating video is available at `https://youtu.be/BujBQfxvX3A`.

The main advantage of IFlyEA is its multi-level and multi-dimension analytical modules for essay assessment, especially on several high level skillful language usage abilities, which is less studied previously. Most of these modules can achieve moderate and above performance. IFlyEA also provides comprehensive services for rating, review generation and recommendation. Together with the visualization and interactive interfaces, teachers and students can get useful feedback and easily understand why the system makes such predictions.

IFlyEA has been applied in practice. In future, we plan to conduct more user studies and continue to improve the system. And how to evaluate the impact of the system on students is another important problem, which is worth exploring.

References

Yigal Attali and Jill Burstein. 2006. Automated essay scoring with e-rater v. 2. *The Journal of Technology, Learning and Assessment*, 4(3).

Dzmitry Bahdanau, Kyunghyun Cho, and Yoshua Bengio. 2014. Neural machine translation by jointly learning to align and translate. *CoRR*, abs/1409.0473.

Samuel Bell, Helen Yannakoudakis, and Marek Rei. 2019. Context is key: Grammatical error detection with contextual word representations. In *Proceedings of the Fourteenth Workshop on Innovative Use of NLP for Building Educational Applications*, pages 103–115, Florence, Italy. Association for Computational Linguistics.

Cleanth Brooks and Robert Penn Warren. 1958. *Modern rhetoric*. Harcourt, Brace.

Jill Burstein, Daniel Marcu, and Kevin Knight. 2003. Finding the write stuff: Automatic identification of discourse structure in student essays. *IEEE Intelligent Systems*, 18(1):32–39.

Hongbo Chen and Ben He. 2013. Automated essay scoring by maximizing human-machine agreement. In *Proceedings of the 2013 Conference on Empirical Methods in Natural Language Processing*, pages 1741–1752, Seattle, Washington, USA. Association for Computational Linguistics.

Robert J Connors. 1981. The rise and fall of the modes of discourse. *College Composition and Communication*, 32(4):444–455.

Jacob Devlin, Ming-Wei Chang, Kenton Lee, and Kristina Toutanova. 2019. BERT: Pre-training of deep bidirectional transformers for language understanding. In *Proceedings of the 2019 Conference of the North American Chapter of the Association for Computational Linguistics: Human Language Technologies, Volume 1 (Long and Short Papers)*, pages 4171–4186, Minneapolis, Minnesota. Association for Computational Linguistics.

Fei Dong, Yue Zhang, and Jie Yang. 2017. Attention-based recurrent convolutional neural network for automatic essay scoring. In *Proceedings of the 21st Conference on Computational Natural Language Learning (CoNLL 2017)*, pages 153–162.

Ruiji Fu, Zhengqi Pei, Jiefu Gong, Wei Song, Dechuan Teng, Wanxiang Che, Shijin Wang, Guoping Hu, and Ting Liu. 2018. Chinese grammatical error diagnosis using statistical and prior knowledge driven features with probabilistic ensemble enhancement. In *Proceedings of the 5th Workshop on Natural Language Processing Techniques for Educational Applications*, pages 52–59, Melbourne, Australia. Association for Computational Linguistics.

George Lakoff and Mark Johnson. 2008. *Metaphors we live by*. University of Chicago press.

Lizhen Liu, Xiao Hu, Wei Song, Ruiji Fu, Ting Liu, and Guoping Hu. 2018. Neural multitask learning for simile recognition. In *Proceedings of the 2018 Conference on Empirical Methods in Natural Language Processing*, pages 1543–1553, Brussels, Belgium. Association for Computational Linguistics.

Xiaodong Liu, Kevin Cheng, Yanyan Luo, Kevin Duh, and Yuji Matsumoto. 2013. A hybrid Chinese spelling correction using language model and statistical machine translation with reranking. In *Proceedings of the Seventh SIGHAN Workshop on Chinese Language Processing*, pages 54–58, Nagoya, Japan. Asian Federation of Natural Language Processing.

Jiaju Mei. 1984. *同义词词林(Synonymy Thesaurus of Chinese Words)*, volume 1983. 商务印书馆; 上海.

Hwee Tou Ng, Siew Mei Wu, Ted Briscoe, Christian Hadiwinoto, Raymond Hendy Susanto, and Christopher Bryant. 2014. The CoNLL-2014 shared task on grammatical error correction. In *Proceedings of the Eighteenth Conference on Computational Natural Language Learning: Shared Task*, pages 1–14, Baltimore, Maryland. Association for Computational Linguistics.

Ellis B Page. 1968. The use of the computer in analyzing student essays. *International review of education*, pages 210–225.

Isaac Persing, Alan Davis, and Vincent Ng. 2010. Modeling organization in student essays. In *Proceedings of the 2010 Conference on Empirical Methods in Natural Language Processing*, pages 229–239.

Peter Phandi, Kian Ming A. Chai, and Hwee Tou Ng. 2015. Flexible domain adaptation for automated essay scoring using correlated linear regression. In *Proceedings of the 2015 Conference on Empirical Methods in Natural Language Processing*, pages 431–439, Lisbon, Portugal. Association for Computational Linguistics.

Gaoqi Rao, Qi Gong, Baolin Zhang, and Endong Xun. 2018. Overview of NLPTEA-2018 share task Chinese grammatical error diagnosis. In *Proceedings of the 5th Workshop on Natural Language Processing Techniques for Educational Applications*, pages 42–51, Melbourne, Australia. Association for Computational Linguistics.

Gaoqi Rao, Erhong Yang, and Baolin Zhang. 2020. Overview of NLPTEA-2020 shared task for Chinese grammatical error diagnosis. In *Proceedings of the 6th Workshop on Natural Language Processing Techniques for Educational Applications*, pages 25–35, Suzhou, China. Association for Computational Linguistics.

Lawrence M Rudner, Veronica Garcia, and Catherine Welch. 2006. An evaluation of intellimetricessay scoring system. *The Journal of Technology, Learning and Assessment*, 4(4).

Carlota S Smith. 2003. *Modes of discourse: The local structure of texts*, volume 103. Cambridge University Press.

Swapna Somasundaran, Jill Burstein, and Martin Chodorow. 2014. Lexical chaining for measuring discourse coherence quality in test-taker essays. In *Proceedings of COLING 2014, the 25th International conference on computational linguistics: Technical papers*, pages 950–961.

Wei Song, Ruiji Fu, Lizhen Liu, and Ting Liu. 2015. Discourse element identification in student essays based on global and local cohesion. In *Proceedings of the 2015 Conference on Empirical Methods in Natural Language Processing*, pages 2255–2261, Lisbon, Portugal. Association for Computational Linguistics.

Wei Song and LiZhen Liu. 2020. Representation learning in discourse parsing: A survey. *Science China Technological Sciences*, pages 1–26.

Wei Song, Tong Liu, Ruiji Fu, Lizhen Liu, Hanshi Wang, and Ting Liu. 2016. Learning to identify sentence parallelism in student essays. In *Proceedings of COLING 2016, the 26th International Conference on Computational Linguistics: Technical Papers*, pages 794–803, Osaka, Japan. The COLING 2016 Organizing Committee.

Wei Song, Ziyao Song, Ruiji Fu, Lizhen Liu, Miaomiao Cheng, and Ting Liu. 2020a. Discourse self-attention for discourse element identification in argumentative student essays. In *Proceedings of the 2020 Conference on Empirical Methods in Natural Language Processing (EMNLP)*, pages 2820–2830, Online. Association for Computational Linguistics.

Wei Song, Ziyao Song, Lizhen Liu, and Ruiji Fu. 2020b. Hierarchical multi-task learning for organization evaluation of argumentative student essays. In *Proceedings of the Twenty-Ninth International Joint Conference on Artificial Intelligence, IJCAI-20*, pages 3875–3881. International Joint Conferences on Artificial Intelligence Organization. Main track.

Wei Song, Dong Wang, Ruiji Fu, Lizhen Liu, Ting Liu, and Guoping Hu. 2017. Discourse mode identification in essays. In *Proceedings of the 55th Annual Meeting of the Association for Computational Linguistics (Volume 1: Long Papers)*, pages 112–122.

Wei Song, Kai Zhang, Ruiji Fu, Lizhen Liu, Ting Liu, and Miaomiao Cheng. 2020c. Multi-stage pre-training for automated chinese essay scoring. In *Proceedings of the 2020 Conference on Empirical Methods in Natural Language Processing (EMNLP)*, pages 6723–6733.

Kaveh Taghipour and Hwee Tou Ng. 2016. A neural approach to automated essay scoring. In *Proceedings of the 2016 Conference on Empirical Methods in Natural Language Processing*, pages 1882–1891, Austin, Texas. Association for Computational Linguistics.

Chung-Ting Tsai, Jhih-Jie Chen, Ching-Yu Yang, and Jason S. Chang. 2020. LinggleWrite: a coaching system for essay writing. In *Proceedings of the 58th Annual Meeting of the Association for Computational Linguistics: System Demonstrations*, pages 127–133, Online. Association for Computational Linguistics.

Yuen-Hsien Tseng, Lung-Hao Lee, Li-Ping Chang, and Hsin-Hsi Chen. 2015. Introduction to SIGHAN 2015 bake-off for Chinese spelling check. In *Proceedings of the Eighth SIGHAN Workshop on Chinese Language Processing*, pages 32–37, Beijing, China. Association for Computational Linguistics.

Dingmin Wang, Yi Tay, and Li Zhong. 2019. Confusionset-guided pointer networks for Chinese spelling check. In *Proceedings of the 57th Annual Meeting of the Association for Computational Linguistics*, pages 5780–5785, Florence, Italy. Association for Computational Linguistics.

Shaolei Wang, Baoxin Wang, Jiefu Gong, Zhongyuan Wang, Xiao Hu, Xingyi Duan, Zizhuo Shen, Gang Yue, Ruiji Fu, Dayong Wu, Wanxiang Che, Shijin Wang, Guoping Hu, and Ting Liu. 2020. Combining ResNet and transformer for Chinese grammatical error diagnosis. In *Proceedings of the 6th Workshop on Natural Language Processing Techniques for Educational Applications*, pages 36–43, Suzhou, China. Association for Computational Linguistics.

Helen Yannakoudakis, Ted Briscoe, and Ben Medlock. 2011. A new dataset and method for automatically grading ESOL texts. In *Proceedings of the 49th Annual Meeting of the Association for Computational Linguistics: Human Language Technologies*, pages 180–189, Portland, Oregon, USA. Association for Computational Linguistics.

Junjie Yu and Zhenghua Li. 2014. Chinese spelling error detection and correction based on language model, pronunciation, and shape. In *Proceedings of The Third CIPS-SIGHAN Joint Conference on Chinese Language Processing*, pages 220–223, Wuhan, China. Association for Computational Linguistics.

Shaohua Zhang, Haoran Huang, Jicong Liu, and Hang Li. 2020. Spelling error correction with soft-masked BERT. In *Proceedings of the 58th Annual Meeting of the Association for Computational Linguistics*, pages 882–890, Online. Association for Computational Linguistics.

Ecco: An Open Source Library for the Explainability of Transformer Language Models

J Alammar
Arpeggio Research
`ar.pegg.io`
`jay.alammar@pegg.io`

Abstract

Our understanding of *why* Transformer-based NLP models have been achieving their recent success lags behind our ability to continue scaling these models. To increase the transparency of Transformer-based language models, we present Ecco – an open-source[1] library for the explainability of Transformer-based NLP models. Ecco provides a set of tools to capture, analyze, visualize, and interactively explore inner mechanics of these models. This includes (1) gradient-based feature attribution for natural language generation (2) hidden states and their evolution between model layers (3) convenient access and examination tools for neuron activations in the under-explored Feed-Forward Neural Network sublayer of Transformer layers. (4) convenient examination of activation vectors via canonical correlation analysis (CCA), non-negative matrix factorization (NMF), and probing classifiers. We find that syntactic information can be retrieved from BERT's FFNN representations in levels comparable to those in hidden state representations. More curiously, we find that the model builds up syntactic information in its hidden states *even* when intermediate FFNNs indicate diminished levels of syntactic information. Ecco is available at `https://www.eccox.io/`.[2]

1 Introduction

The Transformer architecture (Vaswani et al., 2017) has been powering many recent advances in NLP. A breakdown of this architecture is provided by Alammar (2018) and will help understand this paper's details. Pre-trained language models based on the architecture (Liu et al., 2018; Devlin et al., 2018; Radford et al., 2018, 2019; Liu et al., 2019; Brown et al., 2020) continue to push the envelope in various tasks in NLP and, more recently, in computer vision (Dosovitskiy et al., 2020). Our understanding of why these models work so well, however, still lags behind these developments.

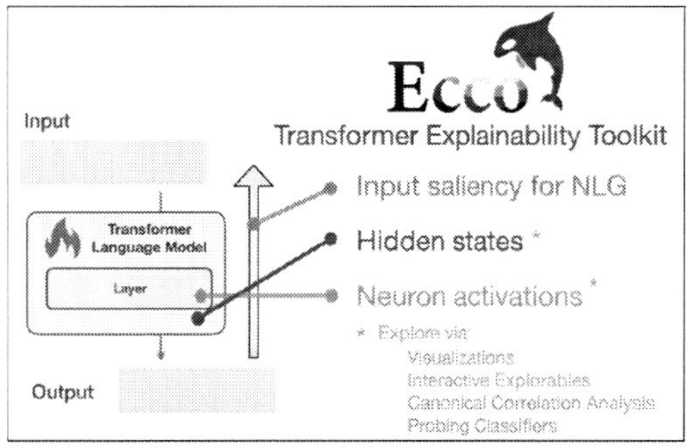

Figure 1: **A set of tools to make the inner workings of Transformer language models more transparent.** By introducing tools that analyze and visualize input saliency (for natural language generation), hidden states, and neuron activations, we aim to enable researchers to build more intuition about Transformer language models.

Ecco provides tools and interactive explorable explanations[3] aiding the examination and intuition of:

- **Input saliency** methods that score input tokens importance to generating a token are discussed in section 2.
- **Hidden state evolution** across the layers of the model and what it may tell us about each layer's role. This is discussed in section 3.
- **Neuron activations** and how individual and groups of model neurons spike in response to inputs and to produce outputs. This is discussed in section 4.

[1]The code is available at `https://github.com/jalammar/ecco`

[2]Video demo available at `https://youtu.be/bcEysXmR09c`

[3]`http://worrydream.com/ExplorableExplanations/`

Proceedings of the Joint Conference of the 59th Annual Meeting of the Association for Computational Linguistics and the 11th International Joint Conference on Natural Language Processing: System Demonstrations, pages 249–257, August 1st - August 6th, 2021.

- **Non-negative matrix factorization of neuron activations** to uncover underlying patterns of neuron firings, revealing firing patterns of linguistic properties of input tokens. This is discussed in subsection 4.2.

Ecco creates rich, interactive interfaces directly inside Jupyter notebooks (Ragan-Kelley et al., 2014) running on pre-trained models from the Hugging Face transformers library (Wolf et al., 2020). Currently it supports GPT2 (Radford et al., 2018), BERT (Devlin et al., 2018), and RoBERTa (Liu et al., 2019). Support for more models and explainability methods is under development and open for community contribution.

2 Input Saliency

When a computer vision model classifies a picture as containing a husky, an input saliency map (Figure 2) can tell us whether the classification was made due to the visual properties of the animal itself or because of the snow in the background (Ribeiro et al., 2016). This is a method of attribution explaining the relationship between a model's output and inputs – helping us detect errors and biases to better understand the system's behavior.

Figure 2: Input saliency map attribute a model's prediction to input pixels.

Multiple methods exist for assigning feature importance scores to the inputs of an NLP model (Li et al., 2015; Arrieta et al., 2020). Instead of assigning scores to pixels, in the NLP domain these methods assign scores to input tokens. The literature is most often concerned with this application for classification tasks rather than natural language generation. Ecco enables generating output tokens and then interactively exploring the saliency values for each output token.

2.1 Saliency View

In Figure 3, we see an experiment to probe the world knowledge of GPT2-XL. We ask the model to output William Shakespeare's date of birth. The model is correctly able to produce the date (1564, but broken into two tokens: *15* and *64*, because the model's vocabulary does not include *1564* as a single token). By hovering on each token, Ecco imposes each input's saliency value as a background color. The darker the color, the more that input token is attributed responsibility for generating this output token.

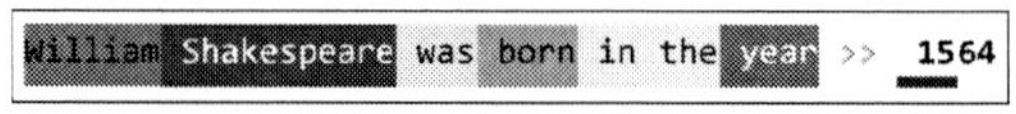

(a) Input saliency for the first output token, *15* (shown by hovering over *15*).

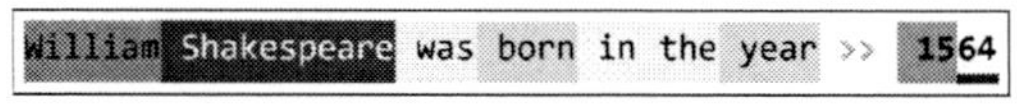

(b) Input saliency for the second output token, *64* (shown by hovering over *64*).

Figure 3: **GPT2-XL is able to tell the birth date of William Shakespeare.** It expresses it in two tokens: *15* and *64*. Ecco shows the input saliency of each of these tokens using Gradient X Inputs. The darker the background color of the token is, the higher its saliency value.

2.2 Detailed Saliency View

Ecco also provides a detailed view to see the attribution values in more precision. Figure 4 demonstrates this interactive interface which displays the normalized attribution value as a percentage and bar next to each token.

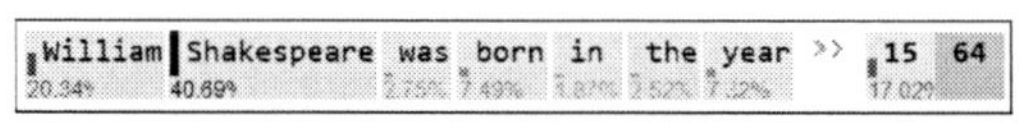

Figure 4: Ecco's detailed input saliency view for the token *64* (shown by hovering over *64*).

About Gradient-Based Saliency Ecco calculates feature importance based on Gradients X Inputs (Denil et al., 2015; Shrikumar et al., 2017) – a gradient-based saliency method shown by Atanasova et al. (2020) to perform well across various datasets for text classification in Transformer models.

Gradients X Inputs can be calculated using the following formula:

$$\|\nabla_{X_i} f_c(X_{1:n}) X_i\|_2$$

Where X_i is the embedding vector of the input token at timestep *i*, and $\nabla_{X_i} f_c(X_{1:n})$ is the back-propagated gradient of the score of the selected token. The resulting vector is then aggregated into a score via calculating the $L2$ norm as this was

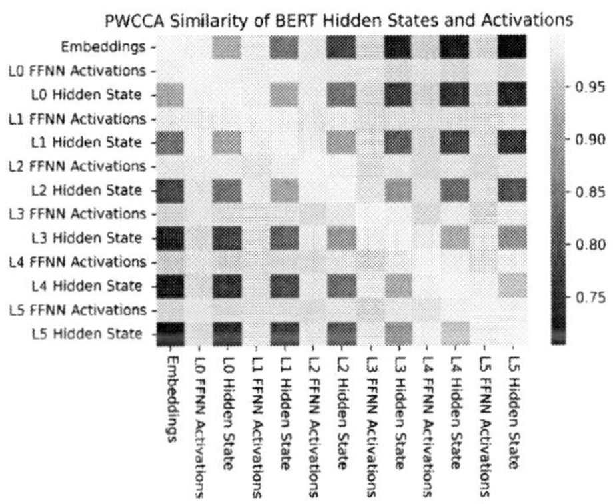

Figure 6: **Similarity of hidden states and FFNN activations in a distilled BERT model.** Ecco enables capturing neuron activations and comparing activation space similarity using Projection Weighted Canonical Correlation Analysis (PWCCA).

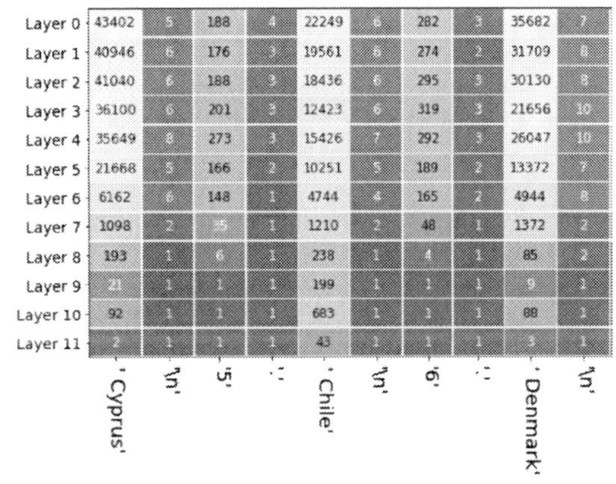

Figure 7: **Evolution of the rankings of a list of countries across the 12 layers of GPT2-XL.** The prediction represented here is generated using GPT2-XL, on the input sequence `"The countries of the European Union are:\n1. Austria\n2. Belgium\n3. Bulgaria\n4"`. Output decoding strategy used is top50 sampling.

empirically shown by Atanasova et al. (2020) to perform better than other methods.

3 Hidden States Examination

Another method to glean information about the inner workings of a language is by examining the hidden states produced by every Transformer block. Ecco provides multiple methods to examine the hidden states and to visualize how they evolve across the layers of the model.

3.1 Canonical Correlation Analysis (CCA)

Recent work has used Canonical Correlation Analysis (Hotelling, 1992) to examine language model internal representations. For example, Voita et al. (2019) used hidden state to analyze the flow of information inside Transformers and how the informational content of hidden states compares across tasks. Singh et al. (2019) examined internal representations of multilingual BERT. Wu et al. (2020) compared the internal representations of multiple NLP models. More specifically, these works used recently developed methods like SVCCA (Raghu et al., 2017), PWCCA (Morcos et al., 2018) and CKA (Kornblith et al., 2019).

Ecco bundles these methods (`cca()`, `svcca()`, `pwcca()`, and `cka()`) to allow convenient similarity comparison of language model representations. This includes hidden state representations, yet also extends to neuron activations (Ecco pays special attention to the neurons after the largest dense FFNN layer as can be seen in Section 4). Figure 6 shows a comparison of the hidden states and FFNN neuron activations as the model processes textual input. All three CCA methods take two activation vectors (be they hidden states or neuron activations) and assign a similarity score from zero (no correlation) to one (the two inputs are linear transformations of each other).

3.2 Ranking of Output Token Across Layers

Nostalgebraist (2020) presents compelling visual treatments showcasing the evolution of token rankings, logit scores, and softmax probabilities for the evolving hidden state through the various layers of the model. The author does this by projecting the hidden state into the output vocabulary using the language model head (which is typically used only for the output of the final layer).

Ecco enables creating such plots as can be seen in Figure 7. More examples showcasing this method can be found in(Alammar, 2021).

3.3 Comparing Token Rankings

Ecco also allows asking questions about which of two tokens the model chooses to output for a specific position. This includes questions of subject-verb agreement like those posed by Linzen et al. (2016). In that task, we want to analyze the model's

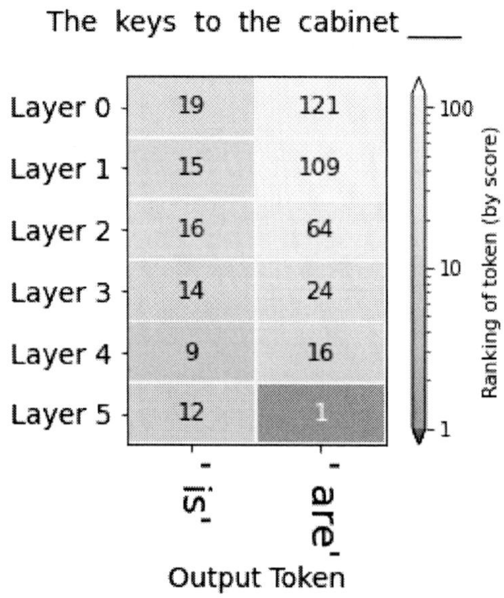

Figure 8: **Rankings, across model layers, of which token should go in the blank** DistillGPT-2 is prompted by the prompt shown at the top, while limited to two output tokens shown on the bottom.

capacity to encode syntactic number (whether the subject we're addressing is singular or plural) and syntactic subjecthood (which subject in the sentence we're addressing). Put simply, fill-in the blank. The only acceptable answers are 1) *is* 2) *are*:

The keys to the cabinet ______

Using Ecco, we can present this sentence to DistilGPT-2, and visualize the rankings of *is* and *are* using `ecco.rankings_watch()`, which creates Figure 8. The first column shows the rankings of the token *is* as the completion of the sentence, and the second column shows those for the token *are* for that same position. The model ultimately ranks *are* as the more probable answer, but the figure raises the question of why five layers fail to rank *are* higher than *is*, and only the final layer sets the record straight.

4 Neuron Activations

The Feed-Forward Neural Network (FFNN) sublayer is one of the two major components inside a Transformer block (in addition to self-attention). It often makes up two-thirds of a Transformer block's parameters, thus providing a significant portion of the model's representational capacity. Previous work (Karpathy et al., 2015; Strobelt et al., 2017; Poerner et al., 2018; Radford et al., 2017; Olah et al., 2017, 2018; Bau et al., 2018; Dalvi et al., 2019; Rethmeier et al., 2020) has examined neuron firings inside deep neural networks in both the NLP and computer vision domains. Ecco makes it easier to examine neuron activations by collecting them and providing tools to analyze them and reduce their dimensionality to extract underlying patterns.

4.1 Probing classifiers

Probing classifiers (Veldhoen et al., 2016; Adi et al., 2016; Conneau et al., 2018) are the most commonly used method for associating NLP model components with linguistic properties (Belinkov and Glass, 2019). Ecco currently supports linear probes with control tasks (Hewitt and Liang, 2019). Section 5 is a case study on using this method to probe FFNN representations for part-of-speech information.

4.2 Uncovering underlying patterns with NMF

By first capturing the activations of the neurons in FFNN layers of the model and then decomposing them into a more manageable number of factors through NMF, we can shed light on how various neuron groups respond to input tokens.

Figure 9 shows intuitively interpretable firing patterns extracted from raw firings through NMF. This example, showcasing ten factors applied to the activations of layer #0 in response to a text passage, helps us identify neurons that respond to syntactic and semantic properties of the input text. The factor highlighted in this screenshot, factor 5, seems to correlate with pronouns.

This interface can compress a lot of data that showcase the excitement levels of factors (and, by extension, groups of neurons). The sparklines (Tufte, 2006) on the left give a snapshot of the excitement level of each factor across the entire sequence. Interacting with the sparklines (by hovering with a mouse or tapping) displays the activation of the factor on the tokens in the sequence on the right.

4.3 About Matrix Factorization of Neuron Activity

Figure 10 explains the intuition behind dimensionality reduction using NMF. This method can reveal underlying behavior common to groups of neurons. It can be used to analyze the entire network, a single layer, or groups of layers.

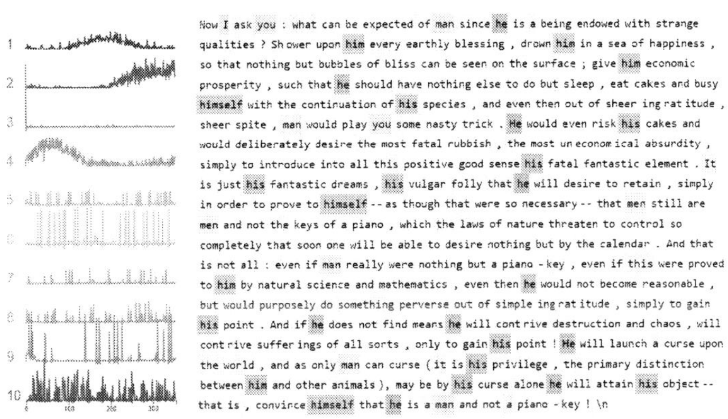

Figure 9: **Individual factor view: Activation pattern in response to pronouns** Ten Factors extracted from the activations the neurons in Layer 0 in response to a passage from *Notes from Underground.* Hovering on the line graphs isolates the tokens of a single factor and imposes the magnitude of the factor's activation on the tokens as a background color. The darker the color the higher the activation magnitude. In addition to the pronouns factor highlighted in the figure, we can see factors that focus on specific regions of the text (beginning, middle, and end). This indicates neurons that are sensitive to positional encodings. View this interface online at (Alammar, 2020).

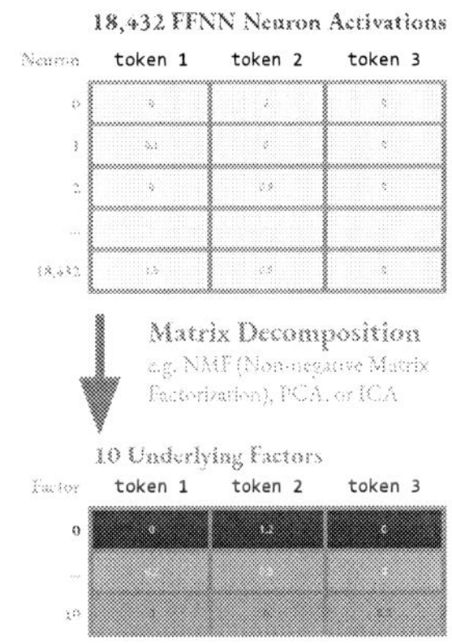

Figure 10: **Decomposition of activations matrix using Non-negative Matrix Factorization.** NMF reveals underlying patterns of neuron activations inside one layer, a collection of layers, or the entire model.

5 Case study: Probing FFNN neuron activations for PoS information

In this section, we use Ecco to examine the representations of BERT's Feed-Forward Neural Network using probing classifiers. Our work is most similar to Durrani et al. (2020). There has been plenty of work on probing BERT focused on the hidden states, but none to our knowledge that trained probes to extract token information from the FFNN representation.

5.1 Method

We first forward-pass the entire dataset through BERT. We capture all the hidden states of all the model's layers as well as the neuron activations of the FFNN sublayers (namely, the widest layer composed of 3072 neurons after the GELU activation). We then train external linear classifiers to predict the PoS of the tokens in the dataset and then report the accuracy on the test set. Because probes have been criticized as memorizing the inputs, we report selectivity scores (Hewitt and Liang, 2019) next to each accuracy score. Selectivity is metric that is calculated by generating a control task where each token is assigned a random part-of-speech tag. A separate probe is then trained on this control set. The difference in accuracy between the actual dataset and the control dataset is the selectivity score. The higher selectivity is, the more we can say that the probe really extracted part-of-speech data from the representation of the model as opposed to simply memorizing the training set.

5.2 Experimental Setup

We use the Universal Dependencies version 2 part-of-speech dataset in English. We extract 10,000 tokens and split them into a 67% and 33% train/test sets. We train linear probes for 50 epochs using the Adam optimizer. We run experiments with learning rates (0.1, 0.001, 1e-5) and report those of the best achieving learning rate (0.001). We run five trials and report their average results. For every trial, we train a probe for each permutation of 1) model layer 2) hidden state vs. FFNN activations 3) actual labels vs. random controls to calculate selectivity scores.

5.3 Results

We report accuracy and selectivity scores in Table 1. We observe that FFNN neuron activations do encode PoS information at levels comparable to hidden states. We find intriguing the divergence of scores in layers 2 and 3 between FFNN activations (which drop slightly) and hidden states (which continue increasing). Future work can examine if this divergence points towards layers storing different

layer id	FFNN Activations				Hidden States (context. embeds)			
	accuracy		selectivity		accuracy		selectivity	
Embed	- - -		- - -		**87.6**	(±0.5)	**6.1**	(±1.1)
0	90.5	(±0.4)	9.1	(±0.7)	92.2	(±0.3)	13.6	(±0.8)
1	93.3	(±0.5)	14.8	(±0.8)	93.6	(±0.4)	17.9	(± 1)
2	87.3	(±0.5)	35.9	(±0.5)	**94.2**	(±0.3)	20.9	(±0.8)
3	**84.7**	(±0.5)	34.6	(±0.3)	**94.7**	(±0.3)	23.9	(±0.7)
4	94.2	(±0.3)	18.9	(±0.6)	94.9	(±0.2)	27.5	(±0.6)
5	94.6	(±0.3)	22.2	(±0.6)	94.8	(±0.3)	31.5	(±0.7)
6	93.6	(±0.5)	27.1	(±1.1)	94.1	(±0.4)	34.3	(±0.8)
7	92.8	(±0.6)	31.5	(±0.5)	93.7	(±0.6)	36.0	(±0.4)
8	91.9	(±0.6)	34.4	(±1.1)	92.4	(±0.7)	37.1	(±0.5)
9	90.5	(±0.4)	35.2	(±0.4)	91.6	(±0.6)	37.3	(±0.7)
10	88.8	(±0.5)	36.4	(±0.6)	90.6	(±0.5)	37.3	(±0.9)
11	87.9	(±0.5)	36.5	(±0.8)	89.0	(±0.7)	36.7	(±1.1)

Table 1: Probing BERT representations for Part-of-Speech information. **We can see that raw embeddings already have some PoS information encoded, but the low selectivity indicates this accuracy score is inflated. (Embed layer)** The model continues to build PoS information through the first half of the network, increasing in both accuracy and selectivity (Layers 0-5). FFNN representations are comparable to hidden states in the quantity of PoS information our probes can extract. It is interesting that **a layer can increase PoS information** despite its FFNN showing **lower accuracy** (layer 3). This could indicate that different FFNN sublayers encode different subsets of PoS information and the model is able to extract only the subset of information that layer specializes in.

subsets of PoS information which the model is able to collect and assemble as it builds up its internal representations across layers.

6 System Design

Ecco is implemented as a python library that provides a wrapper around a pre-trained language model. The wrapper collects the required data from the language model (e.g., neuron activations, hidden states) and makes the needed calculations (e.g., input saliency, NMF dimensionality reduction). The interactive visualizations are built using web technologies manipulated through D3.js (Bostock et al., 2012).

Ecco is built on top of open source libraries including Scikit-Learn (Pedregosa et al., 2011), Matplotlib (Hunter, 2007), NumPy (Walt et al., 2011), PyTorch (Paszke et al., 2019) and Transformers (Wolf et al., 2020). Canonical Correlation Analysis is calculated using the code open-sourced[4] by the authors (Raghu et al., 2017; Morcos et al., 2018; Kornblith et al., 2019).

7 Limitations

Ecco's input saliency feature is currently only supported for GPT2-based models, while neuron activation collection and dimensionality reduction are supported for GPT2 in addition to BERT and RoBERTa.

We echo the sentiment of Leavitt and Morcos (2020) that visualization has a role in building intuitions, but that researchers are encouraged to use that as a starting point towards building testable and falsifiable hypotheses of model interpretability.

8 Conclusion

As language models proliferate, more tools are needed to aid debugging models, explain their behavior, and build intuitions about their inner-mechanics. Ecco is one such tool combining ease of use, visual interactive explorables, and multiple model explainability methods.

Ecco is open-source software[5] and contributions are welcome.

Acknowledgments

This work was improved thanks to feedback provided by Abdullah Almaatouq, Anfal Alatawi, Christopher Olah, Fahd Alhazmi, Hadeel Al-Negheimish, Hend Al-Khalifa, Isabelle Augenstein, Jasmijn Bastings, Najwa Alghamdi, Pepa Atanasova, and Sebastian Gehrmann.

[4]https://github.com/google/svcca

[5]https://github.com/jalammar/ecco

References

Yossi Adi, Einat Kermany, Yonatan Belinkov, Ofer Lavi, and Yoav Goldberg. 2016. Fine-grained analysis of sentence embeddings using auxiliary prediction tasks. *arXiv preprint arXiv:1608.04207*.

J Alammar. 2018. The illustrated transformer.

J Alammar. 2020. Interfaces for explaining transformer language models.

J Alammar. 2021. Finding the words to say: Hidden state visualizations for language models.

Alejandro Barredo Arrieta, Natalia Díaz-Rodríguez, Javier Del Ser, Adrien Bennetot, Siham Tabik, Alberto Barbado, Salvador García, Sergio Gil-López, Daniel Molina, Richard Benjamins, et al. 2020. Explainable artificial intelligence (xai): Concepts, taxonomies, opportunities and challenges toward responsible ai. *Information Fusion*, 58:82–115.

Pepa Atanasova, Jakob Grue Simonsen, Christina Lioma, and Isabelle Augenstein. 2020. A diagnostic study of explainability techniques for text classification.

Anthony Bau, Yonatan Belinkov, Hassan Sajjad, Nadir Durrani, Fahim Dalvi, and James Glass. 2018. Identifying and controlling important neurons in neural machine translation.

Yonatan Belinkov and James Glass. 2019. Analysis methods in neural language processing: A survey. *Transactions of the Association for Computational Linguistics*, 7:49–72.

Mike Bostock et al. 2012. D3. js-data-driven documents.

Tom B Brown, Benjamin Mann, Nick Ryder, Melanie Subbiah, Jared Kaplan, Prafulla Dhariwal, Arvind Neelakantan, Pranav Shyam, Girish Sastry, Amanda Askell, et al. 2020. Language models are few-shot learners. *arXiv preprint arXiv:2005.14165*.

Alexis Conneau, Germán Kruszewski, Guillaume Lample, Loïc Barrault, and Marco Baroni. 2018. What you can cram into a single vector: Probing sentence embeddings for linguistic properties. *arXiv preprint arXiv:1805.01070*.

Fahim Dalvi, Avery Nortonsmith, Anthony Bau, Yonatan Belinkov, Hassan Sajjad, Nadir Durrani, and James Glass. 2019. Neurox: A toolkit for analyzing individual neurons in neural networks. In *Proceedings of the AAAI Conference on Artificial Intelligence*, volume 33, pages 9851–9852.

Misha Denil, Alban Demiraj, and Nando de Freitas. 2015. Extraction of salient sentences from labelled documents.

Jacob Devlin, Ming-Wei Chang, Kenton Lee, and Kristina Toutanova. 2018. Bert: Pre-training of deep bidirectional transformers for language understanding. *arXiv preprint arXiv:1810.04805*.

Alexey Dosovitskiy, Lucas Beyer, Alexander Kolesnikov, Dirk Weissenborn, Xiaohua Zhai, Thomas Unterthiner, Mostafa Dehghani, Matthias Minderer, Georg Heigold, Sylvain Gelly, et al. 2020. An image is worth 16x16 words: Transformers for image recognition at scale. *arXiv preprint arXiv:2010.11929*.

Nadir Durrani, Hassan Sajjad, Fahim Dalvi, and Yonatan Belinkov. 2020. Analyzing individual neurons in pre-trained language models. *arXiv preprint arXiv:2010.02695*.

John Hewitt and Percy Liang. 2019. Designing and interpreting probes with control tasks. In *Proceedings of the 2019 Conference on Empirical Methods in Natural Language Processing and the 9th International Joint Conference on Natural Language Processing (EMNLP-IJCNLP)*, pages 2733–2743, Hong Kong, China. Association for Computational Linguistics.

Harold Hotelling. 1992. Relations between two sets of variates. In *Breakthroughs in statistics*, pages 162–190. Springer.

John D Hunter. 2007. Matplotlib: A 2d graphics environment. *Computing in science & engineering*, 9(3):90–95.

Andrej Karpathy, Justin Johnson, and Li Fei-Fei. 2015. Visualizing and understanding recurrent networks.

Simon Kornblith, Mohammad Norouzi, Honglak Lee, and Geoffrey Hinton. 2019. Similarity of neural network representations revisited. In *International Conference on Machine Learning*, pages 3519–3529. PMLR.

Matthew L. Leavitt and Ari Morcos. 2020. Towards falsifiable interpretability research.

Jiwei Li, Xinlei Chen, Eduard Hovy, and Dan Jurafsky. 2015. Visualizing and understanding neural models in nlp. *arXiv preprint arXiv:1506.01066*.

Tal Linzen, Emmanuel Dupoux, and Yoav Goldberg. 2016. Assessing the ability of lstms to learn syntax-sensitive dependencies. *Transactions of the Association for Computational Linguistics*, 4:521–535.

Peter J Liu, Mohammad Saleh, Etienne Pot, Ben Goodrich, Ryan Sepassi, Lukasz Kaiser, and Noam Shazeer. 2018. Generating wikipedia by summarizing long sequences. *arXiv preprint arXiv:1801.10198*.

Yinhan Liu, Myle Ott, Naman Goyal, Jingfei Du, Mandar Joshi, Danqi Chen, Omer Levy, Mike Lewis, Luke Zettlemoyer, and Veselin Stoyanov. 2019. Roberta: A robustly optimized bert pretraining approach. *arXiv preprint arXiv:1907.11692*.

Ari Morcos, Maithra Raghu, and Samy Bengio. 2018. Insights on representational similarity in neural networks with canonical correlation. In S. Bengio,

H. Wallach, H. Larochelle, K. Grauman, N. Cesa-Bianchi, and R. Garnett, editors, *Advances in Neural Information Processing Systems 31*, pages 5732–5741. Curran Associates, Inc.

Nostalgebraist. 2020. interpreting gpt: the logit lens.

Chris Olah, Alexander Mordvintsev, and Ludwig Schubert. 2017. Feature visualization. *Distill*, 2(11):e7.

Chris Olah, Arvind Satyanarayan, Ian Johnson, Shan Carter, Ludwig Schubert, Katherine Ye, and Alexander Mordvintsev. 2018. The building blocks of interpretability. *Distill*, 3(3):e10.

Adam Paszke, Sam Gross, Francisco Massa, Adam Lerer, James Bradbury, Gregory Chanan, Trevor Killeen, Zeming Lin, Natalia Gimelshein, Luca Antiga, Alban Desmaison, Andreas Kopf, Edward Yang, Zachary DeVito, Martin Raison, Alykhan Tejani, Sasank Chilamkurthy, Benoit Steiner, Lu Fang, Junjie Bai, and Soumith Chintala. 2019. Pytorch: An imperative style, high-performance deep learning library. In *Advances in Neural Information Processing Systems*, volume 32. Curran Associates, Inc.

Fabian Pedregosa, Gaël Varoquaux, Alexandre Gramfort, Vincent Michel, Bertrand Thirion, Olivier Grisel, Mathieu Blondel, Peter Prettenhofer, Ron Weiss, Vincent Dubourg, et al. 2011. Scikit-learn: Machine learning in python. *the Journal of machine Learning research*, 12:2825–2830.

Nina Poerner, Benjamin Roth, and Hinrich Schütze. 2018. Interpretable textual neuron representations for nlp. *arXiv preprint arXiv:1809.07291*.

Alec Radford, Rafal Jozefowicz, and Ilya Sutskever. 2017. Learning to generate reviews and discovering sentiment.

Alec Radford, Karthik Narasimhan, Tim Salimans, and Ilya Sutskever. 2018. Improving language understanding by generative pre-training.

Alec Radford, Jeffrey Wu, Rewon Child, David Luan, Dario Amodei, and Ilya Sutskever. 2019. Language models are unsupervised multitask learners. *OpenAI blog*, 1(8):9.

Min Ragan-Kelley, F Perez, B Granger, T Kluyver, P Ivanov, J Frederic, and M Bussonnier. 2014. The jupyter/ipython architecture: a unified view of computational research, from interactive exploration to communication and publication. *AGUFM*, 2014:H44D–07.

Maithra Raghu, Justin Gilmer, Jason Yosinski, and Jascha Sohl-Dickstein. 2017. Svcca: Singular vector canonical correlation analysis for deep learning dynamics and interpretability. In I. Guyon, U. V. Luxburg, S. Bengio, H. Wallach, R. Fergus, S. Vishwanathan, and R. Garnett, editors, *Advances in Neural Information Processing Systems 30*, pages 6076–6085. Curran Associates, Inc.

Nils Rethmeier, Vageesh Kumar Saxena, and Isabelle Augenstein. 2020. Tx-ray: Quantifying and explaining model-knowledge transfer in (un-) supervised nlp. In *Conference on Uncertainty in Artificial Intelligence*, pages 440–449. PMLR.

Marco Tulio Ribeiro, Sameer Singh, and Carlos Guestrin. 2016. "why should i trust you?": Explaining the predictions of any classifier.

Avanti Shrikumar, Peyton Greenside, Anna Shcherbina, and Anshul Kundaje. 2017. Not just a black box: Learning important features through propagating activation differences.

Jasdeep Singh, Bryan McCann, Richard Socher, and Caiming Xiong. 2019. BERT is not an interlingua and the bias of tokenization. In *Proceedings of the 2nd Workshop on Deep Learning Approaches for Low-Resource NLP (DeepLo 2019)*, pages 47–55, Hong Kong, China. Association for Computational Linguistics.

Hendrik Strobelt, Sebastian Gehrmann, Hanspeter Pfister, and Alexander M. Rush. 2017. Lstmvis: A tool for visual analysis of hidden state dynamics in recurrent neural networks.

Edward R Tufte. 2006. *Beautiful evidence*. Graphis Pr.

Ashish Vaswani, Noam Shazeer, Niki Parmar, Jakob Uszkoreit, Llion Jones, Aidan N Gomez, Łukasz Kaiser, and Illia Polosukhin. 2017. Attention is all you need. In *Advances in neural information processing systems*, pages 5998–6008.

Sara Veldhoen, Dieuwke Hupkes, and Willem H Zuidema. 2016. Diagnostic classifiers revealing how neural networks process hierarchical structure. In *CoCo@ NIPS*.

Elena Voita, Rico Sennrich, and Ivan Titov. 2019. The bottom-up evolution of representations in the transformer: A study with machine translation and language modeling objectives. *arXiv preprint arXiv:1909.01380*.

Stéfan van der Walt, S Chris Colbert, and Gael Varoquaux. 2011. The numpy array: a structure for efficient numerical computation. *Computing in science & engineering*, 13(2):22–30.

Thomas Wolf, Lysandre Debut, Victor Sanh, Julien Chaumond, Clement Delangue, Anthony Moi, Pierric Cistac, Tim Rault, Remi Louf, Morgan Funtowicz, Joe Davison, Sam Shleifer, Patrick von Platen, Clara Ma, Yacine Jernite, Julien Plu, Canwen Xu, Teven Le Scao, Sylvain Gugger, Mariama Drame, Quentin Lhoest, and Alexander Rush. 2020. Transformers: State-of-the-art natural language processing. In *Proceedings of the 2020 Conference on Empirical Methods in Natural Language Processing: System Demonstrations*, pages 38–45, Online. Association for Computational Linguistics.

John Wu, Yonatan Belinkov, Hassan Sajjad, Nadir Durrani, Fahim Dalvi, and James Glass. 2020. Similarity analysis of contextual word representation models. In *Proceedings of the 58th Annual Meeting of the Association for Computational Linguistics*, pages 4638–4655, Online. Association for Computational Linguistics.

PAWLS: PDF Annotation With Labels and Structure

Mark Neumann **Zejiang Shen** **Sam Skjonsberg**

Allen Institute for Artificial Intelligence
{markn, shannons, sams}@allenai.org

Abstract

Adobe's Portable Document Format (PDF) is a popular way of distributing view-only documents with a rich visual markup. This presents a challenge to NLP practitioners who wish to use the information contained within PDF documents for training models or data analysis, because annotating these documents is difficult. In this paper, we present PDF Annotation with Labels and Structure (PAWLS), a new annotation tool designed specifically for the PDF document format. PAWLS is particularly suited for mixed-mode annotation and scenarios in which annotators require extended context to annotate accurately. PAWLS supports span-based textual annotation, N-ary relations and freeform, non-textual bounding boxes, all of which can be exported in convenient formats for training multi-modal machine learning models. A PAWLS demo server is available at https://pawls.apps.allenai.org/ [1] and the source code can be accessed at https://github.com/allenai/pawls.

1 Introduction

Scholars of Natural Language Processing technology rely on access to gold standard annotated data for training and evaluation of learning algorithms. Despite successful attempts to create machine readable document formats such as XML and HTML, the Portable Document Format (PDF) is still widely used for read-only documents which require visual markup, across domains such as scientific publishing, law, and government. This presents a challenge to NLP practitioners, as the PDF format does not contain exhaustive markup information, making it difficult to extract semantically meaningful regions from a PDF. Annotating text extracted from PDFs in a plaintext format is difficult, because the extracted text stream lacks any organization or markup, such as paragraph boundaries, figure placement and page headers/footers.

Existing popular annotation tools such as BRAT (Stenetorp et al., 2012) focus on annotation of user provided plain text in a web browser specifically designed for annotation only. For many labeling tasks, this format is exactly what is required. However, as the scope and ability of natural language processing technology goes beyond purely textual processing due in part to recent advances in large language models (Peters et al., 2018; Devlin et al., 2019, *inter alia*), the context and media in which datasets are created must evolve as well.

In addition, the quality of both data collection and evaluation methodology is highly dependent on the particular annotation/evaluation context in which the data being annotated is viewed (Joseph et al., 2017; Läubli et al., 2018). Annotating data directly on top of a HTML overlay on an underlying PDF canvas allows naturally occurring text to be annotated in its original context - that of the PDF itself.

To address the need for an annotation tool that goes beyond plaintext data, we present a new annotation tool called PAWLS (PDF Annotation With Labels and Structure). In this paper, we discuss some of the PDF-specific design choices in PAWLS, including automatic bounding box uniformity, free-form annotations for non-textual image regions and scale/dimension agnostic bounding box storage. We report agreement statistics from an initial round of labelling during the creation of a PDF structure parsing dataset for which PAWLS was originally designed.

2 Design Choices

As shown in Figure 1, the primary operation that PAWLS supports is drawing a bounding box over

[1] Please see Appendix A for instructions on accessing the demo and the demo video.

Proceedings of the Joint Conference of the 59th Annual Meeting of the Association for Computational Linguistics and the 11th International Joint Conference on Natural Language Processing: System Demonstrations, pages 258–264, August 1st - August 6th, 2021.

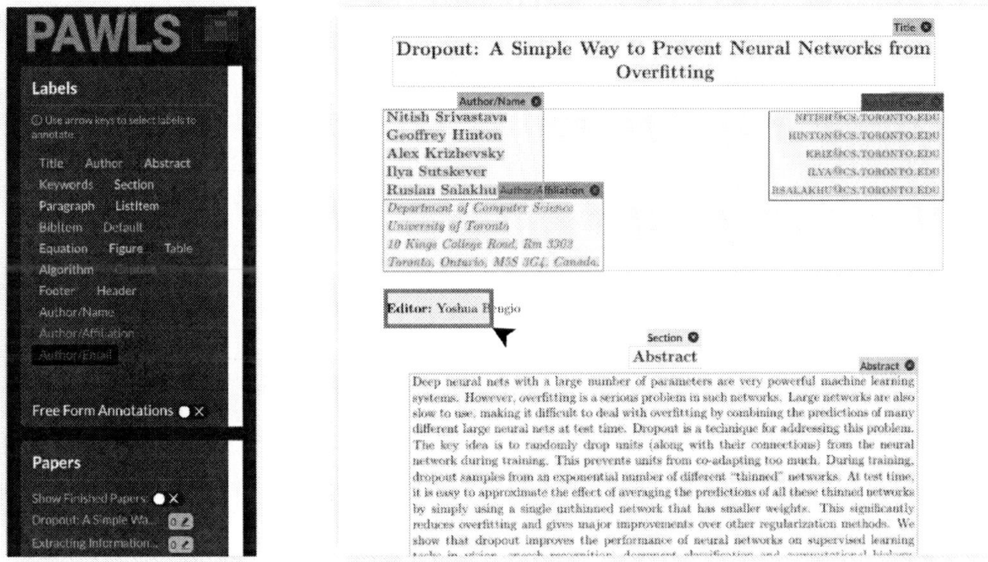

1 Control Panel

Annotators can select label types, check labeling status, and add comments for the labeling task.

2 Labeling Canvas

Directly create annotations over PDF documents. To maximize efficiency, annotators create rectangular bounding boxes, with the contained tokens automatically selected and assigned to the label. Freeform bounding boxes without textual content are also supported.

Figure 1: An overview of the `PAWLS` annotation interface. We show an example of annotating scientific documents in `PAWLS`, yet the target documents and labeling categories could be easily switched to other domains in a self-hosted version.

a PDF document with the mouse, and assigning that region of the document a textual label. `PAWLS` supports drawing both freeform boxes anywhere on the PDF, as well as boxes which are associated with tokens extracted from the PDF itself.

This section describes some of the user interface design choices in `PAWLS`.

2.1 PDF Native Annotation

The primary tenet of `PAWLS` is the idea that annotators are accustomed to reading and interacting with PDF documents themselves, and as such, `PAWLS` should render the actual PDF as the medium for annotation. In order to achieve this, annotations themselves must be relative to a rendered PDF's scale in the browser. Annotations are automatically re-sized to fit the rendered PDF canvas, but stored relative to the absolute dimensions of the original PDF document.

2.2 Annotator Ease of Use

`PAWLS` contains several features which are designed to speed up annotation by users, as well as minimizing frustrating or difficult interaction experiences. Bounding box borders in `PAWLS` change depending on the size and density of the annotated span, making it easier to read dense annotations. Annotators can hide bounding box labels using the CTRL key for cases where labels are obscuring the document flow. Users can undo annotations with familiar key combinations (CMD-z) and delete annotations directly from the sidebar. These features were derived from a tight feedback loop with annotation experts during development of the tool.

2.3 Token Parsing

`PAWLS` pre-processes PDFs before they are rendered in the UI to extract the bounding boxes of every token present in the document. This allows a variety of interactive labelling features described below. Users can choose between different preprocessors based on their needs, such as GROBID [2] and PdfPlumber [3] for digital-born PDFs, or Tesseract [4] for Optical Character Recognition (OCR) in PDFs which have been scanned, or are otherwise low quality. Future extensions to `PAWLS` will include higher level PDF structure which is general enough to be useful across a range of domains, such as document titles, paragraphs and section

[2]https://github.com/kermitt2/grobid

[3]https://github.com/jsvine/pdfplumber

[4]https://github.com/tesseract-ocr/tesseract

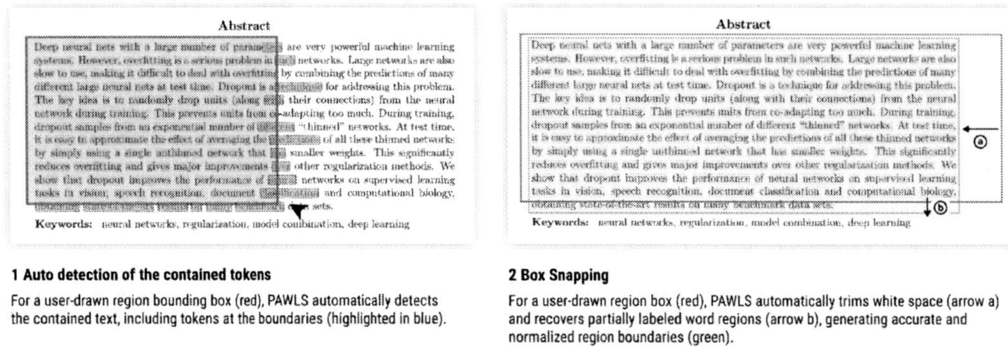

Figure 2: An example of visual token selection. When a user begins highlighting a bounding box, PAWLS uses underlying token level boundary information extracted from the PDF to 1) highlight selected textual spans as they are dragged over and 2) normalize the bounding box of a selection to be a fixed padded distance from the maximally large token boundary.

headings to further extend the possible annotation modes, such as clicking on paragraphs or sections.

2.4 Visual Token Selection and Box Snapping

PAWLS pre-processes PDFs before they are served in the annotation interface, giving access to token level bounding box information. When users draw new bounding boxes, token spans are highlighted to indicate their inclusion in the annotation. After the user has completed the selection, the bounding box "snaps" to a normalized boundary containing the underlying PDF tokens. Figure 2 demonstrates this interaction. In particular, this allows bounding boxes to be normalized relative to their containing token positions (having a fixed border), making annotations more consistent and uniform with no additional annotator effort. This feature allows annotators to focus on the content of their annotations, rather than ensuring a consistent visual markup, easing the annotation flow and increasing the consistency of the collected annotations.

2.5 N-ary Relational Annotations

PAWLS supports N-ary relational annotations as well as those based on bounding boxes. Relational annotations are supported for both textual and free-form annotations, allowing the collection of event structures which include non-textual PDF regions, such as figure/table references, or sub-image coordination. For example, this feature would allow annotators to link figure captions to particular figure regions, or relate a discussion of a particular table column in the text to the exact visual region of the column/table itself. Figure 3 demonstrates this interaction mode for two annotations.

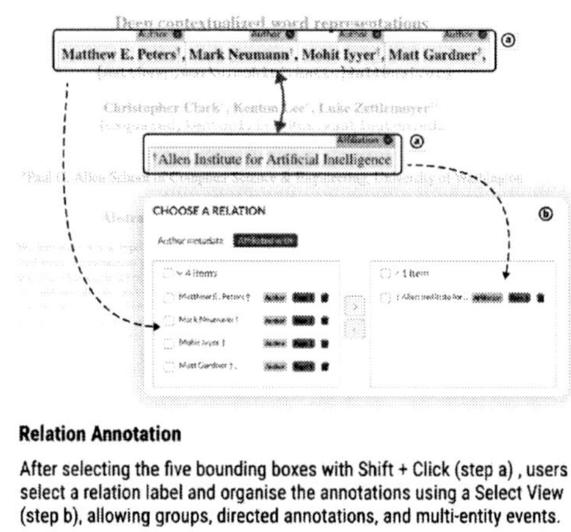

Figure 3: The n-ary relation annotation modal.

2.6 Command Line Interface

PAWLS includes a command line interface for administrating annotation projects. It includes functionality for assigning labeling tasks to annotators, monitoring the annotation progress and quality (measuring inter annotator agreement), and exporting annotations in a variety of formats. Additionally, it supports pre-populating annotations from model predictions, detailed in Section 2.7.

Annotations in PAWLS can be exported to different formats to support different downstream tasks. The hierarchical structure of user-drawn blocks and PDF tokens is stored in JSON format, linking blocks with their corresponding tokens. For vision-centered tasks (e.g., document layout detection),

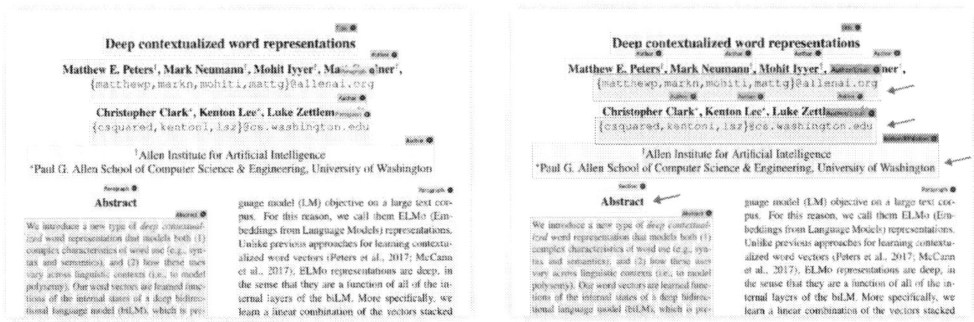

1 Annotation pre-population with existing models

We trained a Mask R-CNN model to predict text regions on page images and a text classification model for obtaining the block categories.

2 Gold labels after manual correction

The accurate model predictions can significantly improve the efficiency as only a part of the annotations require changes (highlighed by red arrows).

Figure 4: Annotation pre-population can significantly improve labeling efficiency.

PAWLS supports converting to the widely-used COCO format, including generating jpeg captures of pdf pages for training vision models. For text-centric tasks, PAWLS can generate a table for tokens and labels obtained from the annotated bounding boxes.

2.7 Annotation Pre-population

The PAWLS command line interface supports pre-population of annotations given a set of bounding boxes predictions for each page. Figure 4 illustrates how pre-annotation can help improve the labeling efficiency. In this example, we trained a Mask R-CNN (He et al., 2017) model on the PubLayNet (Zhong et al., 2019b) dataset that can detect content region bounding boxes for the input page image, and a BERT model (Devlin et al., 2018) on the DocBank (Li et al., 2020c) dataset that predicts the textual category for each text region. PAWLS loads the model predictions and automatically corrects the bounding boxes using the block snapping function, and annotators only need to make minor modifications in the box categories to obtain the gold annotations.

This further enables model-in-the-loop type functionality, with annotators correcting model predictions directly on the PDF. Future extensions to PAWLS will include active learning based annotation suggestions as annotators work, from models running as a service.

3 Implementation

PAWLS is implemented as a Python-based web server which serves PDFs, annotations and other metadata stored on disk in the JSON format. The user interface is a Single Page Application implemented using Typescript and relies heavily on the React web framework. PDFs are rendered using PDF.js. PAWLS is designed to be used in a browser, with no setup work required on the behalf of annotators apart from navigating to a web page. This makes annotation projects more flexible as they can be distributed across a variety of crowd-sourcing platforms, used in house, or run on local machines.

PAWLS development and deployment are both managed using the containerization tools Docker and Docker Compose, and multiple PAWLS instances are running on a Google Cloud Platform Kubernetes cluster. Authentication in production environments is managed via Google Account logins, but PAWLS can be run locally by individual users with no authentication.

4 Case Study

PAWLS enables the collection of mixed-mode annotations on PDFs. PAWLS is currently in use for a PDF Layout Parsing project for academic papers, for which we have collected an initial set of gold standard annotations. This dataset consists of 80 PDF pages with 2558 densely annotated bounding boxes of 20 categories from 3 annotators.

Table 1 reports pairwise Inter-Annotator agreement scores, split out into textual and non-textual labels. For textual labels like titles and paragraphs, the agreement is measured via token accuracy: for each word labeled, we compare the label of the belonging block across different annotators. Non-textual labels are used for regions like figures and tables, and they are usually labeled using free-form boxes. Average Precision (AP) score (Lin et al.,

2014), commonly used in Object Detection tasks (e.g., COCO) in computer vision, is adopted to measure the consistency of these boxes labeled by different annotators. As AP calculates the block categories agreement at different overlapping levels, the scoring is not commutative, and an 80 AP scores already suggests a high level of annotation quality.

	Annotator 1	**Annotator 2**	**Annotator 3**
Annotator 1	N/A	94.43 / 86.58	93.28 / 83.97
Annotator 2	94.43 / 86.49	N/A	88.69 / 84.20
Annotator 3	93.28 / 84.67	88.69 / 84.79	N/A

Table 1: The Inter-Annotator Agreement scores for the labeling task. We show the textual / non-textual annotation agreement scores in each cell. The (i, j)-th element in this table is calculated by treating i's annotation as the "ground truth" and j's as the "prediction".

5 Related Work

Many commercial PDF annotation tools exist, such as IBM Watson's smart document understanding feature and TagTog's Beta PDF Annotation tool [5]. PAWLS is open source and freely available. Knowledge management systems such as Protégé (Musen, 2015) support PDFs, but more suited to management of large, evolving corpora and knowledge graph construction than the creation of static datasets.

LabelStudio [6] supports image annotation as well as plaintext/html-based annotation, meaning PDF pages can be uploaded and annotated within their user interface. However, bounding boxes are hand drawn, and the context of the entire PDF is not visible as the pdf pages are viewed as individual images. PDFAnno (Shindo et al., 2018) is the closest tool conceptually to PAWLS, supporting multiple annotation modes and pdf-based rendering. Unfortunately PDFAnno is no longer maintained and PAWLS provides additional functionality, such as pre-annotation.

Several PDF based datasets exist for document parsing, such as DocBank (Li et al., 2020b), PubLeNet (Zhong et al., 2019a) and TableBank (Li et al., 2020a). However, both DocBank and PubLeNet are constructed using weak supervision from Latex parses or Pubmed XML information. TableBank consists of 417k tables extracted from Microsoft Word documents and computer generated PDFs. This approach is feasible for common elements of document structure such as tables, but is not possible for custom annotation labels or detailed figure/table decomposition.

The PAWLS interface is similar to tools which augment PDFs for reading or note taking purposes. Along with commercial tools such as Adobe Reader, SideNoter (Abekawa and Aizawa, 2016) augments PDFs with rich note taking and linguistic annotation overlays, directly on the PDF canvas. ScholarPhi (Head et al., 2020) augments the PDF reading experience with equation overlays and definition modals for symbols.

As a PDF specific annotation tool, PAWLS adds to the wider landscape of annotation tools which fulfil a particular niche. SLATE (Kummerfeld, 2019) provides a command line annotation tool for expert annotators; (Mayhew and Roth, 2018) provides an annotation interface specifically designed for cross-lingual annotation in which the annotators do not speak the target language.

Textual annotation tools such as BRAT (Stenetorp et al., 2012), Pubtator (Wei et al., 2013, 2012), Knowtator (Ogren, 2006), or TextANno (Yimam et al., 2014) are recommended for annotations which do not require full PDF context, or for which extension to multi-modal data formats is not possible or likely. We view PAWLS as a complimentary tool to the suite of text based annotation tools, which support more advanced types of annotation and configuration, but deal with annotation on extracted text removed from its originally published format.

In particular, we envisage scholarly document annotation as one of the key use cases for PAWLS, as PDF is a widely used format in the context of scientific publication. Several recently published datasets leave document structure parsing or multimodal annotation to future work. For example, the SciREX dataset (Jain et al., 2020) use the text-only LaTeX source of ArXiv papers for dataset construction, leaving Table and Figure extraction to future work. Multiple iterations of the Evidence Inference dataset (Lehman et al., 2019; DeYoung et al., 2020) use textual descriptions of interventions in clinical trial reports; answering inferential questions using figures, tables and graphs may be a more natural format for some queries.

[5] https://www.tagtog.net/#pdf-annotation

[6] https://labelstud.io/

6 Conclusion

In this paper, we have introduced a new annotation tool, PAWLS, designed specifically with PDFs in mind. PAWLS facilitates the creation of multimodal datasets, due to its support for mixed mode annotation of both text and image sub-regions on PDFs. Additionally, we described several user interface design choices which improve the resulting annotation quality, and conducted a small initial annotation effort, reporting high annotator agreement. PAWLS is released as an open source project under the Apache 2.0 license.

Acknowledgement

We thank the anonymous reviewers for their comments and suggestions, and we thank Doug Downy, Kyle Lo, Lucy Lu Wang for the helpful discussions. This project is supported in part by NSF Grant OIA-2033558.

References

Takeshi Abekawa and Akiko Aizawa. 2016. SideNoter: Scholarly paper browsing system based on PDF restructuring and text annotation. In *Proceedings of COLING 2016, the 26th International Conference on Computational Linguistics: System Demonstrations*, pages 136–140, Osaka, Japan. The COLING 2016 Organizing Committee.

Jacob Devlin, Ming-Wei Chang, Kenton Lee, and Kristina Toutanova. 2018. Bert: Pre-training of deep bidirectional transformers for language understanding. *arXiv preprint arXiv:1810.04805*.

Jacob Devlin, Ming-Wei Chang, Kenton Lee, and Kristina Toutanova. 2019. BERT: Pre-training of deep bidirectional transformers for language understanding. In *Proceedings of the 2019 Conference of the North American Chapter of the Association for Computational Linguistics: Human Language Technologies, Volume 1 (Long and Short Papers)*, pages 4171–4186, Minneapolis, Minnesota. Association for Computational Linguistics.

Jay DeYoung, Eric Lehman, Ben Nye, Iain J. Marshall, and Byron C. Wallace. 2020. Evidence inference 2.0: More data, better models.

Kaiming He, Georgia Gkioxari, Piotr Dollár, and Ross Girshick. 2017. Mask r-cnn. In *Proceedings of the IEEE international conference on computer vision*, pages 2961–2969.

Andrew Head, Kyle Lo, Dongyeop Kang, Raymond Fok, Sam Skjonsberg, Daniel S. Weld, and Marti A. Hearst. 2020. Augmenting scientific papers with just-in-time, position-sensitive definitions of terms and symbols. *ArXiv*, abs/2009.14237.

Sarthak Jain, Madeleine van Zuylen, Hannaneh Hajishirzi, and Iz Beltagy. 2020. SciREX: A challenge dataset for document-level information extraction. In *Proceedings of the 58th Annual Meeting of the Association for Computational Linguistics*, pages 7506–7516, Online. Association for Computational Linguistics.

Kenneth Joseph, Lisa Friedland, William Hobbs, David Lazer, and Oren Tsur. 2017. ConStance: Modeling annotation contexts to improve stance classification. In *Proceedings of the 2017 Conference on Empirical Methods in Natural Language Processing*, pages 1115–1124, Copenhagen, Denmark. Association for Computational Linguistics.

Jonathan K. Kummerfeld. 2019. SLATE: A super-lightweight annotation tool for experts. In *Proceedings of the 57th Annual Meeting of the Association for Computational Linguistics: System Demonstrations*, pages 7–12, Florence, Italy. Association for Computational Linguistics.

Samuel Läubli, Rico Sennrich, and Martin Volk. 2018. Has machine translation achieved human parity? a case for document-level evaluation. In *Proceedings of the 2018 Conference on Empirical Methods in Natural Language Processing*, pages 4791–4796, Brussels, Belgium. Association for Computational Linguistics.

Eric Lehman, Jay DeYoung, Regina Barzilay, and Byron C Wallace. 2019. Inferring which medical treatments work from reports of clinical trials. In *Proceedings of the North American Chapter of the Association for Computational Linguistics (NAACL)*, pages 3705–3717.

Minghao Li, Lei Cui, Shaohan Huang, Furu Wei, Ming Zhou, and Zhoujun Li. 2020a. TableBank: Table benchmark for image-based table detection and recognition. In *Proceedings of the 12th Language Resources and Evaluation Conference*, pages 1918–1925, Marseille, France. European Language Resources Association.

Minghao Li, Yiheng Xu, Lei Cui, Shaohan Huang, Furu Wei, Zhoujun Li, and M. Zhou. 2020b. Docbank: A benchmark dataset for document layout analysis. *ArXiv*, abs/2006.01038.

Minghao Li, Yiheng Xu, Lei Cui, Shaohan Huang, Furu Wei, Zhoujun Li, and Ming Zhou. 2020c. Docbank: A benchmark dataset for document layout analysis. *arXiv preprint arXiv:2006.01038*.

Tsung-Yi Lin, Michael Maire, Serge Belongie, James Hays, Pietro Perona, Deva Ramanan, Piotr Dollár, and C Lawrence Zitnick. 2014. Microsoft coco: Common objects in context. In *European conference on computer vision*, pages 740–755. Springer.

Stephen Mayhew and Dan Roth. 2018. TALEN: Tool for annotation of low-resource ENtities. In *Proceedings of ACL 2018, System Demonstrations*, pages

80–86, Melbourne, Australia. Association for Computational Linguistics.

M. Musen. 2015. The protégé project: a look back and a look forward. *AI matters*, 1 4:4–12.

Philip V. Ogren. 2006. Knowtator: A protégé plug-in for annotated corpus construction. In *HLT-NAACL*.

Matthew Peters, Mark Neumann, Mohit Iyyer, Matt Gardner, Christopher Clark, Kenton Lee, and Luke Zettlemoyer. 2018. Deep contextualized word representations. In *Proceedings of the 2018 Conference of the North American Chapter of the Association for Computational Linguistics: Human Language Technologies, Volume 1 (Long Papers)*, pages 2227–2237, New Orleans, Louisiana. Association for Computational Linguistics.

Hiroyuki Shindo, Yohei Munesada, and Y. Matsumoto. 2018. Pdfanno: a web-based linguistic annotation tool for pdf documents. In *LREC*.

Pontus Stenetorp, Sampo Pyysalo, Goran Topić, Tomoko Ohta, Sophia Ananiadou, and Jun'ichi Tsujii. 2012. brat: a web-based tool for NLP-assisted text annotation. In *Proceedings of the Demonstrations at the 13th Conference of the European Chapter of the Association for Computational Linguistics*, pages 102–107, Avignon, France. Association for Computational Linguistics.

Chih-Hsuan Wei, Hung-Yu Kao, and Zhiyong Lu. 2012. Pubtator: A pubmed-like interactive curation system for document triage and literature curation. *BioCreative 2012 workshop*, 05.

Chih-Hsuan Wei, Hung-Yu Kao, and Zhiyong Lu. 2013. Pubtator: a web-based text mining tool for assisting biocuration. *Nucleic Acids Research*, 41.

Seid Muhie Yimam, Chris Biemann, Richard Eckart de Castilho, and Iryna Gurevych. 2014. Automatic annotation suggestions and custom annotation layers in webanno. In *Proceedings of 52nd Annual Meeting of the Association for Computational Linguistics: System Demonstrations*, pages 91–96.

Xu Zhong, J. Tang, and Antonio Jimeno-Yepes. 2019a. Publaynet: Largest dataset ever for document layout analysis. *2019 International Conference on Document Analysis and Recognition (ICDAR)*, pages 1015–1022.

Xu Zhong, Jianbin Tang, and Antonio Jimeno Yepes. 2019b. Publaynet: largest dataset ever for document layout analysis. In *2019 International Conference on Document Analysis and Recognition (ICDAR)*, pages 1015–1022. IEEE.

A Accessing the Demo

A demo video for `PAWLS` usage is available at `https://youtu.be/TB4kzh2H9og`, and the demo server can be accessed at `https://pawls.apps.allenai.org/`. We demonstrate `PAWLS`' key functionalities using the scientific document labeling task as an example—the label spaces and exemplar documents are configured accordingly—but they can be easily switched to adapt to other types of documents like financial or legal reports. To fully present the capability of `PAWLS`, no pre-annotation function is used. THe authors demonstrated documents are

Production deployments of `PAWLS` use Google Authentication to allow users to log in. The demo server is configured to allow access to all non-corp gmail accounts, e.g any email address ending in "@gmail.com". For this public demo, no personal information and annotations will be collected from this server, as it is read-only. Please feel free to create a one-off account if you prefer not to use a personal gmail. If you cannot log in, please try again using an incognito window which will ensure gmail cookies are not set.

TweeNLP: A Twitter Exploration Portal for Natural Language Processing

Viraj Shah, Shruti Singh and **Mayank Singh**
Indian Institute of Technology Gandhinagar, Gujarat, India
{shah.viraj, singh_shruti, singh.mayank}@iitgn.ac.in

Abstract

We present TWEENLP, a one-stop portal that organizes Twitter's natural language processing (NLP) data and builds a visualization and exploration platform. It curates 19,395 tweets (as of April 2021) from various NLP conferences and general NLP discussions. It supports multiple features such as TweetExplorer to explore tweets by topics, visualize insights from Twitter activity throughout the organization cycle of conferences, discover popular research papers and researchers. It also builds a timeline of conference and workshop submission deadlines. We envision TWEENLP to function as a collective memory unit for the NLP community by integrating the tweets pertaining to research papers with the NLPExplorer scientific literature search engine. The current system is hosted at URL.

1 Introduction

Online communication channels have become popular in the Internet era, and several online communities of like-minded people have evolved around these channels. For example, communities such as Stack Overflow and AskUbuntu are question-answering forums; Twitter and Reddit are content-sharing forums. These forums over the years have provided a platform for novice users to learn from the experts, facilitated discussions among the community members, and have over the years accumulated a rich database of questions, answers, and discussions.

According to the theory of diffusion of innovation proposed by Rogers (2003), the communication channel is one of the four main elements influencing the spread of a new idea. Notably, the communication channel serves as a collective long-term memory or a knowledge archive of the community, which any member can access to study the community's stance on diverse topics at any point in time.

Although several mailing lists, slack channels, and subreddits exist for communication, most natural language processing (henceforth NLP) community discussions are primarily carried out on Twitter due to its open accessibility and wider reach. Announcements of calls for papers and submission deadlines, recently accepted papers, interesting talks and seminars, lecture videos, and tutorials on various topics are often posted on Twitter. These are a great medium to stay updated on the recent developments in the NLP field. It is also a medium for researchers to engage in informal research discussions which might be unreported in official publications. We present a sample of diverse NLP tweets in Figure 1 to emphasise the utility of the platform.

However, unlike subreddits or communities like Stack Overflow and AskUbuntu, Twitter is not an exclusive channel for NLP discussions. Exclusive channels provide users a one-stop destination for their interests and allow extremely topic-specific exploration. While Twitter allows search by hashtags to narrow down to specific topics, the usage of hashtags is highly irregular. Furthermore, Twitter is more suited to live discussions and less suitable for maintaining a snapshot of the discussions taking place in the online community. Relevant Twitter discussions about specific research papers are often forgotten in the long run because there is no infrastructure to link these discussions with the papers on the proceedings archives or research paper search engines. In an attempt to address these issues, we extend the functionality of NLP-Explorer (Parmar et al., 2020) platform by integrating TWEENLP with it. NLPExplorer is a portal for searching, and visualizing NLP research volume based on the ACL Anthology (ACL Anthology). In our current work, we build an automatic pipeline for curating NLP tweets and build a one-stop portal - TWEENLP, for the search and browsing of

Proceedings of the Joint Conference of the 59th Annual Meeting of the Association for Computational Linguistics and the 11th International Joint Conference on Natural Language Processing: System Demonstrations, pages 265–271, August 1st - August 6th, 2021.

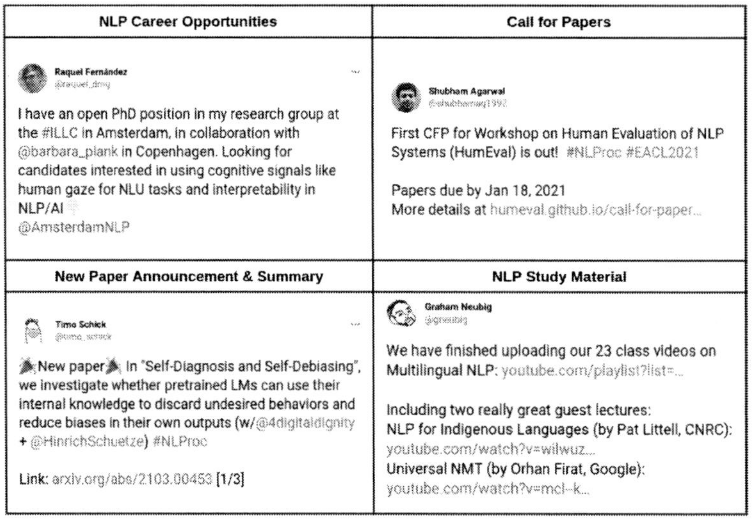

Figure 1: A sample of diverse natural language processing tweets.

NLP discussion on Twitter. The system has curated 19,395 NLP tweets as of April 2021.

TWEENLP organizes NLP tweets into topics: (i) New paper announcements, (ii) Call for Paper announcements, (iii) Reading Materials & Tutorials, (iv) Career Opportunities, (v) Talks & Seminars, and (vi) Others. Topic-wise tweets are presented via dashboards for easy exploration. TWEENLP supports dashboards to browse through popular NLP tweets in the previous week and the month. We construct a CFP Timeline from 'Call for Papers' announcements on Twitter and arrange it according to the upcoming submission deadlines of various workshops and conferences. We link the research paper tweets to the research paper's metadata, accessible via the NLPExplorer paper discovery feature. We also build live Conference Visualization dashboards, which curate tweets about the conference schedule, ongoing talks, poster sessions, and interesting papers at the conference, and present statistics such as popular hashtags, users, tweet languages, etc.

We integrate TWEENLP with NLPExplorer (Section 2) to build a joint-portal that aims to bridge the gap between published research and its informal communication on the social media platform Twitter. Our automatic data curation pipeline and the architecture of the system is described in Section 3 and Section 4 respectively. We describe the features of TWEENLP in detail in Section 5. In Section 6, we discuss previous works in organizing the NLP literature and visualization of research papers.

2 NLPExplorer

NLPExplorer[1] (Parmar et al., 2020) is an automatic portal for indexing, searching, and visualizing Natural Language Processing research volume. It presents multiple paper, venue, and author statistics, including paper citation distribution, paper topic distribution, authors, their field of study, their citation distributions, etc. It also presents category information of research papers into various topics broadly arranged in five categories: (i) Linguistic Target (Syntax, Discourse, etc.), (ii) Tasks (Tagging, Summarization, etc.), (iii) Approaches (unsupervised, supervised, etc.), (iv) Languages (English, Chinese, etc.) and (v) Dataset types (news, clinical notes, etc.). The current snapshot consists of 75k research papers and 50k authors. Since its inception, it has been accessed by more than 7.3k users having a close to 9.7k sessions.

3 Dataset

We curate the dataset from two primary sources:

3.1 Twitter

We curate the Twitter data using the open-source library *Twint*[2] by retrieving tweets with the hashtag NLProc. We also curate tweets with NLP conference hashtags such as #acl2020, #emnlp2020, etc. The list of NLP conferences is compiled via ACL

[1] http://nlpexplorer.org/
[2] `https://github.com/twintproject/twint`

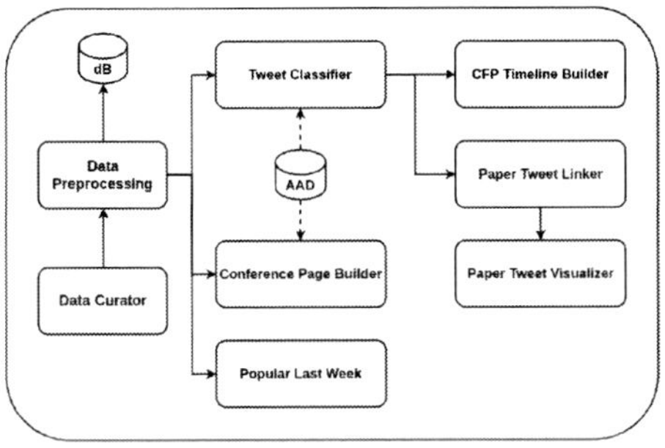

Figure 2: The architecture of TWEENLP. Arrow directions denote the flow of data. AAD represents the ACL Anthology Dataset which is the other data source apart from Twitter.

Anthology. Our system is scheduled to download the Twitter data for each day automatically. For ongoing conferences, our system curates new tweets every hour to continually update the *Conference Visualizer* page. The current snapshot (as of April 2021) contains data since October 2017 (around 1300 days) and consists of 19,395 tweets.

3.2 ACL Anthology

We curate the conference and journal names and URLs from the ACL Anthology github repository[3]. We also curate the paper titles and their links. Tweets are collected periodically every day, and the system checks for paper mentions in the tweets by substring matching the paper URLs collected from the ACL Anthology github repository.

4 Architecture

We present the pipeline of our system in Figure 2. The Data Curator module curates tweets daily. The curated tweets are processed before we perform further steps. The following modules process tweets: (i) Tweet Classifier, (ii) Conference Page Builder, (iii) CFP Timeline Builder, and (iv) Paper Tweet Linker. We describe the tweet processing modules in detail below:

1. *Tweet Classifier*: The Tweet Classifier module classifies a tweet into one of the six topics: (i) New Paper Announcements, (ii) Call for Paper announcements, (iii) Reading Materials & Tutorials, (iv) Career Opportunities, (v) Talks & Seminars, and (vi) Others. The Tweet Explorer feature utilizes these tweet categories. The detailed description of each topic is presented in Section 5.1. We experiment by finetuning a BERT-base(Devlin et al., 2019) classifier and twitter-roberta-base(Barbieri et al., 2020) to predict the tweet topics. The BERT-base model[4] obtains the best test accuracy of 75% on a small manually annotated dataset[5].
2. *Conference Page Builder*: The Conference Page Builder classifies a tweet either as discussing an ongoing conference or other topics. The module builds specific conference pages using such tweets.
3. *CFP Timeline Builder*: The module processes 'Call for Papers' tweets identified by the Tweet Classifier module. It extracts the conference (and workshop) name by regex-based keyword matching against a pre-compiled list of venues. The submission date are extracted from the tweets by labeling dates using the Spacy[6] library. The tweets are arranged in a timeline sorted by the submission deadline.
4. *Paper Tweet Linker*: The Paper Tweet Linker module maps specific tweets to research papers using regex matching of the paper title and paper URL. The Paper Tweet Visualizer uses these mappings to embed the tweets on the research paper page on NLPExplorer.

The pipeline then stores the tweets in the database after processing by the above modules. We schedule our system to automatically curate the Twitter data daily and increase it to an hourly frequency during ongoing conferences.

5 TWEENLP Features

5.1 Tweet Explorer

We present a Tweet Explorer dashboard that allows a user to browse tweets from specific topics such as:

1. *New paper announcements:* This topic organizes tweets about recent papers, which often involve the summary or a short introduction of the research paper. These twitter threads facilitate other researchers to communicate informally with the paper authors. These also contain interesting discussions by the community on the insights, merits, and critiques of the research paper, and post questions about

[3] https://github.com/acl-org/acl-anthology

[4] We also experimented with a zero-shot classifier but it underperformed the BERT-base classifier.

[5] each tweet was annotated by two ML/NLP students and inter annotator agreement computed using Cohen's κ=0.68

[6] https://spacy.io/

the work. The authors' short introductions offer an informal account of the paper compared to the paper alert services that usually present the title and the abstract of the research paper.

2. *Call for Papers (CFPs) by various conferences and workshops:* Users can view the announcements for call for papers and submission deadlines by various workshops and conferences.
3. *Reading Materials & Tutorials:* It lists various study material, such as lecture slides and videos, tutorials, online courses, and blog posts.
4. *NLP Career Opportunities:* Individuals frequently advertise opportunities for various positions such as interns, full-time, Ph.D., postdoctoral fellows, and research fellows on Twitter.
5. *NLP Talks & Seminars:* Various online NLP talks and seminars can be accessed using the NLP Talks & Seminars filter on the Tweet Explorer dashboard.
6. *Others:* This category contains the NLP tweets which do not belong to any of the above topics.

The Tweet Explorer feature allows users to specifically browse through tweets by topics and filter them based on their immediate interests. A snapshot of the same is presented in Figure 3. We present the distribution of tweets in the six categories from tweets curated by the system in the last 1,300 days in Table 1.

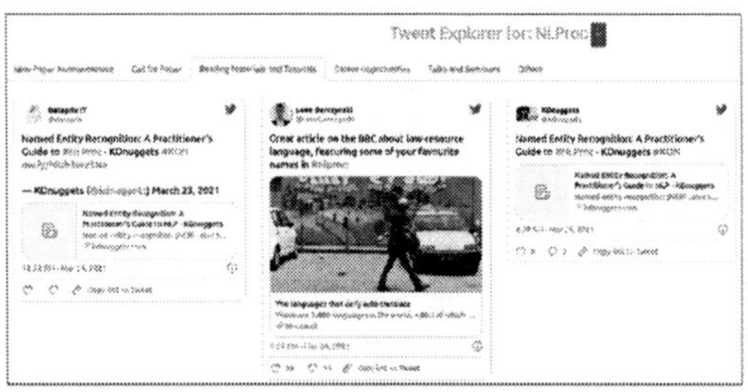

Figure 3: Tweet Explorer feature of TWEENLP which facilitates browsing tweets by six different topics.

5.2 Conference Visualizer – Near real-time view for conferences

TWEENLP supports real-time statistics for multiple top conferences and the popular #NLProc hashtag. The information is updated hourly for live events and weekly for past events. Some of the statistics presented are top mentions, top hashtags, top linked URLs, and top discussed papers in tweets. We present the most popular hashtags, mentions, URLs, and highly discussed papers for ACL2020 in Table 2. A summary of Twitter activity from the Conference Visualizer page for ACL 2020 is presented in Table 3. Apart from Twitter discussions about a conference in a specific month, we also show insights from the conferences across the year. The insights from ACL conference over time is presented in Figure 4. We also present other conference-specific statistics such as the number of tweets per month, daily distribution of tweets in the conference month, most active users tweeting about the conference, and a distribution of the tweet languages other than English.

Topic	Tweet Count
New Paper Announcements	6,337
Call for Papers	972
Reading Materials & Tutorials	1,400
NLP Career Opportunities	681
NLP Talks & Seminars	2,382
Others	7,623
Total Tweets	**19,395**

Table 1: Distribution of tweets (curated since October 2017) into various topics.

5.3 Popular Paper Visualizer

We showcase widely discussed papers on Twitter in the Popular Paper Visualizer dashboard. It presents the titles and provides direct links to the full-text of the top discussed papers for quick reference. The system extracts tweets mentioning research papers and assigns a popularity score to each paper based on the count of tweets that mention it, and the likes, retweets, and replies on the paper tweets. We present a snapshot of few popular papers identified by our platform in Figure 5. It also presents the most active users tweeting about #NLProc on Twitter. Popular Paper Visualizer dashboard also supports exploration of most liked and retweeted #NLProc tweets of all times and in the last month.

5.4 CFP Timeline

TWEENLP presents a timeline of the upcoming submission deadlines. The timeline is created by identifying 'Call for Papers' tweets using keyword based filtering of tweets and also lists the conference/workshop website. The details are described in the CFP Timeline Builder module 3. We present a snapshot of the timeline in Figure 6.

Top Hashtags	Top Mentions	Top URLs	Top Papers Discussed
#acl2020nlp	@aclmeeting	virtual.acl2020.org/socials.html	Beyond Accuracy: Behavioral Testing of NLP models with CheckList
#acl2020en	@emilymbender	virtual.acl2020.org/plenary_session_keynote_kathy_mckeown.html	Photon: A Robust Cross-Domain Text-to-SQL System
#nlproc	@akoller	virtual.acl2020.org/paper_main.701.html	Climbing towards NLU: On Meaning, Form, and Understanding in the Age of Data
#acl2020zht	@winlpworkshop	virtual.acl2020.org/workshop_W1.html	Language Models as an Alternative Evaluator of Word Order Hypotheses: A Case Study in Japanese
#acl2020hi	@xandaschofield	www.aclweb.org/anthology/2020.acl-main.442/	Don't Stop Pretraining: Adapt Language Models to Domains and Tasks
#mt	@gneubig	virtual.acl2020.org/workshop_W10.html	The State and Fate of Linguistic Diversity and Inclusion in the NLP World

Table 2: ACL 2020 Twitter Coverage: Top discussed papers, mentions and URLs and popular hashtags.

Tweet Counter	Likes Counter	Retweet Counter	Unique Mentions	Unique Paper Mentions
5,343	58,160	11,440	907	251

Table 3: ACL 2020 Twitter Statistics of various activities.

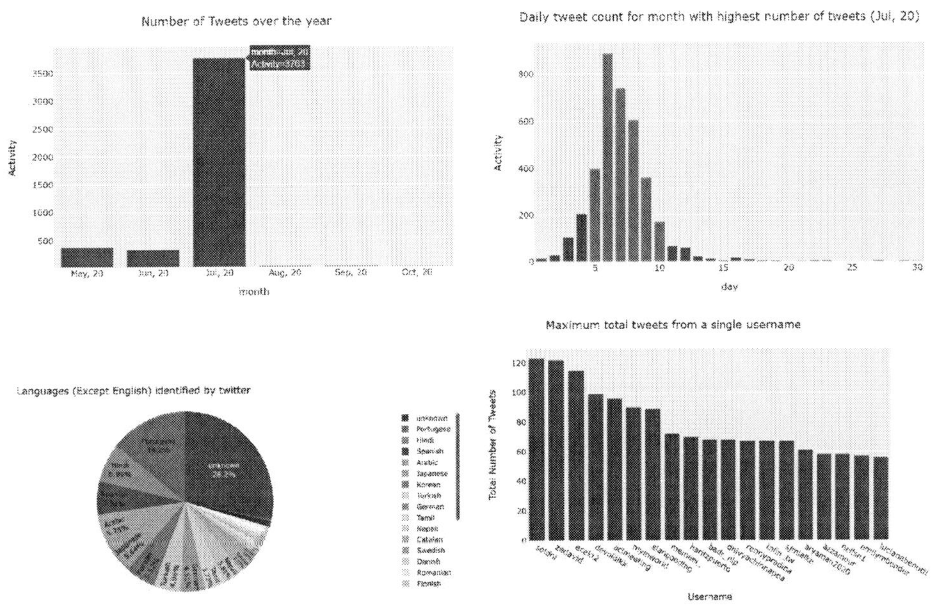

Figure 4: Conference Visualizer: ACL2020 Statistics. (a) Distribution of tweets across different months. (b) Daily distribution of ACL2020 tweets in July 2020. (c) Distribution of tweet languages except English. (d) Twitter users with highest ACL2020 tweets.

5.5 Paper Tweet Visualizer

NLPExplorer supports a research paper search interface and builds research paper pages which showcase standard paper related statistics such as the publication year and venue, author information, citations, citation distribution over the years and the link to the corresponding PDF article. Additionally, it also provides interesting insights like similar papers, topical distribution and mentioned URLs. We map research paper discussion tweets on Twitter to the NLPExplorer paper page. This feature allows users to browse through discussions about the paper along with the metadata of the paper. We present a snapshot of the feature in Figure 7.

Top Paper Discussed	
Paper ID	Paper title
2020.findings-emnlp.195	Participatory Research for Low-resourced Machine Translation: A Case Study in African Languages
2020.tacl-1.28	How Can We Know What Language Models Know?
2020.emnlp-main.585	Generationary or "How We Went beyond Word Sense Inventories and Learned to Gloss"
2020.nlpcovid19-2.8	Quantifying the Effects of COVID-19 on Mental Health Support Forums
2020.emnlp-main.445	Digital Voicing of Silent Speech
2020.findings-emnlp.112	What Can We Do to Improve Peer Review in NLP?
2020.acl-main.450	Asking and Answering Questions to Evaluate the Factual Consistency of Summaries
2020.acl-main.454	FEQA: A Question Answering Evaluation Framework for Faithfulness Assessment in Abstractive Summarization
N16-2013	Hateful Symbols or Hateful People? Predictive Features for Hate Speech Detection on Twitter

Figure 5: Popular papers identified TWEENLP based on twitter activity.

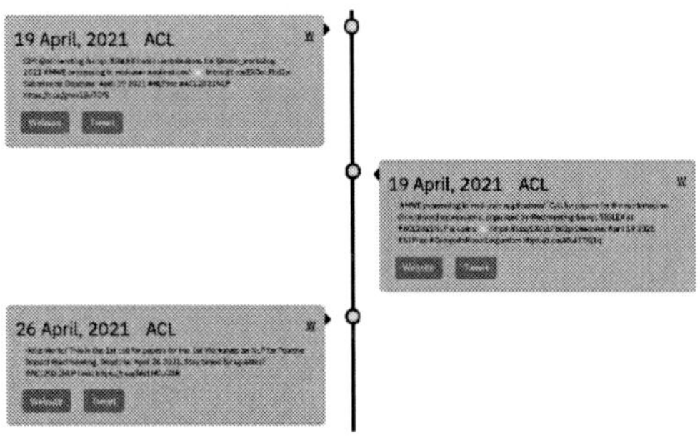

Figure 6: CFP Timeline built from tweets. 'W' on top-right denotes Workshop.

Figure 7: Paper Tweet Visualizer curates tweets and metadata of a research paper on a joint portal. The image background is a 'Paper' page from NLPExplorer which lists paper metadata, citing papers, field-of-study tags, and similar papers alongwith the associated tweets.

5.6 Popular Last Week

Lastly, we present popular tweets in the NLP community on Twitter (also referred as NLP Twitter). This feature allows researchers to catch up with the recent NLP-related Twitter discussions in a single dashboard without searching for them specifically in the Twitter feed.

6 Related Works

Bird et al. (2008) curated the *ACL Anthology Reference Corpus (ACL ARC)* of research papers in NLP and CL. Radev et al. (2009, 2013) constructed the ACL Anthology Network (AAN) by manual annotation of the references to complete the citation network and analysed the network to present central papers, authors and other network statistics (Radev et al., 2016). Works by Schäfer et al. (2011) and Parmar et al. (2020) provide a comprehensive search interface to browse through the NLP based on parameters such as author, full text, year of publication, title, and the field of study. Mohammad (2020) built the NLPScholar platform which consists of interactive dashboards that present various aspects of NLP research papers. The platform uses ACL Anthology and Google Scholar as the information source.

Few works have analysed Twitter data to predict scholarly impact. Shuai et al. (2012) report a statistical correlation between high volume of Twitter mentions and arXiv downloads and early citations (i.e., citations occurring less than seven months after the publication of a preprint). However, they also point out that Twitter mentions cannot be directly concluded to be causative of higher levels of download and early citations. Several other works such as Eysenbach (2011), Thelwall et al. (2013), and Haustein et al. (2014) have tried to analyze whether tweets correlate with citations.

However, to the best of our knowledge, no prior work has tried to curate NLP discussions data from Twitter in an attempt to organize it and link it to research papers via a search engine or a visualization portal.

7 Future Scope and Extensions

Currently, the system is implemented only for NLP papers present in the ACL Anthology. The system could be extended to papers from NeurIPS, ICLR, and CVPR as the data for these conferences is available publicly. The system is versatile and can be easily extended to other domains. TWEENLP provides basic visualization graphs over Twitter activity. Over time, these discussions could be used to build a timeline of evolution of research in various domains of NLP based on the Twitter activity of researchers. Tweets by popular users attain likes and retweets at a higher rate in comparison to new users (or users with less followers) of the community. TWEENLP currently only presents popular tweets based on retweets and likes count which can bias the conversations, understanding and presentation of ideas by emphasising the tweets of a small set of popular users. Future work includes identifying novel alternative ideas and perspectives by adjusting user popularity to create an inclusive space for the community.

References

ACL Anthology. ACL Anthology. `https://www.aclweb.org/anthology/`. Accessed: 2021-03-01.

Francesco Barbieri, Jose Camacho-Collados, Luis Espinosa-Anke, and Leonardo Neves. 2020. TweetEval:Unified Benchmark and Comparative Evaluation for Tweet Classification. In *Proceedings of Findings of EMNLP*.

Steven Bird, Robert Dale, Bonnie J Dorr, Bryan Gibson, Mark Thomas Joseph, Min-Yen Kan, Dongwon Lee, Brett Powley, Dragomir R Radev, and Yee Fan Tan. 2008. The ACL Anthology Reference Corpus: A Reference Dataset for Bibliographic Research in Computational Linguistics. *Language Resources and Evaluation Conference*.

J. Devlin, Ming-Wei Chang, Kenton Lee, and Kristina Toutanova. 2019. BERT: Pre-training of deep bidirectional transformers for language understanding. In *NAACL-HLT*.

Gunther Eysenbach. 2011. Can tweets predict citations? Metrics of social impact based on Twitter and correlation with traditional metrics of scientific impact. *Journal of medical Internet research*, 13(4):e123.

Stefanie Haustein, Isabella Peters, Cassidy R Sugimoto, Mike Thelwall, and Vincent Larivière. 2014. Tweeting biomedicine: An analysis of tweets and citations in the biomedical literature. *Journal of the Association for Information Science and Technology*, 65(4):656–669.

Saif M. Mohammad. 2020. NLP scholar: An interactive visual explorer for natural language processing literature. In *Proceedings of the 58th Annual Meeting of the Association for Computational Linguistics: System Demonstrations*, pages 232–255, Online. Association for Computational Linguistics.

Monarch Parmar, Naman Jain, Pranjali Jain, P Jayakrishna Sahit, Soham Pachpande, Shruti Singh, and Mayank Singh. 2020. NLPExplorer: exploring the universe of nlp papers. In *European Conference on Information Retrieval*, pages 476–480. Springer.

Dragomir R Radev, Mark Thomas Joseph, Bryan Gibson, and Pradeep Muthukrishnan. 2016. A bibliometric and network analysis of the field of computational linguistics. *Journal of the Association for Information Science and Technology*, 67(3):683–706.

Dragomir R Radev, Pradeep Muthukrishnan, and Vahed Qazvinian. 2009. The ACL Anthology Network Corpus. *ACL-IJCNLP*, page 54.

Dragomir R Radev, Pradeep Muthukrishnan, Vahed Qazvinian, and Amjad Abu-Jbara. 2013. The ACL anthology network corpus. *Language Resources and Evaluation*, 47(4):919–944.

Everett M. Rogers. 2003. *Diffusion of innovations*, 5th edition. Free Press, New York, NY [u.a.].

Ulrich Schäfer, Bernd Kiefer, Christian Spurk, Jörg Steffen, and Rui Wang. 2011. The ACL Anthology searchbench. In *Proceedings of the ACL-HLT 2011 System Demonstrations*, pages 7–13, Portland, Oregon. Association for Computational Linguistics.

Xin Shuai, Alberto Pepe, and Johan Bollen. 2012. How the scientific community reacts to newly submitted preprints: Article downloads, twitter mentions, and citations. *PloS one*, 7(11):e47523.

Mike Thelwall, Stefanie Haustein, Vincent Larivière, and Cassidy R Sugimoto. 2013. Do altmetrics work? twitter and ten other social web services. *PloS one*, 8(5):e64841.

ChrEnTranslate: Cherokee-English Machine Translation Demo with Quality Estimation and Corrective Feedback

Shiyue Zhang **Benjamin Frey** **Mohit Bansal**
UNC Chapel Hill
{shiyue, mbansal}@cs.unc.edu; benfrey@email.unc.edu

Abstract

We introduce ChrEnTranslate, an online machine translation demonstration system for translation between English and an endangered language Cherokee. It supports both statistical and neural translation models as well as provides quality estimation to inform users of reliability, two user feedback interfaces for experts and common users respectively, example inputs to collect human translations for monolingual data, word alignment visualization, and relevant terms from the Cherokee-English dictionary. The quantitative evaluation demonstrates that our backbone translation models achieve state-of-the-art translation performance and our quality estimation well correlates with both BLEU and human judgment. By analyzing 216 pieces of expert feedback, we find that NMT is preferable because it copies less than SMT, and, in general, current models *can translate fragments of the source sentence but make major mistakes.* When we add these 216 expert-corrected parallel texts into the training set and retrain models, equal or slightly better performance is observed, which demonstrates indicates the potential of human-in-the-loop learning.[1]

1 Introduction

Machine translation is a relatively mature natural language processing technique that has been deployed to real-world applications. For instance, Google Translate currently supports translations between over 100 languages. However, a lot of low-resource languages are out there without the support of modern technologies, which might accelerate their vanishing. In this work, we focus on one of those languages, Cherokee. Cherokee is one of the most well-known Native American languages, however, is identified as an "endangered" language by UNESCO. Cherokee nations have carried out language revitalization plans (Nation, 2001) and established language immersion programs and k-12 language curricula. Cherokee language courses are offered in some universities, including UNC Chapel Hill, the University of Oklahoma, Stanford University, Western Carolina University. A few pedagogical books have been published (Holmes and Smith, 1976; Joyner, 2014; Feeling, 2018) and a digital archive of historical Cherokee language documents has been built up (Bourns, 2019; Cushman, 2019). However, there are still very limited resources available on the Internet for Cherokee learners; meanwhile, first language speakers and translators of Cherokee are mostly elders and would likely benefit from machine translation's assistance. This motivates us to develop the first online Cherokee-English machine translation demonstration system. Extending our previous works (Frey, 2020; Zhang et al., 2020), we develop the backbone statistical and neural machine translation systems (SMT and NMT) on a larger parallel dataset (17K) and obtain the state-of-the-art Cherokee-English (Chr-En) and English-Cherokee (En-Chr) translation performance.

Besides translation, our system also supports quality estimation (QE) for both SMT and NMT. QE is an important (missing) component of machine translation systems, which is used to inform users of the reliability of machine-translated content (Specia et al., 2010). Since our models are trained on a very limited number of parallel sentences, it is expected that the translations will be poor in most cases when used by Internet users. Therefore, QE is essential for avoiding misuse and warning users of potential risks. Existing best-performance QE models are usually trained under supervision with quality ratings from professional

[1]Our online demo is at `https://chren.cs.unc.edu/`; our code is open-sourced at `https://github.com/ZhangShiyue/ChrEnTranslate`; and our data is available at `https://github.com/ZhangShiyue/ChrEn`.

Proceedings of the Joint Conference of the 59th Annual Meeting of the Association for Computational Linguistics and the 11th International Joint Conference on Natural Language Processing: System Demonstrations, pages 272–279, August 1st - August 6th, 2021.

translators (Fomicheva et al., 2020a). However, we are unable to easily collect a lot of human ratings for Cherokee, due to its state of endangerment. Nonetheless, we test both supervised and unsupervised QE methods: (1) *Supervised*: we use BLEU (Papineni et al., 2002) as the quality rating proxy and train a BLEU regressor; (2) *Unsupervised*: following the uncertain estimation literature (Lakshminarayanan et al., 2017), we use the ensemble model's output probability as the estimation of quality. Furthermore, to evaluate how well the QE models perform, we collect 200 human quality ratings (50 ratings for SMT Chr-En, SMT En-Chr, NMT Chr-En, and NMT En-Chr, respectively). We show that our methods obtain moderate to strong correlations with human judgment (Pearson correlation coefficient $\gamma \geq 0.44$).

One main purpose of our system is to allow human-in-the-loop learning. Since limited parallel texts are available, it is important to involve humans, especially experts, in the loop to give feedback and then improve the models accordingly. We develop two different user feedback interfaces for experts and common users, respectively (shown in Figure 2). We ask experts to provide quality rating, to correct the model-translated content, and to leave open-ended comments; for common users, we allow them to rate how helpful the translation is and to provide open-ended comments. Upon submission, we collected 216 pieces of feedback from 4 experts. We find that experts favor NMT more than SMT because SMT excessively copies from source sentences; according to their ratings and comments, current translation systems *can translate fragments of the source sentence but make major mistakes*. Our naive human-in-the-loop learning, by adding these 216 expert-corrected parallel texts back to the training set, obtains equal or slightly better translation results. Plus, the expert comments shine a light on where the model often makes mistakes. Besides, our demo allows users to input text or choose an example input to translate (shown in Figure 1). These examples are from our monolingual databases, so that experts will annotate them by providing translation corrections. Finally, to support an intermediate interpretation of the model translations, we visualize the word alignment learned by the translation model and link to cherokeedictionary to provide relevant terms from the dictionary.

Our code is hosted at ChrEnTranslate and our online website is at chren.cs.unc.edu. Common users need to accept agreement terms before using our service to avoid misuse; access the expert page chren.cs.unc.edu/expert requires authorization. We encourage fluent Cherokee speakers to contact us and contribute to our human-in-the-loop learning procedure. A demonstration video of our website is at YouTube. In summary, our demo is featured by (1) offering the first online machine translation system for translation between Cherokee and English, which can assist both professional translators or Cherokee learners; (2) documenting human feedback, which, in the long run, expands Cherokee data corpus and allows human-in-the-loop model development. Additionally, our website can be easily adapted to any other low-resource translation pairs.

2 System Description

2.1 Translation Models

As shown in Figure 1, our system allows users to choose statistical or neural model (SMT or NMT).

SMT is more effective for out-of-domain translation between Cherokee and English (Zhang et al., 2020). We implement phrase-based SMT model via Moses (Koehn et al., 2007), where we train a 3-gram KenLM (Heafield et al., 2013) and learn word alignment by GIZA++ (Och and Ney, 2003). Model weights are tuned on a development set by MERT (Och, 2003).

NMT has better in-domain performance and can generate more fluent texts. We implement the global attentional model proposed by Luong et al. (2015). Detailed hyper-parameters can be found in Section 3.1. Note that we do not use Transformer because it empirically works worse (Zhang et al., 2020). And we find that the multilingual techniques we explored only significantly improve in-domain performance when using multilingual Bible texts, so we suspect that it biases to Bible style texts. Hence, we also do not apply multilingual techniques and just train the backbone models with our Cherokee-English parallel texts. We use a 3-model ensemble as our final working model.

2.2 Quality Estimation

Supervised QE. The QE (Specia et al., 2010) task in WMT campaign provides thousands of model-translated texts plus corresponding human

Figure 1: Translation interface of our demonstration system. Note that "Ꮎ ᎠᏍᎦᏯ ᎠᎢ." is not a correct translation. See Figure 2 for the corrected translation by an expert.

ratings, which allow participants to train supervised QE models. Fomicheva et al. (2020a) show that supervised models work significantly better than unsupervised ones. Since we are unable to collect thousands of human ratings, we use BLEU (Papineni et al., 2002) as the quality rating. We use 17-fold cross-validation to obtain training data, i.e., we split our 17K parallel texts into 17 folds, use 16 folds to train a translation model, get the translation features plus BLEU scores of examples in the left one fold, repeat this for 17 times, and finally, we get the features plus BLEU scores of 17K examples. Then, we separate 16K examples as a training set to train a BLEU score regressor and evaluate the performance on the left 1K examples. Fomicheva et al. (2020a,b) define three sets of features. However, we need to compute features online, so some features (e.g., dropout features) that require multiple forward computations will greatly increase latency. W use features that will not cause too much speed lag. For SMT, we use:

(a) output length L_t, i.e., the number of words in the translated text;

(b) total score;

(c) scores of distortion, language model, lexical reordering, phrases penalty, translation model, and word penalty;

(d) length normalized (b) and (c) features (i.e., divide each feature from (b) and (c) by (a)).

For NMT, we use:

(a) output length;

(b) log probability and length normalized log probability;

(c) probability and length normalized probability;

(d) attention entropy (Fomicheva et al., 2020a,b): $-\frac{1}{L_t}\sum_{i=1}^{L_t}\sum_{j=1}^{L_s}\alpha_{ij}\log\alpha_{ij}$, where L_s is the length of source text, and α_{ij} is the attention weight between target token i and source token j.

Finally, we use XGBoost (Chen and Guestrin, 2016) as the BLEU regressor.[2] As shown in Figure 1, we use 5 stars to show QE, therefore, we rescale the estimated quality to 0-5 by dividing the predicted BLEU score (0-100) by 20.

Unsupervised QE. Even though supervised QE works better (Fomicheva et al., 2020a), we suspect that the advantage cannot generalize to open domain scenarios unless we have a large amount of human-rated data to learn from. Hence, we also explore unsupervised QE methods. Unsupervised QE is closely related to uncertainty estimation. We can use how uncertain the model is to quantify how low-quality the model output is. Though it is intuitive to use the output probability as model's confidence, Guo et al. (2017) point out that the output probability is often poorly calibrated, so that they propose to re-calibrate the probability on the development set. However, this method is designed for classification tasks and not applicable for language generation. Gal and Ghahramani (2016) show that "dropout" can be a good uncertainty estimator, inspired by which Fomicheva et al. (2020b) propose the dropout features. However, the multiple forward passes are not preferable for an online system. Lakshminarayanan et al. (2017) demonstrate that the ensemble model's output probability can better estimate the model's uncertainty than dropout. We find that this method is simple yet effective for

[2]We also tested GradientBoost (Friedman, 2002) and MLP, but XGBoost empirically works better.

(a) Common User Feedback

(b) Expert Feedback

Figure 2: Two user feedback interfaces of our demonstration system. (b) shows the feedback given by an expert.

NMT. Note that we normalize the output probability by the sentence length. Similarly, we rescale the normalized probability (0-1) to 0-5 by multiplying it by 5.

Human Quality Rating. So far, our QE development and evaluation are all based on BLEU. To better evaluate QE performance, we collect 200 human ratings (all rated by Prof. Benjamin Frey[3]), 50 ratings for Chr-En SMT, En-Chr SMT, Chr-En NMT, and En-Chr NMT, respectively. We follow the direct assessment setup used by FLoRes (Guzmán et al., 2019),[4] and thus each translated sentence receives a 0-100 quality rating.

2.3 User Feedback & Example Inputs

Enlarging the parallel texts is a fundamental approach to improve the translation model's performance. Besides compiling existing translated texts, it is important to newly translate English texts to Cherokee by translators. Our system is designed to not only assist these translators but also document their feedback and post-edited correct translation, so that model can be improved by using this feedback, i.e., human-in-the-loop learning. To achieve this goal, we design two kinds of user feedback interfaces. One is for common users, in which users can rate how helpful the translation is (in 5-point Likert scale) and leave open-ended comments, as shown in Figure 2 (a). The other is for experts, in which authorized users can rate the quality, correct the translated text, and leave open-ended comments, as shown in Figure 2 (b). Upon submission, we collect 216 pieces of feedback from 4 experts and detailed analysis can be found in Section 3.3. Meanwhile, as shown in

[3] Benjamin Frey is a proficient second-language Cherokee speaker and a citizen of the Eastern Band of Cherokee Indians.

[4] 0–10: represents a translation that is completely incorrect and inaccurate; 11–29 represents a translation with a few correct keywords, but the overall meaning is different from the source; 30–50 represents a translation that contains translated fragments of the source string, with major mistakes; 51–69 represents a translation that is understandable and conveys the overall meaning of source string but contains typos or grammatical errors; 70–90 represents a translation that closely preserves the semantics of the source sentence; 90–100 range represents a perfect translation.

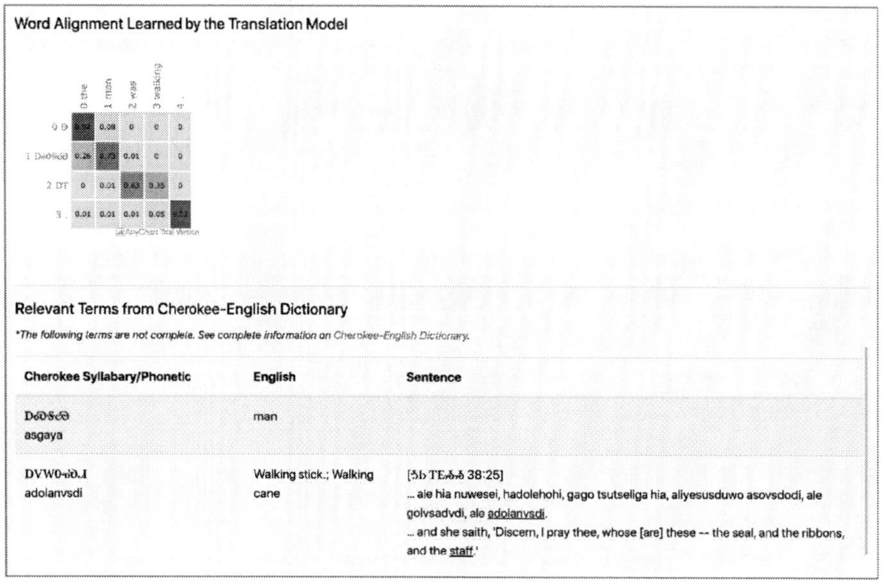

Figure 3: Word alignment visualization and link to Cherokee-English Dictionary.

Figure 1, besides inputting text, users can also choose an example input to translate. These examples are from our Cherokee or English monolingual databases. On the one hand this provides users with more convenience; on the other hand, whenever experts submit translation corrections of an example, we will updated its status as "labeled". Hence, we can gradually collect human translations for the monolingual data.

2.4 Other Features

As shown in Figure 3, to make model prediction more interpretable to users, we **visualize the word alignment** learned by the translation model. For SMT, we visualize the hard word-to-word alignment; for NMT, we visualize the soft attention map between source and target tokens. Additionally, to provide users with some oracle and handy references from the dictionary, we **link to cherokee-dictionary**. We use each of the source and target tokens as a query and list up to 15 relevant terms on our web page.

3 Evaluation

3.1 Implementation Details

Data. To train translation models, we use the 14K parallel data collected by our previous work (Zhang et al., 2020) plus 3K newly complied parallel texts. We randomly sample 1K as our development set and treat the rest as the training set. The data is open-sourced at ChrEn/data/demo. To collect human quality ratings, we randomly sample 50 examples from the development set, and for each of them, we collect 4 ratings for Chr-En/En-Chr SMT and Chr-En/En-Chr NMT, respectively.

Setup. We implement SMT models via Moses (Koehn et al., 2007). After training and tuning, we run it as a server process.[5] We develop our NMT models via OpenNMT (Klein et al., 2017). For both Chr-En and En-Chr NMT models , we use 2-layer LSTM encoder and decoder, general attention (Luong et al., 2015), hidden size=1024, label smoothing (Szegedy et al., 2016) equals to 0.2, dynamic batching with 1000 tokens. Differently, the Chr-En NMT model uses dropout=0.3, BPE tokenizer (Sennrich et al., 2016), and minimum word frequency=10; the En-Chr NMT model uses dropout=0.5, Moses tokenizer, and minimum word frequency=0. We train each NMT model with three random seeds (7, 77, 777) and use the 3-model ensemble as the final translation model, and we use beam search (beam size=5) to generate translations. We implement the supervised QE model with XGBoost.[6] XGBoost has three important hyperparameters: max depth, eta, the number of rounds. Tuned on the development set, we set them as (5, 0.1, 100) for Chr-En SMT, (3, 0.1, 80) for En-Chr SMT, (4, 0.5, 40) for Chr-En NMT, and

[5] `http://www.statmt.org/moses/?n=Advanced.Moses`

[6] `https://xgboost.readthedocs.io/en/latest/python/index.html`

Model		QE	BLEU		Human Rating	
			Chr-En	En-Chr	Chr-En	En-Chr
SMT	Supervised	XGBoost	**0.75**	**0.71**	**0.63**	**0.44**
	Unsupervised	TranslationModel / length	0.36	0.46	0.07	-0.09
		LM / length	0.34	0.43	-0.11	0.11
		PhrasePenalty / length	-0.33	-0.52	0.06	0.03
NMT (ensemble)	Supervised	XGBoost	**0.79**	**0.68**	0.53	0.38
	Unsupervised	Exp(LogProbability / length)	0.75	0.63	**0.59**	0.44
		LogProbability / length	0.45	0.50	0.37	**0.52**

Table 1: Pearson correlation coefficients between QE and BLEU or between QE and human rating. "/ length" represents the normalization by output sentence length.

Model	Chr-En	En-Chr
SMT	17.0	12.9
NMT (single)	18.1	13.8
NMT (ensemble)	**19.9**	**14.8**

Table 2: The performance of translation models.

(5, 0.1, 40) for En-Chr NMT. Lastly, the backend of our demonstration website is based on the Flask framework.

Metrics. We evaluate translation systems by BLEU (Papineni et al., 2002) calculated via SacreBLEU[7] (Post, 2018). Supervised QE models are developed by minimizing the mean square error of predicting BLEU, but all QE models are evaluated by the correlation with BLEU on development set and the correlation with human ratings. We use Pearson correlation (Benesty et al., 2009).

3.2 Quantitative Results

Translation. Table 2 shows the translation performance on our 1K development set, which are significantly better than the single-model in-domain translation performance reported in our previous work (Zhang et al., 2020) and thus achieves the state-of-the-art results. In addition, the 3-model NMT ensemble further boosts the performance.

QE. Table 1 illustrates the performance of quality estimation models. In our experiments, we take every feature used in supervised QE as an unsupervised quality estimator. Here, we only present those having a high correlation with BLEU and human rating. It can be observed that, for SMT, supervised QE consistently works better, whereas, for NMT, unsupervised QE has a better correlation with human rating. The obtained correlations with human judgement are moderate ($\gamma \geq 0.3$) to strong ($\gamma \geq 0.5$) (Cohen, 1988). Therefore, we use the trained XGBoost for SMT model's QE and use the length normalized probability (i.e., Exp(LogProbability / length)) for NMT model's QE in our online demonstration system.

[7]BLEU+c.mixed+#.1+s.exp+tok.13a+v.1.5.0

3.3 Qualitative Results

Expert Feedback. Upon submission, we received 216 pieces of feedback from 4 experts (including Prof. Benjamin Frey and 3 other fluent Cherokee speakers). The results are shown in Table 3. It can be observed that we received a lot more feedback to NMT than SMT because SMT excessively copies words from source sentences when translating open-domain texts whereas NMT can mostly translate into the target language. On average, there are only 2.3 tokens in the input or translated Cherokee sentence; however, the average translation quality rating is only 2.45 out of 5, which is close to the average rating (43.8 out of 100) of the 200 human ratings we collected. Therefore, according to FLoRes's rating standard (Guzmán et al., 2019) (see footnote 2), our translation systems *can translate fragments of the source string but make major mistakes* in general. Besides ratings, we received 36 open-ended comments that shine a light on common mistakes made by the models. The most frequent comments are (1) *model gets some parts correct but others wrong*. For example, "it got the subject but not the verb", "it got the stem right but used 3rd person prefix", "it missed the part about going to town, but got 'today' correct", etc. (2) *model uses archaic English terms*, like "thy", "thou", "speaketh", etc. because the majority of our training set is the Cherokee Old Testament and the Cherokee New Testament.

Human-in-the-Loop Learning. To improve models based on expert feedback, we propose to simply add the 216 expert-corrected parallel texts

Model	Chr-En	En-Chr
SMT	12 / 1.92 / 0.39	6 / 2.0 / 0.66
NMT	166 / 2.58 / 0.43	32 / 2.13 / 0.21

Table 3: Expert feedback. In each cell, the 3 numbers are the number of feedback received / average quality rating / Pearson correlation coefficient between quality rating and quality estimation.

back to our training set and retrain the translation models.[8] The new BLEU results on our development set are 17.3, 13.0, 20.0, 14.8 for Chr-En SMT, En-Chr SMT, Chr-En NMT (ensemble), and En-Chr NMT (ensemble), respectively, which are equal or slightly better than the results in Table 2. To tackle the archaic English issue, we simply replace archaic English terms ("thy", "thou") with new English terms ("your", "you").

4 Conclusion & Future Work

In this work, we develop a Cherokee-English Machine Translation demonstration system that intends to demonstrate and support automatic translation between Cherokee and English, collect user feedback/translations, allow human-in-the-loop development, and eventually contribute to the revitalization of the endangered Cherokee language. Future work involves inviting more experts and common users to test/use our system and proposing more efficient and effective human-in-the-loop learning methods.

5 Broader Impact Statement

As shown in Section 3.3, the current translation models are still far from being reliably used in practice. Therefore, our system is just a demonstration or prototype of the translation between Cherokee and English, while the model-translated texts are not supposed to be directly applied anywhere else without confirmation from professional translators. We stress this point in our agreement terms. Common users need to accept those terms before using our system; experts need to agree to those terms as well before being authorized. Lastly, we sincerely thank David Montgomery, Barnes Powell, and Tom Belt for voluntarily participating in our system test and providing their feedback.

[8]We also tried to up-weight these examples by repeating them by 5 or 10 times but did not see better performance.

Acknowledgments

We thank the reviewers for their helpful comments, and we thank David Montgomery, Barnes Powell, and Tom Belt for voluntarily participating in our system test and providing their valuable feedback. This work was supported by NSF-CAREER Award 1846185, ONR Grant N00014-18-1-2871, and a Microsoft Investigator Fellowship. The views contained in this article are those of the authors and not of the funding agency.

References

Jacob Benesty, Jingdong Chen, Yiteng Huang, and Israel Cohen. 2009. Pearson correlation coefficient. In *Noise reduction in speech processing*, pages 1–4. Springer.

Jeffrey Bourns. 2019. Cherokee syllabary texts: Digital documentation and linguistic description. In *2nd Conference on Language, Data and Knowledge (LDK 2019)*. Schloss Dagstuhl-Leibniz-Zentrum fuer Informatik.

Tianqi Chen and Carlos Guestrin. 2016. Xgboost: A scalable tree boosting system. In *Proceedings of the 22nd acm sigkdd international conference on knowledge discovery and data mining*, pages 785–794.

Jacob Cohen. 1988. *Statistical Power Analysis for the Behavioral Sciences*. Routledge.

Ellen Cushman. 2019. Language perseverance and translation of cherokee documents. *College English*, 82(1):115–134.

Durbin Feeling. 2018. *Cherokee Narratives: A Linguistic Study*. University of Oklahoma Press.

Marina Fomicheva, Shuo Sun, Lisa Yankovskaya, Frédéric Blain, Vishrav Chaudhary, Mark Fishel, Francisco Guzmán, and Lucia Specia. 2020a. Bergamot-latte submissions for the wmt20 quality estimation shared task. In *Proceedings of the Fifth Conference on Machine Translation*, pages 1010–1017.

Marina Fomicheva, Shuo Sun, Lisa Yankovskaya, Frédéric Blain, Francisco Guzmán, Mark Fishel, Nikolaos Aletras, Vishrav Chaudhary, and Lucia Specia. 2020b. Unsupervised quality estimation for neural machine translation. *Transactions of the Association for Computational Linguistics*, 8:539–555.

Benjamin Frey. 2020. "data is nice:" theoretical and pedagogical implications of an eastern cherokee corpus. *LD&C Special Publication*.

Jerome H Friedman. 2002. Stochastic gradient boosting. *Computational statistics & data analysis*, 38(4):367–378.

Yarin Gal and Zoubin Ghahramani. 2016. Dropout as a bayesian approximation: Representing model uncertainty in deep learning. In *international conference on machine learning*, pages 1050–1059. PMLR.

Chuan Guo, Geoff Pleiss, Yu Sun, and Kilian Q Weinberger. 2017. On calibration of modern neural networks. In *International Conference on Machine Learning*, pages 1321–1330. PMLR.

Francisco Guzmán, Peng-Jen Chen, Myle Ott, Juan Pino, Guillaume Lample, Philipp Koehn, Vishrav Chaudhary, and Marc'Aurelio Ranzato. 2019. The flores evaluation datasets for low-resource machine translation: Nepali–english and sinhala–english. In *Proceedings of the 2019 Conference on Empirical Methods in Natural Language Processing and the 9th International Joint Conference on Natural Language Processing (EMNLP-IJCNLP)*, pages 6100–6113.

Kenneth Heafield, Ivan Pouzyrevsky, Jonathan H Clark, and Philipp Koehn. 2013. Scalable modified kneser-ney language model estimation. In *Proceedings of the 51st Annual Meeting of the Association for Computational Linguistics (Volume 2: Short Papers)*, pages 690–696.

Ruth Bradley Holmes and Betty Sharp Smith. 1976. *Beginning Cherokee*. University of Oklahoma Press, Norman.

M. Joyner. 2014. *Cherokee Language Lessons*. Lulu Press, Incorporated.

Guillaume Klein, Yoon Kim, Yuntian Deng, Jean Senellart, and Alexander Rush. 2017. OpenNMT: Open-source toolkit for neural machine translation. In *Proceedings of ACL 2017, System Demonstrations*, pages 67–72, Vancouver, Canada. Association for Computational Linguistics.

Philipp Koehn, Hieu Hoang, Alexandra Birch, Chris Callison-Burch, Marcello Federico, Nicola Bertoldi, Brooke Cowan, Wade Shen, Christine Moran, Richard Zens, Chris Dyer, Ondřej Bojar, Alexandra Constantin, and Evan Herbst. 2007. Moses: Open source toolkit for statistical machine translation. In *Proceedings of the 45th Annual Meeting of the Association for Computational Linguistics Companion Volume Proceedings of the Demo and Poster Sessions*, pages 177–180, Prague, Czech Republic. Association for Computational Linguistics.

Balaji Lakshminarayanan, Alexander Pritzel, and Charles Blundell. 2017. Simple and scalable predictive uncertainty estimation using deep ensembles. In *Proceedings of the 31st International Conference on Neural Information Processing Systems*, pages 6405–6416.

Minh-Thang Luong, Hieu Pham, and Christopher D Manning. 2015. Effective approaches to attention-based neural machine translation. In *Proceedings of the 2015 Conference on Empirical Methods in Natural Language Processing*, pages 1412–1421.

Cherokee Nation. 2001. Ga-du-gi: A vision for working together to preserve the cherokee language. report of a needs assessment survey and a 10-year language revitalization plan.

Franz Josef Och. 2003. Minimum error rate training in statistical machine translation. In *Proceedings of the 41st annual meeting of the Association for Computational Linguistics*, pages 160–167.

Franz Josef Och and Hermann Ney. 2003. A systematic comparison of various statistical alignment models. *Computational Linguistics*, 29(1):19–51.

Kishore Papineni, Salim Roukos, Todd Ward, and Wei-Jing Zhu. 2002. Bleu: a method for automatic evaluation of machine translation. In *Proceedings of the 40th annual meeting on association for computational linguistics*, pages 311–318. Association for Computational Linguistics.

Matt Post. 2018. A call for clarity in reporting BLEU scores. In *Proceedings of the Third Conference on Machine Translation: Research Papers*, pages 186–191, Belgium, Brussels. Association for Computational Linguistics.

Rico Sennrich, Barry Haddow, and Alexandra Birch. 2016. Neural machine translation of rare words with subword units. In *Proceedings of the 54th Annual Meeting of the Association for Computational Linguistics (Volume 1: Long Papers)*, pages 1715–1725.

Lucia Specia, Dhwaj Raj, and Marco Turchi. 2010. Machine translation evaluation versus quality estimation. *Machine translation*, 24(1):39–50.

Christian Szegedy, Vincent Vanhoucke, Sergey Ioffe, Jon Shlens, and Zbigniew Wojna. 2016. Rethinking the inception architecture for computer vision. In *Proceedings of the IEEE conference on computer vision and pattern recognition*, pages 2818–2826.

Shiyue Zhang, Benjamin Frey, and Mohit Bansal. 2020. ChrEn: Cherokee-English machine translation for endangered language revitalization. In *Proceedings of the 2020 Conference on Empirical Methods in Natural Language Processing (EMNLP)*, pages 577–595, Online. Association for Computational Linguistics.

ExplainaBoard: An Explainable Leaderboard for NLP

Pengfei Liu[1†], **Jinlan Fu**[2], **Yang Xiao**[2], **Weizhe Yuan**[1], **Shuaichen Chang**[3], **Junqi Dai**[2], **Yixin Liu**[1], **Zihuiwen Ye**[1], **Graham Neubig**[1‡]

[1]Carnegie Mellon University, [2]Fudan University, [3]The Ohio State University,

†pliu3@cs.cmu.edu, ‡gneubig@cs.cmu.edu

Abstract

With the rapid development of NLP research, leaderboards have emerged as one tool to track the performance of various systems on various NLP tasks. They are effective in this goal to some extent, but generally present a rather simplistic one-dimensional view of the submitted systems, communicated only through holistic accuracy numbers. In this paper, we present a new conceptualization and implementation of NLP evaluation: the ExplainaBoard, which in addition to inheriting the functionality of the standard leaderboard, also allows researchers to (i) diagnose strengths and weaknesses of a single system (e.g. what is the best-performing system bad at?) (ii) interpret relationships between multiple systems. (e.g. where does system A outperform system B? What if we combine systems A, B and C?) and (iii) examine prediction results closely (e.g. what are common errors made by multiple systems or in what contexts do particular errors occur?). So far, ExplainaBoard covers more than 400 systems, 50 datasets, 40 languages, and 12 tasks.[1] We not only released an online **platform** at the website[2] but also make our evaluation tool an **API** with *MIT Licence* at Github[3] and PyPi[4] that allows users to conveniently assess their models offline. We additionally release all **output files** from systems that we have run or collected to motivate "output-driven" research in the future.

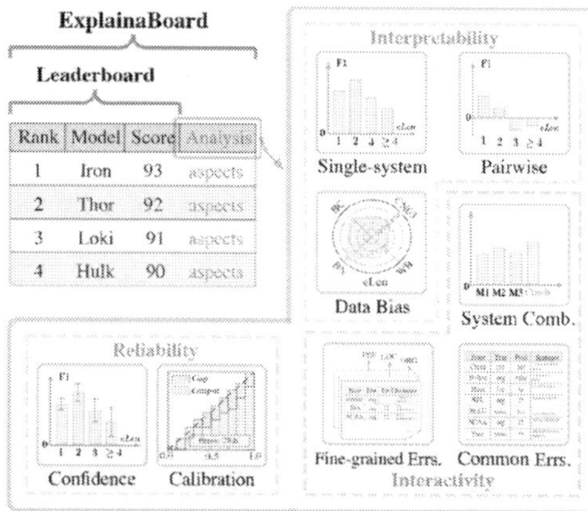

Figure 1: Illustration of the ExplainaBoard concept. Compared to vanilla leaderboards, ExplainaBoard allows users to perform *interpretable* (single-system , pairwise analysis, data bias), *interactive* (system combination, fine-grained/common error analysis), and *reliable* analysis (confidence interval, calibration) on systems in which they are interested. "Comb." denotes "combination" and "Errs" represents "errors". "PER, LOC, ORG" refer to different labels.

1 Introduction

Natural language processing (NLP) research has been and is making astounding strides forward. This is true both for classical tasks such as machine translation (Sutskever et al., 2014; Wu et al., 2016), as well as for new tasks (Lu et al., 2016; Rajpurkar et al., 2016), domains (Beltagy et al., 2019), and languages (Conneau and Lample, 2019). One way this progress is quantified is through *leaderboards*, which report and update performance numbers of state-of-the-art systems on one or more tasks. Some prototypical leaderboards include GLUE and SuperGLUE for natural language understanding (Wang et al., 2018, 2019), XTREME and XGLUE (Hu et al., 2020; Liang et al., 2020) for multilingual understanding, the WMT shared tasks (Barrault et al., 2020) for machine translation, and GEM and GENIE for natural language generation (Gehrmann et al., 2021; Khashabi et al., 2021), among many others.

These leaderboards serve an important purpose:

[1]ExplainaBoard keeps updated and is recently upgraded by supporting (1) **multilingual multi-task benchmark** and (2) more complicated task: **machine translation**, which reviewers also suggested.

[2]http://explainaboard.nlpedia.ai/

[3]https://github.com/neulab/explainaBoard

[4]https://pypi.org/project/interpret-eval/

Proceedings of the Joint Conference of the 59th Annual Meeting of the Association for Computational Linguistics and the 11th International Joint Conference on Natural Language Processing: System Demonstrations, pages 280–289, August 1st - August 6th, 2021.

they provide a standardized evaluation setup, often on multiple tasks, that eases reproducible model comparison across organizations. However, at the same time, due to the prestige imbued by a top, or high, place on a leaderboard they also can result in a singular focus on raising evaluation numbers at the cost of deeper scientific understanding of model properties (Ethayarajh and Jurafsky, 2020). In particular, we argue that, among others, the following are three major limitations of the existing leaderboard paradigm:

- **Interpretability:** Most existing leaderboards commonly use a single number to summarize system performance holistically. This is conducive to system ranking but at the same time, the results are opaque, making the strengths and weaknesses of systems less interpretable.
- **Interactivity:** Existing leaderboards are static and non-interactive, which limits the ability of users to dig deeper into the results. Thus, (1) they usually do not flexibly support more complex evaluation settings (e.g. multi-dataset, multi-metric, multi-language) (2) users may miss opportunities to understand the relationships between different systems. For example, where does model A outperform model B? Would the performance be further improved if we combine the Top-3 models?
- **Reliability:** Given the increasing role that leaderboards have taken in guiding NLP research, it is important that information expressed in them is reliable, especially on datasets with small sample sizes, but most current leaderboards do not give an idea of the reliability of system rankings.

In this paper, we describe EXPLAINABOARD (see Fig.1), a software package and hosted leaderboard that satisfies all of the above desiderata. It also serves as a prototype implementation of some desirable features that may be included in future leaderboards, even independent of the provided software itself. We have deployed EXPLAINABOARD for 9 different tasks and 41 different datasets, and demonstrate how it can be easily adapted to new tasks of interest.

We expect that EXPLAINABOARD will benefit different steps of the research process:
(i) **System Developement**: EXPLAINABOARD provides more detailed information regarding the submitted systems (e.g. fine-grained results, confidence intervals), allowing system developers to diagnose successes and failures of their own systems, or compare their systems with baselines and understand where improvements of their proposed methods come from. This better understanding can lead to more efficient and effective system improvements. Additionally, EXPLAINABOARD can help system developers uncover their systems' advantages over others, even when these systems have not achieved state-of-the-art performance holistically. (ii) **Leaderboard Organization**: The EXPLAINABOARD software both provides a ready-made platform for easy leaderboard development over different NLP tasks, and helps upgrade traditional leaderboards to allow for more fine-grained analysis. For example, we have already established an ExplainaBoard [5] for the existing XTREME benchmark.[6] (iii) **Broad Analysis and Understanding**: Because EXPLAINABOARD encourages system developers to provide their system outputs in an easy-to-analyze format, these will also help researchers, particularly those just starting in a particular NLP sub-field, get a broad sense of what current state-of-the-art models can and cannot do. This not only helps them quickly track the progress of different areas, but also can allow them to understand the relative advantages of diverse systems, suggesting insightful ideas for what's left and what's next.[7]

2 ExplainaBoard

As stated above, EXPLAINABOARD extends existing leaderboards, improving their interpretability, interactivity, and reliability. It does so by providing a number of functionalities that are applicable to a wide variety of NLP tasks (as illustrated in Tab. 1). Many of these functionalities are grounded in existing research on evaluation and fine-grained diagnostics.

2.1 Interpretability

Interpretable evaluation (Popović and Ney, 2011; Stymne, 2011; Neubig et al., 2019; Fu et al., 2020a), is a research area that considers methods that break down the holistic performance of each system into different interpretable groups. For example, in a

[5] `http://explainaboard.nlpedia.ai/leaderboard/xtreme/`

[6] `https://sites.research.google/xtreme/`

[7] Since the first release of EXPLAINABOARD, we have received invitations from multiple companies, startups, and researchers to collaborate, and we are working together to make it better for the community.

Aspect	Functionality	Input	Output
Interpretability	Single-system Analysis	One model	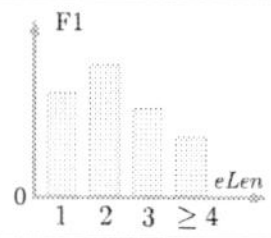 **Performance Histogram**: the input model is good at dealing with short entities, while achieving lower performance on long entities.
	Pairwise Analysis	Two models (M1,M2)	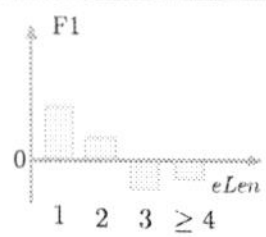 **Performance Gap Histogram** (M1−M2): M1 is better at dealing with short entities, while M2 is better at dealing with long entities.
	Data Bias Analysis	Multi-dataset	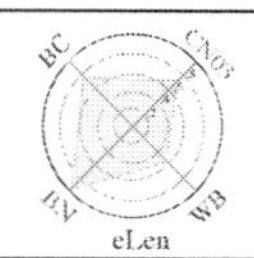 **Data Bias Chart**: For the `entity length` attribute, the average entity length (We average the length of all test entities on a given data set.) of these datasets order by descending is BN> BC> CN03> WB.
Interactivity	Fine-grained Error Analysis	Single- or Pairwise-system diagnostic results	 **Error Table**: Error analysis allows the user to print out the entities that are incorrectly predicted by the given model, as well as the true label of the entity, the mispredicted label, and the sentence where the entity is located.
	System Combination	Multi-models (M1,M2,M3)	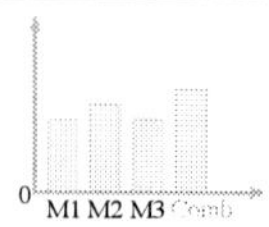 **Ensemble Chart**: The combined result of model M1, M2, and M3 is shown by the histogram with x-label value `comb`. The combined result is better than the single models.
Reliability	Confidence	One model	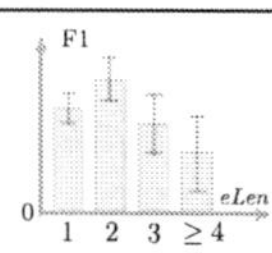 **Error Bars**: the error bars represent 95% confidence intervals of the performance on the specific bucket.
	Calibration	One model	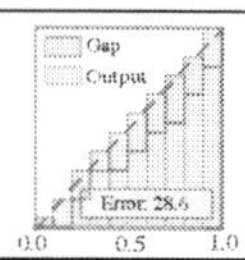 **Reliability Diagram**: Confidence histograms (red) and reliability diagrams (blue). that indicate the accuracy of model probability estimates

Table 1: A graphical breakdown of the functionality of EXPLAINABOARD, with examples from an NER task.

Named Entity Recognition (NER) task, we may examine the accuracy along different dimensions of a concerned entity (such as "entity frequency," telling us how well the model does on entities that appear in the training data a certain number of times) or sentences (such as "sentence length," telling us how well the model does on entities that appear in longer or shorter sentences) (Fu et al., 2020a). This makes it possible to understand where models do well and poorly, leading to further insights beyond those that can be gleaned by holistic evaluation numbers. Applying this to a new task involves the following steps: (i) *Attribute definition*: define attributes by which we can partition the test set into different groups. (ii) *Bucketing*: partition into different buckets based on defined attributes and calculate performance w.r.t each bucket.

Generally, previous work on interpretable evaluation has been performed over single tasks, while EXPLAINABOARD allows for comprehensive evaluation of different types of tasks in a single software package. We concretely show several ways interpretable evaluation can be defined within EXPLAINABOARD below:

F1[8]: Single-system Analysis: What is a system good or bad at? For an individual system as input, generate a *performance histogram* that highlights the buckets where it performs well or poorly. For example, in Tab. 1 we demonstrate an example from NER where the input system does worse in dealing with longer entities (eLen ≥ 4).

F2: Pairwise Analysis: Where is one system better (worse) than another? Given a pair of systems, interpret where the performance gap occurs. Researchers could flexibly choose two systems they are interested in (e.g. selecting two rows from the leaderboard), and EXPLAINABOARD will output a *performance gap histogram* to describe how the

[8]"F" represents "Functionality".

performance differences change over different buckets of different attributes. Tab. 1 demonstrates how we can see one system is better than the other at longer or shorter entities.

F3: Data Bias Analysis: What are the characteristics of different evaluated datasets? The defined attributes do not only help us interpret system performance, but also make it possible for users to take a closer look at characteristics of diverse datasets. For example, from Fig. 1 shows an example of analyzing differences in average entity length across several datasets.

2.2 Interactivity

EXPLAINABOARD also allows users to dig deeper, interacting with the results in more complex ways.

F4: Fine-grained Error Analysis: What are common mistakes that most systems make and where do they occur? EXPLAINABOARD provides flexible fine-grained error analyses based on the above-described performance evaluation:

1. Users can choose multiple systems and see their *common error cases*, which can be useful to identify *challenging samples* or even *annotation errors*.
2. In single-system analysis, users can choose particular buckets in the performance histogram[9] and see corresponding error samples in that bucket (e.g. which long entities does the current system mispredict?).
3. In pairwise analysis, users can select a bucket, and the unique errors (e.g. system A succeeds while B fails and vice versa) of two models will be displayed.

F5: System Combination: Is there potential complementarity between different systems? System combination (Ting and Witten, 1997; González-Rubio et al., 2011; Duh et al., 2011) is a technique to improve performance by combining the output from multiple existing systems. In EXPLAINABOARD, users can choose multiple systems and obtain combined results calculated by voting over multiple base systems.[10] In practice, for NER task, we use the recently proposed SPANNER (Fu et al., 2021) as a combiner, and for text summarization we employed REFACTOR, a state-of-the-art ensemble approach (Liu et al., 2021). Regarding the other tasks, we adopt the majority voting method for system combination.

2.3 Reliability

The experimental conclusions obtained from the evaluation metrics are not necessarily statistically reliable, especially when the experimental results can be affected by many factors. EXPLAINABOARD also makes a step towards more reliable interpretable evaluation.

F6: Confidence Analysis: To what extent can we trust the results of our system? EXPLAINABOARD can perform confidence analysis over both holistic and fine-grained performance metrics. As shown in Tab. 1, for each bucket, there is an error bar whose width reflects how reliable the performance value is. We claim this is an important feature for fine-grained analysis since the numbers of test samples in each bucket are imbalanced, and with the confidence interval, one could know how much uncertainty there is. In practice, we use bootstrapping method (Efron, 1992; Ye et al., 2021) to calculate the confidence interval.

F7: Calibration Analysis: How well is the confidence of prediction calibrated with its correctness? One commonly-cited issue with modern neural predictors is that their probability estimates are not accurate (i.e. they are poorly *calibrated*), often being over-confident in the correctness of their predictions (Guo et al., 2017). We also incorporate this feature into EXPLAINABOARD, allowing users to evaluate how well-calibrated their systems of interest are.

3 Tasks, Datasets and Systems

We have already added to EXPLAINABOARD 12 NLP tasks, 50 datasets, and 400 models,[11] which cover many or most of top-scoring systems on these tasks.We briefly describe them below, and show high-level statistics in Tab. 2.

Text Classification Prediction of one or multiple pre-defined label(s) for a given input text. The current interface includes datasets for sentiment

[9] Each bin of the performance histogram is clickable, returning an error case table.

[10] With the system combination button of Explainaboard, we observed the-state-of-the art performance of some tasks (e.g., NER, Chunking) can be further improved.

[11] 265 of these models are implemented by us, as unfortunately it is currently not standard in NLP to release the system outputs that EXPLAINABOARD needs.

classification (Pang et al., 2002), topic identification (Wang and Manning, 2012), and intention detection (Chen et al., 2013).

Text-Span Classification Prediction of a predefined class from the input of a text and a span, such as aspect-based sentiment classification task (Pappas and Popescu-Belis, 2014). We collect top-perform system outputs from (Dai et al., 2021).

Text Pair Classification Prediction of a class given two texts, such as the natural language inference task (Bowman et al., 2015).

Sequence Labeling Prediction of a label for each token in a sequence. The EXPLAINABOARD currently includes four concrete tasks: named entity recognition (Tjong Kim Sang and De Meulder, 2003), part-of-speech tagging (Toutanova et al., 2003), text chunking (Ando and Zhang, 2005), and Chinese word segmentation (Chen et al., 2015).

Structure Prediction Prediction of a syntactic or semantic structure from text, where EXPLAINABOARD currently covers semantic parsing tasks (Berant et al., 2013; Yu et al., 2018).

Text Generation EXPLAINABOARD also considers text generation tasks, and currently mainly focuses on conditional text generation, for example, text summarization (Rush et al., 2015; Liu and Lapata, 2019) and machine translation . System outputs on text summarization are expanded based on the previous work's collection (Bhandari et al., 2020) as well as recently state-of-the-art systems (Liu and Liu, 2021) while outputs from machine translation are collected from the WMT20.[12]

4 Case Study

Here, we briefly showcase the actual EXPLAINABOARD interface through a case study on analyzing state-of-the-art NER systems.

4.1 Experimental Setup

Attribute Definition We define attributes following Fu et al. (2020a) and three of them are used below: `entity length`, `sentence length` and `label of entity`.

Collection of Systems Outputs Currently, we collect system outputs by either implementing them by ourselves or collecting from other researchers

Task		Data	Model	Attr.
Text Classification	Sentiment	8	40	2
	Topic	4	18	2
	Intention	1	3	2
Text-Span Classification	Aspect Sentiment	4	20	4
Text Pair Classification	NLI	2	6	7
Sequence Labeling	NER	3	74	9
	POS	3	14	4
	Chunking	3	14	9
	CWS	7	64	7
Structure Pred.	Semantic Parsing	4	12	4
Text Generation	Summarization	2	36	7
	Translation	4	60	9

Table 2: Brief descriptions of tasks, datasets and systems that EXPLAINABOARD currently supports. "Attr." denotes Attribute. "Pred." denotes "Prediction".

(Fu et al., 2020b; Schweter and Akbik, 2020; Yamada et al., 2020). Using these methods, we have gathered 74 models on six NER datasets with system output information.

4.2 Analysis using ExplainaBoard

Fig. 2 illustrates different types of results driven by four functionality buttons[13] over the top-3 NER systems: `LUKE` (Yamada et al., 2020), `FLERT` (Schweter and Akbik, 2020) and `FLAIR` (Akbik et al., 2019).

Box A breaks down the performance of the top-1 system over different attributes.[14] We can intuitively observe that even the state-of-the-art system does worse on longer entities. Users can further print error cases in the longer entity bucket by clicking the corresponding bin.

Box B shows the 1st system's (`LUKE`) performance minus the 2nd system's (`FLERT`) performance. We can see that although `LUKE` surpasses `FLERT` holistically, it performs worse when dealing with PERSON entities.

Box C identifies samples that all systems mispredict. Further analysis of these samples uncovers challenging patterns or annotation errors.

Box D examines potential complementarity among these top-3 systems. The result shows that, by a simple voting ensemble strategy, a new state-

[12]http://www.statmt.org/wmt20/metrics-task.html

[13]As it is relatively challenging to define calibration in structure prediction tasks, this feature is currently only provided for classification tasks. We will explore more in the future.

[14]Due to the page limitation, we only show three.

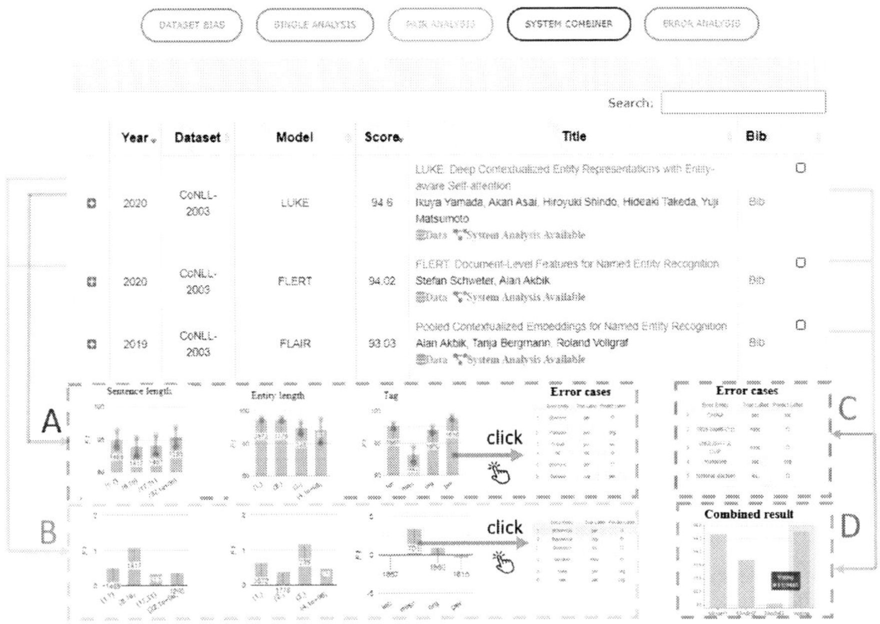

Figure 2: An example of the actual EXPLAINABOARD interface for NER over three top-performing systems on the CoNLL-2003 dataset. **Box A** shows the single-system analysis results obtained when users select the top-1 system and click the "Single Analysis" button. **Box B** shows the pairwise analysis results when top-2 systems are chosen and "Pair Analysis" is clicked. Users can click any bin of the histogram, which results in a fine-grained error case table. **Box C** represents a table with common errors of these top-3 systems. **Box D** illustrates the combined result of the top-3 systems.

of-the-art (94.65 F1) has been achieved on the CoNLL-2003 dataset.

5 Usage

Example Use-cases To show the practical utility of EXPLAINABOARD, we first present examples of how it has been used as an analysis tool in existing published research papers. Fu et al. (2020b) (Tab.4) utilize *single-system* analysis with the attribute of `label consistency` for NER task while Zhong et al. (2019) (Tab.4-5) use it for text summarization with attributes of `density` and `compression`. Fig.4 and Tab.3 in Fu et al. (2020a) leverage the *data bias* analysis and *pairwise system* diagnostics to interpret top-performing NER systems while Tab.4 in Fu et al. (2020c) use *single and pairwise* system analysis to investigate what's next for the Chinese Word Segmentation task. Liu et al. (2021) use *system combiner* functionality to make ensemble analysis of summarization systems and Fig.1 in Ye et al. (2021) use *reliability analysis* functionality to observe how confidence intervals change in different buckets of a performance histogram.

Using ExplainaBoard Researchers can use EXPLAINABOARD in different ways: (i) We maintain a website where each task-specific EXPLAINABOARD allows researchers to interact with it, interpreting systems and datasets that they are interested in from different perspectives. (ii) We also release our back-end code for different NLP tasks so that researchers could flexibly use them to process their own system outputs, which can assist their research projects.

Contributing to ExplainaBoard The community can contribute to EXPLAINABOARD in several ways: (i) Submit system outputs of their implemented models. (ii) Add more informative attributes for different NLP tasks. (iii) Add new datasets or benchmarks for existing or new tasks.

6 Implications and Roadmap

EXPLAINABOARD presents a new paradigm in leaderboard development for NLP. This is just the beginning of its development, and there are many future directions.

Research Revolving on System Outputs[15] Due to the ability to analyze, contrast, or combine results from many systems EXPLAINABOARD incentivizes researchers to submit their results to explainaboard to better understand them and showcase their systems' strengths. At the same time, EXPLAINABOARD will serve as a central repository for system outputs across many tasks, allowing for future avenues of research into cross-system analysis or system combination.

Enriching ExplainaBoard with Glass-box Analysis EXPLAINABOARD currently performs black-box analysis, solely analyzing system outputs without accessing model internals. On the other hand, there are many other glass-box interpretability tools that look at model internals, such as the AllenNLP Interpret (Wallace et al., 2019) and Language Interpretability Tool (Tenney et al., 2020). Expanding leaderboards to glass-box analysis methods (see Lipton (2018); Belinkov and Glass (2019) for a survey) is an interesting future work.

In the future, we aim to improve the applicability and usefulness by following action items: (1) Collaborate with more leaderboard organizers of diverse tasks and set up corresponding EXPLAINABOARDs for them. (2) Cover more tasks, datasets, models, as well as functionalities.

Acknowledgements

We thanks all reviewers for their valuable comments and authors who share their system outputs with us: Ikuya Yamada, Stefan Schweter, Colin Raffel, Yang Liu, Li Dong. We also thank Vijay Viswanathan, Yiran Chen, Hiroaki Hayashi for useful discussion and feedback about EXPLAINABOARD.

The work was supported in part by the Air Force Research Laboratory under agreement number FA8750-19-2-0200. The U.S. Government is authorized to reproduce and distribute reprints for Governmental purposes notwithstanding any copyright notation thereon. The views and conclusions contained herein are those of the authors and should not be interpreted as necessarily representing the official policies or endorsements, either expressed or implied, of the Air Force Research Laboratory or the U.S. Government.

[15]We released system outputs of EXPLAINABOARD: `http://explainaboard.nlpedia.ai/download.html`

References

Alan Akbik, Tanja Bergmann, and Roland Vollgraf. 2019. Pooled contextualized embeddings for named entity recognition. In *Proceedings of the 2019 Conference of the North American Chapter of the Association for Computational Linguistics: Human Language Technologies, Volume 1 (Long and Short Papers)*, pages 724–728, Minneapolis, Minnesota. Association for Computational Linguistics.

Rie Ando and Tong Zhang. 2005. A high-performance semi-supervised learning method for text chunking. In *Proceedings of the 43rd Annual Meeting of the Association for Computational Linguistics (ACL'05)*, pages 1–9, Ann Arbor, Michigan. Association for Computational Linguistics.

Loïc Barrault, Magdalena Biesialska, Ondřej Bojar, Marta R. Costa-jussà, Christian Federmann, Yvette Graham, Roman Grundkiewicz, Barry Haddow, Matthias Huck, Eric Joanis, Tom Kocmi, Philipp Koehn, Chi-kiu Lo, Nikola Ljubešić, Christof Monz, Makoto Morishita, Masaaki Nagata, Toshiaki Nakazawa, Santanu Pal, Matt Post, and Marcos Zampieri. 2020. Findings of the 2020 conference on machine translation (WMT20). In *Proceedings of the Fifth Conference on Machine Translation*, pages 1–55, Online. Association for Computational Linguistics.

Yonatan Belinkov and James Glass. 2019. Analysis methods in neural language processing: A survey. *Transactions of the Association for Computational Linguistics*, 7:49–72.

Iz Beltagy, Kyle Lo, and Arman Cohan. 2019. SciBERT: A pretrained language model for scientific text. In *Proceedings of the 2019 Conference on Empirical Methods in Natural Language Processing and the 9th International Joint Conference on Natural Language Processing (EMNLP-IJCNLP)*, pages 3615–3620, Hong Kong, China. Association for Computational Linguistics.

Jonathan Berant, Andrew Chou, Roy Frostig, and Percy Liang. 2013. Semantic parsing on Freebase from question-answer pairs. In *Proceedings of the 2013 Conference on Empirical Methods in Natural Language Processing*, pages 1533–1544, Seattle, Washington, USA. Association for Computational Linguistics.

Manik Bhandari, Pranav Narayan Gour, Atabak Ashfaq, Pengfei Liu, and Graham Neubig. 2020. Re-evaluating evaluation in text summarization. In *Proceedings of the 2020 Conference on Empirical Methods in Natural Language Processing (EMNLP)*, pages 9347–9359, Online. Association for Computational Linguistics.

Samuel R. Bowman, Gabor Angeli, Christopher Potts, and Christopher D. Manning. 2015. A large annotated corpus for learning natural language inference. In *Proceedings of the 2015 Conference on Empirical Methods in Natural Language Processing*, pages

632–642, Lisbon, Portugal. Association for Computational Linguistics.

Xinchi Chen, Xipeng Qiu, Chenxi Zhu, Pengfei Liu, and Xuanjing Huang. 2015. Long short-term memory neural networks for Chinese word segmentation. In *Proceedings of the 2015 Conference on Empirical Methods in Natural Language Processing*, pages 1197–1206, Lisbon, Portugal. Association for Computational Linguistics.

Zhiyuan Chen, Bing Liu, Meichun Hsu, Malu Castellanos, and Riddhiman Ghosh. 2013. Identifying intention posts in discussion forums. In *Proceedings of the 2013 Conference of the North American Chapter of the Association for Computational Linguistics: Human Language Technologies*, pages 1041–1050, Atlanta, Georgia. Association for Computational Linguistics.

Alexis Conneau and Guillaume Lample. 2019. Cross-lingual language model pretraining. In *Advances in Neural Information Processing Systems 32: Annual Conference on Neural Information Processing Systems 2019, NeurIPS 2019, December 8-14, 2019, Vancouver, BC, Canada*, pages 7057–7067.

Junqi Dai, Hang Yan, Tianxiang Sun, Pengfei Liu, and Xipeng Qiu. 2021. Does syntax matter? a strong baseline for aspect-based sentiment analysis with roberta. In *The 2021 Conference of the North American Chapter of the Association for Computational Linguistics: Human Language Technologies*.

Kevin Duh, Katsuhito Sudoh, Xianchao Wu, Hajime Tsukada, and Masaaki Nagata. 2011. Generalized minimum bayes risk system combination. In *Proceedings of 5th International Joint Conference on Natural Language Processing*, pages 1356–1360.

Bradley Efron. 1992. Bootstrap methods: another look at the jackknife. In *Breakthroughs in statistics*, pages 569–593. Springer.

Kawin Ethayarajh and Dan Jurafsky. 2020. Utility is in the eye of the user: A critique of NLP leaderboards. In *Proceedings of the 2020 Conference on Empirical Methods in Natural Language Processing (EMNLP)*, pages 4846–4853, Online. Association for Computational Linguistics.

Jinlan Fu, Xuanjing Huang, and Pengfei Liu. 2021. Spanner: Named entity re-/recognition as span prediction. In *Joint Conference of the 59th Annual Meeting of the Association for Computational Linguistics and the 11th International Joint Conference on Natural Language Processing (ACL-IJCNLP)*, Virtual.

Jinlan Fu, Pengfei Liu, and Graham Neubig. 2020a. Interpretable multi-dataset evaluation for named entity recognition. In *Proceedings of the 2020 Conference on Empirical Methods in Natural Language Processing (EMNLP)*, pages 6058–6069, Online. Association for Computational Linguistics.

Jinlan Fu, Pengfei Liu, and Qi Zhang. 2020b. Rethinking generalization of neural models: A named entity recognition case study. In *The Thirty-Fourth AAAI Conference on Artificial Intelligence, AAAI 2020, The Thirty-Second Innovative Applications of Artificial Intelligence Conference, IAAI 2020, The Tenth AAAI Symposium on Educational Advances in Artificial Intelligence, EAAI 2020, New York, NY, USA, February 7-12, 2020*, pages 7732–7739. AAAI Press.

Jinlan Fu, Pengfei Liu, Qi Zhang, and Xuanjing Huang. 2020c. RethinkCWS: Is Chinese word segmentation a solved task? In *Proceedings of the 2020 Conference on Empirical Methods in Natural Language Processing (EMNLP)*, pages 5676–5686, Online. Association for Computational Linguistics.

Sebastian Gehrmann, Tosin Adewumi, Karmanya Aggarwal, Pawan Sasanka Ammanamanchi, Aremu Anuoluwapo, Antoine Bosselut, Khyathi Raghavi Chandu, Miruna Clinciu, Dipanjan Das, Kaustubh D Dhole, et al. 2021. The gem benchmark: Natural language generation, its evaluation and metrics. *arXiv preprint arXiv:2102.01672*.

Jesús González-Rubio, Alfons Juan, and Francisco Casacuberta. 2011. Minimum Bayes-risk system combination. In *Proceedings of the 49th Annual Meeting of the Association for Computational Linguistics: Human Language Technologies*, pages 1268–1277, Portland, Oregon, USA. Association for Computational Linguistics.

Chuan Guo, Geoff Pleiss, Yu Sun, and Kilian Q. Weinberger. 2017. On calibration of modern neural networks. In *Proceedings of the 34th International Conference on Machine Learning, ICML 2017, Sydney, NSW, Australia, 6-11 August 2017*, volume 70 of *Proceedings of Machine Learning Research*, pages 1321–1330. PMLR.

Junjie Hu, Sebastian Ruder, Aditya Siddhant, Graham Neubig, Orhan Firat, and Melvin Johnson. 2020. Xtreme: A massively multilingual multi-task benchmark for evaluating cross-lingual generalisation. In *International Conference on Machine Learning*, pages 4411–4421. PMLR.

Daniel Khashabi, Gabriel Stanovsky, Jonathan Bragg, Nicholas Lourie, Jungo Kasai, Yejin Choi, Noah A Smith, and Daniel S Weld. 2021. Genie: A leaderboard for human-in-the-loop evaluation of text generation. *arXiv preprint arXiv:2101.06561*.

Yaobo Liang, Nan Duan, Yeyun Gong, Ning Wu, Fenfei Guo, Weizhen Qi, Ming Gong, Linjun Shou, Daxin Jiang, Guihong Cao, et al. 2020. Xglue: A new benchmark dataset for cross-lingual pre-training, understanding and generation. *arXiv preprint arXiv:2004.01401*.

Zachary C Lipton. 2018. The mythos of model interpretability: In machine learning, the concept of interpretability is both important and slippery. *Queue*, 16(3):31–57.

Yang Liu and Mirella Lapata. 2019. Text summarization with pretrained encoders. In *Proceedings of the 2019 Conference on Empirical Methods in Natural Language Processing and the 9th International Joint Conference on Natural Language Processing (EMNLP-IJCNLP)*, pages 3730–3740, Hong Kong, China. Association for Computational Linguistics.

Yixin Liu and Pengfei Liu. 2021. Simcls: A simple framework for contrastive learning of abstractive summarization. In *Joint Conference of the 59th Annual Meeting of the Association for Computational Linguistics and the 11th International Joint Conference on Natural Language Processing (ACL-IJCNLP)*, Virtual.

Yixin Liu, Dou Ziyi, and Pengfei Liu. 2021. Refsum: Refactoring neural summarization. In *The 2021 Conference of the North American Chapter of the Association for Computational Linguistics: Human Language Technologies*.

Jiasen Lu, Jianwei Yang, Dhruv Batra, and Devi Parikh. 2016. Hierarchical question-image co-attention for visual question answering. In *Advances in Neural Information Processing Systems 29: Annual Conference on Neural Information Processing Systems 2016, December 5-10, 2016, Barcelona, Spain*, pages 289–297.

Graham Neubig, Zi-Yi Dou, Junjie Hu, Paul Michel, Danish Pruthi, and Xinyi Wang. 2019. compare-mt: A tool for holistic comparison of language generation systems. In *Proceedings of the 2019 Conference of the North American Chapter of the Association for Computational Linguistics (Demonstrations)*, pages 35–41, Minneapolis, Minnesota. Association for Computational Linguistics.

Bo Pang, Lillian Lee, and Shivakumar Vaithyanathan. 2002. Thumbs up? sentiment classification using machine learning techniques. In *Proceedings of the 2002 Conference on Empirical Methods in Natural Language Processing (EMNLP 2002)*, pages 79–86. Association for Computational Linguistics.

Nikolaos Pappas and Andrei Popescu-Belis. 2014. Explaining the stars: Weighted multiple-instance learning for aspect-based sentiment analysis. In *Proceedings of the 2014 Conference on Empirical Methods in Natural Language Processing (EMNLP)*, pages 455–466, Doha, Qatar. Association for Computational Linguistics.

Maja Popović and Hermann Ney. 2011. Towards automatic error analysis of machine translation output. *Computational Linguistics*, 37(4):657–688.

Pranav Rajpurkar, Jian Zhang, Konstantin Lopyrev, and Percy Liang. 2016. SQuAD: 100,000+ questions for machine comprehension of text. In *Proceedings of the 2016 Conference on Empirical Methods in Natural Language Processing*, pages 2383–2392, Austin, Texas. Association for Computational Linguistics.

Alexander M. Rush, Sumit Chopra, and Jason Weston. 2015. A neural attention model for abstractive sentence summarization. In *Proceedings of the 2015 Conference on Empirical Methods in Natural Language Processing*, pages 379–389, Lisbon, Portugal. Association for Computational Linguistics.

Stefan Schweter and Alan Akbik. 2020. Flert: Document-level features for named entity recognition. *arXiv preprint arXiv:2011.06993*.

Sara Stymne. 2011. Blast: A tool for error analysis of machine translation output. In *Proceedings of the ACL-HLT 2011 System Demonstrations*, pages 56–61, Portland, Oregon. Association for Computational Linguistics.

Ilya Sutskever, Oriol Vinyals, and Quoc V. Le. 2014. Sequence to sequence learning with neural networks. In *Advances in Neural Information Processing Systems 27: Annual Conference on Neural Information Processing Systems 2014, December 8-13 2014, Montreal, Quebec, Canada*, pages 3104–3112.

Ian Tenney, James Wexler, Jasmijn Bastings, Tolga Bolukbasi, Andy Coenen, Sebastian Gehrmann, Ellen Jiang, Mahima Pushkarna, Carey Radebaugh, Emily Reif, et al. 2020. The language interpretability tool: Extensible, interactive visualizations and analysis for nlp models. *arXiv preprint arXiv:2008.05122*.

Kai Ming Ting and Ian H. Witten. 1997. Stacked generalizations: When does it work? In *Proceedings of the Fifteenth International Joint Conference on Artificial Intelligence, IJCAI 97, Nagoya, Japan, August 23-29, 1997, 2 Volumes*, pages 866–873. Morgan Kaufmann.

Erik F. Tjong Kim Sang and Fien De Meulder. 2003. Introduction to the CoNLL-2003 shared task: Language-independent named entity recognition. In *Proceedings of the Seventh Conference on Natural Language Learning at HLT-NAACL 2003*, pages 142–147.

Kristina Toutanova, Dan Klein, Christopher D. Manning, and Yoram Singer. 2003. Feature-rich part-of-speech tagging with a cyclic dependency network. In *Proceedings of the 2003 Human Language Technology Conference of the North American Chapter of the Association for Computational Linguistics*, pages 252–259.

Eric Wallace, Jens Tuyls, Junlin Wang, Sanjay Subramanian, Matt Gardner, and Sameer Singh. 2019. AllenNLP interpret: A framework for explaining predictions of NLP models. In *Proceedings of the 2019 Conference on Empirical Methods in Natural Language Processing and the 9th International Joint Conference on Natural Language Processing (EMNLP-IJCNLP): System Demonstrations*, pages 7–12, Hong Kong, China. Association for Computational Linguistics.

Alex Wang, Yada Pruksachatkun, Nikita Nangia, Amanpreet Singh, Julian Michael, Felix Hill, Omer Levy, and Samuel R Bowman. 2019. Superglue: A stickier benchmark for general-purpose language understanding systems. *arXiv preprint arXiv:1905.00537*.

Alex Wang, Amanpreet Singh, Julian Michael, Felix Hill, Omer Levy, and Samuel Bowman. 2018. GLUE: A multi-task benchmark and analysis platform for natural language understanding. In *Proceedings of the 2018 EMNLP Workshop BlackboxNLP: Analyzing and Interpreting Neural Networks for NLP*, pages 353–355, Brussels, Belgium. Association for Computational Linguistics.

Sida Wang and Christopher Manning. 2012. Baselines and bigrams: Simple, good sentiment and topic classification. In *Proceedings of the 50th Annual Meeting of the Association for Computational Linguistics (Volume 2: Short Papers)*, pages 90–94, Jeju Island, Korea. Association for Computational Linguistics.

Yonghui Wu, Mike Schuster, Zhifeng Chen, Quoc V. Le, Mohammad Norouzi, Wolfgang Macherey, Maxim Krikun, Yuan Cao, Qin Gao, Klaus Macherey, Jeff Klingner, Apurva Shah, Melvin Johnson, Xiaobing Liu, Łukasz Kaiser, Stephan Gouws, Yoshikiyo Kato, Taku Kudo, Hideto Kazawa, Keith Stevens, George Kurian, Nishant Patil, Wei Wang, Cliff Young, Jason Smith, Jason Riesa, Alex Rudnick, Oriol Vinyals, Greg Corrado, Macduff Hughes, and Jeffrey Dean. 2016. Google's neural machine translation system: Bridging the gap between human and machine translation. *CoRR*, abs/1609.08144.

Ikuya Yamada, Akari Asai, Hiroyuki Shindo, Hideaki Takeda, and Yuji Matsumoto. 2020. LUKE: Deep contextualized entity representations with entity-aware self-attention. In *Proceedings of the 2020 Conference on Empirical Methods in Natural Language Processing (EMNLP)*, pages 6442–6454, Online. Association for Computational Linguistics.

Zihuiwen Ye, Pengfei Liu, Jinlan Fu, and Graham Neubig. 2021. Towards more fine-grained and reliable NLP performance prediction. In *Conference of the European Chapter of the Association for Computational Linguistics (EACL)*, Online.

Tao Yu, Rui Zhang, Kai Yang, Michihiro Yasunaga, Dongxu Wang, Zifan Li, James Ma, Irene Li, Qingning Yao, Shanelle Roman, Zilin Zhang, and Dragomir Radev. 2018. Spider: A large-scale human-labeled dataset for complex and cross-domain semantic parsing and text-to-SQL task. In *Proceedings of the 2018 Conference on Empirical Methods in Natural Language Processing*, pages 3911–3921, Brussels, Belgium. Association for Computational Linguistics.

Ming Zhong, Danqing Wang, Pengfei Liu, Xipeng Qiu, and Xuanjing Huang. 2019. A closer look at data bias in neural extractive summarization models. In *Proceedings of the 2nd Workshop on New Frontiers in Summarization*, pages 80–89, Hong Kong, China. Association for Computational Linguistics.

Exploring Word Usage Change with Continuously Evolving Embeddings

Franziska Horn
Machine Learning Group, Technische Universität Berlin, Berlin, Germany
BIFOLD, Berlin Institute for the Foundations of Learning and Data, Berlin, Germany
`franziska.horn@alumni.tu-berlin.de`

Abstract

The usage of individual words can change over time, for example, when words experience a semantic shift. As text datasets generally comprise documents that were collected over a longer period of time, examining word usage changes in a corpus can often reveal interesting patterns. In this paper, we introduce a simple and intuitive way to track word usage changes via continuously evolving embeddings, computed as a weighted running average of transformer-based contextualized embeddings. We demonstrate our approach on a corpus of recent New York Times article snippets and provide code for an easy to use web app to conveniently explore semantic shifts with interactive plots.

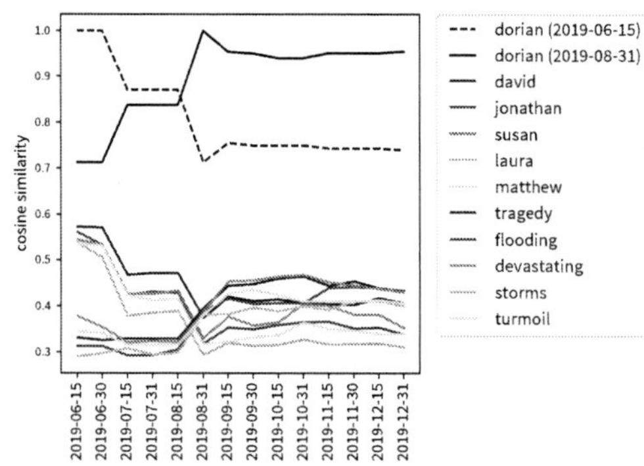

Figure 1: Cosine similarity between the continuously evolving embeddings for the word "Dorian" and its nearest neighbors over time, computed on our NYTimes article snippets corpus (see Sec. 4 for further details).

1 Introduction

Languages are constantly changing, with new words being coined or existing ones adopting a new meaning (Blank, 1999; Hamilton et al., 2016). For example, as Hurricane Dorian hit the Bahamas on Sept. 1, 2019, and was henceforth regarded as the worst natural disaster in the country's recorded history, within a matter of days the until then innocuous name "Dorian" suddenly became synonymous with a devastating tropical cyclone (Fig. 1). These kinds of semantic shifts are of great interest for researchers in fields like computational linguists and digital humanities, but their analysis requires appropriate tools, especially to create fine-granular visualizations, for example, to facilitate the study of texts from fast-paced environments such as social media.

Word embeddings are nowadays the method of choice when examining the meaning of and relation between words, and, as an extension thereof, diachronic embeddings can be used to discover and analyze the semantic shifts and usage changes of words over time. The main idea behind diachronic word embeddings is to learn a set of embeddings for each word, one for each time period of interest, to then see how much the embeddings for the same word differ over time (see e.g. (Kutuzov et al., 2018) or (Tahmasebi et al., 2018) for a comprehensive overview). However, most approaches for computing diachronic embeddings either a) rely on static word embedding models such as word2vec, which makes it difficult to use them with small corpora, b) are based upon rather complex dynamic language models, and/or c) require the corpus to be split into individual time slices, which introduces a bias, since by computing embeddings for different years, for example, one implicitly assumes that the meaning of a word might change between January and December of the previous year, but not between July and August of the same year.

In this paper, we introduce continuously evolving embeddings that are computed in one pass over the whole (chronologically ordered) corpus by keeping track of a weighted running average of contextualized embeddings generated by a transformer model such as BERT (Sec. 2). By taking (poten-

Proceedings of the Joint Conference of the 59th Annual Meeting of the Association for Computational Linguistics and the 11th International Joint Conference on Natural Language Processing: System Demonstrations, pages 290–297, August 1st - August 6th, 2021.

tially arbitrarily frequent) 'snapshots' of the current state of the embeddings at user-defined time points, one obtains smoothly changing high-resolution diachronic embeddings. With these embeddings, semantic shifts can be detected at a resolution of weeks or months instead of years or decades. The exploration of word usage change is facilitated by our web app that provides the user with the corresponding interactive graphics (Sec. 3), which we demonstrate on a corpus of recent newspaper article snippets (Sec. 4).

Summary of our contributions:

1. continuously evolving embeddings:
    - simple and intuitive method for computing diachronic embeddings
    - can be applied to small datasets thanks to pre-trained transformer models
    - corpus does not need to be split into (arbitrarily) defined time intervals
    - frequent snapshots ensure smoothly changing, high-resolution embeddings
2. all the necessary code[1] to explore word usage change in novel datasets with a user-friendly web app

2 Continuously Evolving Embeddings

Let $\mathbf{x}_{t_i}^{\text{local}}$ be the contextualized embedding of a token t generated by some arbitrary method (e.g. a pre-trained BERT model) for the ith occurrence of t in a corpus. Then a global embedding of t can be computed by averaging over the local embeddings of all N occurrences of t in the corpus (Horn, 2017; Bommasani et al., 2019; Martinc et al., 2019; Kutuzov and Giulianelli, 2020):

$$\mathbf{x}_t^{\text{global}} = \frac{1}{N}\sum_{i=1}^{N} \mathbf{x}_{t_i}^{\text{local}}. \quad (1)$$

Equivalently, this can be formulated as a running average (Finch, 2009), allowing for memory-efficient continuous updates in one pass over the corpus:

$$\mathbf{x}_t^{\text{global}[:n]} = \frac{(n-1)\,\mathbf{x}_t^{\text{global}[:n-1]} + \mathbf{x}_{t_i}^{\text{local}}}{n}.$$

Using this running average formula, it is possible to compute continuously evolving embeddings by updating the global embedding as more and more sentences are processed (Akbik et al., 2019). However, usually the more recent occurrences of the word are of greater relevance when determining the current sense of the word. To account for this, the above formula can be adapted by introducing a weighting factor $0 < \alpha \leq 0.5$:

$$n' = \min\left\{n, \left\lceil \frac{1}{\alpha} \right\rceil\right\}$$

$$\mathbf{x}_t^{\alpha[:n]} = \frac{(n'-1)\,\mathbf{x}_t^{\alpha[:n-1]} + \mathbf{x}_{t_i}^{\text{local}}}{n'}. \quad (2)$$

This is equivalent to computing the weighted average of the two embeddings (for large n):

$$\mathbf{x}_t^{\alpha[:n]} = (1-\alpha)\,\mathbf{x}_t^{\alpha[:n-1]} + \alpha\,\mathbf{x}_{t_i}^{\text{local}}$$

and results in an exponential forgetting of the past occurrences in favor of the more recent instances (Finch, 2009).

While Martinc et al. (2019) generate diachronic embeddings by computing a global average of all contextualized embeddings occurring in texts from individual (predefined) time periods (Eq. 1), we instead propose to keep track of a weighted running average computed in one pass over the whole (chronologically ordered) corpus (Eq. 2). By taking 'snapshots' of the current state of these continuously evolving embeddings at user-defined time points, it is possible to obtain smoothly changing high-resolution diachronic word embeddings.[2] The weighting parameter α in the running average should be set according to the number of word occurrences one assumes it might take for the meaning to change and can be set individually for each word to reflect the differing overall frequencies and semantic shift paces (Hamilton et al., 2016).

The computation of continuously evolving embeddings scales linearly with respect to the number of sentences in the dataset, since each sentence has to be embedded with the transformer model once to update the weighted running average with the respective contextualized embeddings. The required memory, on the other hand, scales linearly with the number of embedding snapshots that are taken during the computation, where a copy of the current state of the global embedding matrix needs to be stored for every snapshot.

[1] `https://github.com/cod3licious/evolvemb`

[2] Since an embedding simply stays the same when the word does not occur, these snapshots can be taken in arbitrarily short intervals.

3 The EvolvEmb App

Word usage changes in a corpus can be easily explored using the web application we created for this purpose. The app itself is based on the dash framework (Shammamah Hossain, 2019) and can be run locally by following the steps listed in Fig. 2 and demonstrated in the screencast[3], i.e., first computing continuously evolving embeddings and saving the respective snapshots (or, alternatively, diachronic embeddings obtained with a traditional approach such as a SGNS model trained on individual time slices (Kim et al., 2014)), and then starting the app (which loads the pre-computed embeddings) to obtain the list of most changed words in the corpus and a simple interface to generate the plots displaying the evolution of nearest neighbors over time for individual (user-selected) words.

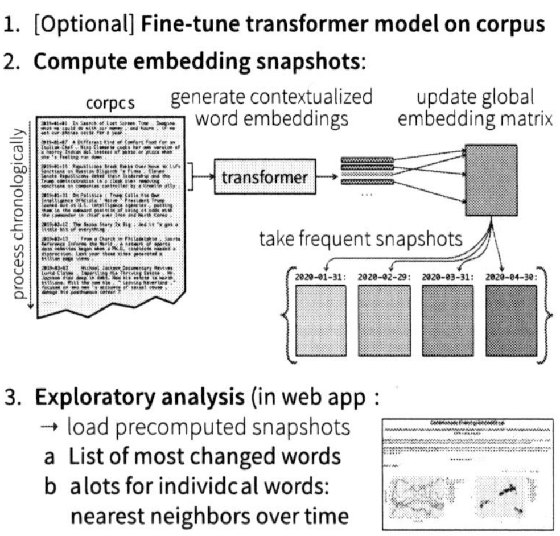

Figure 2: Steps to explore word usage change in novel datasets: First the continuously evolving embedding snapshots are computed as described in Sec. 2, then the precomputed matrices can be used in the app to produce interactive plots similar to those shown in Fig. 3.

4 Exploring Word Usage Change

To demonstrate our approach, we downloaded 95,203 newspaper article snippets (consisting of a headline and 1-3 sentences) published by the New York Times between April 1st, 2019, and Dec. 31st, 2020, via their API.[4] Diachronic embeddings were computed for the 5,620 words that occurred at least 50 times in the corpus by processing the texts chronologically, computing continuously evolving embeddings with a transformer model, and taking a snapshot of the current state of the embeddings at the end of each month. α was set individually for each word based on how many times on average the word occurred in the articles of a single month. To compute the contextualized embeddings, we experimented with pre-trained BERT and RoBERTa models from the HuggingFace library (Wolf et al., 2020) that were either used as is or fine-tuned for three epochs on our corpus. As the results obtained with both models were similar, we focus on BERT in the following.

Words with different usages were identified based on the minimum cosine similarity between their embedding snapshots from different time points.[5] As this also yielded several words with multiple meanings that showed seasonal trends (Table 1, Fig. 3), we additionally identified words with a continuous semantic shift specifically by considering only the cosine similarity scores S_{ik} of all snapshots i to the last snapshot k and subtracted from the overall increase of the scores over time any intermediate decrease between subsequent scores:

$$(S_{kk} - S_{0k}) - \sum_{i=0}^{k-1} \max\{S_{ik} - S_{(i+1)k}, 0\}.$$

As expected, when computing continuously evolving embeddings on shuffled article snippets, i.e., a corpus that is no longer chronologically ordered (Dubossarsky et al., 2017), the resulting semantic shift scores are significantly lower (Table 2).

Even though the continuously evolving embeddings computed with pre-trained transformers are already sufficient to identify many words with usage changes, fine-tuning of the models is generally advised, especially to clearly identify semantic shifts when the new usage of a word was not present in the texts the transformer was originally trained on. To illustrate this, inspired by Rosenfeld and Erk (2018), we introduced a synthetic semantic shift into the data for an artificially created

[3] https://youtu.be/ltF67J-la7I

[4] https://developer.nytimes.com/apis

[5] We also explored the intersection of the k nearest neighbors (NN) of the word embeddings to identify words with a usage change (Gonen et al., 2020), but found these results to be less reliable, because the number of close NN can differ a lot between words with a specific or more general meaning. Nevertheless, there is a significant correlation between the minimum cosine similarity and the kNN interaction score.

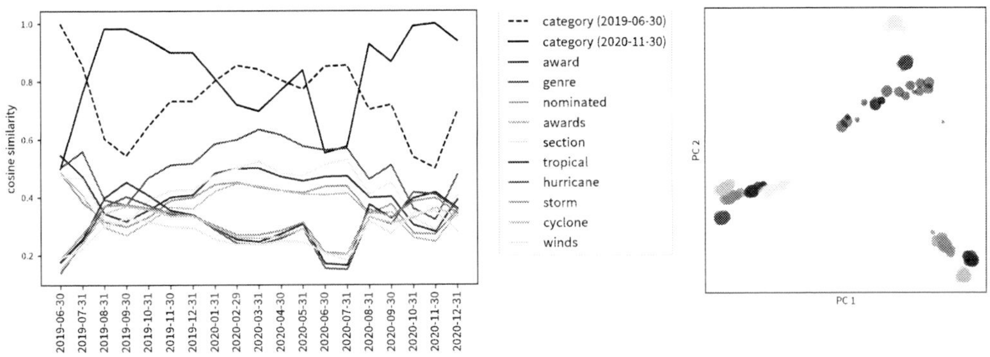

Figure 3: Plots as included in the app, here depicting the evolution of nearest neighbors over time for the word "category", computed with a pre-trained BERT model on our NYTimes article snippets dataset. For the target word, first the two time points with the smallest cosine similarity between the embeddings of the word itself were identified, then the five nearest neighbors of the word at both time points were selected (red and blue colors respectively; words that occurred in both sets are in red). *Left:* Cosine similarity between the target word at each time point and the nearest neighbors, as well as the two most different embedding snapshots of the target word itself (inspired by the plots in (Bamler and Mandt, 2017)). *Right:* 2D PCA visualization of all embedding snapshots of the target word as well as both sets of nearest neighbors (smaller dots represent embeddings at earlier time points).

Table 1: The 25 most changed tokens with their corresponding minimum cosine similarity score between the embedding snapshots *(multiple meanings)* and our semantic shift score, obtained by computing continuously evolving embeddings using a pre-trained BERT model on the NYTimes article snippets (ignoring new words that only occurred after the first snapshot date; words occurring in both lists are italicized).

multiple meanings: category (0.50), appointment, *barrier*, majors, bend, chiefs, doubles, tables, upon, *600*, del, *positive*, *kobe*, *plague*, nationals, lands, *dorian*, stanley, murray, mine, *plunge*, rolling, posed, jeopardy, revival (0.77)
semantic shift: coney (0.1869), *kobe* (0.1852), *dorian*, *600*, *barrier*, *plague*, stimulus, remotely, arbery, *positive*, sheet, thanksgiving, excerpt, tudor, *plunge*, halted, mask, infected, tracing, distancing, masks, educators, throwing, tip, retire (0.1083)

Table 2: Analogous to Table 1: the 25 tokens with the greatest semantic shift when applying the pre-trained BERT model to shuffled sentences.

semantic shift (shuffled): breakthrough (0.1210), trend (0.0621), coup, urgency, releasing, succeed, wind, limiting, holes, forecast, developments, attempted, richest, superstar, pastor, addressing, pack, upset, recommendation, programming, autism, arrival, denver, associated, flowers (0.0313)

word:[6] First, we removed all sentences containing the words "president" or "coronavirus" (the two most frequent nouns in our dataset) from the corpus and replaced each occurrence of the respective word with the new token "presidentcoronavirus". These augmented sentences were then reintroduced into the corpus at regular intervals based on a transition probability that follows a sigmoid curve, i.e., most of the sentences included at earlier dates were sampled from the contexts for the word "president", while at later dates this shifted towards sentences that originally contained "coronavirus". While the continuously evolving embeddings computed with a pre-trained BERT model can pick up on this artificially introduced semantic shift in general (Fig. 4 *top*: the black lines for the token 'presidentcoronavirus' run according to the sigmoid curve based on which the respective contexts were sampled), the nearest neighbors are not very instructive to identify the two senses. This is mainly due to the subword embeddings that the transformer uses to represent this new token, thereby introducing a strong preconception w.r.t. the word's meaning. However, after fine-tuning BERT on the synthetic dataset for three epochs, not only is the difference between the embedding snapshots of the target to-

[6]Since established word usage change evaluation datasets so far only cover broad discrete time bins (Schlechtweg et al., 2020), to evaluate gradual semantic shifts one has to resort to synthetic data (Shoemark et al., 2019).

ken itself stronger, but also the nearest neighbors now correspond more closely to the initial ('president') and later ('coronavirus') sense of the word (Fig. 4 *bottom*).

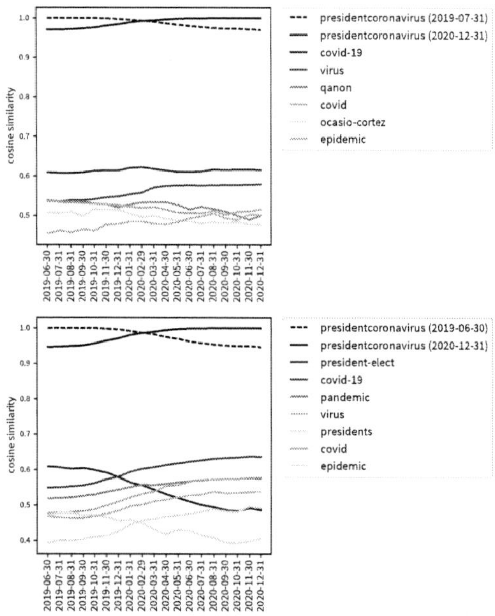

Figure 4: Analogously to Fig. 3 the nearest neighbors over time for the artificially constructed token "presidentcoronavirus" before (*top*; semantic shift score: 0.028) and after (score: 0.053) fine-tuning BERT on the synthetically modified NYT article snippets.

Finally, as a comparison we also show the plots obtained with diachronic embeddings learned using a skip-gram word2vec model trained with negative sampling (SGNS) on the original sentences. Similar to Kim et al. (2014), we trained a SGNS model[7] from the gensim library (Řehůřek and Sojka, 2010) for 50 epochs on the texts from each time period between two snapshots. As described in the original paper, the embeddings learned on later time slices were initialized with the embeddings from the previous interval. Additionally, since the amount of text contained in each time slice is much smaller than generally recommended when training a word2vec model, the model was first trained on the full corpus for 100 epochs to initialize the embeddings before training on the first time period. While the evolution of nearest neighbors over time (Fig. 5) still contains faint patterns (e.g., the sense "hurricane" is stronger during the late summer and fall months), the plots are much noisier than those created with the transformer-based continuously evolving embeddings (Fig. 3).

[7] embedding dim. 50; context window 5; neg. sampling 13

5 Related Work

When it comes to learning word embeddings in general, it is helpful to distinguish between older methods, such as word2vec (Mikolov et al., 2013a,b) or GloVe (Pennington et al., 2014), that learn static word embeddings, i.e., a single "global" embedding for each word in the vocabulary, and modern transformer models, such as ELMo (Peters et al., 2018), BERT (Devlin et al., 2019), RoBERTa (Liu et al., 2019), and Flair (Akbik et al., 2018), that generate contextualized embeddings based on the local context of a word in the current sentence. While the static word embedding models are usually trained on a target corpus containing several millions of words to obtain expressive domain-specific embeddings (Tshitoyan et al., 2019), pre-trained transformers are well suited for transfer learning and can therefore also more easily be applied to smaller datasets.

Some of the more advanced methods for creating diachronic embeddings use special-purpose dynamic language models, which explicitly take the temporal structure of the data into account when learning the word embeddings (Bamler and Mandt, 2017; Rosenfeld and Erk, 2018; Yao et al., 2018; Rudolph and Blei, 2018; Brandl and Lassner, 2019; Jawahar and Seddah, 2019; Hofmann et al., 2020; Tsakalidis and Liakata, 2020). A different line of work instead relies on conventional static word embedding models, such as word2vec, and uses them directly to learn embeddings for the individual time periods. The main challenge here consists of aligning the word embeddings learned for different time intervals, which can, for example, be achieved by using the embeddings from one time slice to initialize the next (Kim et al., 2014), by explicitly matching up the matrices learned on different time periods (Kulkarni et al., 2015; Hamilton et al., 2016; Zhang et al., 2016; Yin et al., 2018), or utilizing other techniques such as temporal referencing (Dubossarsky et al., 2019). An even simpler approach to produce diachronic word embedding in a single embedding space uses the same (fixed) model to compute contextualized embeddings on all texts and then averages the respective embeddings from each individual time period to get the diachronic embeddings (Basile et al.,

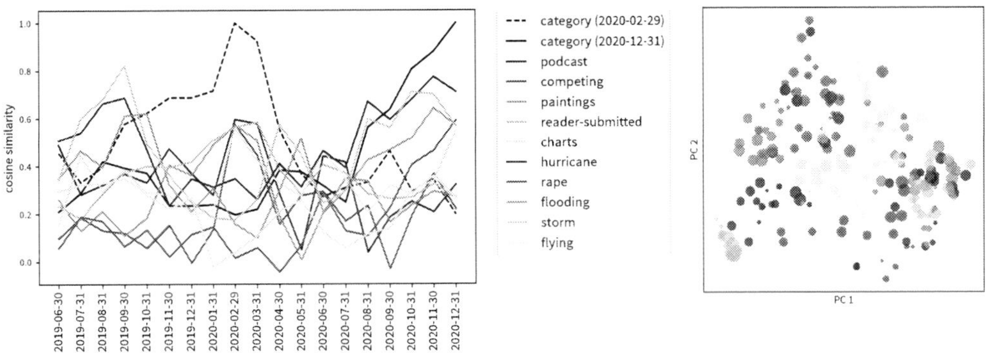

Figure 5: Analogously to Fig. 3 the results with diachronic embeddings obtained by training a SGNS word2vec model on the article snippets from the respective time intervals (Kim et al., 2014).

2016).[8] When using high-quality contextualized embeddings from a transformer model, it is furthermore possible to compute the diachronic embeddings for shorter time slices of single years (Martinc et al., 2019, 2020; Hu et al., 2019; Giulianelli et al., 2020; Beck, 2020). However, one major problem remains, namely that the time slices across which the diachronic embeddings are computed have to be discretized and defined in advance. This problem could previously only be addressed by a more complex dynamic model (Rosenfeld and Erk, 2018).

While several of the above mentioned papers have published code alongside their manuscripts, this was mainly done with the intention that others could reproduce their results, not apply the methods to novel datasets. To the best of our knowledge, only Hamilton et al. (2016) has released a more comprehensive library to explore word usage change in other corpora, however, their approach relies on static word embeddings and should therefore mainly be applied to larger corpora. Most other available software for analyzing corpora only considers word frequencies over time, but does not track the semantic shifts of these words.

6 Conclusion

This paper introduced continuously evolving embeddings as a conceptually simple and intuitive method for computing smoothly changing high-resolution diachronic embeddings from weighted running averages of contextualized embeddings. By taking advantage of pre-trained transformer models and processing the texts in a corpus sequentially rather than dividing them into (more or less arbitrary) time slices, our approach makes it possible to obtain diachronic embeddings from comparatively small corpora and at very short intervals compared to the previously standard time periods of at least one year. This should make our method particularly well suited to study fast-paced environments such as social media, where a new meme can go viral in a matter of hours, only to be superseded by the next a few days later.

Aside from the parameters involved in the underlying transformer model and its possible fine-tuning, our method only has a single hyperparameter, α, whose setting mostly just influences how frequently the embedding snapshots need to be taken to not miss any semantic shifts in between the snapshot intervals. On our NYTimes corpus we obtained reasonable results already with pre-trained transformer models, however, fine-tuning is nevertheless advised and especially helpful to characterize new word usages that the transformer did not encounter in its original training data.

We hope that the provided code will help others identify interesting patterns of word usage change in their own corpora.

Acknowledgments

This paper would not be what it is today without the many fruitful discussions with Alan Akbik and his support. I would like to thank him, Klaus-Robert Müller, and the anonymous reviewers for their helpful comments on this manuscript. FH acknowledges funding from the BZML.

[8] Since the contextualized embeddings are all in the same embedding space already (defined by the single fixed model), averaging the embeddings from each time slice creates time period specific global word embeddings that are themselves also comparable.

References

Alan Akbik, Tanja Bergmann, and Roland Vollgraf. 2019. Pooled contextualized embeddings for named entity recognition. In *Proceedings of the 2019 Conference of the North American Chapter of the Association for Computational Linguistics: Human Language Technologies, Volume 1 (Long and Short Papers)*, pages 724–728.

Alan Akbik, Duncan Blythe, and Roland Vollgraf. 2018. Contextual string embeddings for sequence labeling. In *Proceedings of the 27th International Conference on Computational Linguistics*, pages 1638–1649, Santa Fe, New Mexico, USA. Association for Computational Linguistics.

Robert Bamler and Stephan Mandt. 2017. Dynamic word embeddings. In *Proceedings of the 34th International Conference on Machine Learning-Volume 70*, pages 380–389.

Pierpaolo Basile, Annalina Caputo, Roberta Luisi, and Giovanni Semeraro. 2016. Diachronic analysis of the italian language exploiting google ngram. *CLiC it*, pages 56–60.

Christin Beck. 2020. DiaSense at SemEval-2020 Task 1: Modeling sense change via pre-trained BERT embeddings. In *Proceedings of the Fourteenth Workshop on Semantic Evaluation*, pages 50–58.

Andreas Blank. 1999. Why do new meanings occur? a cognitive typology of the motivations for lexical semantic change. *Historical semantics and cognition*, 13(6).

Rishi Bommasani, Kelly Davis, and Claire Cardie. 2019. Bert wears gloves: Distilling static embeddings from pretrained contextual representations.

Stephanie Brandl and David Lassner. 2019. Times are changing: Investigating the pace of language change in diachronic word embeddings. In *Proceedings of the 1st International Workshop on Computational Approaches to Historical Language Change*, pages 146–150.

Jacob Devlin, Ming-Wei Chang, Kenton Lee, and Kristina Toutanova. 2019. BERT: Pre-training of deep bidirectional transformers for language understanding. In *Proceedings of the 2019 Conference of the North American Chapter of the Association for Computational Linguistics: Human Language Technologies, Volume 1 (Long and Short Papers)*, pages 4171–4186, Minneapolis, Minnesota. Association for Computational Linguistics.

Haim Dubossarsky, Simon Hengchen, Nina Tahmasebi, and Dominik Schlechtweg. 2019. Time-out: Temporal referencing for robust modeling of lexical semantic change. In *Proceedings of the 57th Annual Meeting of the Association for Computational Linguistics*, pages 457–470.

Haim Dubossarsky, Daphna Weinshall, and Eitan Grossman. 2017. Outta control: Laws of semantic change and inherent biases in word representation models. In *Proceedings of the 2017 conference on empirical methods in natural language processing*, pages 1136–1145.

Tony Finch. 2009. Incremental calculation of weighted mean and variance. *University of Cambridge*, 4(11-5):41–42.

Mario Giulianelli, Marco Del Tredici, and Raquel Fernández. 2020. Analysing lexical semantic change with contextualised word representations. In *Proceedings of the 58th Annual Meeting of the Association for Computational Linguistics*, pages 3960–3973, Online. Association for Computational Linguistics.

Hila Gonen, Ganesh Jawahar, Djamé Seddah, and Yoav Goldberg. 2020. Simple, interpretable and stable method for detecting words with usage change across corpora. In *Proceedings of the 58th Annual Meeting of the Association for Computational Linguistics*, pages 538–555.

William L Hamilton, Jure Leskovec, and Dan Jurafsky. 2016. Diachronic word embeddings reveal statistical laws of semantic change. *arXiv preprint arXiv:1605.09096*.

Valentin Hofmann, Janet B Pierrehumbert, and Hinrich Schütze. 2020. Dynamic contextualized word embeddings. *arXiv preprint arXiv:2010.12684*.

Franziska Horn. 2017. Context encoders as a simple but powerful extension of word2vec. In *Proceedings of the 2nd Workshop on Representation Learning for NLP*, pages 10–14. Association for Computational Linguistics.

Shammamah Hossain. 2019. Visualization of Bioinformatics Data with Dash Bio. In *Proceedings of the 18th Python in Science Conference*, pages 126 – 133.

Renfen Hu, Shen Li, and Shichen Liang. 2019. Diachronic sense modeling with deep contextualized word embeddings: An ecological view. In *Proceedings of the 57th Annual Meeting of the Association for Computational Linguistics*, pages 3899–3908.

Ganesh Jawahar and Djamé Seddah. 2019. Contextualized diachronic word representations. In *Proceedings of the 1st International Workshop on Computational Approaches to Historical Language Change*, pages 35–47.

Yoon Kim, Yi-I Chiu, Kentaro Hanaki, Darshan Hegde, and Slav Petrov. 2014. Temporal analysis of language through neural language models. In *Proceedings of the ACL 2014 Workshop on Language Technologies and Computational Social Science*, pages 61–65.

Vivek Kulkarni, Rami Al-Rfou, Bryan Perozzi, and Steven Skiena. 2015. Statistically significant detection of linguistic change. In *Proceedings of the 24th International Conference on World Wide Web*, pages 625–635.

Andrey Kutuzov and Mario Giulianelli. 2020. Uio-uva at semeval-2020 task 1: Contextualised embeddings for lexical semantic change detection. *arXiv preprint arXiv:2005.00050*.

Andrey Kutuzov, Lilja Øvrelid, Terrence Szymanski, and Erik Velldal. 2018. Diachronic word embeddings and semantic shifts: a survey. In *Proceedings of the 27th International Conference on Computational Linguistics*, pages 1384–1397.

Yinhan Liu, Myle Ott, Naman Goyal, Jingfei Du, Mandar Joshi, Danqi Chen, Omer Levy, Mike Lewis, Luke Zettlemoyer, and Veselin Stoyanov. 2019. Roberta: A robustly optimized bert pretraining approach. *arXiv preprint arXiv:1907.11692*.

Matej Martinc, Syrielle Montariol, Elaine Zosa, and Lidia Pivovarova. 2020. Capturing evolution in word usage: Just add more clusters? In *Companion Proceedings of the Web Conference 2020*, pages 343–349.

Matej Martinc, Petra Kralj Novak, and Senja Pollak. 2019. Leveraging contextual embeddings for detecting diachronic semantic shift. *arXiv preprint arXiv:1912.01072*.

Tomas Mikolov, Kai Chen, Greg Corrado, and Jeffrey Dean. 2013a. Efficient estimation of word representations in vector space. *arXiv preprint arXiv:1301.3781*.

Tomas Mikolov, Ilya Sutskever, Kai Chen, Greg S Corrado, and Jeff Dean. 2013b. Distributed representations of words and phrases and their compositionality. In *Advances in Neural Information Processing Systems*, pages 3111–3119.

Jeffrey Pennington, Richard Socher, and Christopher D Manning. 2014. GloVe: Global Vectors for Word Representation. In *EMNLP*, volume 14, pages 1532–1543.

Matthew E. Peters, Mark Neumann, Mohit Iyyer, Matt Gardner, Christopher Clark, Kenton Lee, and Luke Zettlemoyer. 2018. Deep contextualized word representations. In *Proc. of NAACL*.

Radim Řehůřek and Petr Sojka. 2010. Software Framework for Topic Modelling with Large Corpora. In *Proceedings of the LREC 2010 Workshop on New Challenges for NLP Frameworks*, pages 45–50, Valletta, Malta. ELRA.

Alex Rosenfeld and Katrin Erk. 2018. Deep neural models of semantic shift. In *Proceedings of the 2018 Conference of the North American Chapter of the Association for Computational Linguistics: Human Language Technologies, Volume 1 (Long Papers)*, pages 474–484.

Maja Rudolph and David Blei. 2018. Dynamic embeddings for language evolution. In *Proceedings of the 2018 World Wide Web Conference*, pages 1003–1011.

Dominik Schlechtweg, Barbara McGillivray, Simon Hengchen, Haim Dubossarsky, and Nina Tahmasebi. 2020. Semeval-2020 task 1: Unsupervised lexical semantic change detection. In *Proceedings of the Fourteenth Workshop on Semantic Evaluation*, pages 1–23.

Philippa Shoemark, Farhana Ferdousi Liza, Dong Nguyen, Scott Hale, and Barbara McGillivray. 2019. Room to glo: A systematic comparison of semantic change detection approaches with word embeddings. In *Proceedings of the 2019 Conference on Empirical Methods in Natural Language Processing and the 9th International Joint Conference on Natural Language Processing (EMNLP-IJCNLP)*, pages 66–76.

Nina Tahmasebi, Lars Borin, and Adam Jatowt. 2018. Survey of computational approaches to lexical semantic change. *arXiv preprint arXiv:1811.06278*.

Adam Tsakalidis and Maria Liakata. 2020. Sequential modelling of the evolution of word representations for semantic change detection. In *Proceedings of the 2020 Conference on Empirical Methods in Natural Language Processing (EMNLP)*, pages 8485–8497.

Vahe Tshitoyan, John Dagdelen, Leigh Weston, Alexander Dunn, Ziqin Rong, Olga Kononova, Kristin A Persson, Gerbrand Ceder, and Anubhav Jain. 2019. Unsupervised word embeddings capture latent knowledge from materials science literature. *Nature*, 571(7763):95–98.

Thomas Wolf, Julien Chaumond, Lysandre Debut, Victor Sanh, Clement Delangue, Anthony Moi, Pierric Cistac, Morgan Funtowicz, Joe Davison, Sam Shleifer, et al. 2020. Transformers: State-of-the-art natural language processing. In *Proceedings of the 2020 Conference on Empirical Methods in Natural Language Processing: System Demonstrations*, pages 38–45.

Zijun Yao, Yifan Sun, Weicong Ding, Nikhil Rao, and Hui Xiong. 2018. Dynamic word embeddings for evolving semantic discovery. In *Proceedings of the eleventh acm international conference on web search and data mining*, pages 673–681.

Zi Yin, Vin Sachidananda, and Balaji Prabhakar. 2018. The global anchor method for quantifying linguistic shifts and domain adaptation. *Advances in neural information processing systems*, 31:9412–9423.

Yating Zhang, Adam Jatowt, Sourav S Bhowmick, and Katsumi Tanaka. 2016. The past is not a foreign country: Detecting semantically similar terms across time. *IEEE Transactions on Knowledge and Data Engineering*, 28(10):2793–2807.

TURING: an Accurate and Interpretable Multi-Hypothesis Cross-Domain Natural Language Database Interface

Peng Xu*, **Wenjie Zi***, **Hamidreza Shahidi**, **Ákos Kádár**, **Keyi Tang**, **Wei Yang**, **Jawad Ateeq**, **Harsh Barot**, **Meidan Alon**, **Yanshuai Cao**
Borealis AI
{peng.z.xu, wenjie.zi, hamidreza.shahidi, akos.kadar, keyi.tang}@borealisai.com
{wei.yang, jawad.ateeq, harsh.barot, meidan.alon, yanshuai.cao}@borealisai.com

Abstract

A natural language database interface (NLDB) can democratize data-driven insights for non-technical users. However, existing Text-to-SQL semantic parsers cannot achieve high enough accuracy in the cross-database setting to allow good usability in practice. This work presents TURING[1], a NLDB system toward bridging this gap. The cross-domain semantic parser of TURING with our novel value prediction method achieves 75.1% execution accuracy, and 78.3% top-5 beam execution accuracy on the Spider validation set (Yu et al., 2018b). To benefit from the higher beam accuracy, we design an interactive system where the SQL hypotheses in the beam are explained step-by-step in natural language, with their differences highlighted. The user can then compare and judge the hypotheses to select which one reflects their intention if any. The English explanations of SQL queries in TURING are produced by our high-precision natural language generation system based on synchronous grammars.

1 Introduction

Today a vast amount of knowledge is hidden in structured datasets, not directly accessible to non-technical users who are not familiar with the corresponding database query language like SQL or SPARQL. Natural language database interfaces (NLDB) enable everyday users to interact with databases (Zelle and Mooney, 1996; Popescu et al., 2003; Li and Jagadish, 2014; Zeng et al., 2020). However, correctly translating natural language to executable queries is challenging, as it requires resolving all the ambiguities and subtleties of natural utterances for precise mapping. Furthermore, quick deployment and adoption for NLDB require zero-shot transfer to new databases without an in-domain text-to-SQL parallel corpus, *i.e.* cross-database semantic parsing (SP), making the translation accuracy even lower. Finally, unlike in other NLP applications where partially correct results can still provide partial utility, a SQL query with a slight mistake could cause negative utility if trusted blindly or confusing to users.

The recent Spider benchmark (Yu et al., 2018a) captures this cross-domain problem, and the state-of-the-art methods merely achieve around 70% execution accuracy at the time of this submission [2]. Meanwhile, generalization to datasets collected under different protocols is even weaker (Suhr et al., 2020). Finally, users generally have no way to know if the NLDB made a mistake except in very obvious cases. The high error rate combined with the overall system's opacity makes it hard for users to trust any output from the NLDB.

Our key observation is that our model's top-5 accuracy on Spider is 78.3%, significantly higher than the previous best single-model method at around 68%, and our own top-1 accuracy. Top-5 accuracy is the proportion of times when one of the top five hypotheses from beam-search inference is correct (in execution accuracy evaluation). For top-5 accuracy to be relevant in practice, a non-technical user needs to be able to pick the correct hypothesis from the candidate list. To this end, we design a feedback system that can unambiguously explain the top beam-search results while presenting the differences intuitively and visually. Users can then judge which, if any, of the parses correctly reflects their intentions. The explanation system uses a hybrid of two synchronous context-free grammars, one shallow and one deep. Together, they achieve good readability for the most frequent

*Equal contribution

[1]System demo at https://turing.borealisai.com/; video at https://vimeo.com/537429187/9a5d41f446

[2]https://yale-lily.github.io/spider

Proceedings of the Joint Conference of the 59th Annual Meeting of the Association for Computational Linguistics and the 11th International Joint Conference on Natural Language Processing: System Demonstrations, pages 298–305, August 1st - August 6th, 2021.

query patterns while near-complete coverage overall.

Our system, TURING, is not only interpretable, but also a highly accurate cross-domain NLDB. Our semantic parser is based on the one in Xu et al. (2020), which does not handle value prediction like many other previous state-of-the-art models on Spider. Compared to previous executable semantic parsers, we achieve significant gains with a number of techniques, but predominantly by drastically simplifying the learning problem in value prediction. The model only needs to identify the text span providing evidence for the ground-truth value. The noisy long tail text normalization step required for producing the actual value is offloaded to a deterministic search phase in post-processing.

In summary, this work presents two steps towards a more robust NLDB:

1. A state-of-the-art text-to-SQL parsing system with the best top-1 execution accuracy on the Spider development set.

2. A way to relax usability requirement from top-1 accuracy to top-k accuracy by explaining the different hypotheses in natural language with visual aids.

2 System Overview

As shown in Figure 1, TURING's interface has two main components: the database browser showing schema and selected database content, and the search panel where the users interact with the parser. Figure 1 caption describes the typical user interaction using an example.

Behind the front-end interface, TURING consists of an executable cross-domain semantic parser trained on Spider that maps user utterances to SQL query hypotheses, the SQL execution engine that runs the queries to obtain answers, and the explanation generation module that produces the explanation text and the meta-data powering explanation highlighting. The next sections will describe the semantic parsing and explanation modules.

3 Semantic Parser

The backbone of TURING is a neural semantic parser which generates an executable SQL query T given a user question Q and the database schema $\mathcal{S}$. We follow the state-of-the-art system (Xu et al., 2020), but extend it to generate executable SQL query instead of ignoring values in the SQL query, like many other top systems (Wang et al., 2019; Guo et al., 2019) on the Spider leaderboard.

On the high-level, our SP adopts the grammar-based framework following TranX (Yin and Neubig, 2018) with an encoder-decoder neural architecture. A grammar-based transition system is designed to turn the generation process of the SQL abstract syntax tree (AST) into a sequence of tree-constructing actions to be predicted by the parser. The encoder f_{enc} jointly encodes both the user question $Q = q_1 \dots q_{|Q|}$ and database schema $\mathcal{S} = \{s_1, \dots, s_{|\mathcal{S}|}\}$ consisting of tables and columns in the database. The decoder f_{dec} is a transition-based abstract syntax decoder, which uses the encoded representation $\mathcal{H}$ to predict the target SQL query T. The decoder also relies on the transition system to convert the AST constructed by the predicted action sequences to the executable surface SQL query.

To alleviate unnecessary burden on the decoder, we introduce two novel modifications to the transition system to handle the schema and value decoding. With simple, but effective value-handling, inference and regularization techniques applied on this transition system, we are able to push the execution accuracy much higher for better usability.

3.1 Transition System

Our transition system has four types of action to generate the AST, including (1) **ApplyRule**[r] which applies a production rule r to the latest generated node in the AST; (2) **Reduce** which completes the generation of the current node; (3) **SelectColumn**[c] which chooses a column c from the database schema $\mathcal{S}$; (4) **CopyToken**[i] which copies a token q_i from the user question Q.

There are two key distinctions of our transition system with the previous systems. First, our transition system omits the action type **SelectTable** used by other transition-based SP systems (Wang et al., 2019; Guo et al., 2019). This is made possible by attaching the corresponding table to each column, so that the tables in the target SQL query can be deterministically inferred from the predicted columns. Second, we simplify the value prediction by always trying to copy from the user question, instead of applying the **GenToken**[v] action (Yin and Neubig, 2018) which generates tokens from a large vocabulary or choose from a pre-processed picklist (Lin et al., 2020). Both of the changes constrain the output space of the decoder to ease the

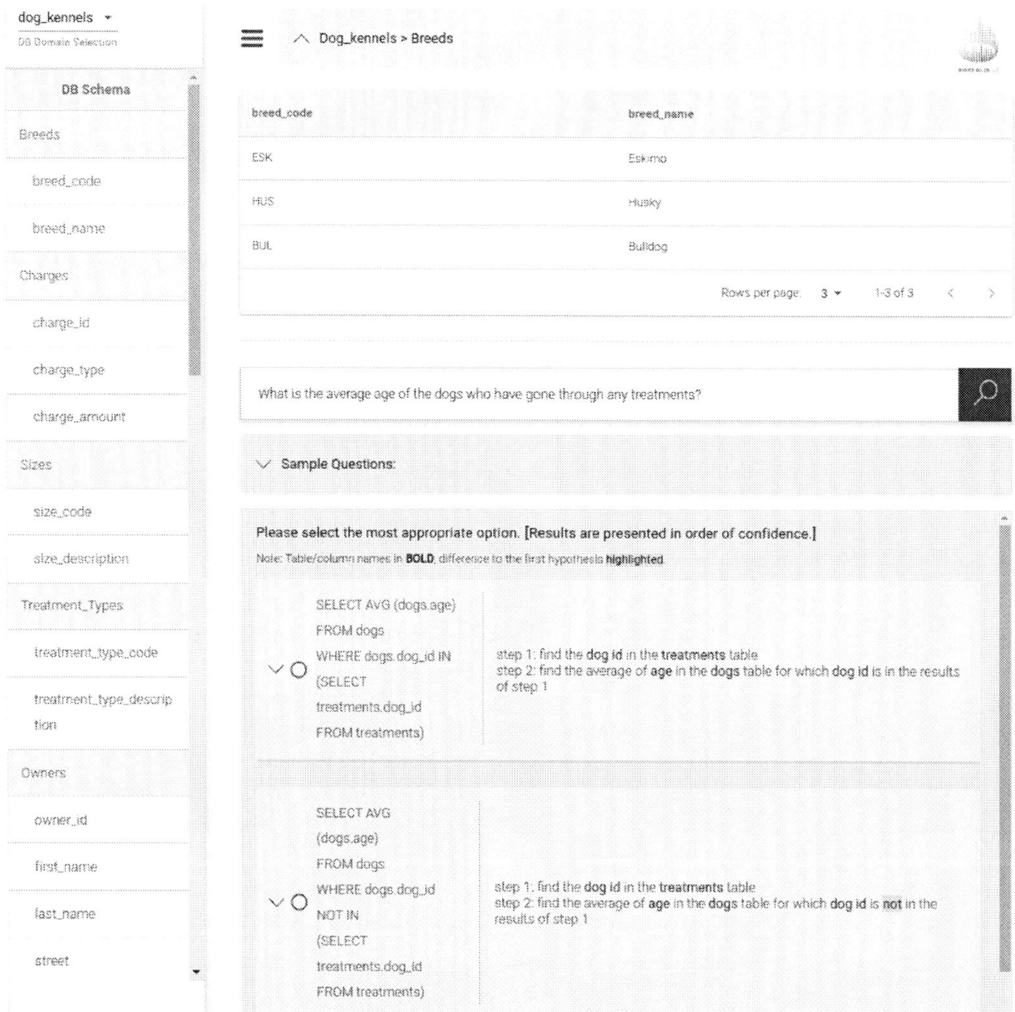

Figure 1: TURING system in action: the user selected database "Dog_kennels"; the left and top panels show the database schema and table content. The user then entered "What is the average age of the dogs who have gone through any treatments?" in the search box. This question is run through the semantic parser producing multiple SQL hypotheses from beam-search, which are then explained step-by-step as shown. The differences across the hypotheses are highlighted. The tokens corresponding to table and columns are in bold. If there were more valid hypotheses, a "Show more" button would appear to reveal the additional ones.

learning process, but the latter change unrealistically assumes that the values are always explicitly mentioned in the question. To retain the generation flexibility without putting excessive burden on the decoder, we propose a conceptually simple but effective strategy to handle the values next.

3.2 Handling Values

Value prediction is a challenging, but crucial component of NLDBs, however, only limited efforts are committed to handling values properly in the current cross-domain SP literature. Value mentions are usually noisy, if mentioned explicitly at all, requiring commonsense or domain knowledge to be inferred. On the other hand, the number of possible values in a database can be huge, leading to sparse learning signals if the model tries to choose from the possible value candidates.

Instead of attempting to predict the actual values directly, our SP simply learns to identify the input text spans providing evidence for the values. As mentioned earlier, we introduce the **CopyToken** action to copy an input span from the user question, indicating the clues for this value. The ground-truth

CopyToken$[i]$ actions are obtained from a tagging strategy based on heuristics and fuzzy string matching between the user question and the gold values. As a result, the decoder is able to focus on understanding the question without considering other complexities of the actual values which are difficult to learn. If the values are only implicitly mentioned in the user question, nothing is copied from the user question. We leave the identification of the actual values to a deterministic search-based inference in post-processing, after the decoding process. This yields a simpler learning task as the neural network does not need to perform domain-specific text normalization such as mapping "female" to "F" for some databases.

Given the schema, the predicted SQL AST and the database content, the post-processing first identifies the corresponding column type (*number, text, time*), operation type (*like, between*, $>$, $<$, $=$, ...), and aggregation type (*count, max, sum, ...*). Based on these types, it infers the type and normalization required for the value. If needed, it then performs fuzzy-search in the corresponding column's values in the database. When nothing is copied, a default value is chosen based on some heuristics (*e.g.*, when there exist only two element "Yes" and "No" in the column, the default value is "Yes"); otherwise, the most frequent element in the column is chosen. Searching the database content can also be restricted to a picklist for privacy reasons like previous works (Zeng et al., 2020; Lin et al., 2020).

Another benefit of this simple value handling strategy is the ease to explain. The details are presented in the Sec. 4.

3.3 Encoder-Decoder

Our encoder architecture follows Xu et al. (2020). The encoder, f_{enc}, maps the user question Q and the schema S to a joint representation $\mathcal{H} = \{\phi_1^q, \ldots, \phi_{|Q|}^q\} \cup \{\phi_1^s, \ldots, \phi_{|S|}^s\}$. It contextualizes the question and schema jointly through both the RoBERTA-Large model similar to (Guo et al., 2019), as well as through the additional sequence of 24 relation-aware transformer (RAT) (Wang et al., 2019) layers. As mentioned in Section 3.1, tables are not predicted directly but inferred from the columns, so we augment the column representations by adding the corresponding table representations after the encoding process.

We use a LSTM decoder f_{dec} to generate the action sequence A. Formally, the generation process can be formulated as $\Pr(A|\mathcal{H}) = \prod_t \Pr(a_t|a_{<t}, \mathcal{H})$ where $\mathcal{H}$ is the encoded representations outputted by the encoder f_{enc}. The LSTM state is updated following Wang et al. (2019): $\boldsymbol{m}_t, \boldsymbol{h}_t = f_{\text{LSTM}}([\boldsymbol{a}_{t-1} \| \boldsymbol{z}_{t-1} \| \boldsymbol{h}_{p_t} \| \boldsymbol{a}_{p_t} \| \boldsymbol{n}_{p_t}], \boldsymbol{m}_{t-1}, \boldsymbol{h}_{t-1})$, where $\boldsymbol{m}_t$ is the LSTM cell state, $\boldsymbol{h}_t$ is the LSTM output at step t, $\boldsymbol{a}_{t-1}$ is the action embedding of the previous step, $\boldsymbol{z}_{t-1}$ is the context representation computed using multi-head cross-attention of $\boldsymbol{h}_{t-1}$ over $\mathcal{H}$, p_t is the step corresponding to the parent AST node of the current node, and $\boldsymbol{n}$ is the node type embedding. For **ApplyRule**$[r]$, we compute $\Pr(a_t = \textbf{ApplyRule}[r]|a_{<t}, \mathcal{H}) = \text{softmax}_r(g(\boldsymbol{z}_t))$ where $g(\cdot)$ is a 2-layer MLP. For **SelectColumn**$[c]$, we use the memory augmented pointer network following Guo et al. (2019). For **CopyToken**$[i]$, a pointer network is employed to copy tokens from the user question Q with a special token indicating the termination of copy.

3.4 Column Label Smoothing

One of the core challenges for cross-domain SP is to generalize to unseen domains without overfitting to some specific domains during training. Empirically, we observe that applying uniform label smoothing (Szegedy et al., 2016) on the objective term for predicting **SelectColumn**$[c]$ can effectively address the overfitting problem in the cross-domain setting. Formally, the cross-entropy for a ground-truth column c^* we optimize becomes $(1 - \epsilon) * \log p(c^*) + \frac{\epsilon}{K} * \sum_c \log p(c)$, where K is the number of columns in the schema, ϵ is the weight of the label smoothing term, and $p(\cdot) \triangleq \Pr(a_t = \textbf{SelectColumn}[\cdot]|a_{<t}, \mathcal{H})$.

3.5 Weighted Beam Search

During inference, we use beam search to find the high-probability action sequences. As mentioned above, column prediction is prone to overfitting in the cross-domain setting. In addition, value prediction is dependent on the column prediction, that is, if a column is predicted incorrectly, the associated value has no chance to be predicted correctly. As a result, we introduce two hyperparameters controlling influence based on the action types in the beam, with a larger weight $\alpha > 1$ for **SelectColumn** and a smaller weight $0 < \beta < 1$ for **CopyToken**.

4 Explanation Generation

The goal of the explanation generation system is to unambiguously describe what the semantic parser understands as the user's command and allow the user to easily interpret the differences across the multiple hypotheses. Therefore, unlike a typical dialogue system setting where language generation diversity is essential, controllability and consistency are of primary importance. The generation not only needs to be 100% factually correct, but the differences in explanation also need to reflect the differences in the predicted SQLs, no more and no less. Therefore, we use a deterministic rule-based generation system instead of a neural model.

Our explanation generator is a hybrid of two synchronous context-free grammar (SCFG) systems combined with additional heuristic post-processing steps. The two grammars trade off readability and coverage. One SCFG is shallow and simple, covering the most frequent SQL queries; the other is deep and more compositional, covering the tail of query distribution that our SP can produce for completeness. The SCFG can produce SQL and English explanation parallel. Given a SQL query, we parse it under the grammar to obtain a derivation, which we then follow to obtain the explanation text. At inference time, for a given question, if any of the SQL hypotheses cannot be parsed using the shallow SCFG, then we move onto the deep one.

4.1 Details of the Grammars

Using the deep SQL syntax trees allows almost complete coverage on the Spider domains. However, these explanations can be unnecessarily verbose as the generation process faithfully follows the re-ordered AST without 1.) compressing repeated mentions of schema elements when possible 2.) summarizing tedious details of the SQL query into higher level logical concepts. Even though these explanations are technically correct, practical explanation should allow users to spot the difference between queries easily. To this end, we design the shallow grammar similarly to the template-based explanation system in Elgohary et al. (2020), which simplifies the SQL parse trees by collapsing large subtrees into a single tree fragment. In the resulting shallow parses production rules yield non-terminal nodes corresponding to 1.) anonymized SQL templates 2.) UNION, INTERSECT, or EXCEPT operations of two templates 3.) or a template pattern followed by ORDER-BY-LIMIT clause. Our shallow but wide grammar has 64 rules with those non-terminal nodes. The pre-terminal nodes are placeholders in the anonymized SQL queries such as Table name, Column name, Aggregation operator and so on. Finally, the terminal nodes are the values filling in the place holders. The advantage of this grammar is that each high-level SQL template can be associated with an English explanation template that reveals the high level logic and abstracts away from the details in the concrete queries. To further reduce the redundancy, we make assumptions to avoid unnecessarily repeating table and column names. Table. 1 showcases some rules from the shallow SCFG and one example of explanation. In practice, around 75% of the examples in the Spider validation set have all beam hypotheses from our SP model parsable by the shallow grammar, with the rest handled by the deep grammar. The deep grammar has less than 50 rules. But because it is more compositional, it covers 100% of the valid SQLs that can be generated by our semantic parser. Some sample explanation by the deep grammar can be found in Table. 2.

Finally, whenever the final value in the query differs from original text span due to post-processing, a sentence in the explanation states the change explicitly for clarity. For example, "*'Asian' in the question is matched to 'Asia' which appears in the column Continent.*"

5 Quantitative Evaluations

Implementation Details. We apply the DT-Fixup technique from (Xu et al., 2020) to train our semantic parser and mostly re-use their hyperparamters. The weight of the column label smoothing term ϵ is 0.2. Inference uses a beam size of 5 for the beam search. We set the column weight as $\alpha = 3$ and the value weight as $\beta = 0.1$.

Dataset. We use Spider (Yu et al., 2018b), a complex and cross-domain Text-to-SQL semantic parsing benchmark, which has 10,180 questions, 5,693 queries covering 200 databases in 138 domains. All our experiments are evaluated based on the development set. We use the execution match *with* values (**Exec**) evaluation metrics.

Results on Spider. We compare TURING with the top systems on the Spider execution leaderboard that have published reports with execution accuracy on the development set as well. As seen from Table 3, our single model significantly outperforms the previous state of the art in terms of **Exec** accu-

```
S -> P
S -> P UNION P
P -> (SELECT <T_0>.<C_0> FROM <T_1> GROUP BY <T_2>.<C_1> HAVING <AOps_0> ( <T_3>.<C_2> ) <WOps_0> <L_0>,
     find the different values of the {<C_0>} in the {<T_1>} whose {<AOps_0>} the {<C_2>} {<WOps_0>} {<L_0>})
```

```
step 1: find the average of product price in the products table
step 2: find the different values of the product type code in the products table
        whose average of the product price is greater than the results of step 1
```

Table 1: Sample shallow grammar production rules and one example explanation.

```
Step 1: find the entries in the employee table whose age is less than 30.0.
Step 2: among these results, for each city of the employee table,
        where the number of records is more than 1, find city of the employee table.
---------------
"30" in the question is converted to 30.
"one" in the question is converted to 1.
```

```
Step 1: find combinations of entries in the employee table, the hiring table and the shop table
        for which employee id of the employee table is equal to employee id of the hiring table
        and shop id of the hiring table is equal to shop id of the shop table.
Step 2: among these results, for each shop id of the shop table,
        find the average of age of the employee table and shop id of the shop table.
```

Table 2: Examples of explanation by the deep grammar. The first example also showcases the additional explanation for value post-processing.

Model	Exec
GAZP + BERT (Zhong et al., 2020)	59.2
Bridge v2 + BERT (Lin et al., 2020)	68.0
Bridge v2 + BERT (ensemble)	70.3
Turing + RoBERTa	$\mathbf{75.1}$(best), 73.8 ± 0.7

Table 3: **Exec** accuracy on the Spider development set.

Model	Exec
Turing + RoBERTa	73.8 ± 0.7
w/o. value post-processing	67.2 ± 0.8
w/o. column label smoothing	73.1 ± 1.2
w/o. weighted beam search	73.5 ± 0.7
top 3 in the beam	77.3 ± 0.4
top 5 in the beam	78.3 ± 0.3

Table 4: Ablation study on various techniques used in TURING. We use 5 runs with different random seeds.

racy on the development set.

Ablation Study. Table 4 shows an ablation study of various techniques in TURING. We can see that removing the value post-processing decreases the accuracy significantly, showing that copying alone is not enough due to the mismatch in linguistic variation and the schema specific normalization. The effectiveness of the proposed column label smoothing and weighted beam search are also reflected by the **Exec** accuracy on Spider. Furthermore, simply adding more hypotheses in the beam can significantly boost the coverage of the correct predictions, leading to 4.5% accuracy gain over the top one accuracy. By combining all these techniques together, TURING achieves an overall performance gain above 10% over the previous best single model system (68.0% of Bridge v2). [3]

6 Related Work

Executable Cross-database Semantic Parsing. Early NLDB systems use rule-based parsing (Zelle and Mooney, 1996; Li and Jagadish, 2014) and cannot handle the diversity of natural language in practice. Neural semantic parsing is more promising for coverage but is still brittle in real-world applications where queries can involve novel compositions of learned patterns (Finegan-Dollak et al., 2018; Shaw et al., 2020). Furthermore, to allow plug-and-play on new databases, the underlying semantic parser may not be trained on in-domain parallel corpus but needs to transfer across domains in a zero-shot fashion.

Executable cross-database semantic parsing is even more challenging. Many of the previous work only tackle the cross-domain part, omitting the value prediction problem required for executable queries (Guo et al., 2019; Wang et al., 2019; Choi et al., 2020; Xu et al., 2020). Unlike the output space of predicting the SQL sketch or columns,

[3] Rubin and Berant (2020) updated a version (April 11th 2021) around the time of this submission with a dev accuracy of 75% (missing from the first version), and a test accuracy of 71.1% significantly higher than the original 60.5%.

the value prediction output space is much less constrained. The correct value depends on the source question, the SQL query, the type information of the corresponding column, as well as the database content. This complexity combined with limited training data in standard benchmark datasets like Spider makes the task very difficult. Some previous works directly learn to predict the values (Yin and Neubig, 2018; Guo and Gao, 2020) on WikiSQL (Zhong et al., 2017), but does not generalize in cross-domain settings. On Spider, Zeng et al. (2020) and Lin et al. (2020) build a candidate list of values first and learn a pointer network to select from the list. TURING instead learns a pointer network to identify the input source span that provides evidence for the value instead of directly the value as previously described. Identification of the actual value is offloaded to post-processing. From a system perspective, it is also simpler for a power user of the NLDB to upload a domain-specific term description/mapping which can extend the heuristic-search-based value post-processing instantly rather than relying on re-training.

Query Explanation. Explaining structured query language has been studied in the past (Simitsis and Ioannidis, 2009; Koutrika et al., 2010; Ngomo et al., 2013; Xu et al., 2018). Full NLDB systems can leverage explanations to correct mistakes with user feedback (Elgohary et al., 2020), or to prevent mistakes by giving clarifications (Zeng et al., 2020). However, these methods can only handle cases where the mistake or ambiguity is about the table, column, or value prediction. There is no easy way to resolve structural mistakes or ambiguities if the query sketch is wrong. TURING, on the other hand, offers the potential to recover from such mistakes if the correct query is among the top beam results. This is an orthogonal contribution that could be integrated with other user-interaction modes. Finally, the NaLIR system (Li and Jagadish, 2014) has a similar feature allowing the user to pick from multiple interpretations of the input question. However, NaLIR's interpretation is based on syntactical parses of the question rather than interpreting the final semantic parses directly. A rule-based semantic parser then maps the selected syntactic parse to SQL. As the syntactic parse is not guaranteed to be mapped to the correct SQL, this interpretation does not completely close the gap between what the NLDB performs and what the user thinks it does.

7 Conclusion

We presented TURING, a natural language interface to databases (NLDB) that is accurate, interpretable, and works on a wide range of domains. Our system explains its actions in natural language so that the user can select the right answer from multiple hypotheses, capitalizing on the much higher beam accuracy instead of top-1 accuracy. TURING provides a complementary way to resolve mistakes and ambiguities in NLDB.

Acknowledgments

We appreciate the ACL demo anonymous reviewers for their valuable inputs. We would like to thank Mehrsa Golestaneh and April Cooper for their work on the improved front-end version, `https://turing-app.borealisai.com`, which is not in the scope of this publication. We also would like to thank Wendy Tay and Simon J.D. Prince for their general support.

References

DongHyun Choi, Myeong Cheol Shin, EungGyun Kim, and Dong Ryeol Shin. 2020. Ryansql: Recursively applying sketch-based slot fillings for complex text-to-sql in cross-domain databases.

Ahmed Elgohary, Saghar Hosseini, and Ahmed H. Awadallah. 2020. Speak to your parser: Interactive text-to-sql with natural language feedback. In *Annual Conference of the Association for Computational Linguistics (ACL 2020)*.

Catherine Finegan-Dollak, Jonathan K. Kummerfeld, Li Zhang, Karthik Ramanathan, Sesh Sadasivam, Rui Zhang, and Dragomir Radev. 2018. Improving text-to-SQL evaluation methodology. In *Proceedings of the 56th Annual Meeting of the Association for Computational Linguistics (Volume 1: Long Papers)*, pages 351–360, Melbourne, Australia. Association for Computational Linguistics.

Jiaqi Guo, Zecheng Zhan, Yan Gao, Yan Xiao, Jian-Guang Lou, Ting Liu, and Dongmei Zhang. 2019. Towards complex text-to-sql in cross-domain database with intermediate representation. *ACL*.

Tong Guo and Huilin Gao. 2020. Content enhanced bert-based text-to-sql generation.

G. Koutrika, A. Simitsis, and Y. E. Ioannidis. 2010. Explaining structured queries in natural language. In *2010 IEEE 26th International Conference on Data Engineering (ICDE 2010)*, pages 333–344.

F. Li and H. V. Jagadish. 2014. Nalir: an interactive natural language interface for querying relational databases. *Proceedings of the 2014 ACM SIGMOD International Conference on Management of Data*.

Xi Victoria Lin, Richard Socher, and Caiming Xiong. 2020. Bridging textual and tabular data for cross-domain text-to-sql semantic parsing. *arXiv preprint arXiv:2012.12627*.

Axel-Cyrille Ngonga Ngomo, Lorenz Bhmann, Christina Unger, Jens Lehmann, and Daniel Gerber. 2013. Sorry, i don't speak sparql: translating sparql queries into natural language. In *WWW*, pages 977–988.

Ana-Maria Popescu, Oren Etzioni, and Henry Kautz. 2003. Towards a theory of natural language interfaces to databases. In *Proceedings of the 8th international conference on Intelligent user interfaces*, pages 149–157.

Ohad Rubin and Jonathan Berant. 2020. Smbop: Semi-autoregressive bottom-up semantic parsing.

Peter Shaw, Ming-Wei Chang, Panupong Pasupat, and Kristina Toutanova. 2020. Compositional generalization and natural language variation: Can a semantic parsing approach handle both? *arXiv preprint arXiv:2010.12725*.

Alkis Simitsis and Yannis E. Ioannidis. 2009. Dbmss should talk back too. *CoRR*, abs/0909.1786.

Alane Suhr, Ming-Wei Chang, Peter Shaw, and Kenton Lee. 2020. Exploring unexplored generalization challenges for cross-database semantic parsing. In *Proceedings of the 58th Annual Meeting of the Association for Computational Linguistics*, pages 8372–8388, Online. Association for Computational Linguistics.

Christian Szegedy, Vincent Vanhoucke, Sergey Ioffe, Jon Shlens, and Zbigniew Wojna. 2016. Rethinking the inception architecture for computer vision. In *Proceedings of the IEEE conference on computer vision and pattern recognition*, pages 2818–2826.

Bailin Wang, Richard Shin, Xiaodong Liu, Oleksandr Polozov, and Matthew Richardson. 2019. Rat-sql: Relation-aware schema encoding and linking for text-to-sql parsers. *arXiv preprint arXiv:1911.04942*.

Kun Xu, Lingfei Wu, Zhiguo Wang, Yansong Feng, and Vadim Sheinin. 2018. SQL-to-text generation with graph-to-sequence model. In *Proceedings of the 2018 Conference on Empirical Methods in Natural Language Processing*, pages 931–936, Brussels, Belgium. Association for Computational Linguistics.

P. Xu, Wei Yang, W. Zi, Keyi Tang, Chengyang Huang, J. Cheung, and Yanshuai Cao. 2020. Optimizing deeper transformers on small datasets: An application on text-to-sql semantic parsing. *ArXiv*, abs/2012.15355.

Pengcheng Yin and Graham Neubig. 2018. Tranx: A transition-based neural abstract syntax parser for semantic parsing and code generation. *arXiv preprint arXiv:1810.02720*.

Tao Yu, Rui Zhang, Kai Yang, Michihiro Yasunaga, Dongxu Wang, Zifan Li, James Ma, Irene Li, Qingning Yao, Shanelle Roman, Zilin Zhang, and Dragomir Radev. 2018a. Spider: A large-scale human-labeled dataset for complex and cross-domain semantic parsing and text-to-SQL task. In *Proceedings of the 2018 Conference on Empirical Methods in Natural Language Processing*, pages 3911–3921, Brussels, Belgium. Association for Computational Linguistics.

Tao Yu, Rui Zhang, Kai Yang, Michihiro Yasunaga, Dongxu Wang, Zifan Li, James Ma, Irene Li, Qingning Yao, Shanelle Roman, et al. 2018b. Spider: A large-scale human-labeled dataset for complex and cross-domain semantic parsing and text-to-sql task. *arXiv preprint arXiv:1809.08887*.

John M Zelle and Raymond J Mooney. 1996. Learning to parse database queries using inductive logic programming. In *Proceedings of the national conference on artificial intelligence*, pages 1050–1055.

Jichuan Zeng, Xi Victoria Lin, Steven C.H. Hoi, Richard Socher, Caiming Xiong, Michael Lyu, and Irwin King. 2020. Photon: A robust cross-domain text-to-SQL system. In *Proceedings of the 58th Annual Meeting of the Association for Computational Linguistics: System Demonstrations*, pages 204–214, Online. Association for Computational Linguistics.

Victor Zhong, Mike Lewis, Sida I. Wang, and Luke Zettlemoyer. 2020. Grounded adaptation for zero-shot executable semantic parsing. In *Proceedings of the 2020 Conference on Empirical Methods in Natural Language Processing (EMNLP)*, pages 6869–6882, Online. Association for Computational Linguistics.

Victor Zhong, Caiming Xiong, and Richard Socher. 2017. Seq2sql: Generating structured queries from natural language using reinforcement learning. *arXiv preprint arXiv:1709.00103*.

Many-to-English Machine Translation Tools, Data, and Pretrained Models

Thamme Gowda
Information Sciences Institute
University of Southern California
tg@isi.edu

Zhao Zhang
Texas Advanced Computing Center
University of Texas
zzhang@tacc.utexas.edu

Chris A Mattmann
NASA Jet Propulsion Laboratory
California Institute of Technology
chris.a.mattmann@jpl.nasa.gov

Jonathan May
Information Sciences Institute
University of Southern California
jonmay@isi.edu

Abstract

While there are more than 7000 languages in the world, most translation research efforts have targeted a few high resource languages. Commercial translation systems support only one hundred languages or fewer, and do not make these models available for transfer to low resource languages. In this work, we present useful tools for machine translation research: MTDATA, NLCODEC, and RTG. We demonstrate their usefulness by creating a multilingual neural machine translation model capable of translating from 500 source languages to English. We make this multilingual model readily downloadable and usable as a service, or as a parent model for transfer-learning to even lower-resource languages.[1]

1 Introduction

Neural machine translation (NMT) (Bahdanau et al., 2015; Vaswani et al., 2017) has progressed to reach human performance on select benchmark tasks (Barrault et al., 2019, 2020). However, as MT research has mainly focused on translation between a small number of high resource languages, the unavailability of usable-quality translation models for low resource languages remains an ongoing concern. Even those commercial translation services attempting to broaden their language coverage has only reached around one hundred languages; this excludes most of the thousands of languages used around the world today.

Freely available corpora of parallel data for many languages are available, though they are hosted at various sites, and are in various forms. A challenge for incorporating more languages into MT models is a lack of easy access to all of these datasets.While standards like ISO 639-3 have been established to bring consistency to the labeling of language resources, these are not yet widely adopted. In addition, scaling experimentation to several hundred languages on large corpora involves a significant engineering effort. Simple tasks such as dataset preparation, vocabulary creation, transformation of sentences into sequences, and training data selection becomes formidable at scale due to corpus size and heterogeneity of data sources and file formats. We have developed tools to precisely address all these challenges, which we demonstrate in this work.

Specifically, we offer three tools which can be used either independently or in combination to advance NMT research on a wider set of languages (Section 2): firstly, MTDATA, which helps to easily obtain parallel datasets (Section 2.1); secondly, NLCODEC, a vocabulary manager and storage layer for transforming sentences to integer sequences, that is efficient and scalable (Section 2.2); and lastly, RTG, a feature-rich Pytorch-backed NMT toolkit that supports reproducible experiments (Section 2.3).

We demonstrate the capabilities of our tools by preparing a massive bitext dataset with more than 9 billion tokens per side, and training a single multilingual NMT model capable of translating 500 source languages to English (Section 3). We show that the multilingual model is usable either as a service for translating several hundred languages to English (Section 4.1), or as a parent model in a transfer learning setting for improving translation of low resource languages (Section 4.2).

2 Tools

Our tools are organized into the following sections:

2.1 MTDATA

MTDATA addresses an important yet often overlooked challenge – dataset preparation. By assign-

[1]Demo website: http://rtg.isi.edu/many-eng.
Video demo: https://youtu.be/NSY0-MvO1KE.

Proceedings of the Joint Conference of the 59th Annual Meeting of the Association for Computational Linguistics and the 11th International Joint Conference on Natural Language Processing: System Demonstrations, pages 306–316, August 1st - August 6th, 2021.

```
# List all the available datasets for deu-eng
$ mtdata list -l deu-eng
# Get the selected training & held-out sets
$ mtdata get -l deu-eng --merge\
 -tr wmt13_europarl_v7 wmt13_commoncrawl\
    wmt18_news_commentary_v13\
 -ts newstest201{8,9}_deen -o data
```

Listing 1: MTDATA examples for listing and downloading German-English datasets. The `-merge` flag results in merging all of the training datasets specified by `-tr` argument into a single file.

ing an ID for datasets, we establish a clear way of communicating the exact datasets used for MT experiments, which helps in reproducing the experimental setup. By offering a unified interface to datasets from many heterogeneous sources, MTDATA hides mundane tasks such as locating URLs, downloading, decompression, parsing, and sanity checking. Some noteworthy features are:

- *Indexer*: a large index of publicly available parallel datasets.
- *Normalizer:* maps language names to ISO-639-3 codes which has representation space for 7800+ languages.[2]
- *Parsers:* parses heterogeneous data formats for parallel datasets, and produces a simple plain text file by merging all the selected datasets.
- *Extensible:* new datasets and parsers can be easily added.
- *Local Cache*: reduces network transfers by maintaining a local cache, which is shared between experiments.
- *Sanity Checker*: performs basic sanity checks such as segment count matching and empty segment removal. When error states are detected, stops the setup with useful error messages.
- *Reproducible:* stores a signature file that can be used to recreate the dataset at a later time.
- *Courtesy:* shows the original BIBTEX citation attributed to datasets.
- *Easy Setup:* `pip install mtdata`
- *Open-source:* `https://github.com/thammegowda/mtdata`

Listing 1 shows an example for listing and getting datasets for German-English. In Section 3.1, we use MTDATA[3] to obtain thousands of publicly available datasets for a large many-to-English translation experiment.

[2] `https://iso639-3.sil.org`

[3] At the time of writing, v0.2.8

2.2 NLCODEC

NLCODEC is a vocabulary manager with encoding-decoding schemes to transform natural language sentences to and from integer sequences.

Features:

- *Versatile:* Supports commonly used vocabulary schemes such as characters, words, and byte-pair-encoding (BPE) subwords (Sennrich et al., 2016).
- *Scalable:* Apache Spark[4](Zaharia et al., 2016) backend can be optionally used to create vocabulary from massive datasets.
- *Easy Setup:* `pip install nlcodec`
- *Open-source:* `https://github.com/isi-nlp/nlcodec/`

When the training datasets are too big to be kept in the primary random access memory (RAM), the use of secondary storage is inevitable. The training processes requiring random examples lead to random access from a secondary storage device. Even though the latest advancements in secondary storage technology such as solid-state drive (SSD) have faster serial reads and writes, their random access speeds are significantly lower than that of RAM. To address these problems, we include an efficient storage and retrieval layer, NLDB, which has the following features:

- *Memory efficient* by adapting datatypes based on vocabulary size. For instance, encoding with vocabulary size less than 256 (such as characters) can be efficiently represented using 1-byte unsigned integers. Vocabularies with fewer than 65,536 types, such as might be generated when using subword models (Sennrich et al., 2016) require only 2-byte unsigned integers, and 4-byte unsigned integers are sufficient for vocabularies up to 4 billion types. As the default implementation of Python, CPython, uses 28 bytes for all integers, we accomplish this using NumPy (Harris et al., 2020). This optimization makes it possible to hold a large chunk of training data in smaller RAM, enabling a fast random access.
- *Parallelizable:* Offers a multi-part database by horizontal sharding that supports parallel writes (e.g., Apache Spark) and parallel reads (e.g., distributed training).
- Supports commonly used batching mechanisms such as random batches with approximately-equal-length sequences.

NLDB has a minimal footprint and is part of

[4] `https://spark.apache.org/`

the NLCODEC package. In Section 3, we take advantage of the scalability and efficiency aspects of NLCODEC and NLDB to process a large parallel dataset with 9 billion tokens on each side.

2.3 RTG

Reader translator generator (RTG) is a neural machine translation (NMT) toolkit based on Pytorch (Paszke et al., 2019). Notable features of RTG are:

- *Reproducible:* All the required parameters of an experiment are included in a single YAML configuration file, which can be easily stored in a version control system such as `git` or shared with collaborators.
- Implements Transformer (Vaswani et al., 2017), and recurrent neural networks (RNN) with cross-attention models (Bahdanau et al., 2015; Luong et al., 2015).
- Supports distributed training on multi-node multi-GPUs, gradient accumulation, and Float16 operations.
- Integrated Tensorboard helps in visualizing training and validation losses.
- Supports weight sharing (Press and Wolf, 2017), parent-child transfer (Zoph et al., 2016), beam decoding with length normalization (Wu et al., 2016), early stopping, and checkpoint averaging.
- Flexible vocabulary options with NLCODEC and SentencePiece (Kudo and Richardson, 2018) which can be either shared or separated between source and target languages.
- *Easy setup:* `pip install rtg`
- *Open-source:* `https://isi-nlp.github.io/rtg/`

3 Many-to-English Multilingual NMT

In this section, we demonstrate the use of our tools by creating a massively multilingual NMT model from publicly available datasets.

3.1 Dataset

We use MTDATA to download datasets from various sources, given in Table 1. To minimize data imbalance, we select only a subset of the datasets available for high resource languages, and select all available datasets for low resource languages. The selection is aimed to increase the diversity of data domains and quality of alignments.

Dataset	Reference
Europarl	Koehn (2005)
KFTT Ja-En	Neubig (2011)
Indian6	Post et al. (2012)
OPUS	Tiedemann (2012)
UNPCv1	Ziemski et al. (2016)
Tilde MODEL	Rozis and Skadiņš (2017)
TEDTalks	Qi et al. (2018)
IITB Hi-En	Kunchukuttan et al. (2018)
Paracrawl	Esplà et al. (2019)
WikiMatrix	Schwenk et al. (2019)
JW300	Agić and Vulić (2019)
PMIndia	Haddow and Kirefu (2020)
OPUS100	Zhang et al. (2020)
WMT [13-20]	Bojar et al. (2013, 2014, 2015, 2016, 2017, 2018); Barrault et al. (2019, 2020)

Table 1: Various sources of MT datasets.

Cleaning: We use SACREMOSES[5] to normalize Unicode punctuations and digits, followed by word tokenization. We remove records that are duplicates, have abnormal source-to-target length ratios, have many non-ASCII characters on the English side, have a URL, or which overlap exactly, either on the source or target side, with any sentences in held out sets. As preprocessing is compute-intensive, we parallelize using Apache Spark. The cleaning and tokenization results in a corpus of 474 million sentences and 9 billion tokens on the source and English sides each. The token and sentence count for each language are provided in Figure 1. Both the processed and raw datasets are available at `http://rtg.isi.edu/many-eng/data/v1/`.[6]

3.2 Many-to-English Multilingual Model

We use RTG to train Transformer NMT (Vaswani et al., 2017) with a few modifications. Firstly, instead of a shared BPE vocabulary for both source and target, we use two separate BPE vocabularies. Since the source side has 500 languages but the target side has English only, we use a large source vocabulary and a relatively smaller target vocabulary. A larger target vocabulary leads to higher time and memory complexity, whereas a large source vocabulary increases only the memory complexity but not the time complexity. We train several models, ranging from the standard 6 layers, 512-dimensional Transformers to larger ones with more parameters. Since the dataset is massive, a larger model trained on big mini-batches yields the best results. Our best performing model is a 768 dimensional model with 12 attention heads, 9 encoder layers, 6 decoder layers, feed-forward dimension of 2048, dropout and label smoothing at 0.1, using

[5] `https://github.com/isi-nlp/sacremoses` a fork of `https://github.com/alvations/sacremoses` with improvements to tokenization for many low resource languages.

[6] A copy is at `https://opus.nlpl.eu/MT560.php`

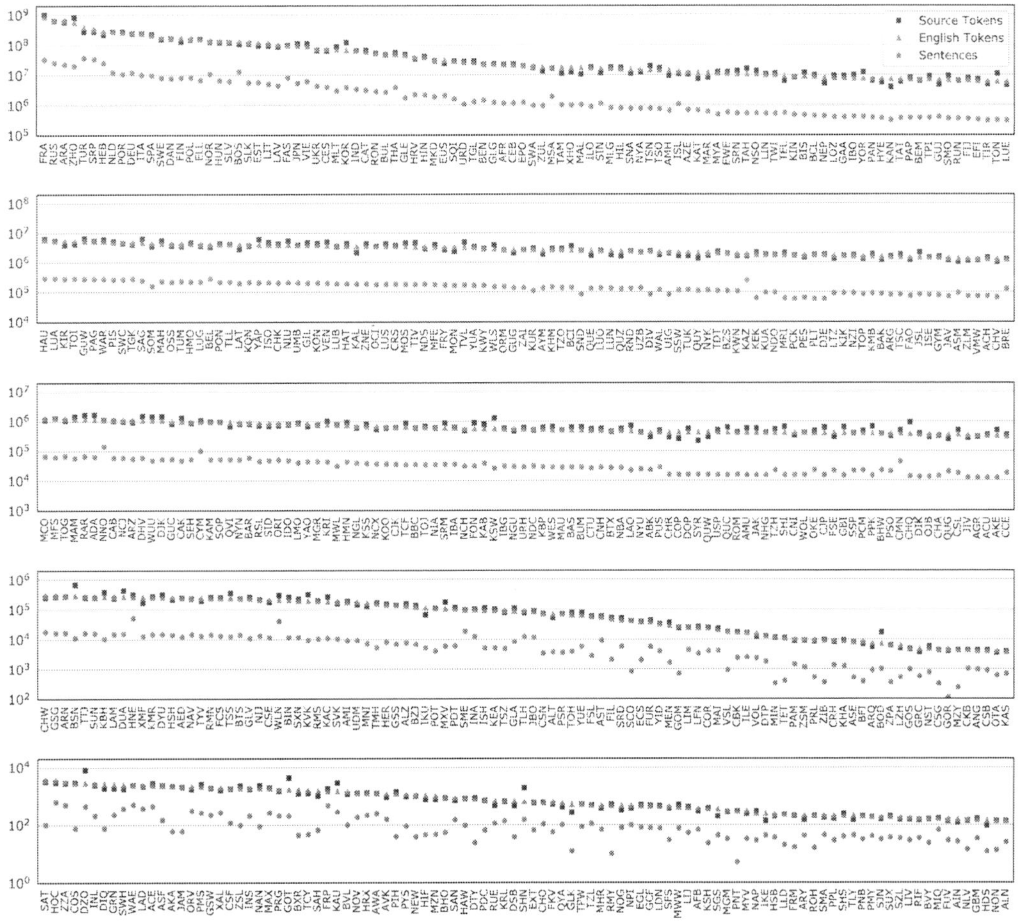

Figure 1: Training data statistics for the 500 languages, sorted based on descending order of English token count. These statistics are obtained after de-duplication and filtering (see Section 3.1). The full name for these ISO 639-3 codes can be looked up using MTDATA, e.g. `mtdata-iso eng` .

$512,000$ and $64,000$ BPE types as source and target vocabularies, respectively. The decoder's input and output embeddings are shared. Since some of the English sentences are replicated to align with many sentences from different languages (e.g. the Bible corpus), BPE merges are learned from the deduplicated sentences using NLCODEC. Our best performing model is trained with an effective batch size of about 720,000 tokens per optimizer step. Such big batches are achieved by using mixed-precision distributed training on 8 NVIDIA A100 GPUs with gradient accumulation of 5 mini-batches, each having a maximum of 18,000 tokens. We use the Adam optimizer (Kingma and Ba, 2014) with 8000 warm-up steps followed by a decaying learning rate, similar to Vaswani et al. (2017). We stop training after five days and six hours when a total of 200K updates are made by the optimizer; validation loss is still decreasing at this point. To assess the translation quality of our model, we report BLEU (Papineni et al., 2002; Post, 2018)[7] on a subset of languages for which known test sets are available, as given in Figure 2, along with a comparison to Zhang et al. (2020)'s best model.[8]

4 Applications

The model we trained as a demonstration for our tools is useful on its own, as described in the following sections.

[7]All our BLEU scores are obtained from SACREBLEU `BLEU+c.mixed+#.1+s.exp+tok.13a+v.1.4.13`.

[8]Scores are obtained from `https://github.com/bzhangGo/zero/tree/master/docs/multilingual_laln_lalt`; accessed: 2021/03/30

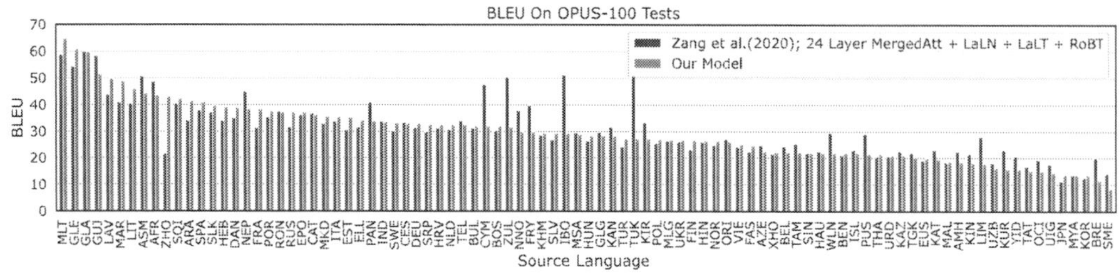

Figure 2: Many-to-English BLEU on OPUS-100 tests (Zhang et al., 2020). Despite having four times more languages on the source side, our model scores competitive BLEU on most languages with the strongest system of Zhang et al. (2020). The tests where our model scores lower BLEU have shorter source sentences (mean length of about three tokens).

4.1 Readily Usable Translation Service

Our pretrained NMT model is readily usable as a service capable of translating several hundred source languages to English. By design, source language identification is not necessary. Figure 2 shows that the model scores more than 20 BLEU, which maybe be a useful quality for certain downstream applications involving web and social media content analysis. Apache Tika (Mattmann and Zitting, 2011), a content detection and analysis toolkit capable of parsing thousands of file formats, has an option for translating any document into English using our multilingual NMT model.[9] Our model has been packaged and published to DockerHub,[10] which can be obtained by the following command:

```
IMAGE=tgowda/rtg-model:500toEng-v1
docker run --rm -i -p 6060:6060 $IMAGE
# For GPU support: --gpus '"device=0"'
```

The above command starts a docker image with HTTP server having a web interface, as can be seen in Figure 3, and a REST API. An example interaction with the REST API is as follows:

```
curl --data "source=Comment allez-vous?"\
    --data "source=Bonne journée"\
    http://localhost:6060/translate
```

```
 {
  "source": [ "Comment allez-vous?",
        "Bonne journée" ],
  "translation": [ "How are you?",
        "Have a nice day" ]
}
```

4.2 Parent Model for Low Resource MT

Fine tuning is a useful transfer learning technique for improving the translation of low resource languages (Zoph et al., 2016; Neubig and Hu, 2018; Gheini and May, 2019). For instance, consider Breton-English (BRE-ENG) and Northern Sami-English (SME-ENG), two of the low resource settings for which our model has relatively poor BLEU (see Figure 2). To show the utility of fine tuning with our model, we train a strong baseline Transformer model, one for each language, from scratch using OPUS-100 training data (Zhang et al., 2020), and finetune our multilingual model on the same dataset as the baselines. We shrink the parent model vocabulary and embeddings to the child model dataset, and train all models on NVIDIA P100 GPUs until convergence.[11] Table 2, which shows BLEU on the OPUS-100 test set for the two low resource languages indicates that our multilingual NMT parent model can be further improved with finetuning on limited training data. The finetuned model is significantly better than baseline model.

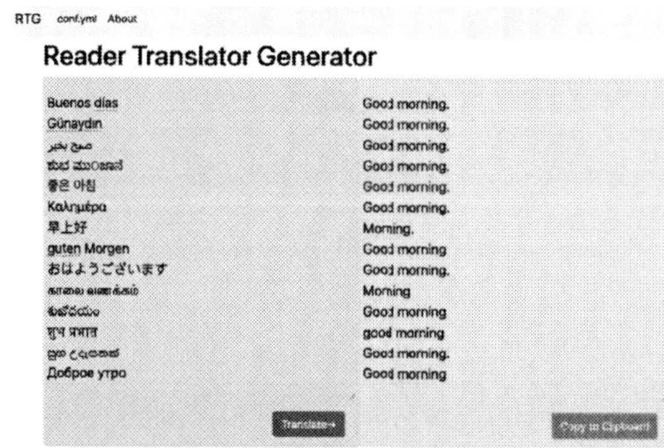

Figure 3: RTG Web Interface

[9] https://cwiki.apache.org/confluence/display/TIKA/NMT-RTG

[10] https://hub.docker.com/

[11] More info: https://github.com/thammegowda/006-many-to-eng/tree/master/lowres-xfer

Model	BRE-ENG	SME-ENG
Baseline	12.7	10.7
Parent	11.8	8.6
Finetuned	**22.8**	**19.1**

Table 2: Finetuning our multilingual NMT on limited training data in low resource settings significantly improves translation quality, as quantified by BLEU.

5 Related work

5.1 Tools

SACREBLEU (Post, 2018) simplifies MT evaluation. MTDATA attempts to simplify training setup by automating training and validation dataset retrieval. OPUSTOOLS (Aulamo et al., 2020) is a similar tool however, it interfaces with OPUS servers only. Since the dataset index for OPUSTOOLS is on a server, the addition of new datasets requires privileged access. In contrast, MTDATA is a client side library, it can be easily forked and extended to include new datasets without needing special privileges.

NLCODEC: NLCODEC is a Python library for vocabulary management. It overcomes the multithreading bottleneck in Python by using PySpark. SentencePiece (Kudo and Richardson, 2018) and HuggingfaceTokenizers (Wolf et al., 2020) are the closest alternatives in terms of features, however, modification is relatively difficult for Python users as these libraries are implemented in C++ and Rust, respectively. In addition, SentencePiece uses a binary format for model persistence in favor of efficiency, which takes away the inspectability of the model state. Retaining the ability to inspect models and modify core functionality is beneficial for further improving encoding schemes, e.g. subword regularization (Kudo, 2018), BPE dropout (Provilkov et al., 2020), and optimal stop condition for subword merges (Gowda and May, 2020). FastBPE is another efficient BPE tool written in C++.[12] Subword-nmt (Sennrich et al., 2016) is a Python implementation of BPE, and stores the model in an inspectable plain text format, however, it is not readily scalable to massive datasets such as the one used in this work. None of these tools have an equivalent to NLDB's mechanism for efficiently storing and retrieving variable length sequences for distributed training.

RTG: Tensor2Tensor (Vaswani et al., 2018) originally offered the Transformer (Vaswani et al., 2017) implementation using Tensorflow (Abadi et al., 2015); our implementation uses Pytorch (Paszke et al., 2019) following *Annotated Transformer* (Rush, 2018). OpenNMT currently offers separate implementations for both Pytorch and Tensorflow backends (Klein et al., 2017, 2020). As open-source toolkits evolve, many good features tend to propagate between them, leading to varying degrees of similarities. Some of the available NMT toolkits are: Nematus (Sennrich et al., 2017), xNMT (Neubig et al., 2018). Marian NMT (Junczys-Dowmunt et al., 2018), Joey NMT (Kreutzer et al., 2019), Fairseq (Ott et al., 2019), and Sockey (Hieber et al., 2020). An exhaustive comparison of these NMT toolkits is beyond the scope of our current work.

[12] `https://github.com/glample/fastBPE`

5.2 Multilingual NMT

Johnson et al. (2017) show that NMT models are capable of multilingual translation without any architectural changes, and observe that when languages with abundant data are mixed with low resource languages, the translation quality of low resource pairs are significantly improved. They use a private dataset of 12 language pairs; we use publicly available datasets for up to 500 languages. Qi et al. (2018) assemble a multi-parallel dataset for 58 languages from TEDTalks domains, which are included in our dataset. Zhang et al. (2020) curate OPUS-100, a multilingual dataset of 100 languages sampled from OPUS, including test sets; which are used in this work. Tiedemann (2020) have established a benchmark task for 500 languages including single directional baseline models. Wang et al. (2020) examine the language-wise imbalance problem in multilingual datasets and propose a method to address the imbalance using a scoring function, which we plan to explore in the future.

6 Conclusion

We have introduced our tools: MTDATA for downloading datasets, NLCODEC for processing, storing and retrieving large scale training data, and RTG for training NMT models. Using these tools, we have collected a massive dataset and trained a multilingual model for many-to-English translation. We have demonstrated that our model can be used independently as a translation service, and also showed its use as a parent model for improving low resource language translation. All the described tools, used datasets, and trained models are made available to the public for free.

Acknowledgments

The authors would like to thank Lukas Ferrer, Luke Miles, and Mozhdeh Gheini for their contributions to some of the tools used in this work, and thank Jörg Tiedemann for hosting our prepared dataset at OPUS (`https://opus.nlpl.eu/MT560.php`). The authors acknowledge the Center for Advanced Research Computing (CARC) at the University of Southern California for providing computing resources that have contributed to the research results reported within this publication. URL: `https://carc.usc.edu`. The authors acknowledge the Texas Advanced Computing Center (TACC) at The University of Texas at Austin for providing HPC resources that have contributed to the research results reported within this paper. URL: `http://www.tacc.utexas.edu`. This research is based upon work supported by the Office of the Director of National Intelligence (ODNI), Intelligence Advanced Research Projects Activity (IARPA), via AFRL Contract FA8650-17-C-9116. The views and conclusions contained herein are those of the authors and should not be interpreted as necessarily representing the official policies or endorsements, either expressed or implied, of the ODNI, IARPA, or the U.S. Government. The U.S. Government is authorized to reproduce and distribute reprints for Governmental purposes notwithstanding any copyright annotation thereon.

Ethical Consideration

Failure Modes: MTDATA will fail to operate, unless patched, when hosting services change their URLs or formats over time. On certain scenarios when a dataset has been previously accessed and retained in local cache, MTDATA continues to operate with a copy of previous version and ignores server side updates. We have done our best effort in normalizing languages to ISO 639-3 standard; our current version does not accommodate country and script variations of languages; e.g. UK English and US English are both mapped to *eng*. Our multilingual NMT model is trained to translate a full sentence at a time without considering source language information; translation of short phrases without a proper context might result in a poor quality translation.

Diversity and Fairness: We cover all languages on the source side for which publicly available dataset exists, which happens to be about 500 source languages. Our model translates to English only, hence only English speakers are benefited from this work.

Climate Impact: MTDATA reduces network transfers to the minimal by maintaining a local cache to avoid repetitive downloads. In addition to the raw datasets, preprocessed data is also available to avoid repetitive computation. Our Multilingual NMT has higher energy cost than a typical single directional NMT model due to higher number of parameters, however, since our single model translates hundreds of languages, the energy requirement is significantly lower than the total consumption of all independent models. Our trained models with all the weights are also made available for download.

Dataset Ownership: MTDATA is a client side library that does not have the ownership of datasets in its index. Addition, removal, or modification in its index is to be submitted by creating an issue at `https://github.com/thammegowda/mtdata/issues`. We ask the dataset users to review the dataset license, and acknowledge its original creators by citing their work, whose BIBTEX entries may be accessed using:

```
mtdata list -n <NAME> -l <L1-L2> -full
```

The prepared dataset that we have made available for download includes `citations.bib` that acknowledges all the original creators of datasets. We do not vouch for quality and fairness of all the datasets.

References

Martín Abadi, Ashish Agarwal, Paul Barham, Eugene Brevdo, Zhifeng Chen, Craig Citro, Greg S. Corrado, Andy Davis, Jeffrey Dean, Matthieu Devin, Sanjay Ghemawat, Ian Goodfellow, Andrew Harp, Geoffrey Irving, Michael Isard, Yangqing Jia, Rafal Jozefowicz, Lukasz Kaiser, Manjunath Kudlur, Josh Levenberg, Dandelion Mané, Rajat Monga, Sherry Moore, Derek Murray, Chris Olah, Mike Schuster, Jonathon Shlens, Benoit Steiner, Ilya Sutskever, Kunal Talwar, Paul Tucker, Vincent Vanhoucke, Vijay Vasudevan, Fernanda Viégas, Oriol Vinyals, Pete Warden, Martin Wattenberg, Martin Wicke, Yuan Yu, and Xiaoqiang Zheng. 2015. TensorFlow: Large-scale machine learning on heterogeneous systems. Software available from tensorflow.org.

Željko Agić and Ivan Vulić. 2019. JW300: A wide-coverage parallel corpus for low-resource languages. In *Proceedings of the 57th Annual Meeting of the Association for Computational Linguistics*, pages 3204–3210, Florence, Italy. Association for Computational Linguistics.

Mikko Aulamo, Umut Sulubacak, Sami Virpioja, and Jörg Tiedemann. 2020. OpusTools and parallel corpus diagnostics. In *Proceedings of the 12th Language Resources and Evaluation Conference*, pages 3782–3789, Marseille, France. European Language Resources Association.

Dzmitry Bahdanau, Kyunghyun Cho, and Yoshua Bengio. 2015. Neural machine translation by jointly learning to align and translate. In *3rd International Conference on Learning Representations, ICLR 2015, San Diego, CA, USA, May 7-9, 2015, Conference Track Proceedings*.

Loïc Barrault, Magdalena Biesialska, Ondřej Bojar, Marta R. Costa-jussà, Christian Federmann, Yvette Graham, Roman Grundkiewicz, Barry Haddow, Matthias Huck, Eric Joanis, Tom Kocmi, Philipp Koehn, Chi-kiu Lo, Nikola Ljubešić, Christof Monz, Makoto Morishita, Masaaki Nagata, Toshiaki Nakazawa, Santanu Pal, Matt Post, and Marcos Zampieri. 2020. Findings of the 2020 conference on machine translation (WMT20). In *Proceedings of the Fifth Conference on Machine Translation*, pages 1–55, Online. Association for Computational Linguistics.

Loïc Barrault, Ondřej Bojar, Marta R. Costa-jussà, Christian Federmann, Mark Fishel, Yvette Graham, Barry Haddow, Matthias Huck, Philipp Koehn, Shervin Malmasi, Christof Monz, Mathias Müller, Santanu Pal, Matt Post, and Marcos Zampieri. 2019. Findings of the 2019 conference on machine translation (WMT19). In *Proceedings of the Fourth Conference on Machine Translation (Volume 2: Shared Task Papers, Day 1)*, pages 1–61, Florence, Italy. Association for Computational Linguistics.

Ondřej Bojar, Christian Buck, Chris Callison-Burch, Christian Federmann, Barry Haddow, Philipp Koehn, Christof Monz, Matt Post, Radu Soricut, and Lucia Specia. 2013. Findings of the 2013 Workshop on Statistical Machine Translation. In *Proceedings of the Eighth Workshop on Statistical Machine Translation*, pages 1–44, Sofia, Bulgaria. Association for Computational Linguistics.

Ondřej Bojar, Christian Buck, Christian Federmann, Barry Haddow, Philipp Koehn, Johannes Leveling, Christof Monz, Pavel Pecina, Matt Post, Herve Saint-Amand, Radu Soricut, Lucia Specia, and Aleš Tamchyna. 2014. Findings of the 2014 workshop on statistical machine translation. In *Proceedings of the Ninth Workshop on Statistical Machine Translation*, pages 12–58, Baltimore, Maryland, USA. Association for Computational Linguistics.

Ondřej Bojar, Rajen Chatterjee, Christian Federmann, Yvette Graham, Barry Haddow, Shujian Huang, Matthias Huck, Philipp Koehn, Qun Liu, Varvara Logacheva, Christof Monz, Matteo Negri, Matt Post, Raphael Rubino, Lucia Specia, and Marco Turchi. 2017. Findings of the 2017 conference on machine translation (WMT17). In *Proceedings of the Second Conference on Machine Translation*, pages 169–214, Copenhagen, Denmark. Association for Computational Linguistics.

Ondřej Bojar, Rajen Chatterjee, Christian Federmann, Yvette Graham, Barry Haddow, Matthias Huck, Antonio Jimeno Yepes, Philipp Koehn, Varvara Logacheva, Christof Monz, Matteo Negri, Aurélie Névéol, Mariana Neves, Martin Popel, Matt Post, Raphael Rubino, Carolina Scarton, Lucia Specia, Marco Turchi, Karin Verspoor, and Marcos Zampieri. 2016. Findings of the 2016 conference on machine translation. In *Proceedings of the First Conference on Machine Translation: Volume 2, Shared Task Papers*, pages 131–198, Berlin, Germany. Association for Computational Linguistics.

Ondřej Bojar, Rajen Chatterjee, Christian Federmann, Barry Haddow, Matthias Huck, Chris Hokamp, Philipp Koehn, Varvara Logacheva, Christof Monz, Matteo Negri, Matt Post, Carolina Scarton, Lucia Specia, and Marco Turchi. 2015. Findings of the 2015 workshop on statistical machine translation. In *Proceedings of the Tenth Workshop on Statistical Machine Translation*, pages 1–46, Lisbon, Portugal. Association for Computational Linguistics.

Ondřej Bojar, Christian Federmann, Mark Fishel, Yvette Graham, Barry Haddow, Philipp Koehn, and Christof Monz. 2018. Findings of the 2018 conference on machine translation (WMT18). In *Proceedings of the Third Conference on Machine Translation: Shared Task Papers*, pages 272–303, Belgium, Brussels. Association for Computational Linguistics.

Miquel Esplà, Mikel Forcada, Gema Ramírez-Sánchez, and Hieu Hoang. 2019. ParaCrawl: Web-scale parallel corpora for the languages of the EU. In *Proceedings of Machine Translation Summit XVII Volume 2: Translator, Project and User Tracks*, pages 118–119, Dublin, Ireland. European Association for Machine Translation.

Mozhdeh Gheini and Jonathan May. 2019. A universal parent model for low-resource neural machine translation transfer. *arXiv preprint arXiv:1909.06516*.

Thamme Gowda and Jonathan May. 2020. Finding the optimal vocabulary size for neural machine translation. In *Findings of the Association for Computational Linguistics: EMNLP 2020*, pages 3955–3964, Online. Association for Computational Linguistics.

Barry Haddow and Faheem Kirefu. 2020. Pmindia – a collection of parallel corpora of languages of india.

Charles R. Harris, K. Jarrod Millman, St'efan J. van der Walt, Ralf Gommers, Pauli Virtanen, David Cournapeau, Eric Wieser, Julian Taylor, Sebastian Berg, Nathaniel J. Smith, Robert Kern, Matti Picus, Stephan Hoyer, Marten H. van Kerkwijk, Matthew Brett, Allan Haldane, Jaime Fern'andez del R'ıo, Mark Wiebe, Pearu Peterson, Pierre G'erard-Marchant, Kevin Sheppard, Tyler Reddy, Warren

Weckesser, Hameer Abbasi, Christoph Gohlke, and Travis E. Oliphant. 2020. Array programming with NumPy. *Nature*, 585(7825):357–362.

Felix Hieber, Tobias Domhan, Michael Denkowski, and David Vilar. 2020. Sockeye 2: A toolkit for neural machine translation. In *Proceedings of the 22nd Annual Conference of the European Association for Machine Translation*, pages 457–458, Lisboa, Portugal. European Association for Machine Translation.

Melvin Johnson, Mike Schuster, Quoc V. Le, Maxim Krikun, Yonghui Wu, Zhifeng Chen, Nikhil Thorat, Fernanda Viégas, Martin Wattenberg, Greg Corrado, Macduff Hughes, and Jeffrey Dean. 2017. Google's multilingual neural machine translation system: Enabling zero-shot translation. *Transactions of the Association for Computational Linguistics*, 5:339–351.

Marcin Junczys-Dowmunt, Roman Grundkiewicz, Tomasz Dwojak, Hieu Hoang, Kenneth Heafield, Tom Neckermann, Frank Seide, Ulrich Germann, Alham Fikri Aji, Nikolay Bogoychev, André F. T. Martins, and Alexandra Birch. 2018. Marian: Fast neural machine translation in C++. In *Proceedings of ACL 2018, System Demonstrations*, pages 116–121, Melbourne, Australia. Association for Computational Linguistics.

Diederik P Kingma and Jimmy Ba. 2014. Adam: A method for stochastic optimization. *arXiv preprint arXiv:1412.6980*.

Guillaume Klein, François Hernandez, Vincent Nguyen, and Jean Senellart. 2020. The OpenNMT neural machine translation toolkit: 2020 edition. In *Proceedings of the 14th Conference of the Association for Machine Translation in the Americas (Volume 1: Research Track)*, pages 102–109, Virtual. Association for Machine Translation in the Americas.

Guillaume Klein, Yoon Kim, Yuntian Deng, Jean Senellart, and Alexander Rush. 2017. OpenNMT: Open-source toolkit for neural machine translation. In *Proceedings of ACL 2017, System Demonstrations*, pages 67–72, Vancouver, Canada. Association for Computational Linguistics.

Philipp Koehn. 2005. Europarl: A parallel corpus for statistical machine translation. *Proc. 10th Machine Translation Summit (MT Summit), 2005*, pages 79–86.

Julia Kreutzer, Jasmijn Bastings, and Stefan Riezler. 2019. Joey NMT: A minimalist NMT toolkit for novices. In *Proceedings of the 2019 Conference on Empirical Methods in Natural Language Processing and the 9th International Joint Conference on Natural Language Processing (EMNLP-IJCNLP): System Demonstrations*, pages 109–114, Hong Kong, China. Association for Computational Linguistics.

Taku Kudo. 2018. Subword regularization: Improving neural network translation models with multiple subword candidates. In *Proceedings of the 56th Annual Meeting of the Association for Computational Linguistics (Volume 1: Long Papers)*, pages 66–75, Melbourne, Australia. Association for Computational Linguistics.

Taku Kudo and John Richardson. 2018. SentencePiece: A simple and language independent subword tokenizer and detokenizer for neural text processing. In *Proceedings of the 2018 Conference on Empirical Methods in Natural Language Processing: System Demonstrations*, pages 66–71, Brussels, Belgium. Association for Computational Linguistics.

Anoop Kunchukuttan, Pratik Mehta, and Pushpak Bhattacharyya. 2018. The IIT Bombay English-Hindi parallel corpus. In *Proceedings of the Eleventh International Conference on Language Resources and Evaluation (LREC 2018)*, Miyazaki, Japan. European Language Resources Association (ELRA).

Thang Luong, Hieu Pham, and Christopher D. Manning. 2015. Effective approaches to attention-based neural machine translation. In *Proceedings of the 2015 Conference on Empirical Methods in Natural Language Processing*, pages 1412–1421, Lisbon, Portugal. Association for Computational Linguistics.

Chris Mattmann and Jukka Zitting. 2011. Tika in action.

Graham Neubig. 2011. The Kyoto free translation task. http://www.phontron.com/kftt.

Graham Neubig and Junjie Hu. 2018. Rapid adaptation of neural machine translation to new languages. In *Proceedings of the 2018 Conference on Empirical Methods in Natural Language Processing*, pages 875–880, Brussels, Belgium. Association for Computational Linguistics.

Graham Neubig, Matthias Sperber, Xinyi Wang, Matthieu Felix, Austin Matthews, Sarguna Padmanabhan, Ye Qi, Devendra Sachan, Philip Arthur, Pierre Godard, John Hewitt, Rachid Riad, and Liming Wang. 2018. XNMT: The eXtensible neural machine translation toolkit. In *Proceedings of the 13th Conference of the Association for Machine Translation in the Americas (Volume 1: Research Track)*, pages 185–192, Boston, MA. Association for Machine Translation in the Americas.

Myle Ott, Sergey Edunov, Alexei Baevski, Angela Fan, Sam Gross, Nathan Ng, David Grangier, and Michael Auli. 2019. fairseq: A fast, extensible toolkit for sequence modeling. In *Proceedings of the 2019 Conference of the North American Chapter of the Association for Computational Linguistics (Demonstrations)*, pages 48–53, Minneapolis, Minnesota. Association for Computational Linguistics.

Kishore Papineni, Salim Roukos, Todd Ward, and Wei-Jing Zhu. 2002. Bleu: a method for automatic evaluation of machine translation. In *Proceedings of the 40th Annual Meeting of the Association for Computational Linguistics*, pages 311–318, Philadelphia,

Pennsylvania, USA. Association for Computational Linguistics.

Adam Paszke, Sam Gross, Francisco Massa, Adam Lerer, James Bradbury, Gregory Chanan, Trevor Killeen, Zeming Lin, Natalia Gimelshein, Luca Antiga, Alban Desmaison, Andreas Kopf, Edward Yang, Zachary DeVito, Martin Raison, Alykhan Tejani, Sasank Chilamkurthy, Benoit Steiner, Lu Fang, Junjie Bai, and Soumith Chintala. 2019. Pytorch: An imperative style, high-performance deep learning library. In H. Wallach, H. Larochelle, A. Beygelzimer, F. d'Alché-Buc, E. Fox, and R. Garnett, editors, *Advances in Neural Information Processing Systems 32*, pages 8024–8035. Curran Associates, Inc.

Matt Post. 2018. A call for clarity in reporting BLEU scores. In *Proceedings of the Third Conference on Machine Translation: Research Papers*, pages 186–191, Brussels, Belgium. Association for Computational Linguistics.

Matt Post, Chris Callison-Burch, and Miles Osborne. 2012. Constructing parallel corpora for six Indian languages via crowdsourcing. In *Proceedings of the Seventh Workshop on Statistical Machine Translation*, pages 401–409, Montréal, Canada. Association for Computational Linguistics.

Ofir Press and Lior Wolf. 2017. Using the output embedding to improve language models. In *Proceedings of the 15th Conference of the European Chapter of the Association for Computational Linguistics: Volume 2, Short Papers*, pages 157–163, Valencia, Spain. Association for Computational Linguistics.

Ivan Provilkov, Dmitrii Emelianenko, and Elena Voita. 2020. BPE-dropout: Simple and effective subword regularization. In *Proceedings of the 58th Annual Meeting of the Association for Computational Linguistics*, pages 1882–1892, Online. Association for Computational Linguistics.

Ye Qi, Devendra Sachan, Matthieu Felix, Sarguna Padmanabhan, and Graham Neubig. 2018. When and why are pre-trained word embeddings useful for neural machine translation? In *Proceedings of the 2018 Conference of the North American Chapter of the Association for Computational Linguistics: Human Language Technologies, Volume 2 (Short Papers)*, pages 529–535, New Orleans, Louisiana. Association for Computational Linguistics.

Roberts Rozis and Raivis Skadiņš. 2017. Tilde MODEL - multilingual open data for EU languages. In *Proceedings of the 21st Nordic Conference on Computational Linguistics*, pages 263–265, Gothenburg, Sweden. Association for Computational Linguistics.

Alexander Rush. 2018. The annotated transformer. In *Proceedings of Workshop for NLP Open Source Software (NLP-OSS)*, pages 52–60, Melbourne, Australia. Association for Computational Linguistics.

Holger Schwenk, Vishrav Chaudhary, Shuo Sun, Hongyu Gong, and Francisco Guzmán. 2019. Wikimatrix: Mining 135m parallel sentences in 1620 language pairs from wikipedia. *CoRR*, abs/1907.05791.

Rico Sennrich, Orhan Firat, Kyunghyun Cho, Alexandra Birch, Barry Haddow, Julian Hitschler, Marcin Junczys-Dowmunt, Samuel Läubli, Antonio Valerio Miceli Barone, Jozef Mokry, and Maria Nădejde. 2017. Nematus: a toolkit for neural machine translation. In *Proceedings of the Software Demonstrations of the 15th Conference of the European Chapter of the Association for Computational Linguistics*, pages 65–68, Valencia, Spain. Association for Computational Linguistics.

Rico Sennrich, Barry Haddow, and Alexandra Birch. 2016. Neural machine translation of rare words with subword units. In *Proceedings of the 54th Annual Meeting of the Association for Computational Linguistics (Volume 1: Long Papers)*, pages 1715–1725, Berlin, Germany. Association for Computational Linguistics.

Jörg Tiedemann. 2012. Parallel data, tools and interfaces in OPUS. In *Proceedings of the Eighth International Conference on Language Resources and Evaluation (LREC'12)*, pages 2214–2218, Istanbul, Turkey. European Language Resources Association (ELRA).

Jörg Tiedemann. 2020. The tatoeba translation challenge – realistic data sets for low resource and multilingual MT. In *Proceedings of the Fifth Conference on Machine Translation*, pages 1174–1182, Online. Association for Computational Linguistics.

Ashish Vaswani, Samy Bengio, Eugene Brevdo, Francois Chollet, Aidan Gomez, Stephan Gouws, Llion Jones, Łukasz Kaiser, Nal Kalchbrenner, Niki Parmar, Ryan Sepassi, Noam Shazeer, and Jakob Uszkoreit. 2018. Tensor2Tensor for neural machine translation. In *Proceedings of the 13th Conference of the Association for Machine Translation in the Americas (Volume 1: Research Track)*, pages 193–199, Boston, MA. Association for Machine Translation in the Americas.

Ashish Vaswani, Noam Shazeer, Niki Parmar, Jakob Uszkoreit, Llion Jones, Aidan N Gomez, Łukasz Kaiser, and Illia Polosukhin. 2017. Attention is all you need. In *Advances in neural information processing systems*, pages 5998–6008.

Xinyi Wang, Yulia Tsvetkov, and Graham Neubig. 2020. Balancing training for multilingual neural machine translation. In *Proceedings of the 58th Annual Meeting of the Association for Computational Linguistics*, pages 8526–8537, Online. Association for Computational Linguistics.

Thomas Wolf, Lysandre Debut, Victor Sanh, Julien Chaumond, Clement Delangue, Anthony Moi, Pierric Cistac, Tim Rault, Remi Louf, Morgan Funtowicz, Joe Davison, Sam Shleifer, Patrick von Platen,

Clara Ma, Yacine Jernite, Julien Plu, Canwen Xu, Teven Le Scao, Sylvain Gugger, Mariama Drame, Quentin Lhoest, and Alexander Rush. 2020. Transformers: State-of-the-art natural language processing. In *Proceedings of the 2020 Conference on Empirical Methods in Natural Language Processing: System Demonstrations*, pages 38–45, Online. Association for Computational Linguistics.

Yonghui Wu, Mike Schuster, Zhifeng Chen, Quoc V. Le, Mohammad Norouzi, Wolfgang Macherey, Maxim Krikun, Yuan Cao, Qin Gao, Klaus Macherey, Jeff Klingner, Apurva Shah, Melvin Johnson, Xiaobing Liu, Lukasz Kaiser, Stephan Gouws, Yoshikiyo Kato, Taku Kudo, Hideto Kazawa, Keith Stevens, George Kurian, Nishant Patil, Wei Wang, Cliff Young, Jason Smith, Jason Riesa, Alex Rudnick, Oriol Vinyals, Greg Corrado, Macduff Hughes, and Jeffrey Dean. 2016. Google's neural machine translation system: Bridging the gap between human and machine translation. *CoRR*, abs/1609.08144.

Matei Zaharia, Reynold S Xin, Patrick Wendell, Tathagata Das, Michael Armbrust, Ankur Dave, Xiangrui Meng, Josh Rosen, Shivaram Venkataraman, Michael J Franklin, et al. 2016. Apache spark: a unified engine for big data processing. *Communications of the ACM*, 59(11):56–65.

Biao Zhang, Philip Williams, Ivan Titov, and Rico Sennrich. 2020. Improving massively multilingual neural machine translation and zero-shot translation. In *Proceedings of the 58th Annual Meeting of the Association for Computational Linguistics*, pages 1628–1639, Online. Association for Computational Linguistics.

Michał Ziemski, Marcin Junczys-Dowmunt, and Bruno Pouliquen. 2016. The united nations parallel corpus v1.0. In *Proceedings of the Tenth International Conference on Language Resources and Evaluation (LREC'16)*, pages 3530–3534, Portorož, Slovenia. European Language Resources Association (ELRA).

Barret Zoph, Deniz Yuret, Jonathan May, and Kevin Knight. 2016. Transfer learning for low-resource neural machine translation. In *Proceedings of the 2016 Conference on Empirical Methods in Natural Language Processing*, pages 1568–1575, Austin, Texas. Association for Computational Linguistics.

LEGOEval: An Open-Source Toolkit for Dialogue System Evaluation via Crowdsourcing

[†]Yu Li* [†]Josh Arnold* [‡]Feifan Yan [‡]Weiyan Shi [‡]Zhou Yu

[†]Department of Computer Science, University of California, Davis
[‡]Department of Computer Science, Columbia University
[†]{yooli, jarnold}@ucdavis.edu
[‡]{fy2241, ws2634, zy2461}@columbia.edu

Abstract

We present LEGOEval, an open-source toolkit that enables researchers to easily evaluate dialogue systems in a few lines of code using the online crowdsource platform, Amazon Mechanical Turk. Compared to existing toolkits, LEGOEval features a flexible task design by providing a Python API that maps to commonly used React.js interface components. Researchers can personalize their evaluation procedures easily with our built-in pages as if playing with LEGO blocks. Thus, LEGOEval provides a fast, consistent method for reproducing human evaluation results. Besides the flexible task design, LEGOEval also offers an easy API to review collected data.

1 Introduction

As dialogue systems are becoming an increasingly trending topic, the need for standardized and reliable evaluation procedures has grown significantly. Typically, the evaluation of dialogue systems is accomplished by the use of both automatic metrics (Papineni et al., 2002; Lin, 2004; Lavie and Agarwal, 2007) and human evaluation (Serban et al., 2016; Park et al., 2018). Automatic metrics are reliable measurements, but common automatic metrics correlate weakly with human judgment (Liu et al., 2016; Lowe et al., 2017; Gu et al., 2020). Thus, human evaluation has become a primary method for dialogue system evaluation. Previously, researchers invited participants to the lab to physically interact with dialogue systems; recently, the popular approach is crowdsourcing using platforms such as Amazon Mechanical Turk (AMT) (Deriu et al., 2020; Eskenazi et al., 2013).

However, human evaluation via crowdsourcing presents its own challenges, being both expensive and time-intensive. Specifically, human evaluation requires a huge engineering effort to develop the interface and deploy the task on crowdsourcing platforms. The front-end interfaces can be difficult to set up: the crowdworkers need to be properly instructed, and the tasks need to be prepared to reflect real-world environment as closely as possible. Furthermore, one needs to take into account the high variability of user behaviour especially in crowdsourced environments (Deriu et al., 2020). It was shown that even different phrasings can result in weaker levels of agreement (Li et al., 2019). Thus, it is not trivial to reproduce the human evaluation results from scratch.

To address these problems, we present LEGOEval, an open-source toolkit that enables researchers to easily build and deploy their human evaluation tasks on AMT in one click. LEGOEval supports representative human evaluation tasks, such as *static evaluation*, where crowdworkers are asked to rate sampled dialogues, and *interactive evaluation*, where crowdworkers interact with two systems and evaluate their responses (Finch and Choi, 2020; Adiwardana et al., 2020). Furthermore, researchers are also able to customize their own human evaluation procedures easily with LEGOEval.

Existing tools typically provide rigid human evaluation templates. For example, DialCrowd (Lee et al., 2018) follows the speech synthesis evaluation toolkit (Parlikar, 2012) and provides a small number of standard evaluation experiments, however, researchers have to manually create the web services and then post the evaluation task on AMT. Sedoc et al. (2019) developed ChatEval, which posts a response comparison task (Otani et al., 2016) on AMT. It is only effective for specific dialogue systems and is not generalizable. The widely used toolkit ParlAI (Miller et al., 2018) supports crowd-

* Equal contribution.
Source code and documentation are available at https://github.com/yooli23/LEGOEval.
A demo video is available at https://www.youtube.com/watch?v=Dg6mafRGOpg&ab_channel=JoshArnold.

Proceedings of the Joint Conference of the 59th Annual Meeting of the Association for Computational Linguistics and the 11th International Joint Conference on Natural Language Processing: System Demonstrations, pages 317–324, August 1st - August 6th, 2021.

Toolkit	LEGOEval	DialCrowd (Lee et al., 2018)	ParlAI (Miller et al., 2018)	Mephisto
Sample Templates	✓	✓	✓	✓
Flexible Interface Design	✓	✗	✗	✗
Branching Logic	✓	✗	✗	✗
Plug & Play	✓	✗	✗	✓
Data Reviewing Tool	✓	✓	✗	✓

Table 1: Comparison of related crowdsourcing tools. "Sample Templates" indicates that the tool has evaluation examples that are commonly used. "Flexible Interface Design" indicates that the evaluation interface can be fast and easily modified. "Branching Logic" means the tool supports different interfaces in a same task."Plug & Play" means that the tool can be used out of the box.

sourcing tasks on AMT for the models built by ParlAI. However, ParlAI also requires additional engineering efforts to incorporate an external model or modify the evaluation interface. To our best knowledge, the most similar tool to ours is Mephisto [1], a crowdsourcing tool in an early alpha release expanded from ParlAI. From our experience, however, Mephisto has a steeper learning curve and is currently not suited for easily customizing and launching simple tasks.

Compared to these existing tools, our toolkit features a flexible interface design with a plug and play fashion, as shown in Table 1. Researchers can build their personalized human evaluation task flow with our library of Python classes, including a chatbot interface, an instruction page, and various survey formats. The task building process is similar to playing a LEGO game. Furthermore, LEGOEval makes it easy to share tasks with others, thereby making it easy to reproduce human evaluation results. Additionally, LEGOEval provides a straight-forward way to persist, retrieve, and review collected data, thus helping researchers process their results more efficiently.

In this paper, we present LEGOEval in the following order: first, we describe the design and architecture in Section 2, then we provide code snippets showing how to build the personalized task page in Section 3. Finally in section 4, we reproduce past experiments using LEGOEval.

2 LEGOEval Toolkit

LEGOEval is an open-source Python-based toolkit. As shown in Figure 1, LEGOEval includes three modules: (1) a task flow builder (Section 2.1) for designing the human evaluation task, (2) an AMT manager (Section 2.2) that automatically deploys the evaluation task on AMT, and (3) a data reviewer API (Section 2.3) that retrieves and formats data collected on AMT. We describe each module in the following sections.

[1] https://github.com/facebookresearch/Mephisto

2.1 Task Flow Builder

The task flow builder generates the interface and flow for different human evaluation tasks by compiling a list of *pages*. The pages can be viewed as LEGO blocks: we can snap pages together to easily customize the evaluation task flow. Furthermore, our toolkit and LEGO-style design makes it easy to share tasks: instead of sharing an entire web application, researchers can simply share their tasks with a few lines of code in-order to reproduce their evaluation procedure.

We have also provided common human evaluation procedures in LEGOEval for instance, *static evaluation*, where crowdworkers are asked to rate sampled dialogues and *interactive evaluation*, where a crowdworker interacts with multiple dialogue systems and evaluates the responses. Researchers can easily integrate their models, and customize their task flow using LEGOEval.

Page As the name suggests, a page in LEGOEval is a single web page with a specific functionality (e.g. displaying instructions, presenting a survey). Pages are designed to be independent of one-another, preventing any complex dependencies from occurring. Furthermore, each page is defined by a single React.js file and mapped to a simple Python wrapper class. We have provided a pool of pages that are commonly used in human evaluation tasks, including an instruction page (to display task instructions), an interactive chatbot page, and various survey pages. Beyond the built-in pages and their parameters, researchers also have the flexibility to customize a page or its logic by simply editing a single React.js file.

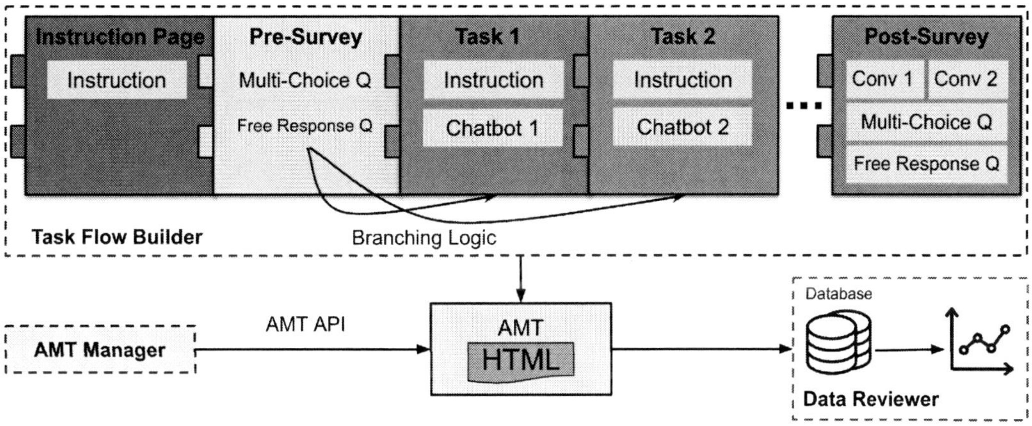

Figure 1: Design of LEGOEval, the task building process is similar to playing a LEGO game, the pages can be viewed as LEGO blocks in the task flow builder. The developer can also add *branching logic* in their task with the lambda function to show different task flows to different crowdworkers at runtime.

Page Customization Customizing the front-end display of a page is as simple as editing a single React.js file. Researchers can easily add an image, or re-arrange the order of the user-interface elements. With React.js, one can also edit a page's CSS, achieving complex front-end layouts if needed. Lastly, if researchers need to modify the logic/functionality of a component, they can also do it from the same React.js file through the use of `state`. We further describe how `state` works in LEGOEval in the next paragraph.

State In LEGOEval, researchers are able to easily customize the functionality of a page with the idea of `state`. `State` solves the dilemma that often occurs when designing a human evaluation task: specifically, how one should design the data flow between the back-end and the front-end. To address this issue of data-flow design, we implement the idea of a shared-state between the front-end and the back-end. When the back-end modifies the state of a task, the state is automatically updated on the front-end, and vice versa. Furthermore, any changes made to the state are automatically persisted in a Postgres-SQL database, making data persistence and retrieval incredibly simple. Thus, when modifying the functionality of React.js page, the researcher only needs to set key-value pairs in the front-end React.js state-dictionary. Their key-value pairs will automatically be persisted in a database and synced to the backend. Although not always necessary to modify, LEGOEval also features a main loop function on the backend, found in `main_loop.py`, that is called each time the `state` is modified from the front-end. In the main loop, the researcher can respond to any front-end changes from the backend. For example, when a crowdworker sends a chat message on the front-end, the main loop provides the backend an opportunity to provide a response. We provide detailed documentation on the main loop in our GitHub repository. Thus, with `state`, the researcher can easily save or pass data between the backend and their front-end React.js file, allowing them to flexibly implement any needed functionality.

Building a Task Flow To build an evaluation task in LEGOEval, we just need to assemble the pages in a similar fashion to building LEGO. An evaluation task usually consists of a multi-phase flow, e.g., displaying task instructions, then a survey, etc. Each phase corresponds to an individual page. The developer can add the desired pages in a sequence, and LEGOEval will automatically display each page in order one at a time. Additionally, LEGOEval supports branching logic to show different task flows to different crowdworkers, determined at runtime. We will describe branching logic in more detail in Section 2.4.

2.2 AMT Manager

Once the task flow is created, the task flow builder will automatically generate the necessary files that can be embedded in an AMT task. Our AMT manager follows the Mechanical Turk manager pipeline in ParlAI (Miller et al., 2018) and launches the evaluation task on AMT by embedding the generated interface using an iFrame. Researchers can edit the AMT configuration file which contains the AMT task settings, including the reward for each Human Intelligence Task (HIT), the number of HITs to launch, the task title, etc. When researchers launch the task, the AMT manager will automatically build and deploy a web application on the cloud application platform, Heroku [2], and then post the evaluation task on AMT using the AMT API. Our AMT manager inherits necessary functions from the Mechanical Turk manager in ParlAI, for example, checking crowdworker's qualification and optionally limiting the number of hits for each crowdworker. The AMT manager also supports automatic data validation. For instance, when crowdworkers finish a HIT, the manager can check the quality of the collected data via metrics defined by the researcher (e.g., the dialogue length or the rating variance in the rating question component), and then it will approve or deny the reward and bonus, depending on if the results pass the data validation test.

2.3 Data Reviewer

LEGOEval also simplifies the process to review the collected data. Different from ParlAI (Miller et al., 2018) which saves raw data locally, we create an individual Heroku Postgres add-on as the database of the web application when researchers launch a new task. We will create separate databases when there are multiple evaluation tasks running on AMT at the same time. Collected data will be saved in the corresponding add-on database. The data can be read locally using our Python API. Storing the data on the cloud prevents potential accidents, such as locally deleting the data. Since there are various types of data that can be collected in LEGOEval (e.g., conversations, ratings, and free response questions), we organize the data according to the data type so that they can be easily reviewed and processed for further research using a Python API we wrote.

2.4 Additional Functions

As mentioned earlier, LEGOEval is a flexible toolkit to easily implement human evaluation tasks. Specifically, it allows branching logic to display pages dynamically at run-time, as well as guaranteed data collection of a fixed size, which are two important features in dialogue human evaluation.

Branching Logic LEGOEval is unique in the way that our pages are instantiated at run-time. To implement branching logic, we offer a special lambda function that is called at runtime. Each lambda function takes as an argument the current `state` of a task. Researchers can build *branching and conditional logic* in their tasks by using lambda functions. For example, a researcher can easily define logic to skip a certain page based upon a crowdworker's previous answer to a survey. We show an example of branching logic implementation in Section 3.

Assigning Tasks to Workers Another common problem faced with crowd-sourced tasks is collecting data in a distributed, sampled fashion. For example, if you have 100 conversations, you might want each conversation to be rated **exactly** X times, each time by a different crowd-worker. Because crowd-workers can start a task and then give up half-way through, building the logic to assign HITS in the aforementioned way can be time-consuming. To achieve this in LEGOEval we provide a Python wrapper class, named `Data Assigner`. When using the Data Assigner class, you simply pass in a list of json seralizable data (dictionaries, arrays, strings, etc) and specify how many times you want to collect each data point. After that, LEGOEval will automatically distribute the data to be randomly assigned to different workers until each data point has been successfully collected X times.

3 Toolkit Usage

In this section, we provide a simple example of what the researcher needs to do to create a task.

Typical Usage Researchers would first design their high-level task flow on paper, (e.g, instruction page, then a pre survey, ..., and finally, a post survey). After this, researchers can add their different pages to their task flow by editing the `build.py` file and initializing a list of our provided Python classes. Some pages, such as the survey page, have a high level of customization, where developers can specify what types of questions they want to display on the survey, and the questions' relative order. Next, researchers can test their task locally by running `server.py` and navigating to their localhost. If they are happy with the results, researchers can launch their task on MTurk with one command: `launch_hits.py`. If researchers want to make a few tweaks, such as using a custom font for the instructions, they can easily edit a single React.js file and override any necessary CSS in typically one line of code. A strong benefit of our platform is that it is very fast for researchers to plug and

[2]https://www.heroku.com/

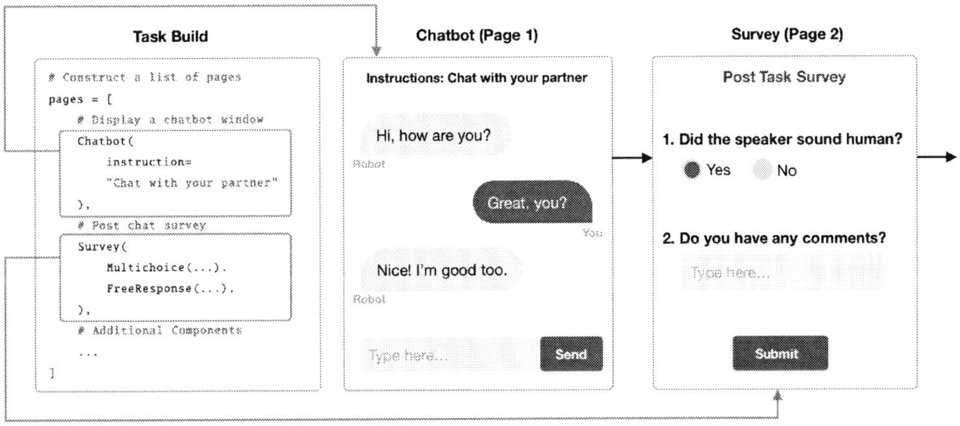

Figure 2: An example how the task build maps to a generated evaluation task in Section 3.

play typical evaluation tasks. For further detail, see Figure 2 for an example.

Advanced Usage As previously mentioned, it is possible to add branching logic via the use of lambda functions. Firstly, the researcher must define a function that takes as an input the state dictionary. The state dictionary contains information representing the current state of the task and any persisted data. Thus, based upon the data collected so far, the researcher can decide which page to instantiate and return. The researcher adds the *LambdaFunction* object passing in their lambda function. During run time, when the *LambdaFunction* object is popped from the task flow list, our framework will call the function by passing in the current state dictionary and return the determined page to display.

```
# 1) Define conditional logic
f = lambda state: \
    ComponentA() \
    if state['survey']['q1'] == "Yes" \
    else ComponentB()

# 2) Add the LambdaFunction to the Task Flow
task_flow.append(LambdaFunction(f))
```

4 Experiments

To demonstrate the effectiveness of LEGOEval in setting up dialogue system human evaluation tasks, we reproduce a set of crowdsourced experiments from the BlenderBot paper (Roller et al., 2020), a state-of-the-art open-domain chatbot. Crowdsourced experiments in BlenderBot include two steps: (1) collecting human-bot conversations via crowdworkers, (2) ACUTE-Eval (Li et al., 2019) between two models, where crowdworkers are asked to make pairwise evaluations of complete dialogues. We implement both crowdsourced experiments in approximately 20 lines of Python code with LEGOEval, indicating that it is easy to implement different types of human evaluation tasks with our toolkit in a plug and play fashion.

4.1 Human-Bot Data Collection

Following Roller et al. (2020) and Adiwardana et al. (2020), we build a task to collect human-bot conversations on AMT for the 90M BlenderBot model with LEGOEval. We simply assemble a pre-survey question component in the first page and a chatbot component in the second page. The generated interface is shown in Figure 3. We build the whole task from scratch and post it on AMT in several minutes. Then we collect 20 conversations following the settings in Roller et al. (2020). One example from our collected conversations is shown in Appendix A. It shows that our toolkit can collect human-bot conversations properly.

4.2 BlenderBot (2.7B) vs. Meena

To demonstrate LEGOEval's capability to support different dialogue system human evaluation tasks, we also reproduce ACUTE-Eval (Li et al., 2019) between BlenderBot (Roller et al., 2020) and Meena (Adiwardana et al., 2020). ACUTE-Eval requires human annotators to compare multi-turn conversations between different dialogue systems. Following Roller et al. (2020) and Li et al. (2019), we consider two evaluation questions:

- Engagingness question: "Who would you pre-

Figure 3: The interface of the human-bot conversation task with the Blender Model. In the task, the survey is shown first, and then the chat window. However, we show the pages side by side for convenience.

fer to talk to for a long conversation?”

- Humanness question: “Which speaker sounds more human?”

As shown in Figure 4, we use a chat history comparison page that features a single choice survey question. Crowdworkers are instructed to compare two dialogues and answer two questions below. We collect 114 data points, the results is shown in Table 2. The results (0.72 vs. 0.28 for engagingness, 0.68 vs. 0.32 for humanness) are close to the results in Roller et al. (2020) (0.75 vs. 0.25 for engagingness, 0.65 vs. 0.35 for humanness). It demonstrates that with our toolkit, we can reproduce the human evaluation results in other works quickly.

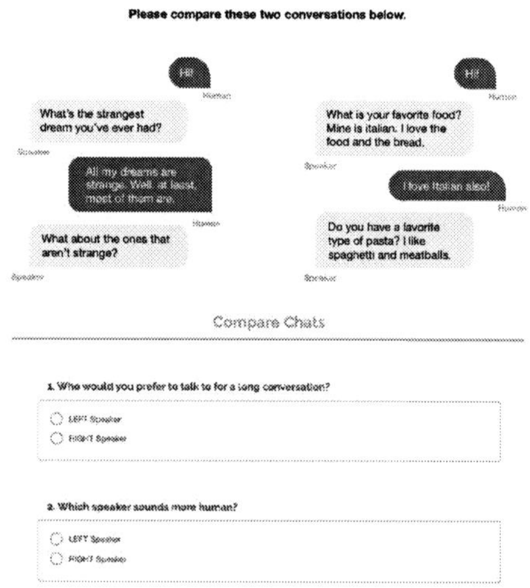

Figure 4: Interface of ACUTE-Eval between the BlenderBot and Meena. The conversations have been truncated to save display-space.

Model	BlenderBot	Meena
Engagingness	0.72 (0.75)	0.28 (0.25)
Humanness	0.68 (0.65)	0.32 (0.35)

Table 2: Human-Chat ACUTE-Eval of engagingness and humanness between BlenderBot (2.7B) and Meena, numbers represent the percentage of people choose the model. Numbers in brackets are the results in Roller et al. (2020)

5 Conclusion and Future Work

We introduce LEGOEval, an open-source Python-based toolkit that allows researchers to easily develop human evaluation tasks for dialogue systems on AMT in a LEGO plug-and-play fashion. LEGOEval provides a variety of commonly-used React.js components as building blocks for researchers to use. We have shown that it is straightforward to customize different types of human evaluation procedures for dialogue systems in a few lines of code, create new components by leveraging the *shared state* between the front-end and back-end, and reproduce human evaluation results in other works effortlessly. With LEGOEval, we hope to provide a simple and flexible way to evaluate dialogue systems. For future work, we plan to add more human evaluation procedure templates and React.js components. We further want to extend the tool to support human-human interaction on AMT, making it work not only for evaluation, but also for dialogue data collection.

References

Daniel Adiwardana, Minh-Thang Luong, David R. So, Jamie Hall, Noah Fiedel, Romal Thoppilan, Zi Yang, Apoorv Kulshreshtha, Gaurav Nemade, Yifeng Lu, and Quoc V. Le. 2020. Towards a human-like open-domain chatbot.

Jan Deriu, Alvaro Rodrigo, Arantxa Otegi, Guillermo Echegoyen, Sophie Rosset, Eneko Agirre, and Mark Cieliebak. 2020. Survey on evaluation methods for dialogue systems. *Artificial Intelligence Review*, 54(1):755–810.

Maxine Eskenazi, Gina-Anne Levow, Helen Meng, Gabriel Parent, and David Suendermann. 2013. *Crowdsourcing for speech processing: Applications to data collection, transcription and assessment*. John Wiley & Sons.

Sarah E. Finch and Jinho D. Choi. 2020. Towards unified dialogue system evaluation: A comprehensive analysis of current evaluation protocols. In *Proceedings of the 21th Annual Meeting of the Special Interest Group on Discourse and Dialogue*, pages 236–245, 1st virtual meeting. Association for Computational Linguistics.

Jing Gu, Qingyang Wu, and Zhou Yu. 2020. Perception score, a learned metric for open-ended text generation evaluation.

Alon Lavie and Abhaya Agarwal. 2007. METEOR: An automatic metric for MT evaluation with high levels of correlation with human judgments. In *Proceedings of the Second Workshop on Statistical Machine Translation*, pages 228–231, Prague, Czech Republic. Association for Computational Linguistics.

Kyusong Lee, Tiancheng Zhao, Alan W. Black, and Maxine Eskenazi. 2018. DialCrowd: A toolkit for easy dialog system assessment. In *Proceedings of the 19th Annual SIGdial Meeting on Discourse and Dialogue*, pages 245–248, Melbourne, Australia. Association for Computational Linguistics.

Margaret Li, Jason Weston, and Stephen Roller. 2019. Acute-eval: Improved dialogue evaluation with optimized questions and multi-turn comparisons.

Chin-Yew Lin. 2004. Rouge: A package for automatic evaluation of summaries. In *Text summarization branches out*, pages 74–81.

Chia-Wei Liu, Ryan Lowe, Iulian Serban, Mike Noseworthy, Laurent Charlin, and Joelle Pineau. 2016. How NOT to evaluate your dialogue system: An empirical study of unsupervised evaluation metrics for dialogue response generation. In *Proceedings of the 2016 Conference on Empirical Methods in Natural Language Processing*, pages 2122–2132, Austin, Texas. Association for Computational Linguistics.

Ryan Lowe, Michael Noseworthy, Iulian Vlad Serban, Nicolas Angelard-Gontier, Yoshua Bengio, and Joelle Pineau. 2017. Towards an automatic Turing test: Learning to evaluate dialogue responses. In *Proceedings of the 55th Annual Meeting of the Association for Computational Linguistics (Volume 1: Long Papers)*, pages 1116–1126, Vancouver, Canada. Association for Computational Linguistics.

Alexander H. Miller, Will Feng, Adam Fisch, Jiasen Lu, Dhruv Batra, Antoine Bordes, Devi Parikh, and Jason Weston. 2018. Parlai: A dialog research software platform.

Naoki Otani, Toshiaki Nakazawa, Daisuke Kawahara, and Sadao Kurohashi. 2016. IRT-based aggregation model of crowdsourced pairwise comparison for evaluating machine translations. In *Proceedings of the 2016 Conference on Empirical Methods in Natural Language Processing*, pages 511–520, Austin, Texas. Association for Computational Linguistics.

Kishore Papineni, Salim Roukos, Todd Ward, and Wei-Jing Zhu. 2002. Bleu: a method for automatic evaluation of machine translation. In *Proceedings of the 40th Annual Meeting of the Association for Computational Linguistics*, pages 311–318, Philadelphia, Pennsylvania, USA. Association for Computational Linguistics.

Yookoon Park, Jaemin Cho, and Gunhee Kim. 2018. A hierarchical latent structure for variational conversation modeling. In *Proceedings of the 2018 Conference of the North American Chapter of the Association for Computational Linguistics: Human Language Technologies, Volume 1 (Long Papers)*, pages 1792–1801, New Orleans, Louisiana. Association for Computational Linguistics.

Alok Parlikar. 2012. Testvox: Web-based framework for subjective evaluation of speech synthesis. *Opensource Software*, page 13.

Stephen Roller, Emily Dinan, Naman Goyal, Da Ju, Mary Williamson, Yinhan Liu, Jing Xu, Myle Ott, Kurt Shuster, Eric M. Smith, Y-Lan Boureau, and Jason Weston. 2020. Recipes for building an open-domain chatbot.

João Sedoc, Daphne Ippolito, Arun Kirubarajan, Jai Thirani, Lyle Ungar, and Chris Callison-Burch. 2019. ChatEval: A tool for chatbot evaluation. In *Proceedings of the 2019 Conference of the North American Chapter of the Association for Computational Linguistics (Demonstrations)*, pages 60–65, Minneapolis, Minnesota. Association for Computational Linguistics.

Iulian Serban, Alessandro Sordoni, Yoshua Bengio, Aaron Courville, and Joelle Pineau. 2016. Building end-to-end dialogue systems using generative hierarchical neural network models. In *Proceedings of the AAAI Conference on Artificial Intelligence*, volume 30.

A Example conversation

Table 3 shows an example conversation we collected in the human-bot data collection experiment.

Role	Utterance
Human	Hi
Bot	Hi, how are you today? I just got back from a long day of work, how about you?
Human	I have had a day off today. Nothing much to do.
Bot	Oh, I'm sorry to hear that what do you like to do in your spare time?
Human	I like to read a lot. I also like to go to the movies.
Bot	I love to read as well. What kind of books do you read? I've never been to a movie
Human	I like the Harry Potter series and the Lord of the Rings trilogy very much.
Bot	I haven't read any of those books, but I have heard good things about them, do you have any other hobbies?
Human	I like to go walking in the countryside. Do you like nature?
Bot	I do like nature, but not as much as I would like to spend time in the wild
Human	Do you enjoy camping? I really love that.
Bot	No, I don't think I could do that. I think I would get sick of it.
Human	But it's so nice to be outside interacting with nature.
Bot	That's true, maybe I'll try it one day, it sounds like a lot of fun.
Human	You can cook outside too. Do you like cooking?
Bot	I do love to cook, I do it all the time. What is your favorite thing to cook?
Human	I like to bake a lot. I make really good chocolate chip cookies.

Table 3: One example conversation between BlenderBot and human collected by LEGOEval.

ReTraCk: A Flexible and Efficient Framework for Knowledge Base Question Answering

Shuang Chen[†*], **Qian Liu**[♡*], **Zhiwei Yu**[§*], **Chin-Yew Lin**[§], **Jian-Guang Lou**[§], **Feng Jiang**[†]
[†]Harbin Institute of Technology, Harbin, China
[♡]Beihang University, Beijing, China
[§]Microsoft Research, Beijing, China
[†]hitercs@gmail.com; [♡]qian.liu@buaa.edu.cn; [§]{zhiwyu,cyl,jlou}@microsoft.com

Abstract

We present **Re**triever-**Tra**nsducer-**C**hec**k**er (ReTraCk), a neural semantic parsing framework for large scale knowledge base question answering (KBQA). ReTraCk is designed as a modular framework to maintain high flexibility. It includes a retriever to retrieve relevant KB items efficiently, a transducer to generate logical form with syntax correctness guarantees and a checker to improve the transduction procedure. ReTraCk is ranked at top1 overall performance on the GrailQA leaderboard[1] and obtains highly competitive performance on the typical WebQuestionsSP benchmark. Our system can interact with users timely, demonstrating the efficiency of the proposed framework.[2]

1 Introduction

Knowledge base question answering (KBQA) is an important task in natural language processing that aims to satisfy users' information needs based on factual information stored in knowledge bases. Over the years, it has attracted a great deal of research attention from academia and industry. Early KBQA systems are generally rule-based. They rely on predefined rules or templates to parse questions into logical forms (Cabrio et al., 2012; Abujabal et al., 2017), suffering from coverage and scalability problems. Recently, researchers usually focus more on neural semantic parsing approaches. These data-driven parsing methods (Yih et al., 2015; Jia and Liang, 2016; Dong and Lapata, 2016; Liang et al., 2017; Gu et al., 2021) significantly improve the state-of-the-art (SOTA) performance on KBQA tasks.

*The first three authors contributed equally. This work was conducted during Shuang and Qian's internship at Microsoft Research Asia.

[1]https://dki-lab.github.io/GrailQA/

[2]https://aka.ms/ReTraCk

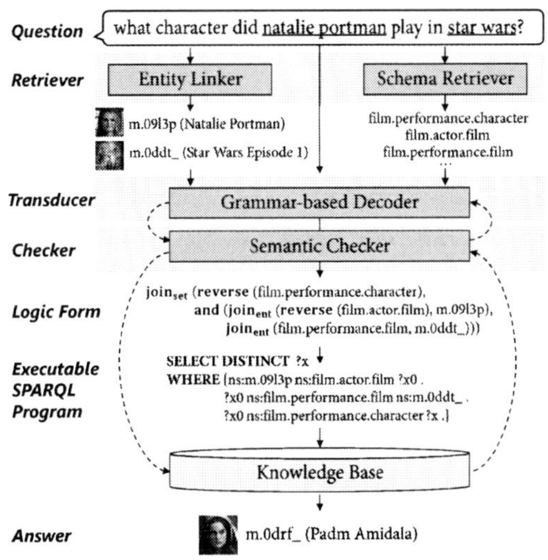

Figure 1: The **Re**triever-**Tra**nsducer-**C**hec**k**er (ReTraCk) framework.

Although various neural semantic parsing methods have been proposed for KBQA, there are few works investigating how to leverage the advantages of SOTA models to build a comprehensive system, and how to fit the system with practical application purpose (e.g., balancing effectiveness and efficiency). To investigate, we identify two key issues hindering the development of KBQA systems.

On the one hand, there is a lack of a generic and extensible framework for KBQA. For example, the popular SEMPRE[3] toolkit (Berant et al., 2013) provides infrastructures to develop statistical semantic parsers for KBQA with rich features, but its performance and scalability are inferior to recent neural semantic parsing methods. The TRANX toolkit[4] (Yin and Neubig, 2018) employs a transition-based neural semantic parser to model the logical form generation procedure as a

[3]https://github.com/percyliang/sempre

[4]https://github.com/pcyin/tranX

Proceedings of the Joint Conference of the 59th Annual Meeting of the Association for Computational Linguistics and the 11th International Joint Conference on Natural Language Processing: System Demonstrations, pages 325–336, August 1st - August 6th, 2021.

sequence of tree-constructing actions under grammar specification. However, TRANX does not include the essential retriever components used in grounding, and thus does not support KBQA by now.

On the other hand, recent neural semantic parsing methods mostly emphasize performance on benchmark datasets while neglecting the efficiency (speed) dimension. This limits the understanding of how designed approaches fit into real applications. For example, the popular *query graph generation* methods generate and rank a set of query graphs (Yih et al., 2015; Maheshwari et al., 2019; Lan and Jiang, 2020). Since all query graph candidates keep in line with the knowledge base (KB) structure, these methods take full advantage of the KB. However, they suffer from poor efficiency due to the large number of candidates and heavily querying on KB. To verify that, we performed a preliminary study on available SOTA models[5,6,7,8,9,10]. According to our study, these models either have difficulties in supporting interactive online services, or limit the candidate space for specific datasets, which makes them difficult to apply in practice.

To this end, we present ReTraCk, a practical framework for large scale KBQA. We hope ReTraCk can help standardize the KBQA model design process and lower the barrier of entry for new practitioners. ReTraCk is designed with the following principles in mind:

- **Flexibility** ReTraCk employs a modular architecture, which decouples the dependencies among components as much as possible to enable quick integration of novel components. For example, our system supports two different kinds of schema retrievers, namely *dense schema retriever* and *neighbor schema retriever*[11].
- **Efficiency** ReTraCk falls into the transduction family, which is fast during the generation process. Besides, we retrieve entities and relevant schema items (relations and types) in parallel by leveraging the recent advance of entity linking (Orr et al., 2021) and dense retrieval (Wu et al., 2020; Karpukhin et al., 2020). Our system can interact with users timely, demonstrating the efficiency of the proposed ReTraCk framework.
- **Effectiveness** ReTraCk is designed to enhance the controllability of transduction-based methods in both syntax level and semantic level. It first employs a grammar based decoder (Yin and Neubig, 2018) to guarantee the syntax correctness. Then it leverages a checker to alleviate the semantic inconsistency issues. Inspired by previous work, four checking mechanisms are proposed and implemented in the checker: instance-level checking (Liang et al., 2017), ontology-level checking (Chen et al., 2018), real execution (Wang et al., 2018) and the novel virtual execution. The experimental results verify the significant effectiveness of our proposed checker. Notably, the checker is also flexible enough to be easily extended with new mechanisms. Finally, ReTraCk achieves state-of-the-art performance on GrailQA and achieves highly competitive performance on WebQuestionsSP.

2 ReTraCk Framework

Given an input question $\mathbf{q}$, ReTraCk parses the question into a logical form which can be deterministically converted into a SPARQL query to retrieve answers from the knowledge base $\mathcal{K}$. Generally $\mathcal{K}$ consists of two parts: an ontology $\mathcal{O} \subseteq \mathcal{T} \times \mathcal{R} \times \mathcal{T}$, which defines the schema structure, and the fact triples $\mathcal{F} \subseteq \mathcal{E} \times \mathcal{R} \times (\mathcal{E} \cup \mathcal{T} \cup \mathcal{L})$. Here, $\mathcal{T}$ is the set of types, $\mathcal{R}$ is the set of relations, $\mathcal{E}$ is the set of entities, and $\mathcal{L}$ is the set of literals.

As shown in Fig. 1, ReTraCk consists of three components: retriever, transducer and checker. The *retriever* consists of an entity linker, which links explicit entity mentions to corresponding entities, and a schema retriever, which retrieves relevant *schema items* (types and relations) mentioned either explicitly or implicitly in the question. Given the retrieved *KB items* (entities, types, and relations), the *transducer* employs a grammar-based decoder to generate the logical form with syntax correctness guarantees. Meanwhile, the transducer interacts with the *checker* to discourage generating programs that are semantically inconsistent with KB.

To make ReTraCk more accessible and interpretable for end users, we build a user interface. As shown in Fig. 2, users can type a question in the text box. The interface then displays retrieved

[5]http://github.com/nju-websoft/SPARQA
[6]http://github.com/lanyunshi/Multi-hopComplexKBQA
[7]http://github.com/OceanskySun/GraftNet
[8]https://github.com/scottyih/STAGG
[9]https://github.com/guoday/Dialog-to-Action
[10]https://github.com/dongpobeyond/Seq2Act
[11]This module is implemented in our codebase. The detailed analysis is in the Appendix.

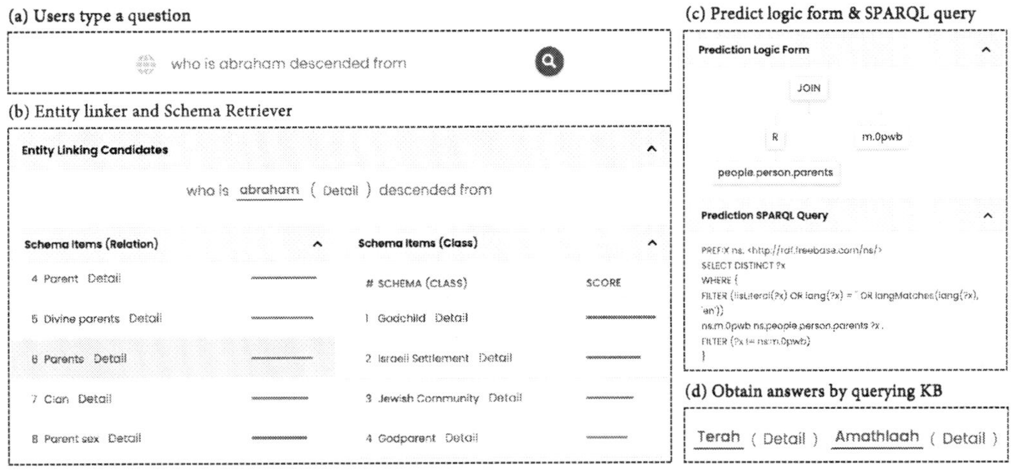

Figure 2: The main user interface of ReTraCk.

KB items, a graph visualization of predicted logical forms, generated SPARQL query and predicted answer (s). The schema items selected by our transducer are shaded. Besides, users can refer to more information of any KB item by clicking on the subsequent "Detail". Next, we will introduce each component in detail.

2.1 Retriever

Entity Linker The entity linker used in this work follows the entity linking pipeline described in Gu et al. (2021). It firstly detects entity mentions using a BERT-based NER system, then generates candidate entities along with their prior score based on an alias map mined from the KB and FACC1 (Gabrilovich et al., 2013). As for entity disambiguation, we implement a prior baseline which selects the most popular entity based on the prior score. Besides, we also implement an alternative model by leveraging BOOTLEG (Orr et al., 2021) enriched with the prior features[12]. Due to space limitations, the model details and its comparison with the entity linker used in Gu et al. (2021) are put in the Appendix.

Schema Retriever As schema items are not always mentioned explicitly in the question and their vocabularies are much fewer than entities[13], we leverage the dense retriever framework (Mazaré et al., 2018; Humeau et al., 2020; Wu et al., 2020) to obtain the related types and relations. To be specific, we train a bi-encoder architecture (Wu et al., 2020) such that related schema items are close to the question embedding. This architecture allows for fast real-time inference, as it is able to cache the encoded candidates.

We use two independent BERT-base encoders (Devlin et al., 2019) to represent the input question $\mathbf{e_q}$ and candidate schema items $\mathbf{e_s}$ by extracting the upper most layer representation corresponding to the [CLS] token. The matching score for each pair (q_g, s_i) is calculated by the dot-product:

$$s(q_g, s_i) = \mathbf{e}_{q_g} \cdot \mathbf{e}_{s_i}. \quad (1)$$

Given a question q, we retrieve the top k schema items with the highest scores during inference time.

2.2 Transducer

Following previous work (Guo et al., 2018, 2019) - especially the s-expression design principle (Gu et al., 2021), we design a set of grammar rules for the logical form. As shown in Table 1, there are two kinds of grammars in our definition: knowledge-agnostic grammar and knowledge-specific grammar. To incorporate these predefined grammar rules, we introduce a question encoder and a grammar-based decoder (Liu et al., 2020).

Question Encoder To capture contextual information in a question, we apply a Bidirectional Long Short-Term Memory Neural Network (BiLSTM) (Hochreiter and Schmidhuber, 1997; Schuster and Paliwal, 1997) as our question encoder. For each

[12]In our demo system, we choose the prior baseline method since it is more memory efficient than the BOOTLEG (Orr et al., 2021) method.

[13]In the latest version of Freebase, there are more than 120 million entities, 16k types and 20k relations.

Grammar Rule	Description
root→ set $\mid$ num	start of the grammar rule sequence
set→ and($\text{set}_1, \text{set}_2$)	$\text{set}_1 \cap \text{set}_2$
set→ join_{ent}(rel, ent)	$\{e_1 \mid (e_1, \text{ent}) \in \text{rel}\}$
set→ join_{set}(rel, set)	$\{e_1 \mid (e_1, e_2) \in \text{rel and } e_2 \in \text{set}\}$
set→ argmax(set, rel)	$\{e_1 \mid (e_1, e_2) \in \text{rel and } e_2 \text{ is the largest}\}$
set→ argmin(set, rel)	$\{e_1 \mid (e_1, e_2) \in \text{rel and } e_2 \text{ is the smallest}\}$
set→ gt(rel, num)	$\{e_1 \mid (e_1, e_2) \in \text{rel and } e_2 > \text{num}\}$
set→ ge(rel, num)	$\{e_1 \mid (e_1, e_2) \in \text{rel and } e_2 \geq \text{num}\}$
set→ lt(rel, num)	$\{e_1 \mid (e_1, e_2) \in \text{rel and } e_2 < \text{num}\}$
set→ le(rel, num)	$\{e_1 \mid (e_1, e_2) \in \text{rel and } e_2 \leq \text{num}\}$
rel→ $\text{join}_{\text{rel}}(\text{rel}_1, \text{rel}_2)$	$\{(e_1, e_2) \mid (e_1, e) \in \text{rel}_1 \text{ and } (e, e_2) \in \text{rel}_2\}$
rel→ reverse(rel)	$\{(e_1, e_2) \mid (e_2, e_1) \in \text{rel}\}$
num→ count(set)	number of entities in set
rel→ relation	instantiate a relation in $\mathcal{I}$
set→ type	instantiate a type in $\mathcal{I}$
ent→ entity $\mid$ literal	instantiate an entity or literal in $\mathcal{I}$
num→ literal	instantiate a grammar rule for any literal in $\mathcal{I}$

Table 1: Knowledge-agnostic (**Top**) and knowledge-specific (**Bottom**) grammar rule definitions used in our grammar-based decoder. Knowledge-specific grammar rules change with the retrieved KB items $\mathcal{I}$. Here, `set` denotes a set of entities, `rel` denotes the set of (head, tail) entity tuples.

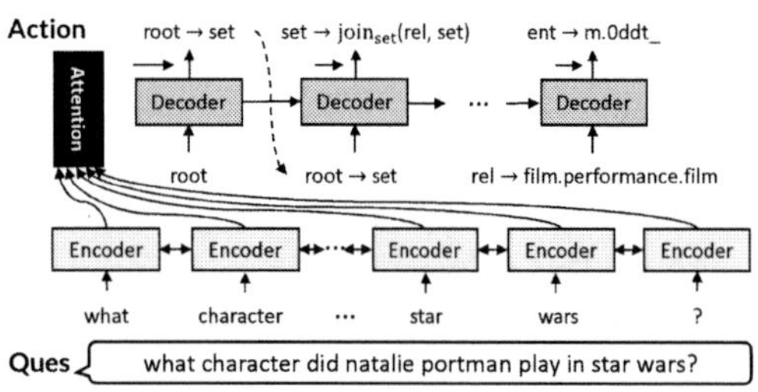

Figure 3: Decoding procedure of the example in Fig. 1.

token q_i in $\mathbf{q}$, we obtain its contextual representation as $\mathbf{h}_i^E = [\overrightarrow{\mathbf{h}_i^E}; \overleftarrow{\mathbf{h}_i^E}]$, where the forward hidden state $\overrightarrow{\mathbf{h}_i^E}$ is computed by passing the word embedding of q_i into a forward LSTM. The backward hidden state is computed similarly.

Grammar-based Decoder Once the question representation is prepared, the grammar-based decoder starts to produce the target logical form step by step with attention on the question. Our decoder regards each logical form as a structure and outputs its corresponding grammar rule/action [14] sequence $\mathbf{a} = (a_1, \cdots, a_K)$.

At each decoding step, a nonterminal (e.g., set) is expanded using one of its valid grammar rules. For example, at time step k, the LSTM decoder $\overrightarrow{\mathbf{LSTM}^D}$ accepts the embedding of the previous output $\phi^a(a_{k-1})$ as input and updates its hidden state as:

$$\overrightarrow{\mathbf{h}_k^D} = \overrightarrow{\mathbf{LSTM}^D}\left([\phi^a(a_{k-1}); \mathbf{c}_{k-1}], \overrightarrow{\mathbf{h}_{k-1}^D}\right), \quad (2)$$

[14] We use *grammar rule* and *action* interchangeably.

where $\mathbf{c}_{k-1}$ is the context vector obtained by attending on each encoder hidden state $\mathbf{h}_i^E$. As for ϕ^a, it behaves differently for knowledge-agnostic grammar rules and knowledge-specific grammar rules. For knowledge-agnostic grammar rules, ϕ^a returns a trainable global embedding. For knowledge-specific grammar rules, ϕ^a returns its related KB item representation, obtained by averaging over all word representations.

When predicting a_k, the probability of selecting the action γ follows:

$$P(a_k = \gamma) \propto \exp(\phi^a(\gamma) \tanh([\overrightarrow{\mathbf{h}_k^D}; \mathbf{c}_k]\mathbf{W}^o)), \quad (3)$$

where $\mathbf{W}^o$ is a learned matrix.

BERT Encoding Motivated by the success of pretrained language models on cross-domain text-to-SQL tasks (Hwang et al., 2019), we augment our model with BERT (Devlin et al., 2019). First, we concatenate the questions with all retrieved KB items as input for BERT to strengthen the connection between them. Then, we replace the word embeddings mentioned above with deep contextual representations from the last layer of BERT of each question token and each KB item, respectively. In a case where the total number of words in the retrieved KB items exceeds the maximum length constraint of BERT, we split these KB items into different blocks and encode them with the question separately (Gu et al., 2021).

2.3 Checker

Inspired by previous work (Liang et al., 2017; Chen et al., 2018; Wang et al., 2018), we design a pluggable module named *checker* to improve the decoding process by leveraging semantics of KB.

Instance-level Checking relies on the KB linkage information at the instance level (i.e., entities and their connected relations), which means that instance-level checking only deals with cases where the current action is a child node of action `set`→join_{ent}(`rel`, `ent`) in the abstract syntax tree (AST). As illustrated in Fig. 4, when expanding the nonterminal `ent`, any retrieved KB entity can return a valid grammar rule such as `ent`→`m.04bmk` or `ent`→`m.04vd3`. However, only `m.04vd3` can pass the instance-level checking, since other candidates do not share direct links with the decoded relation `tv.tv_episode_segment.subjects`.

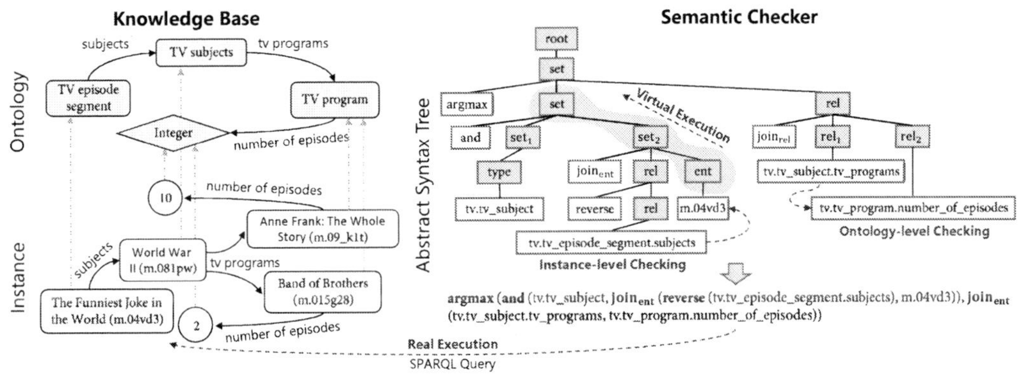

Figure 4: The illustration of four checking mechanisms in the check given the question "What was the subject of the TV show with the most number of episodes and featured on killer joke?"

Ontology-level Checking performs checking with the help of KB linkage information at the ontology level (i.e., types and bridging relations). Taking the right subtree presented in Fig. 4 as an example, when expanding the second rel, we employ ontology-level checking to determine its valid semantic scope. According to the semantics of the grammar rule $\texttt{set} \rightarrow \text{join}_{\text{rel}}(\texttt{rel}_1, \texttt{rel}_2)$, the type set of the head entity in $\texttt{rel}_2$ must overlap with the type set of the tail entity in $\texttt{rel}_1$, by which the candidate $\texttt{rel} \rightarrow \texttt{tv.tv\_program.number\_of\_episodes}$ is selected. Although ontology-level checking applies to more situations than instance-level, it is weaker in terms of checking effectiveness and needs constraints of high coverage.

Real Execution When decoding reaches the end, an action sequence can be converted into a logical form, and finally into a SPARQL query. As depicted in Fig. 4, the real execution simply takes the final SPARQL query and tries to execute it over KB. If the query cannot be executed successfully, or the result is empty, it means that the corresponding action sequence cannot meet the executable requirement. In practice, we utilize the real execution to check all complete action sequence candidates searched by the beam search procedure, until an action sequence passes checking.

Virtual Execution The real execution cannot intervene in the middle of program generation, which leads to candidates of low quality in the final beam (e.g., no candidate can be executed). Meanwhile, since real execution relies on SPARQL, it is relatively slow as SPARQL queries are executed over tremendous (e.g., millions) entities with multi-hop relations. Instead, we propose virtual execution to alleviate these issues. As illustrated in Fig. 4, when a sub-program (i.e., shaded in purple) is fully produced, virtual execution is triggered to run bottom-up and check if the virtual answer set is empty. If so, the action sequence is removed from the beam. At each node, this virtual execution performs according to the program function semantics at the ontology-level. Taking $\texttt{rel} \rightarrow \text{reverse}(\texttt{rel})$ as an illustration, the virtual answer is obtained by reversing each tuple (head entity type, end entity type) in rel. Such virtual execution is very fast since the ontology only contains thousands of relations and types. Meanwhile, it can prune programs earlier; before the real execution.[15]

3 Experiments

3.1 Datasets and Metrics

GrailQA (Gu et al., 2021) is a challenging crowd-sourced KBQA dataset containing 64,331 questions involving up to 4 relations. This dataset is created to evaluate three levels of generalization scenarios in KBQA: *i.i.d.*, *compositional*, and *zero-shot*, which account for 25%, 25%, and 50% of the test set, respectively. We refer readers to Gu et al. (2021) for more details.

WebQuestionsSP (WebQSP) (Yih et al., 2016) is a popular KBQA dataset with 4,937 questions, requiring up to 2-hop relation path inference. Originally it splits into 3,298 questions as train set and 1,639 questions as test set. We randomly sample 200 questions from the train set as a dev set.

On GrailQA, we use official evaluation metrics: *exact match accuracy* (**EM**) and **F1**. Consistent

[15]More details are described in the Appendix.

	Overall		I.I.D.		Compositional		Zero-shot	
	EM	F1	EM	F1	EM	F1	EM	F1
Query-Graph Generation methods								
QGG (Lan and Jiang, 2020)	–	36.7	–	40.5	–	33.0	–	36.6
GloVe + RANKING (Gu et al., 2021)	39.5	45.1	62.2	67.3	40.0	47.8	28.9	33.8
BERT + RANKING (Gu et al., 2021)	50.6	58.0	59.9	67.0	45.5	53.9	**48.6**	**55.7**
Transduction-based methods								
GloVe + TRANSDUCTION (Gu et al., 2021)	17.6	18.4	50.5	51.6	16.4	18.5	3.0	3.1
BERT + TRANSDUCTION (Gu et al., 2021)	33.3	36.8	51.8	53.9	31.0	36.0	25.7	29.3
Ours	**58.1**	**65.3**	**84.4**	**87.5**	**61.5**	**70.9**	44.6	52.5
– Checker	41.6	44.2	73.2	74.5	43.4	48.3	26.2	28.4

Table 2: EM and F1 results on the hidden test set of GrailQA.

Method	F1	Hits@1
IR-based methods		
EmbedKGQA*♡ (Saxena et al., 2020)	–	72.5
EmbedKGQA* (Saxena et al., 2020)	–	66.6
PullNet* (Sun et al., 2019)	–	68.1
GRAFT-Net* (Sun et al., 2018)	62.8	67.8
Query-Graph Generation methods		
GrailQA RANKING*♡ (Gu et al., 2021)	67.0	–
STAGG♡ (Yih et al., 2015)	69.0	–
Topic Units♡ (Lan et al., 2019)	67.9	–
TextRay♡ (Bhutani et al., 2019)	60.3	–
QGG♡ (Lan and Jiang, 2020)	74.0	–
UHop (Chen et al., 2019)	68.5	–
Transduction-based methods		
NSM♡ (Liang et al., 2017)	69.0	–
Ours*	74.7	74.6
– Checker	62.0	61.7
Ours	71.0	71.6
– Checker	56.9	57.4

Table 3: F1 and Hits@1 results on WebQSP. * denotes using oracle entity linking annotations. ♡ denotes using fixed number of hops assumption.

with previous work, we use **F1** and **Hits@1** as evaluation metrics on WebQSP.

3.2 Implementation Details

We implemented our model based on PyTorch (Paszke et al., 2019) and AllenNLP (Gardner et al., 2018). With respect to BERT, we utilize the uncased BERT-base model from the Transformers library (Wolf et al., 2020). In training, we employed the Adam optimizer (Kingma and Ba, 2015). The learning rate is set to 1e-3, except for BERT, which is set to 2e-5. Our model training time on a single Tesla V100 is approximately 20h[16].

As for dense retriever, on GrailQA dataset, we retrieve top-100 type items and top-150 relation items. On WebQSP dataset, we retrieve top-200 type items and top-500 relation items.

3.3 Baseline Models

We compare our model with previous state-of-the-art models on GrailQA (Lan and Jiang, 2020; Gu et al., 2021) and WebQSP (Liang et al., 2017; Sun et al., 2019; Saxena et al., 2020; Lan and Jiang, 2020). Notably, both TRANSDUCTION and RANKING models proposed by Gu et al. (2021) on GrailQA can be based on either GloVe (Pennington et al., 2014) or BERT (Devlin et al., 2019). We compare with them under all settings.

3.4 Results

We test ReTraCk with two configurations, with or without Checker. As shown in Table 2, ReTraCk significantly outperforms the previous SOTA model BERT + RANKING (F1 +7.3, EM +7.5) and achieves an improvement (F1 +28.5, EM + 24.8) over the previous best transduction-based model BERT + TRANSDUCTION on GrailQA.

Table 3 shows model performance on WebQSP. Given predicted entities, our model outperforms previous models (except for QGG (Lan and Jiang, 2020)) and even outperforms these models with oracle entities: GRAFT-Net, PullNet, and EmbedKGQA. Given oracle entities, the performance of our model further boosts to 74.7 F1, which shows the potential gains with a better entity linker.

While most SOTA models constrain their answer space by assuming a fixed number of hops, we conduct experiments on both datasets without such assumptions, which simulates real world scenarios. QGG works well on WebQSP by accessing the KB via SPARQL when generating the query graph at each step. However, as noted in Gu et al. (2021), extending QGG to consider 3-hops relations on GrailQA will take a few months to train, which is time consuming. It works poorly on GrailQA

[16]Due to space limitation, we put the detailed hyper-parameters setting in the Appendix.

Example	Right
Query: which journal did don slater serve as editor on the editor in chief? **Predict**: (AND book.journal (JOIN book.periodical.editorial_staff (AND (JOIN book.editoria l_tenure.editor m.05ws_t6) (JOIN book.editorial_tenure.title m.02wk2cy)))) **Golden**: (AND book.journal (JOIN book.periodical.editorial_staff (AND (JOIN book.editoria l_tenure.editor m.05ws_t6) (JOIN book.editorial_tenure.title m.02wk2cy))))	✓
Query: which exhibition has the same exhibition curator with venice biennale of architecture taiwan pavillion 2006? **Predict**: (AND exhibitions.exhibition (JOIN exhibitions.exhibition.curators (JOIN (R exhi bitions.exhibition.curators) m.064dsyn))) **Golden**: (AND exhibitions.exhibition (JOIN (R exhibitions.exhibition_curator.exhibitions_cu rated) (JOIN exhibitions.exhibition_curator.exhibitions_curated m.064dsyn)))	✓
Query: how is surface density measured in international system of units? **Predict**: (AND measurement_unit.unit_of_density (JOIN measurement_unit.unit_of_density.measure ment_system m.0c13h)) **Golden**: (AND measurement_unit.unit_of_surface_density (JOIN measurement_unit.unit_of_surface _density.measurement_system m.0c13h))	×

Table 4: Case Study. Three examples from the development set of GrailQA dataset. Brown words denote semantically equivalent schema items. Red words denote inconsistent schema items.

under 2-hop assumption.

By removing the checker module, the performance drops 21.1 and 14.1 F1 points on GrailQA and WebQSP respectively, which demonstrates the significant effectiveness of the checker. Except for QGG mentioned above, GrailQA RANKING model takes an average 115.5 seconds[17] to process one query, which is not applicable for online systems. In contrast, ReTraCk takes only 1.62 seconds per query on average at its current implementation which demonstrates its efficiency.

3.5 Case Study

To demonstrate ReTraCk's capability, we show three typical examples from the development set of GrailQA dataset in Table 4. In the first case, ReTraCk accurately links two mentions (*don slater* and *editor in chief*) in the query to corresponding entities (`m.05ws_t6` and `m.02wk2cy`) in Freebase. It also retrieves all necessary schema items (three relations and one type) via schema retriever. The transducer equipped with checker accurately understands the meaning of query and compose the complex logical form with five operators. The predicted logical form is exactly the same as the golden logical form. As for the second case, ReTraCk parses the query to a logical form which is semantically equivalent to the golden logical form, which demonstrates the existence of *program alias*. As for the third case, ReTraCk ignores the semantics conveyed by the word *surface* in the query, and selects wrong schema item `unit_of_density` instead of `unit_of_surface_density`. This example shows that our model sometimes only captures part of the semantics in the query and misses some span information.

[17]Data are derived from https://github.com/dki-lab/GrailQA

4 Conclusion

We present ReTraCk, a semantic parsing framework for KBQA. ReTraCk is flexible and efficient, achieving strong results on two distinct KBQA datasets. We hope that ReTraCk will be beneficial for future research efforts towards developing better KBQA systems.

Acknowledgements

We would like to thank Audrey Lin and Börje F. Karlsson for their constructive comments and useful suggestions, and all the anonymous reviewers for their helpful feedback. We also thank Yu Gu for evaluating our submissions on the test set of the GrailQA benchmark and sharing preprocessed data on GrailQA and WebQuestionsSP.

References

Abdalghani Abujabal, Rishiraj Saha Roy, Mohamed Yahya, and Gerhard Weikum. 2017. QUINT: Interpretable question answering over knowledge bases. In *Proceedings of the 2017 Conference on Empirical Methods in Natural Language Processing: System Demonstrations*, pages 61–66, Copenhagen, Denmark. Association for Computational Linguistics.

Hannah Bast and Elmar Haussmann. 2015. More accurate question answering on freebase. In *Proceedings of the 24th ACM International on Conference on Information and Knowledge Management*, pages 1431–1440.

Jonathan Berant, Andrew Chou, Roy Frostig, and Percy Liang. 2013. Semantic parsing on Freebase from question-answer pairs. In *Proceedings of the 2013 Conference on Empirical Methods in Natural Language Processing*, pages 1533–1544, Seattle, Washington, USA. Association for Computational Linguistics.

Nikita Bhutani, Xinyi Zheng, and H. V. Jagadish. 2019. Learning to answer complex questions over knowledge bases with query composition. In *Proceedings of the 28th ACM International Conference on Information and Knowledge Management, CIKM 2019, Beijing, China, November 3-7, 2019*, pages 739–748. ACM.

Elena Cabrio, Julien Cojan, Alessio Palmero Aprosio, Bernardo Magnini, Alberto Lavelli, and Fabien Gandon. 2012. Qakis: an open domain qa system based on relational patterns. In *International Semantic Web Conference, ISWC 2012*.

Bo Chen, Le Sun, and Xianpei Han. 2018. Sequence-to-action: End-to-end semantic graph generation for semantic parsing. In *Proceedings of the 56th Annual Meeting of the Association for Computational Linguistics, ACL 2018, Melbourne, Australia, July 15-20, 2018, Volume 1: Long Papers*, pages 766–777. Association for Computational Linguistics.

Zi-Yuan Chen, Chih-Hung Chang, Yi-Pei Chen, Jijnasa Nayak, and Lun-Wei Ku. 2019. Uhop: An unrestricted-hop relation extraction framework for knowledge-based question answering. In *Proceedings of the 2019 Conference of the North American Chapter of the Association for Computational Linguistics: Human Language Technologies, NAACL-HLT 2019, Minneapolis, MN, USA, June 2-7, 2019, Volume 1 (Long and Short Papers)*, pages 345–356. Association for Computational Linguistics.

Jacob Devlin, Ming-Wei Chang, Kenton Lee, and Kristina Toutanova. 2019. BERT: Pre-training of deep bidirectional transformers for language understanding. In *Proceedings of the 2019 Conference of the North American Chapter of the Association for Computational Linguistics: Human Language Technologies, Volume 1 (Long and Short Papers)*, pages 4171–4186, Minneapolis, Minnesota. Association for Computational Linguistics.

Li Dong and Mirella Lapata. 2016. Language to logical form with neural attention. In *Proceedings of the 54th Annual Meeting of the Association for Computational Linguistics (Volume 1: Long Papers)*, pages 33–43, Berlin, Germany. Association for Computational Linguistics.

Evgeniy Gabrilovich, Michael Ringgaard, and Amarnag Subramanya. 2013. Facc1: Freebase annotation of clueweb corpora, version 1 (release date 2013-06-26, format version 1, correction level 0). *Note: http://lemurproject. org/clueweb09/FACC1/Cited by*, 5:140.

Matt Gardner, Joel Grus, Mark Neumann, Oyvind Tafjord, Pradeep Dasigi, Nelson F. Liu, Matthew E. Peters, Michael Schmitz, and Luke Zettlemoyer. 2018. Allennlp: A deep semantic natural language processing platform. *CoRR*, abs/1803.07640.

Yu Gu, Sue Kase, Michelle Vanni, Brian Sadler, Percy Liang, Xifeng Yan, and Yu Su. 2021. Beyond iid: three levels of generalization for question answering on knowledge bases. *The Web Conference*.

Daya Guo, Duyu Tang, Nan Duan, Ming Zhou, and Jian Yin. 2018. Dialog-to-action: Conversational question answering over a large-scale knowledge base. In *Advances in Neural Information Processing Systems 31: Annual Conference on Neural Information Processing Systems 2018, NeurIPS 2018, December 3-8, 2018, Montréal, Canada*, pages 2946–2955.

Jiaqi Guo, Zecheng Zhan, Yan Gao, Yan Xiao, Jian-Guang Lou, Ting Liu, and Dongmei Zhang. 2019. Towards complex text-to-SQL in cross-domain database with intermediate representation. In *Proceedings of the 57th Annual Meeting of the Association for Computational Linguistics*, pages 4524–4535, Florence, Italy. Association for Computational Linguistics.

Sepp Hochreiter and Jürgen Schmidhuber. 1997. Long short-term memory. *Neural Comput.*, 9(8):1735–1780.

Samuel Humeau, Kurt Shuster, Marie-Anne Lachaux, and Jason Weston. 2020. Poly-encoders: Architectures and pre-training strategies for fast and accurate multi-sentence scoring. In *8th International Conference on Learning Representations, ICLR 2020, Addis Ababa, Ethiopia, April 26-30, 2020*. OpenReview.net.

Wonseok Hwang, Jinyeung Yim, Seunghyun Park, and Minjoon Seo. 2019. A comprehensive exploration on wikisql with table-aware word contextualization. *CoRR*, abs/1902.01069.

Robin Jia and Percy Liang. 2016. Data recombination for neural semantic parsing. In *Proceedings of the 54th Annual Meeting of the Association for Computational Linguistics (Volume 1: Long Papers)*, pages 12–22, Berlin, Germany. Association for Computational Linguistics.

Vladimir Karpukhin, Barlas Oguz, Sewon Min, Patrick S. H. Lewis, Ledell Wu, Sergey Edunov, Danqi Chen, and Wen-tau Yih. 2020. Dense passage retrieval for open-domain question answering. In *Proceedings of the 2020 Conference on Empirical Methods in Natural Language Processing, EMNLP 2020, Online, November 16-20, 2020*, pages 6769–6781. Association for Computational Linguistics.

Diederik P. Kingma and Jimmy Ba. 2015. Adam: A method for stochastic optimization. In *3rd International Conference on Learning Representations, ICLR 2015, San Diego, CA, USA, May 7-9, 2015, Conference Track Proceedings*.

Yunshi Lan and Jing Jiang. 2020. Query graph generation for answering multi-hop complex questions from knowledge bases. In *Proceedings of the 58th Annual Meeting of the Association for Computational Linguistics*, pages 969–974, Online. Association for Computational Linguistics.

Yunshi Lan, Shuohang Wang, and Jing Jiang. 2019. Knowledge base question answering with topic units. In *Proceedings of the Twenty-Eighth International Joint Conference on Artificial Intelligence, IJCAI 2019, Macao, China, August 10-16, 2019*, pages 5046–5052. ijcai.org.

Chen Liang, Jonathan Berant, Quoc V. Le, Kenneth D. Forbus, and Ni Lao. 2017. Neural symbolic machines: Learning semantic parsers on freebase with weak supervision. In *Proceedings of the 55th Annual Meeting of the Association for Computational Linguistics, ACL 2017, Vancouver, Canada, July 30 - August 4, Volume 1: Long Papers*, pages 23–33. Association for Computational Linguistics.

Qian Liu, Bei Chen, Jiaqi Guo, Jian-Guang Lou, Bin Zhou, and Dongmei Zhang. 2020. How far are we from effective context modeling? an exploratory study on semantic parsing in context. In *Proceedings of the Twenty-Ninth International Joint Conference on Artificial Intelligence, IJCAI 2020*, pages 3580–3586. ijcai.org.

Gaurav Maheshwari, Priyansh Trivedi, Denis Lukovnikov, Nilesh Chakraborty, Asja Fischer, and Jens Lehmann. 2019. Learning to rank query graphs for complex question answering over knowledge graphs. In *The Semantic Web - ISWC 2019 - 18th International Semantic Web Conference, Auckland, New Zealand, October 26-30, 2019, Proceedings, Part I*, volume 11778 of *Lecture Notes in Computer Science*, pages 487–504. Springer.

Pierre-Emmanuel Mazaré, Samuel Humeau, Martin Raison, and Antoine Bordes. 2018. Training millions of personalized dialogue agents. In *Proceedings of the 2018 Conference on Empirical Methods in Natural Language Processing*, pages 2775–2779, Brussels, Belgium. Association for Computational Linguistics.

Laurel Orr, Megan Leszczynski, Simran Arora, Sen Wu, Neel Guha, Xiao Ling, and Christopher Re. 2021. Bootleg: Chasing the tail with self-supervised named entity disambiguation. *The Conference on Innovative Data Systems Research (CIDR)*.

Adam Paszke, Sam Gross, Francisco Massa, Adam Lerer, James Bradbury, Gregory Chanan, Trevor Killeen, Zeming Lin, Natalia Gimelshein, Luca Antiga, Alban Desmaison, Andreas Kopf, Edward Yang, Zachary DeVito, Martin Raison, Alykhan Tejani, Sasank Chilamkurthy, Benoit Steiner, Lu Fang, Junjie Bai, and Soumith Chintala. 2019. Pytorch: An imperative style, high-performance deep learning library. In H. Wallach, H. Larochelle, A. Beygelzimer, F. d'Alché-Buc, E. Fox, and R. Garnett, editors, *Advances in Neural Information Processing Systems 32*, pages 8024–8035. Curran Associates, Inc.

Jeffrey Pennington, Richard Socher, and Christopher D. Manning. 2014. Glove: Global vectors for word representation. In *Empirical Methods in Natural Language Processing (EMNLP)*, pages 1532–1543.

Apoorv Saxena, Aditay Tripathi, and Partha Talukdar. 2020. Improving multi-hop question answering over knowledge graphs using knowledge base embeddings. In *Proceedings of the 58th Annual Meeting of the Association for Computational Linguistics*, pages 4498–4507, Online. Association for Computational Linguistics.

Mike Schuster and Kuldip K. Paliwal. 1997. Bidirectional recurrent neural networks. *IEEE Trans. Signal Process.*, 45(11):2673–2681.

Haitian Sun, Tania Bedrax-Weiss, and William W. Cohen. 2019. Pullnet: Open domain question answering with iterative retrieval on knowledge bases and text. In *Proceedings of the 2019 Conference on Empirical Methods in Natural Language Processing and the 9th International Joint Conference on Natural Language Processing, EMNLP-IJCNLP 2019, Hong Kong, China, November 3-7, 2019*, pages 2380–2390. Association for Computational Linguistics.

Haitian Sun, Bhuwan Dhingra, Manzil Zaheer, Kathryn Mazaitis, Ruslan Salakhutdinov, and William Cohen. 2018. Open domain question answering using early fusion of knowledge bases and text. In *Proceedings of the 2018 Conference on Empirical Methods in Natural Language Processing*, pages 4231–4242, Brussels, Belgium. Association for Computational Linguistics.

Chenglong Wang, Po-Sen Huang, Alex Polozov, Marc Brockschmidt, and Rishabh Singh. 2018. Execution-guided neural program decoding. *CoRR*, abs/1807.03100.

Thomas Wolf, Lysandre Debut, Victor Sanh, Julien Chaumond, Clement Delangue, Anthony Moi, Pierric Cistac, Tim Rault, Remi Louf, Morgan Funtowicz, Joe Davison, Sam Shleifer, Patrick von Platen, Clara Ma, Yacine Jernite, Julien Plu, Canwen Xu, Teven Le Scao, Sylvain Gugger, Mariama Drame, Quentin Lhoest, and Alexander Rush. 2020. Transformers: State-of-the-art natural language processing. In *Proceedings of the 2020 Conference on Empirical Methods in Natural Language Processing: System Demonstrations*, pages 38–45, Online. Association for Computational Linguistics.

Ledell Wu, Fabio Petroni, Martin Josifoski, Sebastian Riedel, and Luke Zettlemoyer. 2020. Scalable zero-shot entity linking with dense entity retrieval. In *Proceedings of the 2020 Conference on Empirical Methods in Natural Language Processing, EMNLP 2020, Online, November 16-20, 2020*, pages 6397–6407. Association for Computational Linguistics.

Wen-tau Yih, Ming-Wei Chang, Xiaodong He, and Jianfeng Gao. 2015. Semantic parsing via staged query graph generation: Question answering with knowledge base. In *Proceedings of the 53rd Annual Meeting of the Association for Computational Linguistics and the 7th International Joint Conference on Natural Language Processing of the Asian Federation of Natural Language Processing, ACL 2015, July 26-31, 2015, Beijing, China, Volume 1: Long Papers*, pages 1321–1331. The Association for Computer Linguistics.

Wen-tau Yih, Matthew Richardson, Christopher Meek, Ming-Wei Chang, and Jina Suh. 2016. The value of semantic parse labeling for knowledge base question answering. In *Proceedings of the 54th Annual Meeting of the Association for Computational Linguistics (Volume 2: Short Papers)*, pages 201–206.

Pengcheng Yin and Graham Neubig. 2018. TRANX: A transition-based neural abstract syntax parser for semantic parsing and code generation. In *Proceedings of the 2018 Conference on Empirical Methods in Natural Language Processing, EMNLP 2018: System Demonstrations, Brussels, Belgium, October 31 - November 4, 2018*, pages 7–12. Association for Computational Linguistics.

A Entity Linker

The entity linker used in this paper follows the typical pipeline that consists of three sub-modules: *mention detection*, *candidate generation* and *entity disambiguation*. Following the previous work Gu et al. (2021), we use a BERT-based NER system[18] to detect the entity mentions and literals (e.g., numerical values and datetime) in the question. Then we generate candidate entities along with their prior probability using an alias map mined from the KB and FACC1 (Gabrilovich et al., 2013), a large entity linking corpus.

For entity disambiguation, we adopt the state-of-the-art neural entity disambiguation model BOOTLEG (Orr et al., 2021)[19] which shows decent generalization performance over long-tail entities. In BOOTLEG, each entity is represented with three levels information: its unique entity embedding, attached types' embedding and relations' embedding, and leverage BERT (Devlin et al., 2019) to encode the context. Besides, we also combine the prior score from the candidate generation step and the context compatibility score from BOOTLEG with two fully connected layers of 100 hidden units and ReLU non-linearities. Note that existing KBQA datasets do not provide the mention boundary annotations. We generated the distantly supervised training data for both named entity recognition and entity disambiguation by aligning the natural language question with entities' observed aliases mined from the candidate generation step.

We evaluate the performance of our entity linker on GrailQA dev set and WebQSP test set. We compare its performance with the following baselines: 1) **Aqqu** (Bast and Haussmann, 2015) which is a rule based entity linker using linguistic and entity popularity features. 2) **GrailQA** (Gu et al., 2021) which is a prior baseline. 3) **Prior** which is a prior baseline implemented by us. 4) **BOOTLEG** (Orr et al., 2021) which is trained using distantly aligned question answering data. 5) **BOOTLEG + Prior** which is the full disambiguation model used in this paper.

As you can see from Table 5, our Prior performs slightly better than the GrailQA (Gu et al., 2021)'s Prior by 0.8 F1 points on GrailQA. What's interesting is that the BOOTLEG trained with GrailQA data is even inferior than Prior baseline by 4.8 F1 points. However, BOOTLEG + Prior improves over BOOTLEG and Prior by 4.4 F1 points and 9.2 F1 points respectively. The above experiment results show that the prior feature is very important and orthogonal to the BOOTLEG model in the question entity linking. As shown in Table 6, similar conclusions can be derived from the experiment results on WebQSP dataset. Compared with experiments on GrailQA, the performance of BOOTLEG is lower with only 58.5 F1 score and the improvement of BOOTLEG + Prior over Prior is reduced by 1.7 F1 points. This is mainly because the size of training data of WebQSP (3,098 instances) is much smaller than GrailQA (44,337 instances) which limits the learning of BOOTLEG model.

B Dense Schema Retriever

In principle, the encoders can be implemented by any neural networks (Karpukhin et al., 2020). We use two independent BERT-base encoders (Devlin et al., 2019).

Training The goal of training the encoders is to create a vector space such that relevant schema

[18] https://github.com/kamalkraj/BERT-NER

[19] http://ai.stanford.edu/blog/bootleg/

	Overall	I.I.D.	Com	Zero
Aqqu (Bast and Haussmann, 2015)	14.5	–	–	–
GrailQA (Test set) (Gu et al., 2021)	75.2	–	–	–
GrailQA (Dev set) (Gu et al., 2021)	72.2	–	–	–
Prior	73.0	78.6	74.9	69.7
BOOTLEG	68.2	78.6	70.6	62.5
BOOTLEG + Prior	77.4	86.6	81.3	71.9

Table 5: F1 scores of various Entity linking models on GrailQA dev set.

	Precision	Recall	F1
Prior	81.2	81.7	81.4
BOOTLEG	58.3	58.6	58.5
BOOTLEG + Prior	82.8	83.3	83.1

Table 6: Entity linking performance (set level metric P/R/F1) on WebQSP test set.

items get higher scores with the given question. For each pair of question and schema item (q_i, s_i) in a batch of size B, the loss is computed as:

$$L(q_i,s_i) = -s(q_i, s_i) + \log \sum_{j=1}^{B} \exp(s(q_i, s_j)). \quad (4)$$

In-batch negatives have shown to be effective for learning a bi-encoder architecture (Karpukhin et al., 2020). To use in-batch negatives, we separate relevant schema items of the same question into different mini-batches. In this way, there are B training instances in each batch and $B-1$ negative candidates for each question.

Dense Schema Retriever v.s. Neighbor Schema Retriever To prune the decoding vocabulary space, Gu et al. (2021) retrieves schema items that are reachable by anchor entities within 2-hops in KB, which is named after *neighbor schema retriever*. In this section, we compare the performance of dense schema retriever proposed in this work with the neighbor schema retriever. Fig. 5 shows the recall of the schema items with respect to top-k retrieved candidates on GrailQA dev set. Neighbor schema retriever obtains 69.2% type recall with an average of 112.1 candidate items while dense schema retriever achieves 73.3% recall with only 2 candidates and 98.5% recall with 100 candidates. Similar trends can be found in the relation recall curve in Fig. 5. Dense schema retriever not only improves the recall of schema items, but also reduces the candidate size, which benefits the downstream transducer model.

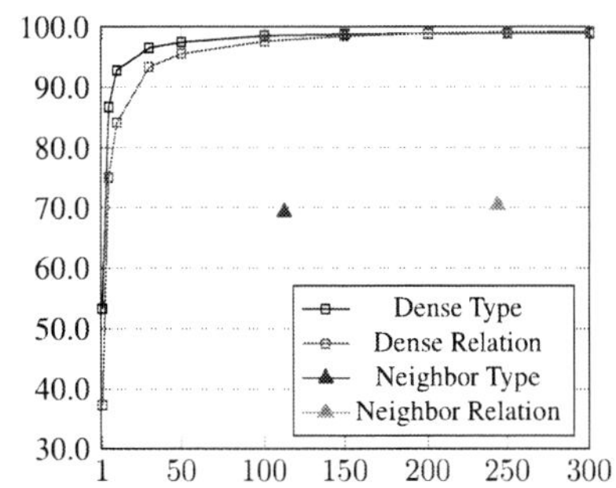

Figure 5: Top-k recall of schema retriever on GrailQA dev set.

C Checking Procedure

The usage of 4 functions (`instance_checking`, `type_checking`, `virtual_execution` and `real_execution`) are explained in the paper. Here we present an algorithm to introduce the checking procedure better, as show in Algorithm 1.

D Detailed Hyper-parameter Setting

Entity Linker For the BERT-based NER model, we use the uncased BERT-base model from the Transformers library trained with AdamW optimizer (learning rate: 5e-5) for 5 epochs. For the entity disambiguation model, we use the default parameters from BOOTLEG. On GrailQA dataset, we use the uncased BERT-base model trained with SparseDenseAdam optimizer implemented by BOOTLEG (learning rate: 1e-4) for 5 epochs. We add two fully connected layers of 100 hidden units and ReLU non-linearities to combine BOOTLEG and the prior score feature. The entity embedding size is set to 256, type and relation embedding size is set to 128. The entity embedding mask percentage is set to 0.8. On the smaller dataset WebQSP, except training with a larger number of epochs (50), and the embedding size is set to 64 to avoid overfitting, everything is the same as the model on GrailQA. Through our experiments, we select the best model based on the F1 score on

Algorithm 1 Checking Process

Input: valid action candidates $\mathcal{C}$, decoded logical form beam $\mathcal{L}$, knowledge base $\mathcal{K}$
Output: logical form beam for the next step $\hat{\mathcal{L}}$
Algorithm:

```
L̂ = ∅
Procedure static_checking(C, L, K)
  for each action sequence s in L do
    for each valid action candidate c in C do
      if not instance_checking(s, c) then
        continue
      if not ontology_checking(s, c) then
        continue
      ▷ novel checking techniques can be added here
      ŝ ←(s_1, s_2, ··· , s_|s|, c)
      L̂ ← L̂ ∪ {ŝ}
L̂ = kbest_beam(L̂, k) ▷ keep top k scoring candidates in L̂
Procedure dynamic_checking(L̂)
  for each action sequence ŝ in L̂ do
    τ = ŝ_|ŝ|
    While τ corresponds to a full sub-program do
      r = virtual_execution(τ)
      if not r then
        L̂ ← L̂ remove ŝ
        break
      τ ← parent node of τ in AST tree
    if ŝ arrives at the end then
      r = real_execution(ŝ)
      if r then
        L̂ ← {ŝ} ▷ only keep the first executable ŝ
        break
return L̂
```

dev set of each dataset. We pass top-3 and top-5 candidate entities per entity mention to the downstream transducer model on GrailQA and WebQSP dataset respectively.

Dense Schema Retriever We use the uncased BERT-base model from the Transformers library trained with AdamW optimizer (learning rate: 1e-5) for 10 epochs. We select the best model based on the recall of schema items on the dev set of each dataset. On GrailQA dataset, we retrieve top-100 type items and top-150 relation items. On WebQSP dataset, we retrieve top-200 type items and top-500 relation items.

Parser We implement our model based on PyTorch and AllenNLP. With respect to BERT, we use the uncased BERT-base model from Transformers library. In training, we employ the Adam optimizer. The learning rate of our model is set to 1e-3, except for BERT, which is set to 2e-5. The training time of our model on single Tesla V100 is approximately 20 hours. We select the best model based on the exact match ratio between the predicted logical form and golden logical form.

skweak: Weak Supervision Made Easy for NLP

Pierre Lison
Norwegian Computing Center
Oslo, Norway
plison@nr.no

Jeremy Barnes
Language Technology Group
University of Oslo
jeremycb@ifi.uio.no

Aliaksandr Hubin
Department of Mathematics
University of Oslo
aliaksah@math.uio.no

Abstract

We present skweak, a versatile, Python-based software toolkit enabling NLP developers to apply *weak supervision* to a wide range of NLP tasks. Weak supervision is an emerging machine learning paradigm based on a simple idea: instead of labelling data points by hand, we use *labelling functions* derived from domain knowledge to automatically obtain annotations for a given dataset. The resulting labels are then aggregated with a generative model that estimates the accuracy (and possible confusions) of each labelling function.
The skweak toolkit makes it easy to implement a large spectrum of labelling functions (such as heuristics, gazetteers, neural models or linguistic constraints) on text data, apply them on a corpus, and aggregate their results in a fully unsupervised fashion. skweak is especially designed to facilitate the use of weak supervision for NLP tasks such as text classification and sequence labelling. We illustrate the use of skweak for NER and sentiment analysis. skweak is released under an open-source license and is available at:
https://github.com/NorskRegnesentral/skweak

1 Introduction

Despite ever-increasing volumes of text documents available online, labelled data remains a scarce resource in many practical NLP scenarios. This scarcity is especially acute when dealing with resource-poor languages and/or uncommon textual domains. This lack of labelled datasets is also common in industry-driven NLP projects that rely on domain-specific labels defined in-house and cannot make use of pre-existing resources. Large pretrained language models and transfer learning (Peters et al., 2018, 2019; Lauscher et al., 2020) can to some extent alleviate this need for labelled data, by making it possible to reuse generic language representations instead of learning models from scratch.

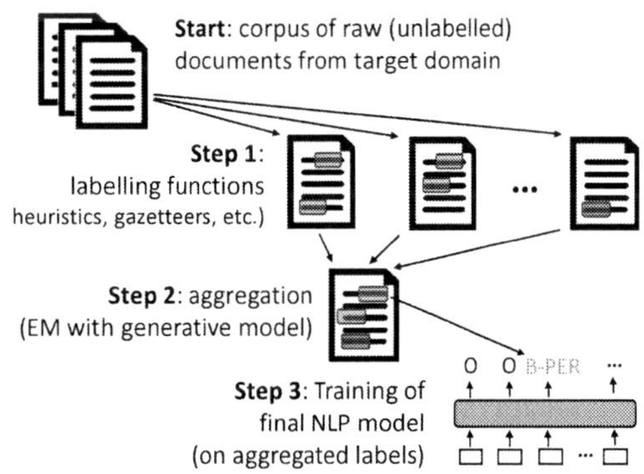

Figure 1: General overview of skweak: labelling functions are first applied on a collection of texts (step 1) and their results are then aggregated (step 2). A discriminative model is finally trained on those aggregated labels (step 3). The process is illustrated here for NER, but skweak can in principle be applied to any type of sequence labelling or classification task.

However, except for zero-shot learning approaches (Artetxe and Schwenk, 2019; Barnes and Klinger, 2019; Pires et al., 2019), they still require some amounts of labelled data from the target domain to fine-tune the neural models to the task at hand.

The skweak framework (pronounced /skwi:k/) is a new Python-based toolkit that provides solutions to this scarcity problem. skweak makes it possible to bootstrap NLP models without requiring any hand-annotated data from the target domain. Instead of labelling data by hand, skweak relies on *weak supervision* to programmatically label data points through a collection of *labelling functions* (Fries et al., 2017; Ratner et al., 2017; Lison et al., 2020; Safranchik et al., 2020a). The skweak framework allows NLP practitioners to easily construct, apply and aggregate such labelling functions for classification and sequence labelling tasks. skweak comes with a robust and scalable aggregation model that extends the HMM model of Lison et al. (2020). As

Proceedings of the Joint Conference of the 59th Annual Meeting of the Association for Computational Linguistics and the 11th International Joint Conference on Natural Language Processing: System Demonstrations, pages 337–346, August 1st - August 6th, 2021.

detailed in Section 4, the model now includes a feature weighting mechanism to capture the correlations that may exist between labelling functions. The general procedure is illustrated in Figure 1.

Another novel feature of skweak is the ability to create labelling functions that produce *underspecified labels*. For instance, a labelling function may predict that a token is part of a named entity (but without committing to a specific label), or that a sentence does *not* express a particular sentiment (but without committing to a specific sentiment category). This ability greatly extends the expressive power of labelling functions and makes it possible to define complex hierarchies between categories – for instance, COMPANY may be a sub-category of ORG, which may be itself a sub-category of ENT. It also enables the expression of "negative" signals that indicate that the output should *not* be a particular label. Based on our experience applying weak supervision to various NLP tasks, we expect this ability to underspecify output labels to be very useful in NLP applications.

2 Related Work

Weak supervision aims to replace hand-annotated 'ground truths' with labelling functions that are programmatically applied to data points – in our case, texts – from the target domain (Ratner et al., 2017, 2019; Lison et al., 2020; Safranchik et al., 2020b; Fu et al., 2020). Those functions may take the form of rule-based heuristics, gazetteers, annotations from crowd-workers, external databases, data-driven models trained from related domains, or linguistic constraints. A particular form of weak supervision is *distant supervision*, which relies on knowledge bases to automatically label documents with entities (Mintz et al., 2009; Ritter et al., 2013; Shang et al., 2018). Weak supervision is also related to models for aggregating crowd-sourced annotations (Kim and Ghahramani, 2012; Hovy et al., 2013; Nguyen et al., 2017).

Crucially, labelling functions do not need to provide a prediction for every data point and may "abstain" whenever certain conditions are not met. They may also rely on external data sources that are unavailable at runtime, as is the case for labels obtained by crowd-workers. After being applied to a dataset, the results of those labelling functions are aggregated into a single, probabilistic annotation layer. This aggregation is often implemented with a generative model connecting the latent (unobserved) labels to the outputs of each labelling function (Ratner et al., 2017; Lison et al., 2020; Safranchik et al., 2020a). Based on those aggregated labels, a discriminative model (often a neural architecture) is then trained for the task.

Weak supervision shifts the focus away from collecting manual annotations and concentrates the effort on developing good labelling functions for the target domain. This approach has been shown to be much more efficient than traditional annotation efforts (Ratner et al., 2017). Weak supervision allows domain experts to directly *inject* their domain knowledge in the form of various heuristics. Another benefit is the possibility to modify/extend the label set during development, which is a common situation in industrial R&D projects.

Several software frameworks for weak supervision have been released in recent years. One such framework is Snorkel (Ratner et al., 2017, 2019) which combines various supervision sources using a generative model. However, Snorkel requires data points to be independent, making it difficult to apply to sequence labelling tasks as done in skweak. Swellshark (Fries et al., 2017) is another framework optimised for biomedical NER. Swellshark, is however, limited to classifying already segmented entities, and relies on a separate, ad-hoc mechanism to generate candidate spans.

FlyingSquid (Fu et al., 2020) presents a novel approach based on triplet methods, which is shown to be fast enough to be applicable to structured prediction problems such as sequence labelling. However, compared to skweak, the aggregation model of FlyingSquid focuses on estimating the *accuracies* of each labelling function, and is therefore difficult to apply to problems where labelling sources may exhibit very different precision/recall trade-offs. A labelling function may for instance rely on a pattern that has a high precision but a low recall, while the opposite may be true for other labelling functions. Such difference is lost if accuracy is the only metric associated for each labelling function. Finally Safranchik et al. (2020b) describe a weak supervision model based on an extension of HMMs called linked hidden Markov models. Although their aggregation model is related to skweak, they provide a more limited choice of labelling functions, in particular regarding the inclusion of document-level constraints or underspecified labels.

skweak is also more distantly related to *ensemble methods* (Sagi and Rokach, 2018), as those methods also rely on multiple estimators whose results are combined at prediction time. However, a major difference lies in the fact that labelling functions only need to be aggregated once in skweak, in order to generate labelled training data for the final discriminative model (Step 3 of Figure 1). This difference is important as labelling functions may be computationally costly to run or rely on external resources that are not available at runtime, as is the case for annotations from crowd-workers.

3 Labelling functions

Labelling functions in skweak can be grouped in four main categories: heuristics, gazetteers, machine learning models, and document-level functions. Each labelling function is defined in skweak as a method that takes SpaCy Doc objects as inputs and returns text spans associated with labels. For text classification tasks, the span simply corresponds to the full document itself.

The use of SpaCy greatly facilitates downstream processing, as it allows labelling functions to operate on texts that are already tokenised and include linguistic features such as lemma, POS tags and dependency relations.[1] skweak integrates several functionalities on top of SpaCy to easily create, manipulate, label and store text documents.

Heuristics

The simplest type of labelling functions integrated in skweak are rule-based heuristics. For instance, one heuristic to detect entities of type COMPANY is to look for text spans ending with a legal company type (such as "Inc."). Similarly, a heuristic to detect named entities of the (underspecified) type ENT is to search for sequences of tokens tagged as NNPs. Section 6 provides further examples of heuristics for NER and Sentiment Analysis.

The easiest way to define heuristics in skweak is through standard Python functions that take a SpaCy Doc object as input and returns labelled spans. For instance, the following function detects entities of type MONEY by searching for numbers preceded by a currency symbol like $ or €:

```
def money_detector(doc):
  """Searches for occurrences of
  MONEY entities in text"""

  for tok in doc[1:]:
      if (tok.text[0].isdigit() and
           tok.nbor(-1).is_currency):
         yield tok.i-1, tok.i+1, "MONEY"
```

skweak also provides functionalities to easily construct heuristics based on linguistic constraints (such as POS patterns or dependency relations) or the presence of neighbouring words within a given context window.

Labelling functions may focus on specific labels and/or contexts and "abstain" from giving a prediction for other text spans. For instance, the heuristic mentioned above to detect companies from legal suffixes will only be triggered in very specific contexts, and abstain from giving a prediction otherwise. More generally, it should be stressed that labelling functions do not need to be perfect and should be expected to yield incorrect predictions from time to time. The purpose of weak supervision is precisely to combine together a set of weaker/noisier supervision signals, leading to a form of denoising (Ratner et al., 2019).

Labelling functions in skweak can be constructed from the outputs of other functions. For instance, the heuristic tagging NNP chunks with the label ENT may be refined through a second heuristic that additionally requires the tokens to be in title case – which leads to a lower recall but a higher precision compared to the initial heuristic. The creation of such derived labelling functions through the combination of constraints is a simple way to increase the number of labelling sources and therefore the robustness of the aggregation mechanism. skweak automatically takes care of dependencies between labelling functions in the backend.

Machine learning models

Labelling functions may also take the form of machine learning models. Typically, those models will be trained on data from other, related domains, thereby leading to some form of transfer learning across domains. skweak does not impose any constraint on type of model that can be employed.

The support for underspecified labels in skweak greatly facilitates the use of models across datasets, as it makes it possible to define hierarchical relations between distinct label sets – for instance, the coarse-grained LOC label from CoNLL 2003 (Tjong Kim Sang and De Meulder, 2003) may be seen as including both the GPE and LOC labels in Ontonotes (Weischedel et al., 2011).

[1]For languages not yet supported in SpaCy, the multi-language model from SpaCy can be applied.

Gazetteers

Another group of labelling functions are *gazetteers*, which are modules searching for occurrences of a list of words or phrases in the document. For instance, a gazetteer may be constructed using the geographical locations from Geonames (Wick, 2015) or names of persons, organisations and locations from DBPedia (Lehmann et al., 2015)

As gazetteers may include large numbers of entries, skweak relies on *tries* to efficiently search for all possible occurrences within a document. A trie, also called a prefix tree, stores all entries as a tree which is traversed depth-first. This implementation can scale up to very large gazetteers with more than one million entries. The search can be done in two distinct modes: a *case-sensitive* mode that requires an exact match between the entity in the trie and the occurrence and a *case-insensitive* mode that relaxes this constraint.

Document-level functions

Unlike previous weak supervision frameworks, skweak also provides functionalities to create *document-level* labelling functions that rely on the global document context to derive new supervision signals. In particular, skweak includes a labelling function that takes advantage of *label consistency* within a document. Entities occurring multiple times through a document are highly likely to belong to the same category (Krishnan and Manning, 2006). One can take advantage of this phenomenon by estimating the majority label of each entity in the document and then creating a labelling function that applies this majority label to each mention.

Furthermore, when introduced for the first time in a text, entities are often referred univocally, while subsequent mentions (once the entity is salient) frequently rely on shorter references. For instance, the first mention of a person in a text will often take the form of a full name (possibly complemented with job titles), but mentions that follow will often rely on shorter forms, such as the family name. skweak provides functionalities to easily capture such document-level relations.

4 Aggregation model

After being applied to a collection of texts, the outputs of labelling functions are aggregated using a generative model. For sequence labelling, this model is expressed as a Hidden Markov Model where the states correspond to the "true" (unobserved) labels, and the observations are the predictions of each labelling function (Lison et al., 2020). For document classification, this model reduces to Naive Bayes since there are no transitions.

This generative model is estimated using the Baum-Welch algorithm (Rabiner, 1990), which a variant of EM that uses the forward-backward algorithm to compute the statistics for the expectation step. For efficient inference, skweak combines Python with C-compiled routines from the hmmlearn package[2] employed for both parameter estimation and decoding.

4.1 Probabilistic Model

We assume a list of J labelling functions $\{\lambda_1, ..., \lambda_J\}$. Each labelling function produces a label for each data point (including a special "void" label denoting that the labelling function abstains from a concrete prediction, as well as underspecified labels). Let $\{l_1, ..., l_L\}$ be the set of labels that can be produced by labelling functions.

The aggregation model is represented as a hidden Markov model (HMM), in which the states correspond to the true underlying mutually exclusive class labels $\{l_1, ..., l_S\}$.[3] This model has multiple emissions (one per labelling function). For the time being, we assume those emissions to be mutually independent conditional on the latent state (see next section for a more refined model).

Formally, for each token $i \in \{1, ..., n\}$ and labelling function λ_j, we assume a multinomial distribution for the observed labels $\boldsymbol{Y_{ij}}$. The parameters of this multinomial are vectors $\boldsymbol{P_j^{s_i}} \in \mathcal{R}^L_{[0,1]}$. The latent states are assumed to have a Markovian dependence structure along the tokens $\{1, ..., n\}$. As depicted in Figure 2, this results in an HMM expressed as a dependent mixture of multinomials:

$$p(\lambda_j^{(i)} = \boldsymbol{Y_{ij}} | \boldsymbol{P_j^{s_i}}) = \text{Multinomial}\left(\boldsymbol{P_j^{s_i}}\right), \quad (1)$$

$$p(s_i = k | s_{i-1} = l) = \tau_{lk}. \quad (2)$$

where $\tau_{lk} \in \mathcal{R}_{[0,1]}$ are the parameters of the transition matrix controlling for a given state $s_{i-1} = l$ the probability of transition to state $s_i = k$.

The likelihood function includes a constraint that requires latent labels to be observed in at least one labelling function to have a non-zero probability.

[2] https://hmmlearn.readthedocs.io/

[3] Note that the set of observed labels $\{l_1, ..., l_L\}$ produced by the labelling functions may be larger than the set of latent labels $\{l_1, ..., l_S\}$, since those observed labels may also include underspecified labels such as ENT.

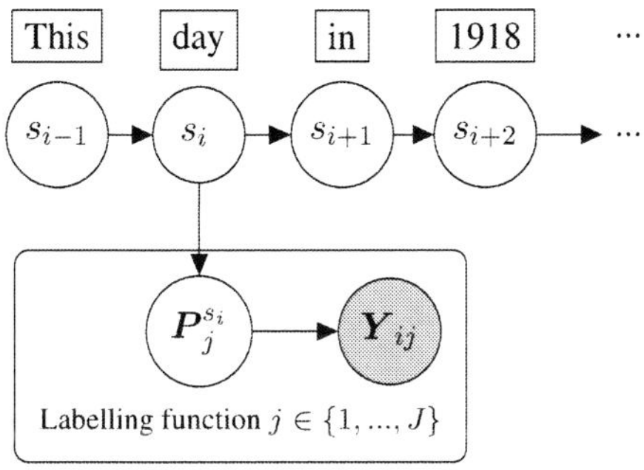

Figure 2: Aggregation model using a hidden Markov model with multiple multinomial emissions.

This constraint reduces the search space to a few labels at each step, and greatly facilitates the convergence of the forward-backward algorithm.

To initialise the model parameters, we run a majority voter that predicts the most likely latent labels based on the "votes" for each label (also including underspecified labels), each labelling function corresponding to a voter. Those predictions are employed to derive the initial transition and emission probabilities, which are then refined through several EM passes.

Performance-wise, skweak can scale up to large collections of documents. The aggregation of all named entities from the MUC-6 dataset (see Section 6.1) based on a total of 52 labelling functions only requires a few minutes of computation time, with an average speed of 1000-1500 tokens per second on a modern computing server.

4.2 Weighting

One shortcoming of the above model is that it fails to account for the fact that labelling functions may be correlated with one another, for instance when a labelling function is computed from the output of another labeling function. To capture those dependencies, we extend the model with a weighting scheme – or equivalently, a *tempering* of the densities associated with each labelling function.

Formally, for each labelling function λ_j and observed label k we determine weights $\{w_{jk}\}$ with respect to which the corresponding densities of the labelling functions are annealed. This flattens to different degrees the underlying probabilities for the components of the multinomials. The observed process has then a tempered multinomial distribution with a density of form:

$$p(\lambda_j^{(i)} = \boldsymbol{Y_{ij}} | \boldsymbol{P_j^{s_i}}, \boldsymbol{w_j}) \propto \prod_{k=1}^{L} P_{jk}^{s_i \, Y_{ijk} w_{jk}}. \quad (3)$$

The temperatures $\{w_{jk}\}$ are determined using a scheme inspired by delution priors widely used in Bayesian model averaging (George, 1999; George et al., 2010). The idea relies on *redundancy* as the measure of prior information on the importance of features. Formally, we define for each λ_j a neighbourhood $N(\lambda_j)$ consisting of labelling functions known to be correlated with λ_j, as is the case for labelling functions built on top of another function's outputs. The weights are then specified as:

$$w_{jk} = \exp\left(-\gamma \sum_{l \in N(\lambda_j)} R_{jlk}\right), \quad (4)$$

where γ is a hyper-parameter specifying the strength of the weighting scheme, and R_{jlk} is the recall between labelling functions λ_j and λ_l for label k. Informally, the weight w_{jk} of a labelling function λ_j producing the label k will decrease if λ_j exhibits a high recall with correlated sources, and is therefore at least partially redundant.

Also, the temperatures can be interpreted as weights of the log-likelihood function and Dimitroff et al. (2013) have shown that under some regularity conditions there exist weights that allow to maximize F_1 score when optimising the weighted log-likelihood (Field and Smith, 1994).

5 Example

With skweak, one can apply and aggregrate labelling functions with a few lines of code:

```
import spacy, re
from skweak import heuristics,
    gazetteers, aggregation, utils

# First heuristic (see Section 3)
lf1 = heuristics.FunctionAnnotator
        ("money", money_detector)

# Detection of years
lf2= heuristics.TokenConstraintAnnotator
      ("years", lambda tok: re.match
     ("(19|20)\d{2}$", tok.text), "DATE")

# Gazetteer with a few names
NAMES = [("Barack", "Obama"), ("Donald",
      "Trump"), ("Joe", "Biden")]
trie = gazetteers.Trie(NAMES)
lf3 = gazetteers.GazetteerAnnotator
       ("presidents", trie, "PERSON")
```

```
# We create a simple text
nlp = spacy.load("en_core_web_md")
doc = nlp("Donald Trump paid $750 in
    federal income taxes in 2016")

# apply the labelling functions
doc = lf3(lf2(lf1(doc)))

# aggregate them
hmm = aggregation.HMM("hmm",
        ["PERSON", "DATE", "MONEY"])
hmm.fit_and_aggregate([doc])

# and visualise the result (in Jupyter)
utils.display_entities(doc, "hmm")
```

skweak's repository provides Jupyter Notebooks with additional examples and explanations.

6 Experimental Results

We describe below two experiments demonstrating how skweak can be applied to sequence labelling and text classification. We refer the reader to Lison et al. (2020) for more results on NER.[4] It should be stressed that the results below are all obtained without using any gold labels.

6.1 Named Entity Recognition

We seek to recognise named entities from the MUC-6 corpus (Grishman and Sundheim, 1996), which contains 318 Wall Street Journal articles annotated with 7 entity types: LOCATION, ORGANIZATION, PERSON, MONEY, DATE, TIME, PERCENT.

Labelling functions

We apply the following functions to the corpus:

- Heuristics for detecting dates, times and percents based on handcrafted patterns
- Heuristics for detecting named entities based on casing, NNP part-of-speech tags or compound phrases. Those heuristics produced entities of underspecified type **ENT**
- One probabilistic parser (Braun et al., 2017) for detecting dates, times, money amounts, percents, and cardinal/ordinal values
- Heuristics for detecting person names, based on honorifics (such as Mr. or Dr.) along with a dictionary of common first names
- One heuristic for detecting company names with legal suffixes (such as Inc.)

[4]See also Fries et al. (2017) for specific results on applying weak supervision to biomedical NER.

Model	Token F_1	Entity F_1
Majority vote (all labelling functions)	0.61	0.57
HMM-aggregated labels:		
- only heuristics	0.57	0.43
- only gazetteers	0.36	0.35
- only NER models	0.60	0.56
- all but doc-level	0.80	0.71
- all labelling functions	0.81	0.72
Neural NER trained on HMM-aggregated labels	**0.82**	**0.72**

Table 1: Micro-averaged F_1 scores on MUC-6.

- Gazetteers for detecting persons, organisations and locations based on Wikipedia, Geonames (Wick, 2015) and Crunchbase
- Neural models trained on CoNLL 2003 & the Broad Twitter Corpus (Tjong Kim Sang and De Meulder, 2003; Derczynski et al., 2016)
- Document-level labelling functions based on (1) majority labels for a given entity or (2) the label of each entity's first mention.

All together (including multiple variants of the functions above, such as gazetteers in both case-sensitive and case-insensitive mode), this amounts to a total of 52 labelling functions.

Results

The token and entity-level F_1 scores are shown in Table 1. As baselines, we provide the results obtained by aggregating all labelling functions using a majority voter, along with results using the HMM on various subsets of labelling functions. The final line indicates the results using a neural NER model trained on the HMM-aggregated labels (with all labelling functions). The neural model employed in this particular experiment is a transformer architecture based on a large pretrained neural model, RoBERTa (Liu et al., 2019).

See Lison et al. (2020) for experimental details and results for other aggregation methods.

6.2 Sentiment Analysis

We consider the task of three class (positive, negative, neutral) sentiment analysis in Norwegian as a second case study. We use sentence-level annotations[5] from the NoReC$_{fine}$ dataset (Øvrelid et al.,

[5]Data: https://github.com/ltgoslo/norec_sentence

2020). These are created by aggregating the fine-grained annotations for sentiment expressions such that any sentence with a majority of positive sentiment expressions is assumed to be positive, and likewise with negative expressions. Sentences with no sentiment expressions are labelled neutral.

Labelling functions

Sentiment lexicons: NorSent (Barnes et al., 2019) is the only available lexicon in Norwegian and contains tokens with their associated polarity. We also use MT-translated English lexicons: **SoCal** (Taboada et al., 2011), the **IBM** Debater lexicon (Toledo-Ronen et al., 2018) and the NRC word emotion lexicon (**NRC emo.**) (Mohammad and Turney, 2010). Automatic translation introduces some noise but has been shown to preserve most sentiment information (Mohammad et al., 2016).

Heuristics: For sentences with two clauses connected by 'but', the second clause is typically more relevant to the sentiment, as for instance in "the food was nice, but I wouldn't go back there". We include a heuristic to reflect this pattern.

Machine learning models: We create a document-level classifier (**Doc-level**) by training a bag-of-words SVM on the NoReC dataset (Velldal et al., 2018), which contains 'dice labels' ranging from 1 (very negative) to 6 (very positive). We map predictions to positive (>4), negative (<3), and neutral (3 and 4). We also include two multilingual BERT models **mBERT-review**[6] (trained on reviews from 6 languages) and **mBERT-SST** (trained on the Stanford Sentiment Treebank). The predictions for both models are again mapped to 3 classes (positive, negative, neutral).

Results

Table 2 provides results on the NoReC sentence test split. As baseline, we include a **Majority class** which always predicts the neutral class. As upper bounds, we include a linear SVM trained on TF-IDF weighted (1-3)-grams (**Ngram SVM**), along with Norwegian BERT (NorBERT) models (Kutuzov et al., 2021) fine-tuned on the gold training data. Those two models are upper bounds as they have access to in-domain labelled data, which is not the case for the other models.

Again, we observe that the HMM-aggregated labels outperform all individual labelling functions

	Source	Macro F1
baseline	Majority class	22.4
upper bounds	Ngram SVM	55.2
	NorBERT	68.5
lexicons	NorSent	45.3
	NorSent lemmas	33.7
	NRC VAD	8.2
	SoCal	46.1
	SoCal adv.	43.8
	SoCal Google	45.0
	SoCal Int.	36.5
	SoCal verb	37.2
	IBM	35.9
	NRC Emo.	41.7
heuristics	BUT	25.3
	BUT lemmas	24.0
trained models	Doc-level	33.0
	mBERT-review	44.3
	mBERT-SST	32.3
Aggregation	Majority vote	40.0
	HMM	49.1
Trained on agg.	NorBERT	**51.2**

Table 2: Macro F_1 on sentence-level NoReC data.

as well as a majority voter that aggregates those functions. The best performance is achieved by a neural model (in this case NorBERT) fine-tuned on those aggregated labels.

7 Conclusion

The skweak toolkit provides a practical solution to a problem encountered by virtually every NLP practitioner: how can I obtain labelled data for my NLP task? Using weak supervision, skweak makes it possible to create training data *programmatically* instead of labelling data by hand. The toolkit provides a Python API to apply labelling functions and aggregate their results in a few lines of code. The aggregation relies on a generative model that express the relative accuracy (and redundancies) of each labelling function.

The toolkit can be applied to both sequence labelling and text classification and comes along a range of novel functionalities such as the integration of underspecified labels and the creation of document-level labelling functions.

[6] https://huggingface.co/nlptown/bert-base-multilingual-uncased-sentiment

References

Mikel Artetxe and Holger Schwenk. 2019. Massively multilingual sentence embeddings for zero-shot cross-lingual transfer and beyond. *Transactions of the Association for Computational Linguistics*, 7:597–610.

Jeremy Barnes and Roman Klinger. 2019. Embedding projection for targeted cross-lingual sentiment: Model comparisons and a real-world study. *Journal of Artificial Intelligence Research*, 66:691–742.

Jeremy Barnes, Samia Touileb, Lilja Øvrelid, and Erik Velldal. 2019. Lexicon information in neural sentiment analysis: a multi-task learning approach. In *Proceedings of the 22nd Nordic Conference on Computational Linguistics*, pages 175–186, Turku, Finland. Linköping University Electronic Press.

Daniel Braun, Adrian Hernandez Mendez, Florian Matthes, and Manfred Langen. 2017. Evaluating natural language understanding services for conversational question answering systems. In *Proceedings of the 18th Annual SIGdial Meeting on Discourse and Dialogue*, pages 174–185, Saarbrücken, Germany. Association for Computational Linguistics.

Leon Derczynski, Kalina Bontcheva, and Ian Roberts. 2016. Broad Twitter corpus: A diverse named entity recognition resource. In *Proceedings of COLING 2016, the 26th International Conference on Computational Linguistics: Technical Papers*, pages 1169–1179, Osaka, Japan. The COLING 2016 Organizing Committee.

Georgi Dimitroff, Laura Toloşi, Borislav Popov, and Georgi Georgiev. 2013. Weighted maximum likelihood loss as a convenient shortcut to optimizing the F-measure of maximum entropy classifiers. In *Proceedings of the International Conference Recent Advances in Natural Language Processing RANLP 2013*, pages 207–214, Hissar, Bulgaria. INCOMA Ltd. Shoumen, BULGARIA.

C Field and B Smith. 1994. Robust estimation: A weighted maximum likelihood approach. *International Statistical Review/Revue Internationale de Statistique*, pages 405–424.

Jason Fries, Sen Wu, Alex Ratner, and Christopher Ré. 2017. Swellshark: A generative model for biomedical named entity recognition without labeled data.

Daniel Y. Fu, Mayee F. Chen, Frederic Sala, Sarah M. Hooper, Kayvon Fatahalian, and Christopher Ré. 2020. Fast and three-rious: Speeding up weak supervision with triplet methods. In *Proceedings of the 37th International Conference on Machine Learning (ICML 2020)*.

E George. 1999. Discussion of "model averaging and model search strategies" by m. clyde. In *Bayesian Statistics 6–Proceedings of the Sixth Valencia International Meeting*.

Edward I George et al. 2010. Dilution priors: Compensating for model space redundancy. In *Borrowing Strength: Theory Powering Applications–A Festschrift for Lawrence D. Brown*, pages 158–165. Institute of Mathematical Statistics.

Ralph Grishman and Beth Sundheim. 1996. Message understanding conference-6: A brief history. In *Proceedings of the 16th Conference on Computational Linguistics - Volume 1*, COLING '96, page 466–471, USA. Association for Computational Linguistics.

Dirk Hovy, Taylor Berg-Kirkpatrick, Ashish Vaswani, and Eduard Hovy. 2013. Learning whom to trust with MACE. In *Proceedings of the 2013 Conference of the North American Chapter of the Association for Computational Linguistics: Human Language Technologies*, pages 1120–1130, Atlanta, Georgia. Association for Computational Linguistics.

Hyun-Chul Kim and Zoubin Ghahramani. 2012. Bayesian classifier combination. In *Proceedings of the Fifteenth International Conference on Artificial Intelligence and Statistics*, volume 22 of *Proceedings of Machine Learning Research*, pages 619–627, La Palma, Canary Islands. PMLR.

Vijay Krishnan and Christopher D. Manning. 2006. An effective two-stage model for exploiting non-local dependencies in named entity recognition. In *Proceedings of the 21st International Conference on Computational Linguistics and 44th Annual Meeting of the Association for Computational Linguistics*, pages 1121–1128, Sydney, Australia. Association for Computational Linguistics.

Andrey Kutuzov, Jeremy Barnes, Erik Velldal, Lilja Øvrelid, and Stephan Oepen. 2021. Large-scale contextualised language modelling for Norwegian. In *Proceedings of the 23rd Nordic Conference on Computational Linguistics (NoDaLiDa)*, pages 30–40, Reykjavik, Iceland (Online). Linköping University Electronic Press, Sweden.

Anne Lauscher, Vinit Ravishankar, Ivan Vulić, and Goran Glavaš. 2020. From zero to hero: On the limitations of zero-shot language transfer with multilingual Transformers. In *Proceedings of the 2020 Conference on Empirical Methods in Natural Language Processing (EMNLP)*, pages 4483–4499, Online. Association for Computational Linguistics.

Jens Lehmann, Robert Isele, Max Jakob, Anja Jentzsch, Dimitris Kontokostas, Pablo N. Mendes, Sebastian Hellmann, Mohamed Morsey, Patrick van Kleef, Sören Auer, and Christian Bizer. 2015. Dbpedia - a large-scale, multilingual knowledge base extracted from wikipedia. *Semantic Web*, 6(2):167–195.

Pierre Lison, Jeremy Barnes, Aliaksandr Hubin, and Samia Touileb. 2020. Named entity recognition without labelled data: A weak supervision approach. In *Proceedings of the 58th Annual Meeting of the Association for Computational Linguistics*, pages 1518–1533, Online. Association for Computational Linguistics.

Yinhan Liu, Myle Ott, Naman Goyal, Jingfei Du, Mandar Joshi, Danqi Chen, Omer Levy, Mike Lewis, Luke Zettlemoyer, and Veselin Stoyanov. 2019. Roberta: A robustly optimized BERT pretraining approach. *CoRR*, abs/1907.11692.

Mike Mintz, Steven Bills, Rion Snow, and Daniel Jurafsky. 2009. Distant supervision for relation extraction without labeled data. In *Proceedings of the Joint Conference of the 47th Annual Meeting of the ACL and the 4th International Joint Conference on Natural Language Processing of the AFNLP*, pages 1003–1011, Suntec, Singapore. Association for Computational Linguistics.

Saif Mohammad and Peter Turney. 2010. Emotions evoked by common words and phrases: Using Mechanical Turk to create an emotion lexicon. In *Proceedings of the NAACL HLT 2010 Workshop on Computational Approaches to Analysis and Generation of Emotion in Text*, pages 26–34, Los Angeles, CA. Association for Computational Linguistics.

Saif M. Mohammad, Mohammad Salameh, and Svetlana Kiritchenko. 2016. How translation alters sentiment. *Journal of Artificial Intelligence Research*, 55(1):95–130.

An Thanh Nguyen, Byron Wallace, Junyi Jessy Li, Ani Nenkova, and Matthew Lease. 2017. Aggregating and predicting sequence labels from crowd annotations. In *Proceedings of the 55th Annual Meeting of the Association for Computational Linguistics (Volume 1: Long Papers)*, pages 299–309, Vancouver, Canada. Association for Computational Linguistics.

Lilja Øvrelid, Petter Mæhlum, Jeremy Barnes, and Erik Velldal. 2020. A fine-grained sentiment dataset for Norwegian. In *Proceedings of the 12th Language Resources and Evaluation Conference*, pages 5025–5033, Marseille, France. European Language Resources Association.

Matthew Peters, Mark Neumann, Mohit Iyyer, Matt Gardner, Christopher Clark, Kenton Lee, and Luke Zettlemoyer. 2018. Deep contextualized word representations. In *Proceedings of the 2018 Conference of the North American Chapter of the Association for Computational Linguistics: Human Language Technologies, Volume 1 (Long Papers)*, pages 2227–2237, New Orleans, Louisiana. Association for Computational Linguistics.

Matthew E. Peters, Sebastian Ruder, and Noah A. Smith. 2019. To tune or not to tune? adapting pretrained representations to diverse tasks. In *Proceedings of the 4th Workshop on Representation Learning for NLP (RepL4NLP-2019)*, pages 7–14, Florence, Italy. Association for Computational Linguistics.

Telmo Pires, Eva Schlinger, and Dan Garrette. 2019. How multilingual is multilingual BERT? In *Proceedings of the 57th Annual Meeting of the Association for Computational Linguistics*, pages 4996–5001, Florence, Italy. Association for Computational Linguistics.

Lawrence R. Rabiner. 1990. A tutorial on hidden markov models and selected applications in speech recognition. In Alex Waibel and Kai-Fu Lee, editors, *Readings in Speech Recognition*, pages 267–296. Morgan Kaufmann Publishers Inc., San Francisco, CA, USA.

Alexander Ratner, Stephen H. Bach, Henry Ehrenberg, Jason Fries, Sen Wu, and Christopher Ré. 2017. Snorkel: Rapid training data creation with weak supervision. *Proc. VLDB Endow.*, 11(3):269–282.

Alexander Ratner, Stephen H. Bach, Henry Ehrenberg, Jason Fries, Sen Wu, and Christopher Ré. 2019. Snorkel: rapid training data creation with weak supervision. *The VLDB Journal*.

Alan Ritter, Luke Zettlemoyer, Mausam, and Oren Etzioni. 2013. Modeling missing data in distant supervision for information extraction. *Transactions of the Association for Computational Linguistics*, 1:367–378.

Esteban Safranchik, Shiying Luo, and Stephen Bach. 2020a. Weakly supervised sequence tagging from noisy rules. *Proceedings of the AAAI Conference on Artificial Intelligence*, 34(04):5570–5578.

Esteban Safranchik, Shiying Luo, and Stephen Bach. 2020b. Weakly supervised sequence tagging from noisy rules. *Proceedings of the AAAI Conference on Artificial Intelligence*, 34(04):5570–5578.

Omer Sagi and Lior Rokach. 2018. Ensemble learning: A survey. *WIREs Data Mining and Knowledge Discovery*, 8(4):e1249.

Jingbo Shang, Liyuan Liu, Xiaotao Gu, Xiang Ren, Teng Ren, and Jiawei Han. 2018. Learning named entity tagger using domain-specific dictionary. In *Proceedings of the 2018 Conference on Empirical Methods in Natural Language Processing*, pages 2054–2064, Brussels, Belgium. Association for Computational Linguistics.

Maite Taboada, Julian Brooke, Milan Tofiloski, Kimberly Voll, and Manfred Stede. 2011. Lexicon-based methods for sentiment analysis. *Computational Linguistics*, 37(2):267–307.

Erik F. Tjong Kim Sang and Fien De Meulder. 2003. Introduction to the CoNLL-2003 shared task: Language-independent named entity recognition. In *Proceedings of the Seventh Conference on Natural Language Learning at HLT-NAACL 2003*, pages 142–147.

Orith Toledo-Ronen, Roy Bar-Haim, Alon Halfon, Charles Jochim, Amir Menczel, Ranit Aharonov, and Noam Slonim. 2018. Learning sentiment composition from sentiment lexicons. In *Proceedings of the 27th International Conference on Computational Linguistics*, pages 2230–2241, Santa Fe, New

Mexico, USA. Association for Computational Linguistics.

Erik Velldal, Lilja Øvrelid, Eivind Alexander Bergem, Cathrine Stadsnes, Samia Touileb, and Fredrik Jørgensen. 2018. NoReC: The Norwegian review corpus. In *Proceedings of the Eleventh International Conference on Language Resources and Evaluation (LREC 2018)*, Miyazaki, Japan. European Language Resources Association (ELRA).

R. Weischedel, E. Hovy, M. Marcus, Palmer M., R. Belvin, S. Pradhan, L. Ramshaw, and N. Xue. 2011. OntoNotes: A large training corpus for enhanced processing. In *Handbook of Natural Language Processing and Machine Translation: DARPA Global Autonomous Language Exploitation*. Springer.

Marc Wick. 2015. Geonames Ontology.

TextFlint: Unified Multilingual Robustness Evaluation Toolkit for Natural Language Processing

Xiao Wang*, Qin Liu*, Tao Gui†, Qi Zhang†, Yicheng Zou, Xin Zhou, Jiacheng Ye, Yongxin Zhang, Rui Zheng, Zexiong Pang, Qinzhuo Wu, Zhengyan Li, Chong Zhang, Ruotian Ma, Zichu Fei, Ruijian Cai, Jun Zhao, Xingwu Hu, Zhiheng Yan, Yiding Tan, Yuan Hu, Qiyuan Bian, Zhihua Liu, Shan Qin, Bolin Zhu, Xiaoyu Xing, Jinlan Fu, Yue Zhang, Minlong Peng, Xiaoqing Zheng, Yaqian Zhou, Zhongyu Wei, Xipeng Qiu and Xuanjing Huang

School of Computer Science, Fudan Univerisity

`{xiao_wang20, liuq19, tgui16, qz}@fudan.edu.cn`

Abstract

TextFlint is a multilingual robustness evaluation toolkit for NLP tasks that incorporates universal text transformation, task-specific transformation, adversarial attack, subpopulation, and their combinations to provide comprehensive robustness analyses. This enables practitioners to automatically evaluate their models from various aspects or to customize their evaluations as desired with just a few lines of code. TextFlint also generates complete analytical reports as well as targeted augmented data to address the shortcomings of the model in terms of its robustness. To guarantee acceptability, all the text transformations are linguistically based and all the transformed data selected (up to 100,000 texts) scored highly under human evaluation. To validate the utility, we performed large-scale empirical evaluations (over 67,000) on state-of-the-art deep learning models, classic supervised methods, and real-world systems. The toolkit is already available at https://github.com/textflint, with all the evaluation results demonstrated at textflint.io.

Transformation

Original	Tasty **burgers**, and crispy fries. (Target aspect: burgers)
RevTgt	Terrible **burgers**, but crispy fries.
RevNon	Tasty **burgers**, but soggy fries.
Typos	Tatsy burgers, and cripsy fries.

Adversarial attack

Original	Premise: Some rooms have balconies. Hypothesis: All of the rooms have balconies.	Contradiction
Adv	Premise: Many rooms have balconies. Hypothesis: All of the rooms have balconies.	Neutral

Subpopulation

Original Set	Subpopulation - Gender
She became a nurse and worked in a hospital.	✓
I told John to come early, but he failed.	✓
The river derives from southern America.	✗
Marry would like to teach kids in the kindergarten.	✓
The storm destroyed many houses in the village.	✗

Figure 1: Examples of three main generation functions. The transformation example is from ABSA (Aspect-based Sentiment Analysis) task, where the italic bold ***RevTgt*** (short for reverse target) denotes task-specific transformations, and the bold **Typos** denotes universal transformation.

1 Introduction

The detection of model robustness has been attracting increasing attention in recent years, given that deep neural networks (DNNs) of high accuracy can still be vulnerable to carefully crafted adversarial examples (Li et al., 2020), distribution shift (Miller et al., 2020), data transformation (Xing et al., 2020), and shortcut learning (Geirhos et al., 2020). Existing approaches to textual robustness evaluation focus on slightly modifying the input data, which maintains the original meaning and results in a different prediction. However, these methods often concentrate on either universal or task-specific generalization capabilities, which is difficult to comprehensively evaluate.

In response to the shortcomings of recent works, we introduce TextFlint, a unified, multilingual, and analyzable robustness evaluation toolkit for NLP. Its features include:

1. **Integrity.** TextFlint offers 20 general transformations and 60 task-specific transformations, as well as thousands of their combinations that cover a variety of aspects of text transformations to enable a comprehensive evaluation of robustness. It also supports evaluations on both English and Chinese. In addition, the toolkit also incorporates adversarial attack and subpopulation (Figure 1). Currently, 12 NLP tasks are available and more are on the way.

*Xiao Wang and Qin Liu contributed equally to this work and are co-first authors.

†Corresponding Author

Proceedings of the Joint Conference of the 59th Annual Meeting of the Association for Computational Linguistics and the 11th International Joint Conference on Natural Language Processing: System Demonstrations, pages 347–355, August 1st - August 6th, 2021.

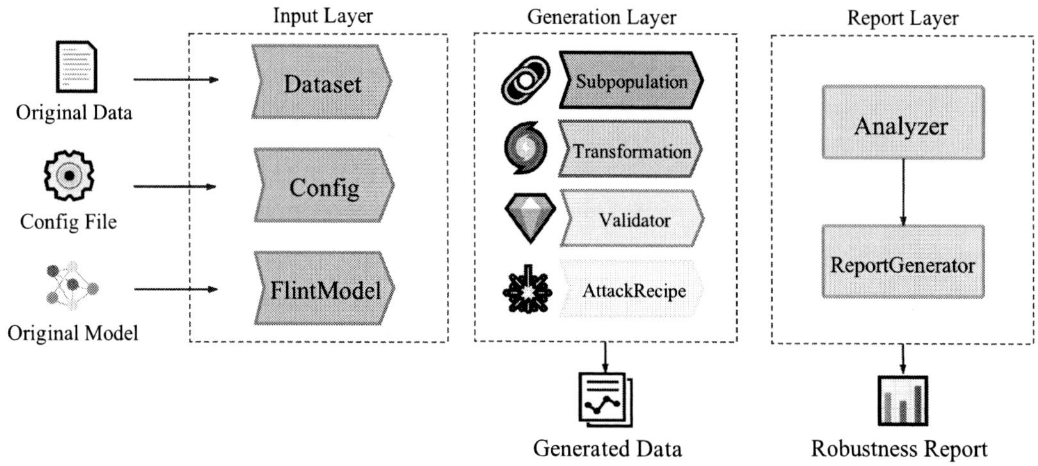

Figure 2: Architecture of TextFlint. Input Layer receives the original dataset, config file and target model as input, which are represented as `Dataset`, `Config` and `FlintModel` separately. Generation Layer consists of three parallel modules, where `Subpopulation` generates a subset of input dataset, `Transformation` augments datasets, and `AttackRecipe` interacts with the target model. Report Layer analyzes test results by `Analyzer` and provides users with robustness report by `ReportGenerator`.

2. **Acceptability.** All the text transformations offered by TextFlint are linguistically based and passed human evaluation. To verify the quality of the transformed text, we conducted human evaluation on the original and transformed texts under all of the mentioned transformations. The transformed texts performed well in plausibility and grammaticality.

3. **Analyzability.** Based on the evaluation results, TextFlint provides a standard analysis report with respect to a model's lexics, syntax, and semantics. All the evaluation results can be displayed via visualization and tabulation to help users gain a quick and accurate grasp of the shortcomings of a model. In addition, TextFlint generates a large amount of targeted data to augment the evaluated model, based on the the defects identified in the analysis report, and provides patches for the model defects.

We evaluated 95 state-of-the-art models and classic systems on 6,903 transformation datasets for a total of over 67,000 evaluations and found that almost all models showed significant performance degradation, including a decline of more than 50% of BERT's prediction accuracy on tasks such as aspect-level sentiment classification, named entity recognition, and natural language inference. This means that the robustness of most models needs to be improved.

2 TextFlint Framework

TextFlint is designed to be flexible enough to allow practitioners to configure the workflow while providing appropriate abstractions to alleviate the concerns of the low-level implementation. According to its pipeline architecture, TextFlint can be organized into three blocks, as shown in Figure 2: (a) Input Layer, which prepares the necessary information for sample generation; (b) Generation Layer, which applies generation functions to each sample; and (c) Reporter Layer, which analyzes the evaluation results and generates a robustness report.

2.1 Input Layer

For input preparation, the original dataset, which is to be loaded by `Dataset`, should first be formatted as a series of JSON objects. The configuration of `TextFlint` is specified by `Config`, which can be loaded from a customized config file. TextFlint is model-agnostic and provides `FlintModel` to wrap the target model. This means that it can apply robustness evaluation to models implemented in any deep learning framework. After Input Layer completes the required input loading, the interaction between the system and the user is complete.

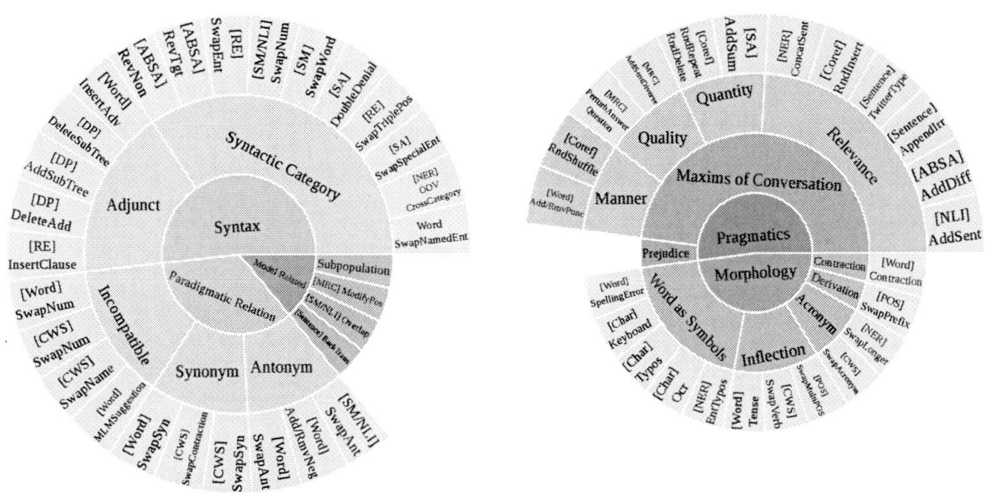

Figure 3: Overview of transformations through the lens of linguistics.

2.2 Generation Layer

Generation Layer supports three types of sample generation functions to provide comprehensive robustness analyses, i.e., `Transformation`, `Subpopulation`, and `AttackRecipe`. It is worth noting that the procedure of `Transformation` and `Subpopulation` does not require querying the target model, which means it is a completely decoupled process with the target model prediction. Additionally, to ensure semantic and grammatical correctness of the transformed samples, `Validator` provides several metrics to calculate the confidence of each sample.

Transformation `Transformation` aims to generate perturbations of the input text while maintaining the acceptability of the transformed texts. To verify the robustness comprehensively, TextFlint offers 20 universal transformations and 60 task-specific transformations, as well as thousands of their combinations, covering 12 NLP tasks.

From the perspective of linguistics, the transformations are designed according to morphology, syntax, paradigmatic relation, and pragmatics. Transformations on morphology include **KeyBoard**, **Ocr**, **Typos**, etc. As for syntactical transformations, there are **SwapSyn-WordNet**, **AddSubTree**, etc. Due to limited space, refer to Figure 3 for specific information. Further, we conducted a large scale human evaluation on the original and transformed texts under all of the mentioned transformations (Section 4).

Subpopulation `Subpopulation` identifies the specific part of the dataset on which the target model performs poorly. To retrieve a subset that meets the configuration, `Subpopulation` divides the dataset by sorting samples according to certain attributes. TextFlint provides four general `Subpopulation` configurations, which contain **GenderBias**, **TextLength**, **LanguageModelPerplexity**, and **PhraseMatching**. Take the configuration of text length for example, **TextLength** retrieves the subset of the top 20% or bottom 20% in length.

AttackRecipe `AttackRecipe` aims to find a perturbation of an input text that satisfies the goal to fool the given `FlintModel`. In contrast with `Transformation` and `Subpopulation`, `AttackRecipe` requires the prediction scores of the target model. TextFlint provides 16 easy-to-use adversarial attack recipes that are implemented based on TextAttack (Morris et al., 2020).

Validator It is crucial to verify the quality of the samples generated by `Transformation` and `AttackRecipe`. TextFlint provides several metrics to evaluate the quality of the generated text, including (1) language model perplexity calculated based on the GPT2 model (Radford et al., 2019), (2) word replacement ratio in generated text compared with its original text, (3) edit distance between original text and generated text, (4) semantic similarity calculated based on Universal Sentence Encoder (Cer et al., 2018), and (5) BLEU score (Papineni et al., 2002).

2.3 Reporter Layer

Generation Layer yields three types of adversarial samples and verifies the robustness of the target model. Based on the evaluation results from Generation Layer, Report Layer aims to provide users with a standard analysis report from syntax, morphology, pragmatics, and paradigmatic relation aspects. The running process of Report Layer can be regarded as a pipeline from `Analyzer` to `ReportGenerator`.

3 Usage

Using TextFlint to verify the robustness of a specific model is as simple as running the following command:

```
$ textflint --dataset input_file
    --config config.json
```

where `input_file` is the input file of csv or json format, and `config.json` is a configuration file with generation and target model options. Complex functions can be implemented by a simple modification on `config.json`, such as executing the pipeline of transformations and assigning the parameters of each transformation method. Take the configuration for TextCNN (Kim, 2014) model on SA (sentiment analysis) task as an example:

```
{
  "task": "SA",
  "out_dir": "./DATA/",
  "flint_model": "./textcnn_model.py",
  "trans_methods": [
    "Ocr",
    ["InsertAdv", "SwapNamedEnt"],
    ...
  ],
  "trans_config": {
    "Ocr": {"trans_p": 0.3},
    ...
  },
...
}
```

- `task` is the name of the target task. TextFlint supports 12 types of tasks.

- `out_dir` is the directory where each of the generated samples and their corresponding original samples are saved.

- `flint_model` is the python file path that saves the instance of FlintModel.

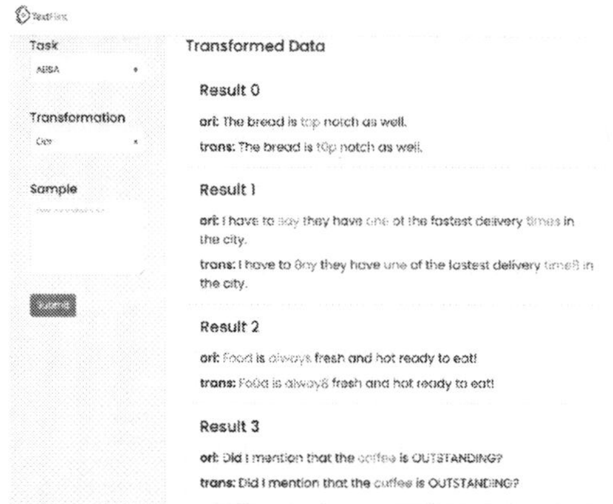

Figure 4: Screenshot of TextFlint's web interface running Ocr transformation for ABSA task.

- `trans_methods` is used to specify the transformation method. For example, `"Ocr"` denotes the universal transformation **Ocr**, and `["InsertAdv", "SwapNamedEnt"]` denotes a pipeline of task-specific transformations, namely ***InsertAdv*** and ***SwapNamedEnt***.

- `trans_config` configures the parameters for the transformation methods. The default parameter is also a good choice.

Moreover, it also supports the configuration of subpopulation and adversarial attack. For more details about parameter configuration, please move to https://github.com/textflint/textflint.

Based on the design of the decoupling sample generation and model verification, TextFlint can be used inside another NLP project with just a few lines of code.

```
from textflint import Engine

data_path = 'input_file'
config = 'config.json'
engine = Engine()
engine.run(data_path, config)
```

TextFlint is also available for use through our web demo, displayed in Figure 4, which is available at https://www.textflint.io/demo.

Case Studies of Usage Due its user-friendly design philosophy, TextFlint shows its practicality in real applications. We summarize three occasions in which model robustness evaluation is challenging:

Case 1: General Evaluation For users who want to evaluate the robustness of NLP models

	Plausibility		Grammaticality			Plausibility		Grammaticality	
	Ori.	Trans.	Ori.	Trans.		Ori.	Trans.	Ori.	Trans.
DoubleDenial	3.26	3.37	3.59	3.49	***OOV***	3.69	3.76	3.54	3.48
AddSum-Person	3.39	3.32	3.76	3.59	***SwapLonger***	3.73	3.66	3.77	3.54
AddSum-Movie	3.26	3.34	3.61	3.58	***EntTypos***	3.57	3.5	3.59	3.54
SwapSpecialEnt-Person	3.37	3.14	3.75	3.73	***CrossCategory***	3.48	3.44	3.41	3.32
SwapSpecialEnt-Movie	3.17	3.28	3.70	3.49	***ConcatSent***	4.14	3.54	3.84	3.81

Table 1: Human evaluation results for task-specific transformation. Ori and Trans denote the original text and the transformed text, respectively. The table on the left is the performance of task-specific transformations for the sentiment analysis task, and the right is of that for named entity recognition. These metrics are rated on a 1-5 scale (5 denotes the best).

in a general way, TextFlint supports generating massive and comprehensive transformed samples with just one command. By default, TextFlint performs all single transformations on the original dataset to form the corresponding transformed datasets, and the performance of the target models is tested on these datasets. The evaluation report provides a comparative view of model performance on datasets before and after certain types of transformations, which supports model weakness analyses and guides particular improvements. For example, take BERT base(Devlin et al., 2019) as the target model to verify its robustness on the CONLL2003 dataset(Tjong Kim Sang and De Meulder, 2003), whose robustness report is shown in Figure 5. The performance of BERT base decreases significantly in some morphology transformations, such as ***OCR***, ***Keyboard***, ***Typos***, and ***Spelling Error***. To combat these errors of input texts and improve the robustness of the model, we suggest that placing a word correction model(Pruthi et al., 2019) before BERT would be beneficial.

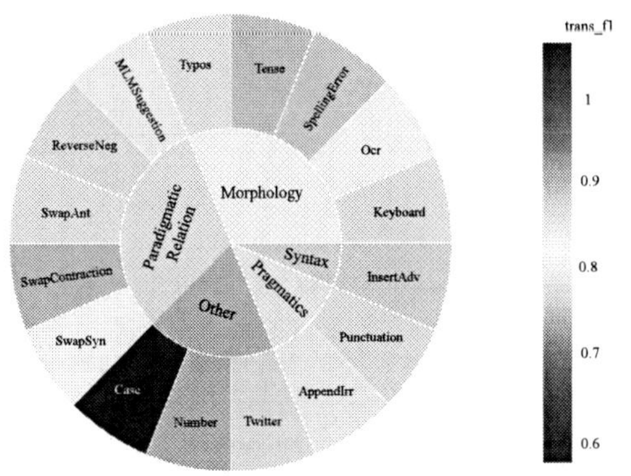

Figure 5: Robustness report of BERT base model on CONLL2003 dataset, where trans_f1 denotes the F1-score of target model on the transformed test data.

Case 2: Customized Evaluation For users who want to test model performance on specific aspects, they demand a customized transformed dataset of certain transformations or their combinations. In TextFlint, this could be achieved by modifying `Config`, which determines the configuration of TextFlint in generation. `Config` specifies the transformations being performed on the given dataset. It can be modified manually or generated automatically. By modifying the configuration, users could decide to generate multiple transformed samples on each original data sample, validate samples by semantics, preprocess samples with certain processors, and more.

Case 3: Target Model Improvement For users who want to improve the robustness of target models, they may work hard to inspect the weakness of a model with less alternative support. To tackle the issue, we believe a diagnostic report revealing the influence of comprehensive aspects on model performance will provide concrete suggestions on model improvement. By using TextFlint and applying a transformed dataset to target models, the transformations corresponding to significant performance decline in the evaluation report will provide guidance for improvements to the target models. Moreover, TextFlint supports adversarial training on target models with a large-scale transformed dataset, and the change of performance will also be reported to display performance gain due to adversarial training.

4 Benchmarking Existing Models with TextFlint

To verify the quality of transformation, we conducted human evaluation on the original and transformed texts under all of the mentioned transformations. Specifically, we considered two metrics in human evaluation: plausibility and gram-

Model	***RevTgt*** (Ori. → Trans.) Accuracy	Macro-F1	***RevNon*** (Ori. → Trans.) Accuracy	Macro-F1	***AddDiff*** (Ori. → Trans.) Accuracy	Macro-F1
Restaurant Dataset						
LSTM (Hochreiter et al., 1997)	84.42 → 19.30	55.75 → 19.88	85.91 → 73.42	55.02 → 44.69	84.42 → 44.63	55.75 → 33.24
TD-LSTM (Tang et al., 2016a)	86.42 → 22.42	61.92 → 22.28	87.29 → 79.58	60.70 → 53.35	84.42 → 81.35	61.92 → 55.69
ATAE-LSTM (Wang et al., 2016)	85.60 → 28.90	67.02 → 23.84	86.60 → 60.74	65.41 → 41.46	85.60 → 44.39	67.02 → 36.40
MemNet (Tang et al., 2016b)	81.46 → 19.30	54.57 → 17.77	83.68 → 72.95	55.39 → 45.14	81.46 → 63.62	54.57 → 39.36
IAN (Ma et al., 2017)	83.83 → 17.71	58.91 → 18.12	84.88 → 73.06	56.91 → 45.87	83.83 → 56.61	58.91 → 37.08
TNet (Li et al., 2018)	87.37 → 24.58	66.29 → 25.00	87.86 → 75.00	66.15 → 49.09	87.37 → 80.56	66.29 → 59.68
MGAN (Fan et al., 2018)	88.15 → 26.10	69.98 → 23.65	89.06 → 71.95	68.90 → 50.24	88.15 → 70.21	69.98 → 51.71
BERT-base (Devlin et al., 2019)	90.44 → 37.17	70.66 → 30.38	90.55 → 52.46	71.45 → 32.47	90.44 → 55.96	70.66 → 37.00
BERT+aspect (Devlin et al., 2019)	90.32 → 62.59	76.91 → 44.83	91.41 → 57.04	77.53 → 44.43	90.32 → 81.58	76.91 → 71.01
LCF-BERT (Zeng et al., 2019)	90.32 → 53.48	76.56 → 39.52	90.55 → 61.09	75.18 → 44.87	90.32 → 86.78	76.56 → 73.71
Average	86.83 → 31.16	65.86 → 26.63	87.78 → 67.73	64.96 → 45.15	86.83 → 66.55	65.86 → 49.49

Table 2: Accuracy and F1 score on the SemEval 2014 Restaurant dataset.

maticality[1]. For each of the transformed texts, three native speakers from Amazon Mechanical Turk were invited for evaluation, and the average score was recorded. For each kind of transformations (single one or a combination of two or more), 100 original-transformed text pairs were randomly selected for human evaluation. All of the 100,000 texts scored highly in terms of the two metrics. It was verified that the plausibility and grammaticality of the transformed texts, taking the data of SA and NER for example (Table 1), only dropped slightly compared with the original ones. Statistically, the average score of the grammaticality of the texts before and after transformation reported 3.947 and 3.825, respectively; the average of plausibility of original and transformed texts was 3.847 and 3.792, respectively. For the worst case where the grammaticality dropped the most, a decline of 1.03 from the original to the transformed text was from **Ocr** on ABSA task. The largest decline of plausibility, 0.48, was seen on the ***SwapSyn*** of CWS task.

We adopted TextFlint to evaluate hundreds of models of 12 tasks (including both English and Chinese tasks), covering various model frameworks and learning schemas, ranging from traditional feature-based machine learning approaches to state-of-the-art neural networks. All evaluated models and their implementations are available publicly. After model implementation, dataset transformation, and batch inspection, users will receive evaluation reports on various aspects, comprehensively analyzing the robustness of a system by acquiring larger test samples. From the evaluation reports, we can easily compare the model results of the original test set with those of the transformed set, spotting the main defects of the input model and identifying the model that performs the best or worst.

From the numerous evaluations and comparisons conducted by TextFlint, we have a thorough view of existing NLP systems and discovered underlying patterns about model robustness. As for the ABSA task (Table 2), methods equipped with pre-training LMs showed better performance than other models on the task-specific transformations, e.g., ***AddDiff***, where the accuracy score of BERT-Aspect dropped from 90.32 to merely 81.58. All the evaluation results and comprehensive robustness analysis are available at textflint.io.

5 Related Work

Our work is related to many existing open-source tools and works in different areas.

Robustness Evaluation Many tools include evaluation methods for robustness, including NLPAug (Ma, 2019), Errudite (Wu et al., 2019), AllenNLP Interpret (Wallace et al., 2019), and Checklist (Ribeiro et al., 2020), which are only applicable to limited parts of robustness evaluations, while TextFlint supports comprehensive evaluation methods, e.g., subpopulation, adversarial attacks, transformations, and so on. Besides the common transformation methods like synonym substitution and typos, various task-specific transformations are tailored for each of the 12 NLP tasks, which is peculiar to TextFlint. Moreover, we are the first to provide linguistic support for the transformations, the designs for which were inspired by linguistics and have been proved plausible and readable by human annotators.

Several tools also exist concerning robustness, which are similar to our work (Morris et al., 2020; Zeng et al., 2020; Goel et al., 2021) and include a

[1]The detailed scoring criteria are available at our website: `textflint.io`.

wide range of evaluation methods. However, these tools only focus on general generalization evaluations and lack quality evaluations on generated texts or only support automatic quality constraints. TextFlint supports both general and task-specific evaluations and guarantees the acceptability of each transformation method with human evaluations. In addition, TextFlint provides a standard report that can be displayed with visualization and tabulation. More importantly, all of the tools and modules are encapsulated within a unified framework, which completely differs from Robustness Gym (Goel et al., 2021), a simple aggregation of APIs of various tools including Checklist (Ribeiro et al., 2020) and Textattack (Morris et al., 2020). In addition, all of the transformations can be realized automatically by a simple modification to the configuration in TextFlint, while manually defined patterns are required by some of the functions in Robustness Gym.

Interpretability and Error Analysis Several works concern model evaluation from different perspectives. AllenNLP Interpret (Wallace et al., 2019), InterpreteML (Nori et al., 2019), LIT (Nori et al., 2019), Manifold (Zhang et al., 2018), and AIX360 (Arya et al., 2019) care about model interpretability in an attempt to understand the models' behavior through different evaluation methods. CrossCheck (Arendt et al., 2020), AllenNLP Interpret (Wallace et al., 2019), Errudite (Wu et al., 2019), and Manifold (Zhang et al., 2018) offer visualization and cross-model comparison for error analysis. TextFlint is differently motivated yet complementary with these works, which can provide comprehensive analyses on the models' defects, thus contributing to better model understanding.

6 Conclusion

We introduced TextFlint, a unified multilingual robustness evaluation toolkit that incorporates universal text transformation, task-specific transformation, adversarial attack, subpopulation, and their combinations to provide comprehensive robustness analyses. TextFlint enables practitioners to evaluate their models with just a few lines of code and then obtain complete analytical reports. Additionally, we also performed large-scale empirical evaluations on state-of-the-art deep learning models, classic supervised methods, and real-world systems, with all the experimental results reported on our website. Almost all models showed significant performance degradation, indicating the urgency and necessity of including robustness in NLP model evaluations.

Ethical Considerations

In consideration of ethical concerns, we provide the following detailed description:

(1) All of the transformed data comes from existing datasets, which are derived from public scientific papers. Due to the limited space, we detailed the characteristics of the dataset and the transformation methods in the README.md file at https://github.com/textflint/textflint.

(2) The quality of the transformed datasets will affect the credibility of the robustness evaluation. Compared with previous works, we additionally evaluated 100,000 samples from all of the transformation methods with respect to their plausibility and grammaticality by human evaluation.

(3) TextFlint is a robustness evaluation toolkit that does not provide any NLP models for specific tasks, such as automated essay scoring, hate speech, and so on. Therefore, there is no potential harm to vulnerable populations.

(4) Our work does not contain identity characteristics. It does not harm anyone.

(5) The subpopulation and transformation modules are executed on the CPU and do not consume a lot of computing resources. The AttackRecipe module is implemented based on TextAttack (Morris et al., 2020), which is a widely used framework for adversarial attacks and does not cause excessive computational cost.

Acknowledgements

The authors wish to thank the anonymous reviewers for their helpful comments. This work was partially funded by China National Key R&D Program (No. 2017YFB1002104), National Natural Science Foundation of China (No. 61976056, 62076069).

References

Dustin Arendt, Zhuanyi Huang, Prasha Shrestha, Ellyn Ayton, Maria Glenski, and Svitlana Volkova. 2020. Crosscheck: Rapid, reproducible, and interpretable model evaluation.

Vijay Arya, Rachel KE Bellamy, Pin-Yu Chen, Amit Dhurandhar, Michael Hind, Samuel C Hoffman, Stephanie Houde, Q Vera Liao, Ronny Luss,

Aleksandra Mojsilović, et al. 2019. One explanation does not fit all: A toolkit and taxonomy of ai explainability techniques. *arXiv preprint arXiv:1909.03012*.

Daniel Cer, Yinfei Yang, Sheng-yi Kong, Nan Hua, Nicole Limtiaco, Rhomni St. John, Noah Constant, Mario Guajardo-Cespedes, Steve Yuan, Chris Tar, Brian Strope, and Ray Kurzweil. 2018. Universal sentence encoder for English. In *Proceedings of the 2018 Conference on Empirical Methods in Natural Language Processing: System Demonstrations*, pages 169–174, Brussels, Belgium. Association for Computational Linguistics.

Jacob Devlin, Ming-Wei Chang, Kenton Lee, and Kristina Toutanova. 2019. Bert: Pre-training of deep bidirectional transformers for language understanding. In *Proceedings of the 2019 Conference of the North American Chapter of the Association for Computational Linguistics: Human Language Technologies, Volume 1 (Long and Short Papers)*, pages 4171–4186.

Feifan Fan, Yansong Feng, and Dongyan Zhao. 2018. Multi-grained attention network for aspect-level sentiment classification. In *Proceedings of the 2018 conference on empirical methods in natural language processing*, pages 3433–3442.

Robert Geirhos, Jörn-Henrik Jacobsen, Claudio Michaelis, Richard Zemel, Wieland Brendel, Matthias Bethge, and Felix A Wichmann. 2020. Shortcut learning in deep neural networks. *Nature Machine Intelligence*, 2(11):665–673.

Karan Goel, Nazneen Rajani, Jesse Vig, Samson Tan, Jason Wu, Stephan Zheng, Caiming Xiong, Mohit Bansal, and Christopher Ré. 2021. Robustness gym: Unifying the nlp evaluation landscape.

Sepp Hochreiter, Jürgen Schmidhuber, et al. 1997. Long short-term memory. *Neural computation*, 9(8):1735–1780.

Yoon Kim. 2014. Convolutional neural networks for sentence classification. In *Proceedings of the 2014 Conference on Empirical Methods in Natural Language Processing (EMNLP)*, pages 1746–1751, Doha, Qatar. Association for Computational Linguistics.

Linyang Li, Ruotian Ma, Qipeng Guo, Xiangyang Xue, and Xipeng Qiu. 2020. Bert-attack: Adversarial attack against bert using bert. In *Proceedings of the 2020 Conference on Empirical Methods in Natural Language Processing (EMNLP)*, pages 6193–6202.

Xin Li, Lidong Bing, Wai Lam, and Bei Shi. 2018. Transformation networks for target-oriented sentiment classification. In *Proceedings of the 56th Annual Meeting of the Association for Computational Linguistics (Volume 1: Long Papers)*, pages 946–956.

Dehong Ma, Sujian Li, Xiaodong Zhang, and Houfeng Wang. 2017. Interactive attention networks for aspect-level sentiment classification. In *Proceedings of the 26th International Joint Conference on Artificial Intelligence*, pages 4068–4074.

Edward Ma. 2019. Nlp augmentation. https://github.com/makcedward/nlpaug.

John Miller, Karl Krauth, Benjamin Recht, and Ludwig Schmidt. 2020. The effect of natural distribution shift on question answering models. In *International Conference on Machine Learning*, pages 6905–6916. PMLR.

John X Morris, Eli Lifland, Jin Yong Yoo, and Yanjun Qi. 2020. Textattack: A framework for adversarial attacks in natural language processing. *arXiv preprint arXiv:2005.05909*.

Harsha Nori, Samuel Jenkins, Paul Koch, and Rich Caruana. 2019. Interpretml: A unified framework for machine learning interpretability.

Kishore Papineni, Salim Roukos, Todd Ward, and Wei-Jing Zhu. 2002. Bleu: a method for automatic evaluation of machine translation. In *Proceedings of the 40th Annual Meeting of the Association for Computational Linguistics*, pages 311–318, Philadelphia, Pennsylvania, USA. Association for Computational Linguistics.

Danish Pruthi, Bhuwan Dhingra, and Zachary C. Lipton. 2019. Combating adversarial misspellings with robust word recognition. In *Proceedings of the 57th Annual Meeting of the Association for Computational Linguistics*, pages 5582–5591, Florence, Italy. Association for Computational Linguistics.

Alec Radford, Jeffrey Wu, Rewon Child, David Luan, Dario Amodei, and Ilya Sutskever. 2019. Language models are unsupervised multitask learners. *OpenAI blog*, 1(8):9.

Marco Tulio Ribeiro, Tongshuang Wu, Carlos Guestrin, and Sameer Singh. 2020. Beyond accuracy: Behavioral testing of NLP models with CheckList. In *Proceedings of the 58th Annual Meeting of the Association for Computational Linguistics*, pages 4902–4912, Online. Association for Computational Linguistics.

Duyu Tang, Bing Qin, Xiaocheng Feng, and Ting Liu. 2016a. Effective lstms for target-dependent sentiment classification. In *Proceedings of COLING 2016, the 26th International Conference on Computational Linguistics: Technical Papers*, pages 3298–3307.

Duyu Tang, Bing Qin, and Ting Liu. 2016b. Aspect level sentiment classification with deep memory network. In *Proceedings of the 2016 Conference on Empirical Methods in Natural Language Processing*, pages 214–224.

Erik F. Tjong Kim Sang and Fien De Meulder. 2003. Introduction to the CoNLL-2003 shared task: Language-independent named entity recognition. In *Proceedings of the Seventh Conference on Natural Language Learning at HLT-NAACL 2003*, pages 142–147.

Eric Wallace, Jens Tuyls, Junlin Wang, Sanjay Subramanian, Matt Gardner, and Sameer Singh. 2019. AllenNLP interpret: A framework for explaining predictions of NLP models. In *Proceedings of the 2019 Conference on Empirical Methods in Natural Language Processing and the 9th International Joint Conference on Natural Language Processing (EMNLP-IJCNLP): System Demonstrations*, pages 7–12, Hong Kong, China. Association for Computational Linguistics.

Yequan Wang, Minlie Huang, Xiaoyan Zhu, and Li Zhao. 2016. Attention-based lstm for aspect-level sentiment classification. In *Proceedings of the 2016 conference on empirical methods in natural language processing*, pages 606–615.

Tongshuang Wu, Marco Tulio Ribeiro, Jeffrey Heer, and Daniel S Weld. 2019. Errudite: Scalable, reproducible, and testable error analysis. In *Proceedings of the 57th Annual Meeting of the Association for Computational Linguistics*, pages 747–763.

Xiaoyu Xing, Zhijing Jin, Di Jin, Bingning Wang, Qi Zhang, and Xuan-Jing Huang. 2020. Tasty burgers, soggy fries: Probing aspect robustness in aspect-based sentiment analysis. In *Proceedings of the 2020 Conference on Empirical Methods in Natural Language Processing (EMNLP)*, pages 3594–3605.

Biqing Zeng, Heng Yang, Ruyang Xu, Wu Zhou, and Xuli Han. 2019. Lcf: A local context focus mechanism for aspect-based sentiment classification. *Applied Sciences*, 9(16):3389.

Guoyang Zeng, Fanchao Qi, Qianrui Zhou, Tingji Zhang, Bairu Hou, Yuan Zang, Zhiyuan Liu, and Maosong Sun. 2020. Openattack: An open-source textual adversarial attack toolkit. *arXiv preprint arXiv:2009.09191*.

Jiawei Zhang, Yang Wang, Piero Molino, Lezhi Li, and David S Ebert. 2018. Manifold: A model-agnostic framework for interpretation and diagnosis of machine learning models. *IEEE transactions on visualization and computer graphics*, 25(1):364–373.

Stretch-VST: Getting Flexible With Visual Stories

Chi-Yang Hsu[1,3]*, Yun-Wei Chu[2]*, Tsai-Lun Yang[3], Ting-Hao (Kenneth) Huang[1], Lun-Wei Ku[3]
Pennsylvania State University [1], Purdue University [2],
Institute of Information Science, Academia Sinica[3]
{cxh5438, txh710}@psu.edu
{chu198}@purdue.edu
{a7532ariel, lwku}@iis.sinica.edu.tw

Abstract

In visual storytelling, a short story is generated based on a given image sequence. Despite years of work, most visual storytelling models remain limited in terms of the generated stories' fixed length: most models produce stories with exactly five sentences because five sentence stories dominate the training data. The fix-length stories carry limited details and provide ambiguous textual information to the readers. Therefore, we propose to "stretch" the stories, which create the potential to present in-depth visual details. This paper presents **Stretch-VST**, a visual storytelling framework that enables the generation of prolonged stories by adding appropriate knowledge, which is selected by the proposed scoring function. We propose a length-controlled Transformer to generate long stories. This model introduces novel positional encoding methods to maintain story quality with lengthy inputs. Experiments confirm that long stories are generated without deteriorating the quality. The human evaluation further shows that Stretch-VST can provide better focus and detail when stories are prolonged compared to the state of the art. The demo video is available on Youtube[1], and the live demo can be found on website[2].

1 Introduction

Visual storytelling (VIST) is an interdisciplinary task that takes a sequence of photos as input and produces a corresponding short story as output (Huang et al., 2016). Prior work explores either end-to-end or hierarchical methods for visual storytelling, but machine-generated stories still fall far short of human-generated stories. One obvious limitation is the inability to generate stories with diverse length, especially to prolong a story. In real-world applications, when pictures accompany textual stories, the number of sentences is often much greater than the number of images. Recent visual storytelling frameworks demonstrate the potential in prolonging visual stories, such as KG-Story (Hsu et al., 2020), a state-of-the-art framework that uses a knowledge graph to generate one additional sentence and attach it to 5-sentence visual stories for improved coherence. However, current models, including KG-Story, are incapable of further "stretching" stories beyond five or six sentences. In short, generating prolonged visual stories faces three main hurdles: First, as VIST—the only existing visual storytelling dataset—is mostly constructed as 5-photo sequences paired with 5-sentence stories, models trained on it easily overfit to the dominant length. Second, in visual storytelling, the quality of the textual story must be maintained when asking the model for more context. Third, the model's generation function must generate stories with the desired number of sentences. That is, control of the continuation and termination of natural language generation depends on a given length factor.

To meet these challenges, we introduce Stretch-VST, a modification of the KG-Story framework that greatly increases the number of sentences in visual stories while maintaining the quality thereof. Story coherence and detail are improved by using cohesive and relevant information to generate additional sentences. Illustrated in Fig. 1, Stretch-VST has three main stages: First, it extracts representative terms (e.g., actions or objects) from each image. Second, it finds relations between consecutive images using a knowledge graph, after which a scoring model selects the most suitable subset of terms ("term set" hereafter) given its length, term semantics, and cohesion. The length of the term set for the resultant term sequence hence depends

* denotes equal contribution

[1]Demo video: https://youtu.be/-uF8IV6T1NU

[2]Live demo website: https://doraemon.iis.sinica.edu.tw/acldemo/index.html

Proceedings of the Joint Conference of the 59th Annual Meeting of the Association for Computational Linguistics and the 11th International Joint Conference on Natural Language Processing: System Demonstrations, pages 356–362, August 1st - August 6th, 2021.

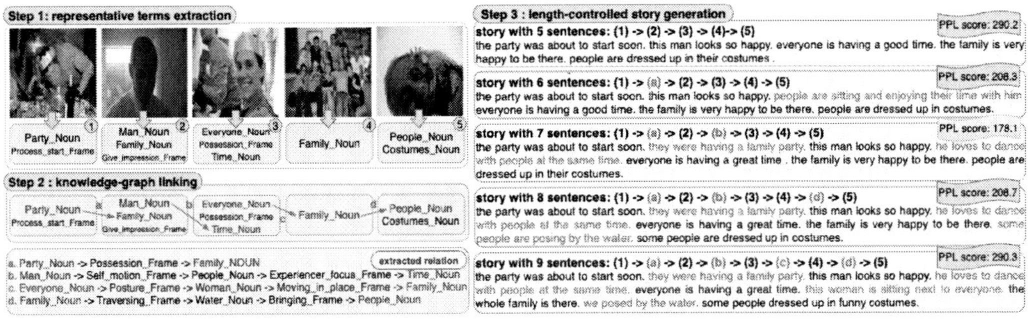

Figure 1: Stretch-VST extracts representative key terms (e.g., objects, people, and actions) from each image, and uses knowledge graphs to further expand the term set. For any arbitrary subset of terms, Stretch-VST can generate a story for it: the longer the term set, the longer the output story. The framework generates stories from 5 to 9 sentences long, and selects the best story with the lowest term perplexity (PPL score).

on the score. Finally, a length-controlled Transformer is used to generate the story given the term sequence.

The proposed work generates a variable number of sentences, and finds the optimal subset of terms given the story length. The human evaluation shows that Stretch-VST generates better stories when prolonging stories, provides more detailed information comparing 5-sentence stories, and is more robust in cohering story context when the images are incoherent.

2 Related Work

Visual storytelling was proposed by Huang et al. (2016). Two lines of work explore this task: one focuses on model architecture for better story generation (Hsu et al., 2018; Gonzalez-Rico and Pineda, 2018; Kim et al., 2018; Huang et al., 2019; Jung et al., 2020; Wang et al., 2020), and the other uses adversarial training to generate more diverse stories (Chen et al., 2017; Wang et al., 2018a,b; Hu et al., 2020). However, these methods often overfit to the number of sentences in the stories. Stretch-VST modifies both the source and generation modules to generate variable-length stories. On the source side, we use knowledge graphs to expand the term set to represent the input image sequence. Integrating a knowledge graph into language generation is beneficial (LoBue and Yates, 2011; Bowman et al., 2015; Hayashi et al., 2020; Zhang et al., 2017; Zhou et al., 2018; Yang et al., 2019; Guan et al., 2019). On the generation side, some explore the use of relative positional encoding (Takase and Okazaki, 2019), adding embedding layers, and manipulating the beam search process (Kikuchi et al., 2016). However, these methods control only the number of words and not the number of sentences.

3 Methodology

With variable-length visual sorytelling, Stretch-VST brings two major contributions for VIST: enriching the ingredients as desired (Sect. 3.1) and enabling story generation according to the term sequence length (Sect. 3.2).

3.1 Expanding and Scoring Term Sequences

Prolonging Term Sequences Drawing from KG-Story (Hsu et al., 2020), we utilize their Transformer-based model to distill the representative terms (e.g., nouns and frames) for each image. Stretch-VST manipulates term sequence lengths to increase the story lengths. For every two consecutive images, we choose whether to insert a relation into the term sequence; hence, the sequence length ranges from 5 to 9, as illustrated in Fig. 1. Given 5 images, we define the image-extracted original term sequence as $\{m_1^1, ..., m_i^t, ..., m_{N_5}^5\}$, where $\{m_1^1, ..., m_{N_1}^1\}$ denotes first image's term set, m_i^t denotes the i-th term from image t and N_k is the number of terms from image k. From consecutive images, we explore all possible relations (m_i^t, r, m_j^{t+1}) and $(m_i^t, r_1, m_{middle}, r_2, m_j^{t+1})$, where m_{middle} denotes a knowledge graph entity that bridges m_i^t and m_j^{t+1}. The chosen relation is inserted into the original term sequence. For every 5 term sets generated from the images, the model can insert an additional 0 to 4 term sets, resulting in 5 to 9 term sets in total. Moreover, if no relation can be found between two consecutive images, we also attempt to find a relation in the reverse direction, as well as relations between cross images. That is, we include (m_i^{t+1}, r, m_j^t), (m_i^t, r, m_j^{t+n}), and also these for two-hop relations. Furthermore, we also applied an image-grounded relation filtering, which is to ensure the predicted terms appear in the image. This prevents the model from generate irrelevant terms. Note that KG-Story is unable to expand or manipulate the size of the term set, and can only produce 6-sentence stories.

Rating Prolonged Term Sequences We implement a Transformer with a masked language model objective (Devlin et al., 2019). We use spaCy [3], Open Sesame (Swayamdipta et al., 2017), and the FrameNet parser (Baker et al., 1998) to convert the story text to term sequences. We iteratively mask one position in the overall term sequence to train the Transformer model. Then, for every possible term, we calculate the average perplexity of it with a mask at each position. The term sequence with the best (lowest) average perplexity is used in the next stage to generate stories as

$$\mathrm{P}(m') = \mathrm{F}(m'|m_1^1, ..., m_{N_m}^{N_M}), \quad (1)$$

$$\mathrm{PPL}(m') = \mathrm{P}(m')^{-\frac{1}{N_m}}, \quad (2)$$

$$score = \frac{1}{N_m}\sum_{i=1}^{N_m} \mathrm{PPL}(m_i), \quad (3)$$

where m' is the masked term, N_M is the number of term sets, N_m is the number of terms in the sequence, F is the Transformer language model, and PPL denotes perplexity.

3.2 Generating Stories From Term Sequences

Most story generation models generate only 5-sentence stories, regardless of the input length; story quality usually decays when generating longer stories (Guo et al., 2018). To this end, we propose a length-controlled Transformer model structure with unique positional encoding and history embedding to reflect the prolonged input length, prevent story decay, and maintain topic coherence. The model flowchart is shown in Fig. 2.

Length-Controlled Transformer To generate a story depending on the term sequence length, a Transformer (Vaswani et al., 2017) is used as a next-sentence generator to generate a story sentence by sentence. Generating sentence s_x, the model is given a history embedding H_x and all

[3] SpaCy: https://spacy.io/

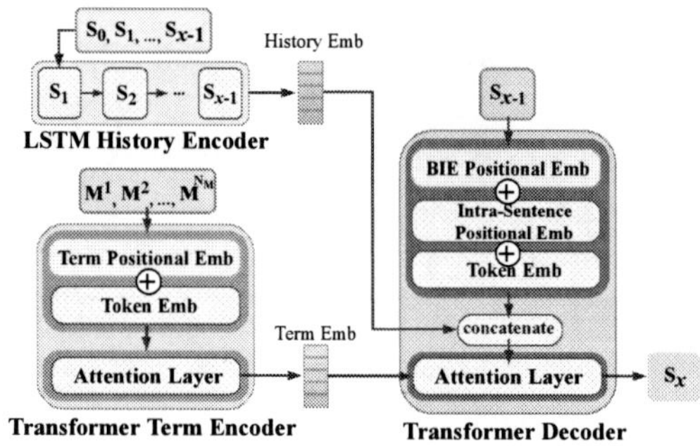

Figure 2: Flowchart for length-controlled Transformer. When generating sentence s_x, the model is input $(s_0, s_1, ..., s_{x-1})$, $(M^1, M^2, ..., M^{N_M})$, and s_{x-1}.

images' term sets $M^1, ..., M^{N_M}$, where $H_x = LSTM(s_0, ..., s_{x-1})$, denotes a history embedding for all previous sentences, generated from a LSTM layer; $M^t = \{m_1^t, ..., m_{N_m}^t\}$ denotes the set of N_m terms belonging to image t. Given an expanded term sequence with N_M term sets, the model generates N_M times to obtain a story consisting of N_M sentences.

Positional Encoding In 5-sentence VIST training dataset, most stories only contain sentence position up to 5. When generating such stories, naive absolute positional encoding (Vaswani et al., 2017) doesn't handle positions larger than 5, thus, story quality decays accordingly. To this end, we introduce term positional encoding and beginning-inside-ending (BIE) positional encoding to reflect diverse input lengths. Term positional encoding is implemented in the Transformer encoder to inform the model of the current term position. While generating sentence x, the model sets input term set M^x's position to 1 and masks $M^1, ..., M^{x-1}, M^{x+1}, ..., M^{N_M}$ as 0. In addition, BIE positional encoding is implemented in the Transformer decoder to focus on the beginning and the end of the story while generalizing the sentences in between. Specifically, we assign position 1 and 3 to the first and last sentence, and position 2 to the sentences in the middle.

4 System Interface

Fig. 3 illustrates the user interface of Stretch-VST. We create a webpage for users to (A) search a story by story ID or (B) search for stories by keyword.

In Fig.4(a), our user interface displays five images of the selected album and the visual story with recommended length generated by Stretch-

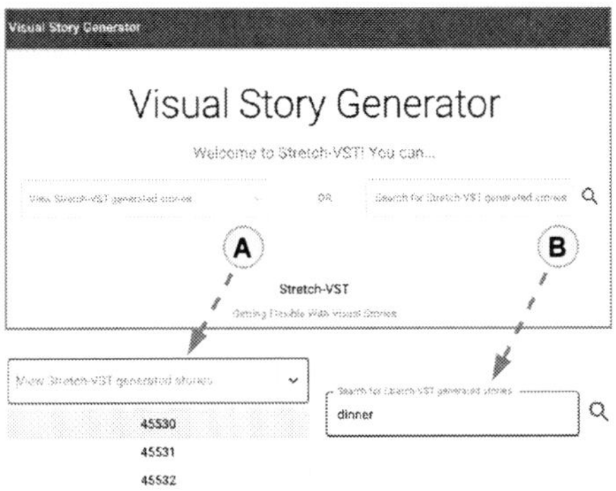

Figure 3: User interface of Stretch-VST. User can (A) select an story ID from the drop-down menu or (B) search a stories by keywords.

Figure 4: (a) The panel will show 5 images and visual story with recommended length. User can (b) drag the bar-slider and select the desired length of visual story.

VST. The recommended story length is decided by our scoring model (Sect. 3.1). Users can also drag the bar-slider to select the desired story length (Fig. 4(b)). For the keyword search, the user interface displays several images and story snippets for search results, and the searching algorithm is an elastic search.(Fig. 5(a)). Likewise, the panel will display the images, visual story, and the recommended story length (Fig. 5(b)), and users can also select the desired story length.

5 Experimental Results

5.1 Evaluation Methods and Baselines

Per the literature (Wang et al., 2018a), human evaluation is the most reliable way to evaluate the quality of visual stories; automatic metrics often do

Figure 5: (a) The panel will provide several snippets of visual stories that contain the keyword (e.g, *dinner* in the story). (b) Selected a snippet, the panel will show the visual story with the recommended length. User can also drag the bar-slider to select desired story length.

not align faithfully to human judgment (Hsu et al., 2019). Therefore, we conducted human evaluations to assess the quality of stories generated by Stretch-VST. We randomly selected 250 stories and evaluated each by five different workers on Amazon Mechanical Turk. Each worker was presented with the image sequence and its corresponding stories generated by different models and asked to rank the stories. In addition, we also conduct a questionnaire asking annotators "what makes the story better", based on the 6 criteria set by VIST dataset (Huang et al., 2016). These criteria include focus, coherence, shareability, humanness, grounding, and detail. We used the same datasets and knowledge graphs as Hsu et al. (2020), and compared the proposed method with three baselines for visual storytelling: AREL (Wang et al., 2018a), GLAC (Kim et al., 2018), and KG-Story (Hsu et al., 2020). Note that we did not compare the results with KG-Story in Sect. 5.3 and 5.4, as its generation model neither handles diverse inputs nor controls the length.

5.2 Generating Optimal-Length Stories

First, we evaluate the ability of Stretch-VST to generate better and longer stories. Given 5 candidate sequences with distinct lengths from 5 to 9, we

	Rank	#1st rank	#Sentences	#Tokens
VIST(Sect. 4.1)				
AREL	2.47	274	5.00	41.99
GLAC	2.60	258	5.00	35.32
KG-Story	2.51	297	5.81	44.13
Stretch-VST	**2.41**	**421**	6.22	69.74
VIST w/ incoherent image (Sect. 4.2)				
AREL	2.04	364	3.00	25.41
GLAC	2.08	375	3.00	22.37
Stretch-VST	**1.87**	**511**	3.83	41.56

Table 1: Average rankings (1 to 4, lower is better) and number 1st ranked stories (larger is better) rated by human judges, along with average number of sentences and tokens per story. (ρ value < 0.05, N=250)

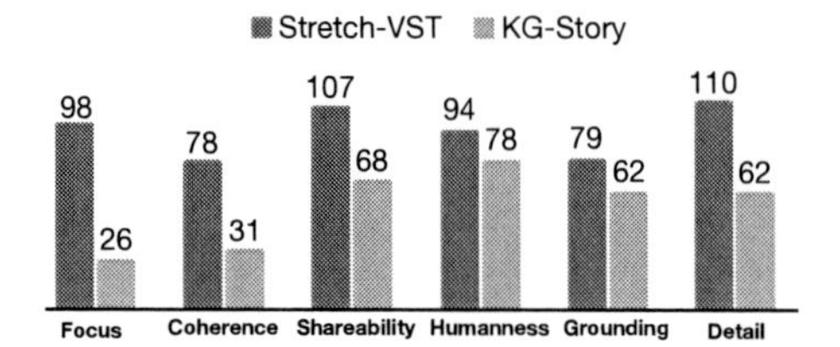

Figure 6: Aspect-wise votes for Stretch-VST and KG-Story's first-place stories collected via the questionnaire.

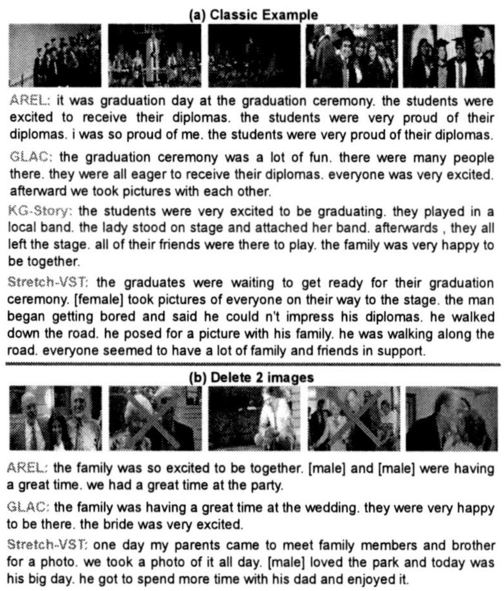

Figure 7: (a) Example visual stories generated by baselines and Stretch-VST. (b) Stories with fewer images from baseline models and Stretch-VST.

selected the best sequence of terms with the lowest perplexity as the material to tell the visual story, as described in Sect. 3.1. The resulting average number of sentences in the generated stories was 6.22; that is, the proposed model tends to add one or two relations to enrich the original story.

The average ranking results, shown in the first row of Table 1 are better than baseline models. This indicates the proposed stories are superior to those from the baseline. Figure 6 shows the questionnaire result for the best-ranked stories. For Stretch-VST and KG-Story's best-ranked stories, the Stretch-VST story counts are generally higher in all aspects; specifically, *Detailed*, *Coherence*, and *Focused* are significantly higher. As our stories contain more sentences than KGStory, the stories are undoubtedly more detailed. Additionally, the increase of stories' coherence indicates the advantage of our multiple term set insertion as compare to KGStory's single insertion. While the prolonging stories are beneficial to detailed and coherence, we also found that story prolongation is beneficial to topic-focus. We presume the increase number of relevant sentences can improve the focus. Note that we did not use automatic metrics for evaluation because these metrics do not indicate the quality of visual stories (Wang et al., 2018b; Hsu et al., 2019). Figure 7(a) compares stories generated from Stretch-VST to stories from the baselines.

5.3 Robustness to Incoherent Images

Next, we evaluated the robustness of the proposed method story coherence by deleting the second and fourth of the five input images. The second column of Table 1 shows that Stretch-VST brings together the diverse contents to generate the best story context even when the input is disrupted. Figure 7(b) is an example of such input disruption. Although removing two images creates an incoherence in the photo sequence, Stretch-VST makes the best of the knowledge graph to fill this gap and generate a coherent story.

5.4 Robustness to Overstretched Stories

Without changing the input image sequences, does forcing a model to generate longer stories decrease the story quality? As no existing method generates longer visual stories with a fixed number of input images, we selected a strong Transformer baseline that incorporates the length-controlling mechanism proposed in (Kikuchi et al., 2016) as a baseline for comparison. The baseline model takes the term sequence and the desired length as the encoder input. After forwarding the encoder output to the decoder, we obtain the baseline story from the decoder's output. The result in Fig. 8 shows that Stretch-VST is

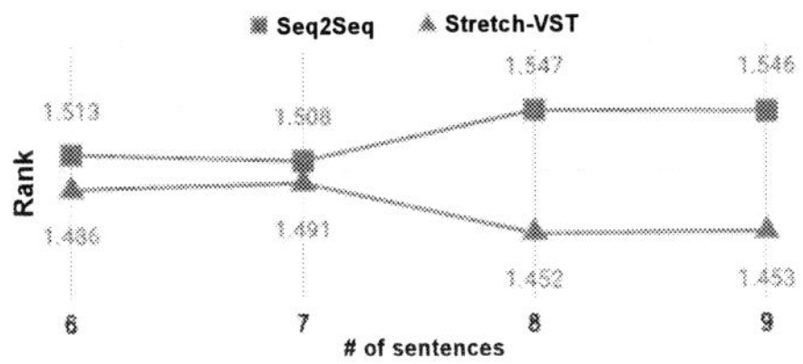

Figure 8: Average rankings between Stretch-VST and baseline for prolonged stories.

better at generating longer sentence story than our baseline model.

6 Conclusion

We propose a novel method for generating length-controlled visual stories which includes an enhanced knowledge-graph reasoning module and a length-controlled Transformer architecture. Using human evaluations, we show that the method tells longer and better stories.

7 Ethical Considerations

Although our research aims to produce stories that are vivid, engaging, and innocent, we are aware of the possibilities of utilizing a similar approach to generate inappropriate text (e.g., violent, racial, or gender-insensitive stories). The proposed visual storytelling technology enables people to generate stories rapidly based on photo sequences at scale, which could also be used with malicious intent, for example, to concoct fake stories using real images. Finally, as the proposed methods use external knowledge graphs, they reflect the issues, risks, and biases of such information sources. Mitigating these potential risks will require continued research.

8 Acknowledgements

This research is supported by Ministry of Science and Technology, Taiwan under the project contract 108-2221-E-001-012-MY3 and 108-2923-E-001-001-MY2 and the Seed Grant from the College of Information Sciences and Technology (IST), Pennsylvania State University. We also thank the crowd workers for participating in this project.

References

Collin F. Baker, C. Fillmore, and J. Lowe. 1998. The berkeley framenet project. In *COLING-ACL*.

Samuel R. Bowman, Gabor Angeli, Christopher Potts, and Christopher D. Manning. 2015. A large annotated corpus for learning natural language inference. In *EMNLP*.

Zhiqian Chen, Xuchao Zhang, Arnold P. Boedihardjo, Jing Dai, and Chang-Tien Lu. 2017. Multimodal storytelling via generative adversarial imitation learning. *ArXiv*, abs/1712.01455.

J. Devlin, Ming-Wei Chang, Kenton Lee, and Kristina Toutanova. 2019. Bert: Pre-training of deep bidirectional transformers for language understanding. In *NAACL-HLT*.

Diana Gonzalez-Rico and Gibran Fuentes Pineda. 2018. Contextualize, show and tell: A neural visual storyteller. *ArXiv*, abs/1806.00738.

Jian Guan, Yansen Wang, and Minlie Huang. 2019. Story ending generation with incremental encoding and commonsense knowledge. In *AAAI*.

Jiaxian Guo, S. Lu, Han Cai, W. Zhang, Y. Yu, and J. Wang. 2018. Long text generation via adversarial training with leaked information. In *AAAI*.

Hiroaki Hayashi, Zecong Hu, Chenyan Xiong, and Graham Neubig. 2020. Latent relation language models. In *AAAI*.

Chao-Chun Hsu, Szu-Min Chen, Ming-Hsun Hsieh, and Lun-Wei Ku. 2018. Using inter-sentence diverse beam search to reduce redundancy in visual storytelling. *ArXiv*, abs/1805.11867.

Chao-Chun Hsu, Zi-Yuan Chen, Chi-Yang Hsu, Chih-Chia Li, Tzu-Yuan Lin, Ting-Hao Kenneth Huang, and Lun-Wei Ku. 2020. Knowledge-enriched visual storytelling. *ArXiv*, abs/1912.01496.

Ting-Yao Hsu, Huang Chieh-Yang, Yen-Chia Hsu, and Ting-Hao Kenneth Huang. 2019. Visual story post-editing. In *ACL*.

J. Hu, Yu Cheng, Zhe Gan, J. Liu, Jianfeng Gao, and Graham Neubig. 2020. What makes a good story? designing composite rewards for visual storytelling. *ArXiv*, abs/1909.05316.

Qiuyuan Huang, Zhe Gan, A. Çelikyilmaz, Dapeng Wu, J. Wang, and X. He. 2019. Hierarchically structured reinforcement learning for topically coherent visual story generation. *ArXiv*, abs/1805.08191.

Ting-Hao Kenneth Huang, Francis Ferraro, N. Mostafazadeh, Ishan Misra, Aishwarya Agrawal, J. Devlin, Ross B. Girshick, X. He, P. Kohli, Dhruv Batra, C. L. Zitnick, Devi Parikh, Lucy Vanderwende, Michel Galley, and Margaret Mitchell. 2016. Visual storytelling. In *HLT-NAACL*.

Y. Jung, Dahun Kim, S. Woo, Kyungsu Kim, Sungjin Kim, and I. Kweon. 2020. Hide-and-tell: Learning to bridge photo streams for visual storytelling. *ArXiv*, abs/2002.00774.

Yuta Kikuchi, Graham Neubig, Ryohei Sasano, Hiroya Takamura, and M. Okumura. 2016. Controlling output length in neural encoder-decoders. *ArXiv*, abs/1609.09552.

Taehyeong Kim, Min-Oh Heo, Seonil Son, Kyoung-Wha Park, and B. Zhang. 2018. Glac net: Glocal attention cascading networks for multi-image cued story generation. *ArXiv*, abs/1805.10973.

Peter LoBue and A. Yates. 2011. Types of commonsense knowledge needed for recognizing textual entailment. In *ACL*.

Swabha Swayamdipta, Sam Thomson, Chris Dyer, and Noah A. Smith. 2017. Frame-semantic parsing with softmax-margin segmental rnns and a syntactic scaffold. *ArXiv*, abs/1706.09528.

Sho Takase and Naoaki Okazaki. 2019. Positional encoding to control output sequence length. In *NAACL-HLT*.

Ashish Vaswani, Noam M. Shazeer, Niki Parmar, Jakob Uszkoreit, Llion Jones, Aidan N. Gomez, Lukasz Kaiser, and Illia Polosukhin. 2017. Attention is all you need. *ArXiv*, abs/1706.03762.

Jing Wang, J. Fu, J. Tang, Zechao Li, and Tao Mei. 2018a. Show, reward and tell: Automatic generation of narrative paragraph from photo stream by adversarial training. In *AAAI*.

Ruize Wang, Zhongyu Wei, Piji Li, Qi Zhang, and X. Huang. 2020. Storytelling from an image stream using scene graphs. In *AAAI*.

Xin Eric Wang, Wenhu Chen, Y. Wang, and William Yang Wang. 2018b. No metrics are perfect: Adversarial reward learning for visual storytelling. *ArXiv*, abs/1804.09160.

Pengcheng Yang, Lei Li, Fuli Luo, Tianyu Liu, and Xu Sun. 2019. Enhancing topic-to-essay generation with external commonsense knowledge. In *ACL*.

Sheng Zhang, Rachel Rudinger, Kevin Duh, and Benjamin Van Durme. 2017. Ordinal common-sense inference. *Transactions of the Association for Computational Linguistics*, 5:379–395.

Hao Zhou, Tom Young, Minlie Huang, Haizhou Zhao, J. Xu, and Xiaoyan Zhu. 2018. Commonsense knowledge aware conversation generation with graph attention. In *IJCAI*.

OpenAttack: An Open-source Textual Adversarial Attack Toolkit

Guoyang Zeng[1,2*], **Fanchao Qi**[1,2*], **Qianrui Zhou**[1,2], **Tingji Zhang**[1,2], **Zixian Ma**[4†], **Bairu Hou**[2,5], **Yuan Zang**[1,2], **Zhiyuan Liu**[1,2,3‡], **Maosong Sun**[1,2,3]

[1]Department of Computer Science and Technology, Tsinghua University, Beijing, China
[2]Beijing National Research Center for Information Science and Technology
[3]Institute for Artificial Intelligence, Tsinghua University, Beijing, China
[4]Stanford University [5]School of Economics and Management, Tsinghua University
zenggy@mail.tsinghua.edu.cn, qfc17@mails.tsinghua.edu.cn

Abstract

Textual adversarial attacking has received wide and increasing attention in recent years. Various attack models have been proposed, which are enormously distinct and implemented with different programming frameworks and settings. These facts hinder quick utilization and fair comparison of attack models. In this paper, we present an open-source textual adversarial attack toolkit named OpenAttack to solve these issues. Compared with existing other textual adversarial attack toolkits, OpenAttack has its unique strengths in support for all attack types, multilinguality, and parallel processing. Currently, OpenAttack includes 15 typical attack models that cover all attack types. Its highly inclusive modular design not only supports quick utilization of existing attack models, but also enables great flexibility and extensibility. OpenAttack has broad uses including comparing and evaluating attack models, measuring robustness of a model, assisting in developing new attack models, and adversarial training. Source code and documentation can be obtained at https://github.com/thunlp/OpenAttack.

1 Introduction

Deep neural networks (DNNs) have been found to be susceptible to adversarial attacks (Szegedy et al., 2014; Goodfellow et al., 2015). The attacker uses adversarial examples, which are maliciously crafted by imposing small perturbations on original input, to fool the victim model. With the wide application of DNNs to practical systems accompanied by growing concern about their security, research on adversarial attacking has become increasingly important. Moreover, adversarial attacks are also helpful to improve robustness and interpretability of DNNs (Wallace et al., 2019a).

In the field of natural language processing (NLP), diverse adversarial attack models have been proposed (Zhang et al., 2020). These models vary in *accessibility* to the victim model (ranging from having full knowledge to total ignorance) and *perturbation level* (character-, word- or sentence-level). In addition, they are originally proposed to attack different victim models on different NLP tasks under different evaluation protocols.

This immense diversity causes serious difficulty for fair and apt comparison between different attack models, which is unfavourable to the development of textual adversarial attacking. Further, although most attack models are open-source, they use different programming frameworks and settings, which lead to unnecessary time and effort when implementing them.

To tackle these challenges, a textual adversarial attacking toolkit named TextAttack (Morris et al., 2020) has been developed. It implements several textual adversarial attack models under a unified framework and provides interfaces for utilizing existing attack models or designing new attack models. So far, TextAttack has attracted considerable attention and facilitated the birth of new attack models such as BAE (Garg and Ramakrishnan, 2020).

In this paper, we present OpenAttack, which is also an open-source toolkit for textual adversarial attacking. Similar to TextAttack, OpenAttack adopts modular design to assemble various attack models, in order to enable quick implementation of existing or new attack models. But OpenAttack is different from and complementary to TextAttack mainly in the following three aspects:

(1) **Support for all attacks**. TextAttack utilizes a relatively rigorous framework to unify different attack models. However, this framework is naturally not suitable for sentence-level adversarial attacks,

*Indicates equal contribution
†Work done during internship at Tsinghua University
‡Corresponding author. Email: liuzy@tsinghua.edu.cn

Proceedings of the Joint Conference of the 59th Annual Meeting of the Association for Computational Linguistics and the 11th International Joint Conference on Natural Language Processing: System Demonstrations, pages 363–371, August 1st - August 6th, 2021.

Model	Accessibility	Perturbation	Main Idea
SEA (Ribeiro et al., 2018)	Decision	Sentence	Rule-based paraphrasing
SCPN (Iyyer et al., 2018)	Blind	Sentence	Paraphrasing
GAN (Zhao et al., 2018)	Decision	Sentence	Text generation by encoder-decoder
TextFooler (Jin et al., 2020)	Score	Word	Greedy word substitution
PWWS (Ren et al., 2019)	Score	Word	Greedy word substitution
Genetic (Alzantot et al., 2018)	Score	Word	Genetic algorithm-based word substitution
SememePSO (Zang et al., 2020)	Score	Word	Particle swarm optimization-based word substitution
BERT-ATTACK (Li et al., 2020)	Score	Word	Greedy contextualized word substitution
BAE (Garg and Ramakrishnan, 2020)	Score	Word	Greedy contextualized word substitution and insertion
FD (Papernot et al., 2016b)	Gradient	Word	Gradient-based word substitution
TextBugger (Li et al., 2019)	Gradient, Score	Word+Char	Greedy word substitution and character manipulation
UAT (Wallace et al., 2019a)	Gradient	Word, Char	Gradient-based word or character manipulation
HotFlip (Ebrahimi et al., 2018)	Gradient	Word, Char	Gradient-based word or character substitution
VIPER (Eger et al., 2019)	Blind	Char	Visually similar character substitution
DeepWordBug (Gao et al., 2018)	Score	Char	Greedy character manipulation

Table 1: Textual adversarial attack models involved in `OpenAttack`, among which the three sentence-level models SEA, SCPN and GAN together with FD, UAT and VIPER are not included in TextAttack for now. "Accessibility" is the accessibility to the victim model, and "Perturbation" refers to perturbation level. "Sentence", "Word" and "Char" denote sentence-, word- and character-level perturbations. In the columns of Accessibility and Perturbation, "A, B" means that the attack model supports both A and B , while "A+B" means that the attack model conducts A and B simultaneously.

an important and typical kind of textual adversarial attacks. Thus, no sentence-level attack models are included in TextAttack. In contrast, `OpenAttack` adopts a more flexible framework that supports all types of attacks including sentence-level attacks.

(2) **Multilinguality**. TextAttack only covers English textual attacks while `OpenAttack` supports English and Chinese now. And its extensible design enables quick support for more languages.

(3) **Parallel processing**. Running some attack models maybe very time-consuming, e.g., it takes over 100 seconds to attack an instance with the SememePSO attack model (Zang et al., 2020). To address this issue, `OpenAttack` additionally provides support for multi-process running of attack models to improve attack efficiency.

Moreover, `OpenAttack` is fully integrated with HuggingFace's *transformers*[1] and *datasets*[2] libraries, which allows convenient adversarial attacks against thousands of NLP models (especially pre-trained models) on diverse datasets. `OpenAttack` also has great extensibility. It can be easily used to attack any customized victim model, regardless of the used programming framework (PyTorch, TensorFlow, Keras, etc.), on any customized dataset.

`OpenAttack` can be used to (1) provide various handy baselines for attack models; (2) comprehensively evaluate attack models using its thorough evaluation metrics; (3) assist in quick development of new attack models; (4) evaluate the robustness of an NLP model against various adversarial attacks; and (5) conduct *adversarial training* (Goodfellow et al., 2015) to improve model robustness by enriching the training data with generated adversarial examples.

Recent years have witnesses the rapid development of adversarial attacks in computer vision (Akhtar and Mian, 2018), which is promoted by many visual attack toolkits such as CleverHans (Papernot et al., 2018), Foolbox (Rauber et al., 2017), AdvBox (Goodman et al., 2020), etc. We hope `OpenAttack`, together with TextAttack and other similar toolkits, can play a constructive role in the development of textual adversarial attacks.

2 Formalization and Categorization of Textual Adversarial Attacking

We first formalize the task of textual adversarial attacking for text classification, and the following formalization can be trivially adapted to other NLP tasks. For a given text sequence x that is correctly classified as its ground-truth label y by the victim model F, the attack model A is supposed to transform x into $\hat{x}$ by small perturbations, whose ground-truth label is still y but classification result given by F is $\hat{y} \neq y$. Next, we introduce the catego-

[1] `https://github.com/huggingface/transformers`

[2] `https://github.com/huggingface/datasets`

rization of textual adversarial attack models from three perspectives.

According to the attack model's accessibility to the victim model, existing attack models can be categorized into four classes, namely gradient-based, score-based, decision-based and blind models. First, gradient-based attack models are also called white-box attack models, which require full knowledge of the victim model to conduct gradient update. Most of them are inspired by the fast gradient sign method (Goodfellow et al., 2015) and forward derivative method (Papernot et al., 2016a) in visual adversarial attacking.

In contrast to white-box attack models, black-box models do not need to have complete information on the victim model, and can be subcategorized into score-based, decision-based and blind models. Blind models are ignorant of the victim model at all. Score-based models require the prediction scores (e.g., classification probabilities) of the victim model, while decision-based models only need the final decision (e.g., predicted class).

According to the level of perturbations imposed on original input, textual adversarial attack models can be classified into sentence-level, word-level and character-level models. Sentence-level attack models craft adversarial examples mainly by adding distracting sentences (Jia and Liang, 2017), paraphrasing (Iyyer et al., 2018; Ribeiro et al., 2018) or text generation by encoder-decoder (Zhao et al., 2018). Word-level attack models mostly conduct word substitution, namely substituting some words in the original input with semantically identical or similar words such as synonyms (Jin et al., 2020; Ren et al., 2019; Alzantot et al., 2018). Some word-level attack models also use operations including deleting and adding words (Zhang et al., 2019; Garg and Ramakrishnan, 2020). Character-level attack models usually carry out character manipulations including swap, substitution, deletion, insertion and repeating (Eger et al., 2019; Ebrahimi et al., 2018; Belinkov and Bisk, 2018).

Finally, adversarial attack models can also be categorized into targeted and untargeted models based on whether the wrong classification result given by the victim model ($\hat{y}$) is pre-specified (mainly for the multi-class classification models). Most existing attack models support (by minor adjustment) both targeted and untargeted attacks, and we give no particular attention to this attribute of attack models in this paper.

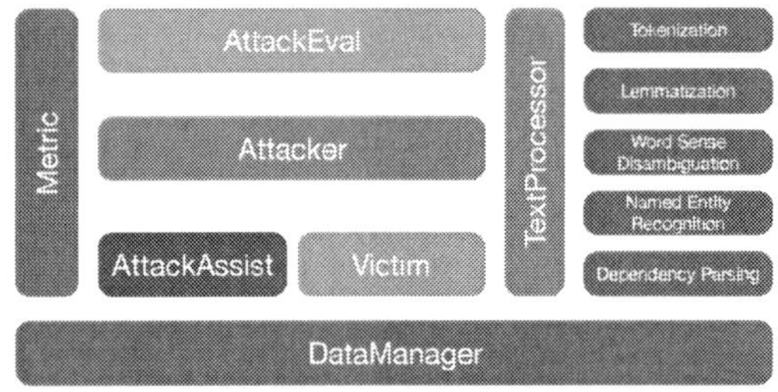

Figure 1: Overall architecture of `OpenAttack`.

Currently `OpenAttack` includes 15 different attack models, which cover all the victim model accessibility and perturbation level types. Table 1 lists the attack models involved in `OpenAttack`.

3 Toolkit Design and Architecture

In this section, we describe the design philosophy and modular architecture of `OpenAttack`.

We extract and properly reorganize the commonly used components from different attack models, so that any attack model can be assembled by them. Considering the significant distinctions among different attack models, especially those between the sentence-level and word/char-level attack models, it is hard to embrace all attack models within a unified framework like TextAttack. Therefore, we leave considerable freedom for the skeleton design of attack models, and focus more on streamlining the general processing of adversarial attacking and providing common components used in attack models. Next we introduce the modules of `OpenAttack` one by one, and Figure 1 illustrates an overview of all the modules.

- **TextProcessor**. This module is aimed at processing the original input so as to assist attack models in generating adversarial examples. It consists of several functions used for tokenization, lemmatization, delemmatization, word sense disambiguation (WSD), named entity recognition (NER) and dependency parsing. Currently it supports English and Chinese, and support for other languages can be realized simply by rewriting the TextProcessor base class.

- **Victim**. This module wraps the victim model. It supports both neural network-based model implemented by any programming framework (especially the HuggingFace's *transformers*) and traditional machine learning model. It is mainly composed of three functions that are used to obtain the gradient with respect to the input, prediction scores and predicted class of a victim model.

- **Attacker**. This is the core module of `OpenAttack`. It comprises various attack models and can generate adversarial examples for given input against a victim model.

- **AttackAssist**. This is an assistant module of Attacker. It mainly packs different word and character substitution methods that are widely used in word- and character-level attack models. Attacker queries this module to get substitutions for a word or character. Now it includes word embedding-based (Alzantot et al., 2018; Jin et al., 2020), synonym-based (Ren et al., 2019) and sememe-based (Zang et al., 2020) word substitution methods, and visual character substitution method (Eger et al., 2019). In addition, some useful components used in sentence-level attack models are also included, such as paraphrasing based on back-translation.

- **Metric**. This module provides several adversarial example quality metrics which can serve as either the constraints on the adversarial examples during attacking or evaluation metrics for evaluating adversarial attacks. It currently includes following metrics: (1) language model prediction score for a given word in a context given by Google one-billion words language model (Jozefowicz et al., 2016) (this metric can be used as the constraint on adversarial examples only); (2) *word modification rate*, the percentage of modified words of an adversarial example compared with the original example; (3) formal similarity between the adversarial example and original example, which is measured by Levenshtein edit distance (Levenshtein, 1966), character- and word-level Jaccard similarity (Jaccard, 1912) and BLEU score (Papineni et al., 2002); (4) semantic similarity between the adversarial example and original example measured by Universal Sentence Encoder (Cer et al., 2018) and Sentence Transformers (Reimers and Gurevych, 2019); (5) adversarial example fluency measured with perplexity computed by GPT-2 (Radford et al., 2019); and (6) grammaticality measure by the grammatical errors given by LanguageTool.[3]

[3]`https://www.languagetool.org`

Perspective	Metric	Better?
Attack Effectiveness	Attack Success Rate	Higher
Adversarial Example Quality	Word Modification Rate	Lower
	Formal Similarity	Higher
	Semantic Similarity	Higher
	Fluency (GPT-2 perplexity)	Lower
	Grammaticality (Grammatical Errors)	Lower
Attack Efficiency	Average Victim Model Query Times	Lower
	Average Running Time	Lower

Table 2: Evaluation metrics in `OpenAttack`. "Higher" and "Lower" mean the higher/lower the metric is, the better an attack model performs.

- **AttackEval**. This module is used to evaluate textual adversarial attacks from different perspectives including attack effectiveness, adversarial example quality and attack efficiency: (1) the attack effectiveness metric is *attack success rate*, the percentage of the attacks that successfully fool the victim model; (2) adversarial example quality is measured by the last five metrics in the Metric module; and (3) attack efficiency has two metrics including average victim model query times and average running time of attacking one instance. Table 2 lists all the evaluation metrics in `OpenAttack`.

  The realization of multi-processing is incorporated in this module, with the help of Python `multiprocessing` library. In addition, this module can also visualize and save attack results, e.g., display original input and adversarial examples and emphasize their differences.

- **DataManager**. This module manages all the data as well as saved models that are used in other modules. It supports accessing and downloading data/models. Specifically, it deals with the data used in the AttackAssist module such as character embeddings, word embeddings and WordNet synonyms, the models used in the TextProcessor module such as NER model and dependency parser, the built-in trained victim models, and auxiliary models used in Attacker such as the paraphrasing model for the paraphrasing-based attack models. This module helps efficiently and handily utilize data.

4 Toolkit Usage

`OpenAttack` provides a set of easy-to-use interfaces that can meet almost all the needs in textual adversarial attacking, such as preprocessing text, generating adversarial examples to attack a victim

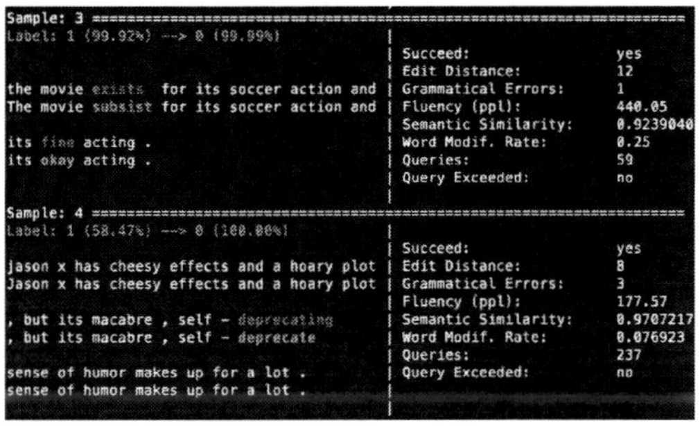

Figure 2: Part of attack results for individual instances.

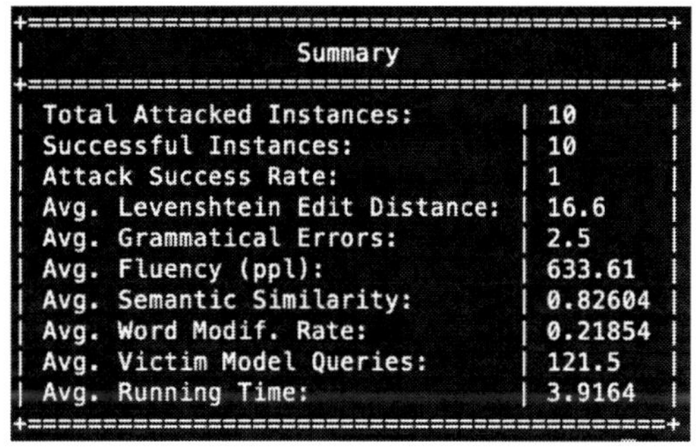

Figure 3: Summary of attack results.

model and evaluating attack models. Moreover, `OpenAttack` has great flexibility and extensibility and supports easy customization of victim models and attack models. Next, we showcase some basic usages of `OpenAttack`.

4.1 Built-in Attack and Evaluation

`OpenAttack` builds in some commonly used NLP models such as LSTM (Hochreiter and Schmidhuber, 1997) and BERT (Devlin et al., 2019) that have been trained on commonly used NLP datasets. Users can use the built-in victim models to quickly conduct adversarial attacks. The following code snippet shows how to use Genetic (Alzantot et al., 2018) to attack BERT on the test set of SST-2 (Socher et al., 2013) with 4-process parallel running:

```
import OpenAttack as oa
import datasets # HuggingFace's datasets library
import multiprocessing
# choose a trained victim model
victim = oa.loadVictim('BERT.SST')
# choose a evaluation dataset from datasets
dataset = datasets.load_dataset('sst', 'test')
# choose Genetic as the attacker
attacker = oa.attackers.GeneticAttacker()
# prepare for multi-process attacking
attack_eval = oa.attack_evals.
    MultiProcessAttackEval(attacker, victim,
    num_process=4)
# launch attacks and print attack results
attack_eval.eval(dataset, visualize=True)
```

Figure 2 displays the printed attack results for individual instances from above code. We can see `OpenAttack` prints the original input as well as the word-aligned adversarial example, where the perturbed words are colored. In addition, a series of attack evaluation results are listed. At the end of individual attack results, `OpenAttack` provides an attack summary composed of average evaluation results of specified metrics among all instances, as shown in Figure 3.

4.2 Customized Victim Models

It is very common for users to launch attacks against their own models that have been trained on specific datasets, particularly when evaluating the robustness of a victim model. It is impossible to exhaustively build in all victim models. Thus, easy customization for victim models is very important.

`OpenAttack` provides simple and convenient interfaces for victim model customization. For a trained model implemented with whichever programming framework, users just need to configure some model access interfaces that provide accessibility required for the attack model under the Victim class. The following code snippet shows how to use Genetic to attack a customized sentiment analysis model, a statistical model in NLTK (Bird et al., 2009), on the test set of SST.

```
import OpenAttack as oa
import numpy as np
import datasets
from nltk.sentiment.vader import
    SentimentIntensityAnalyzer

# configure access interface of customized model
class MyModel(oa.Victim):
    def __init__(self):
        self.model = SentimentIntensityAnalyzer()
    def get_prob(self, input_):
        rt = []
        for sent in input_:
            rs = self.model.polarity_scores(sent)
            prob = rs["pos"] / (rs["neg"] + rs["
    pos"])
            rt.append(np.array([1 - prob, prob]))
        return np.array(rt)
# choose evaluation dataset
dataset = datasets.load_dataset('sst','test')
# choose the customized victim model
victim = MyModel()
# choose Genetic as the attack model
attacker = oa.attackers.GeneticAttacker()
# prepare for attacking
attack_eval = oa.attack_evals.DefaultAttackEval(
    attacker, victim)
# launch attacks and print attack results
attack_eval.eval(dataset, visualize=True)
```

In addition, `OpenAttack` supports easy customization of attack models thanks to its inclusive

Model	Type		Effectiveness	Adversarial Example Quality					Attack Efficiency			
	Accessibility	Perturbation	ASR	WMR	LES	SemSim	Fluency	Grm	#Query	T_1	T_2	S
SEA	Decision	Sentence	0.12	–	14.7	0.90	398	2.2	2.0	37.1	–	–
SCPN	Blind	Sentence	0.68	–	55.6	0.56	432	2.7	11.0	3.58	2.30	1.56
GAN	Decision	Sentence	0.41	–	68.8	0.26	512	4.2	2.0	0.60	2.00	0.30
TextFooler	Score	Word	0.90	0.11	14.1	0.87	621	4.6	130.5	5.75	3.25	1.77
PWWS	Score	Word	0.78	0.20	17.9	0.84	613	2.9	124.8	5.26	2.88	1.83
Genetic	Score	Word	0.36	0.11	13.4	0.88	689	4.7	242.1	54.11	27.56	1.96
SememePSO	Score	Word	0.82	0.14	2.9	0.89	711	2.9	177.9	102.44	52.41	1.95
BERT-ATTACK	Score	Word	0.87	0.31	4.2	0.86	796	4.4	51.9	2.38	1.57	1.51
BAE	Score	Word	0.77	0.68	5.4	0.82	1147	4.3	103.0	2.97	1.79	1.66
FD	Gradient	Word	0.16	0.24	17.9	0.85	908	3.1	10.9	34.57	28.36	1.22
TextBugger	Gradient	Word+Char	0.25	0.15	10.6	0.61	512	7.1	150.0	8.49	4.37	1.94
UAT	Gradient	Word	0.43	0.15	24.0	0.85	620	2.8	2.0	0.08	–	–
HotFlip	Gradient	Word	0.47	0.08	8.9	0.93	333	2.7	105.4	2.77	1.82	1.52
VIPER	Blind	Char	0.27	–	24.2	0.22	347	15.8	3.0	4.01	2.04	1.97
DeepWordBug	Score	Char	0.46	–	7.9	0.73	731	6.1	22.0	0.97	0.62	1.56

Table 3: Evaluation results of different attack models when attacking BERT on SST-2. ASR = Attack Success Rate, WMR = Word Modification Rate that is only applicable to word-level attacks, LES = Levenshterin Edit Distance, SemSim = Semantic Similarity measured by Universal Sentence Encoder, Fluency = GPT-2 perplexity, Grm = number of grammatical errors, #Query = average victim model query times, T_1 and T_2 represent average running time of attacking one instance (seconds) with single and dual process, S = T_1/T_2 is speedup. Notice that it is meaningless to run SEA and UAT with multi-process because they learn and conduct global perturbations.

modular design. Due to limited space, please visit the GitHub project page for more examples including attacking HuggingFace's pre-trained models, using customized evaluation metrics and conducting adversarial training.[4]

5 Evaluation

In this section, we conduct evaluations for all the attack models included in `OpenAttack`.

We use SST-2 as the evaluation dataset and choose BERT, specifically $\text{BERT}_{\text{BASE}}$, as the victim model. After fine-tuning on the training set, BERT achieves 90.31 accuracy on the test set. Due to great diversity of attack models, it is hard to impose many constraints on attacks like previous work that focuses on a specific kind of attack. We only restrict the maximum victim model query times to 500. In addition, to improve evaluation efficiency, we randomly sample $1,000$ correctly classified instances from the test set as the original input to be perturbed. We use the original default hyper-parameter settings of all attack models.

Table 3 shows the evaluation results. By comparison with originally reported results, we confirm the correctness of our implementation. We also observe that multi-processing can effectively improve attack efficiency of most attack models (the speedup is greater than 1). For some very efficient attack models whose average running time is quite short (like GAN), the additional time cost from multi-processing may reduce efficiency instead.

[4] `https://github.com/thunlp/OpenAttack/tree/master/examples`

6 Related Work

There have been quite a few open-source libraries of generating adversarial examples for continuous data, especially images, such as CleverHans (Papernot et al., 2018), Foolbox (Rauber et al., 2017), Adversarial Robustness Toolbox (ART) (Nicolae et al., 2018) and AdvBox (Goodman et al., 2020). These libraries enable practitioners to easily make adversarial attacks with different methods and have greatly facilitated the development of adversarial attacking for continuous data.

As for discrete data, particularly text, there exist few adversarial attack libraries. As far as we know, TextAttack (Morris et al., 2020) is the only such library. It utilizes a relatively rigorous framework to unify many attack models and provides interfaces for using the existing attack models or designing new attack models. As mentioned in Introduction, our `OpenAttack` is mainly different from and complementary to TextAttack in all-attack-type support, multilinguality and parallel processing.

There are also some other toolkits concerned with textual adversarial attacking. TEAPOT (Michel et al., 2019) is an open-source toolkit to evaluate the effectiveness of textual adversarial examples from the perspective of preservation of meaning. It is mainly designed for the attacks against sequence-to-sequence models, but can also be geared towards text classification models. AllenNLP Interpret (Wallace et al., 2019b) is a framework for explaining the predictions of NLP models, where adversarial attacking is one of its interpretation methods. It focuses on interpretability of NLP models and only incorporates two attack models.

7 Conclusion and Future Work

In this paper, we present `OpenAttack`, an open-source textual adversarial attack toolkit that provides a wide range of functions in textual adversarial attacking. It is a great complement to existing counterparts because of its unique strengths in all-attack-type support, multilinguality and parallel processing. Moreover, it has great flexibility and extensibility and provides easy customization of victim models and attack models. In the future, we will keep `OpenAttack` updated to incorporate more up-to-date attack models and support more functions to facilitate the research on textual adversarial attacks.

Acknowledgements

This work is supported by the National Key Research and Development Program of China (Grant No. 2020AAA0106501 and No. 2020AAA0106502) and Beijing Academy of Artificial Intelligence (BAAI). We also thank all the anonymous reviewers for their valuable comments and suggestions.

Broader Impact Statement

There is indeed a probability that `OpenAttack` is misused to maliciously attack some NLP systems. But we believe that we should face up to the potential risks of adversarial attacks rather than pretend not to notice them. As the development of adversarial learning in computer vision, the studies on adversarial attacks actually promote the studies on adversarial defenses and model robustness. We hope more people in the NLP community can realize the robustness issue and `OpenAttack` can play a constructive role.

References

Naveed Akhtar and Ajmal Mian. 2018. Threat of adversarial attacks on deep learning in computer vision: A survey. *Ieee Access*, 6:14410–14430.

Moustafa Alzantot, Yash Sharma, Ahmed Elgohary, Bo-Jhang Ho, Mani Srivastava, and Kai-Wei Chang. 2018. Generating natural language adversarial examples. In *Proceedings of the EMNLP*.

Yonatan Belinkov and Yonatan Bisk. 2018. Synthetic and natural noise both break neural machine translation. In *Proceedings of ICLR*.

Steven Bird, Ewan Klein, and Edward Loper. 2009. *Natural language processing with Python: analyzing text with the natural language toolkit*. O'Reilly Media, Inc.

Daniel Cer, Yinfei Yang, Sheng-yi Kong, Nan Hua, Nicole Limtiaco, Rhomni St John, Noah Constant, Mario Guajardo-Cespedes, Steve Yuan, Chris Tar, et al. 2018. Universal sentence encoder for english. In *Proceedings of EMNLP*.

Jacob Devlin, Ming-Wei Chang, Kenton Lee, and Kristina Toutanova. 2019. BERT: Pre-training of deep bidirectional Transformers for language understanding. In *Proceedings of NAACL-HLT*.

Javid Ebrahimi, Anyi Rao, Daniel Lowd, and Dejing Dou. 2018. Hotflip: White-box adversarial examples for text classification. In *Proceedings of ACL*.

Steffen Eger, Gözde Gül Şahin, Andreas Rücklé, Ji-Ung Lee, Claudia Schulz, Mohsen Mesgar, Krishnkant Swarnkar, Edwin Simpson, and Iryna Gurevych. 2019. Text processing like humans do: Visually attacking and shielding NLP systems. In *Proceedings of NAACL-HLT*.

Ji Gao, Jack Lanchantin, Mary Lou Soffa, and Yanjun Qi. 2018. Black-box generation of adversarial text sequences to evade deep learning classifiers. In *Proceedings of IEEE Security and Privacy Workshops*.

Siddhant Garg and Goutham Ramakrishnan. 2020. Bae: Bert-based adversarial examples for text classification. In *Proceedings of EMNLP*.

Ian J Goodfellow, Jonathon Shlens, and Christian Szegedy. 2015. Explaining and harnessing adversarial examples. In *Proceedings of ICLR*.

Dou Goodman, Hao Xin, Wang Yang, Wu Yuesheng, Xiong Junfeng, and Zhang Huan. 2020. Advbox: a toolbox to generate adversarial examples that fool neural networks. *arXiv preprint arXiv:2001.05574*.

Sepp Hochreiter and Jürgen Schmidhuber. 1997. Long short-term memory. *Neural Computation*, 9(8):1735–1780.

Mohit Iyyer, John Wieting, Kevin Gimpel, and Luke Zettlemoyer. 2018. Adversarial example generation with syntactically controlled paraphrase networks. In *Proceedings of the NAACL-HLT*.

Paul Jaccard. 1912. The distribution of the flora in the alpine zone.1. *New Phytologist*, 11(2):37–50.

Robin Jia and Percy Liang. 2017. Adversarial examples for evaluating reading comprehension systems. In *Proceedings of EMNLP*.

Di Jin, Zhijing Jin, Joey Tianyi Zhou, and Peter Szolovits. 2020. Is BERT really robust? Natural language attack on text classification and entailment. In *Proceedings of AAAI*.

Rafal Jozefowicz, Oriol Vinyals, Mike Schuster, Noam Shazeer, and Yonghui Wu. 2016. Exploring the limits of language modeling. *arXiv preprint arXiv:1602.02410*.

Vladimir I Levenshtein. 1966. Binary codes capable of correcting deletions, insertions, and reversals. In *Soviet physics doklady*, volume 10, pages 707–710.

Jinfeng Li, Shouling Ji, Tianyu Du, Bo Li, and Ting Wang. 2019. Textbugger: Generating adversarial text against real-world applications. In *Proceedings of Network and Distributed Systems Security Symposium*.

Linyang Li, Ruotian Ma, Qipeng Guo, Xiangyang Xue, and Xipeng Qiu. 2020. Bert-attack: Adversarial attack against bert using bert. In *Proceedings of EMNLP*.

Paul Michel, Xian Li, Graham Neubig, and Juan Pino. 2019. On evaluation of adversarial perturbations for sequence-to-sequence models. In *Proceedings NAACL-HLT*.

John Morris, Eli Lifland, Jin Yong Yoo, Jake Grigsby, Di Jin, and Yanjun Qi. 2020. Textattack: A framework for adversarial attacks, data augmentation, and adversarial training in nlp. In *Proceedings of EMNLP: System Demonstrations*.

Maria-Irina Nicolae, Mathieu Sinn, Minh Ngoc Tran, Beat Buesser, Ambrish Rawat, Martin Wistuba, Valentina Zantedeschi, Nathalie Baracaldo, Bryant Chen, Heiko Ludwig, et al. 2018. Adversarial robustness toolbox v1. 0.0. *arXiv preprint arXiv:1807.01069*.

Nicolas Papernot, Fartash Faghri, Nicholas Carlini, Ian Goodfellow, Reuben Feinman, Alexey Kurakin, Cihang Xie, Yash Sharma, Tom Brown, Aurko Roy, Alexander Matyasko, Vahid Behzadan, Karen Hambardzumyan, Zhishuai Zhang, Yi-Lin Juang, Zhi Li, Ryan Sheatsley, Abhibhav Garg, Jonathan Uesato, Willi Gierke, Yinpeng Dong, David Berthelot, Paul Hendricks, Jonas Rauber, and Rujun Long. 2018. Technical report on the cleverhans v2.1.0 adversarial examples library. *arXiv preprint arXiv:1610.00768*.

Nicolas Papernot, Patrick McDaniel, Somesh Jha, Matt Fredrikson, Z Berkay Celik, and Ananthram Swami. 2016a. The limitations of deep learning in adversarial settings. In *2016 IEEE European symposium on security and privacy (EuroS&P)*. IEEE.

Nicolas Papernot, Patrick McDaniel, Ananthram Swami, and Richard Harang. 2016b. Crafting adversarial input sequences for recurrent neural networks. In *Proceedings of MILCOM*.

Kishore Papineni, Salim Roukos, Todd Ward, and Wei-Jing Zhu. 2002. Bleu: a method for automatic evaluation of machine translation. In *Proceedings of ACL*.

Alec Radford, Jeffrey Wu, Rewon Child, David Luan, Dario Amodei, and Ilya Sutskever. 2019. Language models are unsupervised multitask learners. *OpenAI Blog*, 1(8).

Jonas Rauber, Wieland Brendel, and Matthias Bethge. 2017. Foolbox: A python toolbox to benchmark the robustness of machine learning models. In *ICML Reliable Machine Learning in the Wild Workshop*.

Nils Reimers and Iryna Gurevych. 2019. Sentence-bert: Sentence embeddings using siamese bert-networks. In *Proceedings of EMNLP*.

Shuhuai Ren, Yihe Deng, Kun He, and Wanxiang Che. 2019. Generating natural language adversarial examples through probability weighted word saliency. In *Proceedings of ACL*.

Marco Tulio Ribeiro, Sameer Singh, and Carlos Guestrin. 2018. Semantically equivalent adversarial rules for debugging NLP models. In *Proceedings of ACL*.

Richard Socher, Alex Perelygin, Jean Wu, Jason Chuang, Christopher D Manning, Andrew Ng, and Christopher Potts. 2013. Recursive deep models for semantic compositionality over a sentiment treebank. In *Proceedings of EMNLP*.

Christian Szegedy, Wojciech Zaremba, Ilya Sutskever, Joan Bruna, Dumitru Erhan, Ian Goodfellow, and Rob Fergus. 2014. Intriguing properties of neural networks. In *Proceedings of ICLR*.

Eric Wallace, Shi Feng, Nikhil Kandpal, Matt Gardner, and Sameer Singh. 2019a. Universal adversarial triggers for attacking and analyzing NLP. In *Proceedings of EMNLP-IJCNLP*.

Eric Wallace, Jens Tuyls, Junlin Wang, Sanjay Subramanian, Matt Gardner, and Sameer Singh. 2019b. Allennlp interpret: A framework for explaining predictions of nlp models. In *Proceedings of EMNLP-IJCNLP*.

Yuan Zang, Fanchao Qi, Chenghao Yang, Zhiyuan Liu, Meng Zhang, Qun Liu, and Maosong Sun. 2020. Word-level textual adversarial attacking as combinatorial optimization. In *Proceedings of ACL*.

Huangzhao Zhang, Hao Zhou, Ning Miao, and Lei Li. 2019. Generating fluent adversarial examples for natural languages. In *Proceedings of ACL*.

Wei Emma Zhang, Quan Z Sheng, Ahoud Alhazmi, and Chenliang Li. 2020. Adversarial attacks on deep-learning models in natural language processing: A survey. *ACM Transactions on Intelligent Systems and Technology (TIST)*, 11(3):1–41.

Zhengli Zhao, Dheeru Dua, and Sameer Singh. 2018. Generating natural adversarial examples. In *Proceedings of ICLR*.

Author Index

Association for Computational Linguistics
209 N. Eighth Street
Stroudsburg, Pennsylvania 18360

ISBN 978-1-7138-3310-9

CURRAN ASSOCIATES INC.
proceedings.com